BALI & LOMBOK

This eleventh edition was updated by
Zoe Smith

ROUGH GUIDES

Contents

PURA PRASASTI BLANJONG TEMPLE, UNDANG

Introduction to Bali & Lombok

Part of the Indonesian archipelago, Bali and Lombok are fringed by rugged coastlines, glorious sandy beaches and world-class surf. Both islands are small – Bali extends less than 153km at its widest point, Lombok a mere 70km – and dramatically volcanic, graced with swathes of extremely fertile land, much of it sculpted into elegantly terraced rice paddies. Culturally, however, they could not be more different. Bali is Southeast Asia's only predominately Hindu society, and religious observance permeates every aspect of life here; Lombok's Sasak people, on the other hand, are largely Muslim, like the vast majority of Indonesians.

Bali landed on the tourist map in the 1930s and is still an incredibly popular destination, drawing everyone from backpackers to high-end travellers and those seeking spiritual healing. Visitor numbers continue to increase annually placing a strain on existing infrastructure, and traffic congestion and commercialization have affected vast areas of Southern Bali and Ubud. That said, the island's original charm is still very much in evidence once you leave the densely populated areas.

Just to the east of Bali, **Lombok** plays host to far fewer foreign travellers, but numbers are steadily increasing thanks to the island's many unspoilt beaches, terrific surf and forested mountain slopes. Blessed with such natural beauty, Lombok has a burgeoning reputation as a more adventurous destination than its illustrious neighbour.

Until the twentieth century, both Bali and Lombok were divided into small **kingdoms**, each ruled by a succession of Balinese rajas and Sasak princes whose territories fluctuated so much that, at times, parts of eastern Bali and western Lombok were joined under a single Balinese ruler. Both islands endured years of colonial rule under the Dutch East Indies government, which only ended when hard-won **independence** was granted to Indonesia in 1949. (Indonesia celebrates its declaration of independence as August 17, 1945, however, The Netherlands remain committed to the UN-decreed 1949 date.) The

CELEBRATING BEFORE NYEPI

Jakarta-based government has since focused on creating a national identity among its vast array of extraordinarily diverse islands and peoples, both by implementing a unifying five-point political philosophy, Pancasila, and through the use of Bahasa Indonesia, the lingua franca across the whole archipelago. Politically, Bali is administered as a province in its own right with Denpasar as its capital, while Lombok's Mataram city is the capital of West Nusa Tenggara Province, which it shares with Sumbawa Island to the east.

TRADITIONAL DRESS

It is customary for Balinese men and women to wear **traditional dress** to attend temple festivals, cremations, weddings, birth rites and other important rituals; temple dress is also worn if playing in a gamelan orchestra and occasionally for *banjar* (neighbourhood) meetings.

Many **women** wear a vividly coloured bustier under the *kebaya* (blouse), and hair is usually tied neatly in a bun, adorned with flowers or golden ornaments for special occasions. The *kebaya* is worn over a *kamen sarung* (sarong) held in place by two cumberbunds.

Men also wear *kamen sarung*, topped by a *saput* (knee-length hip-cloth) and a formal, collared shirt (generally white but sometimes batik) or a starched jacket-like shirt. The distinctive headcloth (*udeng*) is tied with a triangular crest on top, which symbolically concentrates the mental energies and directs the thoughts heavenwards via the perky cockscomb at the front. Nowadays, some men buy their *udeng* in shops, ready-tied.

Where to go

Bali's best-known beach area, the **Kuta–Legian–Seminyak** strip, is a 6km sweep of golden sand that draws an incongruous mix of holidaying families, weekending Indonesians, backpackers, a loyal gay clientele and design-conscious visitors.

BALI
Pulau Menjangan (Deer Island)
BALI BARAT NATIONAL PARK
Ketapang
Gilimanuk
Cekik
Java
Labuan Lalang
Pemuteran
Pura Agung Pulaki
Lovina Beach
Lovina
Kalibukbuk
Seririt
Dencarik
Brahma Vihara Arama
Munduk
Danau Buyan
Danau Tamblingan
Danau Bratan
Bedugul
Gunung Batukaru
Pupuan
Pura Luhur Batukaru
Sanda
Wongayagede
Jatiluwih
Negara
Perancak
Pura Rambut Siwi
Medewi
Pekutatan
Penebel
Lalang Linggah
Balian Beach
Antosari
Bajera
Krambitan
Tabanan
Mengwi
Yeh Gangga Beach
Pura Tanah Lot
Ubung Bemo Terminal
Sangeh Monkey Forest
Sayan
Pura Taman Ayun
Canggu
Seminyak
Legian
Kuta
DENPASAR
Ngurah Rai Airport
Benoa Harbour
Serangan Island (Turtle Island)
Jimbaran
Tanjung Benoa
Bualu
Nusa Dua
Pura Luhur Uluwatu
Sanur
Batubulan
Sukawati
Batuan
Sakah
Mas
Teges
Gianyar
Bedulu
Pejeng
Ubud
Petulu
Tegalalang
Pujung Kelod
Pelaga
Tampaksiring
Gunung Kawi
Bangli
Semarapura
Sidemen
Padang Bai
Kubutambahan
Air Sanih
Bukti
Singaraja
Ponjok Batu
Bondalem
Tejakula
Sembirenteng
Gunung Batur
Songan
Danau Batur
Kintamani
Toya Bungkah
Penelokan
Kubu
Tulamben
Gunung Agung
Besakih
Culik
Amed
Jemeluk
Lipah Beach
Aas
Tirtagangga
Amlapura
Tenganan
Candidasa
BALI SEA
Bali Strait
Lombok Strait
Badung Strait
Benoa-Gili Gede
Gili Islands (Lombok) &
Senggigi (Lombok)
Lembar (Lombok)
Nusa Lembongan
Jungutbatu
Nusa Ceningan
Ped
Buyuk Harbour
Sampalan
Toyapakeh
Nusa Penida
Bangko Bangko
Lombok
INDIAN OCEAN
N
Feet
9000
7000
5000
3000
2000
1000
500
250
0
Metres
2743
2134
1524
914
610
305
152
76
0
0
20
kilometres
Bali
Lombok
Java

LOMBOK
BALI SEA
INDIAN OCEAN
Lombok Strait
Alas Strait
Sumbawa
Bali
Nusa Penida
Kubu
Tulamben
Amed
Lipah Beach
Culik
Jemeluk
Tirtagangga
Aas
Amlapura
Padang Bai (Bali)
Benoa (Bali)
Nusa Lembongan & Serangan Harbour (Bali)
Sampalan
The Gili Islands
Gili Trawangan
Gili Meno
Gili Air
Gili Lawang
Gili Sulat
Gili Gede
Anyar
Segenter
Batu Koq
Bayan
Kokok Putih
Obel Obel
Senaru
Sendang Gile Waterfall
Tiu Pupus Waterfall
Gangga Waterfall
Gunung Sengkareang (2588m)
Gunung Daya (2941m)
Danau Segara Anak
Gunung Buanmangge (2895m)
Gunung Kondo (2947m)
Gunung Rinjani (3726m)
Gunung Lelonten
Gunung Pusuk (2330m)
Gunung Dundatrum
Sembalun Lawang
Sembalun Bumbung
Labuhan Pandan
Transat
Labuhan Kayangan
Labuhan Lombok
Pringgabaya
Sapit
Pesugulan
Swela
Timbanuh
Jukut Waterfall
Joben Waterfall
Benang Stokel Waterfall
Tetebatu
Pringgasela
Aik Mel
Lenek
Lendang Nangka
Rempung
Masbagik
Selong
Labuhan Haji
Bangsal
Pemenang
Teluk Nara
Mangsit
Senggigi
Ampenan
MATARAM
Cakranegara
Sweta
Narmada
Pemepek
Pancordau
Mantang
Kopang
Banyumulek
Lembar
Bangko Bangko
Pandanan
Tawun
Sekotong Tengah
Pelangan
Sepi
Belongas
Pengantap
Selong Belanak
Keling
Mawun
Tampa
Kuta
Rembitan
Sengkol
Lombok International Airport
Batujai
Praya
Batunyale
Mujur
Ganti
Beleka
Batu Rintang
Batu Nampur
Awang
Awang Bay (Ekas Bay)
Gerupuk
Ekas
Serewe
Sunut
Tanjung Ringgit
Keruak
Gubukdalam
Tanjung Luar
N
Feet
Metres
11000
3353
9000
2743
7000
2134
5000
1524
3000
914
2000
610
1000
305
500
152
0
0
0
10
kilometres

FACT FILE

- **Bali** (almost 5800 square kilometres in size with a population of over 4.3 million) and **Lombok** (just over 5300 square kilometres in size and with a population around 3.8 million, including Sumbawa) make up two of the 34 provinces of the Republic of Indonesia, an ethnically diverse democracy of over 300 million people.
- The Balinese traditionally celebrate their new year, known as **Nyepi** and generally falling in March/April, with a day of silence and meditation. By contrast, the night before features a deafening cacophony designed to scare away evil spirits.
- Every November/December, Muslim and Hindu communities on Lombok take part in the **Perang Topat**, or **Ketupat War**, a ceremonial mock-battle at Pura Lingsar featuring copious rice- and egg-throwing.
- The **Wallace Line** that runs through the 35km-wide Lombok Strait, which separates the two islands, was long thought to mark the boundary between the distribution of Asian and Australasian wildlife.
- Both Bali and Lombok are **volcanic**: large eruptions killed thousands in the twentieth century and occasionally close the islands' airports.

Travellers seeking more relaxed alternatives generally head west to the beaches around and beyond Canggu, across the southern peninsula to **Sanur** or offshore to **Nusa Lembongan**; to sedate **Candidasa** or **Amed** further east; or to Lovina's black volcanic sands on the north coast. Quieter, smarter seaside options can be found at **Jimbaran** and Nusa Dua in the south and **Pemuteran** in the northwest. On Lombok, the trio of white-sand **Gili Islands** in the northwest draw the biggest crowds; there are quieter islands off the southwest **Sekotong** peninsula, a wide range of fading resort accommodation around **Senggigi**, lovely boutique resorts north of Senggigi in **Mangsit** and a series of extraordinarily beautiful beaches and a new high-end holiday development near **Kuta** in the south. All these resorts make comfortable bases for **divers** and **snorkellers** and are within easy reach of the islands' many reefs. **Surfers** have countless swells to choose from, including the famously challenging Uluwatu on Bali and Desert Point on Lombok, as well as many novice-friendly breaks.

Most visitors also venture inland to experience traditional island life. On Bali, Ubud village is a hugely popular cultural centre, still charming but undeniably commercialized, where traditional dances are staged every night and the streets are full of organic cafés, art galleries, yoga studios and myriad purveyors of alternative therapies. **Tetebatu** on Lombok occupies a similarly cool position in the foothills, although, like the island as a whole, it lacks Bali's artistic heritage. In general, the villages on both islands are far more appealing than the towns, but Bali's capital, **Denpasar**, the historic district capital **Semarapura**, and Lombok's **Mataram** conurbation are each worth a daytrip for their museums, markets and temples.

Bali's other big draw is its elegant Hindu **temples**, particularly the Tanah Lot island temple, the dramatically located **Uluwatu** and the extensive **Besakih** complex on the slopes of Gunung Agung. Temple **festivals** are also well worth attending.

Both islands hold a number of **hiking** possibilities, many of them up **volcanoes**. The best is the climb to the summit of Lombok's **Gunung Rinjani**, which at 3726m is one of Indonesia's highest peaks. The ascent of Bali's **Gunung Agung** (3014m) is shorter and

GANESHA STATUE

slightly less arduous. The climb up **Gunung Batur** (1717m) is much less taxing. Bali's sole **national park**, Bali Barat, has few good trails but is good for **birdwatching**, as is the area around **Danau Bratan** in the centre of the island. It's also worth considering a trip to an inland village for the change of scenery, views and refreshing temperatures; **Sidemen**, **Tirtagangga**, **Sarinbuana** and **Munduk** villages are all good bases.

When to go

Just eight degrees south of the equator, **tropical** Bali and Lombok have fairly constant year-round temperatures, averaging 27°C in Bali's coastal areas and the hills around Ubud and 22°C in the central volcanoes around Kintamani. Both islands are hit by an annual **monsoon**, which brings rain, wind and intense humidity from October through to March.

The **best time to visit** is outside the monsoon season, from April to September, though monsoons are, like many other events in Indonesia, notoriously unpunctual, and you should be prepared to get rained on in Ubud at any time of year. However, the prospect of a daily rainstorm shouldn't put you off: you're far more likely to get an hour-long downpour than day-long drizzle. Mountain-climbing, though, is both unrewarding and dangerous at monsoon time (the authorities close Rinjani during the rainy season for safety reasons).

The peak **tourist seasons** between mid-June and mid-September, over the Christmas–New Year period and at Idul Fitry (Eid al-Fitri, usually May–June) see prices rocket.

AVERAGE MONTHLY TEMPERATURES AND RAINFALL

	Jan	Feb	March	April	May	June	July	Aug	Sept	Oct	Nov	Dec
KINTAMANI												
°C	18	18	18	18	18	17	17	17	17	18	18	18
mm	467	378	264	137	77	40	14	11	9	61	110	299
KUTA (BALI)												
°C	27	27	27	27	27	26	26	26	27	27	28	27
mm	340	275	210	89	88	58	50	24	48	110	163	278
MATARAM												
°C	28	28	28	28	28	27	26	26	27	28	28	28
mm	280	223	262	108	94	44	29	19	33	110	163	278
SINGARAJA												
°C	27	27	27	27	27	26	25	26	26	27	27	27
mm	346	294	196	152	128	93	61	28	28	62	128	219
UBUD												
°C	26	26	26	26	25	25	24	24	25	26	26	26
mm	325	292	215	108	124	129	175	90	123	170	201	292

Author picks

Our author covered every corner of Bali and Lombok – from soaring volcanic peaks to underwater havens, bustling city markets to ancient temples – to research this new edition. Here are a few of her favourite experiences.

Beach bars The coastline between Seminyak and Canggu is loaded with fine places for a sundowner, such as the uber-luxe environs of *Potato Head* (see page 70). On Lombok, *Tir Na Nộg* fills the bill (see page 283).

Stunning views On Bali, the jaw-dropping seascape from Pura Luhur Uluwatu is out of this world; views of impossibly green rice terraces don't get much better than around Ubud (see page 108), Sidemen (see page 160) and Tirtagangga (see page 174). Lombok's rice-paddy scenery is impressive too, especially at Tetebatu (see page 261).

Off the beaten track Lombok's southeast peninsula (see page 263) may only be a bumpy ninety-minute drive from the airport, but it feels like the end of the world. The southwest peninsula (see page 246) is better connected but also very remote. On Bali, get your explorer kicks at the narrow and winding Amed coastal road to Ujung (see page 178).

Underwater vision The vibrant coral reefs around Lombok's Gili Islands (see page 274) are perfect both for snorkelling right from the beach and for shallow scuba diving. For dramatic pelagic life, including manta rays, Nusa Penida (see page 101) excels, while Pulau Menjangan (see page 227) has lots of reef sharks.

World-class waves Lombok is a sensational place to surf, whatever your skill level: learn the basics in Kuta's fabulous bays (see page 265) or hit some of the world's best waves at Desert Point (see page 247).

Our author recommendations don't end here. We've flagged up our favourite places – a perfectly sited hotel, an atmospheric café, a special restaurant – throughout the Guide, highlighted with the ★ symbol.

UJUNG WATER PALACE

RICE FIELDS, TIRTA GANGGA

20

things not to miss

It's not possible to see everything that Bali and Lombok have to offer in a single trip – and we don't suggest you try. What follows is a selective taste of the islands' highlights, including memorable places to stay, outstanding beaches and spectacular hikes. All highlights are colour-coded by chapter and have a page reference to take you straight into the guide, where you can find out more.

1

2

3

1 SUNRISE FROM GUNUNG BATUR

See page 186

Climb this ancient volcano before dawn and you'll be rewarded with the most extraordinary panoramas on Bali.

2 TEMPLE FESTIVALS

See page 32

Every one of Bali's thousands of Hindu temples holds at least one annual festival to entertain the gods with processions and offerings.

3 THE AMED COAST

See page 177

Memorable diving and snorkelling and a breathtakingly dramatic coastline are close to Bali's easternmost shore.

4 SOUTH LOMBOK BEACHES

See page 264

The wild and glorious Kuta coastline has some of the most beautiful white-sand bays on the islands.

5 DIVING AND SNORKELLING

See page 36

Wreck dives, submerged canyons, manta rays and oceanic sunfish are just a few of the islands' underwater attractions.

4

5

6

7

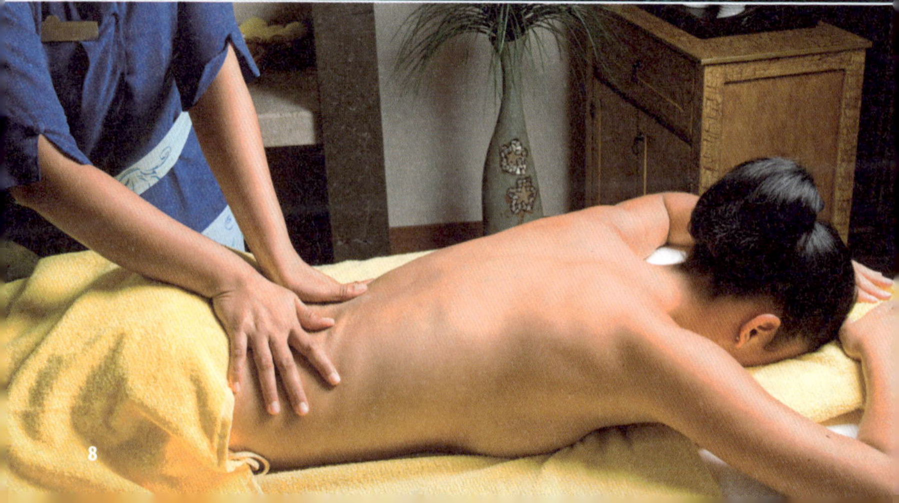
8

6 CLASSICAL KAMASAN ART

See pages 154 and 156

This uniquely Balinese art is at its best on the ceiling of the historic Kerta Gosa in eastern Bali and in the exceptional Nyoman Gunarsa Museum nearby.

7 SURFING

See page 36

Awesome, challenging breaks are at Bali's Uluwatu, Padang Padang and Lombok's Desert Point; beginners' waves at Kuta (Bali), Canggu and around Kuta (Lombok).

8 SPAS

See page 38

Pamper yourself with some of the local beauty treatments, including the spicy Balinese *boreh* deep massage.

9 PURA LUHUR ULUWATU

See page 78

Wonder at the simply spellbinding oceanic vistas from this clifftop temple on the Bukit.

10 THE GUNUNG BATUKARU FOOTHILLS

See page 220

Enjoy breathtaking mountain views, a garden temple and charming accommodation at Wongayagede, Jatiluwih and Sarinbuana.

11 BALI MUSEUM, DENPASAR

See page 86

See traditional architecture and a good ethnological introduction to the island.

12 PURA TANAH LOT

See page 215

Bali's most photographed temple sits atop its own tiny island.

13 UBUD

See page 108

Bali's arty heart has it all: beautifully sited accommodation; great restaurants; shops and galleries; and ricefields in every direction.

14 GAMELAN MUSIC

See page 308

The frenetic syncopations of drums and gongs provide Bali its own soundtrack.

15 CANGGU

See page 62

An engaging mix of surf beaches, organic cafés and paddy field scenery make Canggu a mecca for Bali's creative, leisured crowd.

11

12

13

14

15

16

16 MUNDUK

See page 196

A wonderful area off the beaten tourist track planted with coffee, clove and cacao.

17 BALINESE DANCE

See page 309

From acutely choreographed solo dances to unforgettable choruses of more than fifty men in the Kecak, watching a Balinese dance performance never fails to enchant.

18 CLIMBING RINJANI (LOMBOK)

See page 256

The most challenging and rewarding climb on the islands takes in a dramatic crater lake with its own volcano rising from the waters.

19 NUSA LEMBONGAN

See page 95

Laidback island life, fine coastal scenery and exceptional diving and snorkelling are all just a short boat ride from Bali's mainland.

20 GILI ISLANDS

See page 274

Dazzlingly white sand, turquoise waters and zero road traffic – Lombok's three Gilis are real desert islands.

17

18

19

20

Itineraries

The following itineraries feature a mix of popular and off-the-beaten-path attractions, taking you right across Bali and Lombok, from volcanic foothills and cultural hubs to idyllic tropical islands and bustling cities. You may not have time to complete a full list, but even doing a partial itinerary – or mixing and matching elements from different ones – will give you a wonderful insight into the two islands. The trips below give you a flavour of what the islands' have to offer and what we can plan and book for you at http://roughguides.com/trips.

THE GRAND TOUR

You'll need around three to four weeks to complete this comprehensive trip around Bali and Lombok, though there are numerous places that will tempt you to extend your stay.

❶ **Bukit Peninsula** Expect spectacular views, world-class surf, the magnificent Pura Uluwatu temple and a fine choice of stylish hotels in this emerging region. See page 73

❷ **Kuta–Legian–Seminyak** This busy south Bali conurbation has something for all tastes, with rowdy Kuta, chic Seminyak and the more family-friendly Legian. See page 54

❸ **Canggu** Bali's most fashionable district is a semi-rural region replete with gorgeous bars, restaurants and surf beaches. See page 62

❹ **Pura Tanah Lot** This spectacularly sited temple – perched on a rocky crag overlooking a black-sand, wave-lashed beach – is a favourite sunset spot for tourists. See page 215

❺ **Ubud** Bali's artistic, musical and cultural hub, laidback Ubud has an array of tempting boutique hotels, restaurants, shops and spas that make it an easy place to linger. See page 108

❻ **Gunung Batur** There are stupendous views from the summit of this volcanic peak, especially at sunrise – and after descending, you can sink into one of the hot springs beside the turquoise Danau Batur lake. See page 186

❼ **Gunung Agung and Besakih** Bali's highest peak, the dramatic, 3031m Gunung Agung volcano, is home to a number of important religious sites, most notably Besakih, the Mother Temple. See pages 156 and 157

❽ **The Gili Islands** From Padang Bai hop on a fast boat to Lombok's Gili Islands. This trio of blissfully traffic-free islands has beautiful beaches and reefs. Choose between pumping nightlife on Gili Trawangan, sheer tranquillity on Gili Meno, or the more local feel of Gili Air. See page 274

❾ **Gunung Rinjani** The climb up the 3726m Gunung Rinjani is the most challenging and rewarding trek on either Bali or Lombok. See page 256

❿ **Kuta and south coast Lombok** This fastly developing area is a stunning stretch of coastline with giant white-sand bays. See page 264

SAND, SCUBA AND SURF

You'll need around three weeks to visit all of these destinations, though many people end up staying longer in Lombok's Gili Islands than they originally planned.

❶ **South Bali** Learn to surf on Kuta Beach or in Canggu. If you're more experienced, head to the adrenaline-pumping breaks at Uluwatu, Dreamland, Bingin and Padang Padang. See page 54

❷ **Liberty wreck** Just off the coast of Tulamben, the wreck of the *Liberty*, a US cargo ship torpedoed in 1942, is Bali's most popular dive site. See page 181

❸ **Nusa Lembongan and Nusa Penida** These two relaxed islands have a very different feel to the mainland. Divers regularly encounter manta rays and sunfish. See pages 95 and 101

❹ **The Gili Islands** From Lembongan, catch a boat to the Gilis, Lombok. The dive sites surrounding these islands are some of the best in Lombok – turtles, sharks and moray eels are all common – and there are some great beaches too. See page 274

❺ **Kuta, Lombok** This little town is fast emerging as a prime tourist centre, with some of Indonesia's most spectacular beaches and world-class surf close by. See page 265

❻ **Sekotong, the southwest peninsula** An isolated region, the "other Gilis" are white-sand islets that are a haven for snorkellers, divers, surfers and sunseekers alike. See page 246

ART AND CULTURE

This itinerary can be completed in as little as a week and a half if you have your own vehicle, though a more leisurely timescale allows for a more contemplative exploration and makes it easier to travel by public transport.

❶ **Bali Museum** This museum in Bali's capital, Denpasar, provides an excellent introduction to the island's cultural heritage. See page 86

❷ **Ubud** Watch a traditional dance or gamelan performance, admire paintings by Balinese and expat artists, or learn a new skill – from cooking to silversmithing. See page 108

❸ **Semarapura and the Nyoman Gunarsa Museum** Semarapura is a centre of classical Balinese art, while nearby is the enlightening Nyoman Gunarsa Museum. See pages 153 and 156

❹ **Taman Tirtagangga Water Palace** Built in 1946 by the last Karangasem raja, this palace has a number of sacred pools, moats and fountains. See page 174

❺ **Pura Meduwe Karang** This grand temple on Bali's northern coast features exquisite carvings and reliefs. See page 207

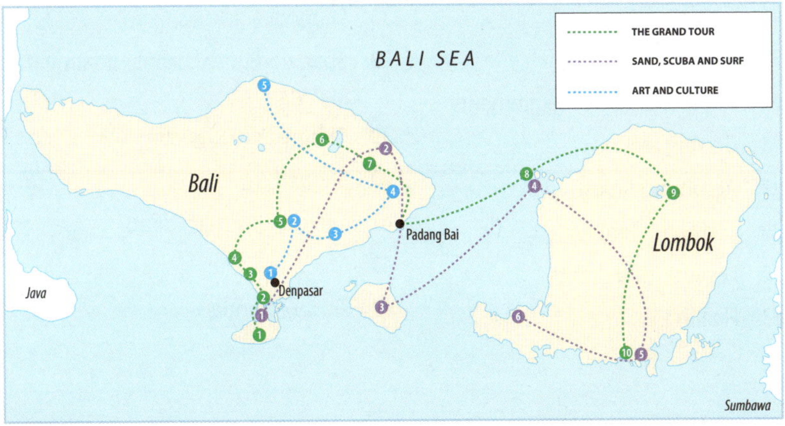

RICE AND CORN FIELDS, UBUD

Basics

Getting there

There's no shortage of international and domestic flights to Bali's only airport, Ngurah Rai International Airport (see page 87) – officially referred to as Denpasar (DPS), though it's actually 3km south of Kuta. Lombok International Airport, listed as LOP or Praya (see page 240), in the south of the island, also has a range of domestic and a few international flights.

The most expensive times to fly to Bali and Lombok are during **high season**, which for most airlines runs from the beginning of July through to the middle or end of August and also includes most of December and the first half of January. During these peak periods, flights should be reserved well in advance.

Note that plans for a new North Bali international airport at Kubutambahan have been approved, although construction is unlikely to begin before 2027, while Lombok Airport is currently undergoing a major redevelopment expected to be completed by 2028.

Flights from the UK and Ireland

There are no nonstop flights **from the UK or Ireland** to Bali or Lombok. Singapore Airlines and Emirates offer some of the fastest London–Denpasar flights; all require a brief transfer but can get you to Bali in as little as seventeen hours. They are often competitively priced against the other major airlines that serve Bali, most of which require longer transit times and can take up to 22 hours.

To Lombok

Lombok is served by a far smaller range of international flights operated by Scoot and Indonesia AirAsia. Alternatively, take the cheapest available flight to Bali or Jakarta, from where you can take an inexpensive domestic flight to Lombok.

Flights from the US and Canada

There's a big choice of flights to Bali **from North America**, although none are direct. Flights leaving from the **west coast** cross the Pacific to Asian hubs such as Taipei, Seoul, Tokyo, Hong Kong, Singapore or Kuala Lumpur, with connections on to Bali. The best journey times are around 24 hours (crossing the Pacific in one hop), although considerably more than this is not unusual; slower journeys touch down midway, perhaps in Honolulu and/or Guam, while some schedules involve overnighting en route. From the **east coast**, airlines take a northern trajectory "over the top"; for example, New York–Tokyo is typically fourteen hours and New York–Bangkok is twenty hours.

Flights from Australia, New Zealand and South Africa

Scores of flights are operated every day **from Australia to Bali** by Qantas, Virgin Australia and Malindo Air, with the best deals on low-cost carriers such as Jetstar and Garuda.

Air New Zealand has (seasonal, May to October) direct flights to Bali from Auckland (9hr). Alternatively, shop around for the cheapest Sydney flight, then change onto one of the budget airlines listed above.

At the time of writing, there were no direct flights to **Lombok**; travel via Bali.

There are no nonstop flights **from South Africa** to Bali or Lombok but it's possible to reach Bali in around 18 to 22 hours with Singapore Airlines via Singapore and Emirates via Dubai.

TRAVEL AGENTS AND TOUR OPERATORS

For most tours, including specialist diving and surfing programmes, it can work out cheaper to contact Bali- and Lombok-based operators direct, thus eliminating the foreign tour operator that will sub-contract to local businesses.

Ampersand Travel UK http://ampersandtravel.com. Specialises in off-beat luxury trips using boutique lodges in extraordinary locations and plenty of cultural interest.

Asian Pacific Adventures US http://asianpacificadventures.com. Small-group tours including "Bali: Through an Artist's Eye", twelve days based mostly in Ubud, concentrating on art, music and culture.

Audley Travel UK http://audleytravel.com. Well-planned luxury tours around Bali and Lombok utilising choice accommodation.

Backroads US http://backroads.com. Cycling tours including an eight-day "Bali Biking" tour that takes in cooking classes, snorkelling and optional yoga.

Bali Bird Walks http://balibirdwalk.com. A variety of bird walks around Ubud.

Bali Cycling http://balicycling.com. Tours for beginners to serious riders hosted by experienced Balinese cyclers.

Bali Golden Tour http://baligoldentour.com. A wide variety of shorter and longer Bali tours (diving, rafting, cycling, fishing and more) organized by the Denpasar-based tour operator.

Intrepid Travel http://intrepidtravel.com. Well-regarded, small-group adventure tour operator, their 12-day Bali & Lombok takes in rafting, hiking and snorkelling. Also offers Bali tours for teenagers.

Perama Tour & Travel http://peramatour.com. Has many outlets on Bali and Lombok. Organizes one-day and several-day tours as

A BETTER KIND OF TRAVEL

At Rough Guides we are passionately committed to travel. We believe it helps us understand the world we live in and the people we share it with – and of course tourism is vital to many developing economies. But the scale of modern tourism has also damaged some places irreparably, and climate change is accelerated by most forms of transport, especially flying. We encourage all our authors to consider the carbon footprint of the journeys they make in the course of researching our guides.

well as trekking tours in Bali and Lombok. Provides transport and accommodation services.

Surf Travel Company Australia http://surftravel.com.au. Flights and accommodation packages – resort-based or aboard boats – to the best surf spots in Bali and Lombok.

Symbiosis Expedition Planning UK http://symbiosis-travel.com. Unusual tailor-made holidays plus small-group specialist trips to Bali focusing on diving and cycling.

Visas

Indonesia **visa laws** change frequently, so always check the latest situation before travelling. All visitors must have a passport that is valid for at least six months from the date of arrival, at least two blank passport pages, and have proof of onward or return passage.

Currently, citizens from more than 90 countries countries qualify for the 30-day single-entry e-**visa** (e-VOA) for tourism purposes, which you can apply for online prior to arrival at https://evisa.imigrasi.go.id. The list includes all European countries, the USA, Canada, Australia, New Zealand, South Africa and India. The e-VOA costs Rp 500,000 and can be applied for up to 48 hours before arrival; it's valid for up to 90 days and is renewable once for a further 30 days. Visa extensions can also be made online and cost a further Rp 500,000. Make sure to use the official immigration website, as unofficial visa websites are common. At best, you'll pay an extra fee; at worst, you'll receive a fraudulent document and be at risk of a fine.

For visits other than tourism (e.g. business or study), you must apply in advance for a visa (30 or 60 days) from an Indonesian embassy; fees vary per country. It's a complicated process and requires a recent bank statement showing a minimum balance and/or a letter from your employer, educational establishment, bank manager, accountant or solicitor certifying your obligation to return home/leave Indonesia by the designated date.

Penalties for **overstaying your visa** are severe, costing Rp 1 million per day overstayed. Note that the day you arrive counts as the first day of your visa.

Additional entry requirements

Since 2024, there are two additional steps required for all international visitors to Bali. Firstly, a one-off payment of the Bali tourism tax, which costs Rp 150,000 and can be purchased online at https://lovebali.baliprov.go.id. Checks may be carried out by local police at any time, so hold on to the QR code issued as proof of payment.

Secondly, a SATUSEHAT health pass, which you can apply for at https://sshp.kemkes.go.id. To save time, apply for both in advance, but as with visas, only use the official websites.

Indonesian embassies and consulates abroad

For comprehensive listings of **Indonesian embassies and consulates** around the world, see the "Mission" page of the website of the Indonesian Ministry of Foreign Affairs at http://kemlu.go.id.

FOREIGN EMBASSIES AND CONSULATES

Most countries maintain an **embassy** in the Indonesian capital, Jakarta, and some also have **consulates** in Bali; there are none on Lombok. Your first point of contact should always be the Bali consulate.

Australia Consulate Jl Letda Tantular 32, Renon, Denpasar 0361 2000100, http://bali.indonesia.embassy.gov.au.

Australia Embassy Jakarta; 021 2550 5555, http://indonesia.embassy.gov.au.

Canada Consulate Contact the Australian consulate in Denpasar.

Canada Embassy Jakarta; 021 2550 7800, https://international.gc.ca/country-pays/indonesia-indonesie/jakarta.aspx.

Ireland Embassy Jakarta; 021 280 943 000, http://dfa.ie.

New Zealand Embassy Jakarta; 021 2995 5800, http://mfat.govt.nz.

South Africa Embassy Jakarta; 021 2991 2500, https://dirco1.azurewebsites.net/jakarta.

UK Consulate Jl. Tantular No. 32, Renon, Denpasar; 021 2356 5200, http://gov.uk/world/organisations/british-consulate-bali.

UK Embassy Jakarta; 021 2356 5200, http://gov.uk/world/organisations/british-embassy-jakarta.

TYING THE KNOT

If you fancy the idea of getting married in Bali, the options are mind-boggling. Many hotels will organize the whole thing for you, as will any number of wedding planners. They will also advise on the paperwork and formalities, which are significant, so start planning early. Prices vary enormously and it is important to check exactly what is included. It's also a good idea to check out postings on travel forums for locations and planners. Attractive **boutique hotels** that host weddings include *Hotel Tugu Bali* and *Puri Taman Sari*. Using a villa as a setting can also be very cost-effective.

US Consulate Jl Hayam Wuruk No. 310, Renon, Denpasar; 0361 233605, http://ld.usembassy.gov.
US Embassy Jakarta; 021 5083 1000, http://id.usembassy.gov.

Customs regulations

Indonesia's **customs regulations** allow foreign nationals to import one litre of alcohol, 200 cigarettes or 25 cigars or 100g of tobacco. Laptops and video cameras are allowed if declared on entry and re-exported on departure. Import restrictions cover the usual banned items, including narcotics, weapons and pornographic material, and foreigners are also forbidden to bring in amounts of Rp100,000,000 or more in any currency. Narcotics trafficking is a serious offense, punishable by death. Indonesia is a signatory to the Convention on International Trade in Endangered Species (CITES), and so forbids import or export of products that are banned under this treaty, which includes anything made from turtle flesh or turtle shells (including tortoiseshell jewellery and ornaments), as well as anything made from ivory. Indonesian law also prohibits the export of antiquities and cultural relics, unless sanctioned by the customs department.

All international visitors to Bali are required to fill out a customs declaration form, which you can fill out online prior to arrival: https://ecd.beacukai.go.id.

Getting around

Bali and Lombok are both small enough to traverse in a few hours by road (there's no rail transport on either island), although the lack of street names, traffic congestion (in Southern Bali and Ubud) and route numbers can make things confusing if you are driving yourself. The major roads are good, carrying at least two-way traffic, and are fairly well maintained, although they see a lot of large trucks. On less-frequented routes, the roads are narrow and more likely to be potholed, while off the beaten track, they may be no more than rough tracks.

The state of the road is a reasonable indication of the frequency of **public transport**, which is generally inexpensive but offers little space or comfort and very few travellers bother with it. **Tourist shuttle buses** operate between major destinations on Bali and Lombok, and although these are more expensive, they are convenient. If you prefer to drive yourself, bicycles, motorbikes and cars are available to rent throughout the islands, or you can rent cars or motorbikes with a driver. App-based taxi services, such as Gojek (motorcycle), GoCar (car), GoRide (car) and Grab (car), operate in Bali and are inexpensive.

Getting **between Bali and Lombok** is easy by plane or boat.

Tourist shuttle buses

Most travellers use private shuttle buses to get around. The most established **operator** is Perama (http://peramatour.com), serving all major tourist destinations. Fares generally work out at least double that of public transport, but the service is usually direct and there's likely to be room for luggage, wheelchairs, buggies and surfboards. It's best to book the day before.

There are several **rival companies** operating on both Bali and Lombok who advertise throughout tourist areas and offer a similar service but are not as high profile. These are worth checking out if, for example, the Perama office is inconveniently far from the town centre (as in Lovina and Ubud).

Bemos and buses

On both Bali and Lombok, public transport predominantly consists of buses and *bemos*. **Bemos** are minibuses of varying sizes. **Buses** operate long-distance routes such as Denpasar to Singaraja, Denpasar to Amlapura, and Mataram to Labuhan Lombok. Because of the rise in motorbike ownership, *bemos* are declining on the islands year on year, making public transport ever more time-consuming. *Bemos* don't really have fixed timetables, generally leaving every hour or so (or when full).

You can pick up a bus or *bemo* from the **terminal** in bigger towns or flag one down on the road. Fares are paid to the driver or conductor, if there is one. You can't buy tickets in advance.

No local person negotiates a **fare**. When they want to get off, they yell "Stop", hop out and pay the fixed fare. Note tourists can be charged several times the local fare, and you may be charged extra for a bulky rucksack. Ask a fellow passenger what the fare should be before getting out.

Ferries and boats

Huge public inter-island **ferries** connect Bali and Lombok with the islands on either side, from Gilimanuk to Java, from Padang Bai to Lembar on Lombok and from Labuhan on Lombok to Sumbawa. They run frequently and regularly, day and night, but aren't particularly concerned with safety standards.

Many private small **boats**, the fastest but most expensive option, connect the Balinese mainland with the Gili Islands, Nusa Lembongan, Nusa Penida and Bangsal in Lombok. There are also smaller, slower boat services to Nusa Lembongan from Bali and from mainland Lombok to all three Gili Islands. A regular ferry runs from Padang Bai on Bali to Nusa Penida.

Taxis

The taxi trade in Bali is notorious, and its workings very complicated. Essentially, there are three kinds of taxi: local drivers who almost never use a meter; taxis like Blue Bird, which always use a meter; and GoCar/Grab app-taxis that you order on your smartphone (and pay for in cash). In some areas, like Kuta or Denpasar, you've a choice of all three kinds of taxi. In Ubud, the local taxi cartel blocks all metered outgoing services, while in other regions it's a grey area. In Lombok there's less hassle. There were no app-taxis in Lombok at the time of research and both Blue Bird and Express Taxi operated freely in tourist areas. Wherever you are, hotel and restaurant staff will know the score and be able to advise.

Local taxi drivers tout for business on street corners, and many villages and towns have an organised cartel of drivers who effectively monopolize the local taxi business (and intimidate cheaper rivals like app-based taxis and Blue Bird). You'll see signs all over Bali with "No Gojek" or "No Grab". These local drivers set their own (high) tariffs, which you'll have to use. Some expats refer to them as 'taxi mafia'. They'll usually allow rival cabs to drop off customers but not pick up from their patch.

Metered **taxis** have a "Taxi" (or "Taksi") sign on the roof. They cruise for business in Kuta, Sanur, Nusa Dua, Jimbaran and Denpasar on Bali, and around tourist areas on Lombok. The best companies are the highly efficient light-blue Bali Taxi on Bali (0361 701 111; http://bluebirdgroup.com) and Blue Bird and Express on Lombok (Blue Bird: 0370 627000, http://bluebirdgroup.com; Express: 1500122; http://expressgroup.co.id). Both have reasonable rates and courteous drivers.

App taxis are quite new in Bali (and not yet available in Lombok). GoCar and Grab are the two main companies. Rates vary on demand but are a lot cheaper than using local drivers and usually quite a bit less than Blue Bird or Express.

Cidomo

The traditional form of transport in Lombok was the horse and cart (*cidomo*). Today, they survive in the Gili Islands (where all motorized vehicles are banned). Prices are fixed and very expensive.

Rental vehicles

There's a big selection of vehicles available for rental on the islands; think about your itinerary before you decide what you need. In the mountains, you need power for the slopes and on rougher terrain, clearance is vital.

Renters must produce an **International Driving Permit**. On major public holidays (like Galungan and Nyepi on Bali and Idul Fitri on Lombok) vehicles are snapped up quickly, so make arrangements in advance. Rental vehicles need to have both Balinese and Lombok registration to travel on both islands, so you must tell the rental agency if you intend to take the vehicle between the islands, and check with them exactly what paperwork is required.

Local and international rental companies operate in resort areas – see the Arrival and departure and Getting around sections for the major resorts in the Guide chapters, or enquire at your hotel. Discounts are available for longer rentals.

Some outfits offer partial **insurance** as part of the fee; if no insurance is included, be sure to get your own policy. When there's a dispute between a foreigner and a local, the local usually wins. The conditions of insurance policies vary considerably, and you should make certain you know what you're signing. Bear in mind that under this system, if there is minor damage – for example, if you smash a light – you'll end up paying the whole cost of the coverage.

Before you take a vehicle, **check** it thoroughly and record any damage that has already been done, or you may end up being blamed for it. Most vehicle rental agencies keep your passport as security, so you don't have a lot of bargaining power in the case of any dispute. Wherever you get the vehicle, take an emergency telephone number to contact if your car breaks down.

On the road

Traffic in Indonesia drives **on the left**, and there's a maximum speed limit (except on tollways) of 70km/hr (though you'll be lucky to average 30km/hr in traffic-choked south and west Bali). Foreign drivers need to carry an **International Driving Permit** and the **registration documents** of the vehicle or are liable for a fine. Seatbelts must be used in front and back seats. The police carry out regular spot checks and you'll be fined for any infringements.

Occasionally police stop foreign drivers for supposed infringements and "fine" them on the spot in what is essentially an extortion racket. If it happens to you, the best advice is to keep calm and have some easily accessible notes separated well away from your main stash of cash if you have to hand some over – it's best to just do so in this scenario as arguing won't get you anywhere.

It's worth driving extremely defensively. **Accidents** are always unpleasant, disagreements over the insurance situation and any repairs can be lengthy, and many local people have a straightforward attitude to accidents involving tourists – the visitor must be to blame. Don't drive at **night** unless you absolutely have to, largely because pedestrians, cyclists, food carts and horse carts all use the roadway without any lights. There are also plenty of roadside ditches.

Note that many **petrol stations** are cash-only.

Hiring a driver

Hundreds of drivers in tourist areas offer **chartered transport** – this means you rent their vehicle (generally cars or jeeps) with them as the driver. *Ojeks* (single-passenger motorbike taxis) are also common. You're expected to pay for the driver's meals on all trips and accommodation if the trip takes more than a day, and you must be very clear about who is paying for fuel, where you want to go and stop, and how many people will be travelling. With somebody driving who knows the roads, you've got plenty of time to look around and fewer potential problems to worry about, but it's very difficult to guarantee the quality of the driving. Typically, the best recommendation of reliable drivers you can get is from your accommodation.

Motorbike and bicycle rental

Motorbikes available for rent vary from scooters through small 100cc jobs to more robust trail bikes. There are discounts for longer rentals. You are required to have an international motorcycle license, which can be obtained at the police station in Denpasar, Bali or Mataram, Lombok. Conditions on Bali and Lombok are not suitable for inexperienced drivers, with poor road signage (usually in Indonesian), heavy traffic on major routes, steep hills and difficult driving off the beaten track. There are many accidents involving tourists, so don't take risks. All motorcyclists, both drivers and passengers, must wear a helmet; these will be provided by the rental outlet, but most aren't of the best quality.

In most tourist areas, it's possible to rent a **bicycle**; check its condition before you set off and carry plenty of water. Helmets, puncture repair kits and locks may or may not be provided so, if you intend to cycle a lot, it would be wise to take your own. There is occasional bag-snatching from bicycles in less populated areas, so attach your bag securely to yourself or the bike. Ubud is a popular area for cycling day-trips and guided rides and they are available in Lombok on the Gili Islands cycling is the only way to get around, other than walking or in a horse cart.

Flights

Tickets for all domestic flights can be booked online, or there are ticket sales counters in airports.

Accommodation

Whatever your budget, the overall standard of accommodation in Bali and Lombok is very high. Even basic lodgings are generally enticing, nearly always set in a tropical garden and with outdoor seating. Interiors can be a bit sparse – and dimly lit – but the verandas encourage you to do as local people do and spend your waking hours outdoors.

Most budget places to stay are classed as *losmen*, a term that literally means homestay but most commonly describes any small-scale and inexpensive accommodation. Some offer the option of hot water and air conditioning, and many include **breakfast** (*makan pagi* or *sarapan*) in the price of the room. *Losmen* rooms are generally designed for two or more people, so solo travellers will normally be given a double room at the same price regardless of whether one or two people stay. Hostels, with dorm beds and

ACCOMMODATION PRICES

Unless stated otherwise, all the accommodation prices in this guide are based on the cost of the cheapest double room in high season, including tax. Rates in low season may be up to fifty percent lower and booking via online agencies at any time may give you significant discounts. Many *losmen* and hotels quote their rates exclusive of government **tax** (ten or eleven percent); many of the more expensive hotels add an extra five or ten percent **service charge** (in hotel-speak, these supplements are usually referred to as "plus-plus").

The smartest hotels quote their rates in **US dollars**, or sometimes in **euros**, and usually accept cash and credit cards, but will also convert to rupiah.

Small establishments are unlikely to have websites and list with online booking sites instead. If no website is listed in the guide, check Instagram and Facebook for information, as both have become popular with small business owners.

ACCOMMODATION PRICES CODES

Throughout the guide, accommodation is categorized according to a price code, which roughly corresponds to the following price ranges. Price categories reflect the cost of a double room, without breakfast, in peak season.

$ under = US$50
$$ = US$51–120
$$$ = US$121–200
$$$$ = over US$200

a social vibe, are also becoming part of the accommodation scene in key backpacker hangouts like Kuta Bali and Gili Trawangan.

Nearly all other accommodation falls into the **hotels** category, most of which offer air conditioning and a swimming pool. Rooms in both *losmen* and hotels are often in "**cottages**" (sometimes known as "**bungalows**"), which can be anything from terraced concrete cubes to detached rice-barn-style chalets (*lumbung*). Bali in particular, does **boutique hotels** very well: small, intimate places, often with gorgeous rural views and tasteful Balinese furnishings. The islands' **super-luxury hotels** tend to give you more for your money than similarly priced hotels in the West, especially when suites come with private plunge pools and living areas.

BALI AND LOMBOK'S TOP 5 PLACES TO STAY

Ubud's green haven, Bali: *Bambu Indah*. See page 127
Stylish seaside resort, Lombok: *Qunci Villas*. See page 252
Fantasy island hotel, Lombok: *Tugu Lombok*. See page 256
Home away from home, Bali: *Griya Valud*. See page 161
Safari elegance, Bali: *Menjangan Dynasty*. See page 228

Villas are luxurious private holiday homes with pools and kitchens; they're especially good for families. They can be rented by the day or week and often include the services of a housekeeper and cook. Be aware, though, that a growing number of villas operate illegally, without government licences, which means they could get closed down at any time; you may be able to check a villa's licence online, and licences must be displayed prominently on the premises. Online villa-rental **agencies** include http://balilongtermrentals.com and http://balivillas.com. Airbnb (http://airbnb.com) also has a wide selection of villas and apartments.

Camping is not popular in Bali. Camping in Bali Barat National Park can only be arranged at the park headquarters and it's considered inappropriate to camp on the slopes of Bali's most sacred mountains; however, camping on Lombok's Gunung Rinjani is normal practice, and tents and sleeping bags can be rented for the climb.

Room rates in all classes of accommodation can vary considerably according to demand. During **low season** (Feb–June and Sept–Nov) many moderate and expensive hotels also offer good discounts on internet and walk-in rates. In **peak season** (July, Aug and the Christmas holidays), however, rates can rise dramatically. All rooms are at a premium during these months and places get booked out so it's advisable to **reserve** well in advance. **Check-out time** is usually noon. Note that during the Idul Fitri (Eid al-Fitri)

BATHROOMS

Most *losmen* and hotel rooms have en-suite **bathrooms** (*kamar mandi*). **Toilets** (*wc*, pronounced *way say*) are usually Western style, though flushing is sometimes done manually, with water scooped from an adjacent pail. The same pail and scoop are used by Indonesians to wash themselves after going to the toilet (using the left hand, never the right, which is for eating), but most tourist bathrooms also have toilet paper.

Many Balinese and Sasak people still **bathe** in rivers, but indoor bathing is traditionally done by means of the scoop and slosh method, or **mandi**, using water that's stored in a huge basin. This basin is not a bath, so never get in it; all washing is done outside it and the basin should not be contaminated by soap or shampoo. Many *losmen* and all hotels in the bigger resort areas provide showers as well as *mandi*. Outside the bigger resorts, the very cheapest rooms may not have hot water (*air panas*).

In the more stylish places, bathrooms can be delightful, particularly if they are designed to be open to the sky and bedecked with plants. These "**garden bathrooms**" often have showers and *mandi* fed by water piped through sculpted flues and floors covered in a carpet of smooth, rounded pebbles. However, they're not to everyone's taste, especially as they can also attract squadrons of bloodthirsty mosquitoes.

holidays (May–June) millions of Indonesians travel, making transportation and hotel reservations difficult to obtain and prices to soar.

Food and drink

Bali and Lombok cuisine is spicy, sweet and incredibly varied with rich curries, fragrant soups, delicious noodle dishes, steamed vegetables and Chinese-style stir-fries all competing for your tummy's attention. The more local you go, the more authentic the meal. In the main tourist regions, most restaurants tend to serve more generic Indonesian food and a multitude of Western and Asian dishes. For really genuine Balinese and Sasak food, head to night markets and *warung* (simple local cafés).

At the inexpensive end of the scale, you can get a bowl of *bakso ayam* (chicken noodle soup) from one of the **carts** (*kaki lima*) on the streets and at night markets after dark. Slightly smarter are **warung** and *rumah makan* (eating houses), ranging from a few tables and chairs in a kitchen to fully fledged **restaurants**. There's usually a menu, but in the simplest places it's just rice or noodle dishes on offer. Most places that call themselves restaurants cater for a broader range of tastes, offering Western, Indonesian and Chinese food, while others specialize in a particular cuisine such as Mexican, Japanese or Italian. The multinational fast-food chains have also arrived in the tourist and city areas.

Vegetarians get a good deal, with tofu (*tahu*) and *tempeh*, a fermented soybean cake, alongside plenty of fresh vegetables.

Restaurant **etiquette** is pretty much the same as in the West, with waiter service the norm. If you're eating with friends, don't count on everyone's meal arriving together.

Prices vary dramatically depending on the location rather than the quality of the meals. Bear in mind that restaurants with more expensive food also have pricier drinks and, in addition, most places add anything up to 21 percent to the bill for tax and service.

In the Language section of the guide there is a menu reader of dishes and a list of common terms (see page 332).

Cooking styles

Throughout Bali and Lombok **Indonesian** rice- and noodle-based meals are most widely available,

EATING PRICES CODES

Throughout the guide, eating out listings are categorized according to a price code, which roughly corresponds to the following price ranges. Price categories reflect the cost of a two-course meal for one with a drink.

$ = under US$7
$$ = US$8–15
$$$ = US$16–25
$$$$ = over US$25

BALI AND LOMBOK'S TOP 5 RESTAURANTS

Mozaic Ubud. See page 128
One Eyed Jack Canggu. See page 70
Sardine Kerobokan. See page 69
Café Wayan Ubud. See page 128
Sage Ubud. See page 128

followed closely by **Chinese** (essentially Cantonese) food, as well as a vast array of other Asian (Thai and Japanese especially) and **Western** food in the resorts. Native Balinese food on Bali, and Sasak food on Lombok, is something you'll need to seek out. Should you wish to learn more about local food, check out the cookery schools for visitors (see page 44).

Indonesian food

Based on rice (*nasi*) or noodles (*mie* or *bakmi*), with vegetables, fish or meat, **Indonesian food** is flavoured with chillies, sweet soy sauce (*kecap manis*), garlic, ginger, candlenut, turmeric and lemongrass. You'll also find chilli sauce (*sambal*) everywhere.

One dish available in even the simplest ***warung*** is **nasi campur**, which is boiled rice with small amounts of vegetables, meat and fish, often served with *krupuk* (huge prawn crackers) and a boiled egg. The accompanying dishes vary from day to day, depending on what's available. Other tourist staples are **nasi goreng** and **mie goreng**, fried rice (*nasi*) or noodles (*mie*) with vegetables, meat or fish, often with fried egg and *krupuk*. The other mainstays of the Indonesian menu are **gado-gado**, steamed vegetables served with a spicy peanut sauce, and **sate**, small kebabs of beef, pork, chicken, tofu, goat or fish, barbecued on a bamboo stick and served with spicy peanut sauce.

Fish is widely available: grilled, skewered, baked in banana leaves or in curries. However, although tasty, by Western standards a lot of it is overcooked.

Inexpensive, authentic and traditionally fiery Sumatran **Padang** dishes are sold in *rumah makan* Padang in every sizeable town. Padang food is pre-cooked, served room temperature and displayed on platters in the *warung*'s front window. There are no menus; when you enter you either select your composite meal by pointing to the dishes on display, or just sit down and let the staff bring you a selection – at the end of the meal, you pay for the food you have taken from the platters. Dishes include *kangkung* (water spinach), *tempeh* (fermented soybean cake), fried aubergine, curried eggs, fried fish, meat curry, fish curry, potato cakes and fried cow's lung.

Balinese food

The everyday **Balinese** diet consists of a couple of rice-based meals, essentially *nasi campur*, eaten whenever people feel hungry, supplemented with whatever snack is handy. The full magnificence of Balinese cooking is reserved for ceremonies. One of the best dishes is **babi guling**, spit-roasted pig, served with *lawar*, a spicy blood mash. Another speciality is **betutu bebek**, smoked duck, cooked very slowly – this has to be ordered in advance from restaurants.

The Balinese rarely eat desserts, but **bubuh injin**, black rice pudding, named after the colour of the rice husk, is available in tourist spots. The rice is sweetened with palm sugar and coconut milk, and occasionally contains mung beans. *Krupuk* (shrimp crackers) play a major part in ceremonial offerings but are also a daily food.

Sasak food

According to some sources, the name "Lombok" translates as "chilli pepper" – highly appropriate considering the savage heat of traditional **Sasak food**. It's not easy to track down, however, and you'll find Indonesian and Chinese food far more widely available on Lombok. Traditional Sasak food uses rice as the staple, together with a wide variety of vegetables, a little meat (although no pork), and some fish, served in various sauces, often with a dish of **chilli sauce** on the side in case it isn't hot enough already. Anything with *pelecing* in the name is served with

BETEL

One habit that you'll notice in villages, mainly among older people, is betel chewing. Small parcels, made up of three ingredients – slices of dried areca nut wrapped in spicy *Piper* betel leaf that has been smeared with lime powder – are lodged inside the cheek. The mixture is a stimulant, and the lime powder produces an abundance of bright red saliva, which is regularly spat out on the ground and eventually stains the lips and teeth red. Other ingredients can be added according to taste, including tobacco, cloves, cinnamon, cardamom, turmeric and nutmeg. You may also come across decorated boxes used to store the ingredients on display in museums.

METHANOL WARNING

Be aware that **methanol-related deaths** occur most years in Bali and Lombok. Incidents are rare but have occurred in bars popular with backpackers, when cheap cocktail buckets have been tainted with methanol. Opt for sealed or bottled drinks or stick to beer if in any doubt.

chilli sauce. *Taliwang* dishes, originally from Sumbawa, are also available on Lombok, consisting of grilled or fried food with, you've guessed it, a chilli sauce. All parts of the animals are eaten, and you'll find plenty of offal on the menu.

Fine dining

Just as it's possible to get by spending a dollar or less for a meal in Bali or Lombok, you can also find some superb **fine dining** experiences on the islands. Plenty of innovative chefs, some Western, some Asian, have imported and adapted modern international gourmet cooking. They offer menus that are creative and imaginative and, best of all, taste great. Restaurants serving this food are invariably stylish, with excellent service.

Fresh fruit

The range of **fresh fruit** available on Bali and Lombok is startling. You'll see **bananas**, **coconuts** and **papaya** growing all year round, and **pineapples** and **watermelons** are always in the markets. Of the citrus fruits, the giant **pomelo** is the most unusual to visitors – larger than a grapefruit and sweeter. **Guavas**, **avocados** (served as a sweet fruit juice with condensed milk), **passion fruit**, **mangoes**, **soursops** and their close relative, the **custard apple**, are all common. Less familiar are seasonal **mangosteens** with a purple skin and sweet white flesh; hairy **rambutans**, closely related to the lychee; **salak** or **snakefruit**, named after its brown scaly skin; and **star fruit**, which is crunchy but rather flavourless. **Jackfruit**, which usually weighs 10–20kg, has firm yellow segments around a large stone inside its green bobbly skin. This is not to be confused with the **durian**, also large but with a spiky skin and a pungent, sometimes almost rotten, odour. Airlines and hotels ban it because of the smell, but devoted fans travel large distances and pay high prices for good-quality durian fruit.

Drinks

Bottled water (see page 35) is widely available throughout the islands, as are international brands of **soft drinks**; you'll pay higher prices in restaurants. There are also delicious **fruit juices**, although many restaurants automatically add sugar to their juices so you'll need to specify *tampa gulah* (without sugar) if you don't want that.

Indonesians are great **coffee** (*kopi*) and **tea** (*teh*) drinkers. Locally grown coffee (*kopi Bali* or *kopi Lombok*) is drunk black, sweet and strong. The coffee isn't filtered, so the grounds settle in the bottom of the glass. If you want milk added or you don't want sugar, you'll have to ask. Increasing numbers of espresso machines have arrived in the smarter tourist restaurants along with imported coffee, so lattes and flat whites are readily available if you want one. One coffee you could consider avoiding is *kopi luwak*, which is an expensive blend made from coffee beans that have been ingested, and then secreted by civets. Most of these captive civets are kept in cramped, inhumane conditions.

Alcohol

Locally produced **beer** includes Bintang, a light, reasonably palatable lager. Draught beer is available in some places. For other locally produced beers – which are cheaper than the imported varieties – look for Bali Hai, Anker, San Miguel and Heineken.

Many tourist restaurants and bars offer an extensive list of **cocktails** and imported spirits; the cheaper cocktails are invariably made with local alcohol.

Wine and spirit lovers should be aware that punitive taxes make drinking extremely expensive in Bali and Lombok. Locally produced **wine** is made from grapes grown in the north of Bali by Hatten Wines – their Aga White, rosé and sparkling wines are very drinkable. Other companies, including Two Islands and Plaga use imported Australian grapes to produce wines. Sababay uses grapes grown on Bali. Imported spirits are available in major tourist areas, where wines from Australia and New Zealand, California and Chile are also generally available but pricey.

Local liquors include *brem*, a type of rice wine, *tuak*, palm wine brewed from palm-tree sap, and powerful *arak*, a palm or rice spirit that is often incorporated into highly potent local cocktails. Be very wary of all three, which – unbeknownst to you – can be mixed with scary stuff, such as insecticides, for a more powerful punch.

Happy hours are common in tourist areas.

Festivals and events

Religious ceremonies and festivals remain central to Balinese life and anyone spending more than a few days on the island is likely to spot local people heading to or from temples. Visitors are welcome as long as they follow certain rules of etiquette (see page 38). Hindus on Lombok adhere to the same customs, and their staunchly Islamic Sasaks have their own ceremonies. On top of these, an array of non-religious festivals are equally appealing.

Balinese festivals

Bali has a complex timetable of religious ceremonies and festivals, both local and island-wide, made even more complicated by Bali having two **traditional calendars**; the *saka* calendar, with 354–355 days, is divided into twelve months and runs eighty years behind the Gregorian year, while the *pawukon* calendar is based on a 210-day lunar cycle. One of the biggest holidays is **Galungan**, an annual event in the *pawukon* calendar. This ten-day festival celebrates the victory of good over evil, and the ancestral souls are thought to visit earth. Elaborate preparations take place: *penyor* – bamboo poles hung with offerings – arch over the road. Galungan day itself is spent with the family. The final and most important day is **Kuningan**, when families once again get together, pray and make offerings as the souls of the ancestors return to heaven.

The main festival of the *saka* year is New Year, **Nyepi**, generally in March or April, the major purification ritual of the year. The night before Nyepi, the evil spirits are frightened away with drums, gongs, cymbals, firecrackers and huge **papier-mâché monsters** (*ogoh-ogoh*). On the day itself, everyone sits quietly at home to persuade any remaining evil spirits that Bali is completely deserted. Visitors are expected to stay quietly in their hotels and the airport is closed.

Every temple has an annual **odalan**, an anniversary and purification ceremony. The majority of these are small, local affairs, but the celebrations at the large directional temples draw huge crowds. There are also local temple festivals related to the moon, some associated with full moon and some with the night of complete darkness.

Another annual event, **Saraswati**, in honour of the goddess of knowledge (see page 303), takes place on the last day of the *pawukon* year. Books are particularly venerated and offerings are made to them in temples, while students attend special ceremonies to pray for academic success. Other annual festivals are **Tumpek Kandang**, when all animals are blessed, and **Tumpek Landep**, a day of devotion to all things made of metal, including tools, motorbikes, cars and buses. On these days you will see colourful offerings adorning animals and machines, indicating that they've been blessed by a priest.

Nonreligious anniversaries that are celebrated in Bali and Lombok include April 21, **Kartini Day**, commemorating the birthday in 1879 of Raden Ajeng Kartini, an early Indonesian nationalist and the first female emancipationist. Parades, lectures and social events are attended by women and children and women in offices often don traditional garb in celebration of their heroine. On Bali, September 20, the anniversary of the **Badung puputan** in Denpasar in 1906 (see page 295), is commemorated each year by a fair in Alun-alun Puputan (town square). Throughout Indonesia November 20 is **Heroes Day**, and in Bali it's celebrated as a remembrance of the defeat of the nationalist forces led by Ngurah Rai at Marga in 1946 (see page 297).

The huge month-long **Bali Arts Festival** celebrates all Balinese arts including traditional music, gamelan recitals and film and documentary screenings with international performers joining in. It's held annually at Denpasar's Taman Werdhi Budaya Arts Centre (Bali Arts Centre) from mid-June. Watersports competitions and parades are the highlights of the **Kuta Karnival**, which runs for a week, usually in October. In Ubud, there's the **Bali Spirit Festival** of world music, dance and yoga every March (http://balispiritfestival.com) and the **Ubud Writers and Readers Festival** (http://ubudwritersfestival.com), with nearly two hundred events, talks and workshops from an international cast of writers, every October.

Lombok's festivals

Lombok's festivals are a mixture of Hindu, Muslim and local folk events. **Ciwaratri** (in Jan) is celebrated by Hindus in West Lombok, where followers meditate without sleeping or eating for 24 hours to redeem their sins. A far more public occasion is **Nyale** (see page 264), which takes place every February or March near Kuta and along the south coast, attracting thousands of people to witness the first appearance of sea worms. **West Lombok's Anniversary**, a formal government event, takes place on April 17. **Harvest festivals** are celebrated by Lombok's Balinese Hindus in March/April at Gunung Pengsong, when they give thanks for the harvest by the ritual slaughter of a buffalo. **Lebaran Topat** occurs seven days after Ramadan, when Sasak people visit family graves at the sacred Loang Baloq Cemetery on the edge of Mataram.

In November or December comes **Perang Topat**, informally known as the **Ketupat War** (see page 245). A riotous and spectacular public rice-throwing battle between local Hindus and Wetu Telu followers that takes place at Pura Lingsar in Mataram. Simultaneously, the **Pujawali** celebration is held at Pura Kalasa temple in Narmada, Pura Lingsar and Pura Meru in Mataram. Also around this time, offerings are made at Gunung Rinjani's crater lake, Segara Anak, to ask for blessings, known as **Pekelem**. December 17 marks the anniversary of the political **founding of West Nusa Tenggara**. **Chinese New Year** (Imlek) sees many Chinese-run businesses throughout Indonesia closing for several days in January or February. Finally, two international sporting events are featured in Lombok annually, the Pertamina Grand Prix of Indonesia in March and the Gunung Rinjani 100 long-distance race in June.

Health

Most travellers to Bali and Lombok experience no health issues. Traveller's diarrhoea ("Bali belly") will affect some. However, serious illness and accidents (including surfers' mishaps) can't be ruled out. All visitors should have travel insurance in case private health care and medical evacuation is needed (see page 46).

Discuss your trip with your **doctor** or a specialist travel clinic (see page 36) as early as possible to allow time to complete courses of **inoculations**. If you've come directly from a country with yellow fever, you'll need to be immunized and you should carry the immunization certificate. Apart from this no inoculations are legally required for Indonesia. However, inoculations against the following should be discussed with your medical adviser: diphtheria, hepatitis A, hepatitis B, Japanese encephalitis, polio, rabies, tetanus, typhoid and tuberculosis.

If you have any medical conditions, are pregnant or are travelling with children, it is especially important to get advice. If you need regular medication, carry it in your hand baggage along with a certificate/letter from your doctor detailing your condition and the drugs, which can be handy for overzealous customs officials.

Treatment in Bali and Lombok

You'll find **pharmacies** (*apotik*), village **health clinics** (*klinik*) and **doctors** across the islands and **public hospitals** in each district capital and in Denpasar, supplemented by **specialist international clinics** in the main tourist areas. In local facilities the availability of English-speaking staff and their ability to tackle accidents and common tourist ailments varies from area to area. Most Balinese use local facilities together with traditional healers (*balian*) as they believe that physical symptoms are a sign of spiritual illness.

If you need an **English-speaking doctor**, seek advice at your hotel (some of the luxury ones have in-house doctors). For more serious problems, you'll want to access private **clinics** in the main resorts. A few places on Bali have international standard facilities. Bali International Medical Centre (BIMC) has a clinic in Ubud and hospitals in Nusa Dua and Kuta and International SOS (see page 72) clinic offer consultations, dentistry, doctor call-out and ambulance service (prices depend on the time of day or night and distance from the clinic). The primary tourist-friendly hospital on Lombok is Rumah Sakit Harapan Keluarga, (0370 617 7000, http://harapankeluarga.co.id, Jl. Ahmad Yani No. 9, Mataram) with medevac and dentistry services. There are two hyperbaric **recompression chambers** on Bali, one located in Denpasar (see page 89) and one in Saba, East Bali (see page 150); there is another on Lombok (see page 277). Details of local medical facilities including **dentists** (*doctor gigi*) are given in the Directory section of each city account in the guide.

Major diseases

Bali and Lombok are home to a range of diseases endemic to tropical Southeast Asia, most of which are not a threat in travellers' home countries. Inoculations are therefore strongly advised.

Most Western travellers will have had inoculations against **polio**, **tetanus**, **diphtheria** and **tuberculosis** during childhood. Travellers should check that they are still covered against these diseases and have booster injections if necessary.

Typhoid can be lethal and is passed through contaminated food or water. It produces an extremely high fever, abdominal pains, headaches, diarrhoea and red spots on the body. Dehydration is a danger here as with all intestinal problems, so drink plenty of fluids, take rehydration salts and get medical help urgently. Inoculation and personal hygiene measures (see page 34) offer the best protection.

Avoid contact with all animals, no matter how cute, especially street dogs and temple monkeys.

Rabies is spread via the saliva of infected animals, most commonly cats, dogs or monkeys; it is endemic throughout Asia and all visitors to Bali should be aware of the disease. Bali was rabies-free for ten years until 2008 but since then the disease has re-established itself and it's now present throughout the island. If you see a suspicious dog you can contact the Bali Animal Welfare Association (http://bawabali.com).

Hundreds of people have died in the last decade despite a major culling and vaccination programme. If you get bitten, wash the wound immediately with antiseptic and get medical help. Treatment involves a course of injections, but you won't need all of them if you have had a course of pre-departure jabs. Lombok was officially rabies-free in 2016, but given its proximity to Bali the same precautions should be taken.

Japanese encephalitis is a serious viral illness causing inflammation of the brain. It is endemic across Asia and is transmitted from infected birds and animals via mosquitoes. Inoculation is available for those planning extended periods in rural areas who are most at risk, although it is rare among travellers. The symptoms are variable but flu-like headache, fever and vomiting are common and the best advice is to seek medical help immediately if you develop these.

There are several strains of **hepatitis** (caused by viral infections) and vaccines can offer some protection against some strains. Symptoms in all of them are a yellow colouring of the skin and eyes, extreme exhaustion, fever and diarrhoea. It's one of the most common illnesses that afflicts travellers to Asia and can last for months and can also lead to chronic illness. Hepatitis A is transmitted via contaminated food and water or saliva. Hepatitis B is more serious and is transmitted via sexual contact or by contaminated blood, needles or syringes, which means that medical treatment itself can pose a risk if sterilization procedures are not up to scratch.

Malaria

Both Bali and Lombok are within **malarial zones**. Information regarding the prevalence, prevention and treatment of malaria is being constantly updated so you must seek medical advice at least a month before you travel. Current advice suggests that there is very little risk of malaria in Bali, but a low risk in Lombok. The latest information shows an increase in the most serious form of malaria across Asia and there are reports of resistance to certain drug treatments by some strains. Pregnant women and children need specialist advice.

Malaria, which can be fatal, is passed into humans in mosquito bites (one is all it takes). The appropriate prophylactic drug depends on your destination but all are taken to a strict timetable, beginning before you enter the malarious area and continuing after leaving. If you don't follow instructions precisely, you're in danger of developing the illness. The symptoms are fever, headache and shivering, similar to a severe dose of flu and often coming in cycles, but a lot of people have additional symptoms. Don't delay seeking help: malaria progresses quickly. If you develop flu-like symptoms at any time up to a year after returning home, you should inform a doctor of your travels and ask for a blood test.

However, none of the antimalarial drugs are a hundred percent effective and it is vital to try to stop the mosquitoes biting you: wear long sleeves and long trousers in infected areas, as malaria-bearing mosquitoes bite at night sleep under a **mosquito net** (preferably one impregnated with an insecticide especially suited to the task), burn mosquito coils, and use **repellent** on exposed skin. The most powerful repellents should be brought from home; DEET is effective but can be an irritant and natural alternatives are available containing citronella, eucalyptus oil or neem oil.

Dengue fever

Another reason to avoid mosquito bites is **dengue fever**, caused by a virus carried by a different species of mosquito, which bites during the day. While malaria is more prevalent in rural settings, dengue fever thrives among urban populations. There is no vaccine or tablet available to prevent the illness – which causes fever, headache and joint and muscle pains among the least serious symptoms, and internal bleeding and circulatory system failure among the most serious – and no specific drug to cure it. Outbreaks occur across Indonesia throughout the year, but particularly during the rainy season. It is vital to get an early medical diagnosis and obtain treatment to relieve symptoms. Most importantly, keep from being bitten by covering up as much exposed skin as possible and using repellent as described above.

AIDS/HIV

Bali has a high rate of HIV/AIDS cases; bear in mind, as well, that other travellers may be infected. Many people with HIV are also infected with hepatitis. **Condoms** can be bought on both islands, but it's advisable to bring your own too.

General precautions

Precautions while you are travelling can reduce your chances of getting ill. Personal hygiene is vital and it pays to use some discretion about choosing where to eat – if the bits you can see are filthy, imagine the state of the kitchen. Avoid **food** that has sat around in the heat in favour of freshly cooked meals; food prepared in fancy tourist places is just as likely to be suspect as that from simple street stalls. **Ice** is supposedly prepared under regulated conditions in Indonesia, but it's impossible to be sure how it has been transported or stored since leaving the factory. If you're being really careful, avoid ice in your drinks – a lot easier said than done in the heat. Treat even small cuts or scrapes with antiseptic and cover them to prevent infection. Wear flip-flops or thongs in the bathroom rather than walk around barefoot and close-toed shoes when trekking.

Water hygiene

Do not drink untreated tap **water** on Bali or Lombok, as it is likely to contain disease-causing micro-organisms. **Bottled water** is available everywhere and refilling facilities are becoming more widespread (in attempts to cut down on plastic waste and be more environmentally-friendly). Or you can buy **purifying tablets**, **water filters** and **water purifiers** from travel clinics and specialist outdoor-equipment retailers. Note that in some *losmen* drinking water is often served hot in a Thermos indicating that it has been boiled. Indonesians are very much aware of the need to boil water before drinking it and generally water, tea or coffee served hot is safe to drink.

Heat and skin problems

Travellers are at risk of **sunburn** and **dehydration**. It's wise to bring your own sunscreen, which is available in Bali (less so in Lombok) but more expensive than in the West. Limit exposure to the sun in the hours around noon, use high-factor sunscreen (reapplying often) and wear sunglasses and a hat. Make sure that you drink enough as you'll be sweating mightily in the heat. If you're urinating very little or your urine turns dark (this can also indicate hepatitis), increase your fluid intake. When you sweat you lose salt, so add some extra to your food or take oral rehydration salts.

A more serious result of the heat is **heatstroke**, indicated by high temperature, dry skin and a fast, erratic pulse. As an emergency measure, try to cool the patient off by covering them in sheets or sarongs soaked in cold water and turn the fan on them; they may need to go to hospital, though.

Heat rashes, **prickly heat** and fungal infections are also common; wear loose cotton clothing, dry yourself carefully after bathing and use medicated talcum powder or antifungal powder if you fall victim.

Intestinal trouble

The priority with an **upset stomach** is to prevent dehydration. Start drinking **rehydration solution** as soon as the attack starts, even if you're vomiting as well, and worry about a diagnosis later. Rehydration salts (such as Oralit and Pharolit) are widely available in pharmacies but it makes sense to carry some with you. The home-made form of these consists of eight teaspoons of sugar and half a teaspoon of salt dissolved in a litre of clean water. Alternately, drink bottled water containing electrolytes, such as Pocara Sweat and Mizone.

Stomach upsets can either be a reaction to a change of diet or can signal something more serious. You should seek medical advice if the attack is particularly severe, lasts more than a couple of days or is accompanied by constant, severe abdominal pain or fever, blood or mucus in your diarrhoea or smelly farts and burps.

Drugs such as Lomotil and Imodium, which stop diarrhoea, should only be used if you are taken ill on a journey or must travel while ill. They are not a cure, and simply paralyse your gut, temporarily plugging you up, at a time when your insides need to get rid of the toxins causing the problem.

Many travellers find locally available charcoal remedies such as Norit (available locally) effective against diarrhoea.

Cuts, bites and stings

Divers should familiarize themselves with potential **underwater hazards** and the appropriate first aid, although you're more at risk from bad diving practices and coral scrapes than from tangling with sharks, sea snakes, stingrays or jellyfish. All cuts should be cleansed and disinfected immediately, covered and kept dry until healed.

On the land, there are poisonous **snakes** on both Bali and Lombok, although they're only likely to attack if you step on them – they are most often encountered in ricefields or forests, so if you are exploring these look where you're stepping. In jungle areas wear long thick socks to protect your legs when trekking and walk noisily. If you're bitten, try to remember what the snake looked like, move as little as you can and send someone for medical help. Under no circumstances do anything heroic with a Swiss army knife. There are also a few poisonous **spiders** in Bali and Lombok, and if you're bitten by one you should also immobilize the limb and get medical help. If you get **leeches** attached to you while trekking in the jungle in the rainy season, use a dab of salt, suntan oil or a cigarette to persuade them to let go, rather than just pulling them off.

MEDICAL RESOURCES FOR TRAVELLERS

Canadian Travel Clinics http://canadiantravelclinics.ca. List of travel health clinics.

CDC http://cdc.gov/travel. Official US government travel health site.

Hospital for Tropical Diseases Travel Clinic UK https://www.uclh.nhs.uk/our-services/find-service/tropical-and-infectious-diseases/travel-clinic-services.

International Society of Travel Medicine US http://istm.org. Has a full list of travel health clinics.

MASTA (Medical Advisory Service for Travellers Abroad) UK http://masta-travel-health.com.

Tropical Medical Bureau Ireland http://tmb.ie. Lists travel health clinics.

The Travel Doctor Australia http://traveldoctor.com.au. Lists travel clinics in Australia, New Zealand and South Africa.

Outdoor activities

The sea and the mountains are the two great focuses of outdoor activities in Bali and Lombok. Both islands have world-class surf breaks, excellent diving and spectacular volcano hikes.

Surfing

Bali's volcanic reef-fringed coastline has made the island one of the world's great **surfing** centres, with a reputation for producing an unusually high number of perfect and consistent tubes and waves. There are also plenty of gentler beach breaks, which are ideal for beginners.

From April to October, the southeast trade winds blow offshore, fanning the waves off **Bali**'s southwest coast and off Nusa Lembongan. This is both the best time of year for surf and the pleasantest, as it's also the dry season. The best-known and most challenging of the southwestern breaks are around **Uluwatu** on the Bukit Peninsula – at **Balangan**, **Dreamland**, **Bingin**, **Padang Padang** and **Suluban**. These are tough, world-class breaks and get very crowded, particularly from June to August; small, surfer-oriented resorts have grown up around each one. **Nusa Lembongan**'s breaks can be less busy but are also challenging. Novice and less confident surfers generally start with the breaks around **Kuta**, **Canggu** and **Medewi**. From November to March, the winds blow from the northwest, bringing rain to Bali's main beach breaks, though the lesser breaks off eastern Bali, around **Sanur** and **Nusa Dua**, are still surfable at this time of year.

On **Lombok**, Bangko Bangko's **Desert Point** is rated as one of the world's top breaks, but there are plenty of other good breaks for all levels of experience around **Kuta** on the south coast, including at **Gerupuk**, **Mawi**, **Ekas** and **Selong Belanak**.

Bali and Lombok have so many different breaks that it's worth doing your homework and being selective if you're a novice; even pros find the tougher breaks very challenging.

Equipment, lessons and information

The main **surf centres** are located in Kuta, Bali and Kuta, Lombok. In both these areas you'll find shops that rent **boards**, sell new boards and international-brand equipment, and repair boards. Both coastlines are dotted with surf instructors (local guys) and professional **surf schools**. There is also a women-only luxury surf camp, Surf Goddess Retreats (http://surfgoddessretreats.com), in Seminyak. For detailed reviews of surf breaks, see the **book** *Indo Surf and Lingo*, widely available in Bali and from http://indosurf.com.au (this website is also a good source of information), as is Bali Waves (http://baliwaves.com).

Many **airlines** will take boards in the hold for free as long as your total luggage weight doesn't exceed 20kg, but call to check if they require special insurance. Board bags with straps are a good idea, as some breaks are only accessible by motorbike. Some **tourist shuttle buses** on Bali and Lombok refuse to carry boards, though Perama buses will take them for an extra fee. You may be best off renting a car or a motorbike to get to the breaks. In the main centres, it's easy to rent **motorbikes** with special surfboard clips already attached.

Diving and snorkelling

Bali and Lombok are encircled by reefs that offer excellent and varied year-round **diving and snorkelling**. The main **dive resorts on Bali** are at Amed, Candidasa, Nusa Lembongan, Padang Bai, Pemuteran and Tulamben. Sanur beach resort also has many dive operators but is further from the best dive sites. Lombok's Gili Islands are another hugely popular dive destination, with many established schools and diving right offshore. Lombok's southwest peninsula and islands are growing in popularity with divers. There are a few dive sites on the island's south coast for advanced divers only that dive shops in Kuta head to.

Most of these dive sites are also rewarding for **snorkelling**, though obviously the shallowest reefs are best. Many hotels and boat captains offer dedicated snorkelling trips, including gear (check boat captains' gear before the trip). Some dive centres will also take accompanying snorkellers for a reduced rate.

Freediving schools on Bali, based in the Amed area and Nusa Penida/Nusa Lembongan, and on Lombok, the Gili Islands, offer professional tuition and internationally recognized courses for those who want to experience the thrill of breath-hold diving.

Dive centres and courses

There are dozens of **dive centres** on Bali and Lombok. If possible, get recommendations from other divers as well, and check the centre's PADI (http://padi.com) or SSI (http://divessi.com) accreditation. Most are highly professional but there a few dodgy dive operators in Bali and Lombok that fake their PADI credentials, and others that are not PADI dive centres, though their staff may be individually certified.

Technical diving using gases other than compressed air is gaining in popularity in Bali and Lombok; the relevant associations are Technical Diving International (http://tdisdi.com) and IANTD (http://iantd.com). Avoid **booking** ahead online without knowing anything else about the dive centre, and be wary of any operation offering extremely cheap courses. Maintaining diving equipment is an expensive business in Indonesia, so any place offering unusually good rates will probably be compromising your safety. Ask to meet your instructor or dive leader, look at their qualifications, find out how many people will be in your group (four divers to one dive master is a good ratio) and whether they're a similar level to you, and look over the equipment, checking the quality of the air in the tanks yourself and also ensuring there's an oxygen cylinder on board. Dive centres that use their own boats, rather than renting one with a crew, tend to take better care of equipment.

Most dive centres charge similar **rates**. Most dive centres also run PADI's introductory Discover Scuba course for novice and Scuba Review for those needing a refresher.

In Lombok's Gilis all divers contribute a one-off payment to the Gili Eco Trust Fund which goes towards the maintenance of buoys on dive sites, patrols against illegal fishing and reef clean-ups.

Safety and information

When planning your trip, note that as you shouldn't go anywhere that's more than **300m above sea level** for eighteen hours following a dive, you'll have to be careful neither to fly straight after your dive, nor to go into the Bali or Lombok highlands. Specifically, that means nearly all the highlands and mountains on Bali and Lombok are temporarily out of bounds.

Bali has two **recompression chambers,** one at Sanglah Public Hospital in Denpasar (see page 89) and the other at Kasih Ibu General Hospital, Saba, East Bali (see page 150), but any reputable dive centre should organize treatment for you in the very unlikely event that you need it. There is also a recompression chamber on Lombok (see page 277). Make sure your travel insurance covers you and transportation, as treatment can be very expensive.

Hiking

The most challenging **hikes** on Bali and Lombok take you up the islands' towering volcanoes, but there are also lots of gentler treks through ricefields in the interior. The biggest undertaking is the ascent of Lombok's **Gunung Rinjani**, which involves at least one night on the mountain, or more time if you want to reach the summit and the crater lake; guides are obligatory for this. Bali's holiest peak, **Gunung Agung**, also involves a very strenuous guided climb, but the ascent and descent can be managed in one day. **Gunung Batur**, also on Bali, is a much easier proposition and by far the most popular of the volcano walks; don't be put off by this, though, as the sunrise from the top is glorious. **Gunung Batukaru** is less commonly hiked but guides are available at the several starting points.

The most popular centre for **ricefield treks** is Ubud but arguably more rewarding are the smaller and far less busy tourist centres on Bali at Sidemen, Candidasa, Tirtagangga, Munduk, Jatiluwih, Sarinbuana and Mayong. There are good hikes inside the Taman Nasional Bali Barat too. In Lombok, Senaru and Tetebatu are the main hiking centres.

Rafting and kayaking

Whitewater rafting on Bali's rivers ranges from Class 2 to Class 4, so there are routes for first-timers as well as the more experienced; you can book trips in all the major coastal resorts as well as in Ubud. It's also possible to go **kayaking** on the gentler rivers, on Bali. Sea kayaking is a growing sport on Lombok.

Cycling and horseriding

Bali and Lombok are both great for **cycling**, and there are several tour companies that can get you off the beaten track, riding through spectacular volcanic scenery, rice paddies and craft villages. Ubud and Kintamani are hotspots for tours. Bali Bike Baik (http://balibike.com) and Banyan Tree Cycling (http://banyantreebiketours.com) are two good operators. On Lombok, Lombok Biking Tour (http://lombokbikingtour.com) offers a variety of bike tours.

There's good **horseriding** in Kerobokan near Seminyak and at Yeh Gangga, Bali, and on Lombok's Gili Trawangan.

Spas, traditional beauty treatments and yoga

Herbal medicines or *jamu* and massages using oils and pastes made from locally grown plants have long played an important role in traditional Indonesian health care. In the last few years, this resource has been adapted for the international market, with dozens of spas and salons now offering traditional beauty treatments to visitors.

The biggest concentrations of hotel **spas** and **traditional beauty salons** are in Seminyak/Petitenget and Ubud but there are many more across Bali: browse Bali Spa Guide (http://balispaguide.com) for a comprehensive database. Most of Lombok's spas are attached to resorts; The Lombok Guide (http://thelombokguide.com) has a good listing.

Treatments

Indonesia's best known traditional treatment is the Javanese exfoliation rub, **mandi lulur**, in which you're painted and then massaged with a turmeric-based paste. Such is its apparent power to beautify that Javanese brides are said to have a *lulur* treatment every day for the forty days before their wedding ceremonies. Another popular body wrap is the **Balinese boreh**, a warming blend of cloves, pepper and cardamom that improves circulation and invigorates muscles. Most scrub treatments include a gentle Balinese-style massage and a moisturizing "milk bath"; prices (/hr) vary depending on the quality of the venue. On Bali, some massage centres also run massage **courses**, such as in Seminyak.

YOGA AND HOLISTIC THERAPIES

Ubud-based Bali Spirit is an excellent resource for all things **holistic** in Bali; the website (http://balispirit.com) carries a detailed programme of all upcoming yoga retreats. Regular **yoga sessions and courses** are held all over Bali, including Kuta, Seminyak, Canggu, Ubud and Sanur and on Lombok in Gili Trawangan, Gili Air and Kuta. There are also good pilates studios near Canggu and Ubud.

Culture and etiquette

Bali and Lombok's people are extremely generous about opening up their homes, temples and festivals to interested tourists but, though they're long-suffering and rarely show obvious displeasure, they do take great offence at certain aspects of Western behaviour. The most sensitive issues on the islands are Westerners' clothing – or lack of it – and the practice code that's required when visiting holy places.

Religious etiquette

Anyone entering a **Balinese temple** (*pura*) is required to show **respect** to the gods by treating their shrines with due deference (not climbing on them or placing themselves in a higher position) and by **dressing modestly**: skimpy clothing, bare shoulders, midriffs and shorts are all unacceptable, and in many temples you'll be required to wear a sarong (usually provided for a small donation at the gate of the most-visited temples). In addition, you should wear a **ceremonial sash** around your waist whenever you visit a temple, symbolizing the restraint of human urges. These can be bought cheaply at most shops selling sarongs, and can be of any style; they too are provided for visitors at popular temples.

When attending special **temple ceremonies**, cremations and other village festivals, you should try to dress up as formally as possible: sarongs and sashes are obligatory, and shirts with buttons are preferable to T-shirts; all clothing must be freshly washed. Don't walk in front of anyone who's praying, or take their photo, and do not sit higher than the priest or the offerings table. Never use a flash.

At temples, you'll be expected to give a small **donation** towards upkeep and to sign the donation book.

Because the shedding of blood is considered to make someone **ritually unclean** (*sebel*) in Balinese Hinduism, women are not allowed to enter a temple, or to attend any religious ceremonies, during **menstruation**, and the same applies to anyone bearing a fresh wound. Under the same precepts, new mothers and their babies are also considered to be *sebel* for the first 42 days after the birth (new fathers are unclean for three days), and anyone who has been recently bereaved is *sebel* until three days after burial or cremation. These restrictions apply to

BALINESE CASTES AND NAMES

Balinese society is structured around a hereditary **caste system**, which, while far more relaxed than its Indian counterpart, does nonetheless carry certain restrictions and rules of etiquette, as ordained in the Balinese Hindu scriptures. Of these, the one that travellers are most likely to encounter is the practice of **naming** a person according to their caste.

At the top of the tree is the **Brahman** caste, whose men are honoured with the title **Ida Bagus** and whose women are generally named **Ida Ayu**, sometimes shortened to **Dayu**. Traditionally revered as the most scholarly members of society, only Brahmans are allowed to become high priests (*pedanda*).

Satriya (sometimes spelt Ksatriya) form the second strata of Balinese society, and these families are descendants of warriors and rulers. The Balinese rajas were all Satriya and their offspring continue to bear telltale names: **Cokorda**, **Anak Agung**, **Ratu** and **Prebagus** for men, and **Anak Agung Isti** or **Dewa Ayu** for women. The merchants, or **Wesia**, occupy the third most important rank, the men distinguished by the title **I Gusti** or **Pregusti**, the women by the name **I Gusti Ayu**.

At the bottom of the heap comes the **Sudra** caste, the caste of the common people, which accounts for more than ninety percent of the population. Sudra children are named according to their position in the family order, with no distinction made between male and female offspring. Thus, a first-born Sudra is always known as **Wayan**, **Putu**, or **Gede** (male) or **Ilu** (female); the second-born is **Made** (or **Kadek**, or **Nengah**); the third **Nyoman** (or **Komang**) and the fourth **Ketut**. Should a fifth child be born, the naming system begins all over again with Wayan/Putu, and so it goes on. In order to distinguish between the sexes, Sudra caste names are often prefaced by "**I**" for males and "**Ni**" for females, for example, I Wayan. Some Wayans and Mades prefer to be known by their second names, and many have distinctive nicknames, but you will come across many more Wayans than any other name in Bali.

Unlike their counterparts in the far more rigid Indian caste system, the Sudra are not looked down upon or denied access to specific professions (except that of *pedanda*), and a high-caste background guarantees neither a high income nor a direct line to political power.

non-Balinese as well, and are sometimes detailed on English-language notices outside the temple.

Mosques

On the whole, Lombok and Bali's **mosques** don't hold much cultural or architectural interest for non-Muslim tourists, but should you have occasion to visit one, it's as well to be aware of certain Islamic practices. Everyone is required to take off their shoes before entering, and to wear long sleeves and long trousers; women should cover their shoulders and may also be asked to cover their heads (bring your own scarf or shawl). Men and women always pray in separate parts of the mosque, though there are unlikely to be signs telling you where to go. Women are forbidden to engage in certain religious activities during menstruation, and this includes entering a mosque.

During the **Ramadan month** (see page 50), devout Muslims neither eat, drink nor smoke in daylight hours. If visiting Lombok during this time, you should be sensitive to this, although you'll certainly be able to find places to eat; accommodation eateries and fast food outlets are your best bet. Adherence varies across Bali during this time: it is most apparent in the south and the east, but is something you might not even notice in Senggigi or the Gili Islands in Lombok.

At any time of year it's highly offensive to drink alcohol near a mosque, including on the Gili Islands. If you're in a bar or restaurant compound where alcohol is served, that's fine, but drinking on the street outside a mosque is a no-no.

The body

Despite tolerating skimpy **dress** in the beach resorts, most Indonesians are extremely offended by topless and nude bathing, and by immodest attire in their towns and villages, as well as by public displays of affection. You'll command a great deal more respect if you keep your shortest shorts, vests and bare shoulders for the seaside. This is especially true in central, southern and eastern Lombok.

The Balinese and Sasak people themselves regularly expose their own bodies in public when **bathing** in rivers and public bathing pools, but they are always treated as invisible by other bathers and passers-by. As a tourist you should do the same: to photograph anyone who is bathing would be very rude indeed. If you bathe alongside them, do as they do – nearly all Indonesian women wash with their sarongs wrapped around them – and take note of the segregated areas: in public pools, the men's and women's sections are usually clearly defined, but in rivers the borders are less obvious.

According to Hindu beliefs, a person's body is a microcosm of the universe: the **head** is the most sacred part of the body and the feet the most unclean. This means that you should on no account touch a person's head – not even to pat a small child's head or to ruffle someone's hair in affection; nor should you lean over someone's head or place your body in a higher position than their head without apologizing. You should never sit with your **feet** pointed at a sacred image (best to sit with them tucked underneath you) or use them to indicate someone or something. Balinese people will never walk under a **clothes line** (for fear of their head coming into contact with underwear), so you should try not to hang your washing in public areas, and definitely don't sling wet clothes over a temple wall or other holy building. The **left hand** is used for washing after defecating, so Indonesians will never eat with it or use it to pass or receive things or to shake hands.

Social conventions

As elsewhere in Asia, Indonesians dislike **confrontational behaviour** and will rarely show anger or irritation. Tourists who lose their cool and get visibly rattled tend to be looked down on rather than feared. A major source of irritation for foreigners is the rather vague notion of **time-keeping** in Indonesia: lack of punctuality is such a national institution that there is even a word for it – *jam karet*, or rubber time.

Since the downfall of Suharto in 1998, and the subsequent democratic elections, some Indonesian people have become much more confident about discussing **political issues** and voicing critical opinions of the state. This is mirrored by a more open press. Religious beliefs, however, are a much more sensitive issue, and it would be bad form to instigate a debate that questions a person's faith.

You will probably find Balinese and Sasak people only too eager to find out about your **personal life** and habits. It's considered quite normal to ask "Are you married?" and to then express sorrow if you say that you aren't, and the same applies to questions about children: marriage and parenthood are essential stages in the life of most Balinese and Sasaks.

Public **displays of affection** are subdued – you're more likely to see affectionate hand-holding and hugging between friends of the same sex than between heterosexual lovers.

Tipping

It's becoming increasingly common to **tip** on Bali and Lombok, generally about ten percent to waiters (if no service charge is added to the bill), drivers and tour guides; a few thousand rupiah to bellboys and chambermaids in mid-range and upmarket hotels; and a round-up to the nearest Rp5000 for metered-taxi drivers. In non-touristy areas tipping is not expected.

Photography

While Bali and Lombok are both incredibly photogenic, not all local people want to be the subject of visitors' holiday snaps; always ask by word or gesture whether it is OK to take a photograph, and respect the answer. Be especially sensitive during religious events such as cremations and take care never to get in the way of worshippers.

Shopping

Shopping can easily become an all-consuming pastime in Bali: the range and quality of artefacts is phenomenal, and although the export trade has dulled the novelty, the bargain prices are irresistible. Bali also has a well-deserved reputation for its elegant modern designs in everything from fashion to tableware; key locations for contemporary goodies are Legian, Seminyak and Ubud. On Lombok, Senggigi has the widest choice of shops, but the real pleasure is visiting the island's pottery and textile villages.

Remember that touts, guides and drivers often get as much as fifty percent **commission** on any item sold to one of their customers – not only at the customer's expense, but also the vendor's. Many shops will organize **shipping**, but be prepared for a huge bill; the minimum container size is one cubic metre. For parcels weighing under 10kg, use the postal system (see page 50).

Arts and crafts

Locally produced arts and crafts include traditional and modern **paintings**, **pottery**, **textiles**, **basket-**

ware, **stone sculptures** and **woodcarvings**. Though the big resorts stock a wide range of all these artefacts, there's much fun and better bargains to be had, at least on the high-quality versions, at the craft-producing **villages** themselves.

There are a couple of practical points to note when choosing **woodcarvings**. Be warned that not all "sandalwood" (*cendana*), which is an extremely expensive material, is what it seems as the aroma can be **faked** with real sandalwood sawdust or oil. In either case, the smell doesn't last that long, so either buy from an established outlet or assume that it's faked and reduce your price accordingly. **Ebony** is also commonly faked. Compare its weight with any other wood: ebony is very dense and will sink in water. Most tropical woods **crack** when exported to a less humid climate: some carvers obviate this by drying the wood in kilns, while others use polyethylene glycol (PEG) to fill the cracks before they widen. Always check for cracks before buying.

Some **stone carvings** are also not what they seem, though shops rarely make a secret of this. Specifically, the cheapest lava-stone *paras* sculptures are usually mass-produced from moulded lava-stone paste rather than hand-carved. They're sometimes referred to as "**concrete**" statues but can still be very attractive.

Soft furnishings, clothing and jewellery

Designers make beautiful use of the sumptuous local fabrics for luxurious and unusual **soft furnishings**, including cushions, bedspreads, sheets, curtains, drapes and tablecloths. Seminyak, Legian, Canggu, Sanur and Ubud have the best outlets.

Bali also produces some great **clothes**. Kuta–Legian–Seminyak and Canggu have the classiest and most original boutiques, along with countless stalls selling beachwear. Brand-name surfwear and urban sportswear is also good value here, as are custom-made leather shoes, boots and jackets.

Bali's small but thriving **silver** and **gold** industry is based in Celuk village, where silversmiths sell to the public from their workshops. For more unusual jewellery, you're better off scouring the jewellery shops in Kuta, Ubud, Lovina and Candidasa, where designs tend to be more innovative and prices similar, if not lower. Lombok is known for its bargain-priced

WHERE TO SHOP

Basketware Loyok and Beleka villages (Lombok); Tenganan.
Beaded bags, necklaces, shoes Kuta (Bali); Ubud.
Books Ubud.
Ceramics Pejaten; Jimbaran.
Fashion Kuta–Legian–Seminyak; Canggu; Ubud; Sanur.
Furniture Modern furniture in Kerobokan and Seminyak. Repro antique furniture from Batubulan, Mas, Seminyak and Senggigi, Lombok.
Interior decor and soft furnishings Seminyak; Legian; Canggu; Ubud; Sanur; Tegalalang–Pujung road.
Jewellery and silver Celuk is Bali's main silver-producing village; shops in Kuta, Seminyak, Canggu, Ubud, Lovina and Candidasa. Gold shops on Jl Hasanudin, Denpasar. Freshwater and cultured pearls in Mataram and Senggigi.
Leather shoes and jackets Kuta (Bali).
Markets and pasar seni (art markets) Sukawati; Ubud; Denpasar; Mataram; Senggigi.
Masks Mas; Singapadu.
Paintings Ubud area; Batuan; Kamasan.
Pottery Mataram; Senggigi; Banyumulek; Penujak; Penakak.
Puppets Sukawati.
Stone sculptures Batubulan.
Textiles Ikat in Tenganan, Gianyar, Sidemen and Singaraja; *songket* weavings in Sideman, Mataram and Sukarara. Traditional Sumba and Flores textiles in Kuta (Bali) and Ubud. Batik and dress fabrics in Denpasar, especially Jl Sulawesi. Mass-produced and hand-printed batik sarongs in *pasar seni* and tourist shops in Kuta (Bali), Sukawati, Ubud, Lovina, Sanur, Candidasa and Senggigi.
Woodcarvings Unpainted figurines from Mas, Ubud and Nyuhkuning. Painted wooden artefacts from villages along the Tegalalang–Pujung road.

imported freshwater **pearls**, and for its home-grown South Sea pearls; shops in Mataram are best for the latter, while Senggigi vendors sell the imports.

Furniture

Several shops in Bali and Lombok advertise, quite ingenuously, "Antiques made to order". The **antiques** in question generally either come from Java or are **reproductions** of mostly Javanese items, chiefly **furniture**, screens, carved panels, window shutters and doors. Weatherworn or fashionably distressed, most of the furniture is heavy, made from hardwoods like teak. Check items for rot and termite damage (genuine teak is resistant to termites).

There is also a demand for contemporary **modern furniture** on Bali. The best place to browse is the region north of Seminyak, around Kerobokan. Make sure any furniture bought locally is kiln-dried. Otherwise it is likely to crack in drier climates.

Travelling with children

The Balinese make a great fuss of their own and other people's children, and permit them to go pretty much anywhere. One peculiar cultural convention you might encounter, though, is that the Balinese abhor young children crawling on the ground – a practice that's considered far too animal-like for young humans – and so in their early months kids are **carried** everywhere, either on the hip or in slings made from sarongs. Don't be surprised if your child gets scooped off the ground for the same reason.

Activities for kids

There's plenty on Bali and Lombok to appeal to children. Aside from the beach and other water-based activities in the southern resorts, Bali's Waterbom Park (http://waterbom-bali.com) is fun for all ages. In Ubud, there's Swing Heaven (http://swingheavens.com) with jungle swings and beds enjoying stunning views of the Ayung river.

Active children may also enjoy **learning surfing, mountain biking**, **whitewater rafting** and **horseriding**. **Wildlife attractions** such as the Bird and Reptile parks in Batubulan and the Bali Safari and Marine Park in Gianyar will also make for a fun day out. Many **dive centres** teach PADI children's scuba courses: their Bubblemaker programme is open to 8-year-olds and the Junior Open Water course is designed for anyone over 10.

Ubud is especially child-friendly, with a huge number of choices that kids will love, including chances to try their hand at jewellery-making, batik, gamelan and dancing, and a multilingual kids' library. The colour and dynamism of the **dance and music shows** could almost be tailor-made for children – from the beauty and grace of Legong to the drama of the Barong. Older, more fashion-conscious children will relish the varieties of brand-name **clothing** available, while parents will appreciate the bargains to be had in the children's sections of department stores in Kuta and Denpasar and the specialist children's clothing stores.

Practicalities

When choosing a base, beaches in Sanur, the north coast of Bali (including Lovina), and the Gili Islands have calm waters most of the year whereas waves can be huge and potentially dangerous on the ocean-battered shoreline in southern Bali (Kuta-Legion-Seminyak and Canggu) and south Lombok.

Many top-end **hotels** provide extra beds for one or two under-12s sharing a room with their parents and the best ones have a kids' club as well, and may also offer babysitting services. The Tuban area of south Kuta (Bali) is particularly strong on family-oriented hotels, many of which have grounds that run right down to the sea.

On the whole, children who occupy their own seat on **buses** and **bemos** are expected to pay full fare. Most **domestic flight** operators charge two-thirds of the adult fare for children under 14, and ten percent for infants.

Although you can buy **disposable** diapers in Kuta, Sanur, Denpasar and Ubud supermarkets, the Balinese rarely use them, so prices are inflated. Bring a **changing mat**, as there are precious few public toilets in Bali and Lombok, let alone ones with special baby facilities (though posh hotels are always a useful option). For touring, child-carrier **backpacks** are ideal. Opinions are divided on whether or not it's worth bringing a **buggy** or three-wheeled **stroller** – pavements are bumpy at best, and there's an almost total absence of ramps; sand is especially difficult for buggies, though less so for three-wheelers. Buggies and strollers do, however, come in handy for feeding and even bedding small children, as highchairs and cots are only provided in the most upmarket hotels. Taxis and car-rental companies never provide baby seats. A child-sized **mosquito net** might be useful. **Powdered milk** is available in every major tourist centre, but sterilizing bottles is a far more laborious process in Indonesian hotels and restaurants than it is back home.

Food in Bali and Lombok's main areas is generally quite palatable to children as it's toned down for Western tastes and rarely too chilli-hot. In local places (particularly in Lombok) the food is usually much spicier. It's wise to avoid unwashed fruit and salads outside of five-star resorts, as well as dishes that have been left uncovered.

Thundering **traffic** is another hazard, as is the tropical **sun**. Many beaches have little shade so sun hats, sunblock and waterproof suntan lotions are essential, and can be bought in the major resorts (though are usually more expensive than in the West). You should also make sure, if possible, that your child is aware of the dangers of **rabies** (see page 34); keep children away from animals, especially dogs and monkeys, and ask your doctor about rabies jabs.

NGOs and volunteer projects

Despite the glossy tourist veneer, Bali and Lombok have a large poverty-level population with limited resources to provide high-quality education and health care to its citizens, whose opportunities, quality of life and very survival are compromised as a result. Below are some suggestions for non-governmental organizations (NGOs) that welcome help from visitors; most of their websites include information on volunteer work.

CHARITIES AND VOLUNTEER WORK

AdoptASchool http://adoptaschool.org.au. Established in 2002, this volunteer-run NGO links Western Australia and Bali schools to share cultural experiences, sponsors Balinese students and supports professional training for teachers.

Bali Children Foundation http://balichildrenfoundation.org. Helps thousands of Balinese children to complete school and find employment.

Bali Life Foundation http://balilife.org. Pledges to give "hope, purpose and dignity to the unprivileged children and women" of Bali.

BAWA (Bali Animal Welfare Organization) Jl Raya Ubud, Ubud, http://bawabali.com. Works to improve all aspects of animal welfare on Bali including the vaccination, as opposed to culling, of dogs as a response to rabies on the island.

East Bali Poverty Project http://eastbalipovertyproject.org. Helps isolated mountain villages on the arid Gunung Agung and Gunung Abang slopes in a number of ways, including education, nutrition, health and sustainable agriculture.

Gili Eco Trust Gili Trawangan, http://giliecotrust.com. Works to promote sustainable tourism in the Gili islands. Projects include growing new coral reefs, recycling programmes, caring for horses and environmental education in schools. Visitors can participate in their monthly beach clean-up and they run courses on Biorock reef restoration.

IDEP Foundation http://idepfoundation.org. An Ubud-based NGO that promotes sustainable-living programmes across Indonesia, including permaculture, micro-credit, fair trade and disaster response projects.

Kupu-Kupu Foundation http://kupukupufoundation.org. Encourages sponsors and volunteers to help improve the lives of disabled people in Bali. Sells inexpensive, high-quality handicrafts and jewellery made by disabled craftspeople at its shop in Ubud. They also have cottages for rent.

Peduli Anak http://pedulianak.org. Centre set up to help street children, with a health clinic as well as child advocacy and education programmes. Volunteers are needed; the centre is located on the outskirts of Mataram, Lombok.

Pondok Pekak Library and Learning Centre Off Jl Monkey Forest, Ubud, 0361 976 194. A library service in Ubud that offers all local children free access to books and educational activities. Visitors can support the project by using the excellent adult-oriented library of English-language books, by taking cultural classes or Indonesian lessons here and by donating books and funds.

Sjaki-Tari-Us Foundation Off Jl Monkey Forest, Ubud, http://sjakitarius.org. Works with disabled children and their families, offering education, training and job opportunities.

Yayasan Senyum http://senyumbali.org. Dedicated to helping fund operations for Indonesians with craniofacial disabilities such as cleft palate. Visitors can assist by donating secondhand goods to their two Ubud charity outlets, Smile Shop.

Travel essentials

Accessible travel

Indonesia makes few provisions for its disabled citizens, which clearly affects **travellers with disabilities**, although the situation is definitely improving year on year.

At the physical level, kerbs are usually high (without slopes) and pavements/sidewalks uneven, with all sorts of obstacles; access to most public places involves steps (very few have ramps); public transport is inaccessible to wheelchair users (although Perama tourist buses will take them); and the few pedestrian crossings on major roads have no audible signal. On the positive side, many hotels consist of bungalows in extensive grounds and/or have spacious bathrooms, while the more aware are increasingly making an effort to provide the necessary facilities. These hotels are highlighted in the guide. UK-based http://disabledholidays.com carries a roundup of accessible hotels and villas on Bali.

For all of these reasons, it may be worth considering an **organized tour** or holiday – the contacts listed below will help you start researching trips to Bali and Lombok. Note that a medical certificate of your fitness to travel, provided by your doctor, can be extremely useful; some airlines or insurance companies may insist on it.

Be sure to carry your complete supply of **medications** whenever you travel (including on buses and planes), in case of loss or theft. It's also a good idea to carry a doctor's letter about your drugs prescriptions with you at all times, particularly when passing through customs at airports, so you don't get hauled up for narcotics transgressions. Assume that if anything happens to equipment, such as a wheelchair, spares will be hard to find, and a small repair kit may well come in very handy.

CONTACTS FOR TRAVELLERS WITH DISABILITIES

Accessible Indonesia Jl. Pelita Raya Blok A-22 No. 2, Makassar, Sulawesi, http://accessibleindonesia.org. Specialises in travellers with disabilities and seniors in Bali, Jakarta, Yogyakarta and Sulawesi. Part of a Dutch-Indonesian travel company.

Bali Access Travel Jl. Danau Tamblingan No 31, Sanur, http://baliaccesstravel.com. Caters only to disabled tourists.

Addresses

A number of streets in resort areas such as Kuta (Bali) are rather confusingly known by two or more names (see page 65), fluctuating with the popularity of local heroes. Because of haphazard planning, frequent rebuilding and local superstitions about unlucky numbers, street numbers are not always sequential – and sometimes may not be present at all. It's also quite common to use "X" where an adjacent property has been added, with the original building being, say, Jl Raya No. 200 and the new one becoming Jl Raya No. 200X.

Cookery and cultural classes

In Bali, short courses in Indonesian cookery are available in Ubud, Petitenget, Tanjung Benoa, Lovina, Sidemen, Munduk, Alila Manggis near Candidasa. In Lombok, there is an excellent cooking class in Gili Air. Ubud is the most popular place to take workshops in art, dance, music, carving and other Balinese arts and crafts.

Costs

Foreign tourists visiting Bali and Lombok, wherever they come from, invariably find that hotel rooms at all levels of comfort, goods and services are relatively inexpensive when compared with their home countries. However, the range of accommodation, restaurants and other opportunities means that it is just as easy to have a fabulously extravagant experience as a budget one.

Prices have shot up in recent years, but if you're happy to eat in local places, stay off the beer, use the public transport system (or rent a bicycle) and stay in simple accommodation, you can still scrape by on a **daily budget** of £20–25/$30–40 per person if you share a room. For around £80/$100 a day per person if you share a room, you'll get quite a few extra comforts, like the use of a swimming pool, hot water and air conditioning, three good meals and a few beers; and you'll be able to afford tourist shuttle buses or the odd taxi to get around. Staying in luxury hotels, eating at the swankiest restaurants and chartering transport, you're likely to spend from £285/$350 per day. The sky's the limit at this end of the market, with $3000-a-night accommodation, helicopter charters, dive or surf safaris and fabulous gourmet meals all available.

The most popular **temples** charge between Rp50,000 and Rp150,000 per person and other **tourist attractions range from** Rp15,000–200,000. Youth and student **discounts** are rare but can be fifty percent where available. All visitors to any temple are expected to give a small donation (minimum about Rp10,000).

Bargaining

Bargaining is one of the most obvious ways of keeping your costs down. Except in supermarkets, department stores, restaurants and bars, the first price given is rarely the real one, and most stallholders expect to engage in some financial banter before finalizing the sale; on average, buyers will start their counterbid at about thirty to forty percent of the vendor's opening price and the bartering continues from there. Pretty much everything, from woodcarvings to car rental is negotiable, and accommodation rates can often be knocked down outside high season, from the humblest *losmen* through to the top-end places.

Bargaining is an art and requires humour and tact – it's easy to forget that you're quibbling over a few cents or pennies, and that such an amount means a lot more to an Indonesian than to you.

Crime and personal safety

While criminal incidents are relatively rare on Bali and Lombok, tourism's importance to the economy, and the damage that adverse publicity could do, means that the true situation may be kept conveniently obscured. Certainly, the majority of visitors have trouble-free trips, but there have been instances of theft and assault on tourists.

It makes sense to take a few **precautions**. Carry vital documents and money in a concealed money belt: bum-bags (aka fanny packs) are too easy to cut off in a crowd. Make sure your luggage is lockable (there are gadgets to lock backpacks) and be aware that things can quickly be taken from the back pockets of a rucksack while you're wearing it without your knowing. Beware of pickpockets on crowded buses or *bemos* and in markets. They usually operate in pairs: one will distract you while another gets what they can either from your pockets or your backpack.

Check room **security** before accepting one, make sure doors and windows can be locked, and don't forget to check if access could be gained via the bathroom. Make sure there are no peepholes through into neighbouring rooms. Some guesthouses and hotels have safe-deposit boxes, which neatly solves the problem of what to do with your valuables while you go swimming.

Keep a separate **photocopy** of your passport and airline ticket, or scan them in and store them online, so you can prove who you are and where you are going if you need to get replacements.

It's never sensible to carry **large amounts of cash**, and on Bali it's not necessary. However, on Lombok you may need to carry more than you would like because of the scarcity of moneychangers and ATMs outside the resort areas. It's wise to keep a few dollars hidden somewhere away from your main stash of cash so that if you get your money stolen you can still get to the police and buy essentials while you sort everything out. There are a number of potential rip-offs when you're changing money (see page 47).

Something else to watch out for on Bali is being approached on the street by somebody wanting to ask a few questions about your holiday. These seemingly innocuous questionnaires provide information for **time-share companies**, who have a reputation for hassling visitors once they've divulged their details. Another ruse is for the "researchers" to offer you a prize as a reward for participating – usually a free dinner or tour – which invariably involves a trip to the time-share company's office. Advice on this is to never sign anything unless you've thought about it extremely carefully, examined all the small print – and then thought about it some more.

It's also worth being alert to the possibility of **spiked drinks** and to be aware that **gambling** is illegal in Indonesia and problems can arise from foreigners getting involved in this.

EMERGENCY NUMBERS

In an emergency anywhere in Indonesia, call the police (110), ambulance (118) or fire service (113).

It is foolish to have anything to do with **drugs** in Indonesia. The penalties are very tough and include death, even for simple possession, and you won't get any sympathy from consular officials. The horrendous fate that awaits foreigners arrested for drug use is described in *Hotel Kerobokan: The Shocking Inside Story of Bali's Most Notorious Jail*.

If you're arrested, or end up on the wrong side of the law for whatever reason, you should ring the **consular officer** at your embassy immediately (see page 24).

It's worth being aware that if you're **driving** the chance of entanglement with the police increases somewhat (see page 27).

Women travellers

Bali and Lombok do not present great difficulties for **women travellers**, either travelling alone or with friends; basic issues of personal security and safety are essentially the same as they would be at home.

However, an image of Western women as promiscuous and on holiday in search of sex is well established on both islands, although attitudes on Bali are a little more open-minded than most places on Lombok.

While topless sunbathing is popular among tourists – and it's unlikely that local people will say anything directly – it's worth being aware how far outside the local dress code such behaviour is. Whatever you do on the beach, you should cover up when you head inshore, and visits to temples or festivals carry their own obligations regarding dress (see page 38).

There's a large population of **young men** on both Bali and Lombok known variously as Kuta Cowboys, whose aim is to secure a Western girlfriend for the night, week, month or however long it lasts. Check out the documentary *Cowboys in Paradise* (http://journeyman.tv/film/4910) for more on this. Older women are increasingly targeted for attention. The boys vary considerably in subtlety and while the transaction is not overtly financial, the woman will be expected to pay for everything.

Male travellers

In Kuta, Bali there are large numbers of prostitutes touting for business in nightclubs, bars and on the street. Western men can expect to be approached by **sex workers** on scooters late at night in Kuta. Some

ROUGH GUIDES TRAVEL INSURANCE

Looking for travel insurance? Rough Guides partners with top providers worldwide to offer you the best coverage. Policies are available to residents of anywhere in the world, with a range of options whether you are looking for single-trip, multi-country or long-stay insurance. There's coverage for a wide range of adventure sports, 24-hour emergency assistance, high levels of medical and evacuation cover and a stream of travel safety information. Even better, roughguides.com users can take advantage of these policies online 24/7, from anywhere in the world – even if you're already travelling. To make the most of your travels and ensure a smoother experience, it's always good to be prepared for when things don't go according to plan. For more information go to http://roughguides.com/bookings/insurance.

of these sex workers target drunken men for business, and patrol the backstreets of Kuta in the early hours intent on pickpocketing inebriated male tourists.

Reporting a crime or emergency

If you have anything **lost** or **stolen** you must get a **police report** for insurance purposes, so head for the nearest police station (these are marked on the maps in the guide). In areas without local police, such as the Gili Islands off the coast of Lombok, ask for the local village headman, *kepala desa* or *kepala kampung* in smaller villages, whose job it is to sort out the problem and take you to the nearest police. The police will usually find somebody who can speak some English, but it's a good idea to take along someone who can speak both Indonesian and English, if you can. Allow plenty of time for any bureaucratic involvement with the police. If you're unfortunate enough to be the victim of violent crime, contact your consulate (see page 24) at once.

Electricity

Usually 220–240 volts AC, but outlying areas may still use 110 volts. Most outlets take plugs with two rounded pins.

Insurance

It is vital to arrange **travel insurance** before travelling to Bali or Lombok, covering for medical expenses due to illness or injury, the loss of baggage and travel documents plus cancellation or curtailment of your journey. Most exclude so-called dangerous sports unless an extra premium is paid: in Bali and Lombok, this can mean scuba diving, kayaking whitewater rafting and other adventure sports, such as mountain climbing.

Before buying a **policy**, check what cover you may already have. Your home-insurance policy may cover your possessions against loss or theft even when overseas; in addition, many credit cards include some form of travel cover and some private medical schemes, especially in Canada and the US, may include cover when abroad. However, in many cases the coverage from these sources is pretty meagre and you'll need to extend your cover or buy a new policy.

Specialist travel insurance companies usually offer the most comprehensive and competitive policies. Alternatively, consider the travel insurance deal we offer (see page 46). Many policies can be chopped and changed to exclude coverage you don't need. With regard to medical coverage, ascertain whether benefits will be paid as treatment proceeds or only after your return home, and be sure to carry the 24-hour medical emergency number and the policy number with you at all times, along with a blank claim form as most insurance companies will require the signature of the attending physician. Always make a note of the policy details and leave them with someone at home in case you lose the original. When securing baggage cover, make sure that the per-article limit will cover your most valuable possession.

It can be more economical for couples and families travelling together to arrange joint insurance. Older travellers or anyone with health problems is advised to start researching insurance well in advance of their trip.

If you need to make a claim, you should keep receipts for medicines and treatment, and, if possible, contact the insurance company before making any major payment (for example, on additional convalescence expenses). In the event you have anything stolen, you must obtain an official report from the police.

Internet

Free **wi-fi** is common in restaurants, bars and virtually all accommodation options. 5G is now available in all of the main resort areas, including Denpasar, Canggu, Nusa Dua, Sanur, and Kuta. The cheapest way to get mobile internet on your phone in Bali and Lombok is by buying a prepaid local 4G or 5G SIM card.

Language lessons

Indonesian language lessons are available in Denpasar and Ubud.

Laundry

Most hotels and *losmen* have laundry services. In tourist centres there are plenty of laundries outside the hotels as well.

Left luggage

Most *losmen* and hotels will store luggage. Bali's Ngurah Rai Airport has a left-luggage facility and the shuttle-bus operator Perama will store luggage for its customers.

LGBTQ+ travellers

As members of a society that places so much emphasis on marriage and parenthood, the Balinese are generally intolerant of homosexuality within their own culture, to the point where gay Balinese men will often introduce themselves to prospective lovers as hailing from Java, so as not to cause embarrassment to their own people. It's not uncommon for men to lead a gay lifestyle for ten or fifteen years before succumbing to extreme social pressure around the age of 30, getting married and becoming fathers. Lesbians are even less visible, but subject to similar expectations.

On the positive side, it's much more common in Bali and Lombok to show a modest amount of physical affection to friends of the same sex than to friends or lovers of the opposite sex, which means that Indonesian and foreign **gay couples** generally encounter less hassle about being seen together in public than they might in the West. Indonesian law is relatively liberal: the legal **age of consent** for heterosexual sex is 16, for homosexual sex 18.

Despite the indigenous aversion to LGBTQ+ culture, Bali's tourist industry has helped establish the island as one of Indonesia's two main gay centres (the other being Jakarta). Young gay men from islands as far afield as Borneo gravitate to Bali in search of a foreign partner, and most end up in southern Bali, where Seminyak has

MONEYCHANGING SCAMS

Some unscrupulous exchange counters try to rip customers off, and there are several well-known **moneychanging scams** practised in the bigger resort areas, in particular in Kuta and Sanur on Bali.

SOME COMMON RIP-OFFS

- Confusing you with the number of **zeros**. It's easy for staff to give you Rp10,000 instead of Rp100,000.
- Giving you larger amounts in Rp10,000 **denominations**, so that you lose track.
- Tampering with the **calculator**, so that it shows a low sum even if you use it yourself. (use your own calculator.)
- **Folding notes** over to make it look as if you're getting twice as much as you are.
- Turning the lights out or otherwise **distracting** you while the pile of money is on the counter.
- **Palming** some notes as they "check" it for the last time.
- Once you've rumbled them and complained, telling you that the discrepancy in the figures is due to "**commission**".

SOME ADVICE

- **Avoid** anywhere that offers a ridiculously good rate. Stick to banks or to exchange desks recommended by other travellers. Authorized moneychangers should display a green logo with "PVA Berizin" written on it.
- Work out the total amount you're expecting beforehand, and write it down.
- Always ask whether there is commission.
- Ask for at least some notes in **reasonable denominations** (Rp 20,000 and Rp50,000 are better for small purchases than Rp 100,000), and ask to see them first.
- **Count your money** carefully, and never hand it back to the exchange staff, as this is when they whip away some notes without you noticing. You should be the last person to count the money.

become the focus of the island's small but enduring **scene**. Here, Jalan Camplung Tanduk has several established gay bars and clubs (with drag shows, go-go dancers, theme nights and the like). A mixed gay crowd of Indonesians and foreigners congregates in certain other Kuta venues, where they're welcomed without a problem. Everything is a lot quieter and less overt on **Lombok**, where Senggigi clubs offer the best chance of access to the local gay scene.

The Utopia website (http://utopia-asia.com) is an excellent **resource** for LGBTQ+ travellers in Bali and the rest of Indonesia. Bali-based tour agency Gay Bali Travel (https://gaybalitravel.com) recommends gay-owned and LGBTQ+-friendly hotels, spas and package tours, while the umbrella organization for gays and lesbians in Bali and Lombok is Gaya Dewata (http://gayadewata.com).

Living and working in Bali and Lombok

Bali has a large and lively expat community, with significant numbers of foreigners choosing to make their homes in and around Ubud, Seminyak, Canggu and Sanur in particular; on Lombok, Senggigi and Gili Trawangan are the main centres. Visa regulations are complicated (see https://www.imigrasi.go.id) but some expats manage to work as English-language teachers in Kuta (Bali) and Ubud, or as dive instructors in south Bali resorts or on the Gili Islands in Lombok. Others export Indonesian fabric, clothes, jewellery, artefacts and furniture. The *Living in Indonesia* website (http://expat.or.id) is a good resource on expat life, and the *Bali Advertiser* (http://baliadvertiser.biz) has employment adverts.

Maps

Your best bet for current street guides is Google Maps.

The media

Online and updated daily, *The Bali Times* (http://thebalitimes.com) is highly informative; there's a printed version published weekly. For Indonesian news, the English-language daily *Jakarta Globe* (http://jakartaglobe.id) and *The Jakarta Post* (http://thejakartapost.com) are both reliable. For more incisive journalism, check out the weekly **news magazine** *Tempo* (http://en.tempo.co) published in both Indonesian and English versions. The online quarterly *Inside Indonesia* (http://insideindonesia.org) runs hard-hitting articles on social and political change.

Most hotels have satellite TV; channels include CNN, HBO and sometimes BBC World, ABC and National Geographic as well as French, German and Asian channels.

Hard Rock FM Bali (87.8 FM; https://www.radioindonesia.org/hard-rock-fm-878-bali) is a music station with English-speaking DJs.

Money

The Indonesian **currency** is the **rupiah** (abbreviated to Rp or IDR). Notes commonly in circulation are Rp1000, Rp2000, Rp5000, Rp10,000, Rp20,000, Rp50,000 and Rp100,000. They are all clearly inscribed with English numbers. You'll commonly come across Rp100, Rp500 and Rp1000 coins. As new currency is issued, colours of notes and coin sizes change, so be prepared to receive the same denominations in different forms. Don't be surprised if cashiers in supermarkets give you sweets instead of small-denomination coins as change.

At the time of writing the **exchange rate** was $1 to Rp16,351, €1 to Rp16,835 and £1 to Rp20,174. However, the exchange rate does change quite a lot. It might be worthwhile downloading a currency converter app for travellers. XE Currency Converter is recommended for either Android or Apple.

Generally you will use rupiah for day-to-day transactions. Many tourist businesses, including hotels, dive operators, tour agents and car-rental outlets, however, quote for their goods and services in **US dollars** while a few use **euros**; in the guide, where dollars are mentioned they are always US dollars. Even where prices are displayed in US dollars or euros, though, you have the option of paying with cash, credit or debit cards or rupiah in tourist businesses.

Cash

There's no need to get **cash** rupiah before you travel. There are exchange counters and ATMs in both Bali's and Lombok's airports, and while airport exchange rates may be a bit lower than in other places, they are generally safe places to do business and are convenient. Some cash in **US dollars or Euros** is useful to take with you, but take crisp new notes.

In tourist centres, **exchange counters** are the most convenient places to exchange cash. They open daily from around 8am–8/9pm and rates are usually better than those offered by the banks. However, be wary of moneychanging scams (see page 47), particularly in Kuta, Bali.

Normal **banking hours** are Monday–Friday 8am–4/5pm and, in some branches, Saturday 8–11.30am, but these do vary. However, in many banks the foreign-exchange counter only opens for a limited period. Banks in smaller towns don't have foreign-exchange facilities.

MUSLIM EVENT DATES

Ramadan begins February 17, 2026; February 7, 2027; January 27, 2028.
Idul Fitri (Eid al-Fitri) begins March 19, 2026; March 9, 2027; February 26, 2028.
Note that Islamic events depend on local sightings of the moon and some sects calculate moonrise by different methods, meaning that Ramadan and Idul Fitri may begin on two different dates. Actual dates may vary.

Plastic

Major **credit cards**, primarily Visa and MasterCard, are accepted by most mid- to top-end hotels and tourist businesses. However, outlets often add fees for using cards (typically three to five percent), to cover the cost of this service.

ATMs are very widespread in all Bali's and Lombok's biggest tourist centres, towns and some villages. Virtually all accept international Visa and MasterCard credit and **debit cards**.

Be aware that your home bank may well block your card when you initially try to use it abroad, even if you've warned them of your trip, and it may take a couple of phone calls to sort this out – take the relevant telephone number with you.

Be careful when using your card – unlike machines at home, most Bali and Lombok machines only return your card *after* they've dispensed your cash, making it easier to forget it. Prepaid travel cards are useful: they work like a debit card in ATMs, hotels and other businesses and allow you to top up as and when you wish.

Wiring money

If you get into financial trouble, getting money wired to you from home is fast but expensive. Money should be available for collection in local currency from the company's local agent within twenty minutes of being sent via Western Union (http://westernunion.com) or Moneygram (http://moneygram.com). Both charge on a sliding scale, so sending larger amounts of cash is better value. Money can be sent via the agents, by telephone or, in some cases, through the websites themselves. Check the websites for locations and opening hours. Getting money wired from a home bank to a local bank on Bali or Lombok can be tortuous and is best avoided.

Opening hours and public holidays

Opening hours are not straightforward in Bali and Lombok, with government offices, post offices, businesses and shops setting their own timetables.

Generally speaking, **businesses** such as **airline offices** open at least Monday to Friday 8am to 3/4pm, Saturday 8am to 1pm, with many open longer, but have variable arrangements at lunchtime. Normal **banking hours** are Monday to Friday 8am to 4/5pm and, in some branches, Saturday 8am to 11.30am, but these do vary and foreign-exchange-counter opening hours are often shorter.

NATIONAL PUBLIC HOLIDAYS

January 1 New Year's Day (Tahun Baru).
January/Febuary Chinese New Year (Imlek).
February/March Prophet Muhammad's ascension (Isra Mi'raj).
March/April Balinese New Year (Nyepi).
April/May Good Friday (Jumat Agung).
May Labour Day (Hari Buruh).
May/June Anniversary of the birth, death and enlightenment of Buddha (Waisak Day).
May/June Ascension of Jesus Christ (Kenaikan Isa Almasih).
May/June Celebration of the end of Ramadan (Idul Fitri).
June 1 Remembrance of the philosophical foundation of Indonesia (Pancasila Day).
July/August Muslim day of sacrifice (Idul Adha).
August 17 Independence Day (Hari Proklamasi Kemerdekaan).
August/September Islamic New Year (Tahun Baru Islam).
October/November Prophet Muhammad's birthday (Maulid Nabi Muhammad SAW).
December 25 Christmas Day (Hari Natal).

In tourist areas, **shops** open from around 10am until 8pm or later, but local shops in towns and villages open and shut much earlier, with the exception of supermarkets in shopping centres, which are generally open from at least 10am to 10pm. Local **markets** vary; some start soon after dawn with business completed by 10am, others only close up towards the end of the afternoon.

Government offices are widely reported as being open Monday to Friday 8am to 4pm; in fact there is much variability in different areas and departments – most close early on Friday and you'll generally be most successful if you turn up any day between 9am and 11.30am. Official government hours shorten during Ramadan; the best advice is to ring offices at that time to check before you make a long journey.

National public holidays

In addition to **national public holidays** celebrated throughout Indonesia there are frequent local **religious festivals** occurring throughout the Muslim, Hindu and Chinese communities. Each of Bali's twenty thousand or so temples also has an anniversary celebration once every *pawukon* year, or 210 days, local communities host elaborate **marriage** and **cremation** celebrations, and both islands have their own particular secular holidays.

All major **Muslim holy days** are national holidays. These, based on a lunar calendar, move backwards against the Western calendar, falling earlier each year. The ninth Muslim month is **Ramadan**, a month of fasting (*puasa*) during daylight hours. It is much more apparent on predominately Muslim Lombok than on majority Hindu Bali. Followers of the Wetu Telu branch of Islam on Lombok observe a three-day *puasa* ritual rather than fasting the full month. Many Muslim restaurants (although not tourist establishments) shut down during the day so it can be hard to get a meal in central and eastern parts of Lombok where you should not eat, drink or smoke in public at this time. However, in all other areas of Lombok and the Gili Islands you'll find Ramadan much less apparent. **Idul Fitri**, also called Lebaran, the first day of the tenth month of the Muslim calendar, marks the end of Ramadan and is a national holiday. In fact, many businesses and government offices across Indonesia shut for a week and many hotels on Bali and Lombok get booked out with visitors from across the archipelago.

INTERNATIONAL CALLS

To **phone abroad** from Indonesia the international access code varies according to the network you're using; See http://telkomsel.com/en for access codes and rates.

To **call Bali and Lombok land lines from abroad**: dial your international access code + 62 for Indonesia + area code + number (minus its initial zero). Indonesian mobile numbers begin with 08. If calling from abroad, dial your international access code + 62, drop the 0 and begin with the number 8.

Phones

The cheapest way to make **international calls** is generally via apps such as WhatsApp, Facebook Messenger/Facetime or similar. Some local mobile phone networks also offer very inexpensive rates for international calls. If you buy a local SIM card ask the vendor what the best access code is for the cheapest international calls as they vary depending on your network provider.

Bali is divided into several **code zones**, and Lombok has two codes. Calls to **mobile phones** – whose numbers begin 08 – are more expensive.

Mobile phones

Most mobile phones will work fine in Indonesia. Virtually all travellers these days choose not to use international roaming (as costs can be prohibitive) but use a **local SIM card**, which will provide 3G or 4G mobile internet. A local SIM is very cheap. Mobile coverage is excellent in Bali and Lombok and there are phone shops everywhere. Staff may have to unblock your phone first and will also advise on the best SIM card for your needs, bearing in mind local and international coverage. Top-up cards are sold at mobile-phone stalls everywhere.

Post

Every town and tourist centre on Bali and Lombok has a main **Post Office** (*kantor pos utama*) where you can buy stamps (*perangko*) and can post letters (*surat*) and parcels (*paket*). Franchised branch offices are ubiquitous in cities but have fewer services. Most *kantor pos utama* keep old-style government office **hours** (Mon–Thurs 7.30/8am–3pm, Fri 7.30/8am–11am, Sat 7.30am–1pm; closed on public holidays). In larger towns and resorts, you can also buy stamps and send letters and parcels from **postal agents**. Post boxes aren't widespread, so it's best to post letters at *kantor pos utama* or postal agents.

If the *kantor pos utama* doesn't offer a **parcel-packing service** ask if there is somewhere nearby that offers a packing service; don't bother packing it yourself as the contents needs to be inspected first. *Kantor pos* won't handle any parcels over 10kg or more than 1m long, but most shops can arrange **shipping**.

Time

Bali and Lombok are on **Central Indonesian Time** (GMT+8, North American EST+12, Australian EST-2). There's no daylight saving.

Tourist information

Indonesia has a few **tourism offices** scattered around the world; consult https://indonesia.travel.

District capitals across Bali and Lombok all maintain their own local **government tourist office** (Mon–Thurs 8am–3pm, Fri 8am–noon; those in the main tourist centres keep longer hours) but they're generally of limited use to travellers. The Ubud office is an exception, with well-informed staff.

GOVERNMENT TRAVEL ADVICE

Most Western governments maintain websites with travel information detailing some of the potential hazards of countries to be visited and what to do in emergencies.

Australian Department of Foreign Affairs http://dfat.gov.au.
British Foreign & Commonwealth Office http://gov.uk.
Canadian Department of Foreign Affairs http://travel.gc.ca.
Irish Department of Foreign Affairs http://dfa.ie.
New Zealand Ministry of Foreign Affairs http://safetravel.govt.nz.
US State Department http://state.gov.
South African Department of Foreign Affairs http://www.dirco.gov.za.

LISTINGS MAGAZINES AND TOURIST PUBLICATIONS

Plenty of **free tourist magazines** supply information on Bali's and Lombok's sights, activities and events; they're generally available online as well as in hotels and restaurants in the main tourist centres.

Bali http://bali.com. Perhaps the most complete and accurate online info source on sites, restaurants, maps and "best of" listings.
Bali Plus http://baliplus.com. Compact monthly that covers tourist attractions and lists and reviews restaurants, clubs, shops and spas.
The beat http://thebeatbali.com. Bali's premier nightlife listings magazine covers gigs, parties and clubs plus a few bars and restaurants. Fortnightly.
The Lombok Guide http://thelombokguide.com. Runs interesting features and general information on all aspects of visiting Lombok and the Gili Islands.
My Lombok http://facebook.com/mylombokmag. Glossy monthly magazine with articles on culture, events, travel and food.
NOW! Bali Magazine http://nowbali.co.id. An insider's guide to life on Bali, with listings of restaurants and bars, cultural events, activities and more.
Sanur Weekly http://sanurweekly.com. News, events and listings in the Sanur area.
The Yak http://theyakmag.com. Lifestyle quarterly magazine for the Seminyak expat community and visitors.

WEBSITES AND FORUMS

Bali Bible http://myevent.promo. Comprehensive online guide with reviews and useful Top Ten lists.
Bali Discovery http://balidiscovery.com. Weekly tourism-related news from Bali, plus hotel and tour booking.
Bali Travel Forum http://balitravelforum.com. Active forum with lots of expert posters.
Living in Indonesia/Bali http://expat.or.id. Plenty of information for people planning to move to Bali and for tourists.

South Bali

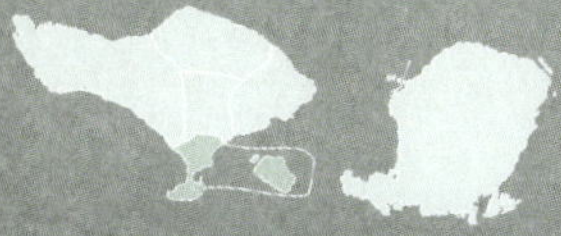

A TRADITIONAL FISHING BOAT ON KARANG BEACH

1

South Bali

The mainly flat land that makes up the south is among the most densely populated in Bali. This is where you'll find the island's major tourist resorts: at Kuta-Legian-Seminyak and Jimbaran in the west, and Sanur, Nusa Dua and Tanjung Benoa in the east. The area is a surfers' paradise, pounded by some of the most famous and challenging breaks in the world. The vast majority of visitors head straight for the brash, commercial coastal sprawl of Kuta–Legian–Seminyak, famous for its shopping and nightlife, while the neighbouring area just to the north, around Canggu, has become one of Bali's most rapidly developing areas and the epicentre of the island's expat and digital nomad crowd.

Bali's administrative capital, **Denpasar**, is also here, and while most tourists treat the city as little more than a transit point for cross-island journeys, it holds the island's best museum and makes an interesting contrast to the more westernised beach enclaves.

Across on the southeast coast, beach life is quieter and less frantic at **Sanur** and more luxurious and manicured at **Nusa Dua** and **Tanjung Benoa**, home to many luxury hotels. Offshore lie three islands: escapist **Nusa Penida**, tiny **Nusa Ceningan**, and resolutely relaxed **Nusa Lembongan**, with exceptional diving and easy access from Sanur. South of Kuta, the **Bukit Peninsula** offers peaceful, upmarket beachfront hotels at **Jimbaran** and fabulous **surf** and lively beach bases beneath the cliffs in and around **Uluwatu**, also the site of an important clifftop temple.

Kuta–Legian–Seminyak

The biggest, brashest resort in Bali, the **KUTA–LEGIAN–SEMINYAK** conurbation expands relentlessly out from its core on the southwest coast, 10km southwest of Denpasar. Packed with thousands of hotels, restaurants, bars, clubs, shops, spas and tour agencies, the 8km-long coastal strip plays host to millions of visitors each year who come to party, shop, surf or simply laze a week away, and sucks in ever-more Indonesians for work. It's a hectic place: noisy, full of touts and busy with constant building work. The area's road network is totally insufficient, so prepare yourself for the horrific traffic: all the main routes are rammed with cars, motorbikes and fumes, and the pollution can be punishing. It's often quicker to walk.

SWIMMING IN KUTA

The waves that make Kuta such a great beach for surfers can make it treacherous for **swimming**, with a strong undertow as well as the rollers to contend with. The current is especially dangerous at the Canggu beaches. This has been compounded by the very real problem of marine debris and plastic waste washing up on the shore, much of it drifting over from Indonesia's other islands. Despite the diligent daily efforts of local volunteers to clear Bali's beaches of rubbish, it's still common to see a fringe of trash along the seafront, and the polluted waters pose a hazard for swimmers. The Indonesian government has pledged to address its waste management issues and move towards a plastic-free future but for now, stick to sunbathing and beach bar-hopping along Kuta's shores.

BINGIN BEACH

Highlights

❶ **Canggu** This rapidly developing rural region, blessed with fine surf beaches, traditional ricefields and an explosion of cool cafes and yoga schools, is Bali at its boho best: it draws a cast of characters from across the globe. See page 62

❷ **Dining in Seminyak and Kerobokan** Top international chefs plus moneyed tourism equals one of Asia's most dynamic dining destinations. See page 69

❸ **Kuta–Legian–Seminyak beach clubs** Choose from style-magazine chic, hipster cool or beach shack and lose a day with sounds, sustenance and sand all in one place. The fun beach holiday in a nutshell. See page 70

❹ **Bingin** Rickety bamboo bars on stilts, surf and a villagey vibe – welcome to the finest escape on the Bukit Peninsula. See page 77

❺ **Surf beaches** Even non-surfers should visit Uluwatu for a view of one of the most legendary waves in the world. Bingin and Padang Padang also offer powerful breaks. See page 78

❻ **Pura Luhur Uluwatu** This important temple complex enjoys an utterly magical clifftop location, particularly at sunset. See page 78

❼ **The Nusas** Nusas Lembongan, Ceningan and Panida are laidback islands offering great diving with manta rays and mola mola, and escapism in spades. See page 94

HIGHLIGHTS ARE MARKED ON THE MAP ON PAGE 56

Infrastructure aside, the area does retain a tropical charm. It's still largely low-rise, and coconut palms and splashes of colour from frangipani trees and bougainvillaea help soften the urban scene. And though Kuta-Legian-Seminyak is very much an international resort – *McDonald's*, Rip Curl, *Hard Rock* and most of the usual corporate suspects are all present – a distinctly Balinese character endures. Villagers still live and work here, making religious offerings, attending *banjar* meetings and holding temple festivals. Each morning and afternoon, women still place **offerings**, which litter the pavements and streets.

The reason everyone is here is the vast **beach**. Even if not quite so glorious as it once was, it is still a gentle curve of pale sand that stretches for 8km from Tuban to Canggu, its breakers luring amateur and experienced surfers alike. It's also the venue for the much-lauded Kuta sunsets; at their blood-red best in April, but streaky-pink at any time of year and the stuff sundowners are made of – whether cocktails in a hip bar or just a cold Bintang on plastic seats.

Brief history

For centuries, Kuta was considered by the Balinese to be an infertile stretch of coast haunted by malevolent spirits and a dumping ground for lepers and criminals. In the seventeenth and eighteenth centuries, it operated as a **slave port** when

the Balinese rajas sold hundreds of thousands of people to their counterparts in Java and beyond. By the mid-nineteenth century, however, life had become more prosperous – thanks in part to the energetic Danish business trader **Mads Lange**, who set up home here in 1839. Lange's political influence was also significant, and, thanks to his diplomatic skills, south Bali avoided falling under Dutch control until 1906.

In 1936 the Americans **Bob and Louise Koke**, spotting Kuta's tourist potential, built a small hotel and, until the Japanese invasion of 1942, the place flourished. World War II and its aftermath stemmed the tourist flow until the 1960s, when young travellers established Kuta as a highlight on the **hippie trail**. Homestays were eventually joined by smarter international outfits, and Kuta–Legian–Seminyak has since evolved into the most prosperous region of the island, drawing workers from across Bali as well as the rest of Indonesia.

Over the years, the popularity of Kuta and Legian beaches has ebbed and flowed. Aging, now more affluent hippies weary of Kuta and Legian's hustle-bustle, began pushing northwest to Seminyak and when it became overcrowded expanded their horizons even further up the coastline, seeking a bigger slice of solitude. Inland, but still wanting to join in tourist gains, Petitenget and Kerobokan began flaunting their rural, relaxed atmospheres. While Canggu is the "new Kuta", attracting raucous

HIGHLIGHTS

1. Canggu
2. Dining in Seminyak and Kerobokan
3. Kuta–Legian–Seminyak beach clubs
4. Bingin
5. Surf beaches
6. Pura Luhur Uluwatu
7. The Nusas

1

KUTA-LEGIAN-SEMINYAK

beer-swilling surfers, the cliffs and shores all the way to Tanah Lot and beyond are dotted with luxurious rental villas.

Kuta and Tuban

Young, fun and frequently trashy, **KUTA** is the original Balinese mass resort area. It's hard to believe that as late as the early 1980s, eating and accommodation options were fairly limited here. Today it's frantic, jam-packed with shops – from tiny outlets to big-brand megastores – and hugely popular with travellers on a budget or visiting for a party – chiefly backpackers, surfers and young Australians. It's almost a surprise to see a temple squeezed between the endless T-shirt and sunglasses outlets in the traffic-choked lanes. The two main lanes, Poppies 1 and 2, and the winding alleys around and between them, are the accommodation hubs. Jalan Legian/Kuta is the 4km-long shopping strip. However, the beach is the real reason everyone is here – often crowded, but a long stretch of fine biscuit-coloured sand.

Just beyond Kuta Square, Kuta Beach officially becomes **Tuban**, often called **South Kuta**, and things quieten down. This area is often the choice of families or older couples, many of whom stay in the resort hotels that have direct access to the beach. The beachfront promenade runs from the lifeguard post near the corner of Jalan Pantai Kuta to the fence of the airport and it's about a thirty-minute walk from Kuta Square to the final Tuban hotel, *Patra Bali Resort & Villas*.

Bali Sea Turtle Society (BSTS)

Kuta beach, access Jl Pantai Kuta • free • http://baliseaturtle.org

Despite the crowds, Olive Ridley and some green **turtles** (see page 82) return to Kuta's shores every year between March and September to lay eggs late at night. To protect them from poachers, a **hatchery** has been established by the Bali Sea Turtle Society who work with local communities throughout Bali. Positioned beside the community police office on the beach near the corner of Jalan Pantai Kuta, the hatchery is basic, just a kiosk with information boards and, in season, sand containers that hold the eggs. The hatchlings are released the following day into the ocean.

Waterbom Park

Jl Kartika Plaza, Tuban • Charge • http://waterbom-bali.com

Tuban's **Waterbom Park** is a hugely popular aquatic adventure park, with water slides, a 150m-long macaroni tube, a lazy river with inner tubes and the Climax ride, which

KUTA–LEGIAN–SEMINYAK ORIENTATION

It's now impossible to recognise the demarcation lines between the once-separate villages of Kuta, Legian and Seminyak. We've used the common perception of the **neighbourhood borders**: Kuta stretches north from the Matahari department store in Kuta Square to Jalan Melasti; Legian runs from Jalan Melasti as far north as Jalan Arjuna; and Seminyak extends from Jalan Arjuna to *The Oberoi* hotel, where Petitenget begins. Petitenget feeds into Kerobokan and then north up to the string of Canggu area beaches, not strictly within the Kuta boundaries but close enough to share facilities. Kuta's increasingly built-up southern fringes, extending south from Matahari to the airport, are defined as south Kuta/Tuban.

The area's **main road**, which begins as Jalan Raya Kuta and becomes Jalan Raya Legian and Jalan Raya Seminyak, runs north–south through all three main districts, a total distance of 5km. The bulk of facilities are packed into the 600m-wide strip between Jalan Legian in the east and the coast to the west, an area crisscrossed by tiny *gang* (alleyways) and larger one-way roads.

The other main **landmark** is a minuscule roundabout at the southern end of Kuta that stands at the Jalan Legian–Jalan Pantai Kuta intersection, formerly known as Bemo Corner.

1

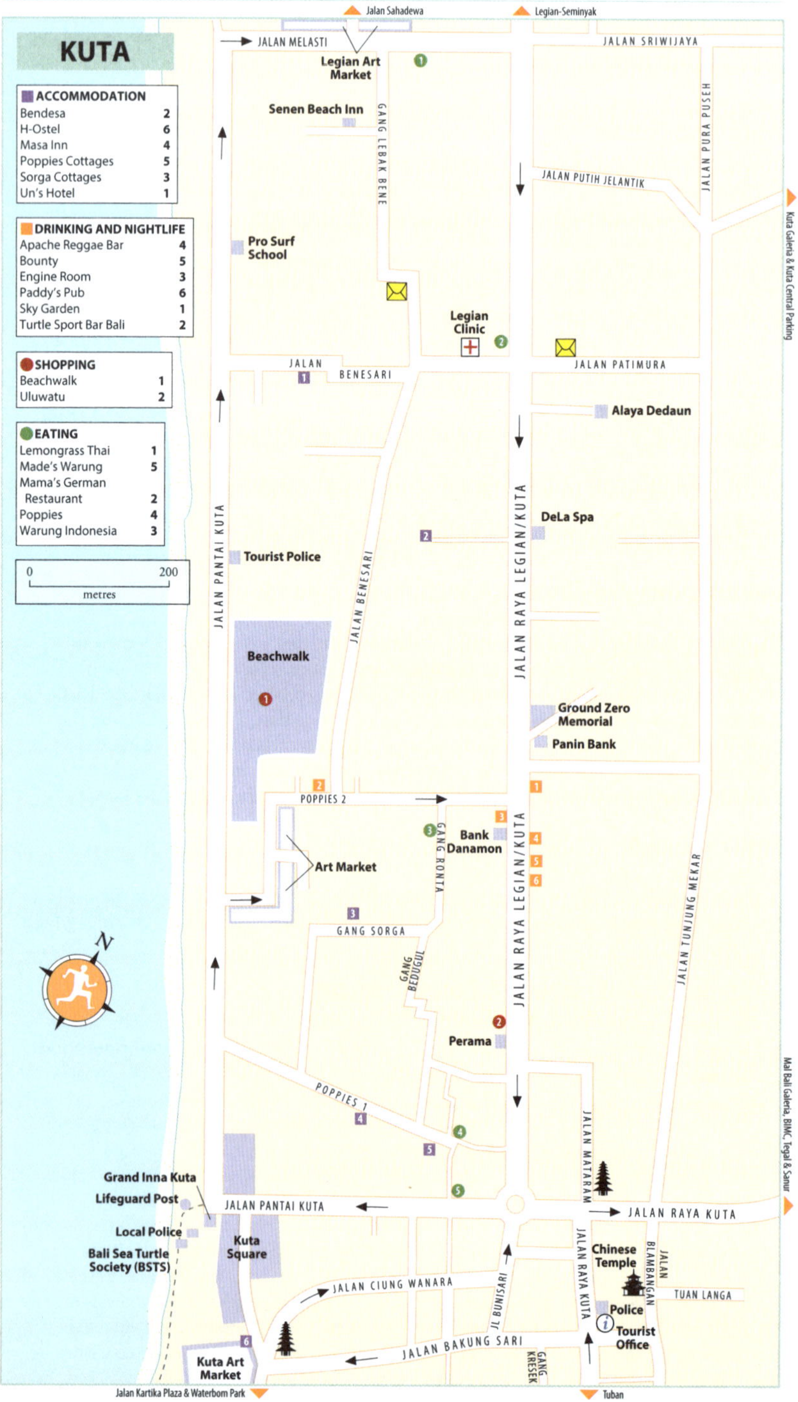
KUTA
ACCOMMODATION
Bendesa 2
H-Ostel 6
Masa Inn 4
Poppies Cottages 5
Sorga Cottages 3
Un's Hotel 1
DRINKING AND NIGHTLIFE
Apache Reggae Bar 4
Bounty 5
Engine Room 3
Paddy's Pub 6
Sky Garden 1
Turtle Sport Bar Bali 2
SHOPPING
Beachwalk 1
Uluwatu 2
EATING
Lemongrass Thai 1
Made's Warung 5
Mama's German Restaurant 2
Poppies 4
Warung Indonesia 3
0 200
metres
N
Jalan Sahadewa
Legian-Seminyak
JALAN MELASTI
JALAN SRIWIJAYA
Legian Art Market
Senen Beach Inn
GANG LEBAK BENE
JALAN PURA PUSEH
JALAN PUTIH JELANTIK
Kuta Galeria & Kuta Central Parking
Pro Surf School
Legian Clinic
JALAN BENESARI
JALAN PATIMURA
Alaya Dedaun
JALAN PANTAI KUTA
DeLa Spa
JALAN BENESARI
Tourist Police
JALAN RAYA LEGIAN/KUTA
Beachwalk
Ground Zero Memorial
Panin Bank
POPPIES 2
Bank Danamon
GANG RONTA
Art Market
GANG SORGA
GANG BEDUGUL
JALAN TUNJUNG MEKAR
Perama
POPPIES 1
JALAN MATARAM
Mal Bali Galeria, BIMC, Tegal & Sanur
Grand Inna Kuta
Lifeguard Post
JALAN PANTAI KUTA
JALAN RAYA KUTA
Local Police
Kuta Square
Bali Sea Turtle Society (BSTS)
Chinese Temple
JALAN BLAMBANGAN
JALAN TUAN LANGA
JALAN CIUNG WANARA
JL BUNISARI
JALAN RAYA KUTA
Police
Tourist Office
JALAN BAKUNG SARI
GANG KRESEK
Kuta Art Market
Jalan Kartika Plaza & Waterbom Park
Tuban

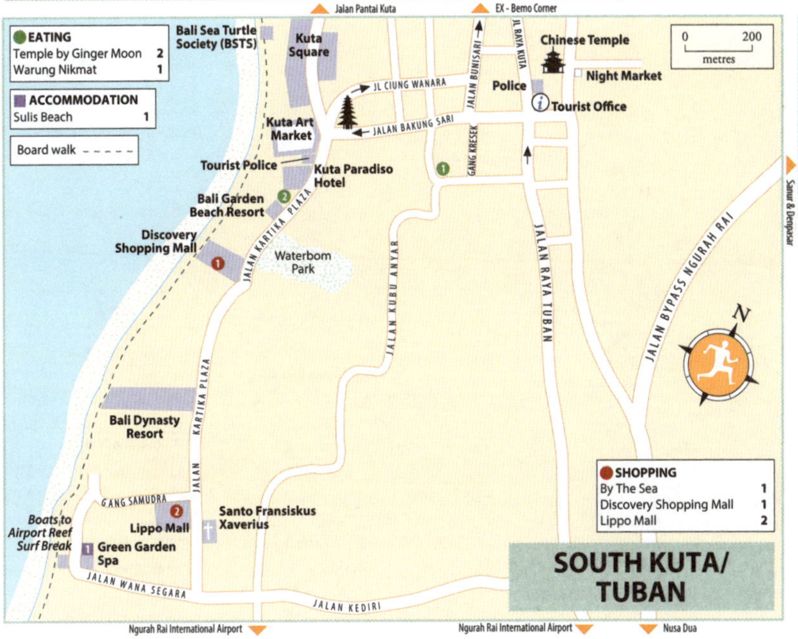

features a 60m near-vertical drop before you slingshot around a tight loop. You top up a pay-wristband first to pay for anything on-site. However, it's not a cheap day out.

Legian

Calmer than Kuta with less-crowded sands, **Legian** is popular with families and tourists who are seeking a more relaxed, easy-going version of Kuta. Geographically and in atmosphere, it is midway between raucous Kuta and more upmarket Seminyak, with plenty of shops (generally more interesting than those in Kuta) and restaurants, and a wider choice of mid-range hotels than Kuta. If you've got your eye on a beachfront hotel in Legian, note that the shorefront road between Jalan Melasti and Jalan Arjuna is open only to toll-paying cars and is very quiet.

Seminyak, Petitenget and Kerobokan

Given the excesses of Kuta and growing development in Legian, expats and style-conscious tourists travelled north to escape the masses. **Seminyak** and **Petitenget** peaked in popularity with the jet set and hipsters around 2005, but over-development and an increasingly Kuta-esque sprawl led to a further exodus and today Seminyak is a pretty mainstream resort area with a slew of mid- to high-end hotels, bars, clubs, restaurants and shops. Most of the style cognoscenti, and the best independent boutiques and bars, have now shifted north to neighbouring **Kerobokan** and on to the Canggu area, a further 7km or so to the north.

That said, Seminyak still has plenty of appeal, particularly for those in need of a good night out or a meal: there's a glut of restaurants along Jalan Kayu Aya (aka Jalan Laksmana) and at the northern end of Jalan Petitenget. Seminyak's Jalan Camplung Tanduk is the area's centre for gay nightlife.

Vegas has arrived on the beach, too, in the form of a smattering of bombastic **beach clubs** north of the temple at Petitenget, providing a venue for rich Jakartans and the

like to lounge around over food and cocktails while DJs spin beats. Here and there you'll also find less swanky beach shacks, for the simpler pleasures of a cool Bintang and local grub.

Canggu

North of Kerobokan, the coastline unfurls in a succession of surfing beaches and dramatic coastal panoramas at Batubelig, Berewa, Batu Bolong, Echo Beach (Batu Mejan) and Pererenan – all can be dangerous for swimming. This area is loosely referred to as **Canggu** and in recent years it has become the name to drop among "connected" visitors: think stylish hotels, uber-luxe villas, *nouveau-warung*, pilates studios and an epidemic of hipster barber shops where beard grooming is an art form. But as all the action is well dissipated, with places scattered among ricefields and behind wild beaches, the Canggu area retains a delightfully (neo)rustic feel – there's no urban sprawl at all.

Echo Beach and Batu Bolong are the real hubs. As ever across southern Bali, traffic can be trying. There's virtually no public transport and even once-quiet backroads

like Jalan Betubelig from Kerobokan can now be traffic clogged. Never take the Tanah Lot highway in the afternoon, which is total roadblock. Locals and resident expats tend to use a bumpy network of little lanes and dirt pathways that are not plotted on maps, but even these can get bumper-to-bumper with mopeds as sunset approaches. A new road currently under construction will hopefully alleviate some of the snarls.

Inevitably, change is happening lightning-fast in Canggu and what was once a surfer bolthole is now developing at a terrifying pace. Get there soon.

ARRIVAL AND DEPARTURE — KUTA–LEGIAN–SEMINYAK-CANGGU

BY PLANE

Bali's only airport, Ngurah Rai International Airport (http://bali-airport.com), is situated 3km south of Kuta. You'll find the usual ATMs and currency exchange booths in the baggage claim hall and just outside the Arrivals building, along with car rental outlets. The 24hr left-luggage offices are tucked away outside, between International Arrivals and Departures, to the right of Domestic Arrivals.

Prepaid taxis The easiest way of getting away from the airport to Kuta–Legian–Seminyak is by pre-paid taxi. The counter is outside International Arrivals to the left, or in the domestic terminal across a pick-up lane at the end of a row of shops.

Metered/app taxis Metered taxis are around twenty

ALTERNATIVE ROAD NAMES

As if the confusion of lanes wasn't enough, the Kuta–Legian–Seminyak area plays fast and loose with **road names**. Many roads were named after their first or biggest hotel or restaurant and although they have been given official names (indeed, often several in succession over the years), many local residents, taxi drivers and maps stick to older versions, and street signs are rarely consistent. The following are the most confusing examples. The **official name** is given in bold.

Jalan Kayu Aya (Petitenget) Previously called Jalan Laksmana and Jalan Oberoi – now sometimes known as "Eat Street" because of its many restaurants.

Jalan Camplung Tanduk (Seminyak) Also known as Jalan Dhyana Pura and Jalan Abimanyu, and sometimes as Jalan Gado-Gado, after the restaurant at the western end.

Jalan Arjuna (Legian) Commonly referred to as Jalan Double Six after a raucous nightclub once located on the beach.

Jalan Yudistira (Legian) In the past this has also been called Jalan Padma.

Jalan Pantai Arjuna (Legian) Also known as Jalan Blue Ocean Beach, after one of its hotels, or Jalan Pantai Legian.

Jalan Werk Udara (Legian) Formerly called Jalan Bagus Taruna, and sometimes known as Jalan Rum Jungle, after a restaurant.

Jalan Bakung Sari (south Kuta/Tuban) Previously known as Jalan Singo Sari.

percent cheaper than prepaid. They're not licensed to pick up inside the compound, so wait on the road outside the airport gates (turn right outside International and walk about 500m). Blue Bird's Bali Taxi is recommended. Gojek/GoCar/GoRide and Grab app-taxis operate to some areas of southern Bali; rates are about half those charged by airport cabs. However, it can be difficult to get one to pick you up from the airport due to opposition by local drivers.

Bemos Dark-blue public *bemos* often wait for customers on Jl Airport Ngurah Rai outside the airport gates during daylight hours, then run to Kuta. However, given that schedules are random and there can be extra charges for bags, very few travellers bother with them.

Hotel pick-ups Many hotels offer pick-up from (and travel to) the airport for prices just above those charged by taxis.

BY SHUTTLE BUS

Private tourist shuttle buses run to all tourist destinations on Bali, including Lombok and the Gili Islands. There are many operators but Perama has the best reputation. Drop-offs are usually at the operator's office at the destination rather than specific hotels.

Perama Based 100m north of the former Bemo Corner at Jl Legian 39 (http://peramatour.com); for an extra fee, you can be picked up (and dropped off) from/at your hotel. Fare to the Gili Islands includes boat transfer.

Destinations Amed (daily; 3hr 15min); Bedugul (daily; 2hr 30min–3hr); Candidasa (4 daily; 2hr 15min); Gili Islands (daily; 9hr 30min); Kintamani (daily; 2hr 30min); Lovina (daily; 4hr); Nusa Lembongan (daily; 2hr 30min); Padang Bai (4 daily; 2hr); Sanur (7 daily; 30min); Senggigi, Lombok (daily; 9hr); Ubud (6 daily; 1hr–1hr 30min).

BY BEMO

Public *bemos* no longer operate in the Kuta to Seminyak area. Replacing them is the sleek green and yellow Kura-Kura Bus system (Jl. Raya Ngurah Rai No. 88, Tuban, http://kura2bus.com). Five lines service all of southern Bali: Line 1 from Galeria Duty Free (DFS) and Bali Shopping Mall to Kuta via Nusa Dua and Legian; Line 2 from DFS to Kuta via Jimbaran and Legian; Line 3 from DFS to Seminyak via Kuta and Legian; Line 4 from DFS to Legian via Seminyak and Kuta, and Line 5 from DFS to Sanur via Ubud.

There are fixed fares for a single journey on a single line; all lines connect through the DFS bus bay.

You can see route maps, prices and ticket sales locations on their website and can download their app to buy one-stop tickets or passes and see schedules on your phone. Kura-Kura also offers airport transfers and tours.

BY BUS

Intended to be south Bali's mass rapid transit system, but without success so far, Trans Sarbagita buses do not have a great reputation for reliability or punctuality, but operate three routes: Nusa Dua–Batubulan; Denpasar–Jimbaran; and Tabanan–Ngurah Rai International Airport. In theory buses run every 30min from 5am–9pm. Flat-rate fares per stop are in place.

BY BOAT

Private agents such as Perama offer integrated bus and boat tickets to Lombok, Nusa Lembongan and other Indonesian islands.

1

GETTING AROUND

By bemo Public *bemos* have been replaced by the efficient Kura-Kura Bus.

By taxi The most reliable taxis are the light-blue Blue Bird-owned Bali Taxi (0361 701111; http://bluebirdgroup.com) which you can order online or via their app. Gojek/GoCar/GoRide and Grab app-taxis also operate in this part of Bali.

By car, bike or motorbike For motorcycle taxis, download the Gojek Bali app to order online. The nearest driver will respond with a price, which you can accept or reject. They are equipped with helmets and rain gear. Gojek also offers food pick-up and delivery and other services. Countless tour agents offer car and motorbike rentals. Many also offer bicycles – arguably the best way to get around, though not for the faint-hearted. Such is the traffic that a car is more hassle than it's worth within the resort area. Where it is legal to park beside the road, attendants charge a small fee to wave you in and out and guard your vehicle.

INFORMATION AND ACTIVITIES

Adventure activities operators Mason Adventure Tours (http://masonadventures.com) and Bali Trekking Tour (http://balitrekkingtour.com) offer mountain-bike trips from the rim of Gunung Batur volcano, plus trekking and elephant tours. Sobek (http://balisobek.com) specialises in cycling and rafting/kayaking tours on the Grade II–III rapids of the Ayung River. All provide free transfers in southern Bali.

Diving AquaMarine Diving, Jl Petitenget 2A, Kuta (http://aquamarinediving.com) runs dive trips to southern Bali sites such as Nusa Penida, including transport from the Kuta–Legian–Seminyak area.

Kitesurfing Operators Sanur (https://sanursurf.com) provide pick-ups from the Kuta area.

Tourist information There's an official tourist office at Jl Raya Kuta 2 (0361 766181).

COURSES AND CLASSES

Once you tire of sea, sun, sand and shopping, you will be able to find more cultural and spiritual pastimes amid the hedonism.

Cookery Classes Cookly (http://cookly.me/cooking-class/indonesia-bali) is a listing of independent chefs and cooks throughout Bali who teach classes, traditional Balinese, organic, vegan, market and farm tours. Family-friendly. Can book online and pay with a credit card.

Massage Jari Menari (Jl Basangkasa No. 47, Seminyak, http://jarimenari.com) is a well-known massage centre offering half-, one- and twelve-day courses.

Yoga, Pilates and meditation There are more than a

SURFING IN KUTA

They say **surfing** was introduced to Bali by American hotel-owner Bob Koke in 1936. Today it is huge in the Kuta strip; the beach, Jalan Poppies 2, Jalan Poppies 1 and Jalan Benesari, are crammed with board rental and repair shops and surfwear outlets. Surf championships are regular events.

As Kuta is a sandy beach with no coral or rocks to wipe out on, it's a **great place to learn** to surf. However, while Kuta may have launched many a surfer's lifetime hobby, don't underestimate the power of waves on bigger days. First-timers should book a preliminary lesson to guarantee their safety. Slightly more advanced breaks can be found further south in Tuban at Airport Reef accessed by boats from the lot at the west end of Jalan Wana Segara. North of Seminyak, in the Canggu area, there are reef breaks at Batu Bolong, Echo Beach and Pererenan. The best **time of year** for surfing off Kuta is during the dry season (April–Oct); at other times surfers head east to Sanur and Nusa Dua.

SURF SCHOOLS

Surfing **lessons** are offered throughout the area, but choose your instructor carefully; personal recommendation is always good, and bear in mind that established **surf schools** are accredited and have insurance. Freelance instructors hang out on all the main beaches (charges include board rental).

Odesseys Surf School Mercure Hotel, Kuta Bali, Jl Pantai Kuta; http://facebook.com/odysseysurfschool. All instructors are fluent in English and Japanese.

Rip Curl School of Surf Jl Arjuna, Legian and Jl. Cemara, Sanur; http://ripcurlschoolofsurf.com. Also offers wakeboarding, kitesurfing, foil and stand-up paddleboard lessons.

UP2U Surf School Jl Pantai Kuta, Legian; http://up2usurfschool.com. Group and private lessons available.

dozen yoga schools in this region. Up to five drop-in sessions a day in numerous styles are run at the *Desa Seni Resort* (Jl Subak Sari No. 13, Pantai Berawa, Canggu, http://desaseni.com) as well as longer retreats and yoga teacher training. *The Art of Body* (Jl Mertanadi 22XX, Kerobokan, http://theartofbody.com) is a professional pilates and holistic wellness studio. Award-winning *Prana Spa* (Jl. Kunti I No. 118X, Seminyak, http://impiana.com.my/spas/prana-spa) has three classes per day of various yoga styles.

ACCOMMODATION

You're spoilt for choice for accommodation here. Most in Kuta is of the cheap and cheerful variety: hostels, *losmen* and somewhat dated mid-range places. The accomoodation in Legian, Seminyak and Kerobokan is more expensive and more chic. Canggu has more villas for rent than hotels or guesthouses, but there are some highly characterful places.

KUTA AND TUBAN, SEE MAPS PAGES 60 AND 61

Bendesa Jl Legian No. 382; 0361 751 358. A cut above most of the competition, with a range of decent-sized rooms in a large, leafy complex around a pleasant pool, and friendly staff. $

★ **H-Ostel** Kuta Square E8; http://h-ostel.com. Very centrally located, this contemporary hostel is close to vibrant nightlife, shopping and 200m from the beach. All dorms (mixed and female) are a/c and bunks are equipped with charging sockets, reading lights and lockers. There's a great roof terrace, cafe, speedy wi-fi and breakfast is included. $

Masa Inn Poppies 1 No. 27; http://masainn.com. With two pools and a pretty garden, this long-running family-owned place has a traditional, Balinese feel with a/c, mid-range rooms and a restaurant. $

Poppies Cottages Poppies 1 No. 19; http://poppiesbali.com. The attention to detail and genuinely warm welcome from the staff (many have worked here for decades) has served this place well, for it's full of visitors who return every year. Twenty charming, traditionally styled thatched cottages are scattered in a tropical garden around a lovely pool. Reserve ahead. $$

★ **Sulis Beach** Jl Wana Segara; http://sulishotelbali.com/. Surrounded by luxurious 5-star resorts, this modern 3-star provides excellent value for money, especially if you book early. The air-con rooms have super-king beds, full-size fridges and balconies, plus there's a large pool and a beach location that feels like it's on another island and not a mere 20min walk to central Kuta. $$

Sorga Cottages Gang Sorga, off Poppies 1; https://hotelsorgacottages.id-indonesia.com/. On a quiet alley, yet within firing range of the clubs on Jl Legian, these dated-but-decent rooms are comfortable, if something of a 1980s timewarp. There's a small pool and restaurant. $

Un's Hotel Jl Benesari No. 16; http://unshotel.com. Antique furnishings, art and traditional architecture, plus a lovely small garden with pool combine to provide a good-value stay with Balinese character. All rooms have hot-water en-suites but you'll pay more for a/c. $

LEGIAN, SEE MAP PAGE 62

Bali Niksoma Jl Padma Utara; http://baliniksoma.com. Crisp Balinese minimalism in an award-winning boutique hotel bang on the beach. Deluxe rooms are worth the extra expense for their style and space. Also has a spa, a pool overlooking the breakers and faultless service. Single traveller rates available. $$$

Boss Legian Hotel Jl Werkudara; http://bosslegianhotel.com. This new hotel right in the heart of Legian has 93 simply furnished rooms. There's a restaurant on site as well as a rooftop terrace with a pool and bar. $

Hotel Kumala Jl Werkudara; https://www.hotelkumala.com/hotelkumala. A five-minute walk from the beach, and with lots of cafes and restaurants close by, this fine-value hotel has real Balinese flavour thanks to a scattering of statuary and carvings. Avoid the standard rooms which are very plain; the others are spacious and well-furnished, all with a/c, hot water and modern bathrooms. There's a pool and restaurant. $

Hotel Kumala Pantai Jl Werkudara; http://kumalapantai.com. Popular with families and couples, this resort hotel has comfortable classic-modern a/c rooms with balconies, cable TV, bath and shower, in three-storey buildings on the seafront road. There are also two pools, one of which is big enough for laps. $$

Padma Resort Jl Yudistira No. 1; http://padmaresortlegian.com. Smart resort hotel whose extensive tropical gardens run down to the beach. Accommodation, all near or with direct access to a pool, is in the hotel wings or larger deluxe "chalets" – some wheelchair-accessible – and there's a fine spread of facilities: restaurants, bars, pools, a spa, a complimentary kids' club and tours office. $$$$

★ **Three Brothers Bungalows** Jl Padma Utara; http://threebrothersbungalows.com.This place, in a mature garden setting with a pool, resembles a temple complex more than a hotel. Airy accommodation (rooms and two-storey cottages) boast Balinese carvings – "Deluxe" have four-poster beds and semi-outside bathrooms (they're worth the extra). $

SEMINYAK, PETITENGET AND KEROBOKAN, SEE MAP PAGE 63

Blue-Zea Resort by Double-Six Jl Camplung Tanduk No. 66; http://blu-zearesort.com. Good-quality resort hotel near the beach, where tasteful modern rooms gather

1

around a split-level lagoon-style pool – the big draw here, especially for families. Also has a tennis court, on-site spa, gym, cinema and daily activities, plus shuttle buses to Legian. $$$

Inada Losmen Gang Bima No. 9, off Jl Camplung Tanduk and Jl Raya Seminyak; 0361 732 269. This cheapie, run by a helpful Indonesian/Japanese couple has a dozen basic rooms: a bed, a desk, a fan, a bathroom with hot water – and that's your lot. $

The Oberoi Jl Kayu Aya; http://oberoihotels.com. The *grande dame* of local luxury hotels provides beautiful, traditional-style rooms and villas – think thatched roofs meet marble bathrooms – all privately secluded in gorgeous beachfront grounds. To its credit, the ambience remains distinctly Balinese despite the finest international standards (to which numerous awards and celebrity guests testify). $$$$

★ **W Bali-Seminyak** Jl Petitenget; http://marriott.com. A kind of resort city for hipsters featuring a blend of glamour and playfulness in open-plan public areas, stylish bars and restaurants, all gathered around a multi-tiered pool of simply staggering dimensions. At night it feels more like an ultraspacious cool club than a hotel. Choose between 159 well-appointed rooms or 79 stunning garden villas with pools. $$$$

CANGGU AND PERERENAN, SEE MAP PAGE 64

★ **Anyar Estate** Gang Brick Lane, off Jl Bumbak Dauh, Kerobokan; http://anyarestate.com. Gorgeous pool villas, with two to five bedrooms, all with stylish Balinese furnishings and a contemporary feel in a tranquil village location on the east side of Kerobokan. Breakfast is cooked to order and there's plenty of space to entertain and relax. $$$$

The Chillhouse Jl Kubu Manyar 22, Canggu; http://bvrbaliholidayrentals.com. Laidback surf-inspired style – think designer lampshades, a crisp colour scheme and surf photos – in a small garden hotel. Accommodation, in rooms, bungalows and a treetop loft, all has a/c and is set in a lovely garden with a pool and restaurant. Offers surfing as well as massage and yoga packages. It's 500m from the beach; bikes are available. $

★ **Hotel Tugu Bali** Jl Pantai Batu Bolong, Canggu; http://tuguhotels.com. Evoking Indonesian tradition like nowhere else on the island, this Canggu original has ambience, class and history. You stay in polished-teak houses set back from the beach, all beautifully furnished with antiques and many with private plunge pools. Communal areas are equally fabulous, from the restaurant set in a seventeenth-century Chinese temple (moved here brick by brick) to the pool and spa. $$$$

Lila Boutik Residence Jl Padang Linjong 25, Canggu; https://lilaboutikresidence.com. With plenty of natural light and plants galore, Lila's spacious bungalows and villas offer a serene getaway at a still-affordable price point. The villas also have a fully equipped kitchens and huge bathtubs. Relaxing in a hammock by the pool with views across the rice terraces, you'll feel a million miles from Bali's bustle. $$

Serenity Jl Nelayan; http://serenitybali.com. This easy-going place built largely from bamboo has a certain ramshackle, rambling charm. The homely rooms have fan or a/c, and massage and yoga are on offer. There's a backpackers' annexe down the road. Free tea and coffee, bikes for rent and horseriding can be arranged. Good value. $

Sesah Beach Villas Jl. Pantai Seseh, Canggu; https://www.sesehbeachvillas.com. Thatched roof villas set around a lush manicured garden and a glistening pool make this swish beachside spot a favourite for weddings and honeymoons. Most enchanting is the setting, far from the crowds on its own secluded slice of coastline. $$$$

Vassani Stay Jl. Munduk Catu No. 1, Canggu; http://vassanistay.com. Minimalist design with a Zen vibe describes this modern guesthouse with a shared kitchen, for coffee/tea, garden and garden pool. Fronts Canggu's main street for those who like to be in the thick of things; a hop, skip and jump away from the beach. Some rooms have lofts, kitchens or private balconies. $$

EATING

This part of Bali is bursting with restaurants: from tiny *warung* to cutting-edge "**dining experiences**". The most sophisticated (and expensive) are in Seminyak, Petitenget, Canggu and especially Kerobokan; there's often little to differentiate the tourist restaurants in Kuta and Legian (we've selected some of the standouts). If rupiah are precious, Kuta's main **night market** (*pasar senggol*), on Jl Blambangan at the southern edge of Kuta, offers affordable mains.

KUTA AND TUBAN, SEE MAPS PAGES 60 AND 61

Lemongrass Thai Jl Melasti; https://wearelemongrass.com. This Bali institution has been whipping up tasty Thai classics for more than 20 years now and has a reputation to prove it. Try the beef massaman curry followed by mango sticky rice, and make sure to check out the cocktail menu. $$

Made's Warung Jl Pantai Kuta; http://madeswarung.com. The original tourist *warung* from 1969, now a Kuta institution that appeals for its simplicity and great classic Indonesian dishes such as *nasi campur* and Balinese specials such as duck. The portions are large, the quality excellent. There's an offshoot on Jl Raya Seminyak in a rather more elegant setting. $$

Mama's German Restaurant Jl Raya Legian. This popular restaurant serves all kinds of German specialities (including sausages and pork knuckle) and German beers.

It's open 24hrs a day and 7 days a week. $$

Poppies Jl Poppies 1; http://poppiesbali.com. A Kuta institution, established in 1973, which christened the road. And this haven from the hustle still packs 'em in for a huge Indonesian menu and international menu of well-cooked and well-presented food, all served beneath bougainvillea-draped pergolas. $$

Temple by Ginger Moon Jl Kartika plaza no.8; https://templebygingermoon.com. Breezy courtyard restaurant with temple-inspired ceilings and pops of lime green that serves the gamut of Asian cuisine. Dishes are too good not to share, so order a selection like pineapple and cashew squid, *babi guling*, or tofu-stuffed half-moon buns. $$

Warung Indonesia Gang Ronta, off Jl Poppies 2; 0812 3811 1913. In the thick of things, this relaxed *warung* is more authentic than most in the area, and attracts Indonesians too – always a good sign. Pick and mix your own veg and non-veg *nasi campur* or order Indonesian staples and great value juices. $

Warung Nikmat Gang Biduri No. 6A (off Jl Bakung Sari), 0361 764 678. Javanese *warung* of the plastic stools persuasion where you can assemble a terrific *nasi campur* from around thirty spicy dishes – fried fish, beans with chilli, curried eggs, *urap* (steamed vegetables with spiced coconut), *tempeh* and much more. $

LEGIAN, SEE MAP PAGE 62

Brunch Club Jl. Legian no.457; http://brunchclubbali.com/. Whether you prefer sweet or savoury, brunch doesn't get much better than this: think eggs benedict, banoffee pie pancakes, or a frozen smoothie bowl topped with homemade granola. There's also an extensive coffee and smoothie menu, and some tasty burgers to placate the late-risers. $$

The Lokal 80361 Jl Sahadewa no.13d; https://instagram.com/thelokal80361. Seafood is the star at this recently renovated restaurant. If you don't fancy splurging on the lobster or the seafood platter to share, the beer-battered fish and chips is a firm favourite. There's also a varied breakfast menu. $$

Warung Kampung Jl Legian 20; 0852 3820 5004. This simple *warung* excels in cheap, unpretentious food, and you can't go wrong with the *nasi goreng special* (fried rice and veg with an egg on top) or *tempe dan tahu goreng* (spicy tempah with rice). $

Warung Murah Jl Pantai Arjuna No. 99; 0361 732 082. This no-frills eatery is perfectly located and very popular. It serves up affordable simple, fresh and tasty local dishes. Try a *nasi campur* medley – really great food for a bargain price. $

Zanzibar Jl Pantai Arjuna; http://zanzibarseminyak.com. Boasts a raised terrace and breezy upper deck with views of the waves and a large, tourist-friendly menu, which includes good breakfasts (try a Spanish omelette), wood-fired pizza, pasta, steak and seafood. $$

SEMINYAK, PETITENGET AND KEROBOKAN, SEE MAP PAGE 63

Barbacoa Jl Petitenget No. 14; http://barbacoa-bali.com. Argentinian-style place with a spectacular warehouse-style dining room, and dishes roasted on an open fire. Highlights include grilled chorizo, charcoal-grilled octopus and the frozen margaritas. $$$

★ **Biku** Jl Raya Petitenget No. 888; http://bikubali.com. Tasty breakfasts and great lunches, high tea and dinners, taking in Indonesian food, posh burgers, salads featuring the likes of rocket, pumpkin, pear and feta and home-made pies. Dining in the old *joglo* provides a wonderful atmosphere, too. Reservations recommended. $$

Café Bali Jl Laksmana; 0361 736 484. With its mildly distressed furniture, pretty lampshades and lace tablecloths, this place has more charm than its cooler neighbours. The long, eclectic menu includes sweets and sushi rolls, pasta and grills, Indian and Indo faves. $$

Corner House Jl Laksmana No. 10A; http://cornerhousebali.com. Stunning café-restaurant in an a/c loft-like space that's great for brunch, grilled meats and salads. $$

La Favela Jl Laksmana; http://lafavelabali.com. This restaurant run by a husband-and-wife team serves excellent Mexican food. Inspired by the jungles of Bali, Rio de Janeiro's favelas and the underground bars of London and New York, *La Favela* has a truly unique décor and the result is very special – you either love it or hate it. There's also a lush indoor garden with a waterfall and ponds. $$$

La Lucciola On beach beside Pura Petitenget car park, off Jl Petitenget; https://lalucciolabali.com/. Saffron risotto with seafood and a dash of chilli typifies the high-end Mediterranean flavours in this open beach restaurant. It's a popular spot for breakfast, Sunday brunch and sunset cocktails as much as romantic dinners. $$

Mama San Jl Raya Kerobokan No. 135; http://mamasanbali.com. A hip warehouse-style space with eclectic retro leanings – love that painted mural. Food-wise it's sizzling Southeast Asian, with Thai, Malay and Indonesian dishes such as crispy salted pork with yellow bean, garlic, chilli and *gailan*. Nice lounge bar above, too. Reservations recommended. $$

★ **Sardine** Jl Petitenget No. 21; https://kclubgroup.com/sardine. Gorgeous imaginative cuisine in a bamboo *bale*-style structure beside a ricefield. Fish and seafood dominate the menu, with the dishes changing daily depending on the catch – miso-grilled mahi-mahi, Jimbaran-style fish and organic salads are typical. $$$

Sarong Jl Petitenget No. 19X; http://sarongbali.com. Sophisticated South Asian flavours to tingle the tastebuds – Aceh lamb cooked over a coconut chargrill and fluffy naan bread – in a consistently excellent high-end Kerobokan restaurant. With its plush neocolonial style and open sides, the elegant dining area is a delight by candlelight. $$$

Taco Beach Grill Jl Kunti No. 8; http://tacobeachgrill.

1

com. This simple but colourful restaurant dishes up tasty Californian-Mexican food, but also Balinese fusion fare such as the *babi guling* burritos and tacos. $

CANGGU, SEE MAP PAGE 64

Avocado Café Jl Batu Mejan; https://instagram.com/theavocadofactory. The epitome of Bali's health-conscious foodie scene is the island's first avocado bar, serving up a nutrient-packed menu that will take you from brunch through to dinner. Think avocado toast, avo burgers, and poké bowls accompanied by a range of smoothies, protein shakes, and matcha lattes. $$

Beach Garden Jl Pantai Batu Bolong No. 103-107; https://instagram.com/beachgarden103. Hip Brit-owned bar and restaurant perfect for cold-pressed juices, smoothies, raw, organic foods and nutritious snacks, mains and sides. Coffee and teas are also available. $$

Good Mantra Jl. Subak Sari No. 77; https://instagram.com/goodmantrabali. This popular vegan restaurant certainly has good vibes and serves up imaginative plant-based dishes using local produce. Almost everything is made in-house. There's also a bar with a long list of drinks inspired by the seasons of the year. $$

★ **One Eyed Jack** Jl Pantai Berawa No. C89; http://oneeyedjackbali.com. Established by an ex-Nobu chef, *One Eyed Jack* features stupendous Japanese fusion cooking. Choose from the small plates menu, with highlights including crispy soft-shell crab sliders, black cod tacos, kelp salad and yakitori bites. There's a good choice of sake, too. The premises are deceptively humble given the quality of the cuisine. $$$

Sate Babi Street Food Warenda off Jl. Pantai Batu Bolong. Serving arguably the best satay in Bali, this blink-and-you'll-miss-it street stall lures in plenty of locals, so get there early (it's open every night from around 5.30pm) as they often sell out. Pull up a plastic stool and tuck into succulent barbecued skewers served with sticky rice – no cutlery required. $

Warung Varuna Jl Batu Bolong 89; https://facebook.com/warungvaruna. Surfers' hangout with chunky wooden tables and paint-smeared walls. Serves up a mean *nasi campur*. There's a useful noticeboard for yoga classes and community events. $

BEACH BARS AND CLUBS

SEE MAPS PAGES 63 AND 64

For lazy days and balmy nights enjoying food and drink beside the breakers, Bali's **beach clubs** are very popular indeed. But choose carefully, as some of these places have become oversized, Vegas-style and soulless. Relaxed little beach **bar-shacks** endure here and there too. **Entrance charges** vary greatly according to the venue and night. The mainstream Kuta clubs are usually free to get in. More upmarket venues in Seminyak and elsewhere tend to charge a moderate entrance fee; it's higher if there's a big DJ or band playing.

707 Beachberm Jl. Pantai Batu Belig, Kerobokan; 0812 398 1356. The perfect beach hangout with bean bags and a shack for a bar serving simple drinks and menu. Musically, it's far more sophisticated than some of the mega beach clubs, with DJs playing deep house, reggae and funk to a boho clientele. $$

Ku Dé Ta Jl Kayu Aya No. 9; http://kudeta.com. Globally famous venue that remains a cut above the competition for sophisticated dining and relaxing beachside. The sea views are as breathtaking as the prices on the dinner menu. Often hosts club nights too. $$$

La Plancha Jl. Mesari Beach, Seminyak; http://laplancha-bali.com. With its blast of colour, this little beach shack feels more Mexico than Bali. Alongside lazy beach vibes and beats, it serves a small menu of tapas favourites, raw plates and pricier grilled mains. Come early to grab a bean bag on the beach. $$

★ **Old Man's** Jl Pantai Batu Bolong No. 177X, Canggu; http://oldmans.net. A no-nonsense, wildly popular Canggu beach bar with tables by the waves that draws an eclectic, incongruous crowd of surfers, expats, boozers, boozing surfer expats, yogis and even the odd local. Check out its "Old Man's Mondays", "Acoustics Tuesdays and Thursdays" and "Beach Clean-up" every Saturday. Beer is cheap and the ambience is social and relaxed. $$

★ **Potato Head** Kerobokan beach, off Jl Petitenget; https://seminyak.potatohead.co. With an exterior clad in old shutters, this effortlessly hip beach club shouts style. Eclectic retro furnishings tap into the glamour of Fifties Miami, but really it's about great modern food, great chilled beats and great views of the waves as you laze by the pool on a day bed. $$$

DRINKING AND NIGHTLIFE

Bali has a vibrant nightlife scene, with the vibe very much depending on the area. **Kuta**'s bars and clubs are loud and laddish – this is the drunken home of the jam jar (pint-sized cocktails of multiple spirits) and countless happy hours. Start at *Paddy's Club* and follow the crowds from one to the next. The scene is more sophisticated in **Legian**, **Seminyak** and **Kerobokan**, with an ever-changing choice of lounge bars, plus occasional nights at beach clubs. Many clubs stage **live music** and special events, detailed in the free fortnightly **magazine** *the beat* (http://thebeatbali.com).

KUTA AND LEGIAN, SEE MAP PAGE 60

Apache Reggae Bar Jl Raya Legian No. 146; 0361 761 210. Tucked in what seems to be a Balinese barn beside

Bounty, Kuta's reggae spot is all heavy bass. Features talented live bands every night, and resident DJs. $$

Bounty Jl Legian, near Poppies 2 junction; 0823 9704 1938. Infamous hub of bare-chested boozy excess, centred around a replica of Captain Bligh's ship. Expect main-stream dance, cover bands on live music stages, themed foam parties and much drunkeness. A love-or-loathe experience. $$

Engine Room Jl Raya Legian No. 66; http://engineroombali.com. Occupying several levels, this established club is the place to come for pumping R&B, hip-hop and house. Drinks are cheap and it's popular with a party-loving international crowd. $$

Paddy's Pub Jl Legian 166, near Jl. Poppies 2 junction; 0361 758 555. This place – part of the *Bounty* complex – is huge and open-sided but still manages to get crammed; think chart sounds, drinking competitions and organised merriment for a young crowd. $$

Sky Garden Jl Raya Legian No. 60; https://baliskygarden.com. Sprawling over four floors, including the rooftop bar, there's a safe bet of dancing into the early hours here. The extended happy hours and all-you-can-drink packages are perennially popular. $$

Turtle Sport Bar Bali Jl Poppies 2; http://turtlesportbarbali.com. This busy bar, apart from a full range of live sports available on the large TV screens, has a restaurant and club, a huge selection of cocktails plus live music on Mon, Wed and Fri. $$$

SEMINYAK, PETITENGET AND KEROBOKAN, SEE MAP PAGE 63

Mirror Jl. Petitenget No. 106, Kerobokan; https://allin.co.id/mirrorbali/. Imagine dancing the night away to deep bass, house and hip-hop music in a gothic cathedral illuminated by neon laser lights, wondering what country you're in. That's Mirror. This pricey club in an up-market neighbourhood has a dress code: casual chic for guys, dress to impress for ladies. Reservations recommended for lounge section seats. $$$

Red Ruby Jl. Petitenget No. 919, Seminyak; http://redrubygroup.com/club. An amalgamation of former underground nightclubs whose legacies live on in the variety of music, from deep bass to jazz, and blues to hip-hop. Snuggle up in an intimate back room, party hard on the terrace or go wild in the main clubbing room. $$

Woobar Jl Petitenget; http://woobarbali.com. The glossy bar of the *W Bali-Seminyak* hotel vis very Ibiza/Miami club-cool – start beachside on the terrace with sunset cocktails, then move into the main bar area, all soundtracked by lounge and disco-house. A small downstairs club opens for occasional international DJs. $$$

SHOPPING

Kuta–Legian–Seminyak is a retail dreamland, especially for clothes, surfing gear, homeware and souvenirs. There's a 6km strip from the Intersection of Jalan Legian and Jalan Pantai Kuta up Jl Legian into Seminyak that takes in everything from cheap, mass-market stuff to style and substance around Seminyak where Jl Kayu Aya has several designer stores. Things get quirkier and more independent the further north you go: Kerobokan and Canggu have many intriguing little stores selling unusual clothing and craft products.

ART AND BOOKS

Biasa Artspace Jl Raya Seminyak No. 34; http://biasagroup.com; see map page 63. Part of the clothing store next door, this light commercial gallery specialises in exhibitions of modern Indonesian art.

Periplus Hardy's Supermarket, Jl. Raya Seminyak No. 17, Seminyak Square Kav. No. 9, Jl. Kayu Aya, airport, international terminal, Tuban; http://periplus.com; see map page 63. This outstanding chain of English-language bookshops has branches throughout the country and features novels and plenty of books about Bali and Indonesia among an eclectic nonfiction range, plus international magazines.

CLOTHES, JEWELLERY AND ACCESSORIES

Stylish boutiques are concentrated on the northern end of Jl Legian, Jl Raya Seminyak and up in Kerobokan and Canggu. Surfwear shops abound, though prices for genuine clothing is rarely any cheaper than in Australia or the UK.

★ **Biasa** Jl Raya Seminyak 36, Jl Raya Seminyak No. 34; http://biasagroup.com; see map page 63. Two adjacent stores with elegant, tasteful clothing from natural fabrics for men and women, plus scarves and a sophisticated take on Indonesian jewellery.

By The Sea Discovery Shopping Mall, Jl. Kartika Plaza; https://bytheseabali.com; see map page 61. Relaxed, casual beach fashions for men, women and children; think loose-fitting, unfussy designs in indigo, white, pale grey and cream. Also has several stand-alone stores and shops in some of the better hotels.

Gaia House of Shades Jl Kayu Aya No. 88, Seminyak; 0812 3676 2266; see map page 63. This uber cool shop stocks a fine range of sunglasses including designs by Le Specs, Ksubi, DITA, House of Holland and Karen Walker.

Paul Ropp Factory Outlet store, Jl. Pengubengan No. 1X, Kerobokan; http://paulropp.com; see map page 63. If you want to make a statement, these zesty boho-chic fashions hand-tailored from brightly coloured silks and cotton are just the ticket.

Uluwatu Jl. Raya Legian/Kuta No. 71/79; http://uluwatu.co.id; see map page 60. Eight stores in Kuta, Kerobokan, Sanur, Nusa Dua and Ubud specialise in white and black handmade Balinese lace and cotton clothes in modern styles that make a virtue of simplicity. Also some bedding.

DEPARTMENT STORES, SUPERMARKETS AND SHOPPING CENTRES

Beachwalk Jl Pantai Kuta; http://beachwalkbali.com; see map page 60. This cathedral to consumer culture is the antithesis of the neighbouring stalls – its multistorey venue has cooling mists, the full gamut of international chains from Adidas to Zara and Gap, plus cafés like *Starbucks* and even a cinema. You'll love it or loathe it.

Discovery Shopping Mall Jl Kartika Plaza, Tuban; http://discoveryshoppingmall.com; see map page 61. A colossal place on the seafront that's a good one-stop shopping destination, with scores of international and local brand-name clothing stores, including Indonesian department stores, a bookshop or two, plus several cafés.

Lippo Mall Jl Kartika Plaza, Tuban; http://facebook.com/lippomall.kuta; see map page 61. This three-storey shopping centre groups around 150 international brands under one roof. Clothing stores, food court, supermarket, entertainment venues and more.

HANDICRAFTS, SOUVENIRS AND HOMEWARES

The so-called art markets and stalls in Kuta are generally full of tourist tat; mass-produced batik and handicraft souvenirs from all over Indonesia. As with clothing, the better-made items are in Legian and Seminyak. The cheapest places to buy everyday rayon and mass-produced cotton sarongs are the street stalls and art markets in Kuta and on Jalan Arjuna.

Ashitaba Jl Raya Seminyak No. 6; 0361 737054; see map page 63. Intricate *ata*-grass goods crafted in the Bali Aga village Tenganan in east Bali, fashioned into everything from place mats and bowls to baskets and clutches, all sold at fixed prices.

Bungalow Living Jl. Pantai Berawa No. 35A, Canggu; http://bungalowlivingbali.com; see map page 64. A delightfully eclectic house cum shop filled to the brim with homewares, bags, hats and photo art, much of it ethnic and in earthy hues. Also has a café serving organic breakfast and lunch.

Deus ex Machina Jl Batu Mejan 8, Canggu; http://deuscustoms.com; see map page 64. Way of life store-café-hangout, which sells surfboards, skatewear, art and the coolest customised motorcycles in Asia. Grab a coffee, a cocktail or a bite while you browse.

★ **Lucy's Batik** Jl Raya Basangkasa 88, Seminyak; http://lucysbatik.com; see map page 63. Stunning Javanese batik sarongs and scarves, from stamped cotton wraps up to exquisite hand-drawn silk versions (which cost millions), plus some homeware (from recycled wood and shells), accessories and kids' clothing.

★ **Makassi** Jl Raya Basangkasa No. 31; see map page 63. Colourful, kitsch bags, clutches, gifts and some clothing. Items can be customised to your own design from a photo for example.

SPAS AND BEAUTY TREATMENTS

Cheap and cheerful **day spas** abound, offering massages, pedicures and manicures from dawn until well after dark, and you'll doubtless be offered a kneading on the beach from one of Kuta's conical-hatted massage women. In addition, most **high-end hotels** listed in the guide have a spa open to non-residents.

Bodyworks Jl Kayu Jati No. 2, Petitenget; http://bodyworksbali.com. Set around a courtyard, this long-running and well-regarded treatment centre offers an extensive menu of massages, including Balinese, Javanese exfoliation (*mandi lulur*), Thai, hot stone, reflexology and aromatherapy. Beauty treatments are also available.

DaLa Spa Alaya Dedaun, Jl Raya Legian No. 123; http://dalaspa.com. Award-winning spa offering fabulous pampering in plush, luxurious surroundings just a short walk from Jl Legian. The signature two-hour treatment takes in foot massage, aromatherapy and a facial.

Jari Menari Jl Raya Basangkasa No. 47, Seminyak; http://jarimenari.com. *Jari Menari* means "dancing fingers" and this all-male massage centre certainly lives up to that, with professional massages and courses. Also has a location in Nusa Dua. Reservations advisable.

SUNDARI Wellness Jl Petitenget 7, Seminyak; http://sundari-wellness.com. Luxury levels up at this opulent day spa, where traditional Balinese treatments are combined with the latest in modern healing and wellness. The comprehensive spa menu has everything from ayurvedic massages to oxygen facials.

DIRECTORY

Banks, exchanges and ATMs are everywhere. Be careful at exchange counters: there are several well-known scams (see page 47). A recommended moneychanger is PT Central Kuta, which has many bureaux in the Kuta–Legian–Seminyak region, including several on Jl Legian. If you do get caught in a moneychanging scam, contact the community police (see page 44).

Embassies and consulates See page 24.

Hospitals and clinics Three reputable, private 24hr medical facilities used by expats have English-speaking staff, general, dental, A&E facilities, ambulance and medical evacuation services: BIMC (Bali International Medical Centre) Hospital Kuta, Jl ByPass Ngurah Rai No. 100X (0361 761 263, http://bimcbali.com), which also owns BIMC Hospital Siloam Nusa Dua (Jl. Kawasan IDC Blok D, 0361 300 0911) and International SOS, Jl ByPass Ngurah Rai No. 505X (0361 720 100, http://internationalsos.com).

Immigration office Jl. Perum Taman Jimbaran No. 1,

Jimbaran http://imigrasingurahrai.kemenkumham.go.id/web.

Left luggage Hotels and *losmen* will store your luggage if you reserve a room for your return; some charge a nominal fee. There's also left luggage at the airport and, for Perama customers, at the Perama office, Jl Legian 39, Kuta (free for most pieces; enquire for rates for long periods; 0361 751875).

Police There are three tourist police posts on or near the beaches: Jl. Kartika Plaza No. 170 in front of Kuta Square south of the lifeguard post; Jl. Pantai Kuta north of *Beachwalk* shopping centre and Jl. Pantai Arjuna where it meets Jl. Arjuna, Legian. All are open 24hr with English-speaking attendants.

Post offices The General Post Office is in Denpasar. Smaller postal agents elsewhere in the area can handle parcels and postcards (remember them?); see maps for other locations.

The Bukit Peninsula

After it narrows to a sliver of land at Jimbaran, the **Bukit Peninsula** dangles off the south of Bali. Officially called **Bukit Badung** (*bukit* means "hill" in Bahasa Indonesia), the high limestone plateau has more in common with infertile Nusa Penida than with the lush paddies elsewhere. Known for its dry climate and thin dusty soils, the typical **Bukit landscape** is one of cracked earth and kapok trees, brightened only by the occasional bougainvillaea, perhaps a strip of cassava tubers (used to make tapioca flour) and grass-like sorghum, whose seeds are also pounded into flour.

Given that farming is almost impossible here, its discovery by **surfers** in the late 1960s was a godsend for the local economy. An alchemy of open-ocean swell and coastal alignment produces Bali's most famous and most challenging breaks. And in the last decade or so everyone else has caught on to the extraordinary beauty of the coastline. While most beaches remain nicely ramshackle, development is expanding at a crazy pace as **luxury resorts** and **villas** take advantage of the glorious clifftop views. No one begrudges poor farmers the chance to cash in as their infertile land is re-evaluated as prime retail estate. The sustainability – and sensitivity – of such development is another matter.

Fishing town-turned-resort **Jimbaran**, a couple of kilometres south of the airport, kicks off the luxury hotels, spread behind a fine beach. Continuing beyond, the **surf beaches** begin on the east coast: **Balangan**, **Dreamland**, **Bingin**, **Impossibles**, **Padang Padang**, then **Uluwatu**, the latter a world-class left-hander that is as legendary as any break in Hawaii. Uluwatu is also home to one of Bali's major clifftop temples, perched on the island's tip. On the east coast is **Nusa Dua**, a purpose-built resort that is deluxe and quiet, and **Tanjung Benoa**.

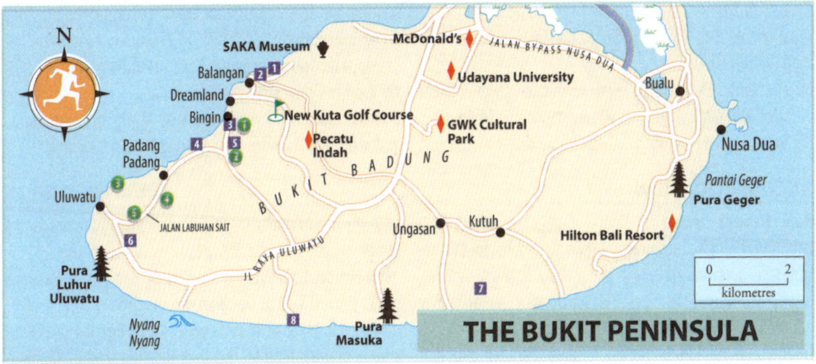

ACCOMMODATION

Alila Villas Uluwatu	8
Balangan Sea View Bungalow	2
BoHo Bingin Beach Bali	3
Flower Bud Bungalows I and II	2
The Gong	6
La Cabane	1
Medori Putih Homestay	5
Mu	3
Ocho Bali Surf Camp	7
Pink Coco	4
The Temple Lodge	3

EATING

The Cashew Tree	1
Drifter Surf Shop Cafe and Gallery	2
La Baracca	5
Single Fin	3
Shaka Rika	2
Yeye's Warung	4

1

SURFING OFF THE BUKIT PENINSULA

Views aside, the greatest assets of the Bukit are its **surfing beaches**. Heavy ocean swells strike the gorgeous craggy shoreline to produce the most revered breaks in Bali. Balangan, which receives the most shelter, is generally the most forgiving wave, while Uluwatu, the most exposed, is for advanced surfers only – it's a wave that demands respect. Board rental is widely available throughout the area and the **breaks** are at their best from April to October. Finally, a word of warning: while the beaches are stunning, **swimming** can be dangerous because of rips and reefs. If swell directions play ball, Balangan provides shelter at its southern end, Bingin has lifeguards in season and Padang Padang is calm since waves detonate on the reef outside.

GETTING AROUND — THE BUKIT PENINSULA

Public transport in the Bukit is sporadic at best and to see it properly you'll need your **own wheels**. Incidentally, be aware that there are parking charges to access Bukit beaches.

Jimbaran

With its crescent of golden sand and upmarket hotels, **JIMBARAN** is a quieter alternative to Nusa Dua. Easy access to the airport makes it a handy first- or last-night destination.

Tourism aside, its raison d'être, however, is **fish**. Every morning at dawn the town's fishermen return from the sea with hundreds of kilos for sale at an enjoyable covered **fish market** in Kedonganan, at the northern end of Jimbaran beach. It's at its best around 6–7am, but stays open all day – the stallholders are used to sightseers. Even if you don't see it, you can taste the day's catch when it is served at the plethora of beach *warung* and cafés that specialise in **grilled seafood** along, what's locally called, Muaya Beach.

Other than lazing in the sun by day and watching sunsets while eating fish at night, there's little to do in Jimbaran, although you can rent boogie boards on the beach or surf the Airport Reef **surf break** in Tuban, halfway down the Jimbaran side of the airport runway; most surfers access it from Kuta, but you should be able to charter a fishing boat from the beach.

ARRIVAL AND INFORMATION — JIMBARAN

By plane You can take a taxi from the airport to Jimbaran.

By bemo There's a sporadic *bemo* service from Denpasar's Tegal terminal to Jimbaran, via Kuta's eastern fringes and then on to Nusa Dua.

Destinations Denpasar (Tegal terminal; 20min); Kuta (30min); Ngurah Rai Airport (30min); Nusa Dua (40min).

By bus Kura Kura minibuses (http://kura2bus.com), hourly until 10pm, connect Jimbaran with Kuta and onto other destinations in Southern Bali. Trans Sarbagita also provides an irregular hourly bus service to Batubulan *bemo* terminal in Denpasar and on to Sanur, Kuta and Jimbaran.

By taxi You can take a taxi from Kuta.

Banks, exchange and internet ATMs, moneychangers and internet places are strung along Jl Raya Uluwatu.

ACCOMMODATION — SEE MAP PAGE 75

Bali Breezz Hotel Jl Pantai Sarai No. 23; http://balibreezzhoteljimbaran.com. While Standard rooms are compact, accommodation in this family hotel is modern, bright and clean. The pool is surrounded by attractive gardens and the beach is less than 100m away. $

Balquisse Heritage Hotel Jl Raya Uluwatu No. 18X; http://balquisse.com. A gem of a place filled with antiques and hand-crafted amenities with garden hideaways for relaxing and, of course, a spa. Take your pick of a room, family bungalow or a restored vintage Javanese teak house. $$$

★ **Belmond Jimbaran Puri Bali** Gang Yoga Perkanti off Jl. Uluwatu; http://belmond.com. Contemporary, well-designed hotel with 42 cottages and 21 gorgeous villas with pools, all with marble and teak interiors and in fabulous grounds – understated sophistication rules here. There's also a large pool and spa. $$$$

EATING AND DRINKING — SEE MAP PAGE 75

Muaya Beach in Jimbaran is lined with seafood places, but the *warung* called *Jimbaran Bay Seafood Club* (Jl. Pantai

Kendonganan, south of the Kendonganan fish market; https://instagram.com/jimbaranbayseafoodresto) is the most popular. There is another cluster of a dozen seafood *warung* further south next to the *InterContinental Bali Resort*. The setup is the same in both places – tables on the sand and a menu of lobster, prawns, fish, squid and crab grilled in the *warung* behind. Some offer set prices, while others price dishes by weight. The *warung* are at their liveliest while crimson sunsets light the skies. Some also serve simple Indonesian dishes and grilled meat.

★ **Cuca** Jl Yoga Perkanthi; http://cucabali.com. With a "globally inspired, locally sourced" menu, *Cuca* is a

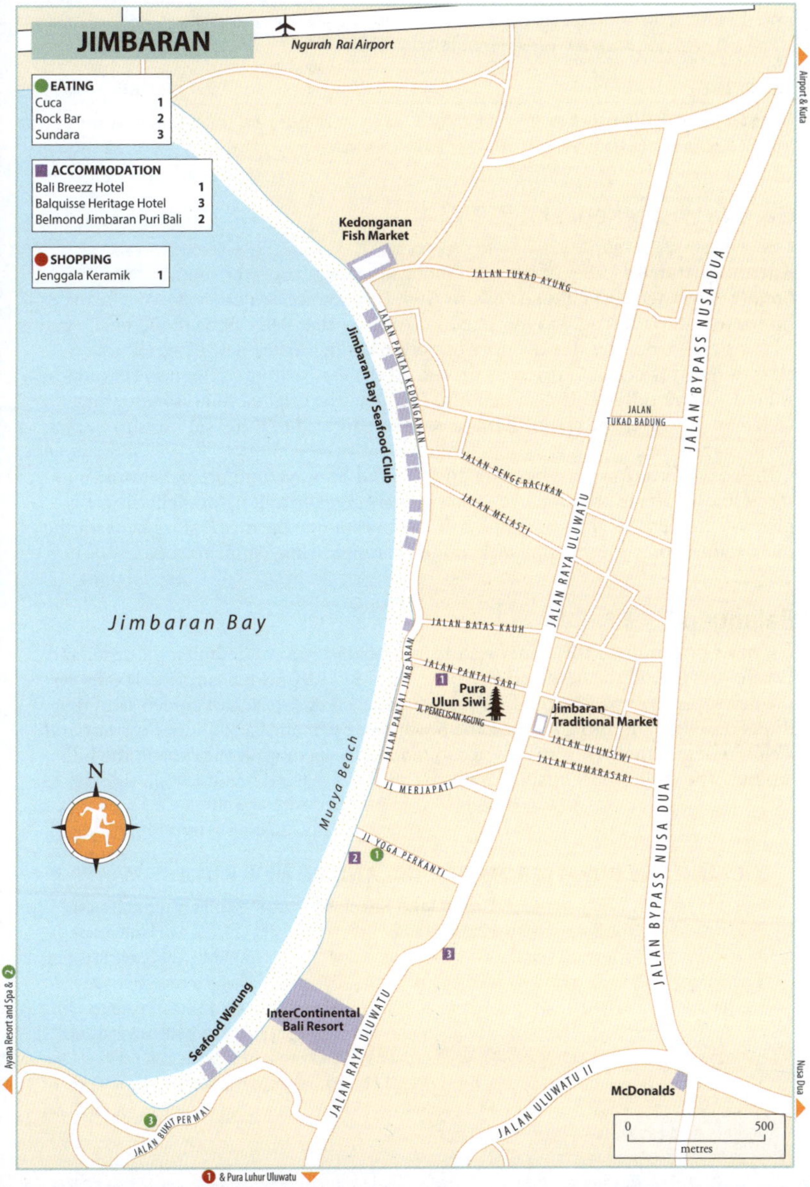

1

thoroughly modern culinary experience – its acclaimed Canadian chef has worked in three-star Michelin restaurants including Spain's *El Bulli*. Think fine dining from a tapas-style menu – ceviche or black squid risotto – and expect to eat three plates/person. The garden is a lovely spot for a pre- or post-meal drink. $$$

Rock Bar Ayana Resort and Spa, Jl Karang Mas Sejahtera; http://ayana.com/bali/dining/rock-bar-bali. Perched 14m above the waves at the base of the Bukit cliffs, this is one of Bali's most celebrated bars – with queues to match. And since access is via a lift, there are also queues to leave. Still, it's impressively arranged over several terraces with DJs stoking the atmosphere later on. $$$$

Sundara Four Seasons Resort Bali at Jimbaran Bay; http://sundarabali.com. A spectacularly sited beach club; there's a 57m infinity pool above the waves, a bar for cocktails, live music five days a week, and international cuisine in a spectacular restaurant including great seafood and Bali's longest Sunday brunch (book ahead). $$$$

SHOPPING

SEE MAP PAGE 75

Jenggala Keramik Jl Uluwatu II house; http://jenggala.com. The flagship store and factory of this ceramic specialist offers sophisticated and simple designs, as well as table linen and cutlery.

Garuda Wisnu Kencana (GWK)

Jl Raya Uluwatu, Ungasan • Charge, plus parking fee • http://gwkbali.com

After nearly three decades of on-again off-again construction the monumental ***Garuda*** **Wisnu Kencana Cultural Park**, or **GWK** (pronounced *ga way kah*), off the main Jimbaran–Uluwatu road, has morphed into a space that Bali can be proud of. Dotted with art and sculptures, the majority of the park is in a valley hewn from limestone cliffs, some of which are intricately carved. At the top, soaring 120m into the clouds, is Lord Vishnu riding half-man half-bird Garuda. The original unfinished statues, which sat idly since the early 1990s, have been relocated to other summits to decorate a performance area.

The park can be traversed by rental bicycles and Segways, and upmarket cafes and shops line a street at the entrance which is charming when lit up at night. There is plenty to do here, so allow at least a half day to explore. The observatory beneath the main statue closes at 6pm, but stick around for night-time performances.

Balangan

Given its proximity to the luxury resorts in Jimbaran – even the hulking Dreamland Beach, just around the headland (see page 76) – **BALANGAN** is a surprise. It's the bit the developers haven't got round to yet; a wonderful cove beach of golden sand that draws travellers and surfers. Above the beach are some ramshackle surfer *warung* and a cluster of guesthouses, with new accommodation opening all the time in the hills around. The shallow reef offshore powers a speedy left-hand break at high tide but can

KICKING THE BUKIT: FROM DREAMLAND TO NEW KUTA

Around Balangan's southern point, **Dreamland Beach** sums up the perils of unregulated development on the Bukit Peninsula for many Balinese and expats. Once it was known solely for its great surf – a fast left and right peak with long rides – and gloriously white sands. Yet like much of the surrounding land, its raw nature was "improved" in 2009 with concrete walkways and restaurants, masseurs and spas, in a multimillion-rupiah project by a government development company. The company rebranded it as New Kuta Beach in 2010. A focus for the controversy is the huge *Pecatu Indah Resort* which stacks against the cliff behind the eighteen-hole New Kuta Golf Course (http://newkutagolf.co.id). An ostentatious development which blights the coast, say critics. A valuable source of income and employment for the Bukit, counter its supporters.

make swimming dicey; depending on the swell direction, the far southern end of the beach usually provides most shelter.

ARRIVAL AND DEPARTURE — BALANGAN

By car or motorbike Road access to Balangan is via 6km of twisting lanes from the main Jimbaran–Uluwatu road. There's no public transport.

Saka Museum

At the Ayana Bali resort, Jl. Karang Mas Sejahtera, Jimbaran • Charge

Sleek contemporary architecture hemmed in by flower-filled gardens create a rousing backdrop for the Saka Museum, the latest addition to Bali's art and cultural scene. Open since 2024, the museum's permanent exhibitions do a deep dive into Balinese culture, and you can learn about Nyepi Day, the Balinese philosophy of Tri Hita Karana, and Tika, the Balinese calendar. The gigantic sculptures of Balinese Gods are mesmerising and the museum also hosts temporary exhibitions and cultural performances.

ACCOMMODATION — SEE MAP PAGE 73

Balangan Sea View Bungalow Jl Pantai Balangan No. 2; http://balanganseaviewbungalow.com. This attractive place has lovely thatched *lumbung* cottages, ethnic bungalows and decent fan or a/c rooms that draw a young crowd who come to loaf around its pool. $

Flower Bud Bungalows I and II Jl. Pantai Balangan; http://flowerbudbalangan.com. From the rusty hurricane lanterns hung on the gate to the verdant gardens, this Balinese-owned spot ticks all boxes for rustic escapism. You stay in traditional bungalows with large verandas; the cheapest are cold water-only. *Flower Bud I* has family-sized accommodation; both sections have a restaurant and a pool. $

La Cabane Jl Pantai Balangan; http://lacabanebali.com. With a spectacular cliff-top location looking out over an expanse of ocean, a palm-fringed infinity pool and a hidden beach just a short stroll away, there's a lot to love at this tropical hideaway. Check into one of the six thatched-roof, timber-beamed bungalows, each with its own terrace and indulge in extras like a private yoga class, floating breakfast or flower bath. $$$$

Bingin

Though fast developing into the liveliest of the Bukit surf beaches, **BINGIN** remains an oversized village of quiet lanes and astonishing scenery, whether you are admiring the superb coastal views from the cliffs or from the rickety *warung* that line the beach. It's a lovely backwater, which has its own rewarding **surf breaks** – the short left-hand tubes close to shore and the long and peeling left-handers of "Impossibles" surf break further out are the reason to come for many visitors. There's even a dedicated lifeguard in season. And where it trumps surrounding destinations is in its choice of accommodation. Access to the beach is via two sets of steep steps.

ARRIVAL AND DEPARTURE — BINGIN

By car Take the coastal road, Jl Labuhan Sait, which is signed west off the main Uluwatu road, then turn right onto a side road marked Pantai Bingin for the 2km drive to the parking area.

ACCOMMODATION — SEE MAP PAGE 73

Bingin has a burgeoning number of accommodation options, mostly midrange and above, with several boutiquey places opening in recent years. The cheapest places to stay are the beach *warung*, many of them built hard against the rock.

BoHo Bingin Beach Bali Jl. Pantai Bingin; https://bohobeachbali.com. Just a 5min walk from Bingin's beach and surf breaks, this laid-back, friendly hotel nails bohemian chic. Rooms come with a sea or garden view, air-conditioning, and minibars, plus you can enjoy the two infinity pools, extensive book library, and breakfast on request. $$

Medori Putih Homestay Jl Pemutih No. 1A, 1km inland from beach; http://medoriputihhomestay.com. A ten-minute walk from the beach, this fine-value place has twenty clean, orderly rooms, all with a/c and hot-water en-suites and a small pool for chilling. Breakfast is not included. $

Mu Jl. Pantai Bingin, Pecatu; http://mu-bali.com. This

1

French-run boutique place has a touch of castaway cool in its gorgeous, individually furnished thatch huts (all with a/c) spread behind a saltwater pool (and jacuzzi) on the cliff. Facilities include a spa, a small resort shop and a resident troupe of (wild) monkeys! $$

★ **The Temple Lodge** Jl. Pantai Bingin, Pecatu; http://thetemplelodge.com. Romance, eclecticism and a stunning location combine in this hideaway, where reclaimed pieces and Indonesian antiques lend bohemian flair to the seven bungalows – some boasting sea views, and a villa with a private pool that is perfect for a family or a group. There's an infinity pool, yoga sessions (extra cost), a spa, and Mediterranean cuisine in a superb restaurant serving fresh healthy dishes. $$

EATING SEE MAP PAGE 73

More and more new places are opening all the time, many with menus that raid the globe for inspiration.

The Cashew Tree Jl. Pantai Bingin; http://facebook.com/thecashewtree.collective. A relaxed garden café that serves creatively prepared healthy food, with lots of options for vegans and veggies: *Budha Bowl* with cashew nuts and tofu, greens and brown rice is deeply satisfying. Also offers detox juices and less saintly cocktails. *The Cashew Tree* hosts a weekly party with live acts and DJs, plus yoga sessions. $$

Drifter Surf Shop Cafe and Gallery Jl Labuan Sait No. 52, 1km inland from the beach; http://driftersurf.com. Huge surf store well stocked with boards and wave essentials, plus yoga mats and lots of clothing. There's a great organic cafe for espresso coffee, cakes, snacks and meals. Browse their books while you're here. $$

Padang Padang and Uluwatu

Padang Padang is a gorgeous cove notched in the Bukit's high cliffs that's safe for swimming. Notwithstanding its use as a location in the film *Eat, Pray, Love* (Julia Roberts meets her beau here), its fame – and the reason for all the restaurants and guesthouses – is the eponymous **surf break**, one of the most exciting waves in Indonesia, not least because of a kink in the final section. Access to the waves and beautiful sands is via steps by the bridge.

Arguably the most impressive break hereabouts, however, is at **Pantai Suluban** (Blue Point), 2km beyond Padang Padang. The **Uluwatu surf breaks** (named after the nearby temple) that wrap around the cliffs on the Bukit's tip are legendary. There are five left-handers, all consistent and surfable from two to fifteen feet, though crowds can be heavy and locals' priority enforced – this is no place for a novice. Even if you don't access the breaks via the steep steps beside the *Blue Point Resort and Spa*, you can head to the *warung* that cling to the cliff for an astonishing grandstand view of turquoise water and crashing white surf.

Pura Luhur Uluwatu

2km east of Uluwatu surf breaks • **Temple**: Charge, including sarong and sash rental, **Kecak and Fire Dance** daily 6–7pm (weather permitting): Charge • No public transport, but this is a fixture on many tourist agency tours in south Bali (including sunset dance)

One of Bali's holiest temples and most iconic sights, **Pura Luhur Uluwatu** is superbly sited on the edge of a sheer promontory that juts out 70m above the foaming surf at the island's tip. Views over the serrated coastline are stunning and this is a favourite spot at sunset, especially with coach-tour groups. Indeed, the setting is all: the temple itself is relatively small and for the most part unadorned.

Accounts of Uluwatu's early **history** are vague, but the Javanese Hindu priest Empu Kuturan almost certainly constructed a *meru* (multitiered thatched shrine) here in the tenth century. Pura Luhur Uluwatu is now sanctified as one of Bali's sacred **directional temples**, or *kayangan jagat* – state temples that have influence over all the people of Bali, not just the local villagers or ancestors. It is the guardian of the southwest, dedicated to the spirits of the sea and its festivals are open to all; during the holy week-long period of Galungan, Balinese from all over the island come here to pay their respects.

Climbing the frangipani-lined stairway to the temple's **outer courtyard**, you're likely to meet Uluwatu's resident troupe of macaques, brazen thieves of many a pair of earrings and sunglasses, even cameras. Images of the elephant god Ganesh flank the temple entrance. Only worshippers are allowed inside but the temple extends to the cliff edge and the famous three-thatched *meru* is visible from along the cliff. A tiny courtyard in the temple contains a locked shrine housing an ancient statue which is thought by some to be Nirartha, the influential sixteenth-century priest from Java, who possibly achieved his own spiritual liberation (or *moksa*) on this spot.

You'll get some of the best **views** of Pura Luhur Uluwatu's dramatic position from the tracks that wind along the cliff edge to the left and right of the temple for a few hundred metres, affording fine, silhouetted vistas of the three-tiered *meru* perched atop the massive, sheer wall of limestone.

ACCOMMODATION

PADANG PADANG AND ULUWATU, SEE MAP PAGE 73

PADANG PADANG

Pink Coco Jl Labuan Sait, about 400m before bridge; http://pinkhotels.com. "La casa del surfero" reads the sign, which may explain the hint of Mexico about this place; think rust-red colours in international-standard rooms with chunky moulded shelves and polished concrete floors. Also has a spa and two pools. $$

ULUWATU

★ **Alila Villas Uluwatu** Jl. Belimbing Sari; http://alilahotels.com. On the cliff at the southern end of the Bukit with stunning contemporary villas and a sublime infinity pool that merges into the horizon (and has graced the cover of many a glossy magazine). Check out the yoga deck, which is suspended above the ocean. Non-guests can enjoy the unique setting in one of its restaurants: *The Warung* for Indonesian dishes or *Cire*, serving "MediterAsian" food. $$$$

The Gong Jl Labuan Sait, 1km west of Pantai Suluban; 0361 769976. Long-running family-run budget place that remains a good choice: relaxed and with twelve clean rooms (including bunks), some with distant sea views, and a pool. There's a popular *warung* here serving big portions at low rates. $

Ocho Bali Surf Camp Kutuh; http://ochobalivilla.com. You won't get more bang for your buck than this tranquil 2-star hotel. The tradeoff is the remote location, but it's still only a 30-minute walk from Pandawa Beach. A pool, a decent breakfast and airport shuttle services make this the ideal place for penny-pinching travellers to escape the crowds. $

EATING

SEE MAP PAGE 73

PADANG PADANG

Shaka Riki Jl. Labuansait; http://shakarikibukit.com. All your favourite sushi staples are on the menu at this elegant Japanese restaurant, including some creative vegan options and delicious fresh seafood. Snag a seat on the garden terrace and save room for the home-made ice cream. $$

Yeye's Warung Jl. Labuan Sait 500m beyond bridge; https://instagram.com/warung_yeyes. Popular for a beer or a bite, this Balinese place with an attractive terrace has good local and western food (try the beer-battered calamari) and fresh-pressed juices. Service can be slow when busy – all dishes are cooked to order – but this is a fine spot to spend an evening. $

ULUWATU

La Baracca Jl Labaunsait no.10; http://labaraccabali.com. The verdant canopy and twinkling fairy lights overhead make this garden restaurant an atmospheric choice for a lunch or dinner date. If you like hearty, perfectly executed Italian cuisine then you'll leave with a full tummy and a smile. Gluten-free and vegan options are also available. $$

★ **Single Fin** Pantai Suluban, Jl. Labuan Sait; http://singlefinbali.com. There are other options for wave gazing, but none has the credentials of this surfer-owned place that spreads over several terraces. The extensive menu takes in pizzas, pasta and Indo curries, and their cocktails and sangría go down a treat. There's a great acoustic night on Wednesdays while the Sunday session rolls and rolls until 1am. $$$

Nusa Dua and Tanjung Benoa

Bali's most carefully designed high-end beach resort luxuriates along a coastal stretch of reclaimed mangrove swamp some 14km southeast of Kuta. A manicured, gated enclave, **NUSA DUA** was purpose-built to indulge upmarket tourists while simultaneously protecting local communities from the impact of mass tourism. Though it has succeeded, it feels fairly soulless after the colour of genuine island life. What draws most visitors here is the **beach**: a long ribbon of mostly pale gold sand, though a reef is exposed at low tide. Halfway down the shoreline, the land blossoms out into two little clumps, or "islands" (Nusa Dua means "Two Islands"), with a temple standing on each one.

1

Real life of a sort resumes north of Nusa Dua on the narrow sand bar known as **Tanjung Benoa**, though this, too, is a strip of yet more swanky hotels, tourist restaurants, shops and watersports facilities. Continue on to the very top of the peninsula, however, and village life returns in areas that can be fun to explore.

Pasifika: Museum Pacific Asia

Complex Indonesia Tourism Development Corporation (ITDC) Area Block P • Charge • http://museum-pasifika.com

To venture beyond Nusa Dua's beach, you could pay a visit to **Pasifika: Museum Pacific Asia**, north across the access road from the Bali Collection, which houses a wide-ranging and reasonably interesting display of art and artefacts from Asia and the Pacific, including a decent gallery of Balinese paintings.

Water Blow Park

Complex Indonesia Tourism Development Corporation (ITDC) • Daily 24hrs • Free

On the peninsula behind the *Hyatt Regency Bali* is Water Blow Park, a chance to see the force of nature at its fiercest. You enter through a landscaped park with statues of Rama and Laksmana as greeters and walk along a paved path until you reach the sea where the Indian Ocean crashes against jagged limestone rocks sending towers of water as high as 30 metres in the air. A spectacular sight, the best time to go is at high tide. Be prepared to protect your camera gear from the mist.

Bualu

Just outside the gates of Nusa Dua, **Bualu** village is where you'll find the densest concentration of *banjar*, temples, *warung*, family homes and commerce, particularly along Jalan Srikandi. It's the sort of scene common to any small Balinese town, but a worthwhile target if you want to explore beyond the rarefied confines of Nusa Dua itself. To the west, on Jalan Kuruksetra is *Puja Mandala*, a unique complex where a Buddhist and a Hindu temple, a Protestant and a Catholic church, and an Islamic mosque stand side by side in harmony on two hectares of land. Only worshippers may enter the buildings but if you fancy a quiet place to reflect, this is it.

Pantai Geger

About a 1km drive from the *Bali National Golf Club* or a 20min walk along the beach from *Ayodya Resort* – without your own transport take a metered taxi to Pantai Geger; an informal service will take you back

For a day out from the beach that fringes Nusa Dua head south towards the *Hilton Bali Resort* and follow signs for **Pantai Geger**. The broad, white-sand beach is quieter than that in Nusa Dua, although much of the southern end, below the clifftop temple, Pura Geger, is given over to seaweed farming.

Tanjung Benoa

Not to be confused with **Benoa Harbour** just north of **TANJUNG BENOA**'s tip, the beach here is more activity-based than the groomed stretches of Nusa Dua, somewhere for the happy hordes to go banana-boating, parasailing or windsurfing.

At Tanjung Benoa's northern tip stand three houses of worship in one area worth seeing if for no other reason than their juxtaposition to tourism nearby. In addition to a nearby mosque, the impressive Pura Dalem Ning dan Taman Beji is actually two temples. Pura Dalem Ning was erected in another era by the Pemecutan royal family and Taman Beji is a community temple where Balinese Hindus come to cleanse their deities on holy occasions. Three gold-coloured wooden doors are surrounded by majestic white limestone gates, and Taman Beji's shrine is carved from coral. The temples are only open on holy days, but villagers coming with daily offerings might help with the temples' histories.

Just a few hundred metres away is Caow Eng Bio Chinese temple (Jl. Segara Ening No. 14), likely built by Hainan trading communities 300 years ago. Painted in Chinese red with intricate ornaments, its unique feature is that the central shrine houses two deities rather than the usual one. There's a glass case outside housing the temple's mask collection used for lion dances.

ARRIVAL AND DEPARTURE

NUSA DUA AND TANJUNG BENOA

By taxi If you've splurged on a few nights' luxury here you're unlikely to be hauling your bags on a *bemo* or bus – you can take a prepaid taxi from the airport or use a metered taxi from Kuta.

1

TANJUNG BENOA AND THE TURTLE TRADE

Indonesia is one of the world's most important countries for **marine turtles** and home to six out of the seven sea turtle species, all endangered due to the destruction of habitat and **nesting sites**, illegal trade and accidental capture by fishing nets. Female turtles only lay eggs on the beaches where they were born; on Bali these include those at **Kuta**, **Sanur**, **Nusa Dua**, **Tanjung Benoa**, **Jimbaran** and **Pemuteran**. All of these have been affected by tourist development; turtles will not come ashore if there's too much light or noise, and hatchlings can get confused by the bright lights and head inshore rather than out to sea.

Traditionally, turtles were slaughtered on Bali for human consumption and religious sacrifice. However, in 1999 Indonesia implemented a **turtle trade ban**; subsequently the Hindu Dharma Council of Indonesia decreed that substitutes could be used for any endangered species in religious rituals.

Two groups have established **turtle hatcheries** on Bali, one on Kuta Beach (see page 59) and another by Reef Seen Divers' Resort in Pemuteran (see page 230).

GETTING AROUND

The resorts, restaurants and shops are strung over some 6km from the northern tip of Tanjung Benoa to southern Nusa Dua, so getting around can be a hot business.

By shuttle bus A free shuttle bus to the Bali Collection shopping centre loops around the big hotels and shops (approximately hourly, http://bali-collection.com/shuttle-bus). Some hotels also run their own free transport.

By taxi Metered taxis circulate constantly.

By bike The flat terrain makes cycling a good option; large hotels provide rental.

On foot The shortest route between hotels is nearly always via the paved beachfront walkway; it takes around 2hr to walk the entire length.

ACTIVITIES

Birdwatching An early morning at the ponds around the mangrove swamp to the north and west of Nusa Dua's North Gate can yield several species of kingfisher, as well as lots of water birds including white-vented Javan mynahs, Sunda teals and white-browed crakes.

Diving There are several PADI Dive Centres: Bali Scuba Masters is at Jl Pratama 85 (http://baliscubamasters.com) and runs day-trips to Nusa Penida.

Paragliding and paratriking You can soar with the eagles off Nusa Dua or Uluwatu cliffs with professional tandem pilots or take courses: Bali Paragliding Tours (http://baliparaglidingtours.com); Timbis Aero Club (http://flybali.info). 15–30min, weather permitting.

Snorkelling The area's calm seas make it a great place for beginners and kids to don flippers and explore. Geger Beach, south of Nusa Dua, is recommended.

Surfing The main Nusa Dua surf break is a right-hander about 1km offshore (accessible by boat from a signposted point south of the Bali National Golf Club), while further north, a short paddle beyond the *Club Med Bali*, "Sri Lanka" is a short, speedy right-hander.

Watersports Tanjung Benoa is south Bali's watersports playground, with kiteboarding, water-skiing, jet-skiing, kayaking, wakeboarding, banana-boating and all the rest offered by at least a dozen shorefront watersports centres. Discounts available for booking online.

ACCOMMODATION

SEE MAP PAGE 81

NUSA DUA

Hotel Sofitel Bali Nusa Dua Beach Resort http://all.accor.com. There's a real sense of contemporary style evident at this landmark resort, which boasts three restaurants, two bars, a gorgeous pool, fine spa and kids' club. Rooms are beautifully appointed, many with oblique seaviews and some have private plunge pools. $$$

TANJUNG BENOA

Conrad Bali Jl Pratama No. 168; http://hilton.com/en/hotels/bpncici-conrad-bali. Modern architecture, strong, uncluttered lines, pale cream stone and dark wood give this deluxe chain hotel enormous style. A 33m lagoon pool dominates a complex that has numerous restaurants, a spa, kids' club, daily yoga and tennis among many other offerings. Some rooms are wheelchair-accessible. $$$$

Novotel Bali Benoa Jl Pratama; http://novotelbalibenoa.com. Offers the best value in the area, though it's not the newest, with accommodation in a low-rise hotel spread over both sides of the road. Cheaper non-beachside rooms, all with a balcony or small garden, are near a quiet pool. Beachside options include tropical terrace bungalows with gardens and fabulous bathrooms by a larger pool. $$

Pondok Agung Bed & Breakfast Jl. Pratama No. 99X; http://pondokagung.com. A treasure on Banoa's quieter end but across the street from a watersports beach. Excellently maintained Balinese-style cottages and rooms (some with kitchenettes) in a lovely garden with a small pool. $

EATING AND DRINKING **SEE MAP PAGE 81**

Bumbu Bali Jl Pratama, Tanjung Benoa; http://artcafebumbubali.com. Founded and managed by renowned expat chef and food writer Heinz von Holzen, this famous courtyard restaurant serves classy Balinese cuisine such as marinated minced seafood and shrimps grilled in banana leaf, and there's lot of choice for vegetarians. The *Bumbu* empire includes a second restaurant *Bumbu Bali 2*, 500m away, and a cooking school. $$

Secret Café Jl. Siligita No. 27, Tanjung Benoa; 0812 3613 3809. Start your day with great coffee or drop in for lunch for a yummy selection of vegetarian, vegan or salad choices topped off with a slice of freshly baked cake. Indoor a/c or outdoor seating. $

Surya Café Jl Segara Lor No. 21, Tanjung Benoa; https://instagram.com/suryacafebali/. Fish and seafood priced by weight and fresh from the tank in a restaurant open to the theatre of boats whizzing past. Try the crab served with chilli and black pepper sauce. Not cheap, but fun to sit and watch the life on the water. $$

DIRECTORY

Banks and exchange ATMs are on Jl Pratama in Tanjung Benoa. Big hotels offer exchange.

Hospitals and clinics Most Nusa Dua hotels provide 24hr medical service; BIMC Hospital Siloam Nusa Dua (Kawasan ITDC Blok D, http://bimcbali.com) is a full-service international standard facility.

Denpasar

Despite the traffic congestion, despite the ever-expanding sprawl, Bali's capital remains a rather pleasant city at heart. Downtown **DENPASAR** is centred on a grassy square, **Alun-alun Puputan**, and has just a few major shopping streets in its core. Department stores and air-conditioned malls are mushrooming in southern districts – modern Denpasar is epitomized by **Jalan Teuku Umar**, a neon-lit strip crammed with restaurants and shopping centres – which leaves these central older neighbourhoods rather bereft of modern life. Maybe that's the appeal – these areas are still dominated by family compounds grouped into traditional *banjar* (village association) districts. There is also a marked influence of the sizeable immigrant communities, notably Javanese Muslims, Sasaks from Lombok and Chinese-Indonesians, who together constitute a **large minority** of the city's population of around 900,000.

Most tourists whizz in on a day-trip from the southern resorts, lingering just long enough to tour the **Bali Museum** and neighbouring state temple, **Pura Agung Jagatnata**, and perhaps to browse the traditional **markets** such as **Pasar Badung**, a huge covered affair beside the Badung River. Very few stay overnight. While these are its main sights as such, handily all within walking distance of each other, the relative dearth of tourists – and accompanying hoopla – is appealing in itself.

Sunday is a particularly good day to visit as traffic is light and many main streets are closed in a car-free initiative that sees joggers and cyclists reclaim the city.

Brief history

Until the early twentieth century, control of the city – then known as **Badung**, like the regency it governed – was divided among several rajas, most notably those at the courts of Pemecutan (southwest Denpasar) and Kesiman (east Denpasar). Supremacy was wrested from them, however, by the insatiably expansionist Dutch. On the pretext of alleged piracy in Sanur, the colonizers marched on the raja on September 20, 1906, and massacred the local court. After Indonesia won independence in 1949, the island's administrative **capital** was moved to Badung from the north-coast town Singaraja and the city was renamed Denpasar. Almost fifty years later Denpasar's status was upgraded again when, in 1992, it became a self-governing municipality, no longer under the auspices of Badung district.

1 Since 2000 the city has continued to sprawl in every direction, and its southern suburbs now merge into the Kuta-Legian-Seminyak district, forming a huge conurbation.

Alun-alun Puputan

At the corner of Jl. Surapati and Jl. Udayana

Grassy **Alun-alun Puputan** or Taman Puputan (Puputan Square), commemorates the fateful events of September 20, 1906, when the Badung Raja marched out of his palace gates, followed by hundreds of his subjects, and faced the invading Dutch. Dressed entirely in holy white, with each man, woman and child clasping a golden *kris* (dagger), the people of Badung had psyched themselves up for a **puputan**, or ritual fight to the death (see page 295). The final death toll was reported to be somewhere

1 between four hundred and two thousand. The palace itself, just across Jalan Surapati on the north edge of the modern square, was razed and has since been rebuilt as the official residence of Bali's governor. The huge bronze statue depicting figures bearing sharpened bamboo staves and *kris* on the northern edge of the park is a memorial to the citizens who died in the *puputan*; it's an image that you'll see across the island. The traffic island here is topped with a huge stone **statue of Catur Muka**, the four-faced, eight-armed Hindu guardian of the cardinal points, indicating the exact location of the city centre.

Puputan Square hosts a commemorative **fair**, with food stalls and *wayang kulit* shows, every year on September 20.

Bali Museum

Jl Mayor Wisnu No. 1 • Charge

The great repository of Balinese culture, the **Bali Museum** (Museum Negeri Propinsi Bali) is Denpasar's top attraction and provides an excellent introduction to the island's culture, past and present. Instigated, ironically, by the very Dutch colonial settlers who spelt the demise of traditional lifestyles, the ethnography museum is housed in an appealing compound divided into traditional courtyards, complete with *candi bentar* (split gates), *kulkul* (bell) tower, shrines patterned by lichen and flower gardens. You don't really need one of the guides who approach as you arrive – labels within are in English.

Much of the appeal of a visit is going on a treasure-hunt through island culture. The two-storey **Gedung Timur** at the back of the entrance courtyard features archaeological finds downstairs, including a massive second-century BC **stone sarcophagus**, and an upstairs gallery given over to traditional **paintings and woodcarvings**. Through the traditional gateway left off the entrance courtyard, the **Gedung Buleleng** holds fine Balinese **textiles**, including the rare Kain *geringsing*, a complicated fabric created through an intricate dyeing and weaving technique called ikat. In Indonesia, double ikat weavings are only found in Tenganan (see page 169).

Built to resemble the long, low structure of an eighteenth-century Karangasem-style palace, the **Gedung Karangasem** introduces Balinese **spiritual and ceremonial life** – the cornerstone of an islander's day-to-day existence – and is the most interesting section of the museum since it details the religious ceremonies of Balinese Hinduism. The Balinese **calendars** on the right-hand wall are immensely complex and still widely used to determine events from temple festivals to when to start building a new house.

Music and dance is tackled in the **Gedung Tabanan**, a replica of a Tabanan regency palace. Exhibits include masks, shadow puppets and costumes, including Barong costumes like the shaggy **Barong Ket**, a cross between a lion, a pantomime horse and a Chinese dragon, that symbolizes the forces of good.

Pura Agung Jagatnata

Jl Surapati • Daily dawn–dusk • Entry by donation includes sarong and sash

Just over the north wall of the Bali Museum, the modern state temple **Pura Agung Jagatnata** is set in a garden of pomegranate, hibiscus and frangipani trees. Founded in 1953, it is dedicated to the supreme god, Sanghyang Widi Wasa, who is here worshipped in his role as "Lord of the World", or Jagatnata.

Carvings of lotus flowers and frogs adorn the tiny stone bridge that spans the moat around the temple's central gallery (access at festival times only) and scenes from the Hindu epics the Ramayana and Mahabharata decorate the gallery's outer wall. The temple's focal point is the looming five-tiered **padmasana** tower in the inner courtyard, balanced on a huge cosmic turtle. Built from blocks of white coral, it is carved with demons' heads and the bottom level displays the face and hands of Bhoma, the son of the earth, whose job is to repel evil spirits from the temple. The lotus throne at its summit is left empty for Sanghyang Widi Wasa to fill when descending to earth at festival times – the god is represented in a gold relief embossed on the back. In the southeast corner of the outer compound stands the **kulkul** tower, its split wooden bell still used to summon locals to festivals, meetings and temple-cleaning duties.

Twice a month, on the full moon and new (or dark) moon, **festivals** are held here and *wayang kulit* shows are sometimes performed, from around 9pm to 11pm; ask at the nearby tourist office for details.

Taman Werdhi Budaya Arts Centre

Jl Nusa Indah No. 1

Marooned in the suburbs of east Denpasar, the **Taman Werdhi Budaya Arts Centre** was designed in 1973 by one of Indonesia's most renowned architects, Ida Bagus Tugur. It consists of a number of performance spaces and is the location of the spectacular annual **Bali Arts Festival** (usually between mid-June and mid-July) with a spectacular array of special exhibitions, competitions and shows.

That aside, the reason to visit is a small **museum** (same hours; free) on the history of Balinese arts. On show is an overview of Balinese **painting**, including the classical *wayang* style plus works from the Ubud, Batuan and Young Artists styles (see page 118) and modern works, as well as a small display of woodcarving, masks, dance costume, shadow puppets and jewellery.

Bajra Sandhi

Jl. Raya Puputan No. 142, Renon • Charge

The government administrative district, **Renon**, on the southeastern edge of the city, is another world from downtown Denpasar, all landscaped gardens, broad tree-lined boulevards and space galore. Among the offices is the huge grey lava-stone **Bajra Sandhi** ("Balinese People's Struggle") monument, at the heart of the **Lapangan Puputan Margarana** (Renon Square) park. Designed by Taman Budaya's architect, Ida Bagus Tugur, to resemble a priest's bell, the monument's structure also symbolizes the date of Indonesia's Declaration of Independence – August 17, 1945 – with its eight entrances, seventeen corners and height of 45m. The upper floor contains a series of 33 dioramas illustrating edited episodes from Balinese history. Climb the spiral stairs and you're rewarded with a panoramic view across Denpasar's rooftops. The park has a jogging track and fitness area.

ARRIVAL AND DEPARTURE — DENPASAR

BY PLANE

Ngurah Rai International Airport is 13km south of Denpasar. You can take a prepaid taxi from the airport to Denpasar.

BY BEMO

Bemos from outside Denpasar arrive at one of three terminals on the edge of town. All times are (very) approximate depending on traffic, and prices listed are a guide only. As most Balinese prefer motorbikes, frequencies on all these routes is falling due to low demand.

Batubulan Batubulan terminal, on the far-flung northeast fringes in Batubulan village (7am–1pm only), runs services to Ubud (40min–1hr 20min), and points in central and eastern Bali: Besakih, Candidasa, Kintamani, Klungkung and Padang Bai.

Tegal Located off Jl. Imam Bonjol on Gang Imbora, Tegal Harum, in the southwest corner (6am–5pm only), Tegal covers routes south of Denpasar, including Kuta (25min), Legian, Jimbaran (50min), Nusa Dua and Uluwatu and Sanur (25min).

Ubung Ubung (Jalan HOS Cokroaminoto, northwest of the city on the main road to Tabanan) runs transport to north and west Bali, Gilimanuk, Negara, Singarja and Tabanan.

BY BUS

Denpasar's main bus terminal for points beyond is Mengwi

(Jl. Mengwi, Mengwitani, 17km northwest of Denpasar). Most buses to and from Java stop here. To get to/from Mengwi terminal, take a Trans Sarbagita Mengwi-Ubang bus which leaves 5–6 times/day.

GETTING AROUND

By bemo Very few tourists bother to take *bemos* within the city because their routes are mega-complicated, they don't depart until they're full, which can mean hours of waiting time (except in the mornings when demand is high), and prices are unregulated causing foreigners to pay up to ten times the normal price. In the long run it could work out cheaper and certainly a lot easier to order an app-based motorcycle or car taxi.

Although some of the terminals in outlying areas also make runs locally, three terminals in Denpasar exclusively service local routes: Gunung Agung, Sanglah and Kareneng.

Routes, times and prices change often, so if you are determined to travel by *bemo*, the best advice is to tell a local (at your accommodation is ideal) where you want to go, ask which terminal to go to, what route to take, what is the best time to go and what price to pay.

By taxi Metered taxis and app-taxis circulate around the city. Blue Bird's Bali Taxis (0361 701111, http://bluebirdgroup.com) and Gojek/Grab are all reliable.

By bus Trans Sarbagita buses (which were meant to be a mass rapid transit system to alleviate traffic, but it didn't turn out that way) run from Denpasar, though it's not a very reliable or punctual service. There are two routes in Denpasar. Corridor 1: Ngurah Rai Stadium to GWK Cultural Park via Jl. Surapati, Udayana University, and Jimbaran. Corridor 2: Batubulan to Nusa Dua via Sanur, Kuta Central Parking, airport and Jimbaran. In theory buses run every 30min from 6am–6pm.

INFORMATION AND ACTIVITIES

Tourist office Near the Bali Museum at Jl Surapati 7 (0361 754092). Useful for transport and festival information, and they've a decent city map, but don't expect much more.

Dance performances Tourist performances (about 2hr) of the Barong (daily 9.30am) take place at the Catur Eka Budhi on Jl Waribang, in Denpasar's eastern Kesiman district, while the Kecak (daily 6.30pm) is performed at the Stage Uma Dewi, also on Jl Waribang, about 300m south of the Barong dance stage.

Music and dance lessons Lessons and workshops in gamelan and Balinese dance at Mekar Bhuana Conservatory, Jl Gandapura III No. 501X, Kesiman Kerthalangu (http://balimusicanddance.com).

Indonesian language IALF (Jl. Raya Sesetan, Denpasar, http://ialf.edu), one of the leading Indonesian language schools, has a two-week intensive language and culture program with an option to stay with a local family.

ACCOMMODATION

SEE MAP PAGE 84

Grand Mirah Boutique Hotel Jl. Kaliasem No. 1; http://grandmirah.com. A huge surprise in the heart of Denpasar: a small, modern Balinese family-owned hotel within walking distance of Alun-Alun Puputan. 32 rooms, a restaurant and full-sized pool make it ideal. $$

★ **Nakula Familiar Inn** Jl Nakula No. 4; http://nakulafamiliarinn.com. Eight well-maintained rooms with a balcony and either a fan or a/c in a welcoming family-style *losmen*. It's less than a 10min walk from the Bali Museum and about a 15min walk from Tegal *bemo* terminal. The only downside is traffic noise at rush-hour. $

EATING

SEE MAP PAGE 84

There are few tourist-oriented restaurants in Denpasar, so this is a good chance to sample Bali's cheap, authentic neighbourhood places to eat. Note that smaller restaurants generally shut by 7pm. Renon is the eating destination of choice for middle-class locals and expats, but it's a fair haul from the hotels in the city centre.

Babi Guling Candra Jl. Teuku Umar No. 140; 0361 221278. While this simple *warung* isn't much to look at, it's one of the last places in Denpasar to sample *babi guling*, Bali's renowned suckling pig. Rice is topped with pork slices and served (quickly) with *sate lilit*, crispy pork skin, soup and veggies. $

Bhineka Jaya Kopi Bali Jl Gajah Mada No. 80; http://kopibali.com. At this modest-looking outlet of Indonesia's Butterfly Globe Brand, you can sample a cappuccino or Bali coffee, then choose which grade of island beans to take home. $

River Walk Pasars Badung and Kumbasari Jl. Gajah Mada on the Badung River. Two bustling markets by day are transformed into a pasar malam (night market) on both sides of the river. At dusk the illuminated bridge and shops transform the usual food stalls into a new adventure. Super-cheap soups, noodle and rice dishes and cold beer are the norm here. $

Warung Be Pasih Renon Jl Pemuda III No. 24; 0361 237755. Renowned for delicious Balinese-style fish and seafood, this local place is inexpensive and has good *paket* (set meals). Try the *ikan goreng* (fried fish) which comes with soup and sambal sauce or one of Bali's celebrated duck dishes. $$

Warung Wardani Jl Yudistira No. 2; 0361 224398. The finest *nasi campur* you'll eat in Denpasar – a delicious, complete feed that might take in *sate lilit*, beef curry, salted egg and a vegetable dish or two. Other options including *nasi soto ayam* and *gado-gado* are also available. No pork though. $$

SHOPPING

Perhaps the second-best reason to visit Denpasar, after the museum, is the city's selection of **markets**. Tourists find them picturesque; to locals they're for mundane day-to-day purchases, and Balinese who can afford it prefer the growing number of **shopping malls**.

MARKETS

The gold quarter Not far from Jl Sulawesi is the city's gold quarter. Centred on the stretch of Jl Hasanudin that runs west from Jl Diponegoro to the river, this market has lots of jewellery outlets, but designs cater to local tastes rather than tourist ones. Daily world gold prices are posted in every shop (mostly 18–22k is sold here), but bargaining is still expected.

Jalan Sulawesi Just to the east of Pasar Badung, this narrow thoroughfare, running from Jl Hasanudin in the south to Jl Gajah Mada in the north, is devoted to fabric of all descriptions, much imported by Middle Eastern and Indian merchants but including batik, *songket* brocades and sari silks.

★ **Pasar Badung** The biggest market and the best occupies a three-storey covered *pasar* beside the river. Trading takes place almost 24hr a day – the main action is around 4–6am, and there's a lull in early afternoon – with buyers and sellers pouring in from all over Bali. You'll find fruit, veg and spices on lower floors, while those upstairs sell everything from buckets to boots and shoes to shovels.

Pasar Kumbasari Directly across the Badung River from Pasar Badung. This four-storey art market stocks clothes, souvenirs, textiles, woodcarvings, paintings and sarongs – all the stuff on sale in Kuta but generally at cheaper prices.

DIRECTORY

Embassies and consulates See page 24.

Hospitals, clinics and dentists Sanglah Public Hospital (Rumah Sakit Umum Propinsi Sanglah, or RSUP Sanglah) at Jl Kesehatan Selatan No. 1 near Jl. Diponegoro, Sanglah (0361 227 911) is the main provincial public hospital, with an emergency ward and some English-speaking staff. It also has one of only two divers' hyperbaric recompression chambers. BaliMed Hospital is a private hospital at Jl Mahendradatta 57X (0361 484748). Most expats use BIMC Hospital in Kuta or Nusa Dua or International SOS clinic near Kuta (see page 72).

Immigration office Jl Panjaitan No. 3 at the corner of Jl Raya Puputan, Renon (0361 227828).

Police There are police stations on Jl. Supratman and Jl. Prof. Ida Bagus Mantra; the main police station is in the far west of the city on Jl Gunung Sanghiang (0361 424346).

Post office Denpasar's main post office is on Jl Raya Puputan.

Sanur

If Kuta–Legian–Seminyak is too frantic and Nusa Dua too manufactured, **SANUR** could well be your sort of place. It's a low-key destination strung behind 5km of fine beach, with a laidback atmosphere and an appealing lack of hustle. Traffic is light, there's little air pollution to content with, it's leafy and boasts a fine promenade. While it's true Sanur is somewhat lacking in clubbing and all-night partying venues (some nickname it "Snore"), for many visitors that is decidedly a good thing. With calm shallow water it's a safe spot for the kiddies, and there are also two surf breaks and some so-so diving. You could use it as a base to explore nearby – Kuta is 15km (about 45min) southwest and Ubud around an hour's drive north, while easy-going Nusa Lembongan, Ceningan and Penida are a short boat ride away.

It could all have ended so differently. Sanur was the site of Bali's first major beach hotel in the 1960s. The lumpish, concrete **Grand Bali Beach** (currently part of the *Inna* hotel group) did not go down well locally and led to a Bali-wide edict against building anything higher than a coconut tree. That edict has slipped (or there are some seriously high coconut trees in Bali), but the ethos against high-rises remains. Sanur's other claim to fame is as the source of some of Bali's most powerful **black magic** and as the home of the most feared sorcerers and respected healers, or *balian*. Not so long ago it was not uncommon to hear stories of police enquiries that used Sanur's black-magic practitioners to help track down criminals.

1

SANUR
ACCOMMODATION
Artotel Sanur 8
Griya Santrian 5
Inna Sindhu Beach Hotel & Resort 1
Little Pond Homestay 2
Ning Homestay 6
Sudamala Suites & Villas 7
Tandjung Sari 4
Yulia Homestay 1 3
EATING
ABC (Artotel Beach Club) 3
Café Batu Jimbar 7
Café Smorgas 6
Juicy & Crispy 11
Luhtu's 1
Massimo 10
The Porch Café 5
The Village Cucina Italiana 4
Warung Hanabi 9
Warung Kecil 8
Warung Little Bird 2
SHOPPING
A-Krea 3
Biasa 1
Hardy's 4
ON'KOR 3
Periplus 4
Uluwatu 1
DRINKING AND NIGHTLIFE
Casablanca 1
Tree Bar 2
Denpasar
Warung Pojok/ Perama
Private fast boats to the Nusas and Lombok
JALAN HANG TUAH
Bemo stop
Museum Le Mayeur
Prime Plaza Hotel Sanur – Bali
Police
Bali Beach Golf Course
JALAN DANAU BATUR
JALAN DANAU BERATAN
JALAN PEMAMORAN
Grand Inna Bali Beach Hotel
Public boats to the Nusas
Tourist Police
JALAN DANAU BUYAN
JALAN SEGARA AYU
GPO
Segara Market
Pura Segara
Sindhu Beach
JALAN TANDAKAN
JALAN PANTAI SINDHU
Sindhu Beach Market
Night Market
Sindhu Market
JALAN DANAU TOBA
JALAN DANAU TAMBLINGAN
GANG BUMI AYU
BATU JIMBAR
JALAN PUNGUTAN
JALAN BYPASS
JALAN PANTAI KARANG
Crystal Divers
Banjar Batu Jimbar
Hyatt Regency Bali
Tourist Police
Supermarket
JALAN DUYUNG
Dune Atlantis Bali
JALAN DANAU POSO
JALAN SUDAMALA
JALAN KESUMA SARI
Pura Blanjong
Bali Scuba
JALAN PANGEMBAK
JALAN SEKAR WARU
JALAN TANJUNG
Blue Season Bali
Bemo Terminal
JALAN CEMARA
Puri Santrian Hotel
JALAN MERTASARI
Mercure Resort
Prama Sanur Beach Hotel
Bali Kitesurfing School
Mertasari Beach
Kuta & Airport
Serangan Harbour
N
0 400
metres

The beach

The length of Sanur's 5km **shoreline** is fronted by a shady, paved esplanade. There are far worse ways to while away a day than to wander (or cycle) down the coast in search of your personal paradise, stopping off for lunch at the abundant *warung* and restaurants, then pausing for a cool sunset Bintang on the return. The busy patches of beach are around the *Grand Inna Bali Beach* in the north and, further south between the Sindhu Beach Market and the *Tandjung Sari* hotel. The empty stretch just south of Batu Jimbar is the quietest. Wherever you end up, the **views** are great: on a clear day, Gunung Agung's profile soars northeast while out to sea you might just make out Nusa Penida's cliffs.

A huge expanse of Sanur's shore is exposed at low tide and a reef lies about 1km offshore at high tide. This offers three mid- to high-tide surf breaks – one in front of the *Grand Inna Bali Beach* hotel, one opposite the *Tandjung Sari* hotel and another 2km offshore at the *Hyatt Regency Bali* – but the **currents** beyond it are strong. They're all at their best Sept–March, when the northwest winds blow offshore.

The shallows within are fine for paddling at low tide and swimming at other times, as well as providing a venue for numerous watersports.

Pulau Serangan

An island south of Sanur once reachable only by wading across at low tide or by boat, Pulau Serangan is best known as a place favoured by egg-laying sea turtles, earning it the nickname Turtle Island. Sadly, development disturbed the habitat which the Turtle Conservation and Education Center (Jl. Tukad Punggawa, http://tcecserangan.jimdofree.com, daily 9am–5pm) is trying to rectify. For a small donation you can adopt and release a hatchling in season, primarily June–October.

The east side of the island is dedicated to watersports such as surfing and windsurfing. On the western shore is Pura Sakenan where thousands of Balinese-Hindu pilgrims visit twice yearly to cleanse their holy relics. The harbour on the north shore hosts boats to and from Lombok, Nusa Lembongan, Ceringan and Penida.

Museum Le Mayeur

Entrance from beach 50m south of Jl Hang Tuah • Sat–Thurs 8am–3.30pm, Fri 8.30am–12.30pm • Charge • 0361 286 201

Sanur's cultural sight, the **Museum Le Mayeur**, is former home of artist **Adrien-Jean le Mayeur de Merprés** (1880–1958). Having arrived in Singaraja in 1932, the 52-year-old Belgian settled in Sanur and set up his easel, painting canvases of 16-year-old beauty Nyoman Pollok and her friends; "the beauty and splendid figure of Ni made the painter enjoy his stay", the museum notes drily. Married three years later, the couple lived in the floridly carved house where around eighty of his works now hang: Impressionist early paintings from his travels in Europe, North Africa and India and romanticized canvases of Ni and her friends from the 1950s. Imagine French Impressionism channelled by Gauguin and you're close. The 1930s house is also interesting for its carving and for the couple's furniture – Ni donated the property to the government on her death in 1985.

ARRIVAL AND DEPARTURE — SANUR

By plane From Ngurah Rai Airport you can take a prepaid taxi to Sanur.

By shuttle bus The fastest, most direct transport is usually tourist shuttle bus. The drop-off point for the biggest operator, Perama, is their office at Warung Pojok, Jl Hang Tuah No. 39 in north Sanur (http://peramatour.com); you can pay an extra fee for a hotel drop-off (or pick-up), or *bemos* or taxis will take you onward.

Destinations Amed (daily; 3hr); Bedugul (daily; 2hr–2hr 30min); Candidasa (4 daily; 2hr 30min–3hr); Gili Islands (daily; 9hr); Kintamani (daily, min 2 people; 2hr 30min–3hr); Kuta (6 daily; 40min–1hr); Ngurah Rai Airport (3 daily; 40min–1hr); Lovina (daily; 3–4hr); Padang Bai (3 daily; 2hr–2hr 30min); Senggigi, Lombok (daily; 8hr 30min);

1

Ubud (7 daily; 45min–1hr).

By bemo Arrival and departure by *bemo* is from the Denpasar terminals at Kereneng or Tegal. Dark-green *bemos* from Kereneng run to the Jl Bypass/Jl Hang Tuah junction in north Sanur, then Jl Danau Beratan and Jl Danau Buyan, before continuing down Jl Danau Tamblingan to Semawang. Dark-blue *bemos* from Tegal run direct to Sanur then follow the same route as the Kereneng ones. Leaving is easy – *bemo* drivers along Jl Danau Tamblingan and the Jl Bypass will honk, signal the driver if you want them to stop and pick you up.

By bus Kura Kura minibuses (http://kura2bus.com) connect Sanur with Kuta and Ubud several times daily, but times vary so check the latest schedule.

By boat An amazing number of scheduled, private fast boats leave from the end of Jl. Hang Tuah or from Serangan harbour headed for Nusa Lembongan, stopping at either Jungubatu and/or Mushroom Bay (both 30min–2hr); Nusa Penida, arriving at Toyapakeh, Buyuk and/or Sampalan; Padang Bai and Kusumba, East Bali; and/or to the Gili islands or Senggigi, Lombok. Tickets for fast boats can be booked either online or at their offices, usually located at departure points. Public slow and fast boats depart from the beach in front of the *Grand Inna Bali Beach* hotel (if tide permits) and although they're cheap, they are not recommended due to lack of safety standards.

Benoa Harbour (Pelabuhan Benoa), 5km southwest of southern Sanur, is the arrival and departure point for many cruise ships, sailing trips and tourist boats, as well as fast boats to the Gili Islands on Lombok and day-trips to the Nusas, as well as for Pelni ferries from elsewhere in Indonesia.

By taxi You can take a taxi from central Kuta or Denpasar or a Gojek/Grab.

GETTING AROUND

By bemo The green and blue public *bemos* to and from Denpasar's terminals can be useful for buzzing up and down the main streets.

By taxi Blue Bird's Bali Taxis (https://bluebirdgroup.com) are reliable and affordable. If you're planning a long trip, consider negotiating a fee with one of the roadside transport touts.

By car or motorbike Transport touts also rent cars and motorbikes, as do many hotels and tour agencies.

By bike Sanur is a good bet for cyclists; most hotels and travel agents along Jl Danau Tamblingan have them for rent.

INFORMATION AND ACTIVITIES

Information Check out the website http://sanurweekly.com for reviews, information and all things Sanur.

Kitesurfing Bali Kitesurfing School, Pantai Mertasari (http://bali-kitesurfing.org) on Sanur beach offers lessons for beginners and advanced pupils, plus gear rental and kitesurf tours.

Spas and beauty treatments Most of Sanur's more expensive hotels have luxurious spas open to the public and offer a range of treatments including aroma-therapy, reflexology, traditional Balinese massages, the Javanese *mandi lulur* exfoliation scrub, facials and hair treatments. Alternatively, there's always the massage-and-manicure ladies who hang out on the beach.

Surfing There is little in the way of surfboard and boogie board rental; a couple of stalls south of the Sindhu beach market provide rental gear.

Watersports Parasailing, glass-bottomed boats, banana boat rides, jet skis, sit-on kayaks, even fishing trips in traditional boats – there's little that Sanur's enterprising agents won't offer. Beachfront outlets rent out equipment, or contact one of the larger operators such as Matsu Bali Service (https://facebook.com/MatsuBaliServices/) and Fusion Freedive and Spearfishing (http://fusionfreedive.com).

Yoga Power Of Now Oasis at Jl Merta (http://powerofnowoasis.com) offers up to four hatha and vinyasa flow classes Wed–Sun, retreats and Yoga Alliance-accredited teacher training courses.

ACCOMMODATION

SEE MAP PAGE 90

There are beds to suit every budget in Sanur and few dud stays – quality is generally high and you get more space and better facilities for your rupiah or dollar here than in Kuta–Legian–Seminyak. Obviously, places with direct access to the beach command a premium.

Artotel Sanur Jl. Kusuma Sari No. 1; http://artotelgroup.com. A quirky little place dedicated to contemporary art and its Bali-based creators, the *Artotel* is a hub for happenings of all kinds. Each room is uniquely artistic and the rooftop pool and bar are as eclectic as the rest of the property. $

Griya Santrian Jl Danau Tamblingan No. 47; http://santrian.com. There's plenty of space and no shortage of beach views at this large well-run hotel, with spacious rooms in a garden compound that runs down to the shore. You'll also find an art gallery, good seafront restaurant and three pools (one shoreside). $$$

Inna Sindhu Beach Hotel & Resort Jl. Pantai Sindhu No. 14; http://hig.id/hotels/inna-sindhu-beach. Right on the beach, this two-storey Balinese-décor hotel is ideal for families. It even has a kids' swimming pool. $$

★ **Little Pond Homestay** Jl Danau Tamblingan No. 19, Sindhu beach; http://littlepondbali.com. The fifteen small bright rooms grouped around a pool have a choice of fan or a/c and are a cut above the usual *losmen*, each with verandas, hot-water bathrooms and a homely feel. Once you factor in that this is quiet and close to the main road

DIVING AND SNORKELLING AROUND SANUR

Despite the abundance of diving operators, Sanur's **reef dives** are only really of interest for beginners or as a refresher. The coral is unspectacular, the visibility so-so, and dives rarely descend beneath 12m. However, dive trips to Nusa Penida and Amed are offered by several schools and **snorkelling** trips (including gear) are also popular. Recommended dive centres in Sanur include:

Bali Scuba Jl Danau Poso No. 46, Sanur; http://baliscuba.com. PADI five-star IDC centre that's known for its technical diving.

Blue Season Bali Gang Wanasari, off Jl. Danau Poso; http://baliocean.com. PADI CDC centre. Also runs snorkelling trips.

Crystal Divers Gang Griya No. 6 off Jl. Bypass Ngurah Rai; http://crystal-divers.com. PADI CDC centre. Established for 20 years and also runs tailored dive safaris all over Bali.

Dune Atlantis Bali Jl. Bypass Ngurah Rai No. 96E, Sanur; http://atlantis-bali-diving.com. PADI five-star IDC Centre. Operates courses in English, French, Chinese and Indonesian.

and beach, you'll realize you've got a bargain. $

★ **Ning Homestay** Gang 3, off Jl Kesari 1; 0823 3910 7639. Sanur's best hostel is well-organized, with clean accommodation and a sociable vibe: the eight-bed dorm is a/c and bunks have reading lights, lockers and power sockets while the double room is fine value for Sanur. There are plenty of spots to relax and chat with other guests around the garden, the restaurant has well-priced drinks and meals, there's free drinking water and communal bathrooms are kept tidy. $

Sudamala Suites & Villas Jl. Sudamala No. 29; http://sudamalaresorts.com. Elegantly furnished with Kamasan style paintings. Although the resort isn't located on the sea it has a private area on one of Sanur's quieter beaches, Mertasari, just a few minutes away by leisurely stroll or free-for-guests bicycle. A spa and daily yoga complete the serenity. $$$

Tandjung Sari Jl Danau Tamblingan No. 41, Sindhu beach; http://tandjungsarihotel.com. Today a delightful, intimate and classy hotel, this was once a private beach house for an English/Javanese couple. There are beautifully furnished cottages of varying sizes, each with a courtyard garden; expect antique floor tiles and tasteful batik furnishings. Add in a large pool, fitness centre, library, a garden that runs to the shore and faultless service and this is a fine choice for a relaxing stay. $$$$

Yulia Homestay 1 Jl Danau Tamblingan No. 38, Sindhu beach; http://facebook.com/yulia1homestay. A very welcoming family-run cheapie with twenty fan-cooled or a/c rooms, some with hot water, all well maintained and comfortable if a little old-fashioned. Owner Ketut is a mine of information about Bali and there's a small pool to enjoy. $

EATING

SEE MAP PAGE 90

Beachfront café-restaurants abound between Sindhu and Batujimbar but none stands out for cuisine, so stroll to the promenade and take your pick. The most authentic Indonesian food and cheapest eats are beyond the main drag; the night market (6pm–midnight) inside the Sindhu Market at Jl Danau Tamblingan/Jl Danau Toba, and the surrounding lanes, are good hunting grounds.

ABC (Artotel Beach Club) Jl Danau Tamblingan No. 35; http://artotelgroup.com/restaurants-bars/artotel-beach-club. *ABC* provides family entertainment on the beach. Start with a breakfast burrito for brunch/lunch or dine on seafood for dinner. A lagoon pool, playground, bars and a lounge complete the picture. $$

Café Batu Jimbar Jl Danau Tamblingan No. 75; 0361 284103. This popular Sanur street-side spot specialises in Italian, Mexican as well as Indonesian food. They also serve healthy salads. On Sundays the café hosts a market selling fresh produce and a breakfast buffet with mouthwatering Balinese dishes. $$

Café Smorgas Jl Danau Tamblingan No. 56; http://cafesmorgas.com. This relaxed Swedish family-run café/restaurant serves up salads, sandwiches, burgers, wraps and main dishes, some of them inspired by Swedish cuisine. The family make their own home-made bread, cakes, pastries and jams. $$

★ **Juicy & Crispy** Jl Tirta Nadi No. 5; http://juicyandcrispy.com. A meat feast par excellence – buzzing, busy *JnC* has a mercifully short menu, specializing in super-succulent spareribs and rotisserie chicken. It's a tiny, cramped space so book ahead for seating, or grab and go. $$

Luhtu's Sindhu Beach; 0812 4605 0576. Likeable beachfront cafe that serves up great breakfasts, sandwiches and salads and a mean *soto ayam* (chicken soup). There's also a counter of fresh cakes to go with it – try the lemon cheesecake. $$

Massimo Jl Danau Tamblingan No. 228; 0811 399 9727. The finest Italian cooking in Sanur, produced by a native chef: excellent antipasti such as *frittura de calamari* (squid with alioli) thin-crust pizza and pasta plus mains including barramunda, Italian style.There's a kids' menu and takeaway *gelato* are a lifesaver on hot days. $$

The Porch Café Jl Danau Tamblingan No. 110; http://www.flashbacks-chb.com/Cafe. A well-run Aussie-owned cafe with a/c interior and small front terrace that offers a

1

good range of breakfasts, home-made fresh pies, veggie dishes, the full gamut of espresso coffee combinations and endless varieties of fresh juice. $$

The Village Cucina Italiana Jl Danau Tamblingan No. 47; http://thevillage-bali.com. This is a great place to try authentic Italian food and wine in Sanur. Everything is home-made from the pasta to the gelato. $$$

Warung Hanabi Jl Jl. Bet Ngandang II No.21; https://www.instagram.com/warung_hanabi. Good value Japanese food served in a welcoming *warung* just off the main drag. Choose from sushi, sashimi, or a selection of udon and rice dishes paired with sides like edamame and *kushiyaki*. $

Warung Kecil Jl Duyung No. 1; http://facebook.com/warungkecilbali. Tiny modern *warung* with both Indo and Western food. Grab a panini, salad or a *nasi goreng ayam* and slurp on a fresh juice. There are a few books to browse too. $

Warung Little Bird Jl Danau Tamblingan No. 34; 0877 3038 2428. This unpretentious little place serves up affordable, authentic local food with live music in the evenings. Great value for money. $

NIGHTLIFE AND ENTERTAINMENT

SEE MAP PAGE 90

There's not much here – this is "Snore", remember? If you don't fancy the cover bands at beachside restaurants on the main drag, you'll have to make do with so-so sports bars and "Irish" pubs favoured by expats.

Casablanca Jl Danau Tamblingan No. 120; http://casablancasanur.com. It's certainly not hip, but the self-styled "most colourful place in Sanur" is definitely lively with live rock, reggae, indie and soul bands entertaining the holiday crowds. $$

Tree Bar Jl Danau Tamblingan No. 89M at Maya Sanur Resort & Spa; http://mayaresorts.com/sanur/restaurant/tree-bar. This sophisticated beachfront restaurant and bar has a long list of wines, beers and exotic cocktails which are served in a lovely setting. The three-level bar and restaurant is centred around a lovely shady tree and apart from drinks it offers a great variety of tapas, but also pasta, salads and international dishes. $$

SHOPPING

SEE MAP PAGE 90

A-Krea Jl Danau Tamblingan No. 51; 0361 286 101. Great little outlet of a Balinese mini-chain whose woven and batik handmade bags and purses, homewares, clothes and cute kidswear and toys are all crafted tastefully in simple modern designs.

Biasa Jl Danau Tamblingan No. 37, http://biasagroup.com. Elegant, tasteful clothing made from natural fabrics for men and women, plus scarves.

Hardy's Jl Danau Tamblingan No. 136; 0361 281 915. You'll find mass-produced crafts if you rummage among the souvenir tat on the top floor of *Hardy's Supermarket*. In addition to food and spirits, there's a Periplus book store and the ground floor sells more Bali souvenir T-shirts than you knew possible.

ON'KOR Jl Danau Tamblingan No. 51; https://www.instagram.com/onkor.sanur. Tucked away in a small shopping arcade alongside A-Krea, this preloved clothing boutique focuses on quirky, unique pieces. Look out for designer finds, bold prints and accessories.

Periplus Jl Danau Tamblingan No. 136; http://periplus.com. The excellent English-language Periplus bookstore has a branch in *Hardy's Supermarket*. It sells a good selection of national and international media, plus a wide selection of fiction and nonfiction, including much on island life and culture.

Uluwatu Jl Danau Tamblingan No. 94; http://uluwatu.co.id. A large outlet of the Balinese chain, which sells elegant white or black handmade lace and flowing cotton clothes – plus bed linen and some jewellery.

DIRECTORY

Banks and exchange There are ATMs and exchange counters all over Sanur.

Embassies and consulates See page 24.

Hospitals and clinics All the major hotels provide 24hr medical service. Guardian Pharmacy by *Hardy's Supermarket* also has a doctor on call. For major international clinics, see Kuta–Legian–Seminyak.

Pharmacies Several on Jl Danau Tamblingan.

Police There's a 24hr Tourist Police post on Jl Danau Tamblingan, just south of the *Hyatt Regency Bali* hotel. The police station (0361 288597) is on Jl Bypass in north Sanur, just south of *Prime Plaza Hotel Sanur*.

Post office Sanur's General Post Office is on Jl Danau Buyan No. 28, Sindhu.

The Nusas

It's amazing what 12km of sea will do. Even compared to Sanur, **Nusa Lembongan**, **Nusa Ceningan** and **Nusa Penida** islands across the Badung Strait seem a throwback to the Bali of twenty years ago – the Bali of laidback villages and bumpy lanes winding through mangroves; of fine white sand and turquoise water; of spectacular sunsets on the beach as time slips by at a lovely lazy pace. Small wonder many people go there for two days and find themselves on the return boat two weeks later.

Of course, there's more to these islands than idle days scrunching white sand between your toes. Encircled by superbly clear water and healthy reef, they offer outstanding **diving** – Nusa Penida's sites are world-class – and challenging **surfing**. There's even industry of sorts – seaweed farming is a major source of income for many islanders.

Of the trio, **Nusa Lembongan** has nearly all the facilities. Even though it's developing rapidly, it remains relaxed, with most accommodation slotted in between homes. Activity providers offer trips both on foot and on two wheels. Tiny, relatively undeveloped **Nusa Ceningan** can be reached on foot or by bicycle from Nusa Lembongan and is a trekker's paradise. **Nusa Penida** is the largest of all and more rugged than Nusa Lembongan. Except for a couple of resorts, bungalows and guesthouses are the name of the game here, but its unique terrain makes it ripe for a few days' exploration for the adventurous.

Nusa Lembongan

Yes, there are now boutique hotels. And each visit reveals a new patch of scrub cleared for yet another homestay or more motorbikes on the lanes. But apart from the ever-growing number of tourists **NUSA LEMBONGAN** retains its village ambience – you can sense the island atmosphere as soon as you wade off the boat. Even the hawkers are half-hearted. Tourism has most definitely arrived – around seventy percent of the seven thousand population are engaged in tourism to some degree – yet it's largely restricted to **Jungutbatu** village in the north (which has the most accommodation), **Mushroom Bay** on the west side and the **Lembongan** area in the south, where the hotels tend to be more upmarket.

The islanders earn a crust by **seaweed farming** in the aquamarine shallows. A source of **agar** vegetable gel and **carrageenan** used in cosmetics and foodstuffs, seaweed is grown on chequerboard bamboo frames and harvested after 45 days – hard, physical work with unpredictable financial rewards. Mangroves, meanwhile, fringe much of the north and east coast. This makes much of the coast so-so for swimming, but there are some pretty white-sand bays that are good for a dip so long as you heed local warnings about currents.

There are near zero cars, so **getting around** means joining villagers on motorbikes or bicycles, which are widely available for rent. The island is just 4km long and less than 3km wide, so if you are supremely keen you could walk around it in a long hot day. Good luck with that.

Jungutbatu and Mushroom Bay

Strung out along the northwest coast, the slightly scruffy **JUNGUTBATU** village spreads out along the beachfront from its core of accommodation and restaurants. The sandy **beach** is lovely and though it is no great shakes for swimming, it looks gorgeous at low tide, a strip of coarse golden sand that arcs before an aquamarine

A MANGROVE SAFARI

Given Nusa Lembongan's focus on diving and surf, a trip into the **mangrove swamps** that fringe the northeast coast is one of the more unusual diversions on a visit. It's an eerie experience: boats are punted with bamboo, so there's no engine noise to disturb the crabs and birds that inhabit the muddy forest floor – the trip is best at low tide when the roots are exposed.

sea filled with wooden boats. It's an ideal place for sunset drinks or for losing days gazing out to Gunung Agung on the northwestern horizon. For a bit more activity, you can walk 1km south to Mushroom Bay in 30–45 minutes via a scenic **west-coast path** that begins at the steps at the far southern end of the beach. You'll have to improvise a path at points – just keep the coast on your right – but the reward is a couple of small beaches en route. A crescent of white sand behind a turquoise bay, **Mushroom Bay** is small and charming. The downside is that before around 5pm it's crowded with boats, huge offshore party pontoons and day-trippers. If you

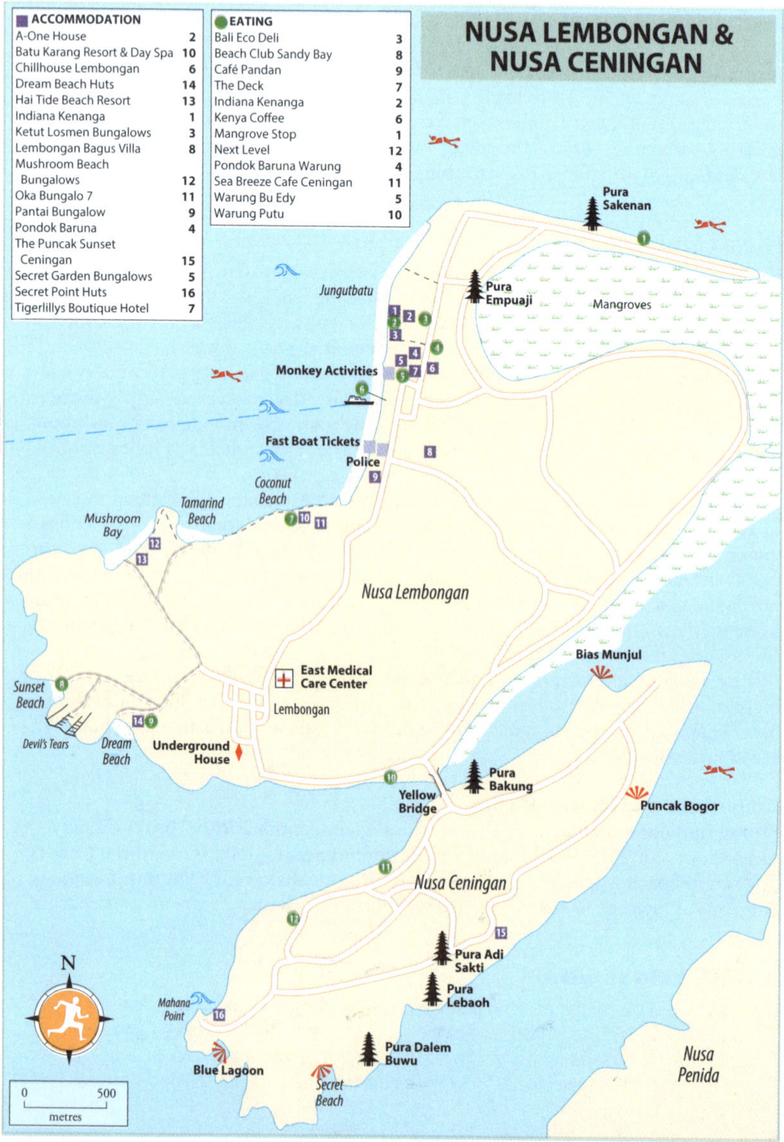

ask locally, you should be able to find a path to Sunset Beach and its beach club, though the easiest access is by road via Lembongan village.

The north coast

Village life and seaweed farming dominates on the **northern tip of the island**, a flat 3km that's easily covered by bicycle from central Jungutbatu. There's also the possibility of exploring the mangrove forest that fringes the northeast coast. Most of the *warung* beyond the unremarkable sea temple, **Pura Sakenan**, will organize a paddle through the mangroves for (20-minute trip).

The east coast

A fork in the road 200m west of Pura Sakenan takes you down the **east coast**, past **Pura Empuaji** (700m southwest; dawn till dusk; free, own sash and sarong required) and its two monumental ficus trees – this is the most venerated temple on the island and you'll need a sarong and sash if you want to visit. The road wends its way between mangrove forest and the occasional house, and after another 5.5km reaches the turn-off for the bridge to Nusa Ceningan. From here it's 2km up to Lembongan village, then another 3km back to Jungutbatu.

Lembongan village

At the top of a steep hill 3km southwest of central Jungutbatu the tidy **LEMBONGAN** settlement is the largest on the island and the location of the **Underground House** (open on request; charge). Reminiscent of France's troglodyte caves and dug between 1961 and 1976 by Made Byasa, a local man who is said to have been inspired by the Mahabharata (see page 311), it consists of several dank rooms, a well and ventilation shafts.

The southwest coast

Two of Bali's loveliest beaches lie on the southwest coast. From Lembongan, follow the main road west through to a T-junction and signs for Mushroom Bay, 750m down a side road. A left turn here leads 1km to **Dream Beach**, one of the island's most beautiful bays with its white sand and clear, turquoise water – beware though, the currents are dangerous. Adrenaline junkies might want to try cliff jumping at Dream Beach, being cautious of tide levels, of course. There's accommodation and eateries here, a great spot for sundowner cocktails. It's just a few minutes' walk beyond to pretty little **Sunset Beach**, with its own resort. At both beaches, it can be too risky for a swim but you can use the pools for a fee.

Between Dream and Sunset beaches is Devil's Tears, aptly named for the mist that forms from blowholes spewing water into the stratosphere with mighty force. During the day, this spot is packed with day-tour folk talking selfies but after they leave at around 5pm, stick around for magnificent crimson sunsets that reflect in the tidepools below. The adventurous can test their cliff-jumping skills here too.

ARRIVAL AND DEPARTURE — NUSA LEMBONGAN

What with the private fast boats, tourist shuttles and slow boats, there are over twenty **daily services** to Jungutbatu and eight to Mushroom Bay. All leave from either the end of Jl Hang Tuah in north Sanur or from Serangan harbour. In Lembongan, offices are on the seafront of southern Jungutbatu. Note that all boats anchor just off the beach, so you're required to **wade** ashore; a porter may offer to carry your luggage. On arrival at Lembongan "beach guides" may offer to show you to accommodation for free (hotels pay commission). They'll also offer motorbikes to transport you between bays for steep fees, though if you reserve ahead hotel staff should meet you.

FROM AND TO SANUR

By fast boat Several private operators run speedy boats from Sanur to Lembongan. Operators include Scoot (http://scootcruise.com) and Rocky (http://rockyfastcruise.com), which run up to four times a day in each direction (30min). Scoot, which departs from Jl. Hang Tua, also has a combination ticket with Gili Trawangan and Lombok.

1

DIVING AND SNORKELLING AROUND THE NUSAS

Protected as a marine conservation area, the reefs around Nusa Lembongan and Nusa Penida attract **divers** from all over the world, not least for the chance to swim with manta rays and the one-tonne legendary local giant, the **mola mola** (oceanic sunfish; see page 101), from early July to the end of October. The diving here is unquestionably the most dramatic in Bali, but also rarely benign, as currents and waves can be fierce. Many of the reefs are rewarding for **snorkelling**, too.

Of the fourteen main dive sites, the most famous are **off Nusa Penida** and can get very crowded in peak season. The aptly named **Manta Point** is renowned for manta rays and pelagics (whale sharks are occasionally encountered here) and is the site that everyone wants to experience. It's also the most exposed, being subject to huge swells and currents, and should only be dived when conditions are favourable – choose a reputable dive company. The famous manta "cleaning station" is at 5m in depth, and if you're lucky you'll encounter a procession of mantas banking in the water (like airplanes circling the sky waiting to land) and then swooping down to the station to get cleaned of parasites by waiting reef fish. Alternatively, juvenile manta rays (still over 2m!) can often be encountered at neighbouring **Manta Bay** where the sea is usually calmer. **Crystal Bay** is known for its clear waters – visibility can be 40m – and is one of the sites which attracts pelagic mola mola or sunfish from late July to October. Mola mola, manta rays and tuna also frequent the huge coral boulders and pillars of **Toyapakeh** reef, which is an incredibly rich site, teeming with fish, macro interest such as nudibranches and other curiosities (stonefish included). **Sekolah Dasar** is an excellent drift dive past the healthy reefs of north **Nusa Penida**, particularly rich in sponges, and where white-tip reef sharks and huge schools of damselfish are present.

Prime **snorkelling** spots off **Nusa Lembongan** that are accessible from the shore if the tide is right are **Mangrove Corner** and **Mushroom Bay**. Off **Nusa Penida** they include **Crystal Bay** (see page 104, the **Toyapakeh Wall**, Manta Bay and **Gamat Bay**. Virtually every guesthouse and hotel on the Islands can organize trips or contact one of the several dive centres on either island.

DIVE CENTRES

The seas around Penida and Lembongan are affected by cold upswells (down to 18°C) and are known for treacherous **currents**, so dive with experts – some sites are for experienced divers only. There are a number of reputable **dive centres** on Nusa Lembongan and Nusa Penida (and one in Ceningan) including those listed below. Cheaper deals are available for longer dive packages. All centres offer tuition.

Big Fish Diving Secret Garden Bungalows, Jungutbatu, Nusa Lembongan; http://bigfishdiving.com. Five-star PADI dive school plus yoga.

Ceningan Divers Ceningan Resort, Jl. Raya Ceningan Kangin, Nusa Ceningan; http://ceningandivers.com. Five-star PADI dive school.

Monkey Activities Beachfront Jungutbatu; http://monkeyactivities.com. SSI freediving training and snorkelling excursions.

Sanctum Dive Ped Village, Nusa Penida; http://sanctumdiveindonesia.com PADI dive courses and yoga.

World Diving Lembongan Pondok Baruna, Jungutbatu, Nusa Lembongan; http://world-diving.com. Five-star PADI dive school with dive and stay packages.

Rocky departs from Serangan harbour. Perama (http://peramatour.com) operates a shuttle boat from Sanur that connects with its island-wide shuttle bus services from Sanur, Kuta and Ubud. It runs to Nusa Lembongan and Nusa Penida (3 times daily); book a day in advance. All three provide pick-up/drop off to hotels in tourist areas. Public fast boats run from Serangan and Sanur to Lembongan (several times daily, http://baliferry.com).

By slow boat From Sanur there are irregular slow boats for Jungutbatu (2hr) and Mushroom Bay (90min), but they are unreliable and unsafe.

FROM AND TO EAST BALI

Demand willing, there are scheduled (in theory) services between Padang Bai and Jungutbatu, Lembongan.

GETTING AROUND

By bike or motorbike Not necessary around the villages but a good bet around Nusa Lembongan. Set off in a clockwise direction to avoid a killer climb south of Jungutbatu if cycling; the road is tarmac, although very broken in places. Both bikes and motorbikes can be rented through your accommodation.

By golf buggy A couple of places rent 4- or 6-seat electric golf carts for 5 or 10 hrs (http://thelembongantraveller.com or https://rickyrajabuggy.biz.id).

By pick-up Some isolated restaurants in the south offer free transport with a reservation.

On foot None of the best west-coast beaches is more than 90min from Jungutbatu.

ACTIVITIES

Spa and massage Su B (0812 3675 7214, by appointment), behind the shore at the south end of Jungutbatu, is the expats' tip for the best massage on the island – he or his wife offer aromatherapy massage and reflexology. For more of a luxe spa environment, Lulur Spa Lembongan (http://lulurspalembongan.com) in the *Batu Karang Resort & Day Spa* offers scrubs, aromatherapy and massages.

Surfing Surfing around Nusa Lembongan is famously challenging. The best months for surfing are from May to September when southeast winds blow offshore. The breaks peel off the reef before Jungutbatu – from south to north: Playgrounds (the most forgiving break); the well-named, heavy Lacerations; and Shipwrecks. You can paddle out the 200m or so to Playgrounds, then on to Lacerations but for Shipwrecks rent a boat. Board rental is available on the seafront at Jungutbatu; Lembongan Surf Lesson (Jungutbatu beach, http://lembongansurflesson.com) has surfing lessons, board rental and snorkelling trips.

ACCOMMODATION

SEE MAP PAGE 96

Accommodations are prolific on the west and south coasts, much of them fronting the beach, ranging from budget to luxe. But you'll also find options on other parts of the island. A word of warning: the island is packed from April to October so reserve ahead during this time.

JUNGUTBATU

A-One House 0812 3615 2422. Cosy bamboo huts with balconies near the beach with your choice of a/c or fan. Large pool, spa center and a bar. $$

Batu Karang Resort & Day Spa http://batukarang lembongan.com. Set on the hillside overlooking the bay of Jungutbatu, these luxurious suites and villas are all limestone floors and outdoor bathrooms and contemporary cool around the pools (there are three). Facilities include a small gym and lovely spa. Minimum stay of three nights in high season. $$$$

★ **Chillhouse Lembongan** Jl Dusun Kelod 1; 0821 4500 6892. Set back from the shore in the village, these neat, very clean and well-presented a/c rooms have good king-sized beds, hot-water bathrooms, flat-screen TVs and verandas. The owner Gede is a super-helpful soul who will arrange snorkelling trips, scooter rentals and is full of island info and history. $

★ **Indiana Kenanga** Jl Pantai Jungutbatu No. 56; http://indiana-kenanga-villas.com. A design-conscious boutique resort right on the beach, with vaguely baroque-meets-contemporary decor. Standard suites are in private garden compounds, while family villas sleep four in two bedrooms. Has two pools, a spa and is home to a yummy French restaurant. $$$$

Ketut Losmen Bungalows Jl Pelabuhan Jungutbatu; 0813 3784 6555. There's a wide choice of bungalows (some very smart with a/c and hot water) at this locally owned place which has a traditional Balinese feel thanks to carved furnishings and doors, plus paintings in rooms. There's a small beachside pool but no restaurant. $

Lembongan Bagus Villa 0812 3746 7740. A fine-value setup run by local Made and his family, with five lovely a/c wooden bungalows that feature outdoor bathrooms and either twin or double beds. It's on the edge of the village, 400m from the sea, pool and restaurant. $$

Oka Bungalo 7 0813 3705 0030. Five rooms and a couple of *lumbung* cottages, all with a/c, that enjoy sweeping bay views and represent good value for the location. There's a plunge pool for cooling off. $$

Pantai Bungalow http://pantaibungalow.com/. Good-value budget rooms with a/c and 24-hour hot water within a short walk of the beach and the Gili Islands ferry terminal. Free surfboards and bikes are available for guests. $

Pondok Baruna Jl Jungutbatu; 0823 4130 4320.There are three options in this local empire: simple yet attractive fan-cooled beachfront rooms with full-frontal sea views; just behind, smarter a/c "Garden" rooms around a pool; and the newer *Pondok Baruna Frangipani* with modern international-hotel-standard a/c accommodation around a large pool down the street. $–$$

★ **Secret Garden Bungalows** http://bigfishdiving.com/stay. A relaxed hideaway, this small, peaceful place has spacious fan- or a/c-cooled bungalows set around a pool in the garden, 100m from the beach. Also hosts the YogaShack and conservation-focused Big Fish Diving (see page 98). Great value; ask about low season discounts. $

Tigerlillys Boutique Hotel http://tigerlillyslembongan.com. The romance of a simple Balinese beach hut meets boutique style in an Australian-owned retreat amid lush

1

tropical gardens. Expect floaty drapes and pops of colour in pretty thatched cottages with semi-outdoor bathrooms. No children under 12. $$

THE REST OF THE ISLAND

Dream Beach Huts Dream Beach; https://dreambeach-lembongan.com. Above the fantastic Dream Beach, these 28 *lumbung*-style thatch-roof huts have bamboo beds, a/c and cold-water garden bathrooms; Deluxe offer the most romance and space. There's also a two-bed family house, two-tier pool over the breakers and a restaurant/bar. Quite isolated, though that's half the point. $$

Hai Tide Beach Resort Mushroom Bay; https://balihaicruises.com/haitidebeachresort-nusa-lembongan-beachfront-accommodation. A beautifully designed, small-scale resort with 24 charming thatched *lumbung* (some with ocean views) and 3 two-bed villas (with private pool). All Bali Hai Beach Club facilities are available to guests, there are two good restaurants and the resort can arrange pickup from your Bali hotel and transfer via its Bali Hai Cruises catamaran. $$

Mushroom Beach Bungalows Mushroom Bay; 0877 5199 9311. Good-quality, spacious rooms with cold-water showers in a splendid location on the headland at the eastern end of Mushroom Bay, just a 2min walk from a pretty small beach. Has an infinity pool, restaurant and a spa. $

EATING AND DRINKING

SEE MAP PAGE 96

JUNGUTBATU

Bali Eco Deli http://baliecodeli.net. Attractive open-sided roadside café with plenty of space to enjoy a coffee and chat. Famous for its cakes (try the chocolate, cashew and coconut) which are all baked on the premises. Healthy meals, fruit salads and ice-pops are also offered and you can refill drinking water bottles here for free. $$

The Deck http://thedecklembongan.com. This café-bar-resto in the hillside *Batu Karang Resort & Day Spa* is the spot in town for a sundowner when cocktails and beers are discounted. It's also a good bet for grub such as gourmet baguettes, paninis and fish tacos. Their Sunday Session features live DJs spinning funky house and lounge vibes. $$

Indiana Kenanga Jl. Pantai Jungutbatu No. 56; http://indiana-kenanga-villas.com. Run by a French chef, there's a casual day menu with dishes such as shrimp ceviche or gourmet burgers while the evening menu really delivers a punch with winning plates such as scallops with a parsley coulis, gnocchi and parmesan sauce. $$$$

Kenya Coffee Beachfront, Gang Nusa Indah; 0819 9985 5535. Great little café offering well-made espresso, cappuccino and fancy options such as green tea lattes. Tables enjoy perfect bay views and the wi-fi is relatively speedy for Lembongan. $

Mangrove Stop Beachfront, Mangrove Point. This rustic Robinson Crusoe-style restaurant is located at the eastern end of the spit of land that runs through the northern mangrove forest. It serves up authentic Indonesian dishes as well as simple Western staples. *Mangrove Stop* also offers a wide variety of water sports (snorkelling, diving, jet skis, stand up paddle and much more) and tours. $$

Pondok Baruna Warung Jl Jungutbatu 0812 394 0992. Popular for Indonesian cooking in more comfortable surrounds than your average *warung*: the menu takes in well-cooked dishes including tasty pork sate with sweet soy sauce and chicken curry with cumin, cardamom and coconut milk. $$

Warung Bu Edy Jl Jungutbatu 0813 3968 7366. Famous for its *nasi campur*, this simple place attracts a stream of expats and locals who come for a feast that might include spicy chicken, yellow rice and stir-fried veg. $

THE REST OF THE ISLAND

Beach Club Sandy Bay Sunset Beach, a 5min walk from Dream Beach; http://sandybaylembongan.com. This chic spot is a fine place to spend a day. Seafood is good or try the Peking duck salad with shredded Asian vegetables. SMS or phone for free transport. $$$

Café Pandan at Dream Beach Huts; https://dreambeach-lembongan.com/experience. This casual open-air cafe and restaurant enjoys the breathtaking views of Dream Beach and serves up a good selection of Balinese, Thai and Western dishes. It's a good idea to ask for the catch of the day. The list of cocktails is imposing. $$

Warung Putu https://instagram.com/warung_putu_lembongan. A great spot around sunset, this *warung* serves burgers and inexpensive local nosh. Try the spicy beef rendang. It's on the south side of the island, 150m west of the suspension bridge. $

DIRECTORY

Banks and exchange There are several ATMs dotted around Jungutbatu. Moneychangers, guesthouses and hotels will change money (at poor rates) and offer credit card advances (eight percent commission, passport required).

Health centre East Medical Care Center (EMMC), Jl. Mushroom Beach No. 247, 0813 3955 5515, http://eastmedicalcarecenter.com. The island's only modern medical care facility with a multilingual staff, ambulance, pharmacy, lab, med evac and home visits. Daily 24hrs.

MOLA MOLA

Between July and October the waters around Nusa Lembongan and Nusa Penida offer the best chance most people will ever have of spotting a **mola mola** (oceanic sunfish), one of the most elusive and startling of underwater creatures. The heaviest bony fish in the world, it has an average weight of 1000kg. Some specimens weigh more than double that and grow up to 3m long, roughly the size of a small car. *Mola* is Latin for millstone, which it resembles in being huge, grey, rough and rounded in shape – it has no tail. Fortunately it is docile and no danger to divers, as it eats jellyfish, squids, crustaceans, small fishes and other marine life. Much remains unknown about this gentle giant but it is thought to spend most of its life well below 200m.

For some reason the annual shift of ocean currents brings mola mola up to shallower waters for a few months each year, which is when enthusiasts and the merely curious head to the seas around these small islands in the hope of spotting one. They are usually encountered when upswells bring cool water from the depths to the surface, so if sea temperatures are balmy they are very rarely seen.

Nusa Ceningan

At the point where the channel between Nusa Lembongan and **NUSA CENINGAN** is narrowest, a suspension bridge (aptly called the Yellow Bridge thanks to its sunshine colour) links the islands. You can cycle or ride a motorbike across for a look at this totally rural island, just 4km long by 1km wide, but it's quite a challenge: the road is very rough in places, there are no signs and gradients are steep, including one killer climb. Or you can walk across. Ceningan is small enough that you easily walk its perimeter in a day and in doing so you might discover hidden treasures. Forested and hilly, the island depends on seaweed farming and lacks swimmable beaches, though there is an exquisite surf break, Mahana Point. Only the brave dare to cliff-jump here as well as at Blue Lagoon further south. (It can't be stressed enough – follow local guidance and do not attempt this alone, watch the tides, and wear reef shoes for climbing out.) Sitting idly by while the foolhardy do their thing is recommended, particularly for the sunsets. Another chance to test your meddle is at Driftwood Bar, where you can quickly zipline over the bay (charge). Reward yourself with a smoothie or a beer afterwards while soaking in the infinity pool. There's also a PADI dive school, Ceningan Divers (http://ceningandivers.com), in a very peaceful location in the mangroves.

ACCOMMODATION AND EATING NUSA CENINGAN, SEE MAP PAGE 96

Tourism has indeed arrived on Ceningan, where accommodations range from homestays to cottages to villas. Likewise, simple *warung* with cheap eats abound but there are now some upscale food and bar choices too, and more are coming soon. Here are a few options.

Next Level Just off Jl. Nusa Ceningan 0822 3636 4574. This small café offers tasty local dishes, snacks, salads and international staples like pizza. Smoothie bowls are particularly worth a try. Great sea views. $

The Puncak Sunset Ceningan Jl. Nusa Ceningan, Jungubatu; 0812 4693 6797. This privately-owned hilltop villa with two bedrooms and infinity pool overlooks the sea. The welcoming hosts and the rare bonus of a fresh-water shower are a great addition. Breakfast included. $$$

Sea Breeze Cafe Ceningan Jl. Nusa Ceningan; 0812 3956 7407. Eat, drink, or simply chill in this colourful café on the beach that provides bean bags and even swings to help you relax. Nice menu ranges from smoothie bowls to chicken satays and happy hour are two-for-the-price-of one. $$

Secret Point Huts A 3min. walk from Blue Lagoon; 0859 5412 4593. With an ideal location, these a/c *lumbung*-style huts with outdoor showers excel for their ocean-view terraces. There's also a restaurant serving seafood and Indonesian dishes. Breakfast included. $

Nusa Penida

Dominated by a dry central limestone plateau either side of beaches in the north and by towering sea cliffs in the south, the handsome **NUSA PENIDA** island feels quite different from mainland Bali. It was once used as a penal colony, a sort of Siberia for transgressive Balinese, and is renowned as the home of the legendary demon Ratu Gede Mas Macaling; its temple, **Pura Dalem Penataran Ped**, is an important pilgrimage site for Hindus from all over Bali. Islanders have their own dialect and many live off seaweed farming, fishing and growing tough crops such as corn; it's too dry for rice.

With its first-class diving (see page 98), superb scenery and a chance to see the endangered Bali starling in the wild, tourism in Nusa Penida is growing by leaps and bounds. Although infrastructure remains relatively poor, it's improving, and adventurous visitors will find reward in the opportunity to visit a destination almost free of tourist glitz – the welcome in villages is genuinely warm.

On a day-trip from nearby Nusa Lembongan you can get a taste of Penida on a circuit that takes in Pura Dalem Penataran Ped, **Pura Goa Giri**, a view of the south-coast cliffs and **Crystal Bay**, as well as the island's main towns, **Toyapakeh** and **Sampalan**. Ideally, at least two days' exploration provides a better impression of an island that feels far larger than its 20km by 16km because of the steep inclines and dizzy back roads. Take to the latter and you'll get lost, of course. But maybe that's half the point.

Toyapakeh

Boats from Nusa Lembongan dock at **TOYAPAKEH**, spread behind a crescent of white-sand beach. There's nothing particular to see, just a small daily market and a tiny mosque, but there are a couple of basic *warung* and usually a hawker or two to meet you. Still, it's a mellow spot – or is unless one of the day-tripper party boats from Sanur has moored to a pontoon just offshore.

Pura Dalem Penataran Ped

Ped village, main road • free; own sash and sarong required to visit

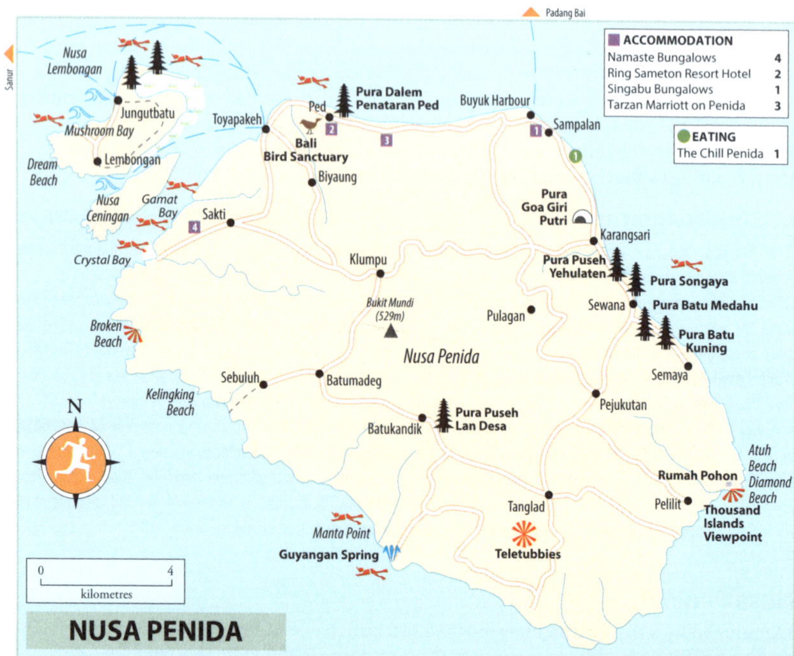

Every day **Pura Dalem Penataran Ped** attracts worshippers from across Bali, bearing copious offerings. The temple complex is always dressed to receive them, its dazzlingly smooth white limestone walls and fantastic carvings draped in ceremonial cloths of black-and-white *poleng* and gold-brocade *songket*. The temple is regarded as *angker*, a place of evil spirits; it is the home of the dreaded **Ratu Gede Mas Macaling**, also known as **I Macaling** and **Jero Gde**, who brings disease, floods and ill-fortune to the mainland and requires regular appeasement. There are actually four temples within the compound, one of which is dedicated to Ratu Gede Mas Macaling; another has a dramatic sculpture of the half-fish, half-elephant deity of the sea, Gajah Mina.

Bali Bird Sanctuary

Western edge of Ped, a few hundred metres west of the temple • daily dawn–dusk • donation appreciated • http://fnpf.org

Thanks to an innovative, community-focused programme run by the Friends of the National Parks Foundation (FNPF) the endangered, fluffy white **Bali starling** (*jalak putih Bali*) and Rothschild's mynah (*Leucopsar rothschildi*) are now flourishing on Nusa Penida, with over a hundred birds microchipped and free to flutter around the island. The easiest place to spot them and other endangered rescued birds is at the **Bali Bird Sanctuary**, where they congregate for food; staff will lead you round the small site. The foundation also accepts volunteers for its bird programmes and other island conservation projects.

Sampalan

The largest village on the island, **SAMPALAN**, 4km from Ped, is a metropolis by local standards, with several ATMs, *warung*, shops and a central **market** all spread out behind the coast. The bemo terminal is in the middle of the village.

Pura Goa Giri Putri

Jl. Ped-Buyuk, Karangasari • Donation, includes sash and sarong

It's a spectacular ride south from Sampalan on a coast-hugging road that offers views of *prahus* on beaches and seaweed-farming plots, as well as vistas of Lombok ahead. About 10km south, in the **Karangasari**, a steep flight of steps leads up to the limestone bat-cave temple **Pura Goa Giri Putri**. Squeeze through a narrow gap in the rock and you enter a 300m-long cavern which houses several small shrines, countless bats and a meditation cave. Walk past the lot and you'll emerge blinking into sunlight at the far end having walked right through the hill. Balinese people consider this a very powerful spiritual site so it's important that you dress and behave accordingly.

The east coast

Though difficult to reach over loose gravel pathways, there's a lot to be said for including eastern Penida. Three beaches with mind-blowing views of the Indian Ocean will make the effort worthwhile. South of Goa Giri Putri, on the left side of Atuh Beach a natural arch juts up from the sea and is spectacular at sunrise when the orange glow peeks underneath. Beach-side vendors provide breakfast at around 8am. Adjacent is Diamond Beach, named for a diamond-shaped rock beyond a sugar-sand beach. Once inaccessible, there is now a staircase leading to the sea. Swimming isn't advised due to strong currents, but sitting in awe on the beach is enough. Next in line is Thousand Islands (Pulau Seribu) Viewpoint. A 10-minute descent down a steep staircase takes you to the first viewpoint, enclosed in a fence for safety. There's a second viewpoint, finally the legendary Rumah Pohon (Tree House) that's available for rent. A parking and beach entry fee is charged at all three, but from the parking lot at Diamond Beach you can walk to Atuh and the viewpoint. The final stop on the east coast is inland Teletubbies, a group of big,

1

round hills that are particularly otherworldly looking in the rainy season when they're green.

The south coast

Not to be overlooked, the south coast has more wonders to behold. Manta Point is a prime diving and snorkelling spot for a year-round chance to swim among these giant, gentle creatures and a recorded 250 fish species. If you're not up for getting wet, you can sometimes spot them from Kelingking Beach, where a rock bearing a close resemblance to a T-Rex breaches the sea and Broken Beach with its wrap-around arch eroded over eons. From Broken Beach you can walk to Angel's Billabong for a dip in a calm tide pool. Do stick close to the shore when swimming or snorkelling and be aware that there are strong currents further out.

Crystal Bay

A postcard-perfect nook of white-sand beach and outstandingly clear water, Crystal Bay is a popular dive and snorkel site but it's crowded with day-trippers in the mornings. Go in the afternoon for a better chance of enjoying it peacefully, but check locally for currents at certain tide states. It's a gorgeous spot simply to admire the view in the shade beneath palms. Less popular due to the difficulty of access is nearby Gamat Bay, so you might find more peace there if you don't mind the trek.

ARRIVAL AND DEPARTURE — NUSA PENIDA

From Nusa Lembongan Public slow boats run from Jungutbatu and the Yellow Bridge between Nusa Lembongan and Nusa Ceningan to Toyapakeh beginning at 6am, ending around 5pm (30min) and have dubious safety standards. Fast boats go roughly hourly (dependent on passenger numbers) from the Yellow Bridge (20 min). For all trips, bear in mind that swells and currents in the channel can disrupt sailing.

From Bali From Sanur there are many daily scheduled boats (though again heavy seas can mean cancellations). The best service is Maruti Express (http://marutigroupfastboat.com), leaving up to four times a day (30min) to Toyapakeh. Gili Transfers (http://gilitransfers.com) are also fairly reliable, sailing three times daily (35min) to Sampalan. Perama (http://peramatour.com) runs to Penida three times daily. Other companies operate boats to Toyapakeh and Buyuk harbour which is very close to Sampalan. From Padang Bai to Toyapakeh there's one daily ferry at 3pm (1hr 30min) and occasional fast boats according to demand (30min).

GETTING AROUND

By bemo A sketchy public *bemo* service operates between Toyapakeh and Sampalan, via Ped, between about 6am and 9pm.

By motorbike The best way to get around is by motorbike. Motorbike drivers/guides wait at Toyapakeh harbour to meet arrivals from Lembongan, and will offer to guide. You can also rent your own bike here, but it's not recommended for inexperienced drivers. The island is a maze of broken, remote lanes and signposts are few. That said, getting lost may be half the fun. Nova Nusa Penida Tour & Travel in Toyapakeh (https://novanusapenida.com) rents reliable motorbikes with or without driver, new model car and driver/guides and offers tours.

ACCOMMODATION AND EATING — SEE MAP PAGE 102

Accommodations can be found on all shores except the rugged south, most of which are simple fan-cooled affairs. Eating options are largely limited to restaurants in the hotels and simple *warung*. Be warned: the further south you go, the more limited your options for food – it's packet snacks with an occasional vendor in the deep south.

The Chill Penida Jl. Batumulapan, Batununggul; http://thechillpenida.com. This lovely restaurant/bar is open for breakfast, lunch and dinner and specialises in Indonesian dishes based on locally-sourced ingredients. The excellent cocktails are also worth a try. It opens directly to the beach and has lovely ocean views. $$

Namaste Bungalows Jl. Raya Sakti, Sakti; http://namaste-bungalows.com. A small French-owned retreat with a pool, en route to Crystal Bay. Rough luxe is the style in the ten bungalows, with artfully repurposed furniture, fine bed linen and minimalist bathrooms – "deluxe" come with a/c. Prices drop in the low season. $

Ring Sameton Resort Hotel Jl. Ped, Ped; http://ringsameton-nusapenida.com. Well-kept business-style hotel with large rooms that make up in space and mod cons for what they lack in character; all have a/c and hot water. The restaurant serves a good seafood curry. $$

Singabu Bungalows Jl. Ped, Buyuk; 0858 5811 6148.

Clean comfortable rooms with a/c, terraces, outdoor bathrooms and pool and garden views. Walking distance from Sampalan Harbour. Scooter rental possible. The on-site *Coco Leaf* restaurant serves a variety of international fare and there's also a bar. $̲

Tarzan Marriott on Penida Jl. Ped, Buyuk; 0853 3745 0331. Apparently unconcerned with 'borrowing' an international hotel chain name, owner Tarzan and family run a very nice a/c place with exceptional customer service. Tucked away from traffic noise but near the north beach with pool and bar/restaurant that serves Asian, pizza and steaks. Breakfast included. $̲

Ubud and central Bali

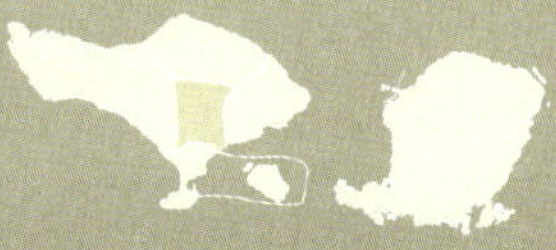

GUNUNG KAWI SEBATU TEMPLE

Ubud and central Bali

2 Inland Ubud and its surrounding area form Bali's cultural heartland, home to a huge number of temples, museums and art galleries, where Balinese dance shows are staged nightly, a wealth of craft studios provide absorbing shopping, and traditional ceremonies and rituals are observed daily. The town centre is increasingly congested but once you get away from the main thoroughfares, Ubud's lovely location is apparent, set amid lush, terraced rice paddies, and there's plenty of scope for hikes and bicycle rides. To get a real sense of traditional Bali, visit the nearby Penestanan and Peliatan, for example, or Pejeng, which still houses relics from the Bronze Age.

Ubud lies within the boundaries of **Gianyar regency**, formerly an ancient kingdom. Gianyar itself (see page 144), 10km east of Ubud, lies on the main route into east Bali. Roads around Ubud tend to run north–south down river valleys, making it difficult in places to travel east–west, and subsequently traffic jams and pollution affect Ubud's centre.

Ubud and around

Ever since the German artist Walter Spies arrived here in 1927, **UBUD** has been a magnet for any tourist with the slightest curiosity about Balinese arts and traditions. It is now a fully fledged tourist destination, visited by nearly every holidaymaker on the island, even if only as part of a day-trip.

Although it's fashionable to characterize Ubud as the "real" Bali, especially in contrast with Kuta, it bears little resemblance to a typical Balinese town. The core village has expanded to take in several neighbouring hamlets and there are now dozens of organic cafés, riverside bungalows and craft shops, spas and alternative treatment centres, chic expat homes and boutique hotels overlooking panoramic scenery. There's even a Starbucks.

That said, traditional practices are still fundamental to daily life and the atmosphere is an appealing blend of ethnic integrity and tourist-friendly comforts. The local people really do still paint, carve, dance and make music, and hardly a day goes by without some kind of religious festival. Appropriately, Ubud is a recognized centre of **spiritual tourism**, a place where visitors can get stuck into yoga and meditation, and visit local healers.

Shopping is a major pastime too, with Balinese carvers and painters selling their wares alongside expat fashion designers and artists. Ubud's **restaurants** and **accommodation** set the town apart as well: imaginative menus are the norm here, and hotels and homestays tend to be small and charming. The surrounding region, meanwhile, gives ample opportunity for exploration and more and more five-star resorts are springing up.

Sadly the town's new prosperity has led to one of Bali's worst traffic problems and Ubud is in desperate need of a pedestrianization programme and bypass before clouds of exhaust fumes suffocate the town's appeal and drive away the yogis and healers to somewhere less polluted.

Brief history

Ubud's emphasis on the arts really evolved at the beginning of the twentieth century; before then its energy had been concentrated on fighting other Balinese kingdoms and then the Dutch. In 1900 the Ubud court was obliged to join its neighbour, the Gianyar royal family, in asking for the protection of the Netherlands Indies government against

MAKING BATIK

Highlights

❶ **A walk through the rice paddies** Enjoy classic vistas of emerald terraces and coconut groves, framed by distant volcanoes, on this walk through the countryside surrounding Ubud. See page 114

❷ **Neka Art Museum** This museum houses the finest collection of Balinese paintings on the island. See page 114

❸ **Cultural classes** Return home with a new skill in batik painting, silversmithing, Balinese cookery or innumerable other activities. See page 125

❹ **Traditional dance performances** Gods and demons flirt and fight by torchlight, to the sounds of the gamelan, at these evocative shows in and around Ubud. See page 129

❺ **Mind, Body and Spirit** Ubud is one of Asia's leading yoga centres and you can also visit a local healer, have a massage or learn to meditate. See page 131

❻ **Bali Bird Park** This vast and beautifully landscaped aviary has elusive Bali starlings in residence. See page 136

❼ **Gunung Kawi** Descend 315 steps to reach these impressive eleventh-century rock-cut "tombs" in the valley of the sacred Pakrisan River. See page 141

HIGHLIGHTS ARE MARKED ON THE MAP ON PAGE 110

UBUD & CENTRAL BALI
HIGHLIGHTS
1 A walk through the rice paddies
2 Neka Art Museum
3 Cultural classes
4 Traditional dance performances
5 Mind, Body and Spirit
6 Bali Bird Park
7 Gunung Kawi
Pelaga
Batur
Penelokan, Gunang Batur
Belong
Taro
Temen
Punggang
Bonjaka
Pura Gunung Kawi Sebatu
Pujung Kaja
Lebah
Pakrisan
Sebatu
Pujung Kelod
Manukaya
Tirta Empul
Tiyingan
Besangambu
Bayao
Kedisan
Gunung Kawi
Tampaksiring
Lebe
Petang
Ayung
Payangan
Wos
Ceking
Manuaba
Yeh Tengah
Keliki
Tegalalang
Bangli
Tanggayuda
Jempeng
Sanding
White Heron Sanctuary
Sangeh Monkey Forest
Sangeh
Kedewatan
Petulu
Sanggingan
Tarukan
Petanu
Pakrisan
Real Bali Swing
Campuhan
Sayan
Galiang
Ubud
Pura Pusering Jagat & Pura Kebo Edan
Pejeng
Penestanan
Abiansemal
Peliatan
Pura Penataran Sasih
Nyuhkuning
Singakerta
Bedulu
Museum Arkeologi Gedung Arca
Aseman
Njana Tilem Museum
Dukuh Kedongan
Pengosekan
Teges
Goa Gajah
Yeh Pulu
N
Gianyar
Setia Darma House of Masks and Puppets
Lodtunduh
Mas
Mambal
Silakarang
Bona
Mawang
Sakah
Blahbatuh
The Green School
Sibang Kaja
Sibang Gede
Negari
Batuan
Bali Bird and Reptile Parks
Singapadu
Sukawati
Celuk
Tebune
Palak
Pinda
Saba
Barong Statue
Pura Puseh
Putrawan Museum of Art
Petanu Cape
Pantai Saba
Batubulan
Penatih
Batuyang
Tabanan & Gilimanuk
Pabean
0
5
kilometres
DENPASAR
Batubulan Bemo Terminal
Tohpati
Kuta & Kerobokan
Sanur

other land-hungry rajas. As a Dutch protectorate with no more wars to fight, the ruling Sukawati family and the Ubud villagers were free to follow creative and musical pursuits. **Cokorda Gede Agung Sukawati** (1910–78) cultivated the arts, and actively encouraged foreign artists to live in his district. The most significant of these was the artist and musician **Walter Spies**, who established himself in Campuhan in 1927. Over the next decade or so, Spies introduced fresh ideas to Ubud's already vibrant **artistic community**. A crowd of other Western intellectuals followed in his wake, including the Dutch artist Rudolf Bonnet and the Canadian musician Colin McPhee, who between them injected a new vigour into the region's arts and crafts, which have thrived ever since.

Central Ubud

Covering the area between Jalan Raya Ubud in the north and the Monkey Forest in the south, and between the Campuhan bridge in the west and the General Post Office in the east, **Central Ubud**'s chief draws are its restaurants and shops. However, it does hold a few notable sights, including Ubud's oldest art museum, **Puri Lukisan**, and the **Threads of Life** textile gallery.

Museum Puri Lukisan

Jl Raya Ubud • Charge, children under 15 accompanied by an adult free • https://www.purilukisanmuseum.com • Kura Kura minibuses (http://kura2bus.com) stop by the museum with routes to Kuta and central Ubud

The **Museum Puri Lukisan** is best visited as an adjunct to the far superior Neka Art Museum, just over 2km west in Sanggingan. Set in well-maintained gardens, Puri Lukisan ("Palace of Paintings") was founded in 1956 by the Ubud *punggawa* (local administrator) Cokorda Gede Agung Sukawati, the member of the Ubud royal family who focused his energies on developing the arts, and the Dutch artist Rudolf Bonnet.

The **North Pavilion**, Pitamaha Gallery, located at the top of the garden, is largely given over to prewar Balinese paintings, mostly black-and-white **Batuan-style** and early **Ubud-style** (see page 118) pictures depicting local scenes. There's also a good selection of distinctive drawings by I Gusti Nyoman Lempad (see page 113). Several fine **woodcarvings** from the 1930s to the 1950s are also here, including the surreal earth-goddess *Dewi Pertiwi* by Ida Bagus Nyana (see page 135), the sinuous *Dewi Sri* by I Ketut Djedeng and I Cokot's much-emulated *Garuda Eating Snake*.

In the **West Pavilion**, to the left on the way up the garden, the Ida Bagus Made (1915–99) Gallery showcases the artist's work alongside other postwar Balinese paintings, including those in the naive expressionist **Young Artists** style that originated in nearby Penestanan in the 1960s. Also in this pavilion, you'll find paintings in the **Ubud style**, including *Balinese Market* by Anak Agung Gede Sobrat, as well as works in the so-called **modern traditional** style, such as I Made Sukada's *Battle between Boma and Krishna*.

In the **East Pavilion**, to the right on the way up the garden, the Wayang Gallery houses a collection of **wayang-style** paintings as well as temporary exhibitions.

There's a good cafe for local and Western food in the **South Pavilion**, which is used for temporary exhibitions and a bookshop.

Pura Taman Saraswati

Jl Raya Ubud • Free

FESTIVALS IN UBUD

Ubud hosts an annual literary **festival**, the Ubud Writers and Readers Festival (http://ubudwritersfestival.com), every October, the Bali Spirit Festival of world music, dance and yoga every spring (http://balispiritfestival.com) and the Ubud Food Festival (http://ubudfoodfestival.com) in April/May.

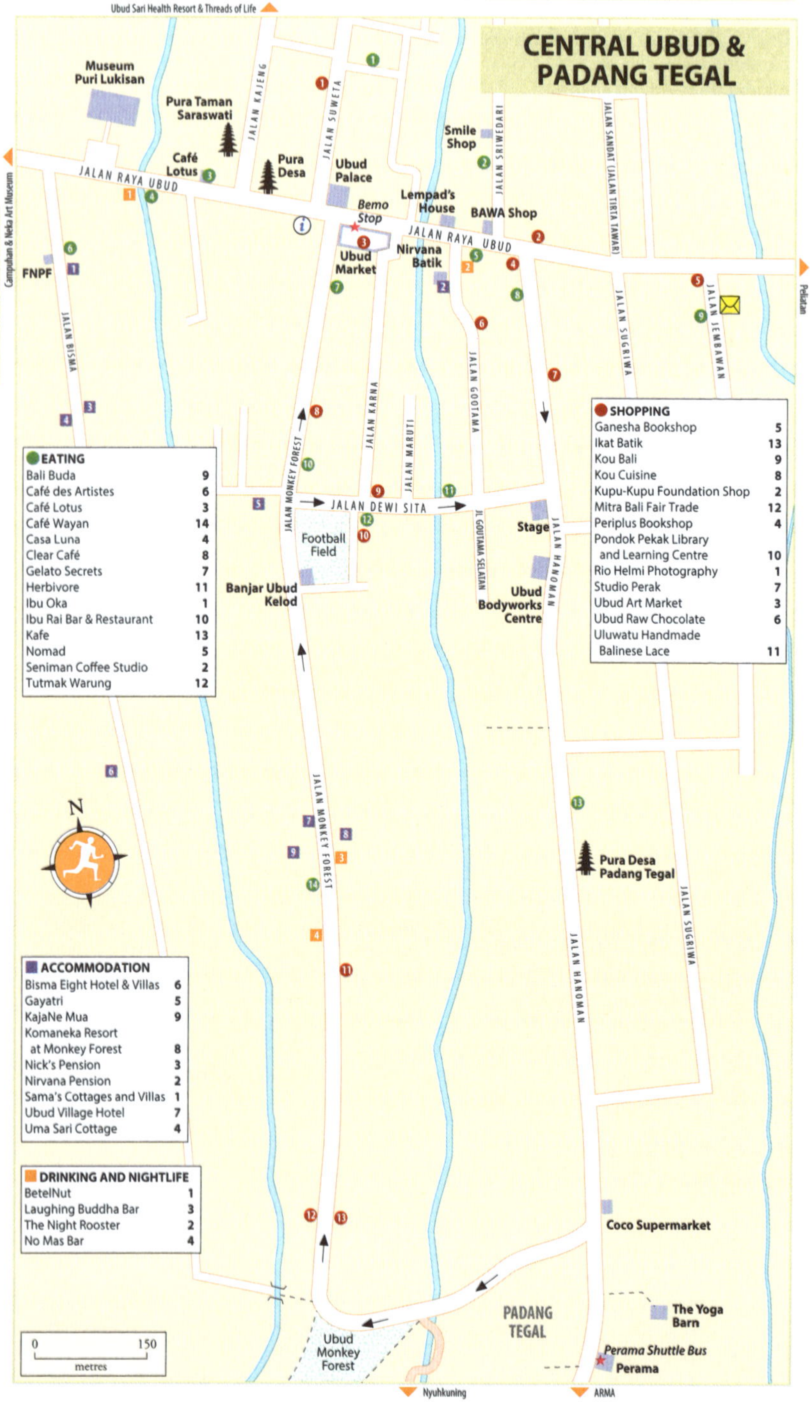
CENTRAL UBUD & PADANG TEGAL
Ubud Sari Health Resort & Threads of Life
Campuhan & Neka Art Museum
Peliatan
Nyuhkuning
ARMA
Museum Puri Lukisan
Pura Taman Saraswati
Café Lotus
Pura Desa
Ubud Palace
Smile Shop
Lempad's House
BAWA Shop
Bemo Stop
Ubud Market
Nirvana Batik
FNPF
Football Field
Banjar Ubud Kelod
Stage
Ubud Bodyworks Centre
Pura Desa Padang Tegal
Coco Supermarket
PADANG TEGAL
The Yoga Barn
Perama Shuttle Bus
Perama
Ubud Monkey Forest
JALAN RAYA UBUD
JALAN KAJENG
JALAN SUWETA
JALAN SRIWEDARI
JALAN SANDAT (JALAN TIRTA TAWAR)
JALAN SUGRIWA
JALAN JEMBAWAN
JALAN BISMA
JALAN MONKEY FOREST
JALAN KARNA
JALAN MARUTI
JALAN GOOTAMA
JL GOUTAMA SELATAN
JALAN DEWI SITA
JALAN HANOMAN
N
0 150 metres
EATING
Bali Buda 9
Café des Artistes 6
Café Lotus 3
Café Wayan 14
Casa Luna 4
Clear Café 8
Gelato Secrets 7
Herbivore 11
Ibu Oka 1
Ibu Rai Bar & Restaurant 10
Kafe 13
Nomad 5
Seniman Coffee Studio 2
Tutmak Warung 12
SHOPPING
Ganesha Bookshop 5
Ikat Batik 13
Kou Bali 9
Kou Cuisine 8
Kupu-Kupu Foundation Shop 2
Mitra Bali Fair Trade 12
Periplus Bookshop 4
Pondok Pekak Library and Learning Centre 10
Rio Helmi Photography 1
Studio Perak 7
Ubud Art Market 3
Ubud Raw Chocolate 6
Uluwatu Handmade Balinese Lace 11
ACCOMMODATION
Bisma Eight Hotel & Villas 6
Gayatri 5
KajaNe Mua 9
Komaneka Resort at Monkey Forest 8
Nick's Pension 3
Nirvana Pension 2
Sama's Cottages and Villas 1
Ubud Village Hotel 7
Uma Sari Cottage 4
DRINKING AND NIGHTLIFE
BetelNut 1
Laughing Buddha Bar 3
The Night Rooster 2
No Mas Bar 4

2

LEMPAD

Many of Ubud's most important buildings – among them Puri Lukisan, Pura Taman Saraswati and Ubud Palace – are associated with the venerable sculptor, architect and artist **I Gusti Nyoman Lempad** (c.1862–1978). Lempad came to Ubud with his family at the age of 13, where he found favour in the Sukawati court, where he worked for most of his life. A versatile **artist** who designed temples, carved stone reliefs, built cremation towers and produced ink drawings, Lempad was an influential figure and an important member of the Pita Maha arts association, which he cofounded with his friends Cokorda Gede Agung Sukawati and Rudolf Bonnet. A **traditionalist** in certain matters, Lempad would only work on propitious days and is said to have waited for an auspicious day on which to die; by that time he was thought to be approximately 116 years old. The best places to see his drawings are the Neka Art Museum and Museum Puri Lukisan.

For more than a century, Lempad lived on Jalan Dewisita, diagonally opposite the market, in a **house** that still belongs to his family, and which is open to the public as a **showroom** for artists working under the "Puri Lempad" by-line (free).

Commissioned in the 1950s by Cokorda Gede Agung Sukawati, **Pura Taman Saraswati** is the work of the prolific royal architect and stonecarver I Gusti Nyoman Lempad, who set the temple complex within a delightful lotus-pond garden. It's dedicated to Saraswati, the goddess of learning, science and literature.

Access to the temple is via a lane between *Café Lotus* and *Starbucks*: walk between the lotus ponds to the red-brick *kori agung* (temple entrance). The straight route into the temple courtyard is blocked by an unusual **aling-aling** (the wall device built into nearly every temple to disorient evil spirits), which is in fact the back of a rotund statue of a *raksasa* (demon guardian). Inside the **courtyard** the main lotus-throne **shrine** is covered with a riot of *paras* (volcanic tuff) carvings, with the requisite cosmic turtle and *naga* (a snake/dragon deity) forming the base, while the tower is a swirling mass of curlicues and floral motifs.

Only visitors in Balinese dress are allowed inside; there's a stall close by which rents out traditional clothing.

Threads of Life Gallery

Jl Kajeng No. 24 • Free • http://threadsoflife.com

The small **Threads of Life** is devoted to exquisite hand-woven textiles from across Indonesia, including Bali, Sumba, Timor, Java and Sulawesi. Though they were all produced using natural dyes and ancient methods, the textiles are modern works, commissioned by the Threads of Life foundation in an attempt to keep Indonesia's historic textile art alive. This is a complex and highly skilled art, and severely endangered, not least because a single weaving can take two years to complete. The gallery displays superb weavings alongside exhibits on natural dyes, spinning and weaving techniques. Beautiful, if pricey, textiles are for sale and there are regular classes and **workshops** on traditional textile appreciation (see page 125), weaving and dyeing. They also have two homestays which support their foundation work (http://rumahroda.com and http://umajati.com).

Campuhan and Sanggingan

Sited at the confluence of the rivers Wos Barat and Wos Timor, **CAMPUHAN** (pronounced *cham-poo-han*) extends west from Ubud as far as the *Hotel Tjampuhan*, and is the home of several of Bali's most charismatic expatriate painters, including the late **Antonio Blanco**, whose house and gallery have been turned into a museum and the late **Walter Spies**, whose villa is inside the *Hotel Tjampuhan* compound.

2

RICE PADDY WALKS

Running east of, and almost parallel to the Campuhan Ridge Walk (see page 116) are two popular rice paddy walks that can be combined into one on an almost circular trek. For the Kajeng walk, from Jalan Raya Ubud go north on Jalan Kajeng west of the palace, a little street paved with graffiti-covered stones placed by villagers who helped "seal" this track. Passing through Kajeng village the path is clearly defined but later it disintegrates. Bearing off to the left you'll pass *Arjuna Bungalows* and rice paddies. Then follow the signs to *Sweet Orange Warung*, an excellent rest stop. If you've had enough for one day you can retrace your steps back through Kajeng village to Jalan Raya Ubud.

For more adventure, continue crossing the ricefields where at times the track becomes totally indistinct, so try to follow the narrow paths along the top of the ricefield dykes, sticking roughly to a northerly direction and keeping the river in view on your left. Don't forget to look back at the amazing Gunung Agung view (cloud cover permitting). With the mountain in the background and the conical-hatted farmers working in the glittering ricefields, these views are perfect real-life versions of the Walter Spies-style paintings you see in Ubud's museums and galleries. Eventually you will see a bridge that crosses the river to the left. Once you're on that path you'll be on your way back to Jalan Raya Ubud on the **Jalan Subak Sok Wayah walk**.

The complete circuit takes 2–3 hours, depending on your speed, and requires scrambling down some rough-cut muddy steps to reach the path, making good walking shoes essential. Sunscreen, mosquito repellent, a hat and water might also come in handy. Early mornings or late afternoons are recommended.

Jalan Subak Sok Wayah is not a proper street but is a stone-covered path through the ricefields to several eateries and a yoga studio; it begins on the west side of Pura Dalem on Jalan Raya Ubud. The entrance to this levee track is a steep, badly paved slope that ends at *Abangan Bungalows*. Pass the car park and continue north following signs to *Café Pomegranate* or *Ubud Yoga House*, about 15–20 minutes away. The path passes art galleries and souvenir stalls, then through verdant paddies where you can see farmers at work and ducks paddling in flooded fields eating insects row after row like vacuum cleaners. Continue north with the river on your right until you reach the bridge, then turn right and walk south back to Ubud if you're game for more adventure. Alternatively, retrace your steps at any point for an easier walk back home.

North up the hill, Campuhan turns into **SANGGINGAN** (though few people bother to distinguish it from its neighbour), and it's here that you'll find Bali's best art collection, the **Neka Art Museum**.

Blanco Renaissance Museum

Just off Jl Raya Campuhan, next to the Penestanan turn-off • Charge (includes drink) • Phone ahead for free transport

The former home of the flamboyant Catalan artist **Antonio Blanco** – complete with gilded pillars and sweeping Spanish balustrades – is open to the public as the enjoyably camp **Blanco Renaissance Museum**. Dubbed "the Bali Dalí", Blanco (1911–99) specialized in **erotic paintings** and drawings, in particular portraits of Balinese women in varying states of abandon. Blanco fell for a local girl, Ni Ronji, soon after arriving in Ubud in 1952, singling her out as his top model and later marrying her. There are sweeping views from the roof, which has four gilded statues.

Blanco's collection also includes multimedia pieces, plus lots of idiosyncratic picture frames created from unorthodox materials. The museum **garden** contains a small aviary and there's a restaurant where you can enjoy your complimentary drink.

Neka Art Museum

Jl Raya Campuhan-Sanggingan, about 2.5km northwest of central Ubud • Charge • http://nekaartmuseum.com • Take any westbound *bemo* from the market in Ubud

Containing the island's most comprehensive collection of paintings from across Bali's various artistic styles (see page 118), the **Neka Art Museum** is housed in a series of pavilions alongside the main Campuhan/Sanggingan road. English-language labels are posted beside the paintings, with Balinese, expatriate and visiting artists all represented. The museum shop sells a couple of recommended **books** about the collection, notably *Neka Art Museum In Modern Balinese History: Art and the Passage of Time by* Garrett Kam, which is essentially a catalogue of the highlights of the collection, and *Perceptions of Paradise: Images of Bali in the Arts* by Garrett Kam.

Real Bali Swing

Jl Dewi Saraswati No.7, about a 25-minute drive from central Ubud • Charge; package including transfers available • https://realbaliswing.com

Art imitates life in Bali thanks to the influx of influencers and snap-happy vacationers leading locals to come up with ever-more inventive photo opportunities to tempt in the masses. The now-ubiquitous **Real Bali Swing** is undoubtedly one of the most popular, affording the opportunity to soar over the rainforest and rice terraces on a gigantic swing while professional photographers work their magic. Get there early or book ahead as the queues can be long. Several similar attractions have now sprung up around Ubud, most notably **Alas Harum** (https://alasharum.com), an entire adventure park developed with photo opportunities in mind.

First Pavilion: Balinese Painting Hall

The first pavilion surveys the three major schools of **Balinese painting** from the seventeenth century to the present day. Some of the earliest works are "puppet style" paintings that depict narrative scenes from Balinese and Javanese literature. Fine examples of **Kamasan style** include works from contemporary artists such as Ida Bagus Rai in *Rajapala Steals Sulasih's Clothes* and *The Pandawa Brothers in Disguise*, in which classical elements are fused with a more modern sensuality. These are followed by art representing the **Ubud style**, including *The Bumblebee Dance* by **Anak Agung Gede Sobrat**. Finally come the dark and densely packed **Batuan-style** canvases, including the dramatic *Busy Bali* by **I Wayan Bendi**, which delineates the effect of tourism on the island, and **I Made Budi**'s 1987 work, *President Suharto and his Wife Visit Bali.*

WALTER SPIES IN CAMPUHAN

The son of a German diplomat, **Walter Spies** (1895–1942) left Europe for Java in 1923, and relocated to Bali in 1927. He set up home in Campuhan and devoted himself to the study and practice of Balinese art and music. He sponsored two local gamelan orchestras and was the first Westerner to attempt to record **Balinese music**. Together with the Canadian composer Colin McPhee, he set about transposing gamelan music for Western instruments, and with another associate, Katherine Mershon, encouraged Bedulu dancer I Wayan Limbak to create the enduringly popular dance-drama known as the **Kecak** (Monkey Dance).

Spies was an avid collector of Balinese **art**, and became one of the founding members of the Pita Maha arts association in 1936. He is said to have inspired, if not taught, a number of talented young Ubud artists, among them the painter Anak Agung Gede Sobrat, and the woodcarver I Tegelan. Characteristic of Spies's own Balinese works are dense landscapes of waterlogged paddies, peopled with conical-hatted farmers – a distinctive style that is still much imitated. There's currently only one Walter Spies painting on show in Bali; it's at the Agung Rai Museum of Art in Pengosekan (see page 122).

In 1937 Spies retired to Iseh village in the east, turning his Campuhan home into a **guesthouse**, the first of its kind in the Ubud area. He died in 1942, drowning when the ship deporting him as a German national in World War II was bombed in the Indian Ocean. The guesthouse became *Hotel Tjampuhan*.

2

THE CAMPUHAN RIDGE WALK

Campuhan means "the place where two rivers meet" and the confluence of the Wos Barat and the Wos Timor is marked by **Pura Gunung Lebah** (also known as Pura Campuhan). The track that extends north along the grassy spine behind Pura Gunung Lebah forms part of a pleasant two-hour circular **walk** around the outskirts of Campuhan and Sanggingan. Alternatively, if you continue the complete length of the ridge, you'll eventually reach **Keliki** (7km) and **Taro** (13km) before joining the Sayan road to **Kintamani** (32km). All routes are feasible on a **mountain bike**, but be prepared for some significant undulations and a few steps.

If you're starting **from central Ubud**, walk (or take a *bemo*) west from Ubud market almost as far as the Campuhan bridge, turning north off the main road about 100m before the bridge, into the entrance of the *Warwick Ibah* hotel, where an immediate left fork takes you down some steps to Pura Gunung Lebah. The track heads right around the temple walls and climbs up onto the ridge, where it curves and slopes for a stretch before levelling out along the flattened **ridgetop** between the two river valleys. The perspective from this section is breathtaking: to the left lie the steep banks of the Wos Barat valley; to the right, the eastern panorama across the Wos Timor valley is of savanna, coconut groves, the rocky river gorge and Gunung Agung in the distance. You'll walk through a seemingly endless carpet of **alang-alang grass** swaying in the breeze – a valuable resource used for thatching houses and shrines.

About twenty minutes from Pura Gunung Lebah, the track passes through the first ridgetop settlement, site of the *Klub Kokos* hotel and, beyond, about 1500m of sculpted ricefields before reaching **Bangkiang Sidem** hamlet. Just beyond the village temple, you arrive at a larger sealed road; turn left on the road for the round trip back to Campuhan road, or continue straight on for Keliki.

Once you've turned left, the road cuts a swathe through ricefields, drops down steeply towards the Wos Barat and then climbs up through **Payogan** and **Lungsiakan** before reaching **Jalan Raya Sanggingan**. From here you can either flag down any *bemo* heading east for the ten-minute ride into Ubud, or continue walking for twenty minutes east down to the **Neka Art Museum**, or twenty minutes west to Kedewatan and the main Kintamani road.

Second Pavilion: Arie Smit Pavilion

The top floor of the second pavilion is devoted to the hugely influential Dutch expatriate artist **Arie Smit**. His work is instantly recognizable by the bold, expressionist tone; many of the paintings, including *A Tropical Garden By the Sea*, have a breathtakingly beautiful Cézanne-like quality.

The ground-floor hall is given over to **contemporary Balinese art**, which includes expressionist, figurative and abstract works – a clear indication of the vibrancy of modern art on the island. The styles range widely from the huge abstract canvases of I Made Sumadiyasa to the unsettling wooden sculptures of I Made Supena.

Third Pavilion: Photography Archive Center

The third pavilion houses an archive of black-and-white **photographs** from Bali in the 1930s and 1940s, taken by the American **Robert Koke**. He and his wife Louise founded the first hotel in Kuta in 1936. His photographic record includes village scenes, temple festivals and cremations, but its highlights are the pictures of the dance performances and the portraits of the Kebyar dancer Mario and of the Kecak choreographer I Wayan Limbak.

Fourth Pavilion: Lempad Pavilion

The late **I Gusti Nyoman Lempad** (see page 113) is the subject of the fourth pavilion, which holds the largest collection of his pictures in Bali. Among his best-known works is a series on **Men and Pan Brayut**, the well-known folk story about a poor couple and their eighteen children (see page 155).

Fifth Pavilion: Contemporary Indonesian Art Hall

The fifth pavilion focuses on works by formally trained Indonesian artists, whose style is often labelled "Academic". Outstanding examples include large oils by Javanese-born **Anton Hwang** (Anton Kustia Widjaja), who moved to Ubud in 1969, and **Abdul Aziz**'s much-reproduced diptych entitled *Mutual Attraction*.

Sixth Pavilion: East–West Art Annex

The upstairs galleries feature the paintings of **foreign artists in Bali**, including the Dutch painter **Rudolf Bonnet**'s sensual portraits: *Temptation of Arjuna* is particularly impressive. The bright Gauguin-esque oils of Swiss-born **Theo Meier** draw on the vivid light and sultry ambience of Bali, in contrast to the Dutch **Willem Gerard Hofker**'s minutely observed crayon studies of temples, such as *Temple at Campuhan, Ubud*. Also on show are some erotically charged portraits by the Catalan-born **Antonio Blanco**, whose studio-gallery is nearby (see page 114); the Australian **Donald Friend**'s charmingly fanciful Chagall-esque evocations of his Sanur home, including *Batujimbar Village*; and the Dutch **Han**. Not all the impressions of Bali come from outside Asia: the dynamic *Gabor-Pendet Dance* is by **J. Elizalde Navarro** from the Philippines, while the striking works *Barong and Rangda Dance* and *Balinese Fishing Boats* are by the Javanese expressionist **Affandi**.

Penestanan

West of Campuhan is the still-traditional **PENESTANAN** hamlet, which became known in the 1960s for its so-called **Young Artists** (see page 118), who forged a naive style of painting that's since been named after them. Some are still painting, but Penestanan's current niche is **bead-making**, and the village has several shops selling intricately decorated items.

Penestanan is accessible from the side road that turns off beside the Blanco Museum, but the most atmospheric approach is via the steep flight of steps a few hundred metres further north along Jalan Raya Campuhan. The steps climb the hillside to a narrow westbound track, which passes several arterial north–south paths leading to panoramic **views** (many of which have been appropriated by new villas), then drops down through ricefields into the next valley, across a river and through a small wooded area, before coming to a crossroads with Penestanan's main street. Go straight across (west) if you're heading for Sayan (600m away), right for *Taman Rahasia* hotel after 200m, or left for the circular walk back through the village to the Blanco Museum in Campuhan (1.5km). There are several places to eat en route.

Petulu's white heron sanctuary

1.5km off Jl Andong • Charge • Follow Jalan Andong north from the T-junction at the eastern edge of Ubud for about 1.5km, then take the left-hand (signed) fork for a further 1.5km; lots of public *bemos* ply Jalan Andong, but you'll have to walk the section from the fork

Every evening at around 6pm, hundreds (sometimes thousands) of herons fly in from far and wide to roost in **PETULU**, immediately northeast of Ubud – quite a spectacle. Birdwatchers might be able to distinguish the four species of wading birds that frequent the heronry – the **Javan pond heron**, the **plumed egret**, the **little egret** and the **cattle egret** – but for everyone else the sheer volume of birds is impressive enough. From the upper floor of the community centre you'll get a good perspective over the scene and local guides are at hand to help you spot the different birds (and sell you beer).

It isn't clear why the birds have chosen to make their home in Petulu, though locally it's claimed that the birds are **reincarnations** of the tens of thousands of men and women who died in Bali's civil war (1965–66). Many of the victims were buried close by, and the birds are said to have started coming here only after an elaborate ceremony was held in the village in memory of the dead.

2

2

BALINESE PAINTING

Art historians group **Balinese painting** into six broad **schools**: *wayang* (also known as classical or Kamasan), Ubud, Pengosekan, Batuan, Young Artists and Modern or Academic.

WAYANG OR KAMASAN STYLE

The earliest Balinese painters drew their inspiration from the *wayang kulit* shadow plays, using two-dimensional figures to depict episodes from the same religious and historical epics that were played out on the stage. Variously known as the **wayang style**, the **classical style** or the **Kamasan style** (after the east Bali village where the most famous *wayang*-style artists came from), this is the most traditional genre of Balinese art, and the one that's been the least influenced by Western techniques and subjects. The oldest surviving examples are the eighteenth-century temple banners, calendars and astrological charts housed in the **Nyoman Gunarsa Museum** near Semarapura (see page 156). To see Kamasan art in situ visit the old palace in Semarapura, where the ceilings of the **Kerta Gosa** and **Bale Kambung** pavilions retain their *wayang*-style painted ceilings; they were done by artists from Kamasan in the early nineteenth century but have been retouched several times.

All *wayang*-style pictures are packed full of people painted in **three-quarter profile**, with caricature-like features and puppet-like poses. There is no perspective, and stylized symbols indicate the location; pictures are often divided into scenes by borders of mountains, flames or walls. Traditional *wayang* artists limit their palette to red, blue, yellow, black and white.

As with the *wayang* puppets, the **characters** in the paintings are instantly recognizable by their facial features and hairstyles and by their clothes, stance and size. Convention requires, for example, that "refined" characters (heroes, heroines and others of noble birth) look slightly supercilious, and that their bodies be svelte and elegant. "Coarse" characters, on the other hand, such as clowns, servants and demonic creatures, have bulbous eyes, prominent teeth and chunky bodies.

The *wayang* style is still popular with modern artists and continues to be centred on **Kamasan**, which has many studios open to the public.

UBUD STYLE

By the 1930s, Balinese painters were starting to experiment with more **naturalistic techniques**, including perspective and the use of light and shadow, and to reproduce what they saw at the market, at the temple and in the ricefields. Ubud was at the heart of this experimentation so the style has been dubbed **Ubud style**. Expatriate artists **Walter Spies** and **Rudolf Bonnet**, both resident in the Ubud area in the 1930s, are said to have had a big influence; they also helped set up the **Pita Maha arts foundation**, whose mission was to promote innovation and individual expression.

Though the Ubud style is more naturalistic than *wayang* art, the pictures are still unrealistically crammed with busyness and **activity**, every corner filled with detail. Every palm leaf and blade of grass is painstakingly delineated, every sarong pattern described, but people are rarely given much individuality, their faces usually set in a rather stylized expression.

Most of the best-known Ubud-style artists are represented in the major Ubud art museums, among them the highly rated **Anak Agung Gede Sobrat**.

PENGOSEKAN STYLE

During the 1960s, a group of young painters working in the Ubud style and living in the Pengosekan on the outskirts of Ubud came up with a new approach, subsequently known as

Ubud Monkey Forest

Jl Monkey Forest; the entrance is a 15min walk south of Ubud's central market • Charge • http://monkeyforestubud.com

Ubud's best-known tourist attraction is the **Monkey Forest**, which occupies the land between the southern end of Jalan Monkey Forest and the northern edge of Nyuhkuning.

the **Pengosekan style**. From the Ubud-style pictures, the Pengosekan school isolated just a few components, specifically the **birds**, **butterflies**, **insects** and **flowering plants** and magnified them to fill a whole canvas. The best Pengosekan paintings look delicate and lifelike, generally depicted in soothing pastels, and reminiscent of classical Japanese flower and bird pictures.

BATUAN STYLE

In contrast to the slightly romanticized visions of events being painted by the Ubud-style artists in the 1930s, a group of painters in nearby Batuan were taking a more quizzical approach. Like the *wayang* artists, **Batuan-style** painters filled their works with scores of people, but on a much more frantic scale. A single Batuan-style picture might contain a dozen apparently unrelated scenes – a temple dance, a rice harvest, a fishing expedition, an exorcism and a couple of tourists taking snapshots – all depicted in fine detail that strikes a balance between the naturalistic and the stylized. By clever juxtaposition, the best Batuan artists, such as the Neka Art Museum exhibitors **I Wayan Bendi**, **I Made Budi** and **Ni Wayan Warti**, can turn their pictures into amusing and astute comments on Balinese society. Works by their precursors, the original Batuan artists **Ida Bagus Made Togog** and **Ida Bagus Made Wija**, focused more on the darker side of village life, on the supernatural beings that hang around the temples and forests, and on the overwhelming sense of men and women as tiny elements in a forceful natural world.

YOUNG ARTISTS STYLE

A second flush of artistic innovation hit the Ubud area in the 1960s, when a group of teenage boys from **Penestanan** started producing unusually expressionistic works, painting everyday scenes in vibrant, non-realistic colours. Encouraged by Dutch artist and Penestanan resident **Arie Smit**, who gave them materials and helped organize exhibitions, they soon became known as the **Young Artists**, a tag now used to describe work by anyone in that same style. The style is indisputably childlike, even naive: the detailed, mosaic-like compositions of scenes from daily life are crudely drawn with minimal attention to perspective, outlined in black like in a child's colouring book, and often washed over in weird shades of pink, purple and blue.

All the major museums have works by some of the original Young Artists from the 1960s, the most famous of whom include **I Ketut Tagen**, **I Wayan Pugur**, **I Nyoman Londo**, **I Nyoman Mundik** and **I Nyoman Mujung**. The Neka Art Museum in Ubud devotes a whole gallery to Arie Smit's own work (see page 114).

ACADEMIC AND BALI MODERNISM

Bali's Modern artists, both indigenous and expatriate, are sometimes labelled as **Academic**, meaning that they've studied and been influenced by Western modernism but have settled in Bali and paint Balinese subjects. Many of the best-known are graduates from the Indonesia Institute of the Arts (ISI) in Yogyakarta, Java, and some are or have been part of the **Sanggar Dewata Indonesia** art movement, whose style – loosely defined as Balinese Hindu abstract expressionism – has been the dominant form of modern Balinese painting since the 1970s. Although the style has been somewhat devalued by the countless poor-quality abstracts sold in souvenir shops across Bali, works by the best-known Academics – including **Affandi**, **Anton H** and **Abdul Aziz**, all from Java, the Sumatran-born **Rusli** and **Made Wianta**, **Nyoman Gunarsa**, **Nyoman Erawan** and **Made Budiana** from Bali – are on show at the Ubud museums and the Nyoman Gunarsa Museum near Semarapura (see page 156). Of these important modern artists, Made Wianta is probably the best known internationally; he represented Indonesia in the Venice 2003 Biennale, with a video installation on the Kuta bombings.

It is the focus of numerous day-tours because of its more than seven hundred malevolent but photogenic **long-tailed macaques** (they will swiftly hunt out any food or drink you might have on your person, and bites and scratches are not uncommon, so beware). There is a first-aid station in the sanctuary, and note that plastic bags are officially banned.

2

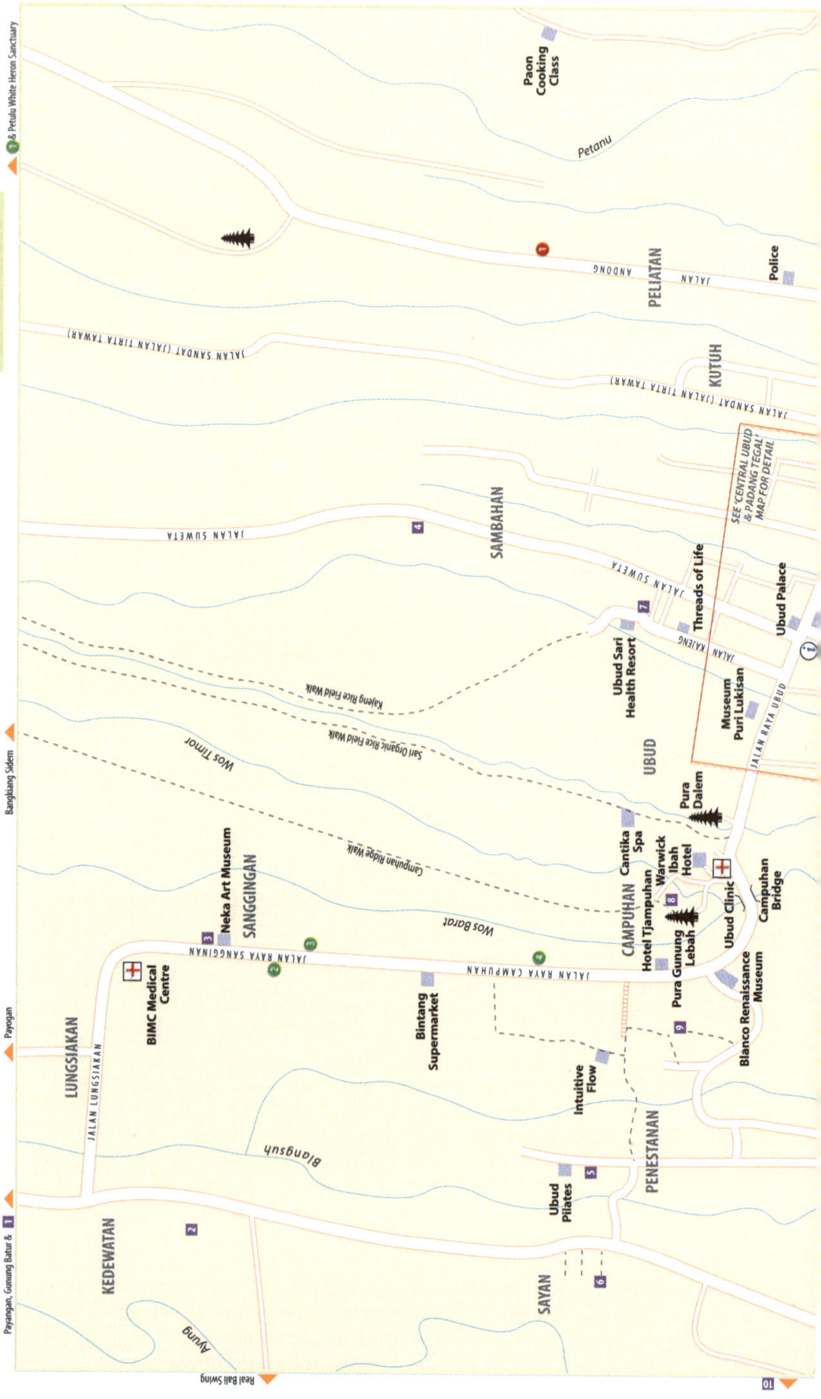

Paon Cooking Class
Petanu
PELIATAN
JALAN ANDONG
Police
KUTUH
JALAN SANDAT (JALAN TIRTA TAWAR)
SEE 'CENTRAL UBUD & PADANG TEGAL' MAP FOR DETAIL
SAMBAHAN
JALAN SUWETA
Threads of Life
Ubud Palace
Ubud Sari Health Resort
JALAN KAJENG
Museum Puri Lukisan
JALAN RAYA UBUD
UBUD
Kajeng Rice Field Walk
Sari Organic Rice Field Walk
Wos Timor
Campuhan Ridge Walk
Pura Dalem
Cantika Spa
Warwick Ibah Hotel
Ubud Clinic
Campuhan Bridge
CAMPUHAN
Hotel Tjampuhan
Pura Gunung Lebah
Blanco Renaissance Museum
Neka Art Museum
SANGGINGAN
Wos Barat
JALAN RAYA SANGGINGAN
JALAN RAYA CAMPUHAN
BIMC Medical Centre
Bintang Supermarket
Intuitive Flow
LUNGSIAKAN
JALAN LUNGSIAKAN
Blangsuh
PENESTANAN
Ubud Pilates
KEDEWATAN
SAYAN
Ayung
1 & Petulu White Heron Sanctuary
Bangkiang Sidem
Payogan
Payangan, Gunung Batur & 1
Real Bali Swing
10

UBUD & NEIGHBOURING VILLAGES
ACCOMMODATION
Alam Jiwa 16
Alila Ubud 1
Amandari 2
The Aruna House 11
Bambu Indah 13
Byasa Ubud 15
COMO Uma Ubud 3
Four Seasons Resort at Sayan 6
Londo Bungalows 9
Menzel Villas Ubud 12
Nur Guest House 8
Rumah Roda Homestay 7
Taman Rahasia Tropical Sanctuary 5
Tegal Sari 14
Uma Capung Mas Cottage 10
Wapa di Ume 4
EATING
The Elephant 4
Indus 3
Mozaic 2
Sage 6
Warung D'Atas Grill & BBQ 1
Warung Makan Pak Sedan 5
SHOPPING
Above the Clouds Natural Wear 2
The Drum Factory 1
Sari Api Gallery 3
0
1
kilometre
11, 12 & Peliatan
Goa Gajah & Gianyar
Batuan & Denpasar
Lodtunduh
13 (200m)
Bank Danamon
Stage
Pura Dalem
TEBESAYA
JALAN PELIATAN
Bale Banjar
PELIATAN
Puri Agung Stage
Pura Agung
Bale Banjar
Stage
JALAN RAYA TEGES
TEGES
Bale Banjar
Museum Rudana
JALAN SUKMA
JALAN RAYA UBUD
JALAN HANOMAN
Stage
PADANG TEGAL
Market
Football Field
Banjar Ubud Kelod
JALAN MONKEY FOREST
Bale Banjar
JALAN BISMA
UBUD MONKEY FOREST
Pura Dalem Agung
Perama Shuttle Bus
Perama
JALAN MADE LEBAH
ARMA
PENGOSEKAN
JALAN RAYA PENGOSEKAN
JALAN NYUH BULAN
Museum Pendet
NYUHKUNING
JL RAYA NYUH KUNING
Outpost
SINGAKERTA
N

The forest itself is small and has many mature trees, with nearly two hundred species present including the *majagan* tree used for the building of Balinese shrines, areca palms and mahogany. A stroll around the forest works well with an exploration of Nyuhkuning. Five minutes into the forest, you'll come to **Pura Dalem Agung Padang Tegal**, the temple of the dead for the Padang Tegal *banjar* (you can borrow the requisite sarong and sash at the temple entrance, for which a small donation is requested). You'll find half a dozen stonecarved images of the witch-widow **Rangda** (see page 310) flanking the main stairway – hard to miss with her hideous fanged face, unkempt hair, metre-long tongue and pendulous breasts. Two of the Rangda statues are depicted in the process of devouring children – a favourite occupation of hers.

Nyuhkuning

South of the Pura Dalem Agung Padang Tegal is the woodcarvers' village **NYUHKUNING**, a pleasingly quiet place for a wander and the site of several charming hotels and cafes. The road is dotted with shops selling the carvers' handiwork, but the atmosphere is relaxed and more workshop-oriented than in the more famous Mas woodcarving centre – and prices are better too. Many of the carvers will give woodcarving lessons to interested tourists. Other arts are also represented here. The paintings and sculptures of well-known Nyuhkuning maestro, the late I Wayan Pendet, are exhibited in the tiny **Museum Pendet** (daily 2–5pm; free). From the museum continuing south you'll pass walled family compounds for the 600m to the main road, Jalan Nguhkunung-Pengosekan. A left turn here leads into the next village, **Pengosekan** (1km to the east).

Peliatan

East of Nyuhkuning at **PELIATAN** is another art museum hosting a different collection of genres.

Museum Rudana

Jl. Cok Rai Pudak No. 44, Peliatan about 3km south of the Ubud Monkey Forest • Charge • http://museumrudana.org

A collection of classical and contemporary art across three floors set in expansive gardens includes plenty of works by the big hitters of the contemporary scene. They include Nyoman Gunarsa, Made Budhiana and Made Wianta, all of whom are associated with the influential Sanggar Dewata Indonesia style. Antonio Blanco and expressionist Affandi are also represented. Rotating exhibitions showcasing emerging artists are held throughout the year.

Pengosekan

You can also reach **PENGOSEKAN** from the southern end of Jalan Hanoman in central Ubud, about a thirty-minute walk or a short hop on an Ubud–Batubulan *bemo*, which is home to the excellent ARMA (**Agung Rai Museum of Art**), as well as an interesting artist community. The Pengosekan painters developed a distinct style in the 1960s (see page 118) and their art also features on carved picture frames, boxes and small pieces of furniture.

ARMA (Agung Rai Museum of Art)

Jl Raya Pengosekan • Charge (includes drink) • http://armabali.com

Pengosekan's main attraction is the impressive ARMA (**Agung Rai Museum of Art**). Founded by Ubud art dealer Anak Agung Rai, its collection nearly matches that of the Neka Art Museum; there's also an excellent public-access **library** and research centre here, plus an open-air dance stage, spa, bookstore, restaurants and hotel.

If you drop by in the mid-afternoon you may chance upon a Balinese dance practice or a gamelan orchestra rehearsal. There are also regular evening dance performances, check the ARMA website for details.

Bale Daja pavilion

From the main entrance, pass through the temporary exhibition hall and across the garden to the large **Bale Daja pavilion**. The downstairs area celebrates the life and work of Walter Spies (see page 115) and includes life-size reproductions of his work along with some typical Ubud-style paintings such as I Ketut Sepi's *Cremation Ceremony* and Anak Agung Gede Sobrat's *Baris Dance*. The upstairs gallery gives a brief survey of the development of Balinese art, though the labels aren't that helpful. Historically speaking, you should begin with the **wayang-style** canvases that are hung high up on the walls overlooking the central well; they are in typical seventeenth-century style, though experts think that they date from much later. Ida Bagus Belawa's *Cock Fighting* is thought to have been painted in the 1930s and is a good example of a modern subject done in traditional two-dimensional style.

Also on this floor, the **Batuan-style** art focuses on real life too; the works are instantly recognizable by their extraordinary detail. *The Island of Bali* by the popular I Wayan Bendi is a fine example: crammed with archetypal Balinese scenes, it's also laced with satire, notably in the figures of long-nosed tourists poking their camera lenses into village events. If you look closely you'll find a surfer in the picture too. Look out also for the pen-and-ink cartoons of I Gusti Nyoman Lempad, an important Ubud character (see page 113).

Bale Dauh pavilion

Across the garden, the **Bale Dauh pavilion** is dedicated to works by expatriate artists, including Rudolf Bonnet, Miguel Covarrubias, Donald Friend, Theo Meier, Antonio Blanco, Arie Smit, Malaysia's Chang Fee Ming and Damas Mangku of Java. The highlight is *Calonarang* (1930) by **Spies** himself, a dark portrait of a demonic apparition; this is the only Spies painting currently on show in Bali. The other major work is the *Portrait of a Javanese Nobleman and his Wife* (1837) by the Javanese artist **Raden Saleh**, considered to be the father of Indonesian painting whose works primarily hang in the Netherlands galleries. The rest of the floor is given over to modern Indonesian painting, including works by **Affandi** and some strikingly powerful abstracts by I Made Sumadiyasa.

ARRIVAL AND DEPARTURE — UBUD AND AROUND

Most Ubud **travel agents** sell Perama bus and boat tickets for the Gili Islands and Lombok, as well as international and domestic airline tickets. Ubud Center (https://ubudcenter.com/) provides transport and tours, as does Perama.

BY PLANE

The easiest way to get to/from Ngurah Rai Airport is by shuttle bus or taxi.

BY SHUTTLE BUS

Perama Bali's ubiquitous shuttle-bus operator, Perama, serves all major tourist destinations on Bali and Lombok. Perama's Ubud office (Jl. Raya Pengosekan, http://peramatour.com; tickets are also available from the tourist office and some travel agencies) is inconveniently located in Padang Tegal at the far southern end of Jl Hanoman, 2.5km from the central market. There's no local *bemo* or metered taxi service from here; you can either take your chances with touts offering free transport to whichever accommodation they are promoting or pay one of the drivers that hang about outside.

Destinations airport (3 daily; 1hr 15min–1hr 45min); Amed (1 daily; 2hr 30min); Bedugul (1 daily; 1hr 30min); Candidasa (3 daily; 1hr 30min–2hr); Gili Islands (daily; 8hr); Kintamani (1 daily; 45min); Kuta (6–7 daily; 1hr–1hr 30min); Lovina (1 daily; 1hr 45min–2hr); Nusa Lembongan (1 daily; 2hr 30min); Padang Bai (3 daily; 1hr–1hr 30min); Sanur (6 daily; 45min–1hr); Senggigi (Lombok; 2 daily; 7hr 30min–11hr 30min).

Kura Kura minibuses (http://kura2bus.com) connect Ubud to Sanur and Kuta several times daily, picking up from the Coco Supermarket at the junction of Jl Raya Pengosekan and Jl Monkey Forest. Times vary so check the latest schedule.

Other services Other shuttle-bus companies may offer more convenient services: the tourist office keeps an up-to-date list of operators and sells tickets. The alternative is the transfer service offered by transport touts and some *losmen*

2

and hotels. For Pemuteran, Gilimanuk and other parts of northwest Bali, take a shuttle bus to Lovina and then change on to a westbound *bemo* for the last coastal stretch.

BY BEMO

Only a limited number of direct *bemo* services run from Ubud, normally departing every 30min or so from about 6am until around 2pm, then at least hourly until about 5pm. They all leave from the central market on Jl Raya Ubud. If coming from Batubulan (Denpasar) you can alight in Peliatan en route; if heading for Campuhan, Sanggingan or Penestanan, you can connect on to a westbound service at the market. For Nyuhkuning, you'll either have to walk from the market (about 30min) or negotiate a ride with a transport tout. Change in Batubulan for services across Denpasar and convoluted connections to southern resorts, the southwest and Java. Change in Gianyar for connections to Candidasa.

Destinations Campuhan/Sanggingan (5–10min); Celuk (40min); Denpasar (Batubulan terminal; 50min); Gianyar (20min); Goa Gajah (10min); Kedewatan (10min); Kintamani (1hr); Mas (15min); Peliatan (5min); Pujung (25min); Sukawati (30min).

GETTING AROUND

By bemo It's possible to use the public *bemos* for certain short hops: to get to the Neka Art Museum, flag down any *bemo* heading west; for Pengosekan or Peliatan take any *bemo* heading for Batubulan; and for Petulu use the orange *bemos* to Pujung or the brown *bemos* to Tegalalang and Kintamani.

By taxi There are no metered taxis in Ubud (the local transport touts prevent them from operating), so you have to bargain with the transport touts who hang around on every corner. Most outlying hotels provide free transport in and out of central Ubud.

By car or motorbike Most transport touts and tour agencies in central Ubud offer car and motorbike rental. A reputable and efficient place is Bali Ari Tours & Driver (Jl Raya Mawang (https://facebook.com/baliaritours/). Note that if you're driving northwards, i.e. uphill, to Kintamani or to the north coast, it's worth getting something more powerful than the cheapest Jimny.

By bike Bicycles are an excellent way to get around if you avoid the busier roads; they can be rented from numerous outlets along Jl Raya Ubud, Jl Monkey Forest and Jl Hanoman and through some accommodation.

On foot The most enjoyable way of seeing Ubud and its immediate environs is on foot via the tracks through the rice paddies and the narrow *gang* that weave through the more traditional *banjar*.

INFORMATION

Tourist information Ubud's tourist office (daily 8am–8pm; 0361 973285) is centrally located just west of the Jl Raya Ubud/Jl Monkey Forest intersection across from the Ubud market. Staff provide schedules of dance performances and festivals, sell tickets for dance shows, run inexpensive day-trips to local sights and sell shuttle-bus tickets for Perama and their competitors. You can pick up useful local magazines here.

Maps and specialist guides If you're planning to do any serious walking or cycling around the area, buy the worthwhile *Bali Pathfinder* map from any local bookstore or the widely available *Bali Street Atlas* (Periplus). Another good investment, though less widely available, is the slim volume, *Bali Bird Walks*, written by the local expat ornithologist Victor Mason, whose Bali Bird Club also runs tours.

TOURS

Although the Ubud tourist office and all travel agencies offer programmes of **standard tours** (minimum 2 people), it's usually more rewarding (and no more expensive if there's at least a couple of you) to hire your own driver and **design your own itinerary**. You can arrange one through almost any car-rental outlet or hotel. Most tour agencies advertise inclusive trips to local festivals and cremations, although you can simply check the details at the tourist office and attend independently. Note that whether you go to a temple ceremony with a group or on your own, modest formal dress (sashes and sarongs) is required.

Bicycle tours Downhill rides from Gunung Batur and other areas, via villages, temples and traditional homes, are organised by such recommended operators as Bali Bike Baik Cycling Tours (http://balibike.com); Bali Eco Cycling (http://baliecocycling.com); E-Bike Tour Bali (http://ebiketourbali.com); Bali Go Bike (http://baligobike.com); and Jegeg Bali Cycling Tours (http://jegegbalicycling.com).

Bird walks Bird-spotting walks in the Campuhan area, organized by Bali Bird Club, successors to expat author Victor Mason (http://balibirdwalk.com; charge includes lunch and conservation donation).

Cultural and ecological walks Guided walks with an emphasis on learning about traditions and local life: Bali Nature Walks (http://balinaturewalks.net).

VOLUNTEERING AROUND UBUD

The Ubud area hosts a number of **charitable foundations** that can use a helping hand for varying lengths of time. All welcome volunteers; contact them in advance.

Sunrise mountain treks Gunung Batur and Gunung Agung. Try Bali Sunrise Trekking and Tours (http://balisunrisetours.com) or Jegeg Bali.

Traditional medicine walks Bali Herbal Walks starting in front of Puri Lukisan Museum Ubud (https://nadisherbalbali.com).

Whitewater rafting and kayaking On the Ayung River just west of Ubud, Sobek's 2hr courses cover about 8km and cross Class 2 and 3 rapids. Mason Adventures Bali (https://masonadventures.com/white-water-rafting); Ubud White Water Rafting Adventure (https://ubudraftingadventure.com).

COURSES AND WORKSHOPS

With so many creative types in residence, Ubud is a great place to learn something new: there are tourist-oriented **courses** in everything from batik to yoga. In addition to the more formal venues listed below, it's always worth asking advice from the more traditional homestays, whose managers are often dancers, musicians or painters. Unless otherwise stated, all of the places below are in central Ubud.

ARTS, CRAFTS, MUSIC, DANCE AND TRADITIONAL CULTURE

ARMA Cultural Workshops Jl Raya Pengosekan, Pengosekan; http://armabali.com. Museum-endorsed classes (2–3hr) in ancient Balinese culture, Balinese painting, woodcarving, batik, gamelan, dance and theatre, silver, basket-weaving, traditional architecture, Hinduism, astrology and making offerings.

Five Art Studio Jl Raya Keliki; http://facebook.com/suardana.kojex. Well-regarded batik painting, and wood- and stone-carving classes. Free transport in the Ubud area.

Museum Puri Lukisan Cultural Workshops Jl Raya Ubud; https://purilukisanmuseum.com. Reputable classes at Ubud's oldest art museum covering batik, woodcarving, classical painting, basketry, mask-painting, shadow puppet-making, gamelan and Balinese dance.

Nirvana Batik Course Jl Goutama No. 10; http://nirvanaku.com. Renowned batik artist I Nyoman Suradnya runs one- to five-day courses in batik painting (fee includes materials) and offering-making (2 hr).

Nyuhkuning woodcarving shops Nyuhkuning. There are plenty of willing teachers in this village of woodcarvers; just ask at any of the shops.

Pondok Pekak Library and Learning Centre Jl Dewi Sita east of the football field; https://pondokpekak.com. Beginners' classes in dance, gamelan, painting, woodcarving, making offerings and jewellery. Book ahead.

Sari Api Jl Suweta; https://sariapi.com. Courses in ceramics-making from the Canadian ceramicist Susan Kohlik.

Studio Perak Jl Hanoman; https://instagram.com/studioperak. Courses in silversmithing: in half a day you can produce your own ring or pendant (fee includes 5g of silver).

Threads of Life Jl Kajeng 24; http://threadsoflife.com. Classes (minimum four people; book ahead) on different aspects of Indonesian and Balinese textiles and natural dyes; also hosts regular lectures and workshops. See web for details.

COOKING AND LANGUAGE

Café Wayan/Laka Leke Jl Monkey Forest; http://alamindahbali.com. There are seven choices of lessons (2hr) featuring various menus, given at *Café Wayan* on Jl Monkey Forest and its sister restaurant *Laka Leke* in Nyuhkuning village. *Laka Leke* also runs cultural classes that are great for kids.

Casa Luna Jl Raya Ubud; http://casalunabali.com. Popular, long-running half-day Balinese cooking workshops run by *Fragrant Rice* author Janet deNeefe and her staff.

Paon Cooking Class Jl Raya Laplapan, Petulu village; http://paon-bali.com. Well-regarded classes with free pick-up in the Ubud area.

Pondok Pekak Library and Learning Centre Jl Dewi Sita east of the football field; https://pondokpekak.com. Intensive Indonesian language courses and individual lessons (1hr 30min), plus Balinese lessons.

Tegal Sari Jl Hanoman, Padang Tegal; http://tegalsari-ubud.com. Half-day courses in Balinese and Indonesian cuisine (charge includes lunch).

ACCOMMODATION

SEE MAPS PAGES 112 AND 120

Ubud has an incredible choice of **accommodation**. Most family homestays are in traditional compounds and have real Balinese charm. Midrange hotels often have pools and a dash of artistic style, while upscale options are wonderfully luxurious, many with rice paddy or river views. For a stunning river valley location, the Ayung River hotels, 6km or so west of Ubud, are perfect. For **house rental** opportunities, check the noticeboards at *Bali Buda* café, Jl Jembawan; Bintang Supermarket, Jl Raya Campuhan-Sanggingan No. 45; and *Kafe*, Jl Hanoman.

CENTRAL UBUD

The 1km-long Jl Monkey Forest is the most central and commercial part of town, while the smaller roads, such as Jl Karna, Jl Maruti, Jl Gootama, Jl Kajeng and Jl Bisma, for example, retain a more peaceful atmosphere and have less traffic. Jl Hanoman, to the east, is marginally quieter than Jl Monkey Forest but still has plenty of shops and restaurants.

Bisma Eight Hotel & Villas Jl Bisma No. 68; http://bisma-eight.com. With 38 boutique suites and 12 one- and two-bedroom villas with private pools, this is an unexpected oasis for central Ubud. In addition to several eateries and drinks spots – one of them a library café – at the back of the property is another restaurant and day-pool. $$$

Gayatri Jl. Monkey Forest No. 41 Gang Biji; http://gayatri.org. An eclectic mix of 18 rooms, all with a/c, mostly in the Balinese style of the 1960s but several renovated and decorated with contemporary furnishings in a great location at good value prices. *Gayatri* is particularly proud of being 100% vegan in all aspects, including composting for its permaculture gardens. $

2

★ KajaNe Mua Jl Monkey Forest; http://kajane.com. Popular resort with villa compounds offering one to four rooms, all with private pools in addition to the inviting main pool. The chic modern Balinese or antique-themed interiors come with good facilities, service is excellent and there's a small gym and a DVD library for rainy nights in. $$$

Komaneka Resort at Monkey Forest Jl Monkey Forest; http://komaneka.com. Beautifully designed, this contemporary hotel offers large, fabulously stylish a/c suites and villas, some with private pools. There's also a stunning lap pool and beautiful spa. Three other wonderful resorts are offered in and near Ubud – check the website for details. $$$

Nick's Pension Jl Bisma No. 32; http://nickspensionbali.com. Efficiently run place with a wide choice of rooms (all with private bathrooms, verandas and plenty of space). There's a decent pool, and a bridge that acts as a handy shortcut between Bisma and Monkey Forest streets (guests only). You pay more for a rice paddy view. The same owners also run a couple of other hotels in Ubud (see website for details). $

Nirvana Pension Jl Goutama No. 10; http://nirvanaku.com/pension.html. Artistically decorated and comfortable rooms, all with fans and hot water, in the traditional house compound of renowned batik artist I Nyoman Suradnya. $

Nur Guest House Jl Abangan Sok Wayah, 500m from Ubud market; https://instagram.com/nurguesthouse/. This lovely place has gorgeous traditional wooden bungalows set amongst ricefields. It's a short walk from central Ubud yet feels very rural and the complimentary breakfast is outstanding. $

Rumah Roda Homestay Jl. Kajeng No. 24; http://rumahroda.com. Epitomizing the meaning of homestay, this is the original Balinese family home of the Threads of Life founders. Nine simple rooms with a/c or fan, all with hot water, a small pool and restaurant. The bonus is the genuine hospitality found in a real Balinese home. Breakfast included. $

Sama's Cottages and Villas Jl Bisma; http://samascottagesubud.com. Tranquil hideaway, just 10min from central Ubud with charming cottages (with either fans or a/c) built on steep tiers in a river gully. There's a small pool, and breakfast is brought to your private veranda each morning. Also owns two villas (see website for details). $

Ubud Village Hotel Jl Monkey Forest; http://theubudvillage.com. This elegant, medium-priced hotel offers 62 comfortable rooms, suites and luxury villas. Two swimming pools, spa, gym and four different dining options. $$

Uma Sari Cottage Jl Bisma no.35; 0361 981 538. The cottage has 10 comfortable Balinese-style rooms with fans or a/c in a quiet but convenient location. All rooms have balconies overlooking tropical gardens. There's also a small pool and a restaurant. $

PELIATAN, PENGOSEKAN, NYUHKUNING, PADANG TEGAL AND SAMBAHAN

Peliatan, 1.6km southeast of the Ubud market, harbours a couple of excellent places to stay. Nyuhkuning, Padang Tegal and Pengosekan are peaceful southern settlements. Sambahan is just north of central Ubud.

★ Alam Jiwa Nyuhkuning; http://alamindahbali.com. Run by the hospitable Café Wayan family, the spacious accommodation here is located by a small river, affording dramatic views of ricefields and Gunung Agung. There's a pool, and free transport into Ubud. This is one of five delightful *Alam* hotels. $$

The Aruna House Jl. Gunung Sari, Peliatan, 1.7km from Ubud Market; 0821 4521 0171. Away from the bustle of central Ubud and close to nature, The Aruna House has two a/c rooms with pool views and excellent service by a caring host. Ideal for those seeking serenity. $

Byasa Ubud Jl Made Lebah No.12, Peliatan; 0821 4431 1500. Set off the road, this small hotel has nine plush rooms in a delightfully peaceful location overlooking paddy fields and a lovely pool. Staff really go the extra mile here. $$

Menzel Villas Ubud Jl Yudistira, Peliatan; http://menzelubud.com. An escape from the city noise, rooms and villas available in one-, two- and three-bedrooms, all individually decorated, with rice paddies on the premises. Villas have plunge or private pools. Spa, bar, and restaurant serving tasty cuisine and a cooking school. $$

★ Tegal Sari Jl Pengosekan, Padang Tegal; http://tegalsari-ubud.com. An excellent, ecologically conscious place that's solar-powered and has a waste-recycling programme. Rooms are fine value and tastefully furnished, all with terraces and a/c; the deluxe options are very stylish indeed. Service is thoughtful and there are massage facilities, a pool, free local transport and opportunities for cookery classes, day-treks and village visits. Book well ahead. $

★ Wapa di Ume Jl. Suweta, Sambahan, 1.8km north from Ubud market; http://wapadiume.com. The attention to detail is flawless at this beautiful natural chic hotel where each room has a rice paddy view. There's a fine pool, spa, restaurant with stunning vistas and free daily yoga class. Regular shuttles into central Ubud are available. $$

SANGGINGAN, PAYANGAN AND KELIKI

West of central Ubud, the hotels in Sanggingan are reached via busy Jl Raya Ubud; some hotels offer free transfers. If you're staying in Keliki or Payangan you'll probably need transport.

Alila Ubud Desa Melinggih Kelod, Payangan; http://alilahotels.com. A wonderful position overlooking the jungle-rich Ayung Valley with spacious and stylish rooms and bungalows that make the most of the stunning views. There's

2

PLASTIC FREE BALI

Discarded plastic bottles don't decompose and are wasteful and expensive to manufacture. The Bali Cantik Tanpa Plastik (**Plastic Free Bali**) Campaign is working to get rid of all plastic, including single-use bags and straws. Their Facebook page is http://facebook.com/groups/44297661289. In the meantime, to help minimize the rubbish problem, you can **refill** your plastic water bottle at certain clued-up outlets in Ubud for less than what it would cost to buy a replacement. These include:

Jl Dewi Sita *Tutmak* restaurant.
Jl Dewi Sita (east of the football field) Pondok Pekak Library and Learning Centre.
Jl Hanoman *Kafe* restaurant.
Jl Jembawan *Bali Buda* café.

a superb restaurant, professional spa with an extensive range of treatments, and perhaps Ubud's best infinity pool. $$$

Amandari Jl Raya Kedewatan, Kedewatan; http://aman.com. A true temple of luxury, *Amandari's* design evokes Balinese architecture and its bungalows and suites are wonderfully opulent, some with private pools. There's a library and glorious jungle views from its idyllic main pool. $$$$

COMO Uma Ubud Jl Raya Sanggingan, Sanggingan; http://comohotels.com. Fabulous resort of white-walled compounds containing Japan-influenced accommodation set along the side of the Wos River. Part of the top-end *COMO* group, they put an emphasis here on wellbeing, with complimentary daily yoga classes and morning walks. $$$$

SAYAN, PENESTANAN AND SINGAKERTA

Sayan, Penestanan and Singakerta, west and south of central Ubud, are dotted with ultra-luxe resorts and villas but there are some good mid-range accommodation options here, too. Getting back to nature surrounded by village life is the name of the game here.

★ **Bambu Indah** Sayan; http://bambuindah.com. Probably Bali's most unique place to stay, and the antithesis of the corporate five-star hotel. This is perhaps the most environmentally conscious hotel in Indonesia, built entirely from natural materials, while the 30m pool is river-fed and chlorine-free, and there are organic vegetable patches rather than manicured gardens. Guests get to revel in the epic views over the Ayung valley and stay in traditional Javanese teak houses, or startling mod-meets-trad bamboo creations. There's fine food, attentive service and a wonderful chillout zone by the riverbank below. $$$

Four Seasons Resort at Sayan Jl Raya Sayan, Sayan; http://fourseasons.com. One of Bali's top hotels, the Four Seasons is built on several levels in the Ayung valley; the two-tier pool and other communal areas are stunning. Its suites and villas are beautifully appointed and fabulously comfortable, and villas have private pools. $$$$

Londo Bungalows Penestanan; http://londobungalows.com. Five large budget cottages and another one under construction; each sleep four and are equipped with a kitchenette. $

Taman Rahasia Tropical Sanctuary Penestanan Kaja; 0812 3902 2153. A classy, family-run boutique hideaway in the heart of the village. The large a/c rooms here are attractively furnished with tasteful artworks and local fabrics and have deep verandas or balconies. There's a restaurant, small pool, good spa and charming garden. Also has a cooking school for in-house guests. Not recommended for children. $$

Uma Capung Mas Cottage Jl. Katiklantang, Singakerta, 1.7km from Ubud market; 0812 3889 9758. At *Uma Capung Mas* you have the advantage of a tranquil setting plus free shuttle to Ubud centre. Spotlessly clean rooms, pool and ricefields as your neighbour. Rates include breakfast served on your terrace or balcony. $

EATING

SEE MAPS PAGES 112 AND 120

If you like your food vegan, organic and raw, Ubud will be heaven: it's probably Asia's healthy eating epicentre. Or if barbecued meats and pizza are more to your taste, you'll eat well here too. Factor in Japanese, Chinese, Italian, French, a slew of delis, and of course, Indonesian and Balinese restaurants and there's an amazing selection. Many restaurants outside central Ubud offer free pick-ups if you call up advance.

CENTRAL UBUD

Bali Buda Jl Jembawan No. 1; http://balibuda.com. Offers a vast menu of healthy drinks, sandwiches made with traditional or rye, spelt and red-rice breads, raw-food meals, pizza and salads, soups and main courses, as well as cakes and pastries. There's a shop around the corner, plus a noticeboard for yoga and language classes and houses for rent. $$

Café des Artistes Jl Bisma No. 9X; http://cafedesartistesbali.com. Sophisticated place with exhibitions by local artists and a tasty menu that features half a dozen steak dishes (try tenderloin with blue cheese), pastas, *escargots* and pate plus a good-value monthly four-course special. It also offers a good imported wine list and aperitifs. $$

Café Lotus Jl Raya Ubud; https://thecafelotusubud.com. Inaugurated almost 40 years ago, this restaurant has become a real Ubud institution over the years. It has a unique setting: it is situated over a lotus pond; a frame of frangipani trees with a temple backdrop completes the picture. Try their delicious pastas and desserts. $$

★ **Café Wayan** Jl Monkey Forest; http://cafewayan.com. An Ubud visit is not complete without at least one stop at the iconic Café Wayan which has served scrumptious food for over 30 years. The breakfast, lunch and dinner menus contain everything you're hungry for, from traditional cuisine to sandwiches and cocktails. Sunday evenings there's a mouth-watering Balinese buffet and there are cooking classes too. $$

Casa Luna Jl Raya Ubud; http://casalunabali.com. Long-running, justly popular restaurant-bakery serving fine international cuisine. The weekend brunch is particularly good and there's live jazz on Friday and Sunday evenings. However service can be distracted at times. *Casa Luna*'s owners also run cooking classes (see page 125). $$

Clear Café Jl Hanoman No. 8; http://clearcafebali.com. Offers an excellent range of organic raw, vegan, vegetarian and seafood dishes, drawing culinary inspiration from across the globe (though many ingredients are sourced in Bali). The design (bamboo screens, high ceiling, wonderful aged wooden door) is eye-catching too. $$

Gelato Secrets Jl Raya Ubud; http://gelatosecrets.com. Serving the best gelato and sorbets in central Ubud, this gelateria sources its ingredients from across the Indonesian archipelago and makes its cones in-house. $$

Herbivore Jl Dewi Sita; https://locavorenxt.com/family/herbivore. Ubud's acclaimed Locavore restaurant has been superseded by this all-vegan counterpart. Raising the bar for serious gastronomic cuisine in Ubud, there's no à la carte menu; instead, you'll be treated to a highly innovative (and expensive by local standards) three-, five- or seven-course menu inspired by locally sourced ingredients and elevated to a world-class dining experience. Foodies can also check out the new LocavoreNXT restaurant south of town. $$$$

★ **Ibu Oka** Just off Jl Suweta; 0361 976 345. Another Ubud icon, this open-sided *warung* attracts queues of diners for it's always flavoursome *babi guling* (suckling pig). There are a couple of other branches around town too. Get there early. $$

Ibu Rai Bar & Restaurant Jl Monkey Forest No. 72; https://instagram.com/iburairestaurant. Serves up artfully presented Indonesian, Asian and international dishes in bustling surroundings. $$

Kafe Jl Hanoman No. 44B; http://kafe-bali.com. The vast and enticing "organically inspired" menu includes Mexican dishes, stir-fries, noodles and sandwiches supplemented by healthy juices and smoothies, top coffee, and scrumptious cakes and desserts. *Garden Kafe* is a small branch at The Yoga Barn. $$

Nomad Jl Raya Ubud No. 35; http://nomadubud.com. Serves local, Asian fusion and international dishes with style from a small but inviting menu including satay, Malaysian *laksa* and Balinese-style tapas. There are plenty of cocktails, too. $$

Seniman Coffee Studio Jl Sriwedari No. 5; http://senimancoffee.com. Coffee is elevated to an art form at this hip café-roastery-design shop, which has a range of equipment that would look more in place in a science lab. The menu features five regular, single-origin coffees, plus weekly "guest beans", as well as British- and Indonesian-style breakfasts, top cakes and pleasing oddities like Argentine *alfajores* (*dulce de leche*-filled biscuits). $$

Tutmak Warung Jl Dewi Sita; 0361 975754. This friendly cafe-style restaurant serves great sandwiches, burgers, dips, snacks and full meals, including Indonesian specialities. There is also a children's menu. $$

NYUHKUNING AND PELIATAN

★ **Sage** Jl Nyuh Bulan No. 1, Nyuhkuning; http://facebook.com/sagerestobali. Located on a corner plot, this vegan-vegetarian place has an outstanding selection of healthy dishes including "Go Jolly Green salad" (with kale, spinach and tempeh), great jackfruit tacos and wonderful juices. The attractive premises are light and airy and staff are sweet. $$

Warung D'Atas Grill & BBQ Jl Gunung Sari No. 777; Peliatan, 0361 908 0345. Sizzling up a storm, this unpretentious, open-sided place is a carnivore's delight with expertly spiced pork ribs, home-made sausages and kebabs at moderate prices. Their meat combo plate is almost enough for two. $$

CAMPUHAN, SANGGINGAN AND PENESTANAN

The Elephant Jl Raya Sanggingan, Sayan in Hotel Taman Indrakila; http://elephantbali.com. Offering vistas over the Campuhan ridge, this vegetarian-vegan restaurant with an international menu is a wonderful spot to enjoy a delicious meal. Mains include *polenta alla griglia* (grilled polenta with pesto) and there are tasty smoothies, coolers and juices. $$

Indus Jl Raya Sanggingan No. 88, Campuhan; http://casalunabali.com. Promises great daytime views across to the Campuhan Ridge and draws a loyal clientele for its eclectic menu: healthy breakfasts, Balinese, Asian and Western cuisine and a fresh fish dish on Fridays. There's free transport from *Casa Luna*, a daily happy hour with free tapas and Monday night salsa dancing. $$

Mozaic Jl Raya Sanggingan, Sanggingan; http://mozaic-bali.com. This multi-award-winning restaurant showcases the talents of French-American chef Chris Salans. The French- and Asian-inspired dishes change regularly but include favourites such as Kintamani suckling pork with Javanese pomelo purée or splash out on a 6-course *grand menu*. Reservations essential. $$$$

Warung Makan Pak Sedan Jl Made Lebah No. 3; https://instagram.com/wr_paksedan. Some of the most economical food around Ubud is served at this low-key establishment: try the tasty house speciality, nasi campur ayam. $

DANCE AND DRAMA IN UBUD

The Ubud region is an important centre of **Balinese dance** (see page 309) and **gamelan** and boasts dozens of village-based performance groups. Between them they stage up to nine different dance shows every night in the area; the tourist office publishes the schedule (which is also available at http://balitaksu.com) and arranges **free transport** to outlying venues. **Ticket prices** are fixed. Performances generally start between 7pm and 8pm, and there's unreserved seating so arrive early for the best spot.

The **Kecak** (Monkey Dance) and the **Barong** (Lion Dance) are the most accessible and visually interesting, while the **Legong** is more refined and understated. Unusual shows worth seeking out include the unique **all-female** Kecak Srikandi.

If you have only one evening to catch a show, consider seeing whatever is playing at **Puri Saren Agung (Ubud Palace)**, opposite the Ubud market. The setting is atmospheric, with the courtyard gateway and staircase furnishing a memorable backdrop. The Kecak Rina that's staged twice a month on full and dark moon nights at **ARMA** in Pengosekan (see page 122) is also worth a special effort to catch, as it's an unusually fiery and humorous version.

2

DRINKING AND NIGHTLIFE

SEE MAP PAGE 112

Ubud is no hotbed of hedonistic nightlife. Most tourists go to an early-evening **Balinese dance performance** before catching last orders at a restaurant at around 9pm. The bar scene is pretty sedate, so choose a **live music night** at one of the town's restaurants or bars to be sure of a decent crowd.

BARS AND LIVE MUSIC VENUES

BetelNut Jl Raya Ubud; http://dekco.com/betelnut. Lounge-type establishment with live music, live events, movie nights, documentary screenings and excellent food and drinks. Indoor and outdoor seating. $$

Laughing Buddha Bar Jl Monkey Forest; http://laughingbuddhabali.com. There's regular live music (from blues to reggae) at this small, relaxed bar in the heart of Jl Monkey Forest. You'll find a long drinks menu plus plenty of nibbles and tapas. $$

The Night Rooster Jl. Goutama Sel. No.5; http://locavore.co.id. Sleek second floor lounge bar from the *Locavore* team, with outstanding cocktails, fine wine by the glass, and superb sharing platters: try their charcuterie spread. $$

No Mas Bar Jl Monkey Forest; http://nomasubud.com. Stylish bar with a social vibe, vintagey decor, rotating live bands and DJs and killer cocktails (try a Pickleback – whisky and homemade juice). $$

SHOPPING

SEE MAPS PAGES 112 AND 120

Shopping for arts and crafts is a major pastime in Ubud: there are outlets in all its neighbourhoods, but if you're short on time the art **market** in central Ubud is a good one-stop venue and overflows with stalls. For a shopping excursion around the central area, Jl Monkey Forest, Jl Hanoman and Jl Dewi Sita are the best roads. You might also want to explore the specialist "craft villages" of Celuk, Sukawati, Batuan and Mas that lie south of Ubud along the Denpasar–Ubud road. The 24hr **minimarts** that dot the Ubud streetscape stock essentials, from suntan lotion to beer. Many Ubud shops can organize shipping if required. Unless otherwise stated, all of the places below are in central Ubud.

ART AND PHOTOGRAPHY

Rio Helmi Photography Jl Suweta No. 6B; http://riohelmi.com. Gallery of the respected Indonesian photographer. Limited edition and mass-market prints. By appointment only.

Sari Api Gallery Jl Raya Pengosekan; http://sariapi.com. This gallery in the heart of Ubud shows contemporary ceramics made at Sari Api Ceramics Studio, the first professional ceramic studio in Ubud. There are also silk and batik products available. By appointment only.

BOOKS

Ganesha Bookshop Jl Raya Ubud, corner of Jl Jembawan; http://ganeshabooksbali.com. The best bookshop in Ubud, with a huge stock of new books on all things Balinese and Indonesian, plus maps and fiction.

Periplus Bookshop Jl Raya Ubud no.88; http://periplus.com. This well-stocked Indonesia-wide chain has three branches in Ubud, each with a good collection of novels, non-fiction, coffee-table books, magazines and newspapers.

Pondok Pekak Library and Learning Centre Jl Dewi Sita east of the football field; 0361 976194. A great resource with around 30,000 books available for sale, rent and part-exchange.

CLOTHING, JEWELLERY AND ACCESSORIES

Above the Clouds Natural Wear Jl. Nyuh Bojog No. 13,

TOO MUCH LUGGAGE?

Need to make room in your luggage for new purchases? Donate unwanted clothes, books, bric-a-brac and anything else "so long as it's not alive" to the Yayasan Senyum **charity shop**, the Smile Shop at Jalan Nyuhkunung, Pengosekan (http://senyumbali.org). Profits help fund operations for Balinese people with craniofacial disabilities such as cleft palate. You can, of course, also buy cheap secondhand stuff at the shop too. There's also a Smile Shop in Sanur.

Nyuhkuning; http://abovetheclouds.store. Men's clothing designed and produced in Bali made from cotton and linen, some handwoven natural dyed pieces.

Studio Perak Jl Hanoman No. 15; https://instagram.com/studioperak. Stylish silver jewellery to suit all tastes from the folks who run the silversmithing courses. It's also possible to purchase jewellery here produced by inmates at Kerobokan jail.

CRAFTS, TEXTILES AND SOUVENIRS

The Drum Factory Jl. Raya Andong, Peliatan; http://bali-treasures.com. The largest African djembe hand-drum manufacturer in Indonesia offers more than two hundred percussion instruments, gongs and gamelan of all shapes and sizes. Some will even fit in your luggage.

Ikat Batik Jl Monkey Forest; http://facebook.com/kadekwiraubud. Gorgeous ikat and contemporary batik, many are hand-spun and hand-dyed pieces.

Kupu-Kupu Foundation Shop Jl Tirta Tawar No. 22; http://kupukupufoundation.org. Inexpensive and beautiful works produced by disabled woodcarvers, kite-makers, painters, bead-workers and weavers, under the auspices of the Kupu-Kupu Foundation. Staffed by the artists themselves.

Mitra Bali Fair Trade Jl Monkey Forest; http://mitrabali.com. Support local craftspeople at this little shop, where a changing range of crafts is on offer that includes homewares, small gifts and jewellery.

Ubud Art Market Jl. Raya Ubud. Ubud's central market has transformed over the years from a humble fruit and veg street market to a one-stop shop for traditional art, handicrafts and souvenirs in a purpose-built market hall. You can still find quality crafts in-between the more touristy souvenirs, but sharpen your haggling skills if you want to secure a good price. Note that a fire devastated the market building in 2024; the market has partly reopened but works are ongoing.

Uluwatu Handmade Balinese Lace Jl. Monkey Forest No. 14; http://uluwatu.co.id. Exquisite handmade English cutwork fashioned into casual- and nightwear, table and bed linens. There are several outlets throughout Bali.

FOOD AND DRINK

Kou Cuisine Jl Monkey Forest; https://facebook.com/koucuisine.jam/. Stocks a fabulous range of home-made jams, with milk caramel a favourite. Its sister shop, Kou Bali, around the corner on Jl Dewi Sita sells wonderful handmade soaps and sea salts.

Ubud Raw Chocolate Jl. Goutama No. 8; http://ubudraw.com. Made from organically grown Balinese cacao, heavenly raw organic chocolate in the form of bricks, bites, powders and beans produce drools from the aromas when you first open the shop doors. Try their tester plate of four kinds of chocolate before deciding what to take home. You can also visit their factory on Jl. Raya Sayan No. 74, Sayan to see it being lovingly made and to restock supplies.

SPA TREATMENTS AND ALTERNATIVE THERAPIES

Arty, spiritual-minded Ubud is Bali's centre for holistic practices and **alternative therapies**, and also offers plenty of traditional spa and **beauty treatments**. For more information on holistic activities and therapies in Ubud and the rest of Bali, visit the Bali Spirit network website (http://balispirit.com), which also runs Ubud's annual Bali Spirit Festival of world music, dance and yoga every March (http://balispiritfestival.com). Unless otherwise stated, all of the places below are in central Ubud.

Bali Botanica Day Spa Jl Raya Sanggingan, Sanggingan; http://balibotanica.com. Cute little day spa overlooking a small flower garden and river where the signature treatments are Ayurvedic and herbal massage. Packages are available.

Cantika Alami Jl Sok Wayah; http://cantikazestbali.com. Located on the ricefield walk. Massages, facials, hair treatments, manicures and pedicures are also available using their own natural products. With two other Ubud outlets, they also run workshops on making your own beauty products at Cantika Zest in Penestanan.

Jaens Spa Ubud Jl Raya Pengosekan; http://jaensspa.com. An excellent day spa offering a wide assortment of wellness treatments, including traditional Balinese massages, facials, hair treatments, manicures and pedicures.

Karsa Spa Campuhan Ridge; http://karsaspa.com. Accessed via backroads or the Campuhan Ridge Trail, this professional spa and reiki centre has great massages and tempting packages. Pre-booking recommended.

Ubud Bodyworks Centre Jl Hanoman No. 25; http://ubudbodyworks.com. Well-respected centre for massage and spiritual healing where you can book an appointment with master healer Ketut Arsana or with one of his staff. Also offers traditional baths and massages, beauty treatments, acupressure, energy balancing, herbal healing, reflexology and yoga sessions, and sells essential oils.

Ubud Sari Health Resort Jl Kajeng No. 35; http://ubudsari.com. Boasts an on-site swimming pool and health restaurant. Treatments (30mins) include massage, reflexology, reiki, sports massage and yoga. You can also book an all-inclusive healing week.

YOGA, PILATES & MEDITATION

Ubud is one of Asia's foremost **yoga communities**, with many resident and visiting devotees. You'll find over a dozen schools in the area and there are possibly hundreds of instructors. Check websites for exact schedules.

Intuitive Flow Jl. Raya Campuhan, Sayan; http://intuitiveflow.com. Many yoga styles are taught here, as well as meditation and healing therapies. Classes are at the centre on the Penestanan ridgetop with brilliant views from the studio windows. Also runs yoga teacher-training courses.

Taksu Yoga Jl Goutama Selatan; http://taksuyoga.com. Offers vinyasa, hatha gentle yoga and private classes. Package discounts available.

Ubud Aura Retreat Jl Hanoman No 888; http://ubudaura.com. This retreat, with a pool, is affiliated with the Ubud Bodyworks Centre and offers a tranquil base for yoga and treatments. Four-night yoga packages available.

Ubud Pilates Jl. Cempaka Putih No. 13, Sayan, off Jl Raya Campuhan; http://ubudpilates.com. Offering small-group classes (from beginners to advanced) from an experienced instructor in a beautiful location.

Ubud Yoga House Jl Subak Sok Wayah; http://ubudyogahouse.com. Located in the ricefields leading to the Campuhan Ridge, the Yoga House offers a busy programme of hatha, vinyasa flow and gentle yoga sessions. Guided meditation classes are also available.

The Yoga Barn Southern Jl Hanoman, Padang Tegal; http://theyogabarn.com. Runs a big programme of yoga classes in various disciplines along with pilates, capoeira, dance and meditation. It also offers yoga retreats and yoga teacher-training.

DIRECTORY

Banks and exchange There are ATMs and money-changers throughout central Ubud. Be aware of some ongoing scams (see page 47). PT Central Kuta is a recommended exchange counter in the Circle K supermarket opposite Museum Puri Lukisan.

Cinema Paradiso Ubud (Jl Goutama Selatan; https://

JAMU: HERBAL TONICS FOR HEALTH AND BEAUTY

Ubud has long been renowned for its **herbal medicine** – *ubad* means "medicine" in Balinese – known both for the medicinal plants that flourish around the Campuhan river gullies and for the local healers who know how to use them.

The pills, pastes and potions distilled from medicinal herbs are collectively known as **jamu** and are widely used throughout Bali (and the rest of Indonesia), both in the treatment of serious ailments and for general wellbeing. Healers usually make their own *jamu* from herbs they may have picked or even grown themselves and will have a standard range of special, secret, mixtures to prescribe to their patients as pills or for use in infusions; often they'll custom-make *jamu* for particular conditions as well. Commonly used mainstream plants include turmeric, ginger, galangal and garlic, but there are countless others. Some *jamu* makers don't offer healing sessions but simply hawk their home-brews around the market in old glass bottles or drive by neighbourhoods on bicycles. Several Ubud spas and cafés also serve ready-made *jamu* drinks to tourists, including *Bali Buda*.

Commercially produced *jamu* is also a huge industry and tends to focus more, but not exclusively, on the wellbeing side of things. Sex and beauty enhancers for men and women are predictably big sellers, as are diet and breast-enlargement elixirs, but there are also plenty of products for cleansing the blood, easing joint pain and muscle ache, improving circulation and dealing with skin conditions. The reputable brands use entirely natural ingredients, often to recipes that are familiar to those who make their own and, like home-made *jamu*, should have no side effects at all (though it's always best to seek local advice first). Pharmacies sometimes sell these commercial powders and pills but there are also dedicated *jamu* shops, like the one towards the eastern end of Ubud's Jalan Raya. Commercial *jamu* is distinctively packaged, often carrying a helpful graphic, like a pulsating knee joint (arthritis) or a smiling, muscular male (better sex), and the most vital information is usually also given in English.

facebook.com/paradisoubud) screens classics, documentaries, cult movies and kids' flicks on an HD projector with an organic vegan café attached.

Embassies and consulates See page24.

Hospitals, clinics and dentists Ubud Clinic at Jl Raya Campuhan No. 36 (0361 974911) and BIMC's Ubud Medical Centre (a branch of BIMC Clinic in Kuta and BIMC Siloam hospital in Nusa Dua) at Jl. Raya Sanggingan No. 21, Kedewatan are open 24hr, staffed by English-speakers and will respond to emergency call-outs. Ubud Clinic also has dental service. For anything serious, the nearest hospitals are in south Bali (see page 72).

2

Libraries ARMA (Agung Rai Museum of Art; https://armabali.com/museum) has the island's best library of books about Bali, including notable esoteric works and language books.

Police The main police station is on the eastern edge of town, on Jl Andong. There's a more central police booth at the Jl Raya Ubud/Jl Monkey Forest crossroads.

Post office The main office, at Jl Jembawan 1, has a parcel-packing service at the back. There are postal agents throughout Ubud where you can buy stamps and send mail and parcels.

South of Ubud

The stretch of road running 26km **south from Ubud** to Denpasar links a string of arts- and crafts-producing towns, all with long histories of creative activity: Mas, for example, is famed for **woodcarvings**, Celuk for **silverwork**, and Batubulan for **stone sculptures**. If you have private transport, these towns are easily visited as a day-trip from Ubud or from the southern resorts; access by *bemo* from Sanur is particularly easy, with the Batubulan terminal halfway between Sanur and Ubud (total 26km).

There are two north-south routes between Denpasar and Ubud. The principal artery and *bemo* route from south to north turns east at Batubulan and travels through Celuk, Sukawati and Mas. If continuing straight (north) the prong narrows into a scenic back road which cuts through a series of traditional villages as far as Sayan, four kilometres west of Ubud, passing through Singapadu and Batuan before eventually continuing to Kintamani. In addition, there are several other pleasantly rural and peaceful side roads

CARVED IN STONE: FOR GODS, RAJAS AND TOURISTS

The traditional function of **stonecarved statues and reliefs** was to entice and entertain the gods and to ward off undesirable spirits and evil forces. The **temples** in south Bali generally do this in a restrained way, being built mainly from red brick with just a few flourishes of carved volcanic tuff or *paras* (though Batubulan's Pura Puseh is an exception), but the northern temples, which are often built entirely from the easy-to-carve *paras*, are a riot of vivacious curlicues. Outstanding northern examples include the Pura Dalem in Jagaraga, Pura Beji and the Pura Dalem in Sangsit and, most interestingly, Pura Meduwe Karang at Kubutambahan. In the east, Bangli's Pura Kehen is not to be missed.

Rajas and high-ranking nobles also commissioned fantastic carvings for their **palaces** (*puri*). Few outlasted the early twentieth-century battles with the Dutch, but one notable survivor is Puri Saren Agung in Ubud, the work of Bali's most skilful stonecarver, **I Gusti Nyoman Lempad** (see page 113). These days, **hotels** are the modern *puri*, and many of the older, grander ones were built in the Bali-baroque *puri-pura* style, with plenty of high-spirited stonecarved embellishments. **Gateways** normally feature the most elaborate carvings, in keeping with their function as both a practical and symbolic demarcation between the outer and the inner world, whether they're leading to the inner temple courtyard or giving access to palace compounds or hotels.

Sculptures of *raksasa* (Hindu demon-giants) often guard temple and hotel gates, and most other freestanding stonecarvings destined for homes and gardens in Bali and abroad still take their inspiration from traditional subjects, including Hindu deities and mythological characters and creatures. The vast majority are made in Batubulan workshops, which is the best place to buy small or large sculptures. Many shops can arrange shipping.

TRADITIONAL DANCE SHOWS IN BATUBULAN

The spectacular **Barong dance**, which sees the lion-like Barong Ket pitted against the widow-witch Rangda, is performed for tourists at various venues around Batubulan including the stage next to Pura Puseh and the Denjulan Barong and Kris stage, 300m south down the main Denpasar road from the Pura Puseh junction. Both stages are served by Ubud–Batubulan *bemos*. Additionally, in the evenings, there's a double bill of the **Kecak** and the **Fire Dance** at the Barong Sahadewa stage on Jalan SMKI No. 25 (0361 4711 015), signed off the main road about 500m south of the Pura Puseh junction.

that take in some of the area's other attractions, such as *PUMA* (Putrawan Museum of Art) north of Penatih and the *Bali Bird Park* and Bali Reptile Park outside Batubulan.

Batubulan and around

Barely distinguishable from Denpasar's northeastern suburbs, **BATUBULAN** is the capital's terminal for public transport heading east and northeast, the home of outstanding Barong **dance troupes**, and respected across the island for its **stonecarvers**. There's also a **bird park** and a **reptile park** here. The town is strung out over 3km along the main road, bound by the *bemo*/bus station in the south and the huge **Barong statue** at the Singapadu/Celuk junction in the north.

Roadsides throughout Batubulan are crowded with ranks of **stone statues** in front of dozens of workshops and galleries. Most of these shops deal in a range of images and stone types. Some sell carvings imported from Java, and most also deal in cheaper, mass-produced artworks that are moulded (rather than carved) from lava-stone "concrete".

Pura Puseh

250m east off the main road, from a signed junction about 250m south of the Barong statue • free

As you'd expect in a town so renowned for stonecarving, the main temple, **Pura Puseh**, is exuberantly decorated. Its unusual design features a five-tiered gateway tower inspired by Indian religious architecture, as well as a number of Buddha images not normally associated with Bali's Hindu temples. The rest of the iconography, however, is characteristically and flamboyantly Balinese: a grimacing Bhoma head overlooks the main gateway and, to his right, the god Wisnu poses astride a bull; to the right of him, Siwa stands ankle-deep in skulls and wears a string of them around his neck.

PUMA (Putrawan Museum of Art)

Jl. Trenggana No. 108, Penatih village, 4.6 km west of Batubulan • Charge • 0361 463737 • Situated inside the Alam Puri Resort, about 3km north of Denpasar

West of the main road to Ubud, **PUMA** (**Putrawan Museum of Art)** is a remarkable – though largely ignored – collection of tribal sculpture from across Indonesia including works from Flores, Nias, Kalimantan and Sumba, supplemented by jewellery and other artefacts. The *ana deo*, ancestral figures from Flores, and *tau tau*, effigies of the dead from Sulawesi, are especially compelling. Given that tourist shops are awash with reproductions of these, this is a fabulous chance to see the real thing.

ARRIVAL AND DEPARTURE — BATUBULAN AND AROUND

By bus and bemo Batubulan's bus and *bemo* station runs services across Denpasar and to destinations around Ubud. It's at the far southern end of town and has clearly signed bays for each destination, including Amlapura via Candidasa, Kintamani, Nusa Dua, Padang Bai, Singaraja (for Lovina) and Ubud. All services run every 30min or so; after about 2pm services are sporadic at best; travel as early in the day as possible. Note that for rucksacks and other bulky baggage there's usually an extra charge on *bemos*.

Destinations Amlapura (2hr 30min); Bangli (2hr 30min); Candidasa (2hr); Celuk (10min); Gianyar (1hr); Kintamani (1hr 30min); Klungkung (1hr 30min); Mas (35min); Nusa

Dua (1hr); Padang Bai (for Lombok; 1hr 45min); Peliatan (45min); Semarapura (1hr 20min); Singaraja (Penarukan terminal; 3hr 15min); Sukawati (20min); Tegalalang (1hr 15min); Ubud (50min).

Celuk

2

Known as the "silver village", **CELUK** is a major centre for **jewellery** production, and the silversmiths welcome both retail and wholesale customers – though designs are often less innovative than in Ubud or southern resort shops. Many of the outlets have workshops or factories where visitors can watch the silversmiths at work. The smaller, lower-key Celuk outlets are along Jalan Jagaraga (a back road to Singapadu), which runs north from the western end of the main road, Jalan Raya. Batubulan–Ubud **bemos** pass through Celuk, but the shops and workshops are spread out over a 3km stretch.

Sukawati

SUKAWATI is a lively market town and a major arts-and-crafts shopping destination. It's convenient for public transport as Ubud–Batubulan **bemos** stop in front of the town's **art market** (*pasar seni*), which trades every day from dawn till dusk inside a traditional two-storey building on the main road, Jalan Raya Sukawati. Here you'll find a tantalizing array of artefacts, paintings, fabrics, clothing and basketware, piled high on stalls that are crammed together. The scrum, and parking, are so bad that a second market, **Pasar Seni Guwang**, operates about 1km to the south, offering the same range of stuff but in slightly less frenetic surroundings. Bargaining is essential; both places are accustomed to busloads of tourists.

Sukawati is also known for its *wayang kulit*, or **shadow puppetry**, a traditional form of entertainment that's still popular across the island. The puppets (*wayang*) are made out of animal hide, perforated to let the light shine through in intricate patterns, and designed to traditional profiles that are instantly recognizable to Balinese audiences. To visit the workshops inside the homes of the makers look for signs on Jalan Padma (the road that runs east off Jalan Raya, one block south of the *pasar seni*) and Jalan Yudisthira, which runs parallel to Jalan Raya a few hundred metres to the east.

Batuan

A ribbon-like roadside development, **BATUAN** was the original home of the **Batuan style of painting** (see page 118) and is now a commercial centre for all styles of Balinese art.

Batuan is dominated by large **galleries** lining the main road, while smaller studios are tucked away in the traditional neighbourhoods to the west; look for "painter" signboards above their gateways. On the west side of the main road, the **I Wayan Bendi Gallery**, named after the most well-known exponent of the Batuan style of painting, displays some of the great man's work, while the sprawling **Dewa Putu Toris** (https://instagram.com/dewapututorisgallery), another large commercial enterprise, is also worth a visit; it's located 250m west off the southern end of the main road, in Tengah *banjar* – turn west at the *raksasa* (demon-giant) statue and follow the signs. Just before the gallery you'll pass Batuan's main temple, **Pura Desa-Pura Puseh** (dawn–dusk; donation), graced with appropriately elaborate gold-painted woodwork. At the northern limit of Batuan, a plump stone statue of a well-fed baby Brahma (officially known as Brahma Rare and unofficially as the **Fat Baby statue**) marks the Sakah turn-off to Blahbatuh and points east, while the main road continues north.

Mas and around

Long established as a major **woodcarving** centre as well as for traditional *topeng* and *wayang wong* masks, **MAS** is a rewarding place both to browse and to buy. However, be warned that it stretches 5km from end to end so exploration is gruelling, and its reputation means that prices are high.

Njana Tilem Museum

Jl. Raya Mas No. 162, approximately halfway along the Mas–Ubud road, about 2km north of the baby Brahma statue • Charge • https://instagram.com/njanatilemmuseum/

The **Njana Tilem Museum** is home to one of Bali's most famous woodcarving families. It displays the work of **Ida Bagus Njana** and his son, **Ida Bagus Tilem** (see page 135). On display are some of Njana and Tilem's finest originals from the 1940s to the 1980s along with other art from Tilem's private collection. There is a café here. You can also visit the workshop, shop and gallery at Jl. Raya Mas No. 116, still run by their descendants. The quality and craftsmanship here is breathtaking, and dexterity of the woodcarvers (who use their feet to grip the carved wood) astonishing. Once you've seen the best, you're ready to browse the street, but be aware you'll need to bargain hard.

Setia Darma House of Masks and Puppets

Jl Br Tegan Bingin, Kemenuh village to the east of Mas • free • http://maskandpuppets.com

The **Setia Darma House of Masks and Puppets** houses a huge collection of more than a thousand masks and 5700 puppets from Asia and Africa, with plenty from Bali and Indonesia, including a fine array of *topeng* masks and *wayang kulit* puppets. A good selection is on show in the glorious antique houses from Java that comprise the museum, and there are explanations in English. The only feasible way to get here is with your own transport; it's about a 5km cycle ride from the bottom of Jalan Monkey Forest in Ubud.

ARRIVAL AND DEPARTURE — MAS

By bemo Mas is served by all Ubud–Batubulan *bemos*, which zip through the village and will stop anywhere on request.

ACCOMMODATION AND EATING

Taman Harum Cottages In the compound of Tantra Gallery, Jl Raya Mas, southern Mas, 6km south of Ubud

THE MAS WOODCARVERS

Woodcarving, like all the arts in Bali, was traditionally used only to decorate temples and palaces, but the early twentieth century saw a growing interest in **secular subjects** and a rise in creativity. Artists began to court the burgeoning tourist market with carvings of nudes, lifelike animals and witty portraits, and a whole new genre evolved in just a few years.

By the mid-1930s, however, creativity and standards were slipping, so a group of influential artists and collectors established the **Pita Maha** foundation to encourage Bali's best carvers to be more experimental. One of these carvers was **Ida Bagus Njana**, from Mas, who from the 1930s to the 1960s produced works in a range of innovative styles, including abstract elongated human figures, erotic compositions of entwined limbs, and smooth, rounded portraits of voluptuously fat men and women. His son, **Ida Bagus Tilem**, was particularly known for his highly expressive pieces fashioned from contorted roots and twisted branches. Works by both artists are on show at the Njana Tilem Museum in Mas (see page 135). The Jati artist **I Nyoman Cokot** developed a "free-form" style that turned monstrous branches into weird, otherworldly creatures, while his son, **Ketut Nongos** lets his supernatural beings emerge from the contours of weatherworn logs and gnarled trunks.

The legacy of these trailblazers can be seen in almost every souvenir shop in Bali, many of which sell goods that suffer from the same lowering of artistic standards that those artists sought to combat. Few **contemporary woodcarvers** have attained the same status as the stars of the Pita Maha.

Monkey Forest, http://tamanharumcottages.com. The two-storey villas and suites are the best choice here, affording fine ricefield views from upstairs. All rooms have a/c and hot water and there is a pool, restaurant, spa and free transport to Ubud (20min). Non-guests are welcome to eat at the restaurant. $

Singapadu and around

2

If taking the alternate route north to Ubud from the south, continuing straight (north) from Batubulan the road passes through traditional villages, where daily life goes on the way it always has, and connects to Ubud at Sayan, west of Campuhan.

Charming **SINGAPADU** is a classic central-Bali settlement of house and temple compounds behind low walls. Some of Bali's most expert **mask-carvers** come from this village (see page 136), but there's little to buy locally. West of Singapadu are the Bali Bird and Bali Reptile parks and northwest of the parks are the awesome environmentally-sustainable *The Green School* and internationally-renowned *John Hardy jewellery workshop*.

Bali Bird Park and Bali Reptile Park

Jl. Serma Cok Ngurah Gambir, 5km northwest of Batubulan *bemo* terminal • Bali Bird Park http://balibirdpark.com • Bali Reptile Park http://balireptilepark.id • Charge; joint ticket for both parks; family packages available; book online for discounts • all *bemos* or buses between Batubulan and Ubud or Gianyar can drop you at the Singapadu/Celuk intersection from where it's about 400m west

Both the Bali Bird Park and the neighbouring Bali Reptile Park are great fun. Home to some thousand birds from 250 species, the **Bali Bird Park** is beautifully landscaped around enormous aviaries. Highlights include birds of paradise, bright scarlet egrets, the rhino hornbill and iridescent blue Javanese kingfishers. And you shouldn't miss the severely endangered Bali starling, the Owl House or the daily "free flight" bird shows.

The highlights at the **Bali Reptile Park** include the highly poisonous green tree pit viper, which is very common in Bali, an 8m-long reticulated python and Komodo dragons.

The Green School and Community

Jl. Raya Sibang Kaja, Sibang Kaja village, about 21km north of Sanur or 15min south of Ubud • Daily tours; book in advance • Charge, extended tour packages are available for community projects, some including lunch • http://greenschool.org • Accessible by motorcycle or bicycle (via Silakarang and Mambal Market) • Tour fees help fund their Local Scholars Programme

North from Sanur at Sibang Kaja, The **Green School** makes an enlightening excursion. Opened in 2008 by John and Cynthia Hardy, owners of a successful jewellery business and Bali residents for more than forty years, the school was established to educate pupils (aged 3–17) in emotional, spiritual and environmental issues alongside the more traditional subjects. Interesting from an **educational** point of view, the school is also fabulous architecturally as it consists entirely of open-sided **bamboo structures**; the

MASKS

Carved wooden **masks** play a crucial role in traditional Balinese dance-dramas. Many are treated as sacred objects, wrapped in holy cloth and stored in the temple when not being used, and given offerings before every public appearance. There's even an annual festival day for all masks and puppets, called Tumpek Wayang, at which actors and mask-makers honour their masks with offerings. **Singapadu** and **Mas** are the main centres of mask-making on Bali. Such is the power generated by certain masks that some mask-makers enter a trance while working, as do masked dancers.

Traditional masks fall into three categories: human, animal and supernatural. Most **human** masks are made for performances of the Topeng, literally "Masked Drama", while **animal** masks are generally inspired by characters from the Hindu epic Ramayana. Most sacred of all are the fantastical **Barong** and **Rangda** masks, worn in many dramas by the **mythical creatures** representing the forces of good and evil.

main bridge and multistorey Heart of School are quite simply works of art. There's a great café here too, open to all.

Tours of the school can be extended with visits to other parts of the Green School family. These include an intriguing **bamboo factory** nearby where bamboo, mostly from north Bali, is prepared for construction use (it's boiled, soaked in saltwater, washed, treated and dried) for export across the world. Alternatively, visit **KulKul Farm**, an impressive permaculture operation, or the **Kembali** recycling centre where new objects are made out of discarded materials. Undoubtedly the most spectacular part of the entire operation is the utterly astonishing **Green Valley** (http://greenvillagebali.com), a bamboo community consisting of thirteen dramatic bamboo houses built on a steep slope overlooking the jungle-clad Ayung river valley. Visitors get to enter a couple of these bamboo houses as part of a guided tour.

John Hardy Workshop & Showroom

Banjar Baturning No. 1 Mambal village • https://johnhardy.com/pages/visit-us-in-bali

About 4km north of The Green School is internationally-known, fabulous jewellery designer John Hardy's workshop and showroom. Set on 400 acres with low-impact bamboo architecture, you can tour the grounds to see the artisans at work in the open-air design centre and workshop using techniques handed down from ancient Balinese courts. Book ahead to join the management team, designers and artisans for lunch after the tour. You can also shop in the Kapal Boutique on the grounds. Tours generally by appointment but walk-in guests are welcome.

East of Ubud

Slicing through the region immediately **east of Ubud**, the sacred Petanu and Pakrisan rivers flow down from the Batur crater rim in parallel, framing a narrow strip of land imbued with great spiritual and historical importance. This 15km-long sliver has been settled since the Balinese Bronze Age, around 300 BC, and now has the biggest concentration of antiquities on Bali. From the stone sarcophagi and Bronze Age gong at **Pejeng** to the eleventh-century rock-hewn hermitage at **Goa Gajah** and fourteenth-century **Yeh Pulu reliefs**, these relics all lie within 7km of Ubud; Goa Gajah is crowded, while Yeh Pulu is often deserted. Access to this area by *bemo* is easy from Ubud – take any Gianyar-bound service – and similarly straightforward by bike or motorbike. This area also combines well with Tirta Empul and Gunung Kawi, 11km further north, and direct *bemos* connect the two.

Goa Gajah

Jl. Raya Goa Gajah, 3km east from Ubud's Jl Peliatan • Charge (includes sarong rental)

Thought to have been a hermitage for eleventh-century Hindu priests, **Goa Gajah** (Elephant Cave) is a popular tourist attraction largely because of its proximity to the main Ubud–Gianyar road. Besides the cave itself, there's a traditional bathing pool here and several ancient stone relics.

Descending the steps from the back of the car park, you get a good view of the elegant rectangular **bathing pool**. Such pools were usually built at holy sites, either at the source of a holy spring as at Tirta Empul or, like this one, near a sacred spot, so devotees could cleanse themselves before making offerings or prayers. The pool is now maintained for ornamental purposes only.

The carvings that trumpet the entranceway to the hillside cave are impressive, if difficult to distinguish. The **doorway** is a gaping mouth, framed by the upper jaw of a monstrous rock-carved head that's thought to represent either the earth god Bhoma or the widow-witch Rangda, or a hybrid of the two. It would have served both as a repeller of evil spirits and as a suggestion that on entering you were being swallowed up into a holier world. Early visitors interpreted it as an elephant's head, which is how the cave got its modern name.

Passing into the monster's mouth, you enter the dimly lit T-shaped **cave**, which served as meditation cells or living quarters for the priests or ascetics. Legend describes how the mythical giant Kebo Iwa gouged out the cells and the carvings here with his powerful fingernails in just one night.

Outside the cave, in a small pavilion to the left of the gateway, is a weatherworn statue of a woman surrounded by a horde of kids. This is the folk heroine **Men Brayut**, who has come to epitomize a mother's struggle against poverty (see page 155). Men Brayut is known as the goddess Hariti in Buddhist literature, and this statue, along with several other relics found nearby, has led archaeologists to believe the site has a **Buddhist** as well as a Hindu history.

ARRIVAL AND DEPARTURE — GOA GAJAH

By bemo An Ubud–Gianyar *bemo* will drop you at the entrance.

By car The car park borders the main Ubud–Gianyar road.

On foot You can walk between Yeh Pulu and Goa Gajah through the ricefields, but you'll need to hire a guide.

Yeh Pulu and around

East of Goa Gajah • Charge (including sarong rental)

The rock-cut panels amid the ricefields at **Yeh Pulu** are delightfully engaging, and yet the site is rarely visited. Chipped away from a cliff face, the 25m-long series of **carvings** are said to date back to the fourteenth or fifteenth century. They are thought by some historians to depict a five-part story and while the meaning of this story has been lost, it's still possible to make out some recurring characters and to speculate on the connections between them; local people, however, simply describe the carvings as showing daily activities from times past.

The small **spring** after which the site is named (*yeh* means "holy spring", *pulu* "stone vessel") rises close by the statue of Ganesh that is carved into the final niche and is sacred – hence the need for all visitors to wear temple dress. The Balinese believe that all water is a gift from the spirits, so whenever the spring fails special ceremonies are required to restore a harmonious flow.

ARRIVAL AND DEPARTURE — YEH PULU AND AROUND

By bemo If you're using the Ubud–Gianyar *bemo*, get off at the Yeh Pulu signs just east of Goa Gajah or west of the Bedulu crossroads, then walk the 1km south through Batulumbang to Yeh Pulu.

By car When driving, follow the same signs through Batulumbang until the road peters out, a few hundred metres above the stonecarvings.

On foot The prettiest approach to Yeh Pulu is on foot through the rice terraces behind Goa Gajah, but you'll need a guide – they wait for customers at both sites.

Pejeng

Inhabited since the Bronze Age, and considered a holy site ever since, **PEJENG** and its immediate environs harbour a wealth of religious antiquities, from carvings and rock-cut *candi* to bronze artefacts and massive stone statues. Some of these have been left in their original location, alongside riverbeds or buried in the paddy fields, while others have been housed in local temples. Several have also been carted off to museums, here and in Denpasar, Jakarta and Amsterdam. The remains have rather an esoteric appeal, and the area gets relatively few visitors. Pejeng's three main **temples** all lie within a few hundred metres of each other on the Bedulu–Tampaksiring road and are clearly signposted.

2

Pura Penataran Sasih

Bedulu–Tampaksiring Rd • free, but donation required; sarongs and sashes can be borrowed

Balinese people believe **Pura Penataran Sasih** to be a particularly sacred temple, because this is the home of the so-called Moon of Pejeng – hence the English epithet **Moon Temple**.

The moon in question is a **large bronze gong**, shaped almost like an hourglass, suspended high in its tower at the back of the temple compound. It probably dates from the Balinese Bronze Age, from sometime during the third century BC, and – at almost 2m long – is thought to be the largest such kettledrum ever cast. Legend tells how the gong once served as the wheel of a chariot that transported the moon through the skies, at which time the wheel shone just as brightly as the moon itself. The Balinese treat the Moon of Pejeng as sacred and make offerings to it whenever they need to move it.

The **temple** itself was once the most important in the area, and whatever the origins of the gong, it would have been used for the same purposes as the modern *kulkul* (bell-like drum) – to summon the Pejeng people to ceremonies, to announce war, and also to invite rain to fall.

Pura Pusering Jagat

100m south of Pura Penataran Sasih • free, but donation required; sarongs and sashes can be borrowed

Pura Pusering Jagat, the "Temple of the Navel of the World", is recognized for its elaborately carved 1m-high **stone jar**, used for storing holy water. Carved in the fourteenth century from a single block of sandstone, the jar's reliefs are thought to depict a scene from the Hindu myth "The Churning of the Sea of Milk", in which the gods and the demons compete for the chance to extract, distil and drink the elixir of immortal life.

Housed in a nearby pavilion is another significant icon, the 1m-high phallic lingam and its female receptacle, the yoni – this is an important shrine visited by many newlywed and infertile couples.

Pura Kebo Edan

200m south of Pura Pusering Jagat • free, but donation required; sarongs and sashes can be borrowed

Along with Pura Pusering Jagat, **Pura Kebo Edan** is also considered lucky for childless couples. The attraction here is the massive, lifelike phallus of the huge stone man, nicknamed the **Pejeng Giant**, who is nearly 4m tall and is depicted dancing on a prone female figure thought to represent the earth. He is said to possess six penises in all; aside from the one swinging out for all to see. His principal penis is pierced from front to back with a huge bolt-like pin, probably a realistic reference to an age-old Southeast Asian practice designed to increase women's sexual pleasure. The giant's identity is debatable; he is possibly Bhima, one of the chief characters from the Mahabharata, or the Hindu god Siwa, who harnessed enormous cosmic power whenever he danced.

Museum Arkeologi Gedung Arca

Jl. Raya Tampakisiring, 500m south of Pura Penataran Sasih • free, but a donation to your guide is expected

Pejeng's government-run **Museum Arkeologi Gedung Arca** (also called Gedung Arca) houses an eclectic assortment of artefacts found in the area, ranging from Paleolithic chopping tools to bronze bracelets and Chinese plates, though labels are limited.

The most interesting exhibits are the huge **sarcophagi**. These massive coffins, up to 3m long and fashioned from two fitted sections of hollowed-out stone, probably date back to about 300 BC. They were designed to hold adult skeletons (those placed in the smallest vessels would have been flexed at knees, hips and shoulders), and only the more important members of a community would have merited such an elaborate burial. Bronze jewellery, coins and weapons were found in some of the sarcophagi.

ARRIVAL AND DEPARTURE — PEJENG

By bemo Coming from Ubud, take a Gianyar-bound *bemo* to the Bedulu crossroads and then either wait for a Tampaksiring-bound *bemo*, or walk the 1km to the temples.

By bike The alternative route from Ubud – by bike or

motorbike – is the fairly scenic but severely undulating 5km-long back road that heads east from the Jl Raya Ubud/Jl Peliatan junction at the eastern edge of Ubud, passes the *Maya Ubud Resort & Spa*, and then zigzags through paddies and small villages before finally emerging at the market on the main road, just 25m north of Pura Penataran Sasih (turn right for the temple).

North of Ubud

2

All three major roads **north of Ubud** lead eventually to Gunung Batur and its huge crater. Whether you go via **Payangan** to the west, **Tegalalang** directly to the north, or **Tampaksiring** to the east, the villages and paddyfields along each route make for a pleasant drive. Distances are comparable, about 40km to Batur whichever way you go, but the most significant tourist sights are located along the most easterly route, around the Tampaksiring area.

Although there's little of specific interest on the **westerly route**, which takes you via Campuhan and Payangan, this is the quietest, least congested and prettiest of the three, and the best if you have **private transport**. The villages on the way are picturesque and in Payangan you pass the village's huge roadside banyan tree. The road eventually brings you to Pura Ulun Danu Batur on the Batur–Kintamani road, about 5km west of Penelokan.

The **central route** up to Gunung Batur begins at the eastern edge of Ubud, from the point where Jalan Raya Ubud intersects with Jalan Peliatan (if you're heading up here on a bicycle, you might prefer the more peaceful route that starts on central Ubud's Jalan Suweta).

ARRIVAL AND GETTING AROUND — NORTH OF UBUD

By bemo The most frequent and reliable *bemo* service running north from Ubud is on the central route via Tegalalang and Pujung; there are frequent *bemos* along the first section of the westerly route, as far as Payangan, but only some of them continue as far as Kintamani. For the easterly route via Tampaksiring, you'll need to change *bemos* at the Bedulu crossroads, just over 5km from the market in Ubud by road.

Tegalalang and Ceking

Seven kilometres north of Ubud on the middle road, **TEGALALANG** and its environs produce a wide range of **handicrafts** and **home accessories**, and the entire length of the 12km-long Ubud–Tegalalang–Pujung road is lined with shops displaying their wares and some attractive artefacts. On a clear morning the **views** become increasingly spectacular as you pass through Tegalalang, with Bali's greatest mountains looming majestically ahead – Gunung Batur to the north and Gunung Agung to the east – and rice terraces providing the classic foreground. Just north of Tegalalang is **CEKING**, which also has well-stocked souvenir shops along with several restaurants that make the most of the vistas.

Sebatu

North of Ceking, 18km along the main road you'll reach the Gunung Batur crater rim. Alternatively, a scenic back road takes you to **SEBATU**, 6km beyond, site of the uncrowded **Pura Gunung Kawi Sebatu** water-temple complex.

Pura Gunung Kawi Sebatu

Sebatu • Charge (including sarong rental)

Not to be confused with the quite different and more-visited Gunung Kawi in nearby Tampaksiring, **Pura Gunung Kawi Sebatu** is built on the site of holy springs, whose water is channelled into seven walled **bathing pools** – four for public bathing and three, at the spring itself, for special cleansing rituals. Many of the temple's wooden shrines and *bale* are carved with exquisite, brightly painted floral motifs.

Tampaksiring and around

The most **easterly route** from Ubud to the mountains takes you along the Bedulu–Penelokan road, passing through Pejeng before reaching **TAMPAKSIRING**, 11km further on, a fairly nondescript town that's the access point for nearby **Gunung Kawi** and **Tirta Empul**.

Gunung Kawi

An easy walk north of the market in Tampaksiring; access is signed via Jl Bayubrata, which heads east off the main road a few hundred metres north of the market • Charge, plus donation for sarong rental

Hewn from the rocky walls of the lush, enclosed valley of the sacred Pakrisan River, the eleventh-century royal "tombs" at **Gunung Kawi** occupy a lovely spot and are a lot quieter than most other archaeological sites, not least because you have to descend 315 steps to reach them.

The *candi* are huge reliefs, chiselled from the riverside cliff face to resemble temple facades. Originally the surface would have been decorated with plaster carvings, but now all that's left are the outlines of a single false door on each one. The most likely **theory** about these "tombs", is that they were erected as memorials to the eleventh-century king Anak Wungsu and his queens. The four Queens' Tombs are thought to be for Anak Wungsu's minor consorts, while the five Royal Tombs across the river probably honour the king and his four favourite wives. The slightly higher *candi* at the far left end is believed to be Anak Wungsu's. As there are no signs of bones or ashes in the *candi*, it appears that they weren't actual tombs, yet over the false door of each were found inscriptions (most of them unreadable) thought to be names or titles.

The complex also contains an extensive **cloister**, which probably accommodated the tombs' caretakers. On the way back to the steps you can branch off left through the fields to reach the so-called **Tenth Tomb**, a five-minute walk away. Believed to have been erected in memory of an important member of the royal household, this *candi* stands on its own, framed only by rock-cut cloisters.

Tirta Empul

Signposted off the main Tampaksiring–Kintamani road, about 500m north of the turn-off to Gunung Kawi • Charge • you should be able to charter a *bemo* in the market

Balinese from every corner of the island make pilgrimages to **Tirta Empul** to spiritually cleanse themselves and cure their physical ailments by bathing in the **holy springs**. Legend describes how the springs were first tapped by the god Indra during his battle with the evil Mayadanawa. Indra's spring was named Tirta Empul, and has been considered the holiest in Bali ever since the tenth century, if not longer. A **temple** was built around the springs and the complex is now an extremely popular destination, both for Balinese and foreign tourists.

The **bathing pools** are sunk into the ground of the temple's outer courtyard, the water from the springs in the inner sanctuary. Men, women and priests have segregated sections in which to immerse themselves, though most just splash their faces. However, for pregnant women and anyone who's just recovered from a long illness, Tirta Empul is one of three places in which they must bathe for a special ritual called *melukat*. This ceremony requires immersion in the waters of each of Bali's three holiest springs: the "holy waters of the mountain" at Tirta Bungkah, the "holy springs of the plain" here at Tirta Empul and the "holy springs of the sea" at Tirta Selukat at Pura Dalem Pingit.

ARRIVAL AND DEPARTURE — TAMPAKSIRING AND AROUND

By bemo Gianyar–Bedulu–Tampaksiring *bemos* terminate near the market in the centre of the long settlement. There's no public *bemo* service between Tampaksiring and Penelokan, about 20km north, but you should be able to charter one.

East Bali

PRAYERS AT THE PURA BESAKIH TEMPLE

East Bali

Eastern Bali is dominated both physically and spiritually by Gunung Agung's majestic, picture-perfect volcanic cone. The Balinese orientate their villages and homes towards this holy mountain and after a few days in the region, you'll probably fall under its spell too. Immediately beneath its awesome bulk unfurls a landscape of dense forests, narrow river valleys and sweeping rice terraces, making for a scenic drive or hike, whichever direction you travel in. By contrast, the land in the far east around the coastal centres of Amed and Tulamben is much drier, and their dark-sand beaches are drawing ever-increasing numbers of visitors.

Most of east Bali comes under the administration of **Karangasem regency**, where villagers still follow a traditional way of life, mostly living off the land or from the sea. There are tourist centres, but on a far smaller scale than in the south, and the lack of crowds and refreshingly unadulterated green vistas are a large part of the east's appeal. With Bali being relatively small, you can base yourself in this part of the island without missing any of the highlights.

The main tourist hubs are along the coasts. **Candidasa** is a low-key resort with good facilities and handy transport connections. Nearby, funky little **Padang Bai** is a port for boats to the Gili Islands and Lombok, and also makes a decent base in its own right. The biggest-hitting **dive centres**, though, are on the east coast, at **Amed**, which has lots of accommodation and plenty of reef close to shore, nearby **Tulamben**, site of an accessible shoreside wreck and Kubu, where there's a relatively new reef-building wreck.

Inland, **Gunung Agung** and its Mother Temple, **Besakih**, are major attractions. Climbing this most magnificent of volcanoes is a significant challenge, but a rewarding one. The temple complex itself, however, can disappoint, as much for its persistent touts as for its sometimes misty outlook.

You might find some of the region's other temples more satisfying, especially the venerable Pura Kehen in **Bangli**, with its splendid sculptures. The east also has a rich artistic heritage associated with its ancient courts: **Semarapura** and the nearby **Kamasan painter's village** keep the traditional art of classical *wayang* painting alive, while the unique palace architecture at Puri Agung Karangasem in **Amlapura** is impressive. In the western part of East Bali near Ubud, **Gianyar** is the capital of the regency by the same name and is justly known for its beautiful *endek* weaving. And there's even more exquisite textile art, in the form of the rare double ikat, produced at **Tenganan**, a traditional Bali Aga village that's home to descendants of the early inhabitants of Bali.

For classic rice-terrace vistas and village walks, it's hard to beat a stay in **Tirtagangga** or **Sidemen**, both offering attractive accommodation in tranquil settings.

Gianyar and around

An immensely powerful kingdom from the late seventeenth century, Gianyar became a **Dutch protectorate** in 1900 and, being spared the depredations wreaked on other Balinese kingdoms, flourished as a centre for the arts. The district capital, also called **GIANYAR**, is still known for its handsome *endek* weaving, and for its delicious roasted suckling pig (*babi guling*) served at the night market, both of which merit a detour. But the town sees few tourists, being far outshone by its

WATER PALACE OF TIRTA GANGGA

Highlights

❶ **Gunung Agung** Bali's highest and most important mountain looms majestically over every eastern district – everyone can enjoy the sight, and if you're seriously fit you can climb it. See page 156

❷ **Sidemen** There's great accommodation and classic rice-terrace scenery in this small upland village. It's also well-placed for temple visits, rafting and hiking. See page 160

❸ **Padang Bai** A small port town that has long been a lively backpacker hub, it's fringed by pretty cove beaches. See page 162

❹ **Tenganan** A unique village inhabited by Bali's aboriginal people whose arts, rituals and form of Hinduism are distinctively theirs. See page 169

❺ **Tirtagangga** Delight in glorious mountain and rice-paddy views, an attractive water palace and gentle treks through typical Balinese countryside. See page 174

❻ **The Amed Coast** A dramatic coastline with steep cliffs, black-sand beaches, small bays packed with fishing boats, views of two volcanoes, and prime diving and snorkelling just offshore. See page 177

HIGHLIGHTS ARE MARKED ON THE MAP ON PAGE 146

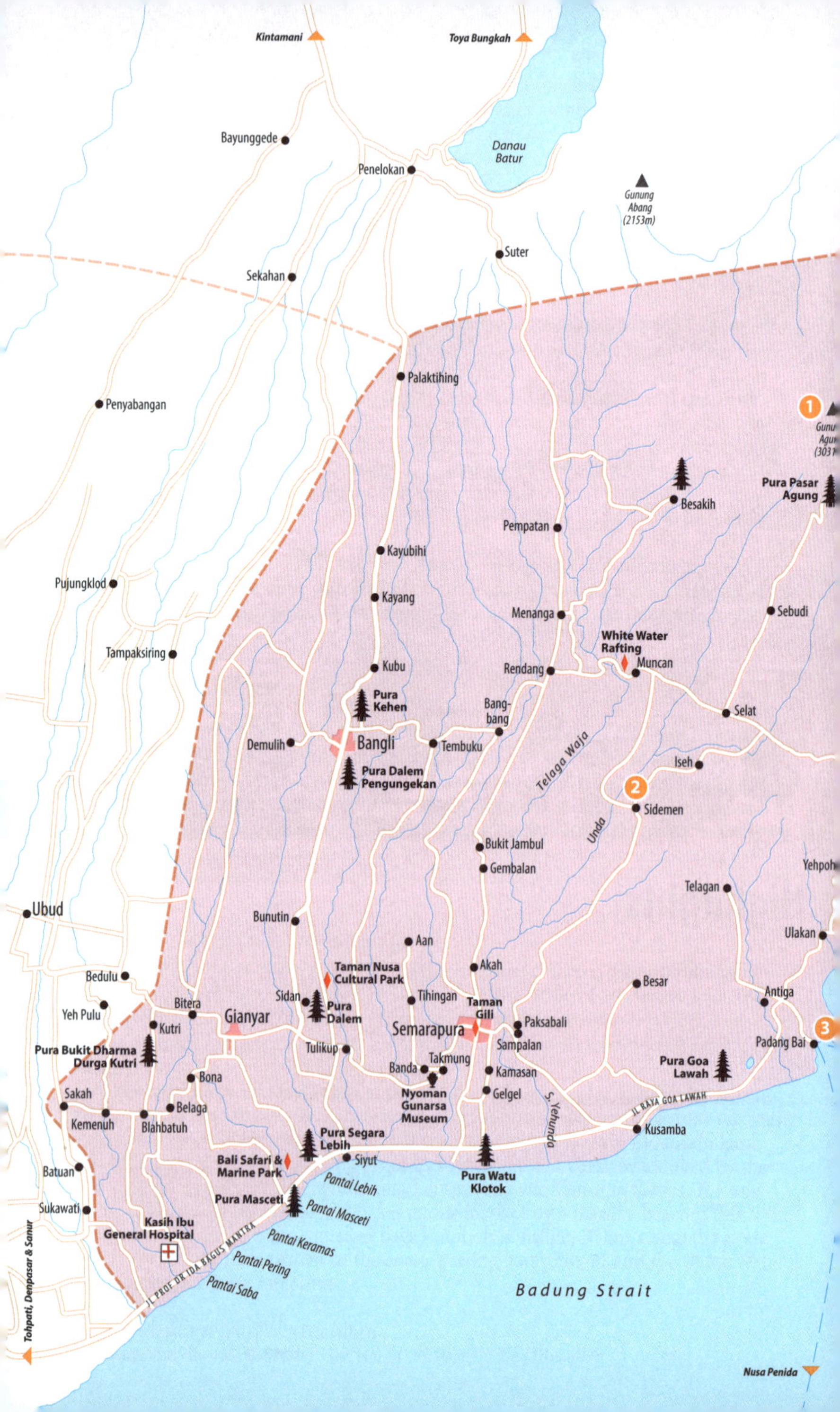

Kintamani
Toya Bungkah
Bayunggede
Danau Batur
Penelokan
Gunung Abang (2153m)
Suter
Sekahan
Palaktihing
Penyabangan
1
Pura Pasar Agung
Besakih
Pempatan
Kayubihi
Pujungklod
Kayang
Menanga
Sebudi
Tampaksiring
White Water Rafting
Muncan
Kubu
Rendang
Pura Kehen
Bang-bang
Selat
Demulih
Bangli
Tembuku
Telaga Waja
Iseh
Pura Dalem Pengungekan
2
Sidemen
Unda
Bukit Jambul
Gembalan
Telagan
Ubud
Bunutin
Aan
Ulakan
Akah
Taman Nusa Cultural Park
Besar
Bedulu
Sidan
Tihingan
Taman Gili
Antiga
Yeh Pulu
Bitera
Gianyar
Pura Dalem
Semarapura
Paksabali
Kutri
Sampalan
3
Padang Bai
Pura Bukit Dharma Durga Kutri
Tulikup
Takmung
Banda
Kamasan
Pura Goa Lawah
Bona
Nyoman Gunarsa Museum
Sakah
Belaga
Gelgel
S. Yehunda
Jl Raya Goa Lawah
Kemenuh
Blahbatuh
Pura Segara Lebih
Kusamba
Bali Safari & Marine Park
Siyut
Batuan
Pantai Lebih
Pura Watu Klotok
Pura Masceti
Pantai Masceti
Sukawati
Kasih Ibu General Hospital
Pantai Keramas
Pantai Pering
Jl Prof Dr Ida Bagus Mantra
Pantai Saba
Badung Strait
Tohpati, Denpasar & Sanur
Nusa Penida

EAST BALI
Baturinggit, Singaraja
Kubu
JL KUBU
Tulamben
Amed
Congkang
Jemeluk
SEE 'THE AMED COAST' MAP
Culik
Bunutan
Lipah Beach
Lean
Selang
Banyuning
Bangle
Aas
Kusambi
Lahangan Sweet Viewpoint
Gunung Lempuyang (1058m)
Gunung Seraya (1175m)
Abang
Ngis
Tista
Ababi
Pura Lempuyang Luhur
Taman Tirtagangga
Tirtagangga
Kelompok Karya Sari Warna Alam
Jungutan
Budakling
Seraya
Lombok Strait
Sibetan
Bebandem
Amlapura
Puri Agung Karangasem
Kastala
Bungaya
Seraya Barat
Ujung
Taman Sukaseda (Ujung Water Palace)
Bakung
Tenganan
Asak
Jasri
Manggis
Perasi
Pasir Putih
Bugbug
Buitan
Candidasa
Pura Gumang
Mendira Beach
Pura Candidasa
Gili Biaha
Gili Mimpang
Gili Tepekong
Gili Trawangan & Lombok
Gili Islands, Lembar & Senggigi (Lombok)
HIGHLIGHTS
1 Gunung Agung
2 Sidemen
3 Padang Bai
4 Tenganan
5 Tirtagangga
6 The Amed Coast
N
0
5
kilometres

much more famous neighbour, Ubud, just 10km to the west. There are several **craft villages** and worthwhile **temples** around Gianyar, but the region's biggest attractions are the **Bali Safari and Marine Park** by the coast to the south of town and the **Taman Nusa Cultural Park** to the north.

Pura Bukit Dharma Durga Kutri

Jl. Raya Buruan, Kutri • donation • 0361 947 873 • Coming from Gianyar, the easiest way to get here is on a *bemo* bound for Denpasar's Batubulan terminal

Kutri, 4km west of Gianyar, is the site of an interesting temple, **Pura Bukit Dharma Durga Kutri**. Head up the 80-step stone staircase from the temple's inner courtyard to the top of the hill, where you'll find the statue of the six-armed goddess **Durga** slaughtering a bull and brandishing a conch shell, flames, bow and arrow, javelin and shield. Many people believe that the carving actually depicts **Mahendradatta**, the alter ego of the legendary widow-witch Rangda (see page 151), and that this is her burial place. An unusual way of visiting Kutri is to walk there from the Yeh Pulu rock carvings east of Ubud (3–5hr), for which you'll need a guide.

The craft villages

South of Gianyar town at Bona, villagers produce baskets and other items woven from rattan, palm and alang-alang grass. At Belaga, the work of bamboo furniture craftsmen lines both sides of the road. **Blahbatuh** village, 5km south of Kutri, is best known for its exceptional gong makers. At **Kemenuh**, west of Blahbatuh, the speciality is **woodcarving**, and there are workshops all along the road to Goa Gajah, further west.

Pura Dalem Sidan

Jl. Sidan-Astina Timur No. 99, Sidan • Only opened on request • Donation • Temple is 2km east of Gianyar then 1km north up the main Gianyar–Bangli road and served by *bemos* between the two towns

Durga, consort of Hindu god Siva, makes an especially gruesome appearance at the **Pura Dalem Sidan**. This temple of the dead, dating from the seventeenth century, drips with grisly carvings and statues of the terrible Durga squashing babies, along with depictions of the punishments that await evildoers in the afterlife – which

TRADITIONAL TEXTILES

Traditional **fabrics** are still fashionable for clothes and furnishings in Indonesia and continue to be hand-woven in some areas of Bali and Lombok. They also have **ritual functions**, with specific weaves used in certain ceremonies, such as the striped *bebali* produced in Pacung. Hand-woven textiles are widely available for sale across Bali and Lombok and are often displayed to their best advantage on the special **carved wooden hangers** sold in some ikat and souvenir shops.

IKAT AND SONGKET

Easily recognized by the fuzzy-edged motifs it produces, **ikat** weaving is common throughout Indonesia, woven on backstrap, foot-pedal or, increasingly, on semi-automatic looms, from either silk, cotton or rayon. The word ikat derives from the Indonesian verb "to tie", and the technique is essentially a sophisticated tie-dye process. Bali is quite unusual in favouring **weft-ikat**, or **endek**, in which the weft yarn (the threads running across the fabric) is tie-dyed into the finished design before the weaving begins. This produces the distinctive blurred edge to the predominantly geometric and abstract designs. **Gianyar** has several excellent *endek* showrooms and workshops (see page 150).

Warp-ikat (in which the threads that run lengthwise are tie-dyed) is more common elsewhere in Indonesia, including on Sumba, where the textiles typically feature bold humanoid motifs and images of real and mythological creatures, and several other small, eastern islands. They are widely sold in Bali's resorts.

Warp- and weft-ikats are complicated enough, but **double ikat**, or **geringsing**, involves dyeing both the warp and the weft threads into their final designs before they're woven together; a double-ikat sarong can take five years to complete. There are just three areas in the world where this method is practised – India, Japan and **Tenganan** in eastern Bali. Not surprisingly, *geringsing* is exceedingly expensive to buy, and has acquired an important ritual significance. At first glance, *geringsing* can look similar to Flores island's warp-ikat, because both use the same dye combinations, but the Tenganan motifs have a highly charged spiritual meaning, and their geometric and floral designs are instantly recognizable to the Balinese.

Embroidered weavings using a supplementary-weft weaving is known as **songket**. This traditionally uses metallic gold and silver yarn to add tapestry-like motifs of birds, butterflies and flowers onto very fine silk, however, today gold and silver-coloured threads and rayon are often used. *Songket* sarongs are worn on ceremonial occasions, and dancers wear *songket* sashes. **Sukarara** in Lombok is the best place to see *songket* being woven.

BATIK AND PERADA

Despite being more common than ikat for everyday and formal wear on Bali and Lombok, nearly all **batik** fabric is imported from Java. The batik process involves drawing patterns on the fabric in dye-resistant wax, then dyeing and re-waxing as necessary to create complex multicoloured designs that look the same on both sides. Screen-printed batik is generally inferior as the dyes don't penetrate to the reverse side.

A special type of batik called **perada** is used for ceremonial outfits and ornaments. This is the gold-painted cloth that you'll see fashioned into temple umbrellas, adorning some sacred statues, and worn in the Legong and other traditional dances. The background colour is nearly always bright green or yellow, sometimes purple, and onto this is painted or stamped a symbolic design (usually birds or flowers) in either gold-leaf paint or, more commonly today, a bronze- or gold-coloured pigment.

include having your head sawn off and being boiled in a vat. As the donation to enter can be quite high, you may want to admire the external carvings, which are also impressive.

GIANYAR'S TEXTILE WORKSHOPS

The outstanding choice and quality of the hand-woven cotton and silk **endek** (tie-dyed weft ikat) produced in the **textile workshops** on the western outskirts of Gianyar town itself are well worth the trip. You'll need about 2.25m for a sarong. You can also buy *endek* shirts, handbags, cushion covers and more. The best-known **showroom** is Setia Cap Cili (Jl Ciung Wanara-Gianyar No. 7, 0361 943 409), which has a dyeing and weaving workshop on-site; over twenty weavers are employed here.

Taman Nusa Cultural Park

Jl Taman Bali, Banjarangka • Charge • http://taman-nusa.com • Located along a minor road leading to Bangli, Taman Nusa is signposted off the Gianyar-Semarapura road

3

The **Taman Nusa Cultural Park** is an impressive open-air museum with more than sixty traditional houses from across the nation and iconic Indonesian buildings overlooking a picturesque gorge. Most buildings are reconstructions including the steep-roofed Sumba houses, while originals include the Minangkabau homes and the Nias house with its earthquake-proof beams. Don't miss the Honai, beehive-like huts of Papua's Dani tribe or the Minangkabau house with its elaborate carvings. You'll also see models of the Dutch-era Kota train station in Jakarta and the Buddhist Borobudur temple in central Java. Tours by enthusiastic guides are included in the price, and there are music and dance shows, plus a couple of museums displaying crafts. You'll find two restaurants and cafés scattered throughout the park.

The coast south of Gianyar

Gianyar's **south coast** is fringed with long, black-sand beaches and offers some fine views of Gunung Agung. For years this area was a surfer haven, but a four-lane coastal highway offering speedy connections to Sanur and the south provided opportunities for development. If you're headed east there are several stops you might wish to include in your plans, most of which are located along Jalan ByPass Prof Dr Ida Bagus Mantra unless otherwise indicated.

Pantai Saba

The **Flamingo Bali Beach Club** (https://flamingobeachclub.com) is family-friendly with kids' playground and menu, but adults can relax in the infinity pool facing the beach or on a bean bag sipping on a cocktail. If more exercise is in order, at Bali Horse Riding (http://balihorseriding.net) you can gallop on the beach at sunrise, attend a stable birthday party or enrol the young ones in riding lessons. Of particular interest to those in need is that Saba is home to the **Kasih Ibu General Hospital** (http://kih.co.id) which has one of only two hyperbaric recompression chambers in Bali.

Pantai Keramas

This slim dark-sand beach is one of the best surf spots on this shoreline, with a consistent right-hander that peels over a reef, creating some of the best tubes in Bali. For years Keramas was something of an in-the-know secret, but the arrival of the **Komune Bali Resort**, with its spotlights to enable night surfing, has put Keramas on the map. At **Sababay Winery** (http://sababaywinery.com) you can enjoy a guided winery tour, wine tasting or a picnic lunch experience (charge).

Pura Masceti

Daily 7am–6pm • Charge

RANGDA, QUEEN OF THE WITCHES

Sporting a mane of unkempt hair, tusk-like teeth, a tongue that hangs to her knees and enormous, pendulous breasts, **Rangda**, Queen of the Witches, is a terrifying spectacle wherever you encounter her. And she is everywhere: on stage in religious dance-dramas, as a larger-than-life statue at temples, in paintings and on textiles. To the Balinese, she represents evil, death and destruction.

It's possible that Rangda is based on a real woman, **Mahendradatta**, a Javanese princess who married the Balinese prince Udayana and bore him a son, Airlangga, in 991 AD. According to legend, Udayana later banished Mahendradatta for practising witchcraft. When Udayana died and Airlangga inherited his kingdom, Mahendradatta, now an angry *rangda* (widow) for having been exiled, used her powers to call a plague upon her son's kingdom. Airlangga duly dispatched a troop of soldiers to kill her, but they failed, despite stabbing her in the heart. In desperation, Airlangga asked for assistance from the holy man Empu Bharadah, who used Rangda's book of magic both to restore her victims to life and to destroy the witch by turning her own magic on herself. Both Mahendradatta and Empu Bharadah are thought to be associated with Bali's Mother Temple, Besakih.

The Rangda story is widely enacted across Bali, most commonly during the **Barong** and **Calonarang** dramas. She always speaks in the ancient Kawi language, spiced with plenty of grunts and cackles. Even in performances the figure of Rangda is believed to have remarkable powers, and prayers precede each show to protect the actors from the evil forces they are invoking.

3

One of several important **temples** along the coast, the ornate **Pura Masceti** is the directional temple, or *kayangan jagat*, for the south. The setting on the coast is lovely, and regular festivals see dozens of worshippers setting off for purification rituals on the beach.

Bali Safari and Marine Park

1.5km east of Pura Masceti, 7km southeast of Gianyar and 15km east of Sanur, just off the coastal highway • Charge, kids under 3 free • http://balisafarimarinepark.com

The landscaped grounds at **Bali Safari and Marine Park** draw several thousand visitors a day who come to see animals from Indonesia, India and Africa (white tigers, Komodo dragons, hippos and Sumatra tigers among them). There's also an aquarium, a water park, the "Bali Agung" theatrical extravaganza, animal rides and shows. If animals being treated as photo opportunities doesn't bother you, it's worthwhile spending an entire day here.

"Safari" buses take you around the park, passing the animal enclosures. There's a (somewhat dated) water park here too where you can cool off and take in a slide or two. It's an expensive day out, so check the various packages available (the buffet lunch offered is poor); some of these include a short elephant ride. The park is wheelchair friendly.

Pantai Lebih

Black-sand **Pantai Lebih** is crowded with fishing boats and is popular for its dozen or so *warungs* serving **fresh seafood** (most are open daily until 10pm). Menu highlights include the local speciality *sate languan* (fish grilled with green coconut leaves, spices and brown sugar), *ikan bakar* (charcoal-grilled fish in banana leaf) and *ikan pepes* (fish steamed in banana leaves).

Pura Segara Lebih

Jl. Raya Pantai Lebih • Donation

Across the highway from the sea, Lebih's **Pura Segara** (Sea Temple) is associated with magical forces, and holds an annual ceremony to placate the demon Ratu Gede Mas Macaling, who is believed to bring disease and ill fortune from Nusa Penida across the Badung Strait.

Pura Watu Klotok

Jl Pantai Klotok • Donation

On its namesake beach, **Pura Watu Klotok** is one of four highly revered state temples in Klungkung district. The sacred statues from the Mother Temple, Besakih, are brought here during the annual cleansing *melasti* ritual. The temple has a spectacular outlook over a black-sand beach towards Lombok and is a fine location to witness sunrise.

ARRIVAL AND INFORMATION — GIANYAR AND AROUND

By bemo Gianyar town has useful *bemo* services to and from Ubud and Denpasar's Batubulan terminal, both of which terminate on the corner of Jl Ngurah Rai-Gianyar and Jl Jata.

Destinations Amlapura (1hr 20min); Bangli (20min); Batur (40min); Blahbatuh (30min); Candidasa (1hr); Denpasar (Batubulan terminal; 1hr); Semarapura (20min); Ubud (20min).

3

ACCOMMODATION AND EATING — SEE MAP PAGE 148

Babi Guling Diirr Jl. Bukit Jati, Gianyar town; https://instagram.com/babigulingdirr. This small local establishment serves up authentic value-for-money Balinese food, including the excellent traditional pork *guling*. $

Keramas Aero Park Jl. ByPass Prof Dr Ida Bagus Mantra Km.28; https://instagram.com/keramasaeropark_official. If you fancy dining in a Boeing 737-400 with bird's eye views of ricefields and sea without ever leaving the ground, here's your chance. Inside, feast on a Mozzarella Chicken Steak, sirloin or seafood, or outside sip cocktails and grab a pizza at the Ground Bar where there's a playground and a kid's menu. $$

Keramas Surf Camp Pantai Keramas; https://instagram.com/keramassurf. Steps from the beach, bordering ricefields, this popular surfers' hangout is run by a friendly family and has attractive a/c bungalows with outdoor bathrooms, a beer garden and restaurant. $

Komune Resort & Beach Club Pantai Keramas; http://komuneresorts.com. Sleek, chic surf lodge with an oceanfront location, yoga sessions, spa, a cool pool, healthy-eating cafe and lights to enable night surfing (book ahead). Accommodation is very stylish and offers all mod cons. $$–$$$

Bangli and around

North of Gianyar **BANGLI**, the capital of Bangli Regency and one of Bali's nine kingdoms until 1907, is a cool and spacious market town whose extravagantly carved **temples** are well worth making the effort to visit. In the pleasant town centre you can shop and eat at the **market**, which mainly sells agricultural produce and crafts from the surrounding villages, or try regional snacks at the small but lively night market with several food stalls just south of the Trimurti statue. During the day, the market south of the Trimurti statue is also worth browsing for street food. The road heading north from Bangli leads to Gunung Batur volcano.

Pura Kehen

Jl Sriwijaya No. 8, 1.5km north of the centre • Donation

Bangli's most notable sight is the ancient **Pura Kehen**, a gem among Bali's temples that is thought to have been founded in 1206. Rising in **terraces**, its mossy stairway is lined with statues of human and mythical creatures, led by a pair of elephants at the base, and crowned by a leering Bhoma above regal red-and-gold carved doors. In the **outer courtyard** a massive banyan tree hides a *kulkul* tower among its branches, and a small compound, guarded by *naga* under an old frangipani tree, houses a stone that reportedly glowed with fire when the site of the temple was decided. The **inner**

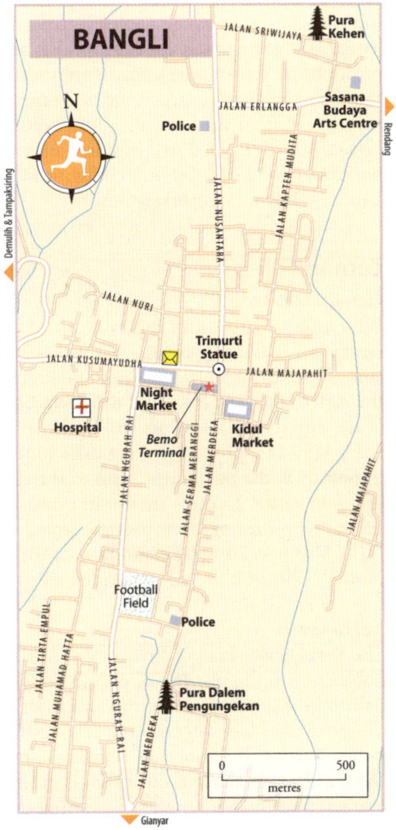

courtyard contains an eleven-roofed *meru* dedicated to Siwa (Shiva), and other shrines dedicated to mountain gods.

Across the road, the lavishly restored **Pura Penyimpenan** (Temple for Keeping Things) contains three ancient bronze inscriptions (*prasasti*) dating from the ninth century, which suggests Pura Kehen could be much older than some believe.

Pura Dalem Pengungekan

Jl Merdeka, 1.5km south of the centre • Donation

From Pura Kehen it's a pleasant walk downhill to the temple of the dead, **Pura Dalem Pengungekan**, at the opposite end of town, where exuberant carvings cover the outside walls. Depicting the fate of souls in hell and heaven as witnessed by Bhima, one of the Pandawa brothers (see page 311), the carvings depict a riot of knives, pleading victims, flames and decapitated bodies. There are also appearances by the widow-witch Rangda and stories of Siwa (Shiva), Ganesh, Uma and Rakshasha.

ARRIVAL AND INFORMATION BANGLI AND AROUND

By bemo Bangli is served by *bemos* from Gianyar and is also on the Denpasar (Batubulan) to Singaraja (Penarukan) route.

Destinations Denpasar (1hr 30min); Gianyar (20min); Singaraja (2hr 15min).

Banks and exchange There are ATMs near the Trimurti statue on Jl Nusantara.

Semarapura and around

Well known as a showcase for classical Balinese art, Klungkung's district capital, **SEMARAPURA** (also frequently referred to as **KLUNGKUNG**), makes an enjoyable day out. The highlight is the rare painted ceiling of the **Kerta Gosa** pavilion inside the **Taman Gili** palace gardens. It overlooks the main crossroads marked by the Kanda Pat Sari statue, guarding the four cardinal directions. The lively **market** opposite is also a fun browse and there's more classical art on the outskirts: in **Kamasan**, home to modern-day artists working in the age-old *wayang* style, and at the **Nyoman Gunarsa Museum** (Museum Seni Lukis Klasik), which houses Bali's best collection of historic Kamasan art as well as its namesake's contemporary paintings.

Brief history

Semarapura became a centre of the arts towards the end of the seventeenth century, when Bali's Majapahit rulers relocated here from their **court** at Gelgel, 4km to the south (Gelgel was believed to have fallen under a curse). The political power of the Majapahits was by then on the wane, with breakaway kingdoms such as Gianyar rising to prominence, but their sophisticated artistic and literary culture endured, its greatest legacy being the classical paintings that adorn the Kerta Gosa and Bale Kambung pavilions in Semarapura's palace grounds. The court remained at Semarapura until the early twentieth century and was one of the last two strongholds against the Dutch invasion. Rather than submit to the colonial power, on April 28, 1908, Semarapura's *dewa agung* (king) led two hundred members of his family and court in the traditional **puputan** (ritual suicide), marching into the line of fire. A monument opposite the Taman Gili commemorates this.

Taman Gili

Jl Untung Surapati • Charge

Built around 1686, and largely destroyed by fighting in 1908, **Taman Gili**, or "Island Gardens", is all that remains of the original **Semarapura palace**. It's an attractive complex of lily ponds, pavilions and graceful statues, and its indisputable highlight is the superb painted ceiling of the **Kerta Gosa** pavilion. This is one of Bali's two examples of *wayang*-style classical art still in situ and was painted by artists from nearby Kamasan (see page 118), probably in the early nineteenth century. Despite its historical importance, the pavilion is open to the elements and located next to the city's busiest junction so the pictures are not in prime condition, though they have undergone several major restorations over the years.

The **Museum Daerah Semarapura** at the back of the Taman Gili grounds contains a motley collection including *kris* (daggers), textiles and Barong costumes.

Kerta Gosa

The **Kerta Gosa** (Hall of Justice) was a criminal court of Bali's highest king, which adds poignancy to the pictures of gruesome punishments on the ceiling. It has nine levels of paintings. **Level one**, nearest the floor, shows scenes from an Indonesian version of the *Thousand and One Nights*, in which a girl, Tantri, weaves tales night after night. **Levels two and three** illustrate the "Bhima Swarga" story (part of the Mahabharata epic), and the punishments meted out to souls in the afterlife, such as having your intestines extracted through your anus for farting in public. Bhima is the aristocratic-looking chap with a moustache, tidy hair, a big club and a long nail on his right thumb. **Level four** shows the "Sang Garuda", the story of the Garuda's search for *amerta*, the

THE TALE OF MEN AND PAN BRAYUT

Blessed – or lumbered – with eighteen children, **Men and Pan Brayut** ("Mother and Father Brayut") may be desperately poor, but their scrapes are typical of any Balinese family. So goes the popular Balinese folk tale that has inspired countless artists, including the mural painters of Semarapura's Bale Kambang hall, the Ubud artist I Gusti Nyoman Lempad (see page 113) and the stonecarvers of Pura Dalem Jagaraga, near Singaraja (see page 206). The fullest account of the couple's story is related in an **epic poem** called *Gaguritan Brayut*, housed in Singaraja's Gedong Kirtya library (see page 204).

According to one version of the **story**, the reason that Men Brayut has so many children is her uncontrollable appetite. When hungry, she gets irritable and rows with her husband, Pan Brayut. After fighting, the couple always make up in the time-honoured fashion – hence the constantly expanding clan. Another version puts the size of the family down to Pan Brayut's insatiable desire for his wife, which he acts upon regardless of place or circumstance.

Men Brayut is both full-time mother and part-time weaver, so her husband does most of the domestic chores; these scenes from daily life – cleaning the yard, cooking ceremonial dishes – feature in many paintings. Eventually, after all their hard parenting, Men and Pan Brayut **renounce the material world** and enter a retreat (still common practice, especially among elderly Balinese men), leaving their home and its contents to be divided among the children.

Although illustrations of the Brayut story always emphasize its **Hindu** elements, with lots of scenes showing offerings and temple ceremonies, Men Brayut is also associated with **Buddhist** lore. In this mythology she is said to have evolved from an evil ogress named Hariti who spent her time devouring children until she converted to Buddhism and became not only a protector of children but also a fertility goddess. Statues of Men Brayut in her Hariti manifestation can be found at Goa Gajah, near Ubud, and at the temple in Candidasa.

water of life. **Level five** is the *palalindon*, predicting the effects of earthquakes on life and agriculture, while **levels six and seven** continue the "Bhima Swarga" story. **Level eight** is the "Swarga Roh", which details the rewards the godly will receive in heaven; unfortunately, it's so far above your head that it's hard to see whether good behaviour is worth it. **Level nine**, the *lokapala*, right at the top, shows a lotus surrounded by four doves symbolizing good luck, enlightenment and salvation.

Bale Kambung

Near Kerta Gosa, **Bale Kambung** (Floating Pavilion), in the middle of the lotus pond, is the other example of in situ Kamasan-style paintings and was the venue for royal tooth-filing ceremonies (see page 321) and other rituals. Its ceiling is slightly less finely drawn; six levels of paintings cover Balinese astrology, the tales of Pan Brayut and, closest to the top, the adventures of Satusoma, a Buddhist saint.

Kamasan

As the home of the original nineteenth-century Kerta Gosa artists, and the source of subsequent generations of restorers and commercial artists, **KAMASAN**, one or two kilometres southeast of Semarapura, has given its name to the classical school of art with which it is so closely associated. Numerous artists have open studios in their homes here, particularly in the **Banjar Sanging** neighbourhood. Among the best-known local names here are **I Nyoman Mandra** and **Ni Made Suciarmi**. Most of the work on sale is either inexpensive small cloth pictures or reproductions of traditional calendars, depicting mythological stories in muted classical colours made with natural pigments. Kamasan's gold- and silversmiths are located nearby in Banjar Pande Mas.

Nyoman Gunarsa Museum

Jl. Pertigaan Banda No. 1, Takmung, 5km south of Semarapura, just beyond Takmung village on the Gianyar road • Charge • 0366 22255 • Any Amlapura–Gianyar *bemo* will drop you outside

Try not to be discouraged by the dilapidated carbuncle of a building or the lack of air conditioning: the **Nyoman Gunarsa Museum** is well worth a lengthy browse. The big attraction is the large and rather special collection of Kamasan **cloth paintings**, some of which probably date back to the eighteenth century. Highlights include several 10m-long *ider ider* – ceremonial banners depicting mythological tales. Labels are informative and the art is supplemented by elaborate antique doors, carved gamelan ornaments and examples of *wayang kulit* puppets that echo the origins of the classical style. There are several paintings by the museum founder, **Nyoman Gunarsa**, one of Bali's foremost modern artists.

ARRIVAL AND INFORMATION — SEMARAPURA AND AROUND

3

By bemo Semarapura is served by *bemo* from Padang Bai, Gianyar and Denpasar. Some Padang Bai *bemos* conveniently terminate on (and pick up from) Jl Nakula, just outside the market, but the main bus and *bemo* terminal, Terminal Kelod (also known as Terminal Galiron), is about 1km south of the town centre. If you're heading up to Besakih via Semarapura, you can pick up a *bemo* going to Rendang or Menanga on Jl Gunung Rinjani just north of the main crossroads in the centre of town.

Destinations Denpasar (1hr 30min); Gianyar (20min); Menanga (for Besakih; 45min); Padang Bai (30min); Rendang (30min); Sidemen (30min).

Banks and exchange There are ATMs east of the market building on Jl Nakula.

ACCOMMODATION AND EATING — SEE MAP PAGE 154

All of the listings below are in central Semarapura.

Klungkung Tower Hotel Jl. Gunung Rinjani No. 18; 0366 25637. A decent affordable hotel, close to the night market, with a restaurant on site. $

Papila's Coffee House Klungkung Jl. Ngurah Rai No. 27. Just because you're in a small town doesn't mean you have to forego your latte or smoothie. Also yummy doughnuts, sandwiches, pizza and beer. $$

Pasar Senggol II night market Jl Arjuna No. 110. The hot-food stalls of the lively night market offer a taste of local flavours after dark. $

Top Kitchen Jl. Diponegoro No. 148; 0812 3857 7773. An affordable and comfortable place with nice views and really tasty Indonesian lunch or dinner. Live music. $

SHOPPING — SEE MAP PAGE 154

Duta Textile Jl Diponegoro 71, 0366 21078. Stocks exceptional textiles including silk and cotton sarongs, and shimmering *kebaya* material; staff are helpful and patient.

Pasar Senggol I (across the street from Taman Gili). Semarapura's main market, Pasar Senggol I, is well worth a browse and is best in the morning. It's essentially a non-touristy affair and at its largest and busiest every three days, but even on normal days it's a fun place to shop. Look out for fine *songket* fabric, as well as the usual sarongs and fruit and vegetables.

Gunung Agung

Visible throughout eastern Bali and even from Nusa Lembongan and west Lombok across the sea, **Gunung Agung's** classic volcanic cone is a majestic presence from any angle. It is the spiritual centre of the island: Balinese people believe the spirits of their ancestors dwell here, and several important temples, including **Besakih**, the Mother Temple, and **Pura Pasar Agung**, are sited on its slopes. Villages and house compounds are oriented towards the mountain, and many people sleep with their heads towards it. At 3031m, Gunung Agung is also Bali's highest peak and the focus of challenging **climbs** to its summit.

Two main **routes** lead up Gunung Agung; both are long and hard. One starts from Besakih and the other from further east, at the mountain's other main temple, Pura Pasar Agung. Whichever route you take, you'll need to set out in the middle of the night to be at the top for the **sunrise** (6am); clouds often obscure the view by late morning. A less-used route, from **Dukuh Bujangga Sakti**, inland from Kubu on the northeast coast, is offered by Mudi. Starting out at an altitude of 300m, the climb is greater but not as steep as the other routes. You begin in the afternoon, camp on the mountain at 1750m and complete the three hours to the summit before dawn. The north of Bali is drier so is less often shrouded in cloud. You can walk round the rim to the absolute summit if you climb from this side and can see the sunrise on the horizon all year round.

The Pura Pasar Agung route

From **Pura Pasar Agung**, at an altitude of 1600m, it's at least a three-hour climb with an ascent of almost 2000m, so you'll need to set out by 2am from the temple, depending on how fit you are. The track initially passes through forest, ascending onto bare, steep rock. It doesn't go to the actual summit, but ends at a point on the rim that is about 100m lower. From here, the summit masks views of part of the island and, between April and September, the sunrise on the horizon, but you'll be able to see Lombok's Gunung Rinjani, the south of Bali and Gunung Batukaru, and look down into the 500m crater.

The Besakih route

From **Besakih** (950m), the climb is longer (5–7hr) and much more challenging; you'll need to leave between 10pm and midnight. This path leads to the **summit** of Agung,

1963

The year **1963** is recalled as a time when the gods were displeased with Bali and took their revenge. Ancient texts prescribe that an immense ceremony, **Eka Dasa Rudra** – the greatest ritual in Balinese Hinduism – should be held every hundred years for spiritual purification and future good fortune. Before 1963, it had only been held a couple of times since the sixteenth century. In the early 1960s, religious leaders believed that the trials of World War II and the ensuing fight for independence were indicators that the ritual was once again needed, and these beliefs were confirmed by a **plague of rats** that overran the entire island in 1962.

The climax of the festival was set to take place at the Besakih temple complex on March 8, 1963, but on February 18, **Gunung Agung**, which had been dormant for centuries, started rumbling; fire glowed within the crater and ash began to coat the area. Initially, this was interpreted as a good omen sent by the gods to purify Besakih, but soon doubts crept in. Some argued that the wrong date had been chosen for the event and wanted to call it off. However, by this time it was too late: President Sukarno was due to attend, accompanied by a group of international guests.

By March 8, black smoke, rocks and ash were billowing from the mountain, but the ceremony went ahead, albeit in a decidedly tense atmosphere. Eventually, on March 17, Agung **erupted** with such force that the top 100m of the mountain was ripped apart. The whole of eastern Bali was threatened by poisonous gas and molten lava, villages were engulfed, between a thousand and two thousand people are thought to have died and the homes of another hundred thousand were destroyed. Roads were wiped out, some towns were isolated for weeks, and the ash ruined crops, causing serious food shortages and great hardship. Some villagers fled as far afield as Lombok.

Despite the force of the eruption and the position of Besakih high on the mountain, a relatively small amount of damage occurred to the temples, and the **closing rites** of Eka Dasa Rudra took place on April 20. Subsequently, many Balinese felt that the mountain's eruption at the time of the ceremony was an omen of the civil strife that engulfed Bali in 1965.

In 1979, the year specified by the ancient texts, Eka Dasa Rudra was held again, this time passing off without incident.

with breathtaking views in all directions, if skies are clear, including both Rinjani in Lombok to the east and Gunung Raung in Java to the west.

The initial climb is through forest, but the path gets very steep, very quickly, even before it gets out onto the bare rock, and you'll soon need your hands to haul yourself upwards. The descent is particularly taxing from this side and feels very precarious when you're already exhausted; allow at least five hours to get down.

INFORMATION — GUNUNG AGUNG

Gunung Agung was recently active in 2017-19. Be sure to check with an experienced local tour operator before making plans. You'll need a **guide**, strong footwear, warm clothes for the summit, a good torch (ideally a headlamp) and water and snacks; for the descent, a stick is handy. Expect muddy conditions at the start of the trek and slippery rocks high up. Climbing is not permitted at **certain times of the year** because of religious ceremonies at Besakih or Pura Pasar Agung. The **dry season** (April to mid-Oct) is the best time to climb (particularly in July and Aug); at other times, especially between Dec and March, wind and rain can render the ascent too dangerous or may mean aborting an attempt. There have been fatalities due to a combination of slippery conditions and poor footwear.

3

TREKKING GUIDES

As this is a serious climb you need to have confidence in your guide and be able to communicate well with them. For these reasons it's strongly advised to climb with an established trekking guide; the freelance guides who hang round Pura Pasar Agung and Besakih tend to have very limited English and may not be as safety-conscious. You'll find a wide choice of scenic accommodation and many guide services in Sidemen village, 18km from Pura Pasar Agung; Selat and Tirtagangga. In the resorts, there's Bali Sunrise Trekking and Tours (https://balisunrisetrekkingandtour.com) in Ubud and Perama (bookable through their offices in most tourist centres or at http://peramatour.com).

Trekking Candidasa http://trekkingcandidasa.com. Somat, an experienced guide who has been living in the area his entire life, offers private treks through the ricefields, villages and hills of Candidasa. There is an easier walk and a more difficult trek. Prices include transport and drinks.

Besakih

Charge; sarong and sash are mandatory and are included in the entrance fee as is a licensed guide

One of the major draws in the east of Bali is undoubtedly the vast **Besakih** temple complex, the most venerated on the island and a pilgrimage place for Balinese Hindus. On a clear day it can be a magnificent sight, the multitiered shrines of the eighteen sanctuaries busy with worshippers in traditional dress bearing elaborate offerings, the whole complex framed against the stark grandeur of the sacred volcano. It is named for the dragon deity that the Balinese Hindus believe inhabits the mountain. The sanctuaries surround three main temples dedicated to Siwa, Brahma and Wisnu, and the complex also houses dozens of temples belonging to various castes and regencies. But Besakih also has a reputation as a place of unpleasant hassle, and many of its inner courtyards are closed to non-Hindus, who must stay outside the low walls; even the towering hulk of Gunung Agung is often invisible behind enveloping cloud. It's best to arrive early morning or late afternoon to avoid the worst of the crowds. Note that there are cheap *warung* on the walk up

CEREMONIES AT BESAKIH

Every temple in Besakih has its timetable of **ceremonies**. The most important annual ceremony is the **Bhatar Turun Kabeh** ("The Gods Descend Together"), which takes place in March or April and lasts a month, with the high point on the full moon of the tenth lunar month. At this time, the gods of all the shrines are believed to come and dwell in Besakih, drawing worshippers from all over the island. Besakih's biggest ceremony is **Eka Dasa Rudra** (see page 157), held every hundred years. The **Panca Wali Krama** occurs every ten years and involves a 42km-long, three-day procession from the coast to the temple.

to Besakih from the car park, but accommodation is very limited.

Brief history

It's likely that Besakih was a religious site long before the start of recorded history. Pura Batu Madeg (Temple of the Standing Stone), in the north of the complex, suggests megalithic connections through its ancient terraced structure based around a central stone. However, the present temple complex's founder is generally believed to be **Sri Markandeya**, a priest who came from eastern Java at the end of the eighth century. An important ceremony occurred in 1007, widely thought to be the cremation rites of **Queen Mahendradatta**, origin of the Rangda legend (see page 151). Already an important temple by the time of the **Majapahit** conquest of Bali in 1343, Besakih then became the **state temple** of the powerful Gelgel and Semarapura courts. An earthquake damaged the buildings in 1917 and renovations were needed after the 1963 eruption of Gunung Agung. As a result, the temples are a mix of old and new, and restoration work is always ongoing.

The temples

The **Besakih complex** consists of eighteen separate **sanctuaries** with courtyards and dozens of lesser **shrines**, spread over a site stretching for more than 3km. It's a good idea to begin with **Pura Penataran Agung** (the Great Temple of State), which is both the largest and the most dramatic. It's built on **six terraces**, with more than fifty *bale*, shrines and stone thrones inside; about half are dedicated to specific gods, while the others are for ceremonial purposes such as receiving offerings or accommodating the gods during festivals. A path skirts Pura Penataran Agung's perimeter wall, from which you can see most of the terraces (the best views are from the west side). A giant stairway, lined by

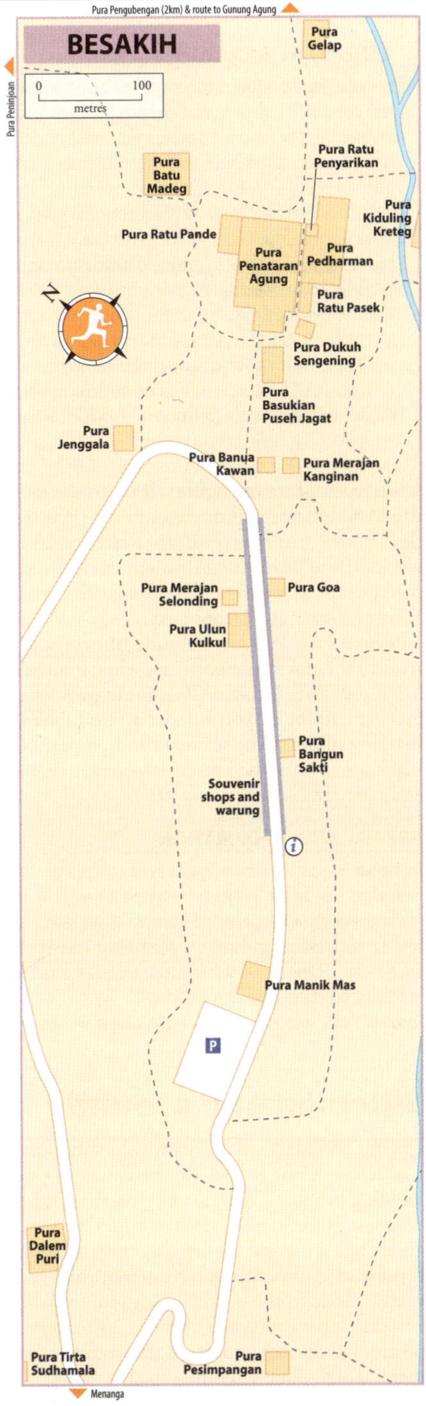

GUIDES AT BESAKIH

Besakih has a terrible reputation as a place of nonstop hassle. The problem stems from the hundreds of local men who style themselves as **guides**, **guardians** or **keepers** of the temple, insistently attaching themselves to tourists and then demanding large sums in payment for their "services". Don't let these touts spoil your chance to learn more about this unique complex. Instead, go directly to the tourist office next to the car park and pay the entrance fee, which includes a licensed guide and a sarong and sash. Ignore everyone else. You can choose to go it alone, of course, but you'll miss the explanations of the vast complex and will be continually hassled to hire a "guide". If on your own, stick to the paths running along the walls outside the temples, wear a sarong and sash, and you'll be in no danger of causing any religious offence. If you're escorted into one of the temples to receive a blessing you'll be expected to make a "donation" to the priest, the amount negotiable through your guide.

If you're with a **tour group**, these matters will be handled for you but if you're alone your driver should be able to offer tips on how to negotiate these pitfalls, but he is forbidden to guide you or translate for you and won't be able to negotiate on your behalf.

seven levels of **carved figures**, leads to the first courtyard; the figures to the left are from the Mahabharata and the ones to the right from the Ramayana. As worshippers process through the first courtyard, they symbolically sever their connection with the everyday world before proceeding through the *kori agung* into the second courtyard, which contains the *padmatiga*, the three-seated lotus throne dedicated to Brahma, Siwa and Wisnu, where all pilgrims pray.

Beyond Pura Penataran Agung, the *meru* of **Pura Batu Madeg**, rising among the trees to the north, are enticing, while **Pura Pengubengan** is a good 2km through the forest and Pura Gelap, a 20-minute walk away, is the most far-flung and rustic with excellent views. As you wander around the complex, look out for representations of the manifestations of the supreme god, in particular differently coloured **flags and banners**: black for Wisnu (the Preserver), red for Brahma (the Creator) and a multicoloured array for Siwa (the Destroyer).

ARRIVAL AND INFORMATION — BESAKIH

By bemo *Bemos* from Semarapura go as far as Menanga, from where you can hire an ojek to the temple. *Bemos* also run from Amlapura (via Selat and Muncan) to Rendang, with some continuing to Menanga. Most *bemos* run in the morning. There are no *bemos* north of Menanga to Penelokan, or between Rendang and Bangli.

Tours Without your own transport, the easiest way of getting to Besakih is to take an organized tour, but check how much time you'll have at the site; anything less than an hour isn't worth it.

Tourist information The Besakih tourist office, on the right just beyond the car park, is staffed by the local guides organization.

Sidemen and around

Upland **SIDEMEN** village sits within a quintessential Balinese setting of tiered rice terraces, coconut groves and the coursing Unda River beneath Gunung Agung's looming profile. It makes a glorious base for a few days, with a burgeoning number of scenic places to stay, opportunities for gentle ricefield treks and easy access to Pura Pasar Agung for the challenging sunrise climb up Gunung Agung. It's also perfectly feasible to explore Besakih from here, and even Batur, which is just 48km, or a ninety-minute drive to the northwest or points further east. Even if you don't intend to stay, you can appreciate some of the area's scenery from the road that begins at **Selat** (8km north of Sidemen) and drops down to Paksabali, 16km southwest of Sidemen on the main Semarapura–Kusamba road.

Artists Walter Spies (see page 115) and Theo Meier both lived in this area in the 1930s and 1940s, 3km to the north in **Iseh**, and Anna Mathews wrote her evocative *The Night of Purnama* about her life in the village before and during Gunung Agung's **1963 eruption**.

The main activity in these parts is relaxation and **ricefield appreciation**, either from the comfort of your veranda or on a walk through the fields to nearby villages and temples. Guesthouses can supply a basic sketch map or you can take a guide for your first outing. Alternatively, swim in the Unda River beneath the much-photographed yellow suspension bridge, take a cooking or yoga class, or head up to the southern end of the main road for Sidemen's excellent **crafts shops**.

ARRIVAL AND DEPARTURE — SIDEMEN AND AROUND

By bemo *Bemos* drop passengers off along the main road through the village.

Destinations Semarapura (30min).

GETTING AROUND

By bemo In the morning, and less frequently in the afternoon, *bemos* connect Rendang with Amlapura and also serve Menanga to the north, for Besakih. Selat is served by *bemos* from Gianyar, Amlapura and Denpasar's Batubulan terminal (mornings only).

By car Your accommodation can recommend a reliable driver.

By scooter Widely available for rent with or without a driver/guide.

3

INFORMATION AND ACTIVITIES

Banks and exchange There are ATMs on Jl. Raya Sideman, the main road.

Walks and trekking Kadek Adita of Sidemen Tour and Trekking (http://sidementourandtrekking.com) leads tours of the region, including ricefield walks and hikes up Gunung Agung.

Whitewater rafting Trips down the Telaga Waja can be organised by Telaga Waja Bali Rafting (http://telagawajabalirafting.com).

Yoga Sidemen Yoga Center at Cepik Villa, Banjar Tabola (http://sidemenyogacenter.com) offers vinyasa flow and other instruction from experienced Balinese teachers in beautiful surrounds.

Classes Several local women offer instruction about making *endek* and *songket* textiles. Sidemen Tour and Trekking can hook you up with local weavers. Wayan Astika (0857 3714 7338) has a small *warung* and runs cooking courses, his wife is an *endek* weaver, and he is also an excellent scooter tour guide.

ACCOMMODATION

The main accommodation area is west off the main road, in Dusun Tabola. The access road forks 400m west of the main road; the following listings give directions from the fork. Many places to stay are located in prime spots scattered across the ricefields. As it's reasonably cool here at night almost none have a/c; few have restaurants, either, but some have kitchenettes. Bring earplugs to muffle the cacophony of the nightly frog chorus. Non-guests can use the pool at *Sawah Indah* if you order a meal.

Giri Carik 800m Banjar Tabola, along the left-hand fork, 0819 3666 5821. Set in a pretty garden with a gorgeous pool, these five bungalows with verandas are excellent value, attractive and popular (book ahead). The in-house restaurant is good and the helpful staff can fix you up with everything from a scooter to a local masseur. $

★ **Griya Valud** along the right-hand fork; http://griyavaludbali.com. Away from the main "hotel street" and across from eye-popping ricefields, two cottages and four attached rooms are a haven away from home. Excellent personal service provided by Made, the caretaker, and the best food anywhere in Bali. $

Khrisna Home Stay Banjar Tabola, 200m along the left-hand fork; 0815 5832 1543. These four well-furnished en-suite rooms are set in a lovely garden, and have open showers, mozzie nets and private terraces. There's a small restaurant, too. Run by Sidemen's English-speaking nurse and his wife. $

Kubu Tani Villas Banjar Tabola, 800m along the left-hand fork; http://kubutani.com. Three beautiful, well-appointed two-storey villas built in wood and thatch to a sophisticated Bali-modern/traditional design. Verandas face a profuse garden and have great ricefield and Agung views. Each villa can sleep four. $

Sawah Indah Villa Banjar Tabola, 1km along the left-hand fork; http://sawahindahvilla.com. Overlooking a fine amphitheatre of rice terraces, the large and stylishly decorated villa-style rooms here have picture windows, colour-washed bathrooms and prettily tiled floors. There's a lovely pool and the restaurant makes the most of the views. $

RIVER RAFTING AND CLIMBING

From **Rendang**, 14km north of Semarapura on the main route to Kintamani, a picturesque **road** heads 32km east to **Amlapura**, running beneath Gunung Agung via ricefields, forest and deep river valleys. The scenery is good but the going is slow, the potholed road crowded with trucks bringing charcoal-coloured sand down from the mountain.

After crossing the Telaga Waja River, whose serpentine 14km-long descent is used by **whitewater rafting** companies such as Bali White Water Rafting (http://baliwhitewaterrafting.info) and Eco Bali Tours (https://ecobalitours.com), you pass through Muncan, a possible base for climbing Gunung Agung (see page 156). From **Muncan**, a further 5km brings you to the western edge of **Selat**, an obvious base for treks up Gunung Agung, and the turn-off to the important **Pura Pasar Agung**, directional temple for the northeast. At 1600m above sea level this is one of the two main starting points for Gunung Agung ascents. The road to the temple is an ear-poppingly steep climb of 10km through bamboo stands and acacia forests, in countryside scored by deep lava-carved gorges. The temple itself, however, is probably not worth a special journey, though on a clear morning you do get fine views.

Wapa di Ume Banjar Tabola; http://wapadiumesidemen.com. The attention to detail is flawless at this chic hillside resort surrounded by ricefields. There's a fine pool, spa, two restaurants as well as yoga and cooking classes. The views are well worth a visit. $$

EATING

Sleeping Gajah Kitchen & Lounge Banjar tabola; https://sleepinggajah.com. Possibly the town's best-situated restaurant, serving local dishes and international classics: think *bebek goreng* (crispy duck), *gado-gado* (tofu with peanut sauce) or vegan lasagna. The views from the open-air terrace are the perfect accompaniment, looking out over the rice fields and the Unda River below. $$

Wapa di Ume Banjar Tabola; http://wapadiumesidemen.com. The *Wapa di Ume* resort has a fine restaurant, *Sleeping Gajah Kitchen & Lounge*, serving up mainly excellent Indonesian fare but there are also several Western dishes available. Booking recommended. There's also the laid-back *Bar57* with an extensive selection of wines and cocktails. $$

Warung Tirta Unda Jl Sideman; https://sleepinggajah.com. Tucked away in the rice fields, this humble local *warung* is the place to go for traditional Balinese home-cooking. Choose from tasty soups, curries, and meat dishes presented on banana leaves instead of plates. $

SHOPPING

Pelangi Jl. Sideman, southern end of Sidemen's main road; 0812 392 3483. Beautiful *endek* and *songket* (gold- and silver-thread) products. All textiles are made in Sidemen, and you can see the production process in the workshop behind the showroom, where the staff dyes and dries threads before weaving the textile using foot-looms.

Padang Bai and around

PADANG BAI, the tiny port village for boats to the Gili Islands and Lombok, is a small, laidback travellers' centre and is also known as a base for **diving**. Its beaches are tiny, but its youthful vibe, funky cafés, cheap accommodation and live music bars may keep you lingering longer than you intended. There's a daily market and shops stocking basic necessities, but for anything major you'll need to head to Candidasa (20min away by *bemo*) or Semarapura (30min). The main local sights are **Blue Lagoon** beach and nearby **Goa Lawah temple**, on the way to Semarapura.

The beaches

Padang Bai's main stretch of **beach** is normally packed with *jukung* (traditional wooden outrigger boats), with the fast boat pier at one end and the ferry terminal at the other. You can swim here and it's often busy with local families on Sundays.

Most tourists head instead for the tiny whiteish-sand coves immediately over the headlands to the east and west, both within walking distance, meaning they get crowded and aren't always too pristine. **Bias Tugal** (also known as **White Sand Beach**) is a fifteen-minute walk south of the port via a steepish trail. Be careful as the beach here is quite exposed to strong waves and has a few tiny *warung*. Vendors here rent snorkel gear.

Alternatively, a five-minute walk along the left fork just east of *Topi Inn* will bring you to the pretty but miniature **Blue Lagoon** beach, less than 100m long. You can snorkel here at high tide but beware the serious undertow and watch the coral (which is just below the surface). Dive boats often stop here for the excellent marine life, which includes Napoleon wrasse, moray eels and nudibranch. The two *warungs* rent snorkel gear as well as sunloungers, and you're sure to find a couple of massage ladies and sarong-sellers in attendance.

Goa Lawah

Jl. Raya Goa Lawah, 7km west of Padang Bai • Donation plus charge for sarong rental • Goa Lawah is located right on the main road; any *bemo* between Padang Bai and Semarapura will drop you at the temple

As Bali's directional temple for the southeast, **Goa Lawah** (Bat Cave), by the coast, is always busy with worshippers who travel here in community groups to perform rites associated with significant life events. Discreetly watching the spectacle of the various **ceremonies**, both in the temple compound and at the shrine on the beach across the road, is part of the appeal of a visit. The other highlight is the **cave** at the base of the cliff, which heaves with fruit bats. It is supposedly the start of a tunnel that stretches 30km inland to Pura Goa in Besakih and is said to contain the cosmic *naga* Basuki. Watch out for pushy souvenir sellers and others offering "gifts" that you're pressured to buy.

DIVING AROUND PADANG BAI

There are half a dozen rewarding dive sites around **Padang Bai** and **Blue Lagoon**, whose hard and soft corals attract everything from eels, wrasses, turtles, lion fish and wobbegong sharks to leaf scorpion fish, ghost pipefish and pygmy sea horses; lobsters and crabs are frequently spotted on night dives. At nearby **Jepun** there's a decent artificial reef and the wreck of a 15m fishing boat, which is great for blue-spotted stingrays and reef fish. It's ideal for novice divers and macro photography, and good for **snorkelling** too. The dive sites at Tulamben, Amed, Candidasa and, further afield, Nusa Lembongan and Nusa Penida, are also within reach.

DIVE CENTRES

There are over a dozen dive outfits in Padang Bai. Fees include equipment, snacks and water. It's well worth choosing a dive centre carefully; below are some long-established outfits.

Geko Dive http://gekodivebali.com. Very professional 5-star PADI centre. Tech dives and training courses are offered.

Ok Divers http://okdiversbali.com. Large school with a training pool that also offers Nitrox diving.

Water Worx http://waterworxbali.com. Well-established German-run dive operator that also offers diving for people with disabilities.

3

ARRIVAL AND DEPARTURE — PADANG BAI AND AROUND

Hundreds of travellers pass through Padang Bai every day, and arranging onward transport is easy. Perama buses link Bali's main towns to Padang Bai, and there are frequent boat departures to the Gili Islands and Lombok. Any number of tour agencies will be keen to sell you tickets, often at highly fluctuating prices.

BY SHUTTLE BUS

Services depart from the Perama office near the port (http://peramatour.com) to major destinations in Bali and Lombok. Other shuttle services are also available.

Destinations Candidasa (3 daily; 30min); Kuta/Ngurah Rai Airport (3 daily; 2hr 30min); Sanur (3 daily; 1hr 30min); Tirtalannga (daily; 1hr); Ubud (3 daily; 2hr).

BY BEMO OR BUS

Bemos and buses from Amlapura, Candidasa, Semarapura and Denpasar's Batubulan terminal terminate at the port entrance about 300m from the main hotel area. Departures (mostly in the morning) run to Amlapura via Candidasa and Semarapura.

Destinations Amlapura (45min); Candidasa (30min); Gilimanuk (3–4hr); Semarapura (30min).

BY BOAT

Car ferry to Lembar, Lombok A more-or-less hourly service operates 24hrs and takes between four and five hours. Perama (http://peramatour.com) runs a cheap and hassle-free daily car ferry-and-bus combo to Senggigi, Lombok using this connection (9am; 6hr). If you have a rental car let your agency know beforehand that you intend to travel between Bali and Lombok to ensure all requirements are met.

Fast boats to the Gili Islands and mainland Lombok Several different operators offer connections to Gili Trawangan (1hr 30min), with some going on to Bangsal, Teluk Kodek or Senggigi on mainland Lombok, most leaving Padang Bai between 8.30am and 9.30am, with additional departures in high season. Some operators stop off at Gili Air as well. Tickets are sold online via the portal Gili Bookings (http://gilibookings.com) or Direct Ferries (http://directferries.com) and operators' websites, in shops and from freelance agents. It's best to check the safety record of unknown operators before purchasing a ticket, especially in rough weather. Sailings are cancelled during heavy seas. Reliable daily services include Blue Water Express (http://bluewater-express.com) and Giligili (http://giligilifastboat.com).

BY TAXI

There are fixed-price taxis from Ngurah Rai Airport (2hr); preordered pick-ups from Padang Bai will usually charge a bit more.

TOURS AND ACTIVITIES

Courses You can do courses in batik, ikat, basket-weaving, Balinese dance, wood carving, cooking and more at *Topi Inn* (https://topiinnbali.com).

Tours Padang Bai Bali Tours (http://padangbaibalitours.com) organises adventure and sightseeing tours of Padang Bai as well as private driver and shuttle services.

ACCOMMODATION — SEE MAP PAGE 163

Except for *Bloo Lagoon Eco Village*, none of Padang Bai's accommodation is more than a 10min walk from the ferry port or jetty, or more than 200m from the sea (which also means that nowhere is out of earshot of the ferry announcements and foghorn blasts).

Bamboo Paradise Jl Penataran Agung; https://facebook.com/bambooparadisebali. A cosy hostel and homestay a 2min walk from Bias Tugel beach with good fan-cooled dorms and a variety of basic private rooms. There's a great lounge for socializing. $

Bloo Lagoon Eco Village http://bloolagoon.com. This village-like compound of 25 eco-conscious villas sits on top of a hill, a 2min walk from Blue Lagoon beach. The two- and three-bedroom villas are all slightly different but all have big decks and coastal views, plus kitchenettes. There's a pool, spa and restaurant and morning yoga classes are included. $$

★ **Lemon House** Gang Melanting No. 5; 0812 4637 1575. Charming budget hotel in a yellow house up a flight of steep steps on the hillside west of the village. There are amazing views of the bay from the communal terrace. Two deluxe rooms enjoy these views as well, but are more exposed to noise; the quieter rooms at the back share facilities. You'll find books, magazines, DVDs and games for rainy nights. $

OK Divers Resort & Spa Jl Silayukti No. 6; http://okdiversbali.com. A well-run place with stylish rooms in a whitewashed, vaguely colonial-looking structure, some with sea views and one disabled-friendly. There's a fine spa, pool (with swim-up bar) and dive shop and restaurant on site. Non-divers are very welcome. $$

Puri Rai Jl Silayukti No. 7X; https://puriraihotels.com/index.html. Good-value hotel with an amazing three pools for its many large, comfortable, if slightly dated a/c rooms; those upstairs are brighter. Wi-fi can be a bit spotty. $

Villa Suari Jl. Penataran Agung Mimba; 081 2364 7434. Private 3-storied villa with accommodation for singles, couples or families. Each floor is unique and there are great sea views from the third storey, which sleeps four. Far enough from the main street to be quiet, but a short walk to all activities. Extremely helpful owners. Higher rates July–Aug. $

EATING

SEE MAP PAGE 163

Fresh seafood is the speciality in Padang Bai's restaurants, especially mahi-mahi, barracuda, snapper and prawns.

The Colonial Jl. Silayukti No. 6; https://okdiversbali.com/resort-restaurant-bar. Located at *OK Divers*, this smart seafront place has good international dishes like South African beef sausages, salads and a few Mexican dishes. There's lots of space to lounge around – just settle into one of their bean bags or sofas. Diners may use the pool. $

Depot Segara Jl. Silayukti Gang Segara No. 10; 0363 438 1666. Beachfront seafood specialists. Choose from the huge catch of the day bowl and watch your fish being grilled right in front of you. The chicken satay is also worth a try. $

Ozone Café Jl. Silayukti; 0831 1446 5255. If it's seafood you're after, *Ozone* serves highly recommended grilled snapper and other seafood: prawns and squid. Also juices, salads and sandwiches. Sit at a regular table or dine *lesehan* (seated on a pillow at a low table) Indonesian-style. Has beer on tap. $$

Warung Sari Laut Jl. Silayukti; 0281 7975 5033. This small family-run *warung* specialises in fresh-off-the-boat barbecued fish, which you can enjoy with a sea view. $

SHOPPING

SEE MAP PAGE 163

Wayan's Bookstore Jl. Penataran Agung, follow the signs into a small gang (alley). This off-the-beaten path little bookshop offers fiction and non-fiction, including some good Indonesian titles, and books in several European languages. Great for browsing and for a coffee or snack with the loquacious owner.

DIRECTORY

Banks and exchange There are exchange counters in the village and several ATMs, with three near the Perama office.

Doctor Highly regarded, English-speaking Dr Nisa can be contacted via Water Worx Dive Centre (0813 3851 1056). The nearest hospitals are at Semarapura and Amlapura.

Candidasa and around

East Bali's main tourist hub, **CANDIDASA** is a relaxed coastal town with plenty of midrange and upmarket accommodation, some good restaurants, rewarding **diving** and lots of opportunities for day-trips. It's not a lively place, though, drawing an older crowd of visitors, and with hardly any nightlife. There's also little or no **beach**, which has eroded away since the reef was destroyed to produce lime for the tourist building boom, and the seafront is fronted by a phalanx of groynes and a sea wall. You can still swim in the sea here, and some hotels do have little patches of sand out front, but for anything approaching a beautiful beach you have to head 9km east to the lovely **Pasir Putih**.

Just 3km north of Candidasa is the well-known traditional Bali Aga village and weaving centre, **Tenganan**, while to the east there's the locally important **Pura Gumang** hilltop temple. Candidasa is also well placed for excursions to Besakih and Tirtagangga, and further afield to Amed.

Pura Candidasa

Jl Raya Candidasa • Donation

Candidasa is an ancient settlement, and its temple, **Pura Candidasa**, opposite the lagoon, is believed to have been founded in the eleventh century. The statue of the fertility goddess Dewi Hariti in the lower section of the temple, surrounded by children, is a focus for pilgrims (the name Candidasa originally derives from "Cilidasa", meaning ten children).

ARRIVAL AND DEPARTURE — CANDIDASA AND AROUND

By plane Candidasa is a 2hr drive from Ngurah Rai Airport; you can take the official airport taxi with a fixed rate.

By shuttle bus Perama (http://peramatour.com) does hotel pick-ups and runs shuttle buses to major Bali and Lombok destinations.

Destinations Amed (daily; 1hr 30min); Kuta/Ngurah Rai Airport (3 daily; 3hr); Lovina (daily; 3hr 30min); Padang Bai (3 daily; 30min); Sanur (3 daily; 2hr); Tirtagangga (daily; 1hr); Tulamben (daily; 2hr); Ubud (3 daily; 1hr 30min).

By bemo or bus Buses and minibuses from Denpasar's Batubulan terminal pass through Candidasa en route to Amlapura. *Bemos* are also handy for travelling around Candidasa and can be flagged down anywhere en route.

Destinations Amlapura (20min); Denpasar (Batubulan terminal; 2hr); Gianyar (1hr); Padang Bai (20min).

GETTING AROUND

By taxi Candidasa Taxi & Tour Service, Jl. Raya Candidasa, 0819 1613 4266. Transportation service provider (English-speaking driver) and tour organiser.

By car or motorbike Cars and motorbikes are best rented through your accommodation.

INFORMATION AND ACTIVITIES

Massage and spas Try Dewi Spa & Salon, (Jl. Raya Candidasa, 0363 41042) one of the few massage places that has a spa and hair salon. For a classy spa head to the *Alila Manggis* hotel in Manggis, west of Candidasa (0363 41011).

Trekking There's good trekking in the Candidasa vacinity. One of the most popular routes begins at Kastala, southwest of Tirtagangga, and takes you downhill to Tenganan Bali Aga village, an easy 2–3hr walk with excellent rice-terrace views. OK Divers Resort & Spa (http://okdiversbali.com) can arrange Kastala trekking tours. (see page 156).

ACCOMMODATION — SEE MAP PAGE 166

Accommodation in central Candidasa is clustered along the main road. Further west, there's a decent beach at Mendira,

beyond which Buitan and Manggis villages have some nice places to stay.

CENTRAL CANDIDASA

Aquaria Jl Puri Bagus; http://aquariabali.com. In a tiny, secluded shorefront compound at the edge of a banana grove, this chic place has twelve contemporary terraced rooms and apartments, a couple of villas and a spa set around a striking little ionized pool. One of Candi's best restaurants is on-site. $$

Ari Homestay & Hot Dog Shop Jl Raya Candidasa; 0817 9707 339. Classic budget guesthouse with well-priced en suites and bungalows, a book exchange and a tiny café that serves Australian-style hot dogs and burgers. Pay for a "superior double" and you'll get a/c and hot water. $

Gedong Gandhi Ashram Jl Raya Candidasa; http://ashramgandhi.com. Occupies a gorgeous location between the lagoon and the ocean and rents out seven simple, attractive bungalows. Guests can take part in the daily *puja*, yoga and meditation as much or as little as they wish; note that there's no TV, wi-fi or a/c, no smoking or drinking, and unmarried couples can't share a room. Volunteer placements are also possible. Rates include three vegetarian or fish meals a day. $

Ida's Homestay Jl Raya Candidasa; 0363 41096. Old-school travellers' lodge in a coconut grove, offering six good-sized timber-and-thatch bungalows with mosquito nets, fans and cold-water garden bathrooms. There's a lovely shore-front deck and breakfast area plus a tiny patch of sandy beach. Book ahead as it's popular. $

Relax Beach Resort Jl Raya Candidasa; http://facebook.com/relaxbeachresortcandidasa. Walk through the

DIVING AND SNORKELLING AROUND CANDIDASA

The local reef is gradually rejuvenating and there is now **snorkelling** just offshore, stretching for about 1km westwards from the beach end of Jalan Puri Bagus. The **currents** can be hazardous, though, so don't venture too far out and stay aware of your position at all times. Jepun, near Padang Bai, is also rewarding. You can arrange snorkelling trips with local boat-owners (including equipment) to the islands off Candidasa or to Pasir Putih.

Just off the coast, the rocky outcrops known as **Gili Tepekong**, **Gili Biaha** and **Gili Mimpang** offer excellent **diving**, although they're not suitable for beginners as the water can be cold and the currents strong. There are several walls, a pinnacle just off Mimpang, dramatic scenery at boulder-lined Tepekong Canyon and a cave at Gili Biaha. The current is too strong for the growth of big coral, but the fish include barracuda, tuna, white-tipped reef shark, mola mola (occasionally between August and October), turtles and sometimes even manta rays. Candidasa is also within day-tripping distance of the reefs at Padang Bai, the wrecks at Tulamben and Amed, and the challenging sites around Nusa Lembongan and Nusa Penida. It's worth choosing a dive centre carefully; listed below are some well-regarded Candidasa options.

Bambu Divers Jl. Raya Candidasa, http://pondokbambu.com. Dutch-run PADI dive school at the *Pondok Bambu Dive Resort*.

Shangrila Scuba Divers http://baliseascapebeachclub.com. British-run centre at *Bali Seascape Beach Club*.

wonderful carved Balinese doors and you'll find an oasis of calm with an oceanfront pool and a selection of pretty a/c bungalows, each with generous veranda, traditional tiled roof and attractive interiors decorated with artistic flair. $

Sagara Candidasa Jl Raya Candidasa; http://sagarabali.com. A small hotel with beautifully arranged and well-equipped spacious rooms, some with balconies. There's a great infinity pool with sea views, a restaurant and bar. $$

★ **Watergarden Hotel & Spa** Jl Raya Candidasa; http://watergardenhotel.com. Yes it's inland, but the Balinese garden setting is a dream, with lush tropical plants and a koi-filled lily pond. Bungalows are in several shallow tiers with the highest ones getting the most light; all have a/c but there are no TVs. There's a pretty swimming pool as well as a spa and a good restaurant. $$

3

MENDIRA

Accommodation in Mendira village fronts some of Candi's nicest beach but is several kilometres from the heart of the area.

Candi Beach Resort & Spa Jl. Raya Mendira; http://candibeachbali.com. If you're up for a bit of a splurge, treat yourself to a room, bungalow or villa set among large palms. Balinese-modern architecture and furnishings, two pools, three restaurants, two bars and a spa. Breakfast and two cocktails included. $$$

Pondok Pisang Resort Jl Raya Mendira; http://pondokpisang.com. A remote but lovely haven at the end of a sandy track, 1km from the main road. The quirky but elegant two-storey fan bungalows are furnished with driftwood, paintings and lovely textiles. Many guests come for yoga and meditation in the large open hall overlooking the sea; the sun can be worshipped from the beautiful decks jutting over the water, and there's good swimming. $

MANGGIS

Around 6km west of central Candidasa, a 20-min walk or 10-mins by bike, Manggis village offers several fine hotels.

★ **Alila Manggis** http://alilahotels.com. Good value given the facilities and attention to detail, this impressive hotel is situated in a shore-side coconut grove with rooms ranged around a gorgeous pool. Though the beach is stony, you can swim in the sea and there are imaginative cultural tours, kids' programmes, a classy spa and a variety of cooking courses. The excellent *Seasalt* restaurant is here and there are free shuttles to central Candidasa and Tenganan. $$$

Lumbung Damuh Jl Pantai Buitan, Manggis; 0363 41553. A totally chilled, traveller-friendly little Balinese/European-owned hideaway of creatively designed *lumbung* beside a tiny patch of shore. Bedrooms are upstairs, with sitting areas and hot-water garden bathrooms below. A good breakfast is included and, though there is no restaurant, there are local *warung*. $

EATING

SEE MAP PAGE 166

There's a good range of restaurants in and around Candidasa, from cheap tourist-oriented *warung* to sophisticated hotel dining. Some offer free transport from hotels around the resort.

CENTRAL CANDIDASA AND JALAN PURI BAGUS

★ **Aquaria** Jl Puri Bagus, http://aquariabali.com. Overlooking the pool, this impressive hotel restaurant serves delicious, inventive food such as mahi mahi with tamarind sauce, ginger-spiced prawns, rye-bread sandwiches and imported cheese. There's a good selection for vegans and a kids' menu; the veggies and herbs are organic. $$

Loaf Cafe Jl Raya Candidasa; 0363 438 1130. Excellent, buzzing a/c cafe with fine pies, sandwiches (with home-made bread), great cakes and all the coffee combos you could wish for, as well as fresh juices and smoothies. $$

Vincent's Restaurant & Lounge Jl Raya Candidasa; http://vincentsbali.com. Very popular with expats, this landmark restaurant has a dining room, garden terrace and separate lounge bar. The menu is extensive and takes in European classics, fresh seafood, salads, Thai and local dishes. Reserve for dinner on Thursday, live jazz night. $$

MENDIRA

Warung Smiley Jl Mendira; 0878 6303 8278. Delicious home-made Indonesian dishes and a warm welcoming atmosphere. No wonder the place is called Smiley. Also offers live music in the evenings. $

BUITAN AND MANGGIS

Sate Bu Rengkeg Sengkidu Jl Mendira; 0852 3785 6425. This small establishment serves probably the best authentic Balinese satay in town. Try the marlin fish satay – it's well worth the visit. $

★ **Seasalt** Alila Manggis Resort; http://alilahotels.com. The setting, in a lovely outdoor pavilion fringed by ponds, is wonderful at this acclaimed hotel restaurant, which features a delectable range of Asian, fusion and vegetarian dishes, with plenty of local specialities – right down to the salt (sourced from flats close by). Try the signature *megibung* eight-dish feast, which includes spicy beef, chicken sate and snapper with ginger, which is more than enough for two. $$$

DRINKING

SEE MAP PAGE 166

Nightlife, mainly consisting of live music at different restaurants through the week, is low-key and things are usually pretty quiet by 10pm. Both of the below are in central Candidasa.

Crazy Kangaroo Jl Raya Candidasa; http://crazy-kangaroo.com. This pub and restaurant has a pool table and an open kitchen serving good Indonesian and Western classics. There's daily live music (covers) or Balinese dancing. Free shuttle service. $$

New Queen Jl Raya Candidasa; 0812 3653 1832. Popular tourist bar and restaurant (there are daily specials) with regular reggae and rock bands, and draught Bintang. $$

SHOPPING

Alam Zempol Jl. Mendira; 0363 41283. Small shop selling scented soaps and other bath products made in Mendira. Herbal ingredients make them suitable for various skin types and sensitivity.

Nadi's Bookstore Jl. Raya Candidasa; 0813 3862 6484. Packed into this tiny store are international novels, travel guides and rare map prints along with vases, statues and tribal art.

DIRECTORY

Banks and exchange There are many ATMs in the central area, as well as a few moneychangers.

Doctor The Pentamedica clinic (Jl Raya Manggis No. 88, http://pentamedica.com) is open 24hr and includes dental services. The nearest hospitals are in Amlapura and Semarapura.

3

Pura Gumang

Daily 7am–7pm • donation • *Bemos* between Candidasa and Amlapura drive by the stalls at the temple staircase

At the top of the pass about 3km northeast out of Candidasa, on the way to Pasir Putih, monkeys crowd around roadside stalls at the point where worshippers begin their hour-long walk up to hilltop **Pura Gumang**. This is one of the most important temples in the area and affords a fine panorama inland to Gunung Agung, down to the coast and across to Gunung Rinjani on Lombok. Every two years, usually at full moon in October, four of the local villages – Bugbug, Bebandem, Jasri and Ngis – participate in a huge ceremony, complete with trance dances, that begins with a procession up to Pura Gumang. It attracts many thousands of people, especially new parents, who bring along hundreds of roast suckling pigs.

Pasir Putih

Everyone in Candidasa bemoans the loss of the beach, but there is a highly satisfying alternative, 9km northeast at the famously beautiful **Pasir Putih** (White Sand Bay). The less than straightforward access, via a steep and rutted track, is part of the appeal (kind of); en route you'll pass a gateway to pay an entrance fee. The pale sand bay feels wild and remote, backed by palms and forest and sheltered by rocky headlands, with aquamarine water perfect for swimming. Offshore, small patches of coral reef offer decent snorkelling. The beach is lined with a dozen or so shacks providing meals and massage plus snorkel and sunloungers (usually free if you order drinks and food).

ARRIVAL AND DEPARTURE — PASIR PUTIH

By car or ojek Access is from the village of Perasi, immediately east of Bugbug on the road to Amlapura, about 6km from Candidasa. There are two routes from here: the first (unsigned) is immediately opposite a temple; the second is a few hundred metres further east and has a tiny sign for White Sand Beach, Jl Pasir Putih. Both lead 3km to the coast via a ticket barrier and a dauntingly rough track. An ojek will drive you there and back from Candidasa, just text him when you want to be picked up; or you can hire a car with a driver.

Tenganan Pegringsingan and around

One of the most accessible Bali Aga villages is **Tenganan Pegringsingan**, a wealthy settlement of over six hundred families set amid forest and hills 3km north of Candidasa. It's a major day-trippers' destination, known not only for its traditional

WHO ARE THE BALI AGA?

When the Javanese Majapahit conquered Bali in 1343, imposing religious reforms and a caste system on the island, those who rejected the Javanization of Bali withdrew to their village enclaves to live a life based around **ritual and ceremony**. Nearly seven centuries later they are still a distinct group, known as the **Bali Aga** or Bali Mula, the "original Balinese", who adhere to a strict, archaic code in their social and religious lives.

According to some, the Bali Aga are followers of the Indra sect of Hinduism and trace their ancestral links to Orissa in India rather than to Java like most Balinese. Among other things, their exacting customary law determines on which of the three village streets they can live and whom they may or may not marry. Most of the daily rites are inaccessible to the public, but there are many **festivals** where visitors are welcome. One of the most dramatic is the month-long **Usaba Sambah**, generally in May and June, which includes ceremonial duelling known as *perang padan* (*mekare-kare* in Balinese language) in which bare-chested men fight each other with thorny pandanus leaves.

architecture but also as the only place in Indonesia that produces the celebrated **geringsing** cloth. It's also the finishing point of a popular and scenic trek that begins in either Kastala or Tirtagangga.

Laid out around three cobbled, vehicle-free avenues that run north–south, the village (admission by donation) rises in a series of terraces, its family compounds hidden behind high walls of thatch, adobe and brick. Communal activities and meetings take place in thatched *bale* on the main street and there are plenty of handicrafts for sale.

The village's most renowned craft is the unique and highly prized **geringsing** or double ikat (see page 149) that gives Tenganan Pegringsingan its name. Dyed in a limited natural palette of brown, deep red, indigo and tan, and designed with deeply symbolic motifs, *geringsing* is revered throughout Bali as a sacred cloth, able to ward off evil and having an important role in tooth-filing and cremation ceremonies. Glossy, golden, tightly woven **basketwork** made from *ata* grass is another painstakingly crafted village product. The grass has to be split, woven, boiled, dried and then smoked, all of which means it can take a month to produce a single item. **Traditional calligraphy** is another attractive Tenganan craft. Pictures and symbols are incised on narrow lengths of *lontar* palm leaf, which are then strung together to create a concertina-like book.

Tenganan Dauh Tukad

West across the river from Tenganan Pegringsingan, the twin Bali Aga settlement **TENGANAN DAUH TUKAD** is smaller, and much less known, but also worth a visit. Part of its appeal is that every visitor is accompanied by a local guide, which is a

THE FOUNDING OF TENGANAN

In the days before the Majapahit invasion of Bali, a Bedulu king ruled the island. Legend has it that one day his favourite horse went missing, and so he offered a large reward for its return. When the horse was discovered – dead – near Tenganan, the king announced that he would give the local people the land within which the stench of the rotting animal could be smelled. One of the king's ministers was sent to adjudicate, and he and Tenganan's headman set out to decide the boundaries. The smell of the horse could be detected over a huge area. The lines were duly drawn and the minister departed. At this point, the devious village headman took out from under his clothes the piece of rotting horsemeat with which he had fooled the minister. The limits of the village lands are still the ones set at that time, and cover more than ten square kilometres.

great chance to learn about village life and customs; their services are free but a tip is appreciated. Tenganan Dauh Tukad looks less traditional than its neighbour but it's also greener and more peaceful. It's also less commercial, because the village forbids inhabitants from displaying wares in the street.

ARRIVAL AND INFORMATION

TENGANAN PEGRINGSINGAN AND AROUND

By car or ojek You can take a car or *ojek* from Candidasa.

On foot The road to Tenganan Pegringsingan is a pleasant 3km walk uphill from the western end of Candidasa. Tenganan Dauh Tukad is off the same road, partway up the hill. To walk between the two villages shouldn't take long but you'll need a guide; going by road, it's about 4km.

Tours To gain insight into daily life in the two Tenganan villages you'll need a guide, provided free of charge in Tenganan Dauh Tukad. Alternatively, consider joining a tour organized through Tenganan Pegringsingan the village ecotourism network, JED (http://jed.or.id).

SHOPPING

Srigading Tenganan Pegringsingan, 0817 162481. High-quality hand-made products including various kinds of bags, wallets and jewellery.

3

Amlapura and around

Formerly known as Karangasem, **AMLAPURA** was renamed after the 1963 eruption of Gunung Agung, when the outskirts of the town were flattened by the lava flow. (Balinese people sometimes change their names after serious illness in the belief that it will bring about a change of fortune.) It's the capital of Karangasem regency, and has a significant history, but the modern town is quiet, tidy and unhurried, with just enough to keep you busy for an hour or two. It also makes a handy pit stop on the popular day-trip circuit from Amed via the scenic coastal route, and there's accommodation and food close by at **Jasri** beach just south of town and **Seraya Barat** 6km east around the coast.

The main sights in and around town are associated with the **Karangasem court**. Once so powerful that in the seventeenth century it established Balinese rule over several Lombok principalities, Karangasem was later severely weakened by feuding between its rival factions and by the mid-nineteenth century was itself ruled from Lombok. Following the Dutch conquest of Lombok in 1894, **Anak Agung Gede Jelantik**, a member of the Lombok ruling family, was appointed regent of Karangasem by the colonialists. He was succeeded in 1908 by his nephew, **Anak Agung Anglurah**, the last raja of Karangasem before Indonesian independence who was well-known as the architect of the water palaces at Tirtagangga and **Taman Sukaseda** in Ujung. Their relatives continue to occupy the **Puri Agung Karangasem** palace in Amlapura and ties with Lombok are still strong: many Balinese in Cakranegara west Lombok have family in Karangasem, and the sizeable Muslim community in Amlapura traces its ancestry back to the period when Karangasem was under Lombok rule.

Puri Agung Karangasem

Jl Sultan Agung • Charge • 0363 21364

Built during the Dutch period at the end of the nineteenth century by the last Karangasem raja, Anak Agung Gede Jelantik, **Puri Agung Karangasem** is still home to descendants of the royal family and offers a rare chance to peek inside a palace. The part of this once-opulent palace that visitors can view is not in great shape today and is in need of renovation, but it does have some intriguing features, particularly its blend of Balinese, European and Chinese architecture that came about during various stages of construction. (Information sheets in English are available.)

3

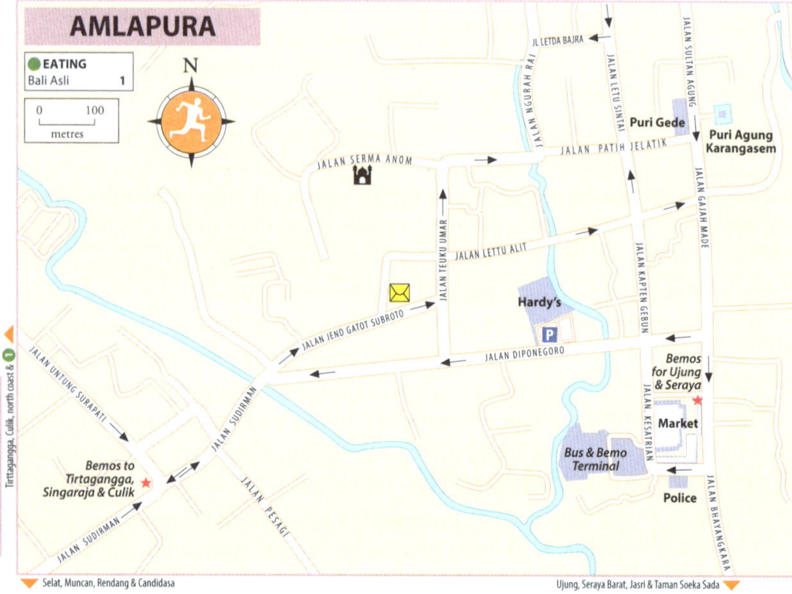

Areas open to the public include elegantly airy **Maskerdam**, the raja's residence, which has beautiful doors carved with three-dimensional reliefs of birds, animals and foliage. Inside there are a few pieces of Dutch furniture, a gift from Queen Wilhelmina, and a gallery of historic photographs. Elsewhere in the compact but artfully tranquil gardens is the **Bale Kambang** (Floating Pavilion), encircled by a lotus pond, which is still used for Balinese dance and gamelan performances today. Wander around the compound, via the edges of the current family quarters in the back for views down over the rest of the town and across to Lombok – at one time under Karangasem rule. The peaks of Gunung Agung and Gunung Lempuyang frame the vista.

Taman Sukaseda (Ujung Water Palace)

5km south of Amlapura • charge

In a rural location 5km south of central Amlapura stands the largest of the three extravagant water palaces conceived by the last Karangasem raja, Anak Agung Anglurah. **Taman Sukaseda** (also spelled Soekasada), familiarly known as the **Ujung Water Palace**, dates from 1901, opened to the public by the Dutch in 1921 but was almost completely destroyed by Gunung Agung's 1963 eruption. Renovations have recreated the stately tranquillity of its ponds, floating pavilions, ornamental bridges and pagodas, but the relief carvings and statuary are concrete. Nonetheless it's a serene spot, served by **bemos** from Amlapura, and worth a visit if you're en route to Amed via the scenic coastal route. Bring a picnic lunch and sit for a while trying to imagine how it must have been in days gone by.

Jasri

Backed by coconut groves and ricefields, the slender shoreline around the beach at **JASRI**, just 2km south of Amlapura, consists of wave-polished grey stones and patches of dark sand. The sea can be choppy and too rough for most swimmers but the area retains a delightfully rural feel and it's a great spot to escape the mass tourism and crowds elsewhere in coastal Bali. A handful of lovely hotels and villas are here.

You don't have to be a chocoholic to get a giggle out of stopping at Bali Chocolate Factory (Jl. Raya Pantai Jasri, http://facebook.com/balichocolat). In fact, when you see the three hobbit-styled huts surrounded by coconut palms you might wonder if you're in a foreign shire instead of Bali. Inside these pointed thatched-roof houses with round windows, divine chocolate is made from locally sourced cacao beans. You can take a tour that includes tasting (yum!) and will also receive a bar of locally made organic soap as a memento of your visit. You can, of course, also buy some chocolate bars or syrup to take home. For a more upmarket experience, Sorga Chocolate (https://sorgachocolate.com) offers chocolate-making workshops and guided tours of its modern purpose-built factory. The on-site serves all-day breakfast with pancakes and freshly baked chocolate chip muffins.

Seraya Barat

The wild, dramatic black-stone shore at **SERAYA BARAT**, 1km east of Ujung, 6km from central Amlapura or 24km from Amed, has a few accommodation options. The sea here is usually too dangerous for reliable swimming but Pasir Putih's gorgeous white sands are a twenty-minute drive away to the southwest and the views to Nusa Penida and Lombok are awesome.

ARRIVAL AND INFORMATION

AMLAPURA AND AROUND

By bemo or bus Amlapura has useful *bemo* services (all most frequent in the morning). From the terminal in town services run to Padang Bai via Jasri and Candidasa (orange and sometimes red), Gianyar, and Rendang via Muncan and Selat (green). *Bemos* to Culik via Tirtagangga (red) leave from the turn-off on the outskirts of town, as do dark-red minibuses to Singaraja. *Bemos* to Ujung and occasional services to Seraya (blue) leave from the southern end of Jl Gajah Made, not far from the terminal.

Destinations Candidasa (20min); Culik (45min); Denpasar (Batubulan terminal; 2hr 30min); Gianyar (1hr 20min); Lovina (3hr 30min); Padang Bai (35min); Seraya (40min); Tirtagangga (20min); Tulamben (1hr); Ujung (20min).

Banks and exchange There are many ATMs in town.

ACCOMMODATION

There are slim pickings for accommodation in Amlapura itself, so base yourself in the coastal towns of Jasri and Seraya Barat where you'll find a wider choice of guesthouses and seaside villas.

JASRI

★ **Aashaya Jasri Resort** Jl Pantai Jasri; http://jasriresort.com. This beautiful guesthouse has real style thanks to the attention to detail evident in its traditional thatched buildings (with up to three bedrooms) which are all decorated with batik textiles and classy wooden furnishings. There's a lovely pool, spa and its fine *Disini* restaurant is open to non-guests. $$

Villa Campuhan Jl Pura Mascima; http://villacampuhanbali.com. An astonishing resort with six traditional structures of timber and thatch (four are Minangkabau-style with upturned boat-shaped roofs), largely built from recycled materials. There's a lovely pool, staff are great and the restaurant serves fine, creative cuisine. Apart from the surging of the waves over the slim pebble beach, it's utterly tranquil here. $$$$

SERAYA BARAT

Kebun Impian Jl Karangasem; http://facebook.com/Kebun-Impian-179365178769894. Attractive bungalows (fan or a/c options) in a garden by the sea, where there's a sliver of a beach at low tide. The restaurant serves good food, including marlin steaks and fresh crayfish, and cooking classes are offered. Diners can also use the swimming pool. $

Seraya Shores Jl Karangasem; https://instagram.com/serayashores_bali. A luxurious hideaway with gorgeous, individually designed Bali-style villas in a great seafront garden. It's popular with yoga groups, and has a lovely deck for practice, plus a beautiful shoreside pool. Breakfast is served any time you choose, but note that the restaurant isn't open to non-guests. $$

Villa Flow http://villaflowbali.com. This elegant, environmentally friendly coastal retreat is the perfect place to get away from it all. Rooms in the main building are large and modern; the deluxe Coconut House beside the pool makes the most of the sea view. There's a spa, yoga classes (check website for packages) and a private beachfront garden just a few minutes' walk away. $$$

EATING

AMLAPURA, SEE MAP PAGE 172

★ **Bali Asli** Jl. Gelumpang, Gelumpang village, north of Amlapura; http://baliasli.com.au. Wonderful Australian-run restaurant and cooking school with stunning views across ricefields to a volcano-filled horizon. The menu changes everyday, depending on the availability of market ingredients. Order the nine-dish *megibung* (family-style) feast for a really authentic taste of Bali. Follow the signs from the traffic lights on the Amlapura–Tirtagangga road. $$$

JASRI

Warung Biker Jl. Raya Perasi; 0821 4552 4888. Quirky *warung* decked out with motorcyclist memorabilia that doubles up as a live music venue come the evening hours. The BBQ ribs are the star dish and there's also an on-site gym to put that extra protein to good use. $

SHOPPING

Sensasatia Botanicals Jl. Pantai, Jasri; http://sensatia.com. Producing natural soaps in a variety of sizes and scents along with bath and body creams and skin care products. You can find them in this shop or you can order them online.

3

Tirtagangga and around

With its mid-twentieth-century **water palace** and its strikingly pretty landscape of plunging rice terraces and dramatic mountain peaks, **TIRTAGANGGA** is a popular day-trip destination and a good base for walkers. It's significantly cooler than on the coast and there are countless possibilities for gentle **treks** or more strenuous full-day hikes or bike trips through the terraced ricefields, rambutan, vanilla and banana plantations, and tiny villages. Much of the accommodation enjoys fine panoramas, especially in neighbouring **Ababi**, 2.5km north. On a clear day you get fine views of Gunung Lempuyang to the east, on whose slopes stands **Pura Lempuyang Luhur**, a worthwhile local trip.

Taman Tirtagangga Water Palace

Charge; extra charge for boat rental and swimming • http://tirtagangga.com

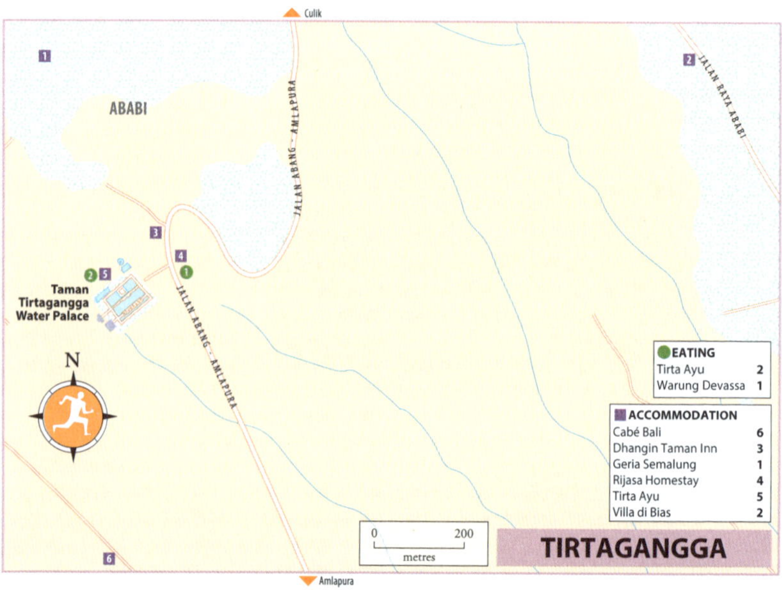

Tirtagangga's only real sight, **Taman Tirtagangga Water Palace** was built in 1946 by Anak Agung Anglurah, the last raja of Karangasem, and is a fine manifestation of his obsession with pools, moats and fountains. Constructed on the site of a holy spring just off the main road, it's actually a water **garden** rather than a palace, a confection of terraced ponds, pretty shrubs and water burbling from the mouths of sculpted water buffaloes and nymphs, the pools flashing orange with very well-fed carp. Balinese-Hindus come here for ritualistic cleansings taking advantage of the "Ganges water" for which the park is named. Two of the upper-level pools are open to the public for **swimming**, mostly used by local kids, and you can also rent a traditional boat to paddle around the Royal Water Park.

Pura Lempuyang Luhur

Gunung Lempuyang • Donation plus charge for renting sarongs • The temple car park is 8km from Abang, itself 3.5km north of Tirtagangga on the Culik road; *bemos* only cover the 2km from Abang to Ngis Tista, but go all the way during festivals

Visible to the northeast from Tirtagangga, less than 12km away, **Gunung Lempuyang** is a sacred peak and site of **Pura Lempuyang Luhur**, one of the *kayangan jagat* or directional temples of Bali, giving spiritual protection from the east. The temple, which is one of Bali's oldest and most venerated, gleams white on the mountain slopes and offers exceptional views. A daunting two-hour climb, up 1700 steps from the car park, will get you to the principal temple, which is believed to be the dwelling place of the god Genijaya, but the vistas, including of Gunung Agung perfectly framed in the temple gateway, make it all worthwhile. The **courtyard** contains a stand of bamboo, and on festival days the priest makes a cut in the bamboo to release holy water. From the temple, a ninety-minute climb up another staircase brings you to the **summit** of Gunung Lempuyang (1058m), where there's another temple.

Festival days are the best time to visit, when the temple swarms with worshippers carrying offerings all the way up the staircase. Pilgrims believe the ascent should be made without complaining, thereby enhancing the spiritual experience.

3

Lahangan Sweet Viewpoint

Gunung Lempuyang • https://lahangansweet.com

Another one of Bali's custom-made viewpoints sits on the slopes of Gunung Lahangan just north of Pura Lempuyang Luhur and affords a magnificent panorama of the east coast with a clear view to **Gunung Agung**. Follow the bumpy road (a 4WD is recommended) to about 1km out, then climb up to the viewpoint, about a 20min walk. Two wooden platforms have been built around a pair of tall trees providing the perfect silhouette for a photograph with Agung's cloud-capped peak looming on the horizon.

ARRIVAL AND INFORMATION — TIRTAGANGGA AND AROUND

By shuttle bus Perama (http://peramatour.com) run daily to/from Candidasa-Tirtagangga (45min) and Candidasa-Amed daily.

By bus Tirtagangga is served by minibuses and buses plying the route between Amlapura and Singaraja.
Destinations Amlapura (20min); Culik (30min); Padang Bai (1hr) Singaraja (2hr 30min); Tulamben (1hr).

By taxi Ask at you're accommodation for car and driver recommendations.

Banks and exchange The nearest ATMs are in Amlapura, 6km south. There are moneychangers in the village but rates are better in Candidasa.

ACTIVITIES

Trekking Every guesthouse can organise hikes. Choose from easy local hikes to longer versions that take you to Tenganan village above Candidasa (2–6hr depending on where you start the walk): the Kastala to Tenganan section (2hr) is a real highlight but can get busy in high season. More strenuous routes take you to Amed (Bunutan) via the mountaintop Pura Lempuyang (9hr), and up Gunung Agung.

ACCOMMODATION

SEE MAP PAGE 174

Staying in central Tirtagangga puts you near a choice of *warung* but also within earshot of the busy road; staying further away means a greener and quieter location. Most accommodation has a restaurant attached.

Cabé Bali Temaga; http://cabebali.com. Encircled by ricefields with views to Gunung Agung and the sea, the four large bungalows enjoy glorious surroundings, including a pool. The genial German-Javanese hosts foster a relaxed atmosphere and the Indonesian food (served to guests only) is great. A 10min easy (flat) walk from Tirtagangga. Discounts for longer stays. $$

Dhangin Taman Inn 0363 22059. Close to the Water Palace, these are the cheapest beds in Tirtagangga. All rooms are simple, those with cold-water bathrooms are very spartan indeed but acceptable for a night, while the hot-water options are smarter. $

Geria Semalung Jl. Tanah Lengis, Ababi; 0851 9011 3001. A forest hideaway of five attractively furnished hot-water bungalows, with fine views across to Gunung Lempu-yang and down to the rice terraces below. It's a steep 15min walk down to Tirtagangga. $

Rijasa Homestay 0363 21873. Located just a few steps away from the Water Palace this friendly no frills family-run homestay has a lovely garden, terrace, restaurant and bar. $

Tirta Ayu 0363 22503. Set inside the Water Palace compound, these five Bali-style villas are fit for a raja with very classy decor and furnishings, sunken bathtubs, grand verandas and a spa. Wake early and you can stroll the palace gardens at dawn before the public is admitted. $$$

Villa di Bias Jl. Raya Ababi, Ababi; http://villadibias.com. This unique and attractively furnished luxury villa has two rooms, a pool, terrace and amazing views of the ricefields and Gunung Agung. Can be rented as a whole or each of the rooms separately. The excellent *Bali Asli* restaurant is in the vicinity. $$–$$$

EATING

SEE MAP PAGE 166

Tirta Ayu https://instagram.com/tirtaayuhotel. For a unique experience head to this upmarket hotel restaurant with lovely views over the Water Palace grounds. Great lunch stop on touring days. The extensive menu offers an

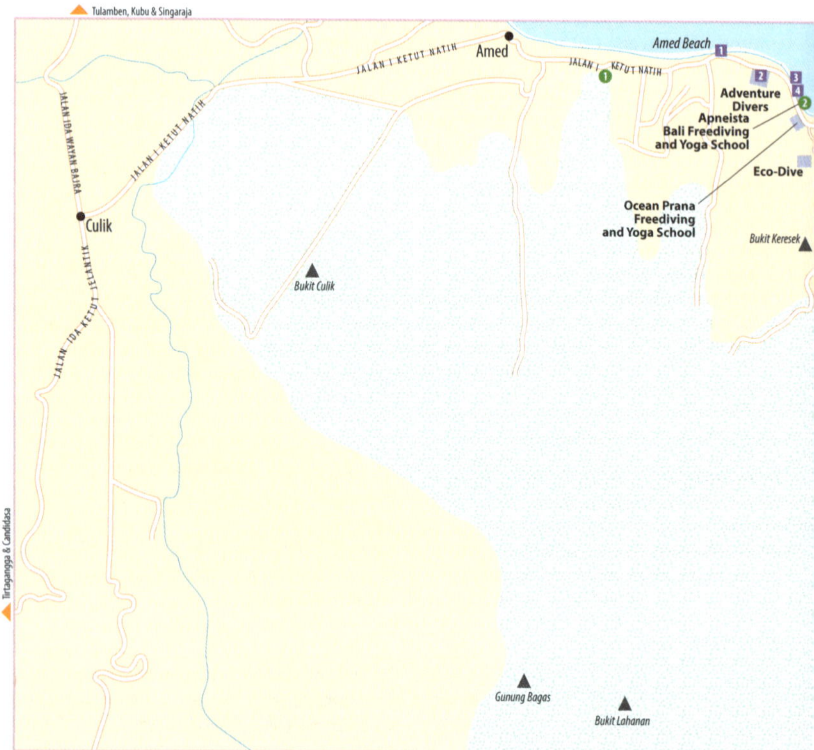

eclectic range of dishes including crispy duck and Balinese *megibung* dishes. $$$

Warung Devassa 0853 3904 9791. An ideal place to have a mouthwatering Balinese lunch before or after visiting the Water Palace. They also have international food. $

The Amed coast

The entire 15km stretch of coast **from Culik to Aas** in the far east of Bali is known as **Amed**, although this is the name of just one of several villages in an area of peaceful bays, clear waters and dramatically undulating topography. Long one of Bali's poorest regions, it is notorious for its dusty soil and subsistence economy based around fishing and salt production. As more people seek to escape crowds, Amed has become an important – yet still rural – tourism centre. Visitors are drawn by the region's impressive offshore reefs, which offer great **snorkelling** and **diving**, and facilities are mushrooming, with accommodation now available in every village bay. Stand-up paddleboarding (SUP) is now a popular pastime and progressive beach outlets rent them. If a more relaxing holiday is what you're after you'll find an abundance of yoga classes.

East of Amed village, **Jemeluk**, with its dive centres, restaurants and travellers' vibe, is a good choice if you don't have your own transport; **Bunutan** has some very nice places to stay; and **Banyuning** is great for snorkelling. If you're not here for the snorkelling or diving, there are several day-tripping possibilities, but be warned that the beaches are not Bali's finest, being mostly black, stony and shadeless (though they do get paler and sandier east of **Lipah** beach, further away from Gunung Agung), and generally busier

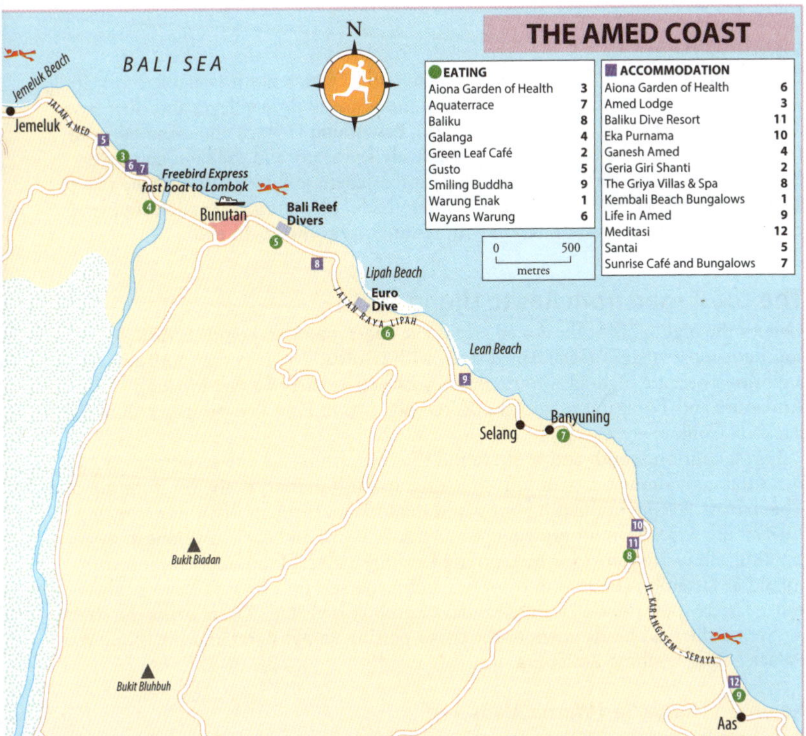

with traditional wooden outriggers (*jukung*) than sunloungers. The scenery, however, is magnificent: as the coast road crests one headland after another, the scalloped bays and aquamarine waters sparkle beneath the folds of the stark volcanic hills behind. It's a joy to explore on two wheels.

Amed, Congkang and Jemeluk

The eponymous **Amed** village, the westernmost of the coastal villages in the area, is just 3km from Culik. Its traditional fishing and salt production are being encroached upon by tourist development, but it retains a local feel.

Offshore at Congkang, Pyramid Reef is popular with snorkellers for its easy access from the beach and together with neighbouring Jemuluk (6km from Culik) there is a decent spread of accommodation, a useful supply of tourist facilities such as restaurants, a good dive shop along the narrow shrub-lined road, and excellent diving. At low tide, a swathe of beach is revealed here, and though there's almost no shade, there are sunloungers for rent. There's good snorkelling in front of many of the hotels, and especially beneath the headland by *Villa Coral Café* bungalows.

Bunutan

Continuing east over the headland from Jemeluk brings you first to **Bunutan**, 8km from Culik, which has some of the nicest accommodation along the Amed coast, many of the establishments enjoying great views. Places are quite spread out though, divided by a steep headland, so you'll probably need transport.

Lipah to Aas

Beyond Bunutan is **Lipah** beach, 10km from Culik, which has reasonable snorkelling. After Lipah, it's headland after headland to the peaceful little villages and their bays at **Lean** (11km from Culik), **Selang** (12km), **Banyuning** (13km) and eventually **Aas** (15km). These eastern beaches get progressively less stony and the sand gets paler; Banyuning has the area's best **snorkelling**, at the Japanese Wreck just offshore (see page 179). The beach at Banyuning also has some shade, plus snorkel rental, a couple of cheap *warung* and accommodation with restaurants at the north end.

The coast road from Aas to Ujung

One of the highlights of the Amed area is the **coast road** that connects **AAS**, the southern-most village on the Amed strip, with **UJUNG**, 25km to the southwest. It's a gloriously scenic high-level route that works well as part of a **day-trip loop** – via Amlapura and Tirtagangga, with a possible side trip to Pura Lempuyang Luhur, then back via Culik.

As you continue south and west around the coast from Aas, the scenery is breathtakingly dramatic, with hills sweeping up for hundreds of metres from the coast. The narrow, steeply undulating but paved road snakes through dry mountain land used in the wet season for growing peanuts, soya beans and corn, overlooked by the hulking silhouettes provided by Gunung Lempuyang and Gunung Seraya. It turns inland at **Kusambi**, about 4km from Aas and is marked by a massive beacon; this is the most easterly point of Bali – on clear days Lombok is visible, 35km across the strait. At Seraya the road heads down to the coast, passing **Seraya Barat** and the **Ujung Water Palace** before reaching **Amlapura**.

Kelompok Karya Sari Warna Alam

Bungin, Seraya Timur • Free • 082 8368 8122

DIVING AND SNORKELLING ALONG THE AMED COAST

Banyuning has the area's best **snorkelling**, at the **Japanese Wreck**, which lies in shallow water (6–12m) just 20m offshore; the small freighter is overgrown with soft corals and is frequented by pygmy seahorses, leaf scorpionfish and a number of nudibranch. If you're staying elsewhere you can charter a boat to the wreck: from Jemeluk it's a forty-minute ride. There's rewarding reef in **Jemeluk** too, especially in the (usually) very clear water around the headland beside *Villa Coral*, and also in a long stretch in front of *Amed Café* and *Ganesh Amed*. **Snorkel sets** can be rented everywhere.

DIVING

Amed's reefs are popular with divers from all over Bali and by late morning can be very crowded with day-trippers. Local dive operators tend to set off early in the day to get a head start on incomers, which is one of several good reasons to base yourself here.

The main diving area is at **Jemeluk**, where a massive sloping terrace of hard and soft coral leads to a wall dropping to a depth of more than 40m. Gorgonian fans, basket sponges and table coral are especially good, and there are plenty of fish (including schools of red-tooth trigger fish and sergeant majors), plus sharks, wrasses and parrotfish. Advanced divers rate **Gili Selang**, an islet off Bali's eastern tip, about 5km south of Aas, with its pristine reef and pelagics (hammerhead sharks are sometimes encountered here), but the currents are nearly always fierce. There are also the Japanese Wreck at **Banyuning** and a dramatic drift dive at **Bunutan**, with schools of barracuda and giant barrel sponges. **Tulamben** is a thirty-minute drive away and most dive centres offer safaris to sites further afield.

There are countless **dive centres** in the Amed area. All the established places will collect you from your accommodation. There are also freediving schools for breathholding athletic types who hate underwater bubbles.

Adventure Divers http://adventurediversbali.com. At *Geria Giri Shanti*, Congkang.

Apneista Bali Freediving and Yoga School http://apneista.com. Jemeluk.

Bali Reef Divers http://diveamed.com. *Puri Wirata* hotel, Bunutan.

Eco-Dive http://ecodivebali.com. Jemeluk.

Euro Dive http://facebook.com/EurodiveBali. Lipah.

Ocean Prana Freediving and Yoga School http://oceanprana.com. Jemeluk.

3

This weavers' cooperative that has worked hard to preserve the nearly-extinct traditional *kain bebali* lies 14km on from Kusambi, on the fringes of the small market centre **Seraya**, and is well worth a stop. They grow their own cotton and dye it in the traditional way with indigo and bark harvested from the workshop garden. You can watch the spinners and weavers at work and then buy their beautiful scarves and sarongs, recognizable by their muted, natural tones.

ARRIVAL AND INFORMATION — THE AMED COAST

Access to Amed is via Culik, 12km northeast of Tirtagangga or 7km southeast of Tulamben. Tourist transport services are offered in almost every village, and through hotels, to all major destinations on Bali including the airport.

By bus Perama (http://peramatour.com) have regular mini-buses to several destinations in Bali from their office in Amed village.

Destinations Airport (daily; 2hr 45min); Candidasa (daily; 1hr 15min); Padang Bai (daily; 1hr 30min); Tirtagangga (2 daily, 30min); Ubud (daily; stops in Candidasa and Padang Bai).

By bemo All public transport between Amlapura and Singaraja passes through Culik. From here, the odd *bemo* runs via Amed to Aas in the morning.

Destinations from Culik Aas (1hr 30min); Air Sanih (1hr 30min); Amed (10min); Amlapura (45min); Bunutan (45min); Jemeluk (30min); Lipah Beach (1hr); Selang (1hr 15min); Singaraja (Penarukan terminal; 2hr 30min); Tirtagangga (20min); Tulamben (20min).

By boat Freebird Express (https://gilibookings.com/freebird-express) runs safe fast boats direct from Amed to the Gili Trawangan (1hr 15min) and Gili Air (1hr 30min) and also to Baangsal, Lombok (2hr), all daily.

Banks and exchange ATMs and moneychangers are in the main villages along the Amed coast.

GETTING AROUND

By car or motorbike Transport along the Amed coast is scant. For transport within the Amed area you'll either need to rent your own motorbike, available in every village, or use an ojek/driver. Car rental, with or without driver, is best arranged through your accommodation.

On a tour The most popular tours on dry land include the sightseeing loop via the spectacular coast road, Pura Lempuyang Luhur and inland hikes. Treks up Gunung Agung can also be arranged from Amed.

ACCOMMODATION

SEE MAP PAGE 176

3

In high season, villagers accommodate backpackers in their homes up tracks off the main road.

JEMELUK AND CONGKANG

Amed Lodge Jl. I Ketut Natih, Jemeluk; http://amedlodge.com. Quirky beach-front place offering a selection of seven bungalows with carefully mismatched furnishings – ceramics, ikat textiles and furniture – that combine Indonesia and Japanese influences. There's a small pool and home-cooked, nutritious and delicious meals in its Suda Café. $

Ganesh Amed Jemuluk; http://ganeshamed.com. *Ganesh Amed* has both the fan-cooled rooms and a/c rooms with private verandas. There's also a small swimming pool and direct beach access. $

★ **Geria Giri Shanti** Jl. Jemuluk, Amed, http://geriagirishanti.com. A tropical garden hideaway, this well-run place has spacious, clean and thoughtfully outfitted bungalows (good mosquito nets, nice fabrics, lots of hangers and long mirrors) just above the road. All have fans and hot water. Also home to Adventure Divers. $

Kembali Beach Bungalows Jl. Jemeluk, Lebah; http://kembalibeachbungalows.nl. Conveniently located on the beach with lots of bars and restaurants within walking distance, this well-managed hotel has eight lovely chalet-style bungalows with sea or garden views, verandas and attractive interiors. There's a pool and restaurant too. $

Sunrise Café and Bungalows Jl. Raya Amed, Jemeluk; 0363 23477. No frills beachside rooms, some of them with terraces enjoying bay views. There's also a restaurant/café serving up Asian cuisine. $

BUNUTAN

Aiona Garden of Health West end of Bunutan; http://aionabali.com. Eco-friendly hotel under coconut palms and mango trees with lovely cottages. The on-site vegetarian restaurant serves lunch and dinner. They also offer all levels of yoga and meditation classes. $

The Griya Villas & Spa Bunutan village; http://thegriya.com. This luxurious resort is perched on a headland so steep that golf carts are used to bring guests to their villas. Each villa has the latest electronic gadgets, a private infinity pool and great views over Lipah bay. The two restaurants and spa are top quality – but you'll need to walk 10–15min to get to the beach. Regularly hosts meditation workshops. $$$

Santai http://santaibali.com. Long-running beachfront resort with various types of a/c rooms in thatched bungalows. The furnishings are perhaps a tad dated in some ways but some have sea views. There's a small beach out front that's safe for children, with good snorkelling, and the on-site *Coconut Restaurant* is worth a visit. $$

LIPAH, LEAN, SELANG, BANYUNING AND AAS

Baliku Dive Resort Banyuning; http://amedbaliresort.com. Luxuriously appointed and indulgently spacious villa-style bungalows – each with kitchenette, a/c, day bed and bathtub – in a steep plot across the road from the Japanese Wreck. The veranda views of the reef, Lombok, and nearby hills are breathtaking. There's a pool and well-regarded restaurant. $$

Eka Purnama Banyuning; http://ekapurnama.com. Family-run, this is an excellent budget choice, especially for snorkellers, with robust bamboo bungalows from whose verandas you can practically see the reef fish across the road. Bungalows each have a single and double bed, mini-fridge, fan, mozzie net and hot-water bathroom. $

Life in Amed Lean; 0363 23152. Petite and pretty little beachside gem, where the a/c bungalows all have traditional carved doors, antique-style furniture, gorgeous, tiled floors and extra beds in the loft. A couple of beachfront villas can sleep bigger groups. There are also a pool, restaurant, yoga, spa and decent snorkelling on your doorstep. $$

Meditasi Aas; http://meditasibungalows.blogspot.com. Lovely, isolated place with a social vibe (daily yoga classes). There are eight large fan-cooled and simply decorated bamboo bungalows with huge sliding screens and private verandas, and four luxury rooms with gorgeous wooden furniture. On-site organic restaurant, *The Smiling Buddha*, is excellent. No wi-fi, phone signal or TVs. $

EATING

SEE MAP PAGE 166

JEMELUK

Green Leaf Café Jl. Raya Jemuluk; http://facebook.com/GreenLeafCafeAmed. A varied menu of Indonesian favourites, burgers, pizza and pasta warrants coming back for more. Free garlic bread and water on arrival are an added bonus as are the homemade breads and cakes. $$

Warung Enak About 750m west of Jukung Dive; 0819 1567 9019. Offers home-style Indonesian cooking including great *gado-gado* and very flavoursome chicken and beef rendang dishes. Expect reasonable prices and generous portions. $

BUNUTAN

Aiona Garden of Health West end of Bunutan; http://aionabali.com. The restaurant at *Aiona Garden of Health* has an excellent vegetarian menu, including salads, home-made pasta, and specialities such as the *Nasi Campur Special*, an Indonesian rice dish. No alcohol is served. Booking required. $

★ **Galanga** Jl. Raya Amed; http://facebook.com/Galanga-restaurant-336719899813199. The sign outside says "fusion food", but don't let that put you off – this is an outstanding cafe-restaurant serving great global food. Try a *nangka* curry (jackfruit cooked with coconut), the perfectly cooked samosas or one of their memorable cakes and desserts (such as shortbread biscuit with pineapple and coconut mousse). There's great (though pricey) coffee and tea too. $$

Gusto Jl. Raya Amed; https://facebook.com/profile.php?id=100063197770346. A nicely designed Hungarian-run restaurant above the road, with great service and a good variety of freshly made Indonesian and central European dishes, including great beef goulash and Wiener schnitzel. *Gusto* also has an excellent bakery. $$

LIPAH, LEAN, SELANG, BANYUNING AND AAS

Aquaterrace Selang; http://aquaterrace-amed.com. Enjoyable little café, which offers authentic Japanese food such as *ebi tempura* (prawns) and teriyaki dishes as well as Balinese and pasta dishes. The dining area has good views over the bay. $

Baliku Banyuning; http://amedbaliresort.com/restaurant. Combine lunch at this hotel restaurant with free use of the pool and premier snorkelling across the road. The (quite pricey) menu is wide ranging and includes steak with peppercorn sauce, rendang and falafel. $$$

Smiling Buddha Aas; http://meditasibungalows.blogspot.com. The restaurant at the *Meditasi* hotel has a gorgeous beach-facing location and offers fine local dishes (including lots of seafood and good veggie choices). Balinese dancers serenade diners on full moon nights. $$

Wayans Warung Jl. Raya Amed, Lipah. Popular with locals and tourists alike, this friendly establishment specialises in seafood. Offers a great variety of excellently prepared fresh seafood at really affordable prices. Live music at night. $

Tulamben and Kubu

North of Amed, the parched landscape is cut with folds and channels, relics of the lava flow from the 1963 eruption of Gunung Agung, which rises dramatically inland. The main focus of tourist attention in these parts is **TULAMBEN**, site of Bali's most popular dive, the **Liberty wreck**, which lies just 30m offshore. Over a hundred divers a day come to explore this most accessible of wrecks and, with several hotels and dive shops nearby, it's perfectly feasible to base yourself here for a few days. That way you can pick your dive times to avoid the crowds of day-trippers who clog the wreck between 11am and 4pm. The beach is black and stony and the village itself is dreary, so you might want to choose one of the hotels just outside central Tulamben, or consider Amed (13km south) as a base.

Continuing north about 5km is **Kubu**, a relatively undiscovered diving centre that's an ideal base for those wishing to be away from the hubub of Tulamben. There's a nice natural reef close to shore, teeming with marine life and also a Dutch cargo ship, the *Boga*, purposely sunk for reef building in 2012. Hard and soft corals and sponges attract small fish, larger ones are spotted nearby and inside are some interesting finds such as someone's long-lost VW Safari.

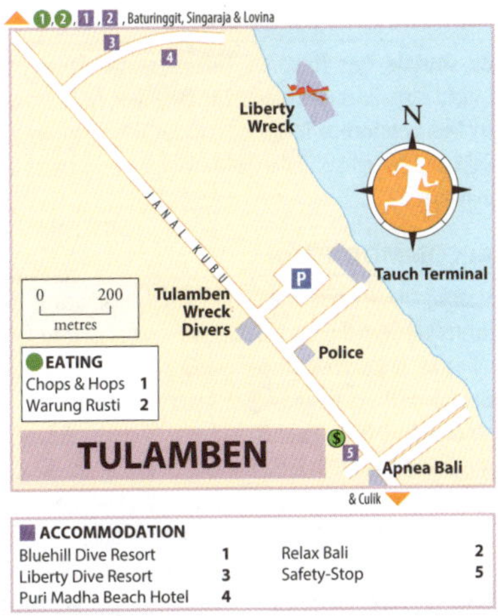

DIVING AT TULAMBEN AND KUBU

Tulamben's underwater treasure trove, the **Liberty wreck**, lies on a sandy slope just 30m offshore, making this one of the most accessible wrecks in Southeast Asia. Some sections are in shallow water, making it a good **snorkelling** site, too. The wreck is encrusted with soft coral, gorgonians and hydrozoans plus a few hard corals, providing a habitat for around three hundred species of resident reef fish and another hundred species that visit from deeper water. Night dives are especially good. Built in 1915 in the US as a steamship, the 120m-long *Liberty* was torpedoed on January 11, 1942, 15km southwest of Lombok. Attempts to tow the ship to port at Singaraja failed and it was beached at Tulamben, where it lay until 1963 when earth tremors accompanying the Gunung Agung eruption shifted it into deeper waters.

There are other sites to explore such as the **Tulamben Wall**, volcanic rock that drops to 60m housing unusual species such as comets, as well as black coral bushes. At **Batu Kelebit**, two huge boulders with coral-covered ridges are frequented by sharks, barracuda, jacks, manta rays and tuna. **Palung Palung** is suitable for beginners and experienced divers and has hard and soft coral from depths of 3m to 40m. **Tulamben Coral Garden** and **Shark Point** are self-descriptive, with black-tip reef sharks the draw at the latter. There's a muck dive site at **Secret Seraya** good for boxer crab, harlequin shrimp, ghost pipe fish and tiger shrimp.

Kubu's reefs are similar to Tulamben's and are easily accessible from the shore, but less crowded. Two metres from the beach are pinnacles of coral heads, also good for snokelling, leading into a ridge covered with staghorn and soft corals sometimes visited by rare porcelain crabs and cowrie snails. Among the scores of reef fish are pygmy seahorses with schools of barracudas and groupers with the occasional batfish dropping by.

The *Boga* wreck lies between 17–36m on a sandy bottom. Hard and soft corals and sponges are occasionally visited by bumphead parrot fish, octopus and barracuda, and there are three cargo holds to explore.

DIVE CENTRES

Scuba dive centres in the area offer dive-and-accommodation packages as well as trips further afield, to Amed, Pemuteran and Nusa Penida. There's also a freediving school. The following centres are well established.

Apnea Bali http://apneabali.com. Freediving school.

Relax Bali http://relaxbali.cz/en.

Tauch Terminal http://tulamben.com.

Tulamben Wreck Divers http://tulambenwreckdivers.com.

ARRIVAL AND INFORMATION — TULAMBEN AND KUBU

By shuttle bus There are Perama shuttle buses from Candidasa to Tulamben (daily; 2hr; minimum two people).

By bus or minibus Tulamben is about 10km northwest of Culik and served by Singaraja–Amlapura public buses and minibuses.

Destinations Air Sanih (1hr); Amlapura (1hr); Culik (30min); Singaraja (2hr); Tirtagangga (1hr).

Banks and exchange There's an ATM in central Tulamben, and several places can change money.

ACCOMMODATION — SEE MAP PAGE 181

Most of the accommodation in central Tulamben is in a cluster between the sea and the Culik–Singaraja road. More upmarket places are scattered within a 5km radius east and west along the coast and will pick you up on request.

★ **Bluehill Dive Resort** half-way between Tulamben and Tukad Dabu; 0813 5308 8444. Undoubtedly the best value around in terms of price and quality of service. Twelve lovingly appointed rooms with private verandas, a/c, hot water, pool, kiddie pool and dive centre. $

Liberty Dive Resort Central Tulamben; http://libertydiveresort.com. Just 200m up the lane from the *Liberty* wreck, the 32 rooms and cottages here have a/c, with large balconies and hot water throughout, plus 3 pools and energetic staff. $

Puri Madha Beach Hotel Central Tulamben, close to the Liberty wreck; http://purimadhabeachhotel.weebly.com. The hotel has a variety of rooms available: some nicely furnished with hot water, a/c and ocean views and some rather basic. There's a shoreside garden, a swimming pool and a restaurant. $

Relax Bali 4km northwest of Tulamben, Kubu; http://relaxbali.cz/en. Surprisingly tucked into a forest by the sea, *Relax Bali* literally has accommodation for everyone: bungalow for one or two or for families and five luxury villas with private pools. There is a dive centre, spa, restaurant and pool bar. $$

Safety-Stop Central Tulamben, close to Tauch Terminal; 0811 3364 222. This German-owned homestay has four comfortable spacious air-conditioned bungalows. Also, there's a popular restaurant and bar. Airport shuttle on request. $

EATING

SEE MAP PAGE 181

Chops & Hops Jl. Raya Kubu at Ocean Sun Dive Resort; https://ocean-sun.com/en/restaurants/chops-and-hops. When you feel ready to tuck into a proper meal, get your wallet ready because this isn't a cheap place. However, the menu makes up for it with schnitzel, sirloin or grilled fish of the day. Kids menu, cocktails, burgers and curries too. $

Warung Rusti Jl Raya Tulamben-Kubu; 0813 3856 2486. While a simple, cheap-food *warung*, there is a good selection of Indonesian food prepared on order by the friendly owner. Good food, great prices. $

3

North Bali and the central volcanoes

HINDU RELIGIOUS PROCESSION ON LAKE BRATAN

North Bali and the central volcanoes

A cool, less populated landscape of morning mists and forest, inland north Bali feels like a different island when compared to the crowded southern plains. The Bedugal highlands is an area defined by mountains, lakes and waterfalls with swathes of clove and coffee plantations around hilltown Munduk. Pura Ulun Danu Bratan, an important temple and a destination for Balinese-Hindu pilgrims, is also here. In the east is the active Gunung Batur volcano where occasional puffs of smoke waft from black rock, one of Bali's most popular sunrise hikes. At its base are other walks over parched, ethereal terrain peppered with giant boulders ejected from the earth's core.

The scenic north-south road from Denpasar to Seririt is winding and hilly, passing through flower and vegetable farms, but is tedious to traverse as it is clogged with trucks headed for the Singaraja port, the gateway for supplies to eastern Indonesia. However, a new toll road from Seririt to the south is under construction which will speed the trucks along a more direct route while allowing pleasure seekers to take in the fabulous views on the old mountain road.

For hundreds of years – possibly thousands – the north of Bali was open to foreign influence as Indian, Chinese and Arab traders landed to do business here via the port and former Balinese capital, **Singaraja**. In 1928 Dutch shipping company KPM, which connected Bali to the rest of Indonesia and to international ports, built a hotel at Singaraja to encourage tourism, making it the island's tourist gateway. It was only when Ngurah Rai Airport opened in 1969 that the south became a focus for tourism and the axis of development shifted away from the north. Today, Singaraja remains north Bali's biggest city as capital of the **Buleleng** administrative district under whose jurisdiction the entire north coast falls.

The **coast** here is markedly quieter than its southern counterpart, receiving fewer visitors than the holiday conurbations in the south. Yet it is a rugged and, in places, impressive landscape, where flanks of the mountains drop steeply to black-sand beaches. The only resort area that warrants the name is **Lovina**, a relaxed beach destination of medium-sized hotels, family-owned guesthouses and funky cafés rather than pounding nightlife. It makes a decent base from which to explore the region on day-trips to the temples and hot springs just west, or to exuberant temple carvings and several large waterfalls around Singaraja.

ARRIVAL AND GETTING AROUND NORTH BALI AND THE CENTRAL VOLCANOES

Plans are underway for a new North Bali international airport and a toll road connecting south and north Bali, both hoped to receive official approval in 2025, but there is currently no such infrastructure in the north. With narrow, hilly roads and traffic congestion, travel time between the north and south can easily amount to three hours or more. As such, it's best to base yourself in the north for a few days rather than attempting to explore on a day trip.

By bemo or bus Public transport regularly serves the Singaraja–Gilimanuk road that runs along the north coast, taking in Lovina, and also the three main southbound roads through the mountains to Denpasar – from Seririt via Pupuan, Singaraja via Bedugul and Kubutambahan via Batur. This makes many of the sights in the north accessible by bus or *bemo*.

By car or motorbike You'll need your own transport to explore the scenic back roads.

Gunung Batur and around

Entry to the Batur area incurs a fee, payable at booths on the access roads from Bangli and Ubud – you'll only pay once, so keep your ticket

SEKUMPUL WATERFALLS

Highlights

❶ **Gunung Batur** The hard-sell of the Kintamani folk can infuriate, but one of Bali's most celebrated (and most active) volcanoes is worth the hassle for the spectacular panorama from its crater rim. To see it close up, trek up to the summit. See page 186

❷ **Danau Bratan area** The Bedugal highlands harbours a trio of sacred crater lakes, a temple that is as beautiful as it is venerated and Bali's best botanical garden. See page 194

❸ **Munduk** A former Dutch colonial highlands getaway, this region has fine accommodation, enjoyable treks and hours to be lost simply enjoying the mesmerising views. See page 196

❹ **Lovina** Although the beaches are not Bali's finest, once merely an escape from the overcrowded south, Lovina remains a laidback place, with a fine selection of hotels and restaurants. See page 199

❺ **Sekumpul Waterfall** Even on an island blessed by waterfalls, seven cascades in one area which tumble into a verdant valley are postcard-perfect. See page 207

❻ **Pura Meduwe Karang** The liveliest example of north Balinese temple carving, depicting vivid scenes from daily life, a Dutch man and Hindu mythology. See page 207

HIGHLIGHTS ARE MARKED ON THE MAP ON PAGE 188

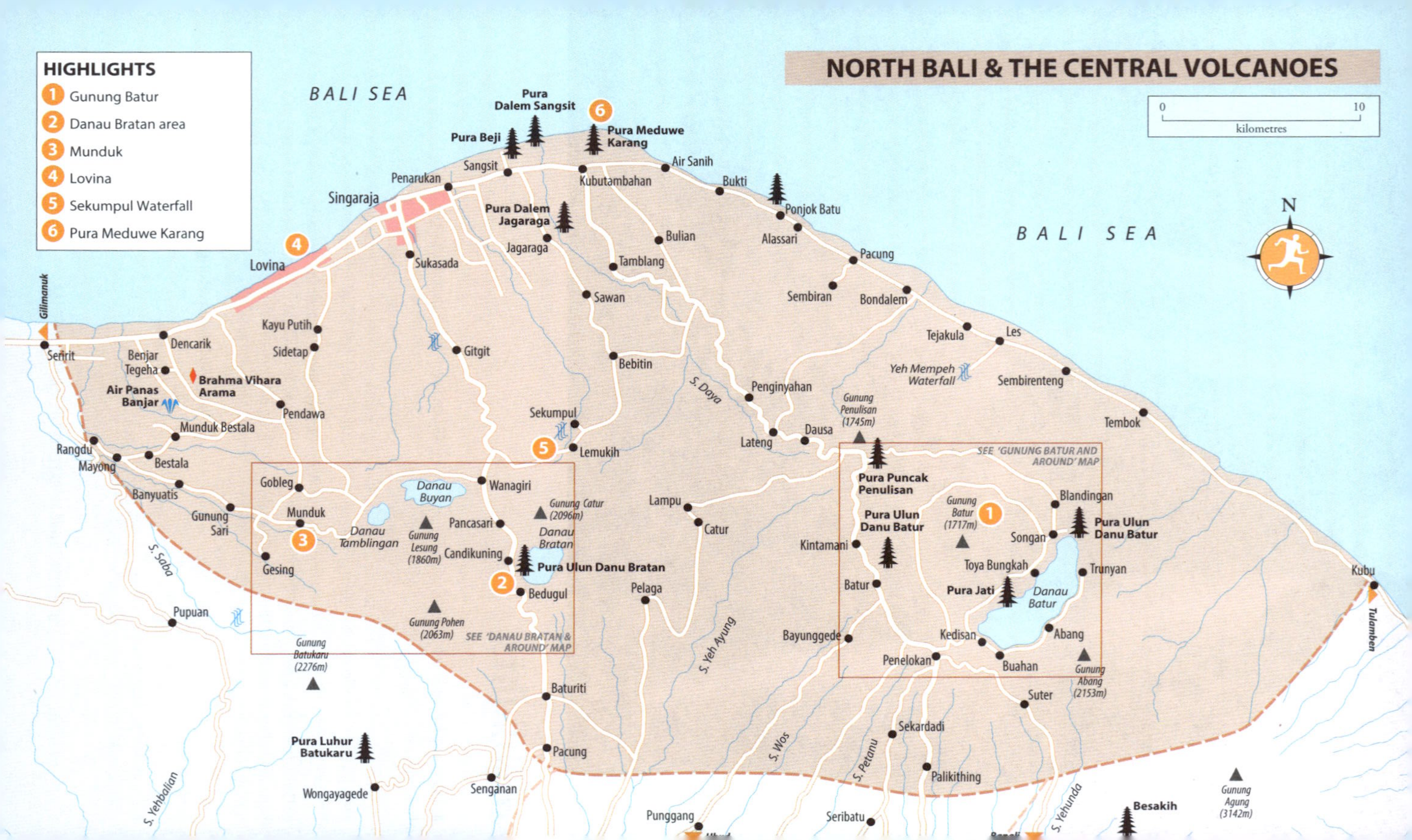
NORTH BALI & THE CENTRAL VOLCANOES
HIGHLIGHTS
1 Gunung Batur
2 Danau Bratan area
3 Munduk
4 Lovina
5 Sekumpul Waterfall
6 Pura Meduwe Karang
0
10
kilometres
N
BALI SEA
BALI SEA
Pura Dalem Sangsit
Pura Beji
Pura Meduwe Karang
Pura Dalem Jagaraga
Sangsit
Penarukan
Singaraja
Lovina
Kubutambahan
Air Sanih
Bukti
Ponjok Batu
Alassari
Bulian
Tamblang
Jagaraga
Sukasada
Sawan
Pacung
Sembiran
Bondalem
Tejakula
Les
Sembirenteng
Tembok
Yeh Mempeh Waterfall
Gilimanuk
Seririt
Dencarik
Benjar
Tegeha
Brahma Vihara Arama
Air Panas Banjar
Kayu Putih
Sidetap
Pendawa
Munduk Bestala
Rangdu
Mayong
Bestala
Banyuatis
Gunung Sari
Gitgit
Bebitin
S. Daya
Penginyahan
Sekumpul
Lemukih
Lateng
Dausa
Gunung Penulisan (1745m)
Pura Puncak Penulisan
Pura Ulun Danu Batur
Gunung Batur (1717m)
Blandingan
Songan
Pura Ulun Danu Batur
Trunyan
Toya Bungkah
Pura Jati
Danau Batur
Kintamani
Batur
Kedisan
Abang
Buahan
Penelokan
Gunung Abang (2153m)
Bayunggede
SEE 'GUNUNG BATUR AND AROUND' MAP
Kubu
Tulamben
Gobleg
Munduk
Danau Buyan
Wanagiri
Danau Tamblingan
Gunung Lesung (1860m)
Pancasari
Gunung Catur (2096m)
Danau Bratan
Candikuning
Pura Ulun Danu Bratan
Bedugul
Gesing
Gunung Pohen (2063m)
SEE 'DANAU BRATAN & AROUND' MAP
Lampu
Catur
Pelaga
S. Yeh Ayung
S. Saba
Pupuan
Gunung Batukaru (2276m)
Baturiti
Pacung
Pura Luhur Batukaru
Wongayagede
Senganan
S. Yehbalian
Punggang
S. Wos
S. Petanu
Sekardadi
Palikithing
Seribatu
Suter
S. Yehunda
Besakih
Gunung Agung (3142m)

ERUPTIONS AT GUNUNG BATUR

Gunung Batur has **erupted more than twenty times** since 1804. In 1917, a major eruption killed over a thousand people, but the lava stopped just outside Batur village's temple, which was then situated in the crater beside the lake. Considering this a good omen, the population stayed put until August 3, 1926, when another eruption engulfed the village and residents were relocated onto the rim. The **longest eruption** started in September 1963, a few months after Gunung Agung's massive explosion (see page 157), and continued for eight months. Along the north coast near Yeh Mampeh, waterfall you'll see lava flows from an eruption in March 1974. The newest crater, Batur IV, was formed during the eruption that began on August 7, 1994, and continues to erupt periodically. It spewed ash 300m above the summit in 2000 and hiking trails were closed in 2009 due to more than a hundred **earthquakes**. It's startling to see the volcano still smoking, but locals believe it's better that Batur lets off a little steam regularly rather than saving it up for a major blow.

On a clear day, no scenery in Bali can match that of the **Batur** area. With its volcanic peaks and silver-turquoise crater lake, the scale and spectacle of this landscape is unrivalled; so much so that UNESCO listed it as a geopark in 2012. It was formed thirty thousand years ago when a gigantic volcano eruption created a vast outer caldera that spans 13.5km. **Gunung Batur** (Mount Batur; 1717m) at its heart is still active – wisps of sulphurous smoke still drift from smaller cones on its slopes. A major trans-Bali road runs along the west side of the crater rim, affording magnificent high-level views, and a side road gives access to the crater lake, **Danau Batur**, on its floor. 4

Given the scenery, it's no surprise that this is one of Bali's most popular tourist destinations. Hundreds of day-trippers come for lunch in **Penelokan** village above the caldera and leave having experienced little except a wraparound panorama and a sloppy buffet lunch in the many coach-tour restaurants. Only by stopping overnight in one of the **villages by the lake** can you drink in the magic of this scenery. Many travellers base themselves locally to make the fairly straightforward sunrise trek up Gunung Batur, Bali's most climbed mountain. **Toya Bungkah** is popular and has some hot springs nearby while **Kedisan** village is an alternative and also the departure point for ethically questionable boat trips to a Bali Aga cemetery at **Trunyan**. South of Kedisan, **Buahan** is the quietest spot of all, while **Songan**, at the northern end of the lake, is the start of other hikes up the crater rim.

The one downside to the awesome scenery is that the Batur area has a reputation for **hassle**. Persistent **hawkers** in Penelokan and aggressive hotel touts make those in Kuta seem relaxed, while a local trekking guide cartel makes it almost impossible to climb the mountain unguided (see page 191). Trust us: the remarkable views are worth it.

Routes up Gunung Batur

Most people ascend up to Batur I from **Toya Bungkah** and **Pura Jati**, a steep climb but not too gruelling if you pace it steadily. The path from Pura Jati is shadeless and largely across old lava fields. From Toya Bungkah, numerous paths head up through the scrub – one starts just south of *Arlina's* guesthouse – before emerging onto bare lava slopes to ascend steeply through black volcanic sand to the tiny *warung* on Batur I's rim. Allow two to three hours to get to the top from either starting point, and about half that time to get back down; sunrise treks up this route depart at about 4am. Though you could just as easily leave later and go for the view from halfway up – it's no less impressive.

A **medium-length trek** takes in Batur I, a walk around its rim, before descending by another route. The **long-trek** option, sometimes called the **Exploration** (about 8hr in total) involves Batur I, walking to the western side, then descending to Batur II, Batur III and down to Toya Bungkah or Pura Jati.

4

Guides are definitely advisable if you're hiking at night and as the hard-sell and pressure from the guides' association is relentless, most hikers do hire one, even if they don't think they need one during the day.

Danau Batur and around

Filling the ancient crater, silver-emerald **Danau Batur** is not just the largest lake in Bali (8km by 3km), it is also one of the most impressive. As the home of Dewi Danu, the goddess of the crater lake, Danau Batur is especially sacred to the Balinese – it is believed to feed springs in other parts of the island that irrigate all fields. Several villages line the lake's shore, notably **Kedisan**, **Buahan** and **Toya Bungkah**, which have tourist accommodation, and **Songan**, site of an important temple and a footpath up the mountain. Nowadays, villagers survive on tourism and the simple things the gods provide: vegetables, which grow in the fertile soils along the shore, and fish.

Kedisan and Buahan

One of the first lakeside villages you'll come to, **KEDISAN** lies among the chilli, tomato, onion and potato plots at the bottom of the steep 3km road from Penelokan into the ancient caldera. The lakeside village is the departure point for boats to Trunyan cemetery and also where you can avail of canoeing, kayaking and cycling trips around the lake.

Turning right at the T-junction in Kedisan brings you to the quietest and most attractive part of the lake, especially around and beyond **BUAHAN** village, 2km from Kedisan, where the eastern shore is lined with market gardens and fish-farming paraphernalia and offers some of the finest lake views of Gunung Batur.

Trunyan

TRUNYAN is among Bali's less edifying tourist destinations. It's one of the few remaining Bali Aga communities, inhabited by descendants of the "original Balinese" who rejected the Javanization of their island when the Majapahit invaded in 1343 and have maintained their distinctive customs ever since. The most unique is the village custom of leaving its dead to decompose in the open rather than cremating or burying them; cadavers are usually covered in a blanket and protected from animals within a bamboo cage (though human bones and even skulls are often visible). If you do decide to visit, expect demands for large donations.

Visiting the **cemetery** is an uneasy experience and it can only be culturally sensitive if you attend with a responsible local guide. It's also not cheap: access is by hired **boat** from a jetty in Kedisan (20min), then expect a hefty fee for a good guide plus another "donation" to enter the village. We recommend that you skip it.

Toya Bungkah and around

The main tourist village on Danau Batur is **TOYA BUNGKAH**; though fairly shabby, it has the most accommodation around the lake and is the starting point for climbs up Gunung Batur, as well as a base of the Association of Mount Batur Trekking Guides (see page 191). It also has a couple of **hot springs** for soaking stiff limbs after a walk. About 4km south of Toya Bungkah, **Pura Jati**, dedicated to the god Wisnu, has some fine carvings. One of the routes up the mountain starts near here.

Songan and around

At the northwestern end of the lake, 4km beyond Toya Bungkah, **SONGAN** village is the location of **Pura Ulun Danu Batur**, not to be confused with the bigger, newer temple on the crater rim. A ceremony is held here every ten years to honour the goddess of the lake, involving the ritual sacrifice of buffaloes, pigs, goats, chickens and geese, all adorned with gold ornaments. Locals speculate that the floor of the lake is littered with riches from hundreds of years of ceremonies – possibly more, since this is said to be built on the site of a pre-Majapahit temple. Not many *bemos* serve Songan and

4

PLANNING A GUNUNG BATUR TREK

Batur remains **active** and the authorities sometimes close the mountain. Check the current situation at http://vsi.esdm.go.id – it's mostly in Indonesian but it is clear if any mountain is on alert. The **dry season** (April–Oct) is best for climbing.

Anyone who makes the ascent to Batur is put under intense pressure to engage a guide from the **Association of Mount Batur Trekking Guides**, or PPPGB (0878 6313 0080), which has offices in Toya Bungkah and at Pura Jati. A guide is essential for all **sunrise treks**, which require route-finding in the dark – one solo foreign walker fell to his death in 2010 – and hugely advisable for longer hikes or less well-trodden paths. These routes are tricky and it's important to stay away from the most active parts of the volcano. If you are doing the climb in daylight either from Serongga or to Batur I from Toya Bungkah or Pura Jati, you don't really need a guide, but you will get intensely hassled, perhaps even intimidated, into hiring one anyway. On the plus side, a good guide will provide historical and cultural context to a walk.

Guide **prices** are displayed in the association's offices. You'll probably have to pay extra for breakfast on the mountain – usually the novelty of boiled eggs cooked by geothermal energy – and transport to the trailhead, if required. Be absolutely clear which route you are doing.

Many **tour agencies** around Bali run sunrise hikes with pick-ups from hotels, albeit at times no tourist should have to see. Try Bali Sunrise Trekking and Tours (http://balisunrisetours.com) or Mudi Goes to the Mountain (http://mudigoestothemountain.com).

However you ascend, you'll need sturdy footwear for the rough track and warm clothing for dawn treks.

you may end up **walking** to or from Toya Bungkah, either along the road or a lakeside track.

Directly behind the temple in Songan, a **footpath** winds up onto the rim of the outer crater – you can follow tracks to explore farming villages populated with bamboo huts. There are some fine views down to the north coast, back to Abang, Agung and even Rinjani on Lombok. With a good supply of food and water, the more intrepid should be able to pick a route down to **Bali's northeast coast** to catch public transport northwest to Air Sanih or southeast to Tulamben.

From the junction in central Songan, a circular **scenic road** runs for 26km around Gunung Batur's western base and back up the hill to Penelokan. It takes you past **Pura Bukit Mentik**, known as Lucky Temple because lava from the 1974 eruption surrounded it but caused no damage. By serendipity, the lava fields are now mined as building stone and sand, which is ferried from the area by a steady procession of trucks.

Pura Ulun Danu Batur

South Kintamani • Charge

The second most important temple on Bali after Besakih, **Pura Ulun Danu Batur** honours **Ida Batara Dewi Ulun Danu** (Dewi Danu for short), the goddess of the crater lake who is believed to control water for the irrigation systems throughout Bali. Her influential representative on earth is the temple's high priest, the Jero Gede, who is appointed on the death of his predecessor by a virgin priestess in a trance. He plays a vital role within Bali's sophisticated *subak* irrigation system and farmers consult him about plans and conflicts – his word is final.

4

Given its status and that it is one of the highly venerated *kayangan jagat*, or directional temples, which protects Bali from the north, it's perhaps surprising to learn that this temple is relatively new. It was relocated from the crater to its present position on the Kintamani–Penelokan border after the 1926 eruption (see page 189). The most significant of its countless shrines is the **eleven-roofed meru** in the inner courtyard dedicated to both the goddess of the lake and the Gunung Agung god. The drum in the *kulkul* tower is beaten 45 times each morning to honour the 45 deities worshipped in the temple. Unfortunately, gangs of aggressive, unholy scammers and guides spoil the experience for many. A sarong and sash are compulsory attire.

Penelokan, Batur and Kintamani

Climbing out of the caldera and up to the main road, spread along the west side of the main road for 11km, the scruffy **Penelokan**, **Batur** and **Kintamani** villages virtually merge; the three are often called Kintamani after the largest settlement. The big attraction, of course, is the view, which is at its most sensational from Penelokan (1450m), literally meaning "Place to Look", and your spot for wraparound views of the volcanic landscape: Gunung Batur (on your left), Gunung Abang (2153m) opposite and between them Danau Batur lake as a shimmering skin of silver. To add context to the view, a **museum** here offers a decent introduction to local geology and there are two very important **temples**, too. As you head north, Batur and Kintamani merge in a seamless sprawl of stalls and shops; the former was moved here from the caldera beneath after it was obliterated in the 1926 eruption. There's a colourful morning market in Kintamani selling produce from Bali's richest fruit and vegetable growing area. Incidentally, bear in mind that you're at about 1400m above sea level up here, so nights are **chilly** – you might be glad of a sweater even in the daytime, especially if the mist descends.

Continuing north on this road takes you to Gunung Penulisan and eventually to the north coast.

Museum Geopark Batur

Jl Raya Penelokan, on Bangli road, just south of the junction with the crater-rim road • Charge • 0366 51088

Housed in a striking building that vaguely resembles a volcano, the **Museum Geopark Batur** summarises the history, mythology and geology of Batur. Scale models show the changing face of the local topography, and there are informative computer animations on volcano systems and an exhibit on the Pacific's "Ring of Fire". From the top floor a telescope is directed at Gunung Batur's smoking cone.

Pura Puncak Penulisan

Sukawana (where road descends to coast) • Donation sometimes requested for admission

Built on the summit of Gunung Penulisan (1745m), 5km north of Kintamani in Sukawana village, **Pura Puncak Penulisan** is the highest temple on Bali and one of the most ancient; it is named in ninth-century inscriptions. There are 333 steps to the top temple, **Pura Panarajon**, which is dedicated to Sanghyang Grinatha, a manifestation of Siwa and god of the mountains. Up here, *bale* shelter ancient lingam and statues from the eleventh to thirteenth centuries. Needless to say, when the clouds clear the views are spectacular.

ARRIVAL AND DEPARTURE — GUNUNG BATUR AND AROUND

By bus or bemo The crater rim road is a main route between the north and south coasts, so public transport is frequent. Perama tourist shuttle buses run to and from Kintamani and Ubud, Kuta and Sanur (minimum 2 people). Occasional public *bemos* from Penelokan go as far as Songan on the western side of the lake and Abang on the eastern side.

Destinations from Penelokan (add/subtract 20min for Kintamani to the north) Bangli (45min); Buahan (30min); Denpasar (Batubulan; 2hr 30min); Gianyar (50min); Singaraja (Penarukan; 1hr 30min); Songan (45min); Toya Bungkah (30min).

ACTIVITIES

Canoeing, kayaking and cycling C Bali in Kedisan, Kintamani (http://c-bali.com) offers morning-only canoeing on Danau Batur, with good cultural input from local guides and free pick-ups from lake accommodation, as well as cycling tours through villages. Toya Devasya's (http://toyadevasya.com) many activities include kayaking (charge includes a soak in hot springs and a swim), cycling and camping.

Mountain-biking Sobek (http://balisobek.com) and Mason Adventures (http://masonadventures.com) both run downhill cycling trips in the Batur area – usually down slopes and through rice paddies – including transport from tourist centres in south Bali. There's not much pedalling involved, mostly freewheeling.

Hot springs For a lovely spa-style experience head to the garden pools in *Toya Devasya* (charge includes hot springs soak and a swim in the resort's pool; http://toyadevasya.com) in the village centre.

ACCOMMODATION AND EATING — SEE MAP PAGE 190

There are simple *warung* in the villages for Indonesian grub like *nasi campur* while the guesthouse restaurants tend to

ROADS LESS TRAVELLED

It's 40km from Kintamani through the foothills to **Kubutambahan** on the **north coast**, from where Singaraja is 7km west and Air Sanih is 6km east. This road is one of Bali's main north–south routes, busy with trucks, cars and tourist buses, but it takes you through some pretty scenery.

If you have time to spare, an attractive quieter alternative route runs northeast via the **back road to Bondalem**, a north coast village that's 15km southeast of Air Sanih and 4km northwest of Tejakula. The *Bondalem Beach Club* (http://bondalembeachclub.com) provides a convenient snack or meal stop.

The junction to the narrow, twisting, very steep and very scenic 16km road is at the main Kubutambahan road at **Lateng**, northwest of Pura Puncak Penulisan, 13km from the Kintamani market, and 500m after the end of Dausa village. This back road is known locally as the **Tejakula road**. It initially descends through vegetable gardens and stands of cloves, cacao, coffee and avocado with great views of neighbouring ridges and west towards Gunung Batukaru. After about 10km the temperature rises significantly, and coconut plantations stretch all the way to the north coast.

4

offer more varied menus, including fresh fish. All are open 8am–9pm. Note that hotels in this highland region, where many owners were subsistence farmers a generation ago, do not have as high standards as those in more mainstream tourist areas.

DANAU BATUR AND AROUND

Batur Volcano Guesthouse Jl. Pendakian Gunung Batur, Kintamani; 0812 462 5447. A spacious property with a great view overlooking the lake, there is a four-bed dorm and a mountain view room with double bed. A natural hot spring pool and responsive host complete the picture. $

Black Lava Hostel Jl. Bunkah, Toya Bunkah; 0813 3755 8998. Owned by a local trekking guide, this impressive, rustic hostel is just the place to hook up with other travellers in the Batur area. There are two mixed dorms (with lockers but shared bathrooms), decent private rooms with en suites and tents with single or double beds. The restaurant serves affordable local food and has sweeping lake views. $

Geopark Village Jl. Bukit Mekar Sari Songan A, Songan; http://geoparkvillage.com. Four wooden villas ideal for sunrise climbs due to the location. Pool, spa and helpful owner are added attractions. $

Songan Homestay Jl. Songan near Pinggan traditional village; https://songanhomestay.blogspot.com. A cosy place with a beautiful garden in front, hot shower and fresh food. Well maintained and great value; owned by the area's midwife. $

Villa Jempana Jl. Raya Songan, Ulun Danu Gang Jempana Indah No. 1; http://villajempana.com. A three-room getaway across from the lake with clean and spacious rooms providing king-sized beds, pool and a restaurant. $$

★ **Volcano Terrace** Jl. Raya Pendakian, Toya Bungkah; https://facebook.com/volcanoterrace. Beautifully designed B&B with wonderful lake views from its four spacious minimalist rooms that feature comfort and imaginative decorative touches. It's run by a friendly local family who provide good meals and can arrange guides for the Batur hike and exploring the area. $$

Danau Bratan and around

At weekends, domestic tourists come by the coachload to munch strawberries, enjoy the cool temperatures and admire the lakes and cloud-capped hills around the **Bedugul** highlands (altitude 700m-plus). The area takes its name from the village of the same name, one of several small settlements (and the most missable, incidentally). But it's also referred to as the **Danau Bratan** area after the largest and most visited of the three spiritually charged crater lakes around Bedugul.

On the lake's shores lies **Pura Ulun Danu Bratan**, not just an exceedingly photogenic temple but also an important pilgrimage site for Balinese Hindus. Temples and fruit and vegetables aside, the other major sight here is the **Bali Botanic Gardens**, with its **Bali Treetop Adventure Park**. Just up the road is *Handara Golf & Resort* whose split gate entrance has become almost as frequently photographed as Pura Ulun Danu Bratan.

For all the fuss made over it by local tourists, **Candikuning** is not Bali's most inspiring base. More appealing for foreign visitors is **Munduk**, 20km northwest; an often misty hilltown, always mellow and a shining example of sustainable village tourism, with several good places to stay and a range of activities to while away a few lazy days. Munduk also offers the opportunity to walk around the area's smaller, less commercial lakes: **Danau Buyan** and **Danau Tamblingan**.

Danau Bratan

Lying just below Candikuning at 1200m above sea level, **Danau Bratan** is thought to be 35m deep in places. It is surrounded by forested hills, with the bulk of **Gunung Catur** (2096m), the caldera's highest peak, rising sheer behind. The trail to the summit begins at Gua Jepang, caves built by Indonesian prisoners of war during World War II, and passes through agricultural fields ending where dense forest and the ascent begins. The last few kilometres require climbing over exposed tree roots on muddy trails so wear appropriate footwear. At the top is Pura Puncak Mangu, a simple temple built by the first Mengwi raja and, of course, spectacular views of the three lakes below.

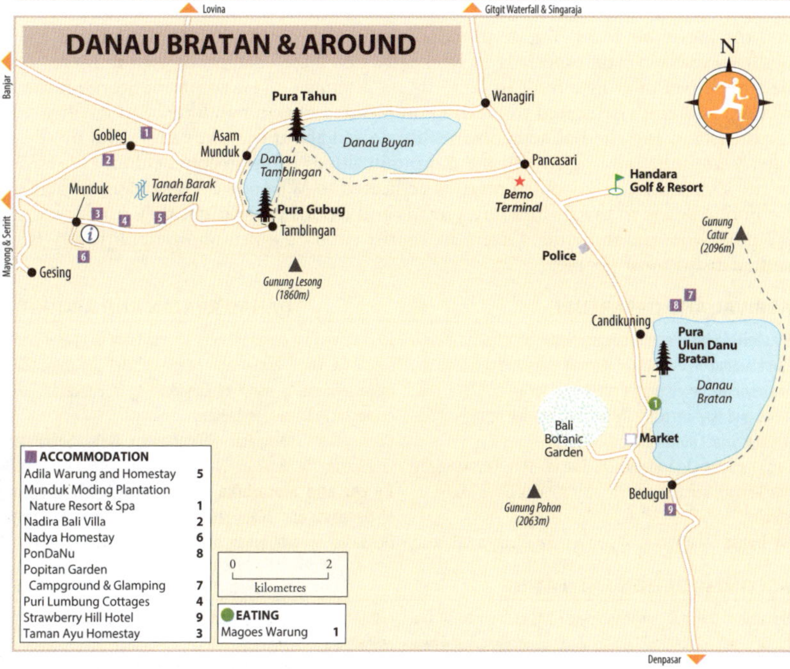

Candikuning

Sliced up by traffic, **CANDIKUNING** village on the western shores of Danau Bratan is the main base for the lake and Bali Botanic Gardens. Accommodation and restaurants line the highway through the village, as well as the side road to the gardens. The daily market in the centre is another fun, if touristy, stop, a mix of fresh local fruit, spices, temple offerings and mass-produced souvenirs. It's a good place to stock up for a picnic in the botanic gardens.

Bali Botanic Gardens

Well signed off a mini-roundabout beside the market, then 700m down a side road • **Bali Botanic Gardens** Jl. Kebun Raya • Charge • https://kebunraya.id/bali

Spread back into the forested slopes, **Bali Botanic Gardens** (Kebun Raya Bali) conserves some two thousand species of tropical montane plants; from ferns and countless orchids to impressive cacti, medicinal plants, bamboo forests and an extensive collection of begonias. It's a tranquil place – often cool and misty due to its altitude of 1250–1450m – and at 1.58 square kilometres is large enough to lose half a day or more exploring. Do so and on one of the hiking trails you may discover birdlife such as brown honeyeaters and grey-cheeked green pigeons – over a hundred species have been recorded here – or see monkeys on upper slopes. Given the park's size, some people drive around the gardens, although you can also wander on foot. The gardens are a lovely spot for a picnic, which is a popular weekend activity. You can also stay in the gardens.

Pura Ulun Danu Bratan

1km north of Candikuning centre • Charge

Lake Danau and its goddess are worshipped in **Pura Ulun Danu Bratan**, a classical Balinese temple situated in a breathtaking lakeside location. Today it's a major tourist attraction, with car parks full of coaches from the coast, souvenir stands and the inevitable touts. Yet, despite the commercialisation, the temple is also highly revered in Bali; especially at weekends, you'll see villagers dressed in their best to deliver offerings. Built in 1633 by the Mengwi raja on a promontory on the western shore, it's dedicated to Dewi Danu, source of water and hence of fertility for the island and the Balinese. Shrines are dotted about the lake's shore and on islets – an impressive sight with the mountain slopes rising steeply behind. Closest to the shore, the eleven-roofed **meru** is dedicated to Wisnu and Dewi Danu. There's no public access to the shrines but, crowds and clouds permitting, they still look fabulous from the shoreline. Given the tourist circus, a quick photo opportunity is sufficient for most people.

ARRIVAL AND DEPARTURE — DANAU BRATAN AND AROUND

By shuttle bus Perama tourist shuttle buses pass through Candikuning on their Ubud–Lovina route and can drop you at any of the hotels on the main road for an extra fee; their office and pick-up point (http://peramatour.com) is at *Sari Artha Inn*, just north of the market.

Destinations Kuta (daily; 2hr 30min–3hr); Lovina (daily; 1hr 30min); Sanur (daily; 2hr–2hr 30min); Ubud (daily; 1hr 30min).

By bemo Candikuning sits on a main north–south road, so is served by *bemo* services to and from Denpasar and Singaraja. Local *bemos* also beetle around the area; the main terminal is north of Candikuning in Pancasari. No *bemos* go to Danau Tamblingan.

Destinations Denpasar (Batubulan; 2hr); Singaraja (Sukasada; 1hr 30min).

By car and motorbike Danau Bratan is 53km north of Denpasar and 30km south of Singaraja on the main Denpasar–Singaraja road; no direct route links it to Batur.

4

ACCOMMODATION AND EATING — SEE MAP PAGE 195

Because of the cool climate up here (it goes down to 10°C at night), fans or air-conditioning aren't generally offered here – you'll be more interested in thick quilts and hot water. A clutch of snazzy glampsites have sprung up around the lake, but many travellers still prefer Munduk as a base. There are a few modern cafés on the main road or for a cheap feed, browse the abundant *warung* in the market, where there are always strawberries for sale.

Magoes Warung Bedugul Jl. Raya Bedugul; 0821 9675 1579. A refreshing, modern alternative to the usual *warungs*, a good variety of pizza, pasta and Balinese dishes appears on the menu alongside iced coffee, cold beer and freshly squeezed strawberry juice. $

PonDaNu Jl.Dajan Danu Kembangmerta; http://pondanu.com. Simple yet comfortable cabins with balconies by the lake alongside several glampsites. There's also a bar, lido restaurant and spa, plus kayak and stand-up paddleboard rentals. $$

Popitan Garden Campground & Glamping Jl. Mawa 2; 0878 6091 1770. Enjoy a warm welcome at this friendly, tranquil campground in a quiet tree-shaded plot with lake views. Choose from A-frame cabins and tents decked out with comfy beds, minimalist furnishings and en-suite bathrooms. $

Strawberry Hill Hotel Jl. Raya Denpasar-Singaraja Km 48, Bedugul; http://strawberryhillbali.com. The best midrange choice for miles, this lovely lodge has seventeen stylish little bungalows kitted out with batik prints and attractive furnishings, while the brilliant pub-like bar-restaurant has a pool table, dart board, books to browse and even a log fire. You'll find Western and Indonesian favourites on the menu and you can pick your own strawberries here too. $

Munduk and around

Strung out amongst clove trees and coffee plantations along a steep valley spur, **MUNDUK** is one of Bali's most appealing hill retreats. It remains a mellow, low-key settlement, with refreshingly cool temperatures and gorgeous vistas; the sort of place where you can arrive for a night and leave a week later. Cloud-gazing aside, days are spent **walking** to nearby villages and waterfalls, while dusks ease into spectacular sunsets and a soundtrack of a million frogs. The **Dutch** administration were the first foreigners to relish Munduk's scenery, as well as its fertile soils and cooler climate at 500–700m above sea level. From 1910 they developed it as a summer retreat and cultivated coffee, cloves, vanilla and cocoa in the surrounding fertile soils. Some of their weekend homes are now used as guesthouses, but colonial **Dutch architecture** along the main street is hardly the point. (The village is barely 500m long, for a start.) Instead, see Munduk as a chance to kick back – slow travel has never been so beautiful.

Tanah Barak waterfall

The most accessible of several falls in the area is pretty **Tanah Barak waterfall**, also known as Red Coral waterfall or simply Munduk waterfall. Take a signposted track off the main road 1km east of Munduk, pay for entry at an ad hoc booth (usually – it's not always manned) and you can take a short rainforest track to reach this impressive cascade which plumes into a lush gorge. There are several other falls in the area, such as Sekumpul and Gitgit to make a half-day trip from central Munduk.

On the main road between the two lakes you'll spot dozens of artistic bamboo structures and swings at scenic overlooks. For the price of a snack or a drink you're allowed to take photographs of the views with these as props.

Danau Buyan

Car park charge, although it's not always staffed

Danau Bratan may receive all the acclaim, but it's not the only lake in this highland region. In **Pancasari**, 4.5km north of Candikuning, at a small *bemo* terminal – it's busiest in the morning and is the junction for travel to Munduk – a turn-off tracks to **Danau Buyan** through allotments and gardens. More pothole than tarmac, the lane peters out at the lake's southern shore; a tranquil spot after the hubbub around Bratan, with little here except a ticket booth for a car park and a few fishermen in dugout canoes. It's a lovely place to relax – or you could embark from here on a good 4km track around the lake's shore and over a saddle to reach Danau Tamblingan.

Danau Tamblingan

Charge, plus parking fee if booth is manned

Danau Tamblingan is the smallest and most atmospheric of Bedugul's three lakes, once contiguous with Danau Buyan to the east (before a landslide in 1818), now separated by a forested shoulder of land. **Trekking** between the two lakes is a popular activity, you don't really need a guide as it's just a matter of keeping the lakes on your left-hand side. The path around the western shore is also renowned for **birdwatching** – sightings of babblers, woodpeckers, ground thrushes and malkohas are possible.

On the shore, **Pura Gubug** has eleven-, nine- and five-roofed *meru* and is dedicated to Dewi Danu, the goddess of the lake. Several other temples overlook the shoreline, including the ancient Pura Dalem Tamblingan on the east side. Villagers grow hydrangeas, marigolds and mandarins in the fertile, lake-watered soils, fish for carp, and rear cattle on the *tunjung* (lotus) that grows on the lake. For a small fee you can hire one of the temple guards to row you around the lake in traditional twin-bodied

4

THE CLOVE TRAIL

It was the search for **cloves**, among other spices, that first drove Europeans to explore the Indonesian archipelago, and for hundreds of years cloves were one of the region's most lucrative exports. Native to certain islands in the Moluccas (Maluku, the original "Spice Islands"), cloves are now grown mainly in Maluku, Sumatra, Sulawesi and Bali. You'll spot the tall trees in the hills around Bedugul, Tamblingan and Munduk and if you're there during **harvest time**, from August to October, you'll see death-defying pickers on rickety ladders and huge piles of drying cloves beside the road – buds must be picked before the petals open, after which the amount of clove oil declines sharply.

Bali's cloves end up in Java for the manufacture of Indonesia's pungent **kretek cigarettes**. These consist of up to fifty percent cloves mixed with tobacco, and demand is so great that the former clove capital of the world now imports them from Madagascar, Zanzibar, Sri Lanka and India to supplement local production.

outrigger canoes for a closer look at the lake's flora and fauna. Prices are posted in the little shed where the guardians sit.

ARRIVAL AND INFORMATION — MUNDUK AND AROUND

Munduk is 8km west of Danau Tamblingan, 20km northwest of Candikuning and 20km southeast of Seririt. Access by public transport is possible but long and circuitous; *bemos* are most reliable in the early morning.

By shuttle bus Coming from southern resorts or Ubud, take the Perama shuttle bus to Bedugul (Pancasari), then change for a *bemo* to Munduk.

By bemo *Bemos* travel up to Munduk from Seririt, itself easily reached by *bemo* from Pemuteran or Lovina on the north coast. There are also *bemos* every couple of hours from Denpasar's Ubung terminal. *Bemos* on all routes are more frequent in the morning.

Destinations Denpasar (Ubung; 2hr 30min); Seririt (1hr).

By taxi Your accommodation can help arrange car and driver.

By motorbike Motorbikes are widely available for rent.

Banks and exchange There are no ATMs in Munduk, though a moneychanger is available.

ACTIVITIES

Activity tours Munduk Wilderness (https://instagram.com/munduk_wilderness) provides a number of off-road driving tours in 4WD vehicles and buggies and two-day wilderness trips. Prices include transfers from major resorts in Bali.

Cooking lessons Both *Puri Lumbung Cottages* (http://purilumbung.com) and *Chez Rico* (0852 0510 7928) offer well-structured Indonesian and Balinese cooking lessons.

Cultural workshops *Puri Lumbung Cottages* has an exceptionally diverse range of cultural workshops: as well as cooking lessons and yoga, it runs sessions in herbal medicine, Indonesian Balinese dance, bamboo-instrument making and offering making.

Trekking and mountain-biking Guesthouses arrange local guides; expert English-speaking guides are more expensive. Most treks are rural hikes through clove and coffee plantations, via market gardens growing blue hydrangeas (used for offerings), vanilla and mandarins, and through ricefields and villages. You're also likely to be offered treks to several waterfalls in the area, the closest being Tanah Barak (Munduk) waterfall (about 1km east of Munduk). Treks to and between lakes Tamblingan and Buyan are also well worth doing, or you could try climbing Gunung Lesung (1860m). Munduk Trekking (http://mundukactivity.wordpress.com) offers good guided walks past waterfalls and clove and coffee plantations. *Puri Lumbung Cottages* runs several half-day guided mountain bike rides including the "Pyramid Trail" past a pyramid made from recycled plastic, ricefields and Danau Tamblingan.

4

ACCOMMODATION AND EATING

SEE MAP PAGE 195

The quality of accommodation in Munduk is generally high. Many places offer superb views and most have an attached restaurant (which is usually OK rather than particularly exciting). *Puri Lumbung Cottages* has the best in the area.

Adila Warung and Homestay Jl Raya Banjar; 0819 3655 1226. Expect a warm welcome at this lovely place, where the four spotless rooms have four-poster beds, hot-water bathrooms and enjoy terrific vistas from their verandas. There's great local food in the *warung* and the owners are full of local information. Book ahead. $

Munduk Moding Plantation Nature Resort & Spa Jl. Asah Gobleg, Gobleg village, 5km west of Danau Tamblingan; http://mundukmodingplantation.com. Hidden within a large working coffee plantation 10km from Munduk, this remote spa retreat is the perfect escape. Modern villas – all rich hardwood floors and crisp, fine cotton – overlook beautiful forest; cheaper suite rooms are also available. Perhaps more impressive is the infinity swimming pool – rightly acclaimed as one of Asia's best – and the spa, gym, library and game room are lovely too. Be sure to try their coffee grown onsite. $$$

Nadira Bali Villa Jl. Gobleg, Gobleg village; http://nadirabalivilla.com. A four-star resort with a/c, TV, restaurant and bar, swimming pool and a welcoming staff that will help you plan your daily activities. Surrounded by nature, all rooms have pool views. Includes breakfast. $$

Nadya Homestay Jl. Pura Puseh; 0819 9993 0085. Rooms in this homestay are simply furnished but clean and comfortable and most have balconies with mountain views. There's a restaurant and a swimming pool. $

Puri Lumbung Cottages Jl. Raya Munduk; http://purilumbung.com. This place has real character and wonderful vistas. Cosy *lumbung*-style cottages or spacious villas are set around ricefields with panoramas to the north coast, though interiors would benefit from some updating. On-site amenities include a spa, a sunset bar and the most extensive menu in the region, serving authentic Indonesian food and Western dishes. It also manages two Dutch-era homestays and eight forest cabins near Lake Tamblingan – if eco-isolation appeals and you don't need electricity, this is your place. $$

Taman Ayu Homestay 0899 015 5357. Traditional, welcoming family homestay, where the simple rooms have mismatched furnishings, balconies over the valley and a basic bathroom with hot water. $

Lovina and around

Northern Bali's primary beach, **LOVINA** remains a low-rise, low-key sort of place, especially when compared to its south Bali counterparts. Its shoreline is not startlingly attractive (the dark sand is not most people's vision of a tropical dream beach and there's some trash about) but Lovina does have a decidedly Balinese, non-international feel and this ensures an enjoyably mellow, local vibe.

Lovina is spread out along 8km of grey-sand beach, encompassing seven merged villages. **Kalibukbuk**, set between two side roads and lined with an oceanfront walkway, is the heart of Lovina, bursting with accommodation, restaurants and facilities. West of Kalibubuk is Kaliasem, where seasonal buffalo races are held. East of Kalibukbuk, the **Banyualit** side road, Jalan Kartika, runs down to the sea and is quiet and green, with banana palms still dotted between the various small *warung* and hotels. It's favoured by long-stay and older tourists from northern Europe. There's more of a backpacker vibe in **Anturan**, 2.2km east of Kalibukbuk, with most places on or very close to the village beach and a snorkellable reef offshore. Finally, after Tukad Mungga, ricefields take over and you're officially in **Pemaron**.

Dolphin-spotting boat trips are wildly popular (though see warning below) and cultural activities including cooking classes are on offer. Lovina's proximity to good **snorkelling** and **diving** sites, and as a base for day-trips to nearby waterfalls and temples are another key appeal. The **Buddhist monastery** and **hot springs** (air panas) at Banjar, 10km west, and temples and waterfalls east of **Singaraja** (see page 203) make a good day out. And with those ticked off, the crater lakes and hikes around Bedugul and Munduk are just under two hours away.

4

Brahma Vihara Arama

Hosts a busy programme of meditation workshops and teachings • Donation for entry includes sarong rental • 0362 92954 • Catch any westbound *bemo* to Dencarik, where *ojek* wait to take you the last, steep 3km; if driving, head as for Air Panas Banjar hot springs and turn left at the central crossroads in Banjar Tegeha village

Bali's largest Buddhist monastery, the **Brahma Vihara Arama** is 10km southwest of Lovina in the hills outside Banjar Tegeha village, so is a good combination trip with the hot springs at Banjar 3km away. (Incidentally, if you ask for directions, bear in mind that locals know it as the "Buddis temple" rather than by its name.)

The monastery is a serene spot after the hurly-burly of everyday Balinese life. It's primarily a place of meditation, yet welcomes well-behaved and modestly dressed casual visitors, and its shrines and prayer halls afford good views to the coast. The

A DAY-TRIP DRIVE FROM LOVINA

For a day-trip from Lovina with your own transport, there's a scenic **inland drive** through the countryside south of Seririt, 12km west of Lovina, initially along the Denpasar road. The road climbs through paddyfields then splits after 7km at **Rangdu**. The right-hand fork heads across the mountains via Pupuan where there's an enormous "sleeping Buddha" statue to the south coast. However, the left goes through Mayong towards Munduk (see page 196) then on to Danau Tamblingan and Danau Buyan.

Just beyond Mayong, take a small left turn for "Desa Bestala", which leads to the **Bestala village**. Turn left by the statue of the independence fighter, then wind down into the valley, across the river and up the other side to **Munduk Bestala hamlet**, renowned for its durians; January and February are the main season. Turn left at the T-junction in the village, and if you have a decent map it's possible to navigate to **Pedawa** and **Sidetapa**, two traditional Bali Aga villages that still retain their narrow lanes and high-walled compounds.

Adjani in Lovina provides guided walks in the Sidetapa area, as well as transport.

ACCOMMODATION	
Bali Paradise Hotel	4
The Damai	7
Frangipani Beach Hotel	2
Kubu Kusuma Guest House	6
The Lovina	3
Mias Jungle House	9
Puri Bagus Lovina	1
Puri Mangga Sea View Resort & Spa	8
Rambutan Boutique Hotel	10
Santhiku Hotel, Villas, Yoga & Spa	5

EATING	
Akar Café	6
Buda Bakery & Resto	4
Cafe Greco	7
The Damai	3
Kakatua Bar & Restaurant	5
Secret Garden	2
Warung Bambu	1

DRINKING AND NIGHTLIFE	
La Costa Beach Lounge	1
Spice Beach Club	2
Zigiz	3

centrepiece of the main temple is a Thai-style gold Buddha, but follow stairs in the peaceful grounds and you'll also find a Nepalese-style stupa (dome-shaped shrine). The most striking section is the (scaled-down) **lava-stone replica** of Central Java's Borobudur temple in serene frangipani gardens at the summit of the complex. It houses a meditation hall with limestone reliefs of the life of the Buddha.

Air Panas Banjar hot springs

Charge • http://banjarhotspring.co.id • Coming from Kalibukbuk in Lovina, take the main road west for 8km, then follow signs south for 2.5km to reach the springs; the springs are also 3km from the Brahma Vihara Arama Buddhist monastery, reached from the village crossroads; there's no public transport

The traditional-style **hot springs** at **Air Panas Banjar** are certainly picturesque: tiered over three pools and fed by water spouting from *naga* dragons' mouths, they sit enclosed in a dell of palm trees and tropical forest, 1.25km south of the market in Banjar Tegeha. The water, however, is another matter. Silky soft and slightly sulphurous, it is a rather murky green, but this doesn't stop the pools from being

hugely popular with locals and tourists alike. Come in the morning to avoid the crowds; weekends are especially busy. There are lockers, (pretty filthy) changing rooms, and a small restaurant overlooking the pools. Note that women have reported being stared at when wearing swimwear, which is considered to be immodest.

ARRIVAL AND INFORMATION

LOVINA AND AROUND

Central Lovina is only 10km west of Singaraja, so there are plenty of transport services to major destinations across Bali, Lombok and Java, including those of Bali-wide Perama tourist shuttle buses.

By shuttle bus Perama tourist shuttle buses connect Lovina with tourist centres across Bali; their office is in Anturan (daily 8am–6pm; http://peramatour.com) but for an additional fee you can be dropped off elsewhere.

Destinations All the following Perama services leave at 9am daily: Bedugul (1hr 30min); Candidasa (3hr–3hr 30min); Gili Islands, Lombok (8hr); Kuta/Ngurah Rai Airport (3hr 15min); Padang Bai (2hr 45min); Sanur (2hr 30min–3hr); Ubud (3hr 30min–4hr).

By bemo or bus From east Bali, you'll come via Singaraja: its Banyuasri terminal is a 20min *bemo* ride away. From Denpasar, there are Ubung–Singaraja services via Pupuan, and minibuses to Seririt for local *bemo* connections. Interisland buses from Java to Singaraja pass through Lovina, as do Gilimanuk–Singaraja and Amlapura–Gilimanuk services and all local buses and *bemos* from west Bali.

Destinations Amlapura (3hr 30min); Gilimanuk (2hr 45min); Seririt (20min); Singaraja (Banyuasri; 20min).

Tourist information Lovina's tourist office (0819 3635 2377) is on Jl Raya Kalibukbuk.

GETTING AROUND

By bemo *Bemos* ply the main Lovina road, Jl Raya, fairly frequently during daylight hours.

By car, motorbike or bike Cars or motorbikes are available everywhere – it's probably easiest to source one through your accommodation. For bicycles, there are several travel agencies on Jl Mawar. Be very careful driving along the main drag Jl Raya Lovina which is the main route for a lot of Bali-Java traffic and is plagued by heavy traffic, including aggressive truck drivers, 24 hours a day.

ACTIVITIES

Buffalo races Lovina has a weakness for buffalo races (*sapi gerumbungan*) in Kaliasem, one of the few places on Bali where this colourful tradition can still be seen. They're usually staged on Independence Day (Aug 17), and in September (along with various other cultural performances) – source information at the tourist office.

Diving and snorkelling The local reef is pretty pedestrian for experienced divers, though there's decent fish life, a small wooden wreck and an artificial reef that's encouraging coral growth. Local dive shops run trips to Pulau Menjangan, Tulamben and Amed but these involve a lot of time on the road. Arrows Dive Centre (http://arrows-dive.com) on Jl. Mawar, Anturan, is a Five Star PADI dive centre. Snorkelling can be arranged through any hotel, with boat skippers on the beach or with dive centres.

Dolphin trips Lovina is famous (or should that be infamous?) for its dawn trips to spot the resident dolphins. And depending on who you talk to, they're either grossly

4

overrated or one of the best things on Bali. A flotilla of traditional *prahu* head out to sea at sunrise, until one skipper spots a dolphin or two. On bad days the entire fleet (dozens of boats) chases after them – and despite regulations many boat owners harass the mammals by driving boats right through the pods and getting far too close. On good days there may be so many dolphins that the atmosphere is less frenetic and the hunt less aggressive. Book directly with skippers on the beach or through your accommodation.

Scooter tours If you've always wanted to buzz about on a motorbike but would prefer someone else do the driving, Bali Vespa Tour (http://bali-vespa-tour.com) offer fun excursions that take in waterfalls, some hiking and superb scenery.

Trekking The most interesting treks are to waterfalls and to nearby villages. Any number of guides will be more than happy to provide a full-day outing. Bali Jungle Trekking (http://balijungletrekking.com) leads tours in the hills around Sidetapa traditional Bali Aga village, including a visit to the Buddhist monastery and hot springs in Banjar.

Watersports Every form of adrenaline-pumping water activity you can think of is here: banana boat, parasailing, jet ski, flyboard and flying fish, to name a few. Krisna Water Sports (Jl. Seririt-Singajaj, Temukus (between Kaliasem and Seririt) https://instagram.com/krisnawatersportslovina).

COURSES AND WORKSHOPS

Cookery classes Lovina has more than its fair share of cookery classes; most include transport to the morning market in Singaraja plus lunch (obviously). Adjani (http://balicookingclass.com) runs classes in Kaliasem, including vegetarian cooking; and *Warung Bambu* restaurant in Pemaron (http://warung-bambu.mahanara.com) offers various classes, including one all about sweets.

Cultural classes *Warung Bambu* restaurant in Pemaron can organize workshops in Balinese dance and gamelan on request.

SPA TREATMENTS

4

As an alternative to the massages offered by women on the beach, there are plenty of hotels and day spas offering treatments.

Kirani Tour and Spa Jl. Raya Lovina, Anturan, https://kiranibalitour.com. Highly recommended for full body, foot or scalp massages or select a facial or eyelash extensions from the spa menu.

Puri Mangga Sea View Resort & Spa (see accommodation section for details). A full resort-style spa menu includes hand and foot treatments, facials, hot stone massage, 60 or 90min. full body massages and more.

ACCOMMODATION

SEE MAP PAGE 200

Bali Paradise Hotel Jl Kartika, Kalibukbuk; http://baliparadisehotel.com. This beachfront hotel in a quiet location has well-appointed colourful rooms and suites featuring local art, a bar, a restaurant and two pools. Most rooms (apart from those on the ground floor) have balconies or terraces with mountain, garden or sea views. $$

★ **The Damai** Jl. Damai, Kayu Putih; http://thedamai.com. Elegance and luxury combine at this fine hotel, blessed with a supremely tranquil hillside location, 4km inland from Kalibukbuk. There are superbly appointed butler-serviced villas, some Bali-style with jacuzzis, others contemporary with a private pool. There's a spa, spectacularly sited pool, superb restaurant and shuttle service to Lovina. $$$

Frangipani Beach Hotel Jl Kartika No. 99, Kalibukbuk; http://frangipanibeachhotelbali.com. Seafront homestay where the rooms, all boasting clean modern lines and sleek bathrooms, are set round a lawn and pool just behind the shore. Located a 10min walk from central Kalibukbuk. $

Kubu Kusuma Guest House Jl. A. A. Pandji Tisna, Kaliasem; http://facebook.com/kubukusuma. An inland private two-bedroom house with infinity pool in tropical gardens beside a mountain stream; excellent service by Australian couple. You can rent one bedroom or the whole house. Cooking classes available. $

The Lovina Jl. Mas Lovina, Kalibukbuk; http://thelovinabali.com. For those whose idea of a holiday leans toward a big resort on the beach, The Lovina fits the bill. With 66 villas and suites, nine plunge and two main pools, kids club, restaurant, beach bar, spa and fitness studio, it has everything. $$

Mias Jungle House Gang Pisang, Kaliasem. In a quiet area away from the crowded beach, free bicycles make to and fro easy. All rooms have a/c, private bath with shower, mini bar and terrace. Shared sitting room with TV. Continental breakfast included. $

Puri Bagus Lovina Jl. Seririt-Singaraja, Pemaron; http://puribaguscandidasa.com. The chicest option in Lovina, offering large, airy, elegantly simple, well-appointed cottages in extensive beachside grounds – "Deluxe" buys a sea view – plus a lovely infinity pool and a wonderful spa. It's some distance from most restaurants and facilities, but the tranquillity really sets the place apart. $$$

Puri Mangga Sea View Resort & Spa Jl. Damai, Kayu Putih; http://puri-mangga.de. With seven villas, a very interesting combo of choices from basic *lumbung*-style with fan to two-bedroom deluxe house ideal for families. Restaurant, spa, pool. Look for promos and off-season discounts on their web. $$

Rambutan Boutique Hotel Jl Mawar, Kalibukbuk; http://rambutan.org. Impressive facilities – two pools, a spa, fitness centre, kids' areas and yoga room – give this UK-Balinese hotel real appeal. Rooms are in Balinese-style buildings and there are three spacious villas suitable for families. Standard fan-only rooms are far less inviting however. $

Santhiku Hotel, Villas, Yoga & Spa Jl Pandji Tisna, Kaliasem; http://facebook.com/santhikuhotel. A quirky, sociable travellers' base with artistic decor and lots of little zones for chilling and chatting. There are four private rooms and one dorm and there are on-site yoga classes, plus a small spa, a tiny pool (a bigger one is planned to be built) for cooling off and a lovely lounge area. All guests are welcomed with a drink, some fruit and a free foot massage. $

EATING

SEE MAP PAGE 200

Akar Café Jl. Pantai Binaria, Kalibukbuk; 0362 343 5636. Green in decor and ethics, this cute vegetarian café has a varied menu of imaginative food that includes Middle Eastern meze plates, outstanding salads, plus health juices (try a "Greenpeace" with mint, lemon and honey), teas and ice creams. There's a garden terrace with river views at the rear. $

Buda Bakery & Resto Jl. I Gede Taman No. 26 off Jl. Damai; http://facebook.com/Budabakeryandresto. Worth the 10min walk from the beach for freshly baked breads (pumpernickel, soft brown) or a gorgeously decorated cake for a special occasion. Upstairs, the café serves salads and soups. Try the Chicken and Vegetable Salad with Focaccia Croutons or Tom Yam Soup. $$

Cafe Greco Jl. Mawar, corner of Jl. Raya Lovina-Singaraja; http://facebook.com/cafegrecolovina. This lovely café-cum-restaurant is popular among the locals and tourists alike. An ideal place to watch the world go by in Lovina. It offers a good selection of pastries and coffee yet there are also sandwiches, burgers and whole meals (schnitzels, kebab, moussaka, chicken satay etc). $$

★ **The Damai** The Damai Hotel, Jl Damai, Kayu Putih; http://thedamai.com. The perfect place for a special meal, this creative, award-winning restaurant uses organic produce from its garden and the menu changes daily. There's an extensive wine list and free transport from the Lovina area. $$$$

Kakatua Bar & Restaurant Jl. Binaria, Anturan; 0362 41344. This popular restaurant specialises in authentic Indonesian and generally Asian fare, but some international staples are also available. Try the fish steak, the mixed fish dish or a wood oven pizza. $$

Secret Garden Jl. Pura Dalem, Anturan; http://secret-garden-restaurant.biz. A charming little find with only five tables tucked away in a… well, secret garden. Presents curries with a flair, fresh seafood, juices, cocktails and a "rice table" (six Balinese dishes with starter and dessert) that must be ordered a day in advance. Pickup/dropoff to hotel is free. $$

★ **Warung Bambu** Pemaron Jl Hotel Puri Bagus, Pemaron; https://warung-bambu.mahanara.com. Overlooking ricefields, this bamboo-built restaurant serves fine Balinese and Indonesian dishes – zingy curries as hot as you request, lots of seafood, traditional "Betutu style" Balinese duck or, for a blow-out, a twelve-dish *rijsttafel*. There's Balinese dancing every Wednesday and Sunday evening and free transport in the Lovina area. Contact them about cooking classes. $$

DRINKING AND NIGHTLIFE

SEE MAP PAGE 200

Clubbing is virtually non-existent in Lovina, where most visitors settle for a cold Bintang at one of the many beach bars while watching the sunset, but there is live music on Friday nights at **Spice Beach Club** (Jl Raya Singaraja-Seririt No. 225, Kaliasem; http://spicebeachclubbali.com) and **La Costa Beach Lounge** (Jl. Singaraja-Seririt, Temukus, next to Krisna Water Sport, 0878 6304 8979) is good for sundowners and tasty food.

Zigiz Jl Pantai Binaria, Anturan, 0877 1558 8766. A tiny, lively bar over two levels – upstairs provides a nice lounge area – with live acoustic music most evenings plus cocktails with local/imported spirits and wine by the glass. Also shows major sports events. $

DIRECTORY

Doctor There are several clinics in the area, including Klinik Kaliasem on Jl Kaliasem and Klinik Lovina, Jl Raya Singaraja-Seririt, Kalibukbuk. The nearest hospitals are in Singaraja.

Immigration office Kantor Imigrasi, Jl Raya Pemaron (0362 32174); visa extensions take around a week.

Police Jl Raya Banyualit (0362 41010).

Singaraja and around

The second-largest city in Bali after Denpasar, with a population of around 150,000, **SINGARAJA** is almost defiantly untouristy. It comes on as a typically Southeast

4

Asian city, with a whirlwind of traffic in its streets and little concession to outsiders. Notwithstanding the occasional monument and the broad avenues, there are few obvious reminders of its past as the capital of Bali or of its role as the former seat of the Dutch administration for the Lesser Sunda Islands (which included Bali and all the islands east to Timor) apart from a few preserved buildings on the waterfront.

Today Singaraja has to content itself instead with being just the capital of the Buleleng district: images of **Singa Ambara Raja**, Buleleng's winged lion symbol, appear all over the city – "Singa Raja" means "Lion King". Sights are few. The traditional market can be fun, while the specialist **Gedong Kirtya library** of books made from *lontar*-palm leaves is worth a visit. As it's very spread out, Singaraja makes for a sweaty, unrewarding time without your own transport.

A trio of otherwise unremarkable villages east of Singaraja – Sangsit, Jagaraga and Kubutambahan – have some of the most engaging **temple carvings** on Bali. Throw in a stop at the **Sekumpul** or **Gitgit waterfalls** to the south, some of Bali's most beautiful falls, and you have the makings of a good day-trip from Lovina. The temple villages are served by *bemos* from Singaraja's Penarukan terminal (which is 3km east along Jalan Surapati from the Pelabuhan Buleleng waterfront).

Brief history

When **Gusti Ngurah Panji Sakti** founded **Buleleng kingdom** in the seventeenth century, he built a new palace called Singaraja at the heart of his north-coast territory, then extended his dominion to Karangasem, Jembrana and parts of East Java. The regency's influence fluctuated over the next 150 years, culminating in eventual defeat at the hands of the **invading Dutch** in 1849, who had launched a series of extended campaigns against the north coast. The victorious colonialists took over the administration of Buleleng and set about building roads, improving irrigation systems and encouraging coffee as a cash crop in the region; European journalists, merchants and scholars began to settle in and around Singaraja, even as the south of the island was still battling the Dutch. As the Dutch strengthened their hold, the administrative importance of the north grew, and when the colonial power combined Bali and Lombok into one regency in 1882, Singaraja was established as the **capital**. During World War II, the invading **Japanese** also made their headquarters here, but Independence saw the Balinese capital move south to Denpasar.

Gedong Kirtya Library

Jl Veteran 20 • Donation • Blue Sukasada–Penarukan *bemos* pass the entrance

Singaraja's best-known attraction is the esoteric **Gedong Kirtya**, the world's only library of **lontar manuscripts**, which was founded in 1928 by a Dutch official. It holds over six thousand of these manuscripts – the text is written on *lontar* (*Borassus flabellifer*) palm leaves and bound between wooden boards – covering Balinese religion, customs, philosophy, folklore, medicine, astrology and black magic. Such is the humidity, the books only last fifty to a hundred years, so decaying manuscripts are transcribed onto new *lontar* leaves, ensuring this ancient art survives. It's an inordinately lengthy process; leaves are soaked then boiled and pressed over many days before the precise, painstaking work of engraving the text can begin – it only becomes visible when rubbed with lamp black, the sooty residue from oil lanterns. The library also conserves *prasasti*, inscribed **bronze plates** from the tenth century, which are among the oldest written records on Bali. It's a scholarly place, but visitors are welcome; a member of the library staff will show you round.

Museum Buleleng

Jl Veteran 23 • Donation welcome • 0362 330 3368

4

The same compound as the Gedong Kirtya – that of the palace of Puri Agung Singaraja – holds the **Museum Buleleng**. It's hard to get excited about its five rooms of local history; the 1930s typewriter formerly owned by Anak Agung Panji Tisna (1908–78), the **last Buleleng raja**, portraits of Buleleng heroes, including the kingdom's founding father, **Gusti Ngurah Panji Sakti** or local Stone Age tools and Bronze Age jewellery are hardly gripping. Moderately more interesting are the eighth-century Buddhist items found in Kalibukbuk in Lovina, which bear testament to north Bali's trading history.

Puri Agung Singaraja

Jl Veteran 23 • entry by donation

Behind the Museum Buleleng are the residential quarters of **Puri Agung Singaraja**, also known as Puri Gede Buleleng, the restored palace of the former Buleleng royal family. Displays summarise the lives of previous rulers, in particular that of Anak Agung Panji Tisna (1908–78), the **last Raja of Buleleng**, founder of Lovina and owner of its first hotel.

Pasar Anyar

Jl Diponegoro • Free

Traditional Singaraja's commercial hub is the covered **market**. It's at its busiest in the very early morning, around 5am, but at any time of day you can buy your live chickens or salted fish and stock up on temple offerings, sarongs and any number of handmade knives.

The waterfront

A few minutes' walk north of the market, **Pelabuhan Buleleng**, the **waterfront** is the site of Buleleng's ancient harbour, although it's hard to imagine that this was once the busiest port on Bali. Today, it's notable for its restaurants on stilts in the water, the statue of freedom fighter I Longtong pointing a defiant finger out to sea, and Chinese temple **Ling Gwan Kiong** (admission by donation), a red-and-white confection of shrines, statues and bridges that date back to 1873. If you're lucky, one of the temple's guardians who speaks English will show you around and point out some interesting artefacts.

Pura Beji and Pura Dalem Sangsit

Jl. Raya Sangsit • Admission by donation (includes sarong rental)

4

Virtually an eastern suburb of the city, **Sangsit**, 2km from Singaraja's Penarukan terminal, is unique for its exuberant north Balinese temple carving. The 15th century pink-sandstone **Pura Beji**, 200m north off the main road, is dedicated to Dewi Sri, the rice goddess, and its every surface seems to writhe with carvings of animals, plants, masks, humans and monsters, both old and new.

From here you can just about glimpse the red roofs atop **Pura Dalem Sangsit**, 500m northeast across a ricefield. Its front wall depicts the rewards that await the godly in heaven and, more luridly, the punishments lined up in hell: stone blocks on the head, women giving birth to strange creatures and sharp spikes descending through skulls.

Jagaraga

Around 4km south of Sangsit off the main road, **JAGARAGA** was the site of two immense battles between the Balinese and the Dutch. In 1848, the Balinese, led by local hero Gusti Ketut Jelantik, won with huge loss of life, their sixteen thousand troops fighting with lances and *kris* against three thousand well-armed Dutch. The two forces met here again in 1849, when the Dutch finally took control of the entire Buleleng regency.

Pura Dalem Jagaraga

1km north of Jagaraga • Charge

Such was the bloodshed at Jagaraga that the sign for the **Pura Dalem Jagaraga** temple greets you with "Welcome to the temple of death". Though badly eroded in places, the lively late nineteenth- and early twentieth-century carvings of daily life before and after the Dutch takeover are among the most photographed in Bali. The best are on the outside front walls: on the left of the main gate is village life before the Dutch invasion – kite-flying, fishing, climbing coconut trees; next to them are the Dutch arriving by car, boat, plane and bicycle, destroying the community. There's also a much-reproduced carving of two Dutchmen in a Model T Ford being held up by bandits. Nearby, a statue of folk character Pan Brayut shows him being crawled over by some of his scores of children (see page 155). And inside the right-hand wall the crocodile eating the man is taken to represent the Dutch conquering Bali.

TREKKING AROUND SEKUMPUL

Without your own transport the easiest way to visit the falls is to arrange **guided treks** between Sekumpul and Lemukih, via the falls, taking in the various plantations and rice terraces as well as a swim. Lovina agents offer this service (all inclusive). If you visit by yourself, contact guide Kadek Ardita, the owner of a coffee stall on the path from Sekumpul (08523 704 4245; https://instagram.com/hanging_resto_bar), who offers trek guiding for two to four hours and charges.

Gitgit Falls

South of Singaraja, 10km along the road to Bedugul • Charge • All buses between Singaraja (Sukasada terminal) and Denpasar via Bedugul pass Gitgit

The three well-signposted **waterfalls** at **Gitgit** are spread over a 3km stretch. Each gets busy and none of them is a patch on Sekumpul falls, but they're worth a look if you're passing by and willing to brave the persistent souvenir hawkers and wannabe guides (you don't need one). There are reports of these faux-guides extorting money from tourists; ignore them. The main **Gitgit Falls**, a 40m single drop, is the one nearest to Singaraja; 2km south, the **Multi-Tiered Falls** has pools for swimming in; and 1km further towards Bedugul are the underwhelming **Twin Falls**.

Sekumpul Waterfall

4

Charge • Access by own transport via Sekumpul, signed 9km south of Jagaraga; guided treks are possible

Of all the stunning waterfalls in northern Bali, the 80m-high Sekumpul Waterfall complex is by far the most impressive. There are two entrances; the most often taken is in the north and begins at Sekumpul village. Within a 10-minute walk from the ticket booth you can stand at the overlook and see all the waterfalls – seven of them in the rainy season (Oct–Mar) – crashing down rugged cliffs. For a closer look and a dip in the pool below, descend several hundred concrete steps (not forgetting you must come up again). Past the bridge at the foot of the steps, on the left is Sekumpul and on the right is Fiji Waterfall. To go to Fiji you'll have to pay the entrance fee a second time since it is governed by a different village.

The other entrance is in the south via Lemukih village. There's a small path off the main road that leads to *Warung Fiji* and from there you'll see a parking lot and an official ticket booth beyond that. To the right is the small Grombon Waterfall. From here you can climb down the steep stairs where the path splits; to the right is the trail to Sekumpul and to the left is Fiji. By using this entrance you show your ticket at the second waterfall without having to pay again.

These can be done on your own without a guide. Another option is to take a tour that will include the waterfalls and other sites. In all cases start early before it gets too hot, wear sturdy walking shoes that you don't mind getting wet and be prepared to protect your camera from heavy mists and sprays.

Pura Meduwe Karang

Jl. Raya Air Sanih, 300m east of the Kintamani road junction at Kubutambahan • donation requested, sarong rental included

Given that it is probably the most arresting temple in north Bali, **Pura Meduwe Karang** is surprisingly little visited. It lies 7km east of Singaraja's Penarukan terminal and is dedicated to Batara Meduwe Karang – the temple ensures divine protection for crops grown on dry land, such as coconuts, maise and groundnuts. It's certainly built on a grand scale: the terraces at the front support 34 figures from the Ramayana (see page 313), including the giant Kumbakarna battling with hordes of monkeys from Sugriwa's army.

Yet what the temple is best known for are the **carvings** of Balinese villagers, including elderly people and mothers with babies. In the inner courtyard, and typical of northern temples, a large rectangular base links the three central shrines, called the *bebaturan*. It is here, on the outer left wall, that you'll find one of the most famous reliefs on Bali: a rather psychedelic cyclist in floral shorts on a bike with a flowerhead wheel. He's sometimes named as W.O.J. Nieuwenkamp, a Dutch artist who explored Bali by bicycle in 1904.

ARRIVAL AND DEPARTURE — SINGARAJA AND AROUND

By bus Singaraja is a major transit hub for travel to Java as well as Bali. Private operator Menggala at Jl Jen Achmad Yani 76 (0362 24374) operates daily "executive" night-buses to Surabaya (10hr) and other cities in Java; book ahead. The city's public bus and *bemo* terminals are in the outskirts: Sukasada (aka Sangket) south of the city and Penarukan in the east.

Destinations from Sukasada Bedugul (1hr 30min); Denpasar (Ubung terminal; 3hr 15min); Gitgit (30min).

Destinations from Penarukan Amlapura (via Tulamben; 3hr); Culik (2hr 30min); Gianyar (2hr 20min); Kintamani, Kubutambahan (20min); Penelokan (1hr 30min; for the Batur area); Tirtagangga (2hr 30min); Tulamben (1hr).

GETTING AROUND

By bemo Small *bemos* ply main routes around town between terminals – cream between Banyuasri and Penarukan, dark-red between Sukasada and Banyuasri, and blue between Sukasada and Penarukan. There are no metered taxis.

EATING — SEE MAP PAGE 205

4

If looking for accommodation, it's better to make for Lovina, which is only 3km or so away.

Rumah Makan Gandi Jl Jen Achmad Yani No. 25; 0362 21163. A dependable, venerable, inexpensive Chinese place where the decor could redefine the word "plain". The menu has dozens of options, but home in on the seafood dishes such as *cap cay udang* (shrimp with stir-fired veggies). $$

Tanjung Alum Dermaga Pelabuhan (waterfront); 0852 3771 1414. There are four restaurants hanging over the sea on the old Dutch pier and this one specialises in fish and seafood. $$

SHOPPING — SEE MAP PAGE 205

Berdikari Jl Dewi Sartika No. 42; 0362 22217. A traditional weaving centre where silk ikat is hand-dyed and woven on foot looms. Fixed prices, cash only.

The northeast coast

Beyond Kubutambahan, the black-sand beaches along the **northeast coast** are quiet and local; they tend to be slim and stony and trash can be an issue. If you have your own transport and fancy some tranquillity, you can check out a number of hotels here, especially in **Air Sanih**, and further east, en route to Tulamben at **Tejakula**, **Sembirenteng** and **Tembok**.

Air Sanih

AIR SANIH, 13km east of Singaraja's Penarukan terminal, is a locals' beach resort with some uninspiring cool **springs** (charge). It's a popular getaway for Balinese couples who want a few private hours away from the village. Close by you'll find *Cilik's Beach Garden*.

Ponjok Batu temple

Free admission, though own sarong and sash required

About 12km east of Air Sanih, the road climbs a headland at **Ponjok Batu** with views along the coast. The impressive **temple** here was founded by the sixteenth-century

Javanese priest Nirartha – the story goes that he used his powers to bring a shipwrecked crew back to life.

Surya Indigo Handweaving Centre

Pacung • Free • 0812 362 6535

Less than 1km east of Ponjok Batu temple, Pecung village is worth a visit for the award-winning cooperative **Surya Indigo Handweaving Centre**, especially in the morning when you have more chance of seeing weavers in action. It's known for its striped *bebali* cloth, used in Balinese rituals, and you can see every stage of the process on site, from dyeing the silk and cotton with natural colours to weaving on *cagcag* (backstrap) looms. The art of hand-weaving *bebali* was revived here in 2000 but now the cooperative supplies cloth around the whole of Bali including some gorgeous indigo-dyed batik fabric from handspun organic cotton. Since the cooperative launched, the owner Nymoman Sarmika has expanded to preserve other traditional handicrafts such as silversmithing, glassware and ceramics.

Yeh Mempeh Waterfall

Charge

A sign directs you inland from Les to **Yeh Mempeh Waterfall**. It's 1.5km through the village to a parking area, then a twenty-minute walk through the forest to the falls and a pool deep enough to swim in during the wet season (Oct–March). Even in the dry season it is picturesque, as the water bounces down the rock face into a cold pool at the bottom.

4

ARRIVAL AND DEPARTURE — THE NORTHEAST COAST

By bemo *Bemos* from Singaraja's Penarukan terminal to Amlapura all pass this way. Similarly all *bemos* from east-coast hubs Amlapura and Candidasa to Singaraja will pass through here.

Destinations from Air Sanih Amlapura (2hr); Culik (1hr 30min); Gilimanuk (3hr); Singaraja (Penarukan; 30min); Tirtagangga (2hr); Tulamben (1hr).

ACCOMMODATION

Alam Anda Ocean Front Resort & Spa Jl. Singaraja-Amlapura, Sembirenteng; http://alam-anda.com. This resort hotel is popular with divers due to its proximity to Tulamben and has a good house reef just offshore; Werner Lau manages the dive centre (http://wernerlau.com). Most accommodation is in a/c bungalows and villas, but there are two pleasant *losmen* rooms as well. There's also a large pool and spa. $$

Cilik's Beach Garden Air Sanih; http://ciliksbeachgarden.com. Down at sea level, set in lush tropical gardens on the black-sand shore, this feels less like a hotel than a private stay, with just two huge Bali-style villas, an octagonal bungalow and one *lumbung*-style cottage, each eclectically furnished with antiques and modern pieces, and each secluded in its own clearing. $$

Gaia-Oasis Tejakula Retreat-Resort, Jl. Raya Singaraja-Amlapura, 4km east of Bondalem; http://gaia-oasis.com. Secluded in a tranquil beachfront garden, eco- and socially conscious *Gaia-Oasis* offers bungalows with kitchenettes and a nice line in romantic decor. Facilities include free yoga sessions, a pool and spa. There's also a hillside retreat 6km inland under the same management. $$

★ **Segara Lestari Villa** Les; http://facebook.com/lesvillagevilla. Owned and managed by the very hospitable Gede Yudarta, these four a/c seafront cottages are attractively decorated and have private verandas and hot-water bathrooms. Guests have access to a kitchen and the owner can arrange transport and snorkelling gear. $

West Bali

TANAH LOT TEMPLE

5

West Bali

Sparsely populated and mountainous in places, west Bali stretches from the outskirts of Denpasar to coastal Gilimanuk, 128km away at the island's westernmost tip, where visitors and cargo-laden trucks cross the Bali Strait to Java. Once connected to that larger island by a long-ago submerged tract of land, the region has always had something of a non-Balinese character. When Java's Hindu Majapahit elite fled to Bali in the sixteenth century, the Javanese priest Nirartha started his influential preaching tour of Bali from the west – leaving the region with a trinity of stunning clifftop temples at Tanah Lot, Rambut Siwi and Pulaki. In the area west of Negara there is a significant Muslim population of migrants from overcrowded east Java, giving it an above-average number of mosques. There is also a Catholic community at Palasari and a Protestant village at Blimbingsari, both resettled to western Bali by Dutch administrators in the 1930s.

Apart from making obligatory visits to a trio of popular sights just west of Denpasar – **Pura Tanah Lot**, Mengwi's **Pura Taman Ayun** and **Sangeh Monkey Forest** are the main draws in this region – few tourists linger in west Bali. You can see why: there aren't many visitor hubs here and few sights per se. Yet for a lazy week's touring, there's much to enjoy. The west's black-sand southern beaches have long been a haven for surfers, while the best of Bali's coral reefs lie off the northwest coast around **Pulau Menjangan**, reachable from quaint **Pemuteran** on the north coast. Bali's only national park, **West Bali National Park**, is also here – a good option if you're feeling adventurous, with its diverse birdlife and attractive coastline.

Inland, the island's second-highest peak, **Gunung Batukaru**, dominates the vistas and its southern slopes hold the most fertile paddies in Bali. None on the island are more spectacular than those around **Jatiluwih** southeast of Batukaru, the focus for a famously scenic drive and heartland of the UNESCO-listed *subak* rice-growing culture, which is celebrated in a museum in nearby **Tabanan**.

And although five-star resorts and Western-menu restaurants aren't the norm in the west they are here, along with several interesting accommodations such as hillside hideaways, rainforest retreats and gorgeous coastal spa stays.

GETTING AROUND — WEST BALI

By bemo or bus West Bali's southwest coast is served by public transport from Mengwi terminal near Denpasar. West Bali's northwest coast is served from Singaraja. Southwest and northwest coast services terminate at Gilimanuk, from where car ferries shuttle across the Bali Strait to Java.

By car or motorbike As the main link between Denpasar and Java, traffic can be exceedingly heavy on the Tabanan–Gilimanuk road (most is single lane), with a higher than average quota of heavy trucks and kamikaze bus drivers. Plan for an average speed of 35km/hr and be very careful of oncoming reckless bus drivers when overtaking.

Tabanan and around

Tabanan regency does little to encourage a protracted stop for tourists and has very few accommodations; however there are several sites here that invite further exploration of the place. The big draw in these parts is of course the one on every tour agenda, Pura Tanah Lot.

SCUBA DIVING AT BALI BARAT NATIONAL PARK

Highlights

❶ **Pura Tanah Lot** Tour groups and souvenir stalls do nothing to cultivate spirituality, yet come early and you'll discover why Tanah Lot is Bali's most visited temple. See page 215

❷ **Pura Luhur Batukaru** Situated on Bali's second-highest mountain, Gunung Batukaru, this is one of the island's most atmospheric temples; all mossy carvings and *meru*, birdsong and bells, among tropical forest. See page 221

❸ **Jatiluwih road** Ancient rice paddies, farmers in straw hats and views to the coast – this sinuous route provides quintessential Balinese scenery. See page 221

❹ **Rainforest retreats** Eco-hillstays around Sarinbuana let you experience rural tranquillity. Take two nights or a week. See page 222

❺ **Balian Beach** Drop off the radar in this surfers' village, with consistent waves to ride, kilometres of beach and a relaxed, tropical ambience See page 222

❻ **Diving and snorkelling off Pulau Menjangan** With vibrant coral reefs and prolific marine life, this tiny island has some of the best diving in Bali. Try not to let on. See page 227

❼ **Pemuteran** The most relaxed resort on the north coast retains its villagey ambience and has great diving and snorkelling, too. See page 229

HIGHLIGHTS ARE MARKED ON THE MAP ON PAGE 214

Heading inland, the former ancient Tabanan kingdom capital and now administrative centre of Bali's most fertile district, **TABANAN** is a midsize town with a traffic problem and is best seen as a quick pit stop if you're interested in local culture: the interesting **Subak Museum** here is dedicated to Bali's rice-growing culture.

To the east, reached on a northbound arterial route towards Bedugul and Singaraja, is the seventeenth-century temple complex at **Mengwi**, with a side road to the **Sangeh Monkey Forest**. To the north of Tabanan, **Alas Kedaton Monkey Forest** offers a quiet diversion. Particularly gripping, however, is the visitor programme in Tunjuk village that gives an excellent insight into everyday rural living and well worth a half day. With your own transport, the modest sights in this area combine into a decent day.

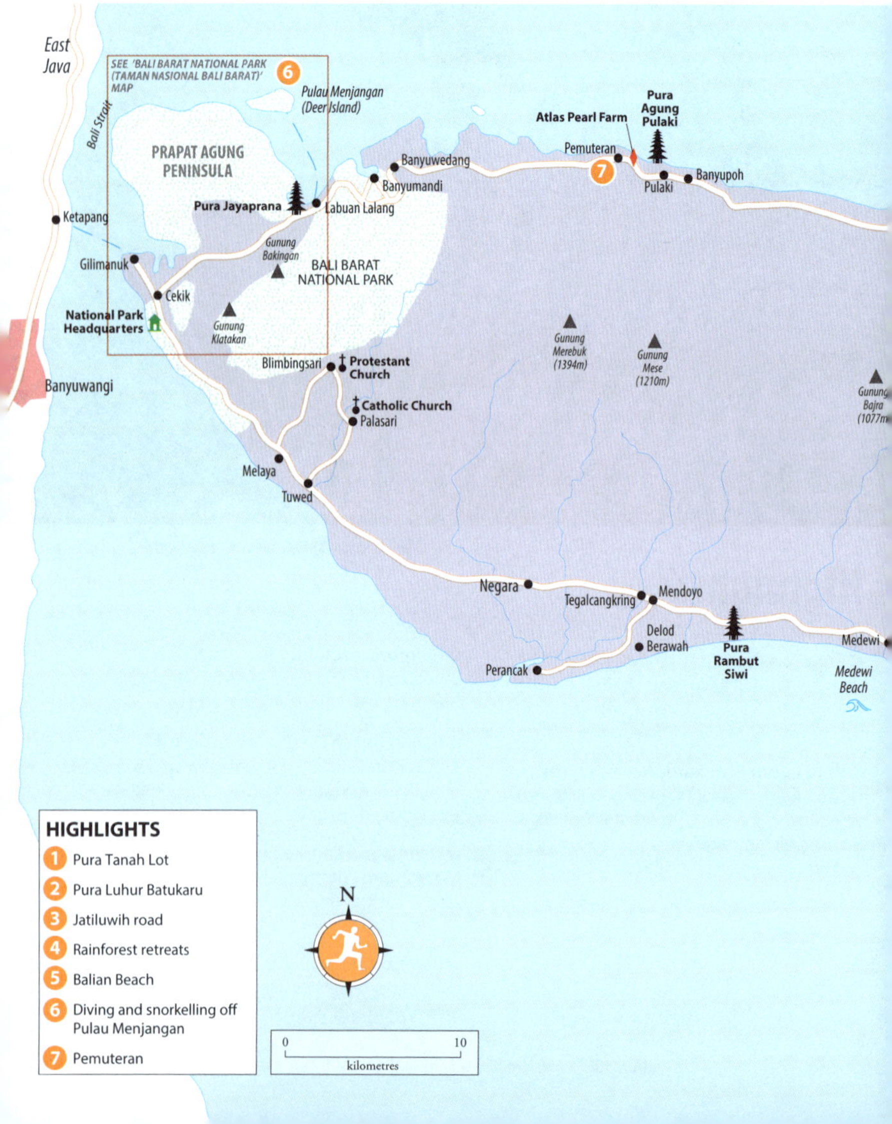

Pura Tanah Lot

Signposted 19km west of Seminyak • Charge; additional fees for parking, photo shoots and drone use • 0361 880361 • You might find a *bemo* direct from Denpasar's Ubung terminal. However, you're more likely to have to go first to Kediri, served by Ubung (Denpasar)–Gilimanuk buses and *bemos*. From Kediri *bemo* station, *bemos* (30–45min) run fairly regularly in daylight hours, more frequently in the morning. Otherwise, you can charter transport around the parking area

Marooned on a craggy, wave-lashed rock just off the southwest coast, **PURA TANAH LOT** exists simultaneously as one of the island's holiest temples for the Balinese and one of its busiest tourist sites. Fringed by white surf and black sand, its multitiered shrines are an unofficial symbol of Bali, appearing on countless souvenirs.

Pura Tanah Lot is said to have been founded by the Hindu priest **Nirartha**, who sailed to Bali from Java during the sixteenth century. Legends describe how he was drawn to

5 the site by a light that beamed from a holy spring. A local priest was less impressed and demanded this rival holy man leave. In response, Nirartha meditated so hard that he pushed the rock he was sitting on out into the sea, creating Tanah Lot "island". They say he dedicated his new retreat to the god of the sea and transformed his scarf into poisonous snakes to protect the place.

The site

Because of its sacred status, only devotees are allowed to climb the stairway carved from the rock face and enter the compounds; everyone else is confined to the grey beach beneath the rock (which gets submerged at high tide). When the waters are low enough, you can take a sip of **holy water** (*air suci*) from the spring that rises beneath the temple rock (donation requested). Otherwise, your best option is to climb up to the mainland **clifftop** for the best viewing angle.

During the day, most people loiter at the cliff-side restaurants immediately above the temple rock, but if you follow a clifftop path northwest instead, you'll get a panoramic view of the Bukit plateau on Bali's southernmost tip. The coast path continues north past small shrines and wild grey sands to eventually reach Yeh Gangga, about two hours' walk away. Every evening (6.30pm; charge) the temple complex hosts a **Kecak dance** performance in its wonderfully atmospheric setting. Anticipate crowds.

There's an **information office** located in the parking area (daily 7am–7pm) and an ATM plus several moneychangers among Tanah Lot's surrounding stalls.

Note that just getting to the site is an exercise in extreme patience, as access roads are woefully inadequate and traffic jams (particularly in the late afternoon) are infamous. The volume of coach tours and sprawl of tawdry souvenir stalls and *warung* around the temple will do nothing for your sense of spirituality either. Then there's the fact that one-third of Tanah Lot's island is artificial, a product of a Japanese-funded renovation programme in the 1980s. So, perhaps the greatest surprise is that Tanah Lot remains a striking sight if you arrive early enough to avoid the coach tours. It might be best to skip the sunset, however.

Yeh Gangga Beach

West of Tanah Lot is a barely developed stretch of black sand notable for weird rock formations offshore. The most appealing (and developed) section is at **YEH GANGGA**, which has emerged into something of a luxury hideaway. The currents make the sea too dangerous for swimming, but it's a dramatic scene punctuated by huge rocks, and the **beach** stretches for kilometres in both directions. If you're really keen, you could walk

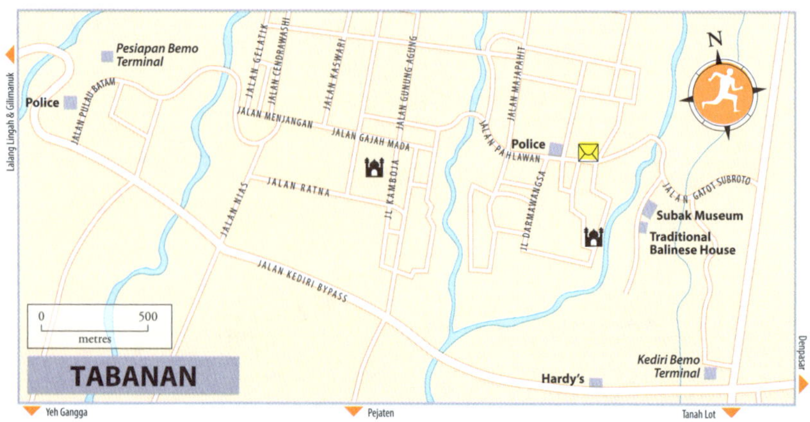

along the coast to Tanah Lot in around two hours. Yeh Gangga and Pantai Gangga are signposted off the main road about 4km west of the Kediri junction, or can be reached via back roads from Tanah Lot.

Pejaten

About 6km northeast of Tanah Lot, **PEJATEN** village is known for manufacturing Balinese roof tiles and roof-crown ornaments (*ketu*). Of more interest to tourists is the Pejaten **ceramic ware**, designed with cute frog, gecko and monkey embellishments and glazed in pastel greens, blues and beiges. You'll find Pejaten ceramics sold in the big resorts in southern Bali, but should get better prices and a bigger choice here. Kilns are all over the village, each fuelled by coconut husks, which lie in piles along the roadside – about as industrial as rural Bali gets. Try the **Tanteri Ceramic outlet** (http://tantericeramicbali.com), a respected producer that also has a museum with four hundred years of pottery on display (charge; http://museumtanteribali.com). It's in Banjar Simpangan in the village centre.

Subak Museum and traditional Balinese house

Jl Gatat Subroto No. 5B, Desa Bajar Anyar • Charge • https://watermuseumsubak.com • Signposted off the main Tabanan road in Banjar Senggulan, 1.5km east of Tabanan town centre and about the same distance west of the Kediri T-junction; if coming by *bemo* from Medewi either alight at the Kediri junction and walk the 1.5km, or switch to a town-centre *bemo* at the Pesiapan terminal

Tabanan district has long been a major rice producer, and the **Subak Museum** or **Mandala Mathika Subak** just outside of Tabanan city celebrates the role of the island's 1200 rice farmers' collectives – the *subak* that control the distribution of irrigation water and shape the landscape. Rice is seen as a gift from the gods, so the *subak* follow a concept of blending the spiritual, human and natural worlds. It's such a distinctly Balinese philosophy that UNESCO added *subak* culture to its World Heritage list in 2012.

While the museum is hardly crammed with exhibits, one interesting display explains the complex **irrigation system** used by every *subak* on the island – an unmechanised process that has been in operation since the eleventh century at least. In a nutshell, a river is channelled to the *subak* area then dispersed by hundreds of small channels, with tiny dams to regulate the water flow and lengths of wood, called *tektek*, to determine the volume and direction of flow, assuring that every field gets an equal share. It's also worth looking out for the **spiked wooden tweezers** used to catch eels from the waterlogged paddies at night, and the **wooden nets** to trap dragonflies, once prized as delicacies by the Balinese.

Less than 100m further along the lane, a purpose-built **traditional Balinese house** complements the Subak Museum by illustrating the layout of a typical village home, comprising a series of thatched *bale* (pavilions) in a walled compound. Each *bale* has a specific function and its location is determined by the sacred Balinese direction *kaja* (towards the revered Gunung Agung mountain) and its counterpoint *kelod* (away from the mountain, or towards the sea).

Mengwi

It's altogether missable today, but **MENGWI**, 8km east of Tabanan and 18km northwest of Denpasar, has a glittering history as the capital of a once-powerful kingdom. From the early seventeenth century until the late nineteenth, the Mengwi rajas held sway over an extensive area comprising parts of present-day Badung, Tabanan and Gianyar districts. Their fortunes eventually waned and in 1885 the Mengwi kingdom was divided between Badung and Tabanan. Descendants of the royal family still live in the Mengwi area – one of their palaces, **Puri Taman Sari** (see Accommodation) in

5

MEET THE FAMILY: TUNJUK

Tunjuk, a tiny, traditional village 9km north of central Tabanan, hosts a wonderful opportunity for visitors to experience life in a typical rural Balinese village. (Book through **Taman Sari Buwana**; charge includes transfers and lunch; reserve ahead on 0361 471 8744, http://balivillagelife.com). You'll have a chance to visit the local elementary school and a family compound that is home to fifteen different families (all related). You can plough a rice field, walk through the village, observe (or help with) cooking your lunch and feast on it afterwards. Overnight stays are also possible. All money contributes directly to the village economy.

nearby Umabian, is now a luxury homestay – while the town is just to the west of the important **Pura Taman Ayun**.

Pura Taman Ayun

Jl Ayoda No. 10, Mengwi. East off main Mengwi–Singaraja road • Donation; sarong not required • The temple is easily reached by *bemo* from Medewi terminal (30min)

The state temple of the former Mengwi kingdom, **Pura Taman Ayun** is thought to have been built by its first raja Tjokerda Sakti Blambangan in 1634. Designed as a series of terraced courtyards, the complex is surrounded by a moat to symbolise the mythological home of the gods, Mount Meru, floating in the cosmic ocean. The **inner courtyard** is encircled by its own little moat and is inaccessible to the public except at festival time, although the surrounding wall is low enough to give a reasonable view of the two-dozen multitiered **meru** within. The most important shrines are the three that honour Bali's holiest mountains; their positions within the courtyard correspond to their locations on Bali in relation to Mengwi. The eleven-roofed structure in the far northwest corner represents Gunung Batukaru; the nine-roofed *meru* halfway down the east side symbolises Gunung Batur; and Batur's eleven-roofed neighbour honours Gunung Agung. The Batur *meru* has only nine tiers because the mountain is significantly lower than the other two.

Alas Kedaton Monkey Forest

Jl. Raya Alas Kedaton, Marga, access is via Kediri: either take a *bemo* from Denpasar's Mengwi terminal to Kediri, then charter one for the final 3km, or drive to Kediri and follow signs for Marga • Charge • 0361 814155

The long-tail macaques at **Alas Kedaton Monkey Forest**, 3km north of the Kediri junction, guard Pura Dalem Kahyanyan Kedaton and are less aggressive than many of their cousins elsewhere in Bali. That said, there's still a lot of monkey business going on so safeguard items like sunglasses, shiny jewellery and mobile phones. The forest here is home to many flying foxes too. Beware of getting landed with a (human) guide – their main concern will be steering you to the souvenir stalls on the edge of the temple car park.

Sangeh Monkey Forest

Jl. Brahamana, Sangeh • https://instagram.com/sangehmonkeyforest • Donation • Sangeh is served by *bemos* from the small Wangaya terminal in central Denpasar; with your own transport it is an easy drive from Mengwi, 15km southwest, or around an hour from Ubud

Monkeys have a special status in Hindu religion, and a number of Balinese temples house a resident troupe, respected by devotees and allowed to roam free. The 14-hectare **Monkey Forest** that surrounds Pura Bukit Sari in **Sangeh**, 21km north of Denpasar on a minor northbound road that connects Denpasar with Kintamani via Petang village, is the most atmospheric. Some of the trees here – mahogany, nutmeg, guava and sapodilla, for example – are said to be over three hundred years old. According to local legend, the forest was created when the monkey king Hanuman attempted to quash Rama's enemy Rawana between two halves of Mount Meru. It is said that part of the mountain fell to earth at Sangeh with hordes of Hanuman's simian retainers still clinging to the trees. The mossy grey-stone **temple** among sacred nutmeg trees was built during the seventeenth century. It's out of bounds to everyone except the monkeys, but beyond the walls you can see a huge Garuda statue, stone-carved reliefs and tiered, thatched *meru*. The place is at its best in late afternoon, when the tour groups leave and the place can assume an almost ghostly aspect. Take heed of the warnings: keep cameras and jewellery out of sight of the monkeys and remove all food from bags and pockets.

Nuanu Creative City

Jalan Pantai Nyanyi, Beraban • https://nuanu.com • Charge; free for children under 12; some activities charged separately • Plenty of parking on-site; free electric shuttle buses run regularly between the different attractions

Among the most recent of Bali's new large-scale developments, the Nuanu Creative City, a sprawling 44-hectare coastal resort and cultural complex just south of Tanah Lot, opened its gates to the public in 2025. Both visually and conceptually, it's an impressive feat, marrying cutting-edge architecture with mesmerising art installations and idyllic natural landscapes, and affording visitors an experience that promises to be entertaining, educational, and sustainable all at the same time.

Entrance tickets allow all-day access to the complex, where you can join yoga and meditation classes, take part in handicraft workshops, attend live music and cultural performances, and explore the various artworks and event venues. Highlights include the unimitable **Luna Beach Club** (https://lunabeachclubbali.com); the **THK Tower**, which features an 11-minute sound and light show; and family-friendly activities such as a Magic Garden and an Alpaca Park. There's also a variety of luxurious, innovative accommodation ranging from glamping in Sungai huts to poolside domed suites.

GETTING AROUND AND INFORMATION — TABANAN AND AROUND

By bemo or bus This area is not worth the hassle of touring without your own transport. However, if you really want to give it a go, then Mengwi (Denpasar)–Gilimanuk buses and *bemos* bypass Tabanan centre to drop passengers at the major Pesiapan terminal on the northwest edge of town (also serving Gilimanuk). Yellow city *bemos* shuttle into the town centre, 1.5km east. Regional services run to Kediri (for Tanah Lot and Taman Ayun in Mengwi), plus Yeh Gangga.

By car or motorbike Be aware that the main road to Pura Tanah Lot from Kuta–Legian–Seminyak via Kerobokan is perpetually clogged with traffic – in particular, trucks loaded with cargo – expect at least an hour, sometimes two to cover the 20km. You could also go direct from central Tabanan via Pejaten.

Information In Tabanan, banks, ATMs and the post office are on Jl Pahlawan and its continuation on Jl Gajah Mada. There's also an ATM plus several moneychangers near Pura Tanah Lot.

ACCOMMODATION — THE BEACHES

A wave of new development around Tabanan has brought several new resorts and eco hotels to the area, but aside from a few decent *warung*, there's little reason to linger in the town itself. Instead, most travellers stay along the coast or in the rural areas around Mengwi.

Soori Bali Kelating Beach 14 km west of Tanah Lot; http://sooribali.com. Gorgeous minimalist villas and "residences", all with private pools and stunning Indian Ocean or mountain and ricefield views. The complex also has three dining options, a 24hr gym, library, luxury spa and a 10-bedroom estate house. $$$$

Waka Gangga Yeh Gangga Beach, Sudimara village; http://wakahotelsandresorts.com. A small, professionally run, Balinese-owned hotel with twenty-one circular villas, most with private pools, scattered across terraced rice paddies, constructed from natural materials (including thatched *alang alang* roofs) and panoramic views of the ocean and ricefields. The restaurant is a large, stunning bamboo structure but sadly the food could be better. $$$

MENGWI

Puri Taman Sari Umabian, Mengwi 5km northwest of Pura Taman Ayun; 0361 894 5475. Situated in a hamlet, this family compound owned by a member of a Mengwi noble family is a chance to get far off the usual tourist trail. The pick of several tranquil accommodation options are the

5

suites overlooking rice terraces. Cultural activities include offering making, gamelan and dance lessons. Access is via Denkayu on the Mengwi–Bedugul–Singaraja road. $$

Gunung Batukaru and around

Much of inland southwest Bali lies in the shadow of massive **GUNUNG BATUKARU** (sometimes spelt Batukau; 2276m), the second-highest mountain on the island after Gunung Agung, and one of the holiest. Beautiful **Pura Luhur Batukaru** temple on the lower slopes is the focus of many pilgrimages.

As the island's largest wetland area, Gunung Batukaru and its hinterland forms Bali's **wettest** region. The dense tropical rainforest on upper slopes has been designated a nature reserve, making this a rewarding area for **birdwatching**. Combine the rainfall with rich volcanic soils on lower gentler slopes and you have some of the most fertile agricultural land on the island. The area could have been tailor-made for rice-growing and the ancient terraces around **Jatiluwih** are some of the most scenic in all of Bali.

As if picture-postcard scenery wasn't reason enough to visit, there are some lovely rural hideaways up here: comfort in **Wongayagede**, eco-chic in **Sarinbuana** or escapism near **Jantiluwih**.

If you don't have a night or two to spend exploring this beautiful landscape but want to see some of it, the north-south road from Seririt to Antosari gives an excellent overview and can be done in one day.

Wongayagede

Remote and scenic, the area around **WONGAYAGEDE** village is a pleasant enough spot to lose a half-day, with opportunities to explore the countryside or even trek up Gunung Batukaru. About 500m from its southern edge, where it merges into **Tengkudak**, lies St. Martinus de Pons Catholic **church** (*gereja*) which draws a congregation from a

CLIMBING GUNUNG BATUKARU

Because of Gunung Batukaru's sacred status, most villagers only make the long trek up the **summit** temple once a year for their village's annual ceremony. A few tourists also **make the ascent** up the extinct volcano, but it's quite an undertaking: a guide is essential and the best months are June to August, with the November–March rainy season usually being too slippery underfoot. A knowledgeable guide will also know the viewpoints in the dense, protected **rainforest** and will be able to point out the flora and fauna, perhaps even elusive pangolins, *luwak* civet cats (of coffee fame) and muntjak (*kijang*) deer. Shade and low cloud make the conditions damp whatever the season, so bring warm clothes, rainwear and decent shoes.

Of the several **routes** up Gunung Batukaru, the most accessible start from hotels in Sarinbuana, Wongayagede and Sanda. The Sarinbuana route is the easiest (about 4hr to the top) and Sanda the most taxing (about 6hr), though all three routes converge at a point known as Munduk Ngandang for the final two-and-a-half-hour slog to the **summit**. On a clear day Batukaru's crater, Bedugal lakes, Mounts Agung and Batur and two volcanic peaks in East Java and Rinjani in Lombok are all visible. **Camping** near the top is an option, giving you the advantage of being there for sunrise. The descent from the summit usually takes three to five hours.

Guides for Batukaru treks are best arranged through local hotels. Would-be guides also hang around Pura Luhur Batukaru but they tend to ask for absurd fees and unnecessary "permits". Bali Jungle Trekking (http://balijungletrekking.com) organises tours, minimum of two people, which include transportation, a breakfast box and a picnic lunch.

handful of local families. It's usually locked, but the facade is an interesting example of Balinese Christian architecture, with Christian motifs carved onto the red-brick facade and a four-tiered Hindu-style *meru* tower instead of a spire.

Pura Luhur Batukaru

Jl Penatahan-Wongayagede. End of the road, 2km north of Wongayagede • Donation, includes sarong and sash

Quiet except for a resident orchestra of cicadas, frogs and cats, **Pura Luhur Batukaru** is one of Bali's nine directional temples (*kayangan jagat*) – the guardian of the west that justifies its epithet of the "Garden Temple". The grassy courtyards are planted with flowering hibiscus, Javanese ixora and cempaka shrubs, and the forests covering Gunung Batukaru press against the compound's perimeters: monuments are encrusted with moss and a web of paths fans out to shrines set in the forest. The proximity of the protected forest means you may see **birds** including green woodpecker-like barbets, scarlet minivets, olive-green grey-headed flycatchers and possibly even scarlet-headed flowerpeckers in the treetops.

Pura Luhur Batukaru is thought to have become a holy site in the eleventh century and was later consecrated by the Tabanan kingdom rajas, who made it into their state temple and dedicated shrines to their ancestral gods. Many of the thatched *meru* inside the **inner sanctuary** still represent a particular branch or ancestor of the Tabanan royal family. The most important shrine, though, is a seven-tiered pagoda dedicated to Mahadewa, the god of Gunung Batukaru. To the east of the main temple compound, a large square **pond** has been dug to represent and honour the gods of nearby Danau Tamblingan, which lies immediately to the north of Gunung Batukaru. Pura Luhur continues to play an important role in the lives of Balinese Hindus. Members of local *subak* groups draw holy water from the pond for agricultural ceremonies, and at the annual Galungan festivities, truckloads of devotees travel long distances to pay their respects and make offerings.

In deference to Pura Luhur's sacred status, strict **rules of admission** are posted at the entrance. Aside from the usual prohibitions against menstruating women and the recently bereaved, Batukaru also bars pregnant women and "ladies whose children have not got their first teeth". A stipulation against "mad ladies/gentleman" has been recently dropped.

Jatiluwih road

Toll

About 2.5km south of Pura Luhur, a road branches east from Wongayagede towards **JATILUWIH**; it's a slow, very rough route through forest that occasionally parts for panoramas over the gently sloping rice terraces. The reason you're here is the oldest and most complex system of rice terraces on the island. Arguably the most beautiful, too – so celebrated is the scenery that the entire three hundred hectare area, which has UNESCO World Heritage status, is called Jatiluwih. Inevitably, it has been designated a tourist site, which means every visitor pays a steep toll to drive through. Yet this is the Bali of postcards: vivid green terraces like contour lines, lush banana trees and palms, fields of chilli peppers and tomato plants, and farmers in pointed woven hats.

Jatiluwih is also a popular rice terrace walking and cycling area, and you can choose from five colour-coded well-marked paths, the shortest being one hour and the longest – for advanced trekkers – around seven hours. If you opt to go, set out early to avoid the heat of the day; a jacket will come in handy until the sun rises.

Eventually the road arrives at the **Senganan** road junction. The quickest route to the north and south coasts is the northeast (left) fork that feeds into the main Denpasar–Bedugul–Singaraja artery at Pacung. For a slower, scenic route back to Tabanan, take the southbound (right) fork via Penebel market town.

5

Sarinbuana

Little **SARINBUANA** village is tucked away on the southwestern slopes of Gunung Batukaru. It's just a few kilometres west of Wongayagede but feels more remote. The relative lack of visitors only adds to the appeal of the **eco- and community-focused accommodation** hereabouts. A climate that is cooler at its 750m altitude than the sweltering plains below helps, too. Rural rainforest retreats are not for everyone – if you value traditional hotel amenities or are nervous in nature, which is omnipresent, they aren't for you. For everyone else they are tiny pieces of paradise; a chance to utterly escape that deserves a few nights at least.

GETTING AROUND

GUNUNG BATUKARU AND AROUND

By car or motorbike This area is inaccessible without your own transport or unless you're on a tour. Be aware that signposts and 3G coverage are both sketchy so try to source a decent map and check routes with locals.

On a tour Many agencies in south Bali resorts offer trips to Pura Luhur Batukaru, usually taking in the Jatiluwih rice terraces. You can take a Jatiluwih electric bike tour (1 hour or 2 hours with lunch) with Green Bikes Bali (http://ebiketourbali.com).

ACCOMMODATION AND EATING

WONGAYAGEDE

Prana Dewi Mountain Resort Signposted 1km north of Wongayagede village, http://balipranaresort.com. If peace and quiet is your thing, then this resort among former rice terraces is your place, with rustic rooms and bungalows with scrumptious views to Gunung Batukaru. There's a 20m spring water pool and the restaurant serves fresh dishes such as *mie goreng* made from home-grown organic red rice and vegetables. Regularly hosts yoga retreats and can provide trekking guides. Cash only. $

JATILUWIH

Batukaru Coffee Estate & Retreat Gunung Sari, Jatiluwih, http://batukarucoffeeestate.com. A unique assortment of accommodation on a working coffee plantation ranging from an open-air wall-less suite to an antique Javanese wooden house to single beds in a lodge, all with chic furnishings. Located halfway up Gunung Batukaru overlooking the famed Jatiluwih rice terraces. $$

SARINBUANA AREA

Bali Eco Stay Kanciana village, 5km south of Sarinbuana; http://baliecostay.com. This organic venture has eight open-air wooden bungalows with deep verandas and stunning views, one of snapshot-worthy ricefields. There's a pool for swimming at a nearby waterfall and power is supplied by a small hydroelectric scheme. Offers cultural classes (including cooking or basket-weaving), massage, trekking and mountain-biking, and there's a restaurant with utterly glorious views. $$

Bali Lush Manikyang village, 5km north of Selemadeg junction; http://balilush.com. A lot of care and attention has gone into the design of this rural hideaway, engulfed by rice terraces and featuring a heart-shaped pool. The three traditional-style, beautifully appointed bungalows are built from recycled teak, and there's fine walking during the day and stargazing after dark. $$

★ Sarinbuana Eco Lodge Jl. Arjuna; http://baliecolodge.com. Run by committed environmentalists, this wonderful eco-lodge has jungle-chic bungalows in a rainforest clearing that make the most of the surround-sound of nature and pristine forest views. As a genuinely community-conscious project, it grows organic fruit and veg – meals in the restaurant are fresh and delicious – and organises workshops in massage, permaculture, cookery and woodcarving. Guided walks and mountain-bike trips are also on offer. Yes it's isolated (wi-fi is limited to the restaurant area), but that's entirely the point. $$

Balian Beach and the west

Few tourists venture further west than Tanah Lot, but the stretch of coast beyond Tabanan holds some nice surprises at the black-sand beaches beginning at Soka and on to **Balian** and **Medewi**. Just beyond Medewi, the spectacular cliffside **Pura Rambut Siwi** temple is almost as stunningly located as Tanah Lot but far less crowded with visitors. Inland there are also a few sites that warrant a look. The main coastal road is plagued by very heavy traffic – take extra care – and these stops provide a welcome break from the highway tedium.

The scenery in the **far west** is generally dry and rugged. Cloud-capped, forested mountains hold very few villages and much of the land is protected by Indonesia's Forestry Department, with the most important habitats conserved as **West Bali National Park.** It's the only national park on the island, explored by few tourists, but it can be rewarding for birdwatchers and the diving and snorkelling are among the best on the island, as some of Bali's best coral fringes are around **Pulau Menjangan** (Deer Island) inside the park.

Soka and Balian beaches

Returning to the coast from Tabanan, the road to Gilimanuk, Bali's westernmost tip, follows the shoreline, affording sea views and occasional panoramas of paddy fields inland. The inland highway connects to the beach at Soka, which is usually empty except for fishermen and is a good place to stretch your legs and get a bite to eat at one of the *warung*. There's also the Museum Ogoh-Ogoh Soka (0823 3629 0777, daily 7am–5pm) if you'd like a closer look at some of the giant hand-crafted effigies that are paraded through the streets to deter evil spirits during certain ceremonies.

From Soka the road to Gilimanuk zips through **Lalang Linggah**, the village closest to **Balian Beach**, a spiritually charged spot at the mouth of the Balian river (Sungai Balian). Its caves and headlands are frequented by priests and shamans for rituals (*balian* means healer or shaman in Bahasa Indonesia) – and now tourists.

As ever, **surfers** got here first – Balian Beach has the most consistent left-hand breaks in west Bali, with larger waves breaking behind off a shelf and gentler peaks inshore. Board rental is widely available. But whether you're a surfer or not, you may well find this mellow village the most relaxed escape on the west coast. There's no hustle, no tourist shops – just low-key accommodation ranging from budget to villas, a few *warungs* and beach bars, and the sense of a shared secret. Get here soon, though, as construction is increasing.

The caveat to all this is that a vicious **rip** inshore makes most of the beach too dangerous for casual swimmers; heed local advice or be content to paddle at low tide. Surfers should also be aware that in 2017 a man was attacked by a bull shark here, the fifth incident in as many years. Caution is advised. After heavy rainfall the beach can be a mess, the gushing river depositing lots of plastic rubbish from inland along the coast.

Ocean aside, there are a few tracks to explore inland through rice and banana plantations; you could also enjoy hiking up the Balian river or just heading west along 30km of grey-sand wild beach – **Mejan Beach**, 1km west, could define escapism. Yoga and meditation retreats are also operating in Balian with groups hiring local hotels or villas. Note that there's a "tourism admission" **fee** to enter the beachfront road at Balian.

Further west 8.4km from Balian the undeveloped boulder-strewn beach at Yeh Leh is magnificent at sunset.

ARRIVAL AND INFORMATION — BALIAN BEACH

By bemo or bus All Mengwi (Denpasar)–Gilimanuk buses pass through Lalang Linggah; they take about 1hr 15min from Mengwi or about 30min from Medewi. Coming from the north coast you can take any Seririt–Mengwi *bemo* as far as Antosari and then change onto the Mengwi–Gilimanuk service. It's about 800m from the main road to the beach.

By car There's plenty of free parking close to the beach if you arrive with your own vehicle.

Banks and exchange There's an ATM on the highway and several places, including *Pondok Pitaya hotel,* change money.

ACCOMMODATION AND EATING

All the following are accessed via the side road that turns sharply south off the Gilimanuk highway. Most are signposted and none are more than a 5min walk from the sea. All hotels except homestays have restaurants, and there are also a few *warung* behind the beach and on the highway.

5

Gajah Mina Lalang Linggah Side road right off descent to beach; http://gajahminabeachresort.com. This spa hotel is a good upmarket option on a private beach, with twelve rough-walled antique-furnished bungalows secluded in tropical garden compounds that include a 27m pool. The in-house *Secret Bay* restaurant serves French cuisine, Indonesian and Thai dishes. $$

Istana Balian Jl. Pantai Balian No. 64. On descent to beach; http://istanabalian.com. Australian/Balinese-owned place with a selection of very well-presented rooms, some above the restaurant with sweeping coastal views and others in the garden. There's a pool and the popular bar-restaurant (a busy hangout for TV sports events) serves great western grub. $

Pondok Pisces Jl. Pantai Balian No. 74. On descent to beach; 0813 3879 7722. Long-running place with real character thanks to the use of natural materials, including antique doors and traditional furniture. There are two locations: just above the beach and in a garden beside the Balian river. Also home to *Tom's Garden Cafe* which offers good international dishes, fresh tropical juices and wine by the glass. $

★ **Pondok Pitaya** Jl. Pantai Balian. On the beach; http://pondokpitaya.com. This attracts surfing couples and families for its unbeatable location overlooking the waves – a great spot to laze by the lovely pool or enjoy the relaxed restaurant – and a range of accommodation. Basic "River Suite" rooms have hut-style castaway cool; the better bungalows, which have been imported from Java then rebuilt here and a "Happy House" that sleeps up to eight. Also runs yoga classes twice daily. Note that during surfing season the bar gets really noisy at night. $–$$

★ **Surya Homestay** Side road right off descent to beach; http://suryahomestaybali.wordpress.com. This is a pleasant place just off the hill to the beach with accommodation facing onto a garden of banana trees and chickens. The fan-cooled rooms, all with verandas, offer modest style and modern(ish) cold-water bathrooms. $

Tekor Bali Jl. Pantai Balian, 100m from the beach; 0815 5832 3330. This restaurant specialises in authentic Balinese food including many vegan options but also serves up such international staples like burgers and pasta. $

Medewi

At **MEDEWI** you have entered Jembrana regency leaving behind the districts formerly ruled by mighty kingdoms and are entering Bali's "wild" west: arid, isolated and a place where Buginese and Javanese families coexist with a low Balinese population. Medewi village sits on the main Denpasar–Gilimanuk road at kilometre-stone 72 and is notable for its surf – a left-hand wave peels off a cobblestone point, larger at the back with a smaller inshore wave for novices. Its black-sand **beach** is used primarily by local fishermen, but is fronted by a small enclave of accommodation catering mainly to **surfers**: the light current and fairly benign waves make this a popular spot for novices. That said, since the village is effectively just a 300m street, there's little else here for non-surfers save for the appeal of the wild beach. But even here, development is underway with villas and hotels beginning past Balian at Pekutatan and onward to Medewi.

As it skirts the coastline, the 25km stretch of road between Lalang Linggah and Medewi Beach crosses more than a dozen rivers which stream down from the Batukaru mountains to water kilometre after kilometre of lush land. **Rice paddies** dominate the landscape, some even dropping to the shoreline, but this area is also a big producer of coconuts, and inland are vanilla pods, cloves, cocoa beans and coffee.

ARRIVAL AND DEPARTURE — MEDEWI

By bemo or bus Medewi is served by frequent *bemos* and buses (about 2hr from Denpasar) – those that head towards Gilimanuk can drop you at the turn.

ACCOMMODATION AND EATING

Aga Living Villa B&B Jl. Hiu No. 3, Pesinggahan, Medewi; http://agalivingvilla.com. A three-storied villa on the beach with rooms and a suite that has amazing surf break views from the two upper floors. Rooms are spacious and modern, and staff defines "hospitality". Scooter and board rental. $

The Galuh Pekutatan Pekutatan, 5km east of central Medewi; 0811 399 5499. Simple, no-frills accommodation in a small family-owned hotel very close to the beach yet located in a quiet area. All rooms have balconies or terraces overlooking the garden or mountains. $

Kelapa Retreat & Spa Pekutatan, 5km east of central Medewi; http://kelaparetreat.com. This all-amenities beach resort and its one- and two-bed villas offer comfortable minimalism and modern furnishings with excellent

BULL RACES IN BALI

Bull races or *makepung* (literally "chasing around"), using carts like chariots, is a sport introduced to Bali by migrant Madurese farmers and now celebrated by statues island-wide. In western Bali, race tracks on beaches, village tracks, even football fields, are cleared in late July and competitions are staged most Sundays until mid-November. There are **seven tracks** spread across the district: Tuwed, on the main road 10km west of Negara, has one of the main circuits. For details, try the Jembrana Government Tourism Office in Negara (Jl. Dr. Setia Budi No 1, Negara; Mon–Fri 8am–4pm; 0365 41060) but be aware that sourcing information can be as much of an adventure as seeing a race. And prepare for an early start; races begin between 7am and 9am.

services. Two pools (one with a slide!) and spa, surfing lessons and tours arranged. $$$

Medewi Beach Inn & Restaurant Jl. Pantai, Medewi; 0857 3872 1103. Located just 3 minutes from the beach, this inn offers pleasant, minimalistic rooms and is popular with surfers. In the evenings, you can enjoy watching surf movies in the open-air restaurant on a big screen. The on-site restaurant serves up Indonesian fare, including tasty seafood and salads. $

Puri Dajuma Beach Eco Resort & Spa Pekutatan, 3km east of central Medewi; http://dajuma.com. This seafront hotel has suites and roomy modern-rustic bungalows; not luxurious but all with a/c, hot water and garden bathrooms, the best sited just behind the beach. The whole place is set in a tropical garden, with a pool, spa, yoga and wellness packages. $$$

West Break Jl. Pantai No. 7, Yeh Sumbul (west of Medewi village); https://westbreakbalimedewi.com. Situated right in front of the beach 100m from the surf break. Unlike the growing crowds at Medewi, West Break offers a secluded getaway spot but within walking distance of the surf point. Lovely massage bale and garden huts to relax in, spacious a/c rooms, restaurant, bar and pool. $

Pura Rambut Siwi

Sixteen kilometres west of Medewi • Donation; including sarong • Reached via Denpasar–Gilimanuk *bemos* or buses, which drop you at the head of the 750m access road to the temple

When the sixteenth-century Hindu priest Nirartha sailed across from Java, he paused at this spot and pronounced it a holy site. On leaving, he donated a lock of his hair to the villagers, who duly erected a temple and named it **Pura Rambut Siwi**, "the temple for worshipping the hair", which is now highly revered by the Balinese. It's not unusual to see truck drivers stop here to pray before making the ferry crossing to Java.

Nirartha's hair along with some of his clothing is enshrined in a sandalwood box deep inside the central three-tiered *meru* in the inner courtyard; it's inaccessible to casual visitors but can be seen from the south-facing **kori agung** (gateway). Built in tiers of red brick and ornamented with fierce stonecarvings of open-mouthed Bhoma who guard against malevolent spirits, the gateway gives direct access to the cliff face and frames a superb view of the Bali Strait. The figure that stands in the stairway, staring out to sea with an arm raised, is said to be looking sorrowfully at Java to bemoan the ascendance of Islam over the Hindu Majapahit kingdom. Gently stepped garden terraces of frangipani and palm trees connect the outer gateway with the **shrine to Dewi Sri**, goddess of rice and of water (and hence prosperity), which balances on the cliff edge. Descending the rock-cut steps to the charcoal-black-sand beach, you'll find a string of tiny **cave temples** tucked into the cliff face to the left of the stairway.

If in need of a break from the traffic, there are some spots near Pura Rambut Siwi to stop. One Is at Batu Agung village where there's a red suspension bridge spanning the gorgeous Gelar River, a great place to take a swim and cool off. Not far away Is Jembrana Green Cliff at Yeh Embang village where a bamboo canopy walk gives an aerial view of the canyon below. If you've ever wished to see a Boeing 737 up close without flying to another destination, turn onto Jl. Mayor Sugianyar next to the temple and continue on until you pass a stadium. Beyond that is an unfinished development and in the middle of nowhere rests a "ghost" airplane that is rumoured to be renovated into a villa. You can't enter the cabin but you can go into the cargo hold and get some pretty interesting photos of this anomaly.

Negara and around

If the coastal region from Tabanan to Medewi is little seen, that beyond is practically terra incognita, with most tourists hurrying towards ferries at Gilimanuk then on to Java. This is the least populated area of Bali, with only one town of any significance, **NEGARA**. Formerly the home of the Jembrana royal family, it remains the administrative capital of Jembrana regency, as its wide boulevards suggest. Its other claim to fame is as the heartland of Balinese **bull races**.

Continuing west 8.5km, turn north at Tuwed for a closer look at a unique part of Bali. In 1939 Dutch colonists, desirous of keeping the Balinese-Hindu culture "pure" for tourism purposes, relocated a Protestant and a Catholic community to the most remote region imaginable: west Bali's arid, unsettled mountainous region. Ten kilometres inland at Palasari is the Catholic community whose cathedral is in Gothic-Balinese style, the usual bell replaced by a Balinese *kulkul* (warning drum) and its carved angels looking very Balinese. Goa Maria 100m away is a pilgrimage site. Three kilometres further north at Blimbingsari is Bali's largest Protestant community, also a missionary training centre. Although its church isn't as exotic as Palasari's, it's interesting to see as this village is literally in the middle of nowhere. The short drive up passes through beautiful scenery and you can return south via a different road with lovely views.

West Bali National Park

Charge • https://btnbalibarat.com

There are two gateways to **West Bali National Park** (Taman Nasional Bali Barat), where permits must be obtained and fees paid to enter the park. The headquarters are at Cekik, about two kilometres southeast of Gilimanuk; the other, more popular entrance, is at Labuan Lalang on the north coast.

While the rest of Bali seems to be caught up in a frenzy of development, 190 square kilometres at the westernmost tip has been protected since 1941 thanks to the nearly extinct Bali starling (*Leucopsar rothschild*), Bali's one true endemic creature. The park's amazing biodiversity encompasses dry savanna, montane, lowland and monsoon forest, mangrove swamp and coral reef, with a corresponding diversity of life. The roll call of animals here is impressive with 160 species of birds, including a small but growing population of **Bali starlings**. This was also the habitat of the Bali tiger until the last one was shot in 1937.

By far the biggest attraction is **Pulau Menjangan** (Deer Island), whose

DIVING IN WEST BALI NATIONAL PARK

The clear, shallow water between the mainland and Pulau Menjangan is protected from excessive winds and strong currents by the Prapat Agung Peninsula, and its **reefs** are in pretty good health, despite some damage. The reefs form a band 100m to 150m wide around the coastline, offering plenty of **dive sites** with drop-offs of 40m to 60m and first-class wall dives. Visibility is superb, ranging from 15m to 50m – as so many of the walls top out near the surface, the snorkelling is good too. While larger pelagic species aren't common visitors, the area is phenomenally rich in sea fans, barrel sponges, sea corals and all manner of soft and hard corals, and is a haven for masses of **reef fish**, nudibranchs, moray eels and other reef dwellers. Reef sharks are regularly seen. Popular sites include **Garden Eel Point** and **Pos II**, or **Anker Wreck**, an old wooden *prahu* at 40m, for more experienced divers.

spectacular **coral reefs** draw snorkellers and divers from throughout Bali. However, for birdwatchers and nature enthusiasts a trek through the little-visited mainland park, most of it done on Prapat Agung Peninsula, can reveal some wonderful surprises.

Pulau Menjangan (Deer Island)

Pulau Menjangan is accessed from a pier at Labuan Lalang, where local boats holding up to ten people can be hired from around 7.30am–2pm (visibility is best in the morning). Travel time is 30min each way. First, pay the park entry fee at the ranger station, and you can rent snorkel equipment at one of the *warungs*, where there are also toilets and showers

If you only see one part of the West Bali National Park, make it **Pulau Menjangan** (misnamed Deer Island, as there are no deer here), a tiny uninhabited isle north of Prapat Agung Peninsula. The island is fringed by some of best **coral reefs** in Bali, offering superb snorkelling and wall dives. The easiest way to visit is an organised dive trip from your accommodation at one of the resorts at the park or in Pemuteran (see page 229), although a group of snorkellers could head to Labuan Lalang and club together to rent a boat.

Snorkelling boats anchor off Menjangan's southeastern corner and you could bring food for a picnic on the beach there. There's little to see on the flat sandy island itself save for several small temples (closed to tourists) and a large shrine to the elephant god Ganesh; you could circle the island in an hour or so if you're keen.

ARRIVAL AND INFORMATION — WEST BALI NATIONAL PARK

By bemo or bus All buses and *bemos* on the Mengwi–Gilimanuk and Singaraja–Gilimanuk routes go past the national park headquarters at Cekik, while those on the latter pass Labuan Lalang (for Pulau Menjangan).

Tourist information The national park headquarters (https://btnbalibarat.com; 0365 61060) is in Cekik, beside the Denpasar–Gilimanuk–Singaraja T-junction, 2km south of Gilimanuk. A second office is at Labuan Lalang (same hours as headquarters), where local fishing boats depart for Pulau Menjangan. It has little visitor information besides a topographical map of the park, however the rangers and guides there are very informative.

Guides and permits Anyone who enters West Bali National Park must be accompanied by a park guide and pay for a permit. If you plan to snorkel or dive you'll pay an additional fee. Guides don't need to be booked in advance and all speak English. We recommend Idris (0823 4018 5768), who will personalise your experience. Guide fees are negotiable.

ACTIVITIES

BIRDWATCHING

If your main interest is birdspotting, your guide will steer you towards the Prapat Agung Peninsula, where the monsoon forest harbours a large bird population, including flocks of the common yellow-vented bulbul and the loud-chirping black-naped oriole. Other possible sightings include parakeets and fantails; the green jungle fowl; the pinky-brown spotted dove, which has a distinctive call; the black drongo, completely black save for its red eyes; and the tiny, yellow-breasted sunbird. You might see one of the 200-plus Bali starlings now living in three areas of the park. Treks usually start at dawn. It is also possible to explore the peninsula by boat and walking or by safari tour, taking a vehicle along the beach for 15km each way (3–6hr). All

5

options can be arranged at the park headquarters or Labuan Lalang ranger station. Overnight camping is also possible but must be prearranged.

TREKKING

The toughest hike in the park is the trail between Gunung Klatakan and Gunung Bakingan (7hr). From the Sumber Klampok ranger post, it ascends the slopes of Gunung Klatakan and Gunung Bakingan, before returning to the main road a few kilometres east of Sumber Klampok. For the most part, you're in tropical rainforest thick with ferns, vines, spiky-stemmed rattan and pandanus palms, plus epiphytic orchids. You're unlikely to spot much wildlife, but you'll probably hear the black monkeys in the canopy, and may stumble across a wild boar. The most dramatic of the birdlife here are the hornbills. Other birds include multicoloured banded pitta, dollarbirds, mynah and the red-and-green jungle fowl. Best in dry season, treks generally start at 5/6am or 4pm. Shorter treks (3hr) don't tend to be that rewarding given the limited area covered. Wildlife-spotting on the coastal flats around Teluk Terima bay, west of the Labuan Lalang jetty, can be rewarding: if you start early enough, sea eagles, dollar birds, plus monkeys, deer and metre-long monitor lizards can be seen.

BOAT TRIPS

The most relaxing way to experience the park is on a boat trip around the mangroves at Gilimanuk Bay. Small boats can be rented for two people. Look out for fiddler crabs – they say their claws are so strong they can open a can of beans – and possibly amphibious mudskippers adapted to breathing out of the water and with pectoral fin "legs". Crab-eating or long-tailed macaques hang out along the shore, too, hunting for fruit, mussels, small mammals and crabs (they're very good swimmers and divers). You might also spot some dark-grey Pacific reef egrets.

ACCOMMODATION AND EATING

SEE MAP PAGE 226

The Menjangan Jl Raya Gilimanuk-Singaraja, 17km marker; http://themenjangan.com. Just east of Labuan Lalang, this eco-resort in the national park offers smart rooms in a forest lodge around a pool or more chic beach villas. Its activities include trekking, horseriding, kayaking, snorkelling and diving. There are two restaurants: *Bali Tower Bistro* is a 28m structure with superb forest views to go with regional specialities, while the *Pantai* is on the beach and perfect for seafood. All facilities are also open to non-residents, including the spa and tower lounges. $$

★ **Menjangan Dynasty Resort** overlooking Banyuwedang Bay; http://mdr.pphotels.com. Introducing glamping (glamourous-camping) to Bali – and we're glad they did – fabulous one- and two-bedroom luxury tents are situated on 16ha on a protected bay that is ideal for swimming and sunsets. Its Pasir Putih Beach Club – diving and watersports, spa, beachside pool and restaurant – are also open to non-guests. $$$

Nusa Bay Menjangan Prapat Agunung Peninsula's east coast; http://wakahotelsandresorts.com. Accessed by a 25min boat ride from Labuan Lalang, this lovely hotel is good value considering its sublimely peaceful beachfront location inside the national park. Its well-equipped villas are dotted between trees and you'll have deer, monkeys and monitor lizards for neighbours. There's good snorkelling just offshore and a spa. See web for scheduled boat transfer times. $$

Plataran Ecolodge Jl. Raya Seririt-Gilimanuk; https://plataran.com/property/menjangan-ecolodge. Eighteen eco-lodges in the heart of the Bali Barat National Park. They offer cycling, kayaking, cruises, educational trips and many other experiences. $$

Gilimanuk

On the west tip of Bali, **GILIMANUK** is more of a transit point to Java than a destination. A 24-hour ferry service shuttles across the Bali Strait, so there's no reason to stop except to see the silhouettes of Java's volcanoes across the water or to fry your palate with a spicy plate of *betutu* chicken. The **Bali Strait** is a notoriously difficult stretch of water to negotiate due to treacherous currents. Despite this, it is occasionally swum; the world record, set by a Californian expat in May 2006, is 29

minutes and 30 seconds. During the ice ages, it's likely that a land bridge connected the two islands, which both rest on the continental plate known as the Sunda shelf, enabling humans and other animals to walk between the two. The **Museum Manusia Purba** (donation requested; 0365 61328) displays the skeletons and grave finds from a Neolithic settlement here. Don't get too excited (though the museum staff will be by your arrival).

Pura Jayaprana

Roadside 1km west of Labuan Lalang • entry by donation; includes sash and sarong

Pura Jayaprana temple itself, which lies to the west of Labuan Lalang, is unimpressive, but its location at the top of a long flight of steps is superb, with panoramas of Pulau Menjangan and its aqua seas. Pura Jayaprana enshrines the grave of an eponymous local seventeenth-century folk hero who was murdered because the king wanted to marry the hero's wife; the wife then committed suicide rather than marry the king. The couple's grave is in the inner courtyard.

ARRIVAL AND DEPARTURE — GILIMANUK

By bemo or bus Gilimanuk's bus and *bemo* terminal is opposite the ferry terminal and sees frequent services to and from various destinations: Mengwi terminal via the southwest coast; Singaraja via Lovina; Padang Bai; and Amlapura. Services operate around the clock to Denpasar and Singaraja and from 4am to 4pm to Amlapura.

Destinations Amlapura (5hr); Cekik (10min); Mengwi (3hr); Kediri (for Tanah Lot; 2hr 45min); Labuan Lalang (25min); Lovina (2hr 15min); Medewi (2hr); Negara (1hr); Padang Bai (5hr 15min); Pemuteran (1hr); Seririt (2hr); Singaraja (Banyuasri terminal; 3hr); Tabanan (3hr).

By boat Ferries shuttle between Bali and Ketapang (East Java) 24hr a day (every 10min; around 45min including loading and docking). Ticket prices are cheap. Note nearly all car-rental agencies prohibit their vehicles from leaving Bali. In Ketapang, the Banyuwangi Baru train station is about 100m north of the ferry terminal for services to Surabaya, Probolinggo and Yogyakarta. The long-distance bus terminal is Sri Tanjung, 2km south of Ketapang.

EATING — SEE MAP PAGE 228

There's no reason to overnight in town – it's a grubby port and sleeping options reflect this.

Ayam Betutu Men Tempeh Terminal Lama, 0813 3746 4953. Among the many *warung* serving *ayam betutu* in the old *bemo* station, this smarter restaurant is well worth visiting. Certainly, there's more meat on its chickens – marinated with a mouth-blasting mix of garlic, galangal, turmeric and chilli and served with extra *sambal*. $$

The north coast

It's a lovely drive east from the west tip of Bali; the road tracks along a narrow strip of the **northwest coast** for sea views on one side and mountains on the other. The terrain becomes more interesting with sharp peaks inland as far as **Pemuteran**, a peaceful beach haven offering plenty of opportunities for snorkelling and diving. Continue east and you'll soon reach an even smaller hideaway at **Ume Anyar**, before the road divides: continue east for Lovina (see page 199) and Singaraja (see page 203) or turn south for the cool, refreshing hills around **Sanda** and **Belimbing** or, alternatively, the scenic **Antosari Road** (see page 232).

Pemuteran and around

PEMUTERAN lives a double life as a fishing village and a holiday getaway. It remains a pleasantly low-key area, especially as the shoreside accommodation has made an effort not to upset the village ambience. Alongside idling on the beach – a ribbon of black and biscuit-colour sand which arcs for 1km or so – Pemuteran is known for its **snorkelling** and **diving**. More than a dozen reefs are within easy reach of the shore – Pemuteran has the largest shallow-reef area in Bali – and seas are calm so there's a site to suit all abilities; indeed the number is increasing through an innovative reef-growing

5

programme (see page 278). The marine life is varied, too; from turtles, giant clams and rays at the larger scale down to tiny nudibranchs and glass shrimp via corals, fans, sponges and fish such as grouper, sweetlips, pipefish, surgeonfish, triggerfish and wrasse. Most divers and snorkellers based in Pemuteran will take at least one trip to nearby **Pulau Menjangan**, something offered by every dive centre here.

With its cool sea breezes, temperate climate and moderately fertile soil, the stretch of the northwest coast between Pemuteran and **Seririt**, 40km to the east, is ideal for **vines** (Bali's main wine-producer, Hatten Wines, has a vineyard in this area; see page 231) and **pearl** cultivation.

Reef Seen Divers' Resort's turtle hatchery

Tours daily, every half hour • donation • http://reefseenbali.com

The Reef Seen Divers' Resort runs a **turtle-hatching** project at its dive centre, with young green, Olive Ridley and hawksbill turtles kept in seawater tanks until they are old enough to be released. All species have nesting sites in the Pemuteran area, but are endangered and their eggs are illegally harvested by locals. To combat this, Reef Seen purchases eggs from villagers for a little above market price and the turtles are hatched and reared before being set free off the Pemuteran coast; many thousands have been released in the last two years. However, some environmental organisations are opposed to turtle hatcheries because it's feared that removing turtle eggs from their sandy nests (and preventing them from hatching naturally) could affect their ability to navigate the ocean successfully and ultimately return to their nesting beach. In an ideal world, perhaps in a decade or two, there will be no need for a hatchery in Pemuteran, or anywhere else. If you do drop by, turtle feeding time is at 4.30pm; releases are done 9–10am, if any juveniles are ready to wobble to the sea.

Pura Agung Pulaki

Main road 7km east of Pemuteran • entry by donation; includes sash and sarong

The **Pura Agung Pulaki** temple sits on top of a weathered cliff, making for a good viewpoint. The temple's history dates back to the sixteenth-century Javanese priest

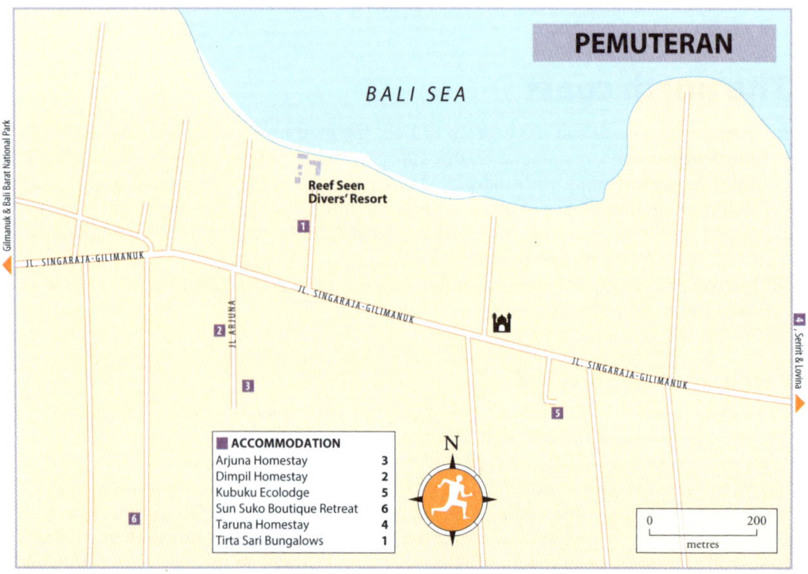

DIVING AND SNORKELLING AROUND PEMUTERAN

Local people and local dive operators have, in recent years, developed a real understanding of the **environmental value** of the reefs and considerable efforts have been made to repair earlier damage caused by the bad practices of local fishermen and unavoidable environmental factors. One initiative was the Karang Lestari Pemuteran project (http://globalcoral.org), just off the Pemuteran shore, using the pioneering "**Biorock**" process (see page 278), which encourages new growth by continuously passing a low electrical current through the stony coral, causing minerals to build up at about four times the normal speed. There are now over seventy separate Biorock reefs in Pemuteran – an incredible coral reef restoration project – though coral bleaching due to El Niño in 2016 has affected growth and visibility can be a bit murky around the installations. **Reef Gardeners** is an initiative to train local people as divers to maintain the Biorock structures, carry out work to maintain the health of the reefs and establish new sites.

Of the naturally occurring sites, **Canyon Wreck**, featuring a 30m wooden Bugis schooner resting in a coral canyon, is among the more dramatic. Of the artificially created sites, Bio-Wreck, where two fishing boats were sunk in 2005 to attract coral growth and fish life, is one area that features Biorock structures and is suitable for snorkellers as well as divers. **Temple Garden** consists of a 4m-high temple gateway and several large statues, which have been submerged to provide a stunning underwater landscape as they are now beautifully covered in fans and attracting all sorts of marine life.

The **map** at the Reef Seen Divers' Resort dive centre gives a good overview of all the sites.

DIVE CENTRES

Pemuteran's **dive centres** cover diving and snorkelling locally and off Pulau Menjangan; some also go to Gilimanuk's Secret Bay, to Puri Jati near Seririt and even to Tulamben on Bali's east coast. Most do night dives, nitrox diving and macro-photography trips.

Bali Diving Academy Pemuteran Taman Sari; http://scubali.com.

Dive Concepts Pemuteran; http://diveconcepts.com.

Kubuku Dive Kubuku Ecolodge; 0813 3857 5384

Reef Seen Divers' Resort http://reefseenbali.com.

Sea Rovers Dive Hotel Adi Assri; http://searovers.net.

Nirartha, but the seven temples are modern and overrun by grey macaques. Most *bemo* drivers stop here on their first trip of the day to make an offering at the temple's roadside shrine and get sprinkled with holy water by the attendant priest.

Atlas Pearl Farm

Jl. Nelayan, Penyabanga village, 10km east of Pemuteran, signposted 700m off the main road • Tours on request (free) • http://atlaspearls.com.au

At the end of a dirt track to the coast, the **Atlas Pearl Farm** is your place should you be in the market for a $2000 necklace, or pretty $250 choker, a $149 pendant, or are just interested in learning about the process through a video of pearl seeding. Tours are available on request – you'll learn about the four-year growing process and how to distinguish fake pearls from the real deal.

Hatten wines

Jl. Raya Seririt–Gilimanuk, Sanggalangit village, 12km east of Pemuteran, signposted 400m off the main road • free tours and tastings • http://hattenwines.com

Bali's biggest winery is spread over 35 hectares near Sanggalangit, and offers a tour of its vineyards and, of course, tastings. Two French grape varieties, Alphonse-Lavallée and Belgia are grown, along with local grapes for sparkling wines.

Ume Anyar

About 1.5km short of Seririt you reach **UME ANYAR**, where signs point you north off the main road to the accommodation, which includes a multitude of villas. The local

5

beach, sometimes known as **Puri Jati**, or PJ, has good **muck-diving** – diving in muddy- or sandy-bottomed bays in search of tiny marine life. It's rich in juvenile fish and rare species and particularly good for macro-photography, so several dive operators around Bali run trips here.

ARRIVAL AND DEPARTURE — PEMUTERAN AND AROUND

By bemo or bus All Gilimanuk–Singaraja buses and *bemos* pass through Pemuteran and will drop you in front of your hotel. If arriving from Ubud or south-coast resorts, it's fastest to take a tourist shuttle bus to Lovina then hop on to a bus or *bemo*.

Destinations Gilimanuk (1hr); Labuan Lalang (for Pulau Menjangan; 30min); Lovina (1hr 45min); Singaraja (Banyuasri terminal; 2hr 15min).

ACCOMMODATION AND EATING

All Pemuteran accommodation is accessed from the Gilimanuk–Singaraja road; the most attractive places occupy beachfront land. Real cheapies worth recommending are very thin on the ground – try the lanes inland from the highway. For eating, there are hotel restaurants, cafés and *warung* on the beachfront and main drag.

PEMUTERAN, SEE MAP PAGE 230

Arjuna Homestay Jl. Arjuna; http://arjuna-homestay.com. Upmarket homestay with sixteen lovely rooms (fan or a/c, hot or cold water) on two levels, with balcony or terrace, which overlook a pool and garden. There's a sense of quality evident (the bedlinen and furnishings are classy) and you'll find a dive shop and restaurant here too. $

Dimpil Homestay Jl. Arjuna; http://dimpilhomestay.blogspot.com. Unbelievable that the price is so low for such a nice place, a 3min walk from the beach. Choose a fan or a/c room and there's a library, sun terrace, bar, pool and excellent hospitality. $

Kubuku Ecolodge Jl. Singaraja-Gilimanuk; 0813 3857 5384. Run by a fun team, this smart place is arranged around a pool that's open to mountain views. Well-maintained rooms have verandas and outdoor showers. There's a good dive school here too. $

Sun Suko Boutique Retreat Jl. Raya Seririt-Gilimanuk; http://sunsukoretreat.com. Ten artistically decorated rooms, some of them in reconstructed Javanese teak houses, within walking distance of the beach, have zen names and colours. Take time to chat with the owner to hear her construction stories. Restaurant is excellent, plus there's a divine swimming pool. spa, and yoga. $$

Taruna Homestay Jl. Raya Seririt-Gilimanuk; https://tarunapemuteran.net. The ten squeaky-clean fan or a/c rooms, all with garden views are only surpassed by the friendliness here. There are also cooking classes in the excellent restaurant, pool and a spa. $

Tirta Sari Bungalows Gerokgak, Singaraja; http://tirtasaribungalow.com. Decent Balinese-style bungalows in a garden plus a restaurant, a pool and a spa. Very close to the Reef Seen Divers' Resort and its turtle hatchery. $

UME ANYAR

Zen Resort Bali http://zenresortbali.com. A short stroll from the beach, with fine views over vineyards to the sea, this place has an extensive programme of Ayurvedic therapies and yoga – book a "Stress Release" package for a blissful week-long recharge. Rooms with a/c are stylishly modern – "Sunset" has large terraces and sunken patio baths – and there's a beautiful pool, plus an in-house diving centre. $$

The Antosari Road

A toll road from Seririt was under construction at the time of writing. The toll road should make traversing the scenic mountain routes more pleasant as it will divert trucks on a more direct path. The old **road from Seririt** to the south coast commands some breathtakingly scenic views as it crosses through the mountains, rice-growing valleys, plantations and small hilltop villages of Bali's central spine. Seven kilometres south of Seririt, the road branches southeast at Mayong to Danau Tamblingan. Mayong village, which has its roots in the sixteenth century, is an excellent starting point for walks through rural villages with mesmerising views of terraced rice paddies. Bali Jungle Trekking (http://balijungletrekking.com) can guide the way for you.

On the southbound road, the first great viewpoint comes 12km south of Seririt, after **Busung Biu**, where you can stop in a lay-by to admire the vista of rice terraces tumbling down into the valley, framed by the peaks of Gunung Batukaru to the southeast.

The road divides at **Pupuan**, 22km south of Seririt, the site of a 100m-high waterfall called **Blahmantung**. Despite the height, the falls are less than spectacular, only really worth visiting in February or March when water levels are high from several months of rain. The 1.7km-long access road is steep and rutted, signed just beyond the southernmost limit of Pupuan; you can walk it in about half an hour. Also at Pupuan is a 10m-long reclining Buddha statue set in lovely gardens at Vihara Dharma Giri (Jl. Raya Pupuan No. 1, https://viharadharmagiri.wordpress.com). Called the "Sleeping Buddha" locally, it's an unexpected sight in primarily Hindu Bali.

Pupuan to Pekutatan (via Tista)

From Pupuan, one route takes you on a slow, twisting course southwest via ridgetop **Kemoning** – where you can veer south, via Ceking, to arrive just west of Balian Beach – and **Tegalasaih**, then south through clove plantations to **Tista**. Beyond Tista, the road parallels the Pulukan River and soon passes through the middle of an enormous sacred banyan tree at **Bunut Bolong**, where Balinese-Hindus often stop to pray before continuing on their journeys. About 10km south of the tree, you arrive at **Pekutatan** on the main Tabanan–Gilimanuk road, 2km east of Medewi Beach.

Pupuan to Antosari (via Sanda and Belimbing)

The easterly branch of the road from Pupuan drops through glorious scenery, affording moutainscapes of Gunung Batukaru to the east. On the way, you'll pass dozens of **coffee plantations**, many protected by spindly-looking *dadap* ("coral") trees – dead leaves fall to act as fertiliser for plants, while the roots prevent soil erosion. **Cacao** is also a big crop here, as are **cloves**, which you may see drying on mats.

Continuing south, the route passes **Sanda** village, about 30km from Seririt, then you roll through **Belimbing**, set in a pretty valley, before hitting the Denpasar–Gilimanuk highway at **Antosari**, 16km west of Tabanan.

100
TELKOMSEL

Lombok

SENGGIGI BEACH

Lombok

6 Located about 40km due east of Bali, Lombok has long been the poor cousin in terms of tourism statistics and global allure compared with its superstar island neighbour. But with southern Bali increasingly gridlocked and overdeveloped, attention has inevitably shifted to Lombok, which can match Bali for physical beauty, if not artistic heritage. Visually it's stunning, with astonishing landscapes defining the north of the island, home to fecund volcanic foothills, and also the deep south, whose staggering coastline of largely untouched surf beaches is a revelation. Culturally, the Lombok Sasak people are predominately Islamic, offering a very different experience for the visitor from Bali; in the west there are Balinese-Hindus, and in the centre and north are large tracts of unadulterated wilderness and a lot less traffic and commerce. The island has undergone rapid changes in recent years, although development is still concentrated in pockets down south around Kuta and overall, the island's essential cultural character remains largely intact. It's likely a taste of things to come: with improved infrastructure, the expansion of Lombok International Airport already underway and the Mandalika International Street Circuit hosting world-class events, there are already whispers of Lombok becoming the "new Bali".

Measuring 80km by 70km, Lombok is slightly smaller than Bali. The mountainous **north** is dominated by the bulk of the sacred volcano **Gunung Rinjani**, at 3726m one of the highest peaks in Indonesia and a popular trekking destination. Most of the population lives in the **central plains**, in a broad, urbanized corridor that runs right across the island from the capital, **Mataram**, in the west, to **Labuhan** port in the east. Lombok's largely agricultural **economy** is focused around this region, producing rice, cassava, cotton, tobacco (a major export), soya beans and chilli peppers. The provincial government is encouraging diversification on Lombok, with **tourism** as one of several potential growth industries.

The main focus of Lombok's tourism has traditionally been along its western coast, with **Senggigi** beach a convenient hub and the Gili islands to the northwest attracting watersports enthusiasts. In recent years, interest in the wild **south coast**, centred on the small but growing surfers' beaches around **Kuta**, has taken off with independent travellers, and new bars and restaurants are popping up each season. Another draw is the upmarket **Mandalika** resort development, home to the lavish Pullman Lombok Mandalika Beach Resort, and the **Mandalika International Street Circuit**, inaugurated in 2021, which pulls in huge crowds of motorsports enthusiasts during annual events. **Sekotong** and **the southwest peninsula**, with its many enticingly tranquil white-sand islets known as the **Southwest Gilis** are also increasingly popular.

Despite its many attractions, the **tourist presence** on Lombok is nowhere near as pervasive as on Bali and it's still easy to find remote villages, unspoilt coastline and locals living traditional lives. That said, foreign tourist numbers topped two million in 2024, proving that travel to Lombok is on the up, albeit still just a fraction of the more than six million annual visitors that descend on Bali. As a result, f**acilities** are improving across the island – you'll find chic and luxurious accommodation in

VIEW OF MOUNT RINJANI

Highlights

❶ **The southwest Gilis** A handful of tropical islands offering excellent snorkelling, diving and plenty of tranquillity. See page 249

❷ **Senggigi** Lombok's main resort still has the best dining and nightlife on the island, a few good beaches nearby and a wild coastline to the north to explore. See page 250

❸ **Gunung Rinjani** The toughest mountain climb in either Lombok or Bali, but you can also just admire the view from the foothills. See page 256

❹ **Tetebatu** A chance to experience Sasak village life on Rinjani's southern slopes, with pretty views and enjoyable waterfall hikes. See page 261

❺ **Lombok pottery** From egg cups to urns, Lombok's beautiful, distinctive pots make great souvenirs. See page 263

❻ **South coast beaches** Blinding curves of white sand against wild green hills, world-class surfing and stunning bays such as Selong Blanak. See page 268

HIGHLIGHTS ARE MARKED ON THE MAP ON PAGE 238

LOMBOK
BALI SEA
The Gili Islands
Gili Trawangan
Gili Meno
Gili Air
Pantai Sire
Pantai Medana
Montong Fal
Gondang
Tanjung
Tiu Pupus Waterfall
Gangga Waterfall
Sire
Bangsal
Pemenang
Autore Pearl Farm
Teluk Nara
Lombok Wildlife Park
Pusak Pass
Benoa Harbour, Serangan Harbour, Nusa Lembongan & Amed (Bali)
Klui
Mangsit
2
Pura Batu Bolong
Senggigi
Lombok Strait
Gunung Sari
Seseot
Pura Segara
Pura Lingsar
Lingsar
Pura Meru
Pura Suranadi
Suranadi
Ampenan
MATARAM
Sweta
Pura Kalasa
Narmada
Pemepek
Padang Bai (Bali)
Cakranegara
Kediri
Labuapi
Gunung Pengsong
5
Rumak
Banyumulek
Puyung
Gerung
Sukarara
Praya
Southwest Gilis
Gili Tangkong
Desert Point
Bangko Bangko
Gili Asahan
Gili Layar
1
Gili Nanggu
Gili Sudak
Lembar
Gili Gede
Pandanan
Gili Kedis
Medang
Selegong
Batu Putih
Labuhan Poh
Batu Leong
Tawun
Tembowong
Batujai
Penujak
Ketara
Lombok International Airport
Pelangan
Sekotong Tengah
Batu Jangkih
Rembi
Sepi
Keling
Teluk Mekaki
Belongas
Pengantap
Selong Belanak Beach
Selong Belanak
Rowok
6
Mawi
Tampa
Mawun
Kuta
Blongas Bay
Belongas diving (extreme)
Are Goleng
Seger
0
10
kilometres
INDIAN OCEAN

N
Labuhan Carik
Anyar
Segenter
Masjid Kuno Bayan Beleq
Bayan
Batu Koq
Kokok Putih
Obel Obel
Senaru
Sindang Gile Waterfall
Gili Lawang
Gili Sulat
Sungian Strait
Belanting
Sembalun Lawang
Mangku Sakti Waterfall
Sambelia
Gunung Daya (2941m)
Danau Segara Anak
Gunung Sengkareang (2588m)
Sembalun Bumbung
Gunung Lelonten
Gunung Rinjani (3726m)
Gunung Buanmangge (2895m)
Gunung Pusuk (2330m)
Gunung Dundatrum
Labuhan Pandan
Transat
Pulo Lampu Beach
Gili Kora
Gili Lampu
Gili Pasaran
Gili Kondo
Gili Bidara
Gili Kapal
Labuhan Kayangan
Labuhan Lombok
Poto Tano (Sumbawa)
Sapit
Pesugulan
Tibu Topat Waterfall
Jukut Waterfall
Timbanuh
Swela
Aik Berik
Joben Waterfall
Tetebatu
Loang Geli
Terutak
Kembang Kuning
Pringgasela
Aik Mel
Pringgabaya
Lendang Nangka
Lenek
Kotaraja
Rungkang
Rempung
Mantang
Loyok
Penakak
Masbagik
Kopang
Terara
Pomotong
Bagik Bontong
Selong
Alas Strait
Labuhan Haji
Mujur
Ganti
Longkhang
Sepapan
Gubukdalam
Keruak
Tanjung Luar
Jerowaru
Gili Indah
Tutuk
Batu Nampur
Ekas
Pemokong
Sunut
Tanjung Ringgit
Awang Bay (Ekas Bay)
Awang
Bumbang
Gerupuk
Gumbang Bay
Kaliantan
Serewe
HIGHLIGHTS
1 The southwest Gilis
2 Senggigi
3 Gunung Rinjani
4 Tetebatu
5 Lombok pottery
6 South coast beaches

Senggigi, Pantai Sire, Southwest Gilis and around the Kuta area – but elsewhere choices are fewer and simpler.

Brief history

6 The majority of Lombok's 3.8 million inhabitants are indigenous Muslim **Sasaks**. Their history is not well documented but many converted to Islam in the sixteenth century under Javanese Majapahit empire rule, with a minority following the animist-influenced Wetu Telu branch (see page 258). About fifteen percent of the population are of **Balinese** origin, practising Balinese Hinduism, introducing themselves as Balinese even though their families may have been on Lombok for several generations, and speaking both Balinese and Sasak.

The history of the two islands has long been interlinked. The east Balinese Karangasem kingdom invaded west Lombok in the seventeenth century and established a Balinese community that still thrives in modern-day Mataram. West Lombok's Balinese rulers extended their dominion over east Lombok, and were later also granted control of Karangasem by the invading Dutch. But the disempowered Sasaks of east Lombok fought back and in 1894 the Dutch seized the chance to take control, bringing all of Lombok island (and Karangasem) under colonial rule until Indonesian independence. In 1958 Lombok and neighbouring Sumbawa became jointly administered as the **Nusa Tenggara Barat** province, or NTB (West Nusa Tenggara), with Mataram the provincial capital.

ARRIVAL AND INFORMATION — LOMBOK

BY PLANE

Lombok International Airport (LOP) Lombok's international airport (https://lombok-airport.co.id/en) is 35km southeast of Mataram, near Praya. At the moment it's served by only two regular international flights: Singapore on Scoot and Kuala Lumpur on Indonesia Air Asia, but has domestic flights to several Indonesian airports, including daily flights to Bali, with AirAsia, Lion Air, Garuda, Citilink and Batik Air. When booking flights, use the IATA code LOP. There's a currency exchange office, ATMs throughout the terminal, a tourist office desk, car rental, taxi stand, hotel and tour desks. The airport is currently undergoing a major redevelopment expected to be completed by 2028.

Destinations Denpasar (Bali; several daily; 30min); Jakarta (Java; several daily; 2hr); Kuala Lumpur (several weekly; 3hr); Singapore (1 daily; 2hr 30min); Surabaya (Java; several daily; 1hr), Yogyakarta (3 daily; 1hr 20min).

Taxis & rideshare The taxi counters all charge

THE WALLACE LINE

Bali and Lombok are separated by the 40km-wide Lombok Strait, which is more than 1400m deep in places. An imaginary boundary, the **Wallace Line**, runs through it, marking a division between the distribution of wildlife of Asian and Australasian origins.

The boundary is named in honour of the nineteenth-century British naturalist **Sir Alfred Russel Wallace**. During his travels described in his book, *The Malay Archipelago*, he suggested that during the Ice Age, when the levels of the world's oceans dropped, animals were able to range overland from mainland Asia through Sumatra and Java to Bali – all connected on the Sunda continental shelf – but were halted by the deep waters at the Lombok Strait. Similarly, animals from Australia could roam only as far as Lombok on the other side of the strait.

While he was only partially correct, it remains true that Bali and the islands to the west have creatures common to **mainland Asia** (eg monkeys, tigers, elephants and large cats). The wildlife on Papua in the east is more characteristic of **Australia** (eg cockatoos, kangaroos, wallabies and cassowaries). Later scientists refined Wallace's theory by describing the islands from Lombok to Timor as a "transition zone" harbouring some species from both continental shelves, those which were able to swim, fly or float across water barriers between islands. Today this area is known as Wallacea.

approximately the same rates for the most popular destinations or you can organise a transfer with Blue Bird Taxi (0370 627000, http://bluebirdgroup.com) or Express (1500122; http://expressgroup.co.id). App-based motorcycle taxi service Gojek is also available on Lombok.

Buses Every 60–90min, DAMRI public buses run from the airport to Mataram (stopping at the Mandalika bus terminal), Senggigi, Ampenan, or Selong; the DAMRI information desk at the exit sells tickets.

BY BOAT

Depending on where you want to go in Lombok, and how well you can cope with the rough seas, flying from Bali is often a much more comfortable option, at approximately the same price.

TOURIST INFORMATION

For local features and current information, consult the fortnightly *The Lombok Guide* magazine (http://thelombokguide.com) or *My Lombok* magazine (https://mylombokmag.com).

West Lombok

West Lombok – stretching from **Sekotong** and the southwest peninsula through **Lembar** port to **Mataram**, then north to **Senggigi** and its satellite beaches including the Gili Islands in the northwest – has Lombok's largest concentration of tourist facilities.

Mataram

MATARAM is Lombok's principal city and the capital of Indonesia's Nusa Tenggara Barat province, or NTB (which comprises Lombok and neighbouring Sumbawa island). A sprawl of half a dozen districts, the city stretches about 8km west to east and is just 5km south of Senggigi. Sights are thin on the ground here and accommodation unappealing, so most visitors come for just a few hours, chiefly to browse the **markets** and perhaps a shopping mall, or to sample some authentic Sasak food.

The administrative centre is **Mataram** itself, a district of broad, tree-lined avenues and imposing government buildings, including the immigration office, but not much else of interest. Immediately to the east, **Cakranegara**, or Cakra (pronounced *chakra*), is the commercial heart of the city and centres around the buzzing **Epicentrum Mall**. Cakra was the capital of Lombok in the eighteenth century, during the height of Balinese ascendancy on the island, and is still the most Balinese area of the island. Two of the city's main sights – **Puri Mayura** and **Pura Meru** – date from the Balinese period. In the far west of the city, closest to Senggigi, the old port town **Ampenan** flourishes around the mouth of the Kali Jangkok river. This is the most traditional and atmospheric part of the city, with narrow streets and a maze of shophouses once inhabited by Chinese and Arab traders, plus the chaotic **Kebon Roek market**. The provincial museum is here.

Museum Negeri Nusa Tenggara Barat

Jl Panji Tilar Negara No. 6, Ampenan • Charge • 0370 632159

The well-maintained **Museum Negeri Nusa Tenggara Barat** focuses on the history, geology and culture of Lombok and Sumbawa and is worth a brief visit; it also hosts rotating exhibitions. Highlights include a scale model of Rinjani, collections of local textiles and sacred *kris* (daggers) and clothing and artefact displays about the daily lives of Lombok's and Sumbawa's people.

Pura Meru and Pura Mayura

Jl Selaparang, Cakranegara • Donation expected; sarong and scarf available

Pura Meru is the largest Balinese-Hindu temple complex on Lombok. It was built in 1720, during the period when the Balinese ruled west Lombok, in an attempt to unite the various Hindu factions on Lombok. The *candi bentar* (split gate) displaying scenes from the Ramayana is well worth lingering over. Watch out for pushy guides requesting

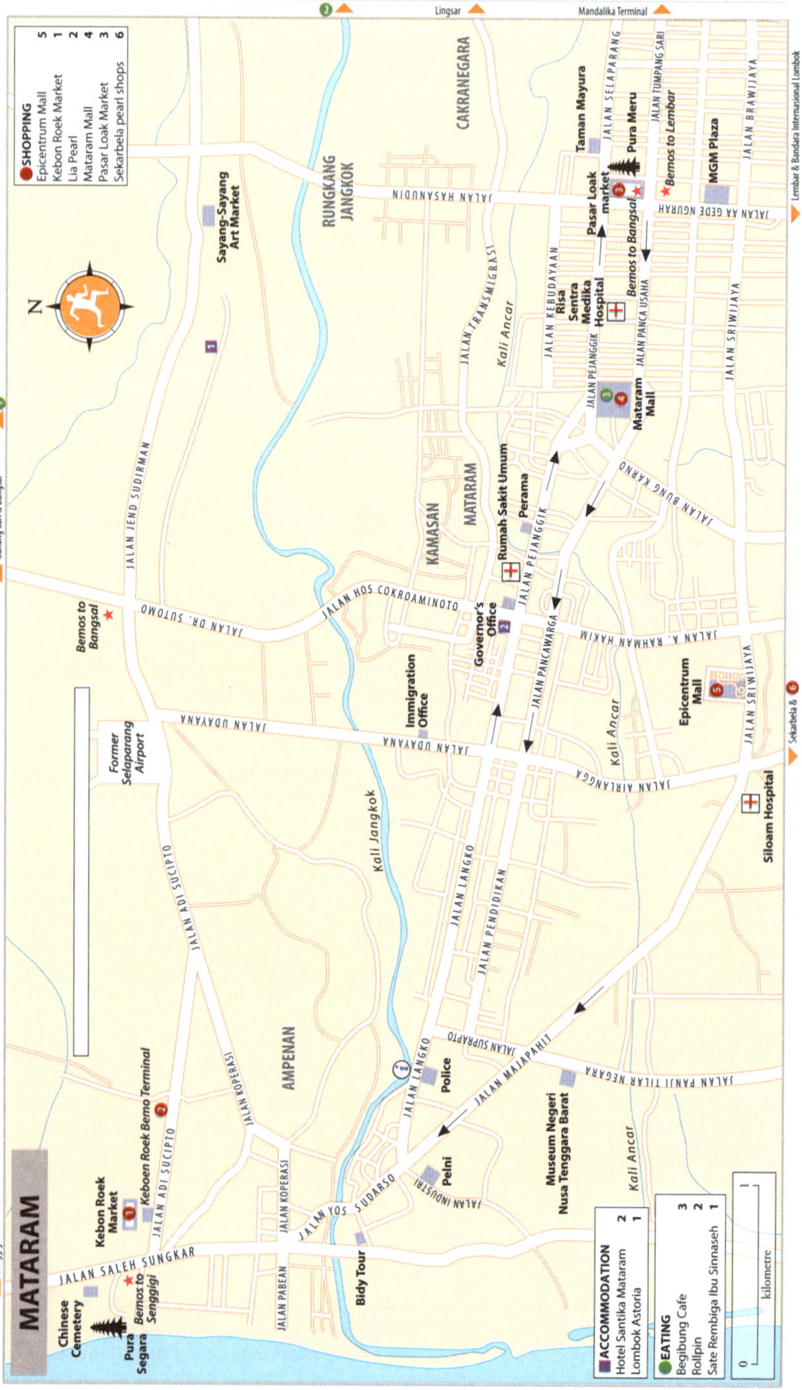
MATARAM
SHOPPING
Epicentrum Mall 5
Kebon Roek Market 1
Lia Pearl 2
Mataram Mall 4
Pasar Loak Market 3
Sekarbela pearl shops 6
ACCOMMODATION
Hotel Santika Mataram 2
Lombok Astoria 1
EATING
Begibung Cafe 3
Rollpin 2
Sate Rembiga Ibu Sinnaseh 1
Lingsar
Mandalika Terminal
Gunung Sari & Bangsal
Senggigi
Sekarbela &
Lembar & Bandara Internasional Lombok
AMPENAN
KAMASAN
MATARAM
CAKRANEGARA
RUNGKANG JANGKOK
Kali Jangkok
Kali Ancar
Chinese Cemetery
Pura Segara
Bemos to Senggigi
Kebon Roek Market
Keboen Roek Bemo Terminal
Bidy Tour
Pelni
Police
Museum Negeri Nusa Tenggara Barat
Former Selaparang Airport
Bemos to Bangsal
Sayang-Sayang Art Market
Immigration Office
Governor's Office
Rumah Sakit Umum
Perama
Mataram Mall
Risa Sentra Medika Hospital
Pasar Loak market
Taman Mayura
Pura Meru
Bemos to Bangsal
Bemos to Lembar
MGM Plaza
Epicentrum Mall
Siloam Hospital
Jalan Saleh Sungkar
Jalan Adi Sucipto
Jalan Pabean
Jalan Koperasi
Jalan Yos Sudarso
Jalan Industri
Jalan Langko
Jalan Majapahit
Jalan Supratio
Jalan Panji Tilar Negara
Jalan Pendidikan
Jalan Udayana
Jalan Dr. Sutomo
Jalan Hos Cokroaminoto
Jalan Jend Sudirman
Jalan Pejanggik
Jalan Pancawarga
Jalan Airlangga
Jalan A. Rahman Hakim
Jalan Bung Karno
Jalan Transmigrasi
Jalan Kebudayaan
Jalan Panca Usaha
Jalan Hasanudin
Jalan Selaparang
Jalan Tumpang Sari
Jalan AA Gede Ngurah
Jalan Brawijaya
Jalan Sriwijaya
kilometre
0
1

inflated fees for their services. Across the street to the north is **Pura Mayura** and its water garden, reminiscent of the Taman Kerta Gosa park and floating pavilions in Bali.

ARRIVAL AND DEPARTURE — MATARAM

By plane See page 240.

By bus or bemo If you're arriving by bus or *bemo* from anywhere except Senggigi, you'll come into Mandalika bus terminal, Lombok's main transport hub. It's in the Bertais suburb on the eastern edge of the city, and is sometimes known as the Bertais terminal or even, confusingly, as the Sweta terminal because that's the suburb where it used to be located. As well as transport to destinations around Lombok, Mandalika also runs long-distance a/c buses from and to major Indonesian cities. For those catching a *bemo* out of Mataram to Lembar (for Sekotong or boats to Bali), there's a conveniently central pick-up point in Cakranegara, just south of the market on Jl AA Gede Ngurah; *bemos* for Pemenang (for onward travel to Bangsal and boats to the Gili Islands) pick up just around the corner, near Pura Meru, on Jl Tumpang Sari. Arriving from Senggigi, you'll come into the Kebon Roek terminal in Ampenan. If travelling to Senggigi or on to Mangsit, there are frequent *bemos* throughout the day until about 6pm; pick them up on Jl Saleh Sungkar, just north of the turn-off to the Kebon Roek terminal.

Destinations Bayan (for Gunung Rinjani; 2hr 30min); Labuhan Lombok (2hr); Lembar (45min); Pemenang (for Bangsal/the Gili Islands; 1hr 20min); Pomotong (for Tetebatu; 1hr 15min); Praya (for Kuta; 40min); Senggigi (30min).

Travel agents Shuttle-bus, tourist-boat and long-distance-bus tickets to destinations on Lombok, Bali and beyond from Perama, Jl Pejanggik No. 66 (http://peramatour.com). Air tickets and tours from Bidy Tour, Jl Ragi Genap No. 17, Ampenan (http://bidytour-lombok.com).

GETTING AROUND

By bemo Bright-yellow city *bemos* ply numerous routes between the Kebon Roek and Mandalika terminals until late evening.

By taxi Blue Bird (0370 627000, http://bluebirdgroup.com) and white Express taxis (1500122, http://expressgroup.co.id) are plentiful.

By bike or motorbike Many places rent out bicycles and motorbikes. Ask for references at your accommodation.

INFORMATION

Tourist office The provincial tourist office (Dinas Pariwisata NTB, Jl Langko No. 70, Ampenan; Mon–Fri 8am–5pm; 0370 637 174) is unfortunately of limited use, only handing out promotional brochures. The tourism desk at the airport is not always staffed.

ACCOMMODATION — SEE MAP PAGE 242

Hotel Santika Mataram Jl. Pejanggik No. 32; http://santika.com. A modern business hotel opposite the governor's office. The rooms are a/c and well designed, if a little bland. There's a small swimming pool. $

Lombok Astoria Jl. Sudirman No. 40; http://lombokastoriahotel.com. Within walking distance of Mataram Mall, this 4-star hotel has all the amenities: restaurant, lobby lounge, spa, gym, infinity pool with jacuzzi and kids' pool. Rooms are minimalist design. $$

EATING — SEE MAP PAGE 242

After dark, a **night market** of food stalls lines Jl Pejanggik, just east of Mataram Mall.

Begibung Cafe Mataram Mall, Jl Pejanggik; 0370 631266. Serves fine Sasak food including spicy *ayam goreng taliwang* (huge portions), veggie dishes and fruit juices. $$

Rollpin Jl. Raya Ahmad Yani, Mataram; https://instagram.com/rollpin.coffee. Unexpectedly contemporary for Mataram, this casual fine dining restaurant overlooking a creek and surrounded by trees has a varied menu that includes juicy steaks, grilled duck, burgers, pasta, soups and yummy deserts. Dine on the outdoor deck or indoors with views. $$

Sate Rembiga Ibu Sinnaseh Jl. Dr. Wahidin No. 11B, Rembiga, Mataram; 0819 1799 1747. If you like your sate spicy and sweet, this is the place. Grilled over coconut husks, you can cool it down with a side of rice or *lontong*. Also serves *pelecing, urap* and *pepes*. Get there early, this place is crowded. $$

SHOPPING — SEE MAP PAGE 242

Epicentrum Mall Jl Sriwijaya No. 333; http://lombokepicentrum.com. This vast mall 1km south of the centre has a huge selection of local and international brands including the likes of Billabong and Levi's, fast food chains and a good food court. There's a cinema and lots of electronic stores in the basement level.

6

6

LOMBOK PEARLS

Lombok is becoming increasingly recognized as a good place to buy cultured pearls (*mutiara*). Ranging in hue from deep gold to champagne, **Golden South Sea pearls** are farmed around the coast, especially in southwest and west Lombok. These saltwater pearls are always expensive and they're sold by the gram (large South Sea pearls often costing $100 apiece), but quality varies considerably, so for these it's best to go to a reputable outlet, in Mataram for example, rather than buying off an itinerant vendor. The Autore Pearl Farm near Bangsal has tours and a reasonably priced shop. Beach hawkers often sell the cheaper imported Chinese **freshwater pearls**, which are available in many colours.

Kebon Roek Market Jl Adi Sucipto. Of Mataram's many markets, Kebon Roek in Ampenan is the most frantic, packed with stalls selling food, household goods and all the necessities of daily life.

Lia Pearl Jl. Adi Sucipto No. 15A, Ampenan; 0819 1600 4007. Locally cultivated South Sea pearls, including the gold ones that are a Lombok speciality, which come with a certificate of authenticity.

Mataram Mall Jl Pejanggik 47. Although it has seen better days, this mall has a department store, Hero supermarket, computer and phone shops, Western fast-food outlets and cafés and (most usefully for anyone about to climb Rinjani) trekking outfitters selling local-brand Rei walking boots, fleeces and sleeping bags.

Pasar Loak Market Jl Selaparang. Slightly less hectic than that at Kebon Roek, Cakranegara's main market selling fruit, vegetables, daily necessities and some crafts is in the heart of the city.

Sekarbela pearl shops For cheaper pearls, try Sekarbela, a suburb 2km south of Mataram, where pearl shops line the main road west from the junction of Jl Gajah Mada and Jl S Kaharudin.

DIRECTORY

Banks and exchange ATMs can be found in the malls and attached to all banks.

Consulates The closest consulates are on Bali (see page 24).

Dentist Dr Darmono, at Jl Kebudayan No. 108, speaks English (0370 664 2385).

Hospital The best hospital is the private Risa Sentra Medik Hospital, close to Mataram Mall at Jl Pejanggik 115 (0370 625560). Siloam Hospital Mataram at Jl. Majapahit No. 10 (0370 600 1100, http://siloamhospitals.com), also privately owned, is newer. The public hospital, Rumah Sakit Umum is at Jl Pejanggik No. 6 (0370 623498).

Immigration office Kantor Imigrasi, Jl Udayana No. 2, Mataram (0370 632520). Expect to have to make two visits for your extension to be finalized; the process can take up to a week.

Around Mataram

Within easy reach of Mataram are several worthwhile attractions, including the monkey-infested forest along the road north to Pemenang, to the east the formal gardens at **Taman Narmada** and the Hindu-Muslim **Pura Lingsar** temple and to the south, the **Banyumulek pottery villages**.

Gunung Sari and Pemenang

Heading north out of Mataram on the Pemenang road, it's a couple of kilometres to **GUNUNG SARI**, the location of a lively morning market. From here the road is very scenic, twisting upwards through lush, towering forest to **Pusuk Pass**, then down again for 10km to the plains and **PEMENANG**, near Bangsal, the port for the Gili Islands. Monkeys gather expectantly in groups along the roadside, and strategically located stalls sell bananas, though it isn't wise to encourage food-begging behaviour.

Pura Lingsar

Admission by donation; optional guides charge • Take a *bemo* from the Mandalika terminal to Narmada, then change on to a Lingsar *bemo*

Pura Lingsar, 11km northeast of Mataram, is used by Hindus as well as the Muslim Wetu Telu and is the site of one of Lombok's most enjoyable **festivals**. The temple was founded around 1714 and rebuilt in 1874; its highest, northernmost courtyard is the Hindu one, guarded by fierce monsters at the *candi bentar*, while the Wetu Telu area has a pond overlooked by a vivid statue of Wisnu, home to well-fed holy eels, which emerge for hard-boiled eggs brought by devotees. On the full moon of the sixth Sasak month (Nov or Dec), the local Hindu, Muslim, Buddhist and Christian communities cement their amicable coexistence and then ritualize their rivalries in a ceremony known as **Perang Topat** or **Ketupat War**. Proceedings open with a procession, the presenting of offerings and prayers, and culminate in a good-humoured mock battle involving the raucous hurling of *ketupat* (steamed rice wrapped in banana leaf packets) and eggs at each other. Everyone participates, most wearing formal dress, and everyone gets splattered. Tourists are welcome to enjoy the spectacle.

Taman Narmada

Jl Raya Narmada • Charge plus charge for optional guide

In **Narmada**, about 13km east of Mataram, the **Taman Narmada** gardens are very popular with local families, especially at weekends. Built in 1727, they include a replica of Gunung Rinjani and its crater lake, made for the raja Anak Agung Ngurah Gede Karangasem when he became too old to climb the real volcano to make his offering to the gods. The design was influenced by rich Dutch merchants of the time, the grounds are extensive, and there are two public swimming pools, a zipline (separate admission charge) and a Balinese temple, **Pura Kalasa**. Performances are also held here on special occasions. The gardens are on the south side of the main Mataram–Labuhan Lombok highway, opposite the *bemo* terminal and daily market.

Benang Stokel falls

Charge includes a guide to escort you to all waterfalls • road access to Benang Stokel is complicated and poorly signed, and may be best done with a local driver; turn north off the main trans-island highway at Pancordau, 17km east of Mataram, and continue uphill via the Terutak village (4km) to Aik Berik, site of the falls car park, 11km from Pancordau

If you're into waterfalls, or need an excuse for a very scenic drive through a landscape of rice terraces and tobacco fields that's reminiscent of Bali several decades ago (with added mosques), head for **Benang Stokel falls**, 30km northeast of Mataram or 21km northeast of Taman Narmada. The trail to the falls is also the opening stretch of a challenging six-hour **hike** up to the **Gunung Rinjani** crater rim, the least frequented of the routes up Lombok's majestic volcano.

An easy ten-minute trail from the car park through light forest gets you to the unexceptional triple 10m-high cascades at Benang Stokel, a hugely popular spot on Sundays, when it's busy with food stalls and probably best avoided. The pool here isn't deep enough for swimming, so for a more spectacular adventure, continue along an undulating forest trail for another 45 minutes to reach the prettier, net-like spray at **Benang Kelambu falls**.

Lembar

Bali's main departures and arrivals seaport is the huge natural harbour at **LEMBAR**, 22km south of Mataram. The port has a reputation for **hassle**, with new arrivals being intimidated by transport touts loitering in the car park, so many tourists find it easier to prebook **through-transport from Bali**, buying tickets that include the ferry and then a shuttle bus to Senggigi, Kuta or elsewhere. The town swarms with traffic; there is no reason to linger.

ARRIVAL AND DEPARTURE — LEMBAR

Ignore the **transport touts** and simply walk straight on through the car park, turning right after 300m at the T-junction for the *bemo* and taxi ranks.

By boat Ferries to and from Padang Bai operate round the clock. If you're buying a ferry ticket for Bali, do so at the checkpoint booths, not from anyone else. Tickets for Pelni ferries can be bought on the day of departure from the port, or in advance from the Pelni office (Jl Industri 1, Ampenan; http://pelni.co.id).

By shuttle bus Perama and other shuttle-bus operators wait for pre-booked guests in the port car park.

By bemo Public *bemos* run from the *bemo* rank just beyond the car park to Mataram's Mandalika terminal (roughly hourly 6am–noon, then less frequently; 40min) and Sekotong (regularly from 6am–5pm; 1hr). For other destinations in the southwest you'll probably have to charter.

By taxi Taxis, whether pre-booked (Blue Bird 0370 627000, http://bluebirdgroup.com; Express 1500122, http://expressgroup.co.id) or for hire, must wait at the rank 300m outside the port, near the *Tidar Home Stay*.

ACCOMMODATION

Bougenville Homestay Jalan Yos Sudarso; 0878 2216 8140. Simple, family-run homestay with friendly hosts, less than a 10-minute drive from the ferry jetty. Rooms are sparsely furnished with faded decor but clean and comfortable enough for a night's stay, and you can't argue with the price. $̱

Banyumulek

Any Lembar harbour-bound *bemo* from Mandalika terminal will drop you at the junction at Rumak, close to the enormous mosque, Masjid Jami' Asasuttaqwa, from where it's 1km west to the Banyumulek showrooms on foot or by *cidomo*

BANYUMULEK, about 7km south of Mataram, is one of the main **pottery** centres on the island, its access road filled with workshops and showrooms including the recommended outlet Berkat Sabar (Jl. Wisata Banyumalek No. 7, 0370 668 0490). The range of designs is impressive – engraved, painted and plain, taking in everything from teacups to metre-high vases – and the pots come from all over Lombok as well as Banyumulek itself, though they're not especially cheap. Potters work on site and packing and shipping services are offered.

The southwest peninsula

Remote and beautiful, with an attractive shoreline and a handful of picture-perfect white-sand islets just offshore, the **southwest peninsula** – sometimes referred to as **Sekotong**, after one of the main settlements – is still little visited. But the **snorkelling** is excellent, with arguably the most pristine coral in Lombok, and there's good **diving** and famously world-class **surfing** at Bangko Bangko's Desert Point. Accommodation is widely dispersed, and most visitors come simply for a day's snorkelling, but there are rooms for every budget and more in the pipeline. The main village centres are **Sekotong Tengah** and **Pelangan**, with **Tawun**, **Tembowong** and **Labuhan Poh** the easiest places to organize boats.

SEKOTONG'S GOLD RUSH

The Sekotong region used to be one of Lombok's poorest, but its fortunes changed in 2008 following the discovery of **gold**. A mining company had found deposits but was scuppered by a bylaw that prohibited gold mining on Lombok, so illegal freelancers immediately moved in, some with experience at mines in neighbouring Sumbawa but most novice chancers from the Sekotong area. At its peak, some three thousand people mined for gold, with makeshift camps popping up on the hillsides and roadside rock-grinding machines in every hamlet. As a result, many households could afford motorbikes or even new concrete houses. But the cost to the environment and public health has been high; tunnel collapses have killed many, and the use of mercury in the filtering process has polluted many sites and led to children with crippling birth defects.

Mining with **mercury** is officially banned but it remains in use and several hundred miners are still active in the mountains. Corrupt police are paid bribes so miners can access gold-rich hillsides. It seems that the exhaustion of the easily reached seams has done more to curb mining activities than any governmental efforts.

ACCOMMODATION

- Bujang Lapuk Hostel & Warung 4
- Cocotinos 2
- Gili Nanggu Cottages & Bungalows 1
- High Dive Gili Gede Resort and PADI Scuba Dive Centre 6
- Ko-Ko-Mo Resort 5
- Krisna Bungalows 8
- Palmyra Indah Bungalows 10
- Papalagi Resort 7
- Silver Fern Beach Retreat 9
- The Suites Lombok 3

EATING

- Warung Bamboo Gili Gede 1

Tawun

Beyond **Sekotong Tengah**, the peninsula's principal settlement, and **Medang**, the views of the **southwest Gilis** become ever more enticing as you reach **TAWUN** (also spelt Taun) harbour village and its sweeping white-sand bay 19km south of Lembar. This is a convenient place to organize boat rides and **snorkelling trips** out to the **islands** that are visible from the shore. Just 1.5km west of Tawun harbour is the Balinese-Sasak village **Batu Leong**, where there's a decent choice of accommodation and good swimming in the calm, shallow waters.

Pandanan and Tembowong

A kilometre west of *Cocotinos* on Jl. Raya Sekotong is **PANDANAN**, where you'll find the blue-roofed *Wyndham Sundancer* resort (https://sundancerofficial.com). About 700m west of *Wyndam Sundancer* (400m east of the Balai Perikanan Budidaya Laut marine research complex), a dirt track snakes seawards, ending at the gorgeous sandy **Elak Elak** peninsula with great swimming and a sand spit at its northern tip that allows you to walk to miniature **Gili Genting** at low tide. **Tembowong**, 5km west of Pandanan, provides access to **Gili Gede**.

Pelangan

PELANGAN, 2km west of Tembowong is the largest village in this part of the peninsula. The coast here is beautifully tranquil, with views to the nearby headland and across to Gili Gede. On the main road at the roundabout, turn left to **Mekaki Beach**, one of the most spectacular, undeveloped shorelines you'll ever see. En route you will have a hilltop view of the mighty Indian Ocean.

Labuhan Poh and around

At the roundabout's right turn, the road skirts the dramatic, crescent-shaped bay, enclosed by forested hills and headlands, and takes in views of islands fringed with white sand. Accommodation is strung out along a 2.5km stretch of road around **LABUHAN POH** and **Batu Putih**, less than 8km from Bangko Bangko. Just offshore is pretty little **Gili Asahan**.

Bangko Bangko and Desert Point

Beyond Batu Putih, the road continues 2km west through a protected forest to Selegong village, where the sealed road ends. It's another 1km to an unsigned junction; the right fork takes you to **BANGKO BANGKO** fishing village, 2.5km down the stony but passable track. Continue through the village to a wild beach with views of Nusa Penida, one hour away by sea. The left fork takes you via a much

6

DIVING AND SNORKELLING IN SOUTHWEST LOMBOK

There's first-class snorkelling and diving in southwest Lombok, with rare never-been-damaged coral and very few people to share them with. With many sites being within the protected bay there are opportunities for all skill levels while Batu Gendang, near Desert Point, rewards experienced divers with eagle rays, sharks and Napoleon wrasse. **Gili Layar** is ideal for snorkelling and also for macro-photographers; it's frequented by turtles, has masses of fish and very good coral. At **Gili Nanggu** there's very good snorkelling right from the beach. **Gili Rengit** (also spellt Ringgit) is good for novice divers and has a lovely beach. **Medang beach**, at the north end of the peninsula, has coral stairs and nudibranchs.

DIVE CENTRES

Snorkelling can be arranged through any accommodation and with boat captains at any of the village harbours. Centres can organize dive-and-stay packages and snorkelling trips. The best season is March to September; the dive centres wind down activities from December to March when visibility is bad.

Odyssea Divers Cocotinos, http://odysseadivers.com. An upmarket dive centre.

Two Fish Divers http://twofishdivers.com.

rougher 2km track to the **surf break** at **Desert Point**. From April to September, hundreds of surfers converge here from across the globe in search of its famously long barrels.

ARRIVAL AND INFORMATION — THE SOUTHWEST PENINSULA

Transport is scarce on the peninsula, and it's less stressful, and sometimes cheaper, to take a taxi or prebook transport via your accommodation; all of them can then arrange motorbike rental locally.

By bemo It's 46km from Lembar to Bangko Bangko at the tip of the peninsula. The route is served by public *bemos* from Lembar, but service is sporadic.

Banks and exchange The closest ATM is in Sekotong, but some hotels will change money for you.

ACCOMMODATION AND EATING — SEE MAP PAGE 247

Staff at most places in this region can arrange motorbike rental and snorkelling trips.

BATU LEONG

Cocotinos Jl. Raya Sekotong Km.51; http://cocotinos-sekotong.com. This luxurious resort fronts its own 300m-long white-sand coral bay 1km west of Batu Leong. It's an attractive set-up, with 36 cheerfully contemporary a/c rooms and villas. There's a sea-view pool, a spa, the Odyssea Divers centre and a restaurant. Rates can drop by half during quiet times. $$

Krisna Bungalows Jl. Raya Sekotong; 0818 0369 4450. Fine value, this beachfront place has modern bungalows around a small garden facing the shore. Four of the six rooms have uninterrupted views of three Gilis from their verandas (you pay more for a/c), while all have cold-water bathrooms. There's a small pool and the restaurant offers Western and Indonesian dishes. $

PANDANAN

Bujang Lapuk Hostel & Warung Jl. Raya Pandanan; 0878 6531 9113. Clean-as-a-whistle accommodation on the beach in a quiet location with *warung*, bar and shared lounge. Rooms have private baths and a/c, some with balconies. Dorms are either mixed or all-female. $

PEKONGAN

Palmyra Indah Bungalows Pekongan; 0877 6007 7714. Five wooden bungalows (including one family-sized) overlooking the sea at the end of a road, thus peaceful and surrounded by nature. Restaurant and grill, beach bar, hammocks, kayaks available and snorkelling right from the beach. $

SEKOTONG

The Suites Lombok Jl. Raya Sekotong; http://thesuiteslombok.com. Lovely contemporary establishment on the beach with 11 garden or ocean view suites and 3 one- and two-bedroom villas, some with private pools. Beachfront infinity pool; restaurant with varied menu and great sunsets. Kayak rental available. $$

TAWUN

Silver Fern Beach Retreat Desa Tawun; 0822 3530 2882.

Paradise in the form of spacious rooms a few steps from the beach, restaurant, pool and bar. Only a short boat ride from Gilis Sudak, Tangkong and Nanggu, which attentive New Zealand owners can arrange. $

The southwest Gilis

Often called "The Secret Islands" because they remain relatively undiscovered, the southwest Gilis are an ideal getaway with good snorkelling from the beaches in crystal-clear azure waters, excellent diving and simply hanging out.

Tawun is the jumping off point for Gilis Nanggu, Tangkong, Sudak and Kedis, which are often visited in a single day-trip. **GILI NANGGU** is a 15min ride from Tawun, where a sign points to the boat hire area, and is the only isle in this group with accommodation. There is decent snorkelling at all and a chance to have a grilled fish beach lunch on **GILI SUDAK**.

Further southwest, **GILI GEDE** is the largest of another island group and has the greatest selection of accommodation. You can hire a local outrigger boat for the crossing at Tembowong. In addition to snorkelling, the attraction here is hiking into the hills with excellent views, deserted beaches and interactions with villagers relatively untouched by tourism.

North of Gili Gede is **GILI RENGIT** (also spellt Ringgit), where a pier permits day-trippers from other areas including Bali, to disembark for day trips. There is good snorkelling on the pier side of the island and also on the west side, reachable by boat. Among the massive hard- and soft-coral gardens, look for Moorish idols and startlingly blue starfish. There is also excellent diving here.

West of Gili Rengit, **GILI LAYAR** offers some of the area's best diving including colourful corals, turtles and squid. There is accommodation on Gili Layar and on the palm-fringed **GILI ASHAN** to the west.

ARRIVAL AND DEPARTURE — THE SOUTHWEST GILIS

By boat from Bali Gili Getaway (http://giligetaway.com) direct from Bali to Gili Gede. They sail daily from Serangan, Bali (2hrs), from Nusa Lembongan (1hr 20min) and from Nusa Penida (1hr).

By boat from Lombok There's a public service from Tembowong to Gili Gede. To get to Tembowong taka a taxi from either Mataram or Lembar, or a public *bemo* from Lembar, with departures between 6am and 3pm. There are day-trips from Tawun taking in three of the islands with a transfer to Gili Nanggu. Local tour operators run one-day trips to Gilis Nanggu, Sudak and Kedis.

ACCOMMODATION AND EATING — SEE MAP PAGE 247

GILI NANGGU

Gili Nanggu Cottages & Bungalows 0878 6458 2020. The only operation in Nanggu, with a dozen small cottages and *lumbung* bungalows on the southern tip of the tranquil island. Renovations are long overdue and facilities are basic, but it's a rare opportunity to truly escape the crowds. Snorkelling gear is available and canoes can be rented for trips to the neighbouring islands. $

GILI GEDE

High Dive Gili Gede Resort and PADI Scuba Dive Centre Gili Gede; http://thehighdiveindonesia.com. The island's leading dive centre offers fun dives as well as various PADI courses, alongside four recently renovated villas. Choose from a beach or garden view or rent out the three-room loft, all with a/c, king-size beds, and hot showers. There's also a beachside restaurant and all-inclusive dive packages available. $$

Ko-Ko-Mo Resort Gili Gede; http://kokomogiligede.com. Really upping the stakes in Gede, this gorgeous, stylish beachfront resort has beautifully built bungalows, villas and a spa. Dining is a delight – the restaurant has amazing seafood (try the grilled calamari) and its menu features imported meats and great salads, while the in-house bakery pumps out perfect croissants. $$

Papalagi Resort http://thepapalagi.com. This place has tiled fan-cooled rooms and two lovely *lumbung* bungalows with a/c and sea views from their front decks. Prices include free use of snorkelling gear and breakfast. $

Warung Bamboo Gili Gede Gili Gede; 0821 4487 7598. Small, family-run *warung* with tables right on the beach so you can dig your toes into the sand as you tuck into a burger, *nasi goreng*, or grilled fish. Try the *ikan bumbu kuning*, a traditional fish stew with rice. $

Senggigi and around

Once Lombok's premier beach resort, **SENGGIGI** is these days in limbo, its greyish beaches trumped by the idyll of the easily accessible white-sand Gili Islands, and the nearby airport closed and replaced by the new one further south near Praya. The resort still attracts a loyal clientele of Australian and European tourists and there's a community of expats, but only in high season is there a bustle about the place. It's not all bad news, however: there are some good hotels and restaurants in central Senggigi, but the outer beaches at **Batu Bolong** (a 10min walk south) and **Mangsit** (about 3km north) are genuinely much more appealing. The coastline is indisputably handsome, its 10km series of sandy, swimmable bays curving deeply between a sequence of dramatic headlands. And Senggigi still has the best tourist facilities on mainland Lombok: its many tour agencies and restaurants, plus its transport connections, dive centres and souvenir shops continue to make it a convenient base, as do Mangsit and Batu Bolong.

Pura Batu Bolong

Jl Raya Senggigi, 2km south of central Senggigi • donation • Any *bemo* to Mataram can drop you off

Senggigi's one sight is the lovely little Balinese-Hindu temple **Pura Batu Bolong**, which crowns a promontory at the southern end of Batu Bolong beach. It's built over an

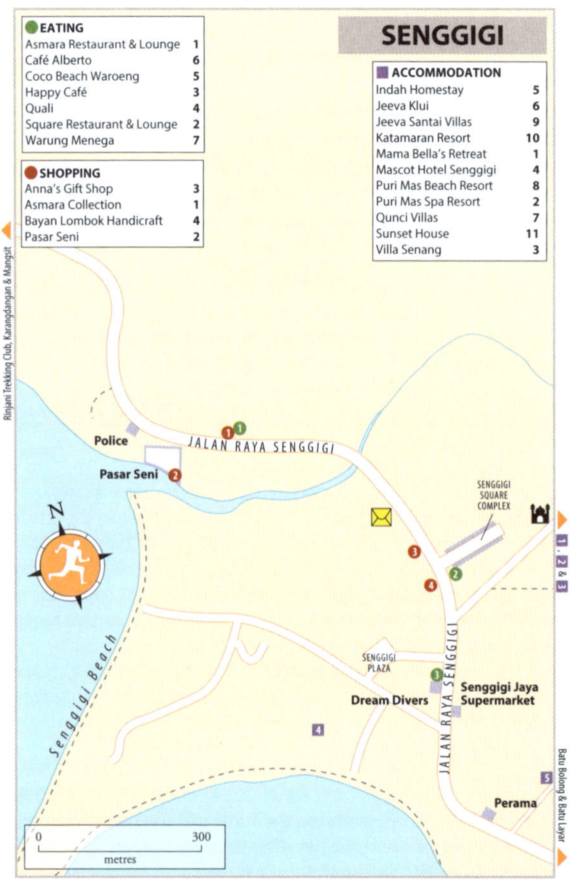

SENGGIGI FESTIVAL

The annual **Senggigi festival** is well worth making the effort to get to, featuring several days of Lombok cultural performances, including classical dances, traditional stickfighting (*peresean*), costumed parades and music. It's usually, but not always, held in September, in Senggigi Square.

archway in the rock (*batu*), the hole (*bola*) through which virgins were once supposedly sacrificed to appease the gods. Nowadays, when the tide is right, it offers access to Batu Layar Beach.

ARRIVAL AND DEPARTURE — SENGGIGI AND AROUND

By plane Senggigi is 50km from Lombok's international airport. Taxis or hotel transfers to Senggigi are available. The DAMRI airport bus stops on the main road by the art market; buses depart every 60–90min, taking 90min to get to the airport.

By shuttle bus For longer-distance travel from tourist centres in Bali and Lombok (including the Gili Islands), tourist shuttle buses and boat/bus combinations are often the most economical option. Perama (http://peramatour.com) offer a good service for a minimum of two passengers. Guesthouses club together with shuttle bus operators to share rides.

Destinations Candidasa (Bali; 3 daily; 6hr); Ngurah Rai Airport & Kuta (Bali; 2 daily; 9hr); Kuta (Lombok; 2 daily; 2hr); Sanur (Bali; 2 daily; 8hr 30min); Tetebatu (2 daily; 2hr); Ubud (Bali; 2 daily; 8hr).

By bemo Coming from Mataram, *bemos* depart at least every 20min from the Kebon Roek terminal in Ampenan until about 6pm and run as far as Mangsit, so are also useful for travelling around the greater Senggigi area.

Destinations Mangsit (10min); Mataram (Ampenan; 20min).

GETTING AROUND

By taxi Blue Bird (0370 627000, http://bluebirdgroup.com) and Express (1500122, http://expressgroup.co.id) metre taxis are plentiful in Senggigi and can be flagged down or booked ahead.

By car or motorbike Rental cars and motorbikes are widely available.

On a tour All agencies offer tours round Lombok – nearly everywhere on the island is accessible on a day-trip – but it's more fun to design your own by hiring a car and driver. Perama (http://peramatour.com) is an excellent outlet for car and motorbike rental and tours to Komodo.

ACTIVITIES

Adventure Lombok (http://adventure-lombok.com) organizes various Lombok cycle day-trips, taking in villages, forests and ricefields.

Diving and snorkelling There's no diving near Senggigi so all dive centres ship their clients to the Gili Islands or Sekotong Bay for the day (1–2hr away). Reputable local dive centres include Blue Marlin (http://bluemarlindive.com) at *Holiday Resort Lombok* on Mangsit Beach and Dream Divers, in central Senggigi (Jl Raya Senggigi No. 15, http://dreamdivers.com). If you're on Lombok primarily for the diving, however, it's cheaper and more time-efficient to base yourself on the Gilis or in Sekotong Bay instead. Most dive centres will take accompanying snorkellers and may provide a dedicated snorkelling guide on request.

Trekking Rinjani Trekking Club, Jl Wisata Alam (http://rinjanitrekclub.com) is a reputable agent for Rinjani trekking packages, and can also arrange much less strenuous hiking day-trips and expeditions to Sumbawa and Flores. Numerous agents in Senggigi (with very similar names) sell trekking packages, but it's worth checking current advice before signing up (see page 259).

ACCOMMODATION — SEE MAP PAGE 250

CENTRAL SENGGIGI

In central Senggigi there are restaurants, bars and tour agents on your doorstep. The two sandy bays, to the north and south of the Senggigi Beach promontory, are fine for swimming at all but the highest tides, though outside July, August and the Christmas holidays you may find it's just you and the indefatigable hawkers.

Katamaran Resort Jl Raya Senggigi, Batu Layar; http://katamaranresort.com. Stunning, modern resort with amazing views, large rooms and excellent service. Select ocean front or pool view suites or villas, family suite, villa or penthouse. $$$

6

TAKE THE ROAD TO PEMENANG

With your own transport, the spectacular **coastal road north** from central Senggigi to Pemenang (24km) makes a great day out, passing through small villages set behind sweeping, invariably empty bays and stands of coconut palm. Wending up and over the steep headlands that separate the bays you get fine views of the Gili Islands – three tiny white-rimmed specks in a turquoise sea – and across to Gunung Agung on Bali. First of the beaches is **Karandangan**, with its charcoal-black sand, seafood *warung* and a good restaurant; **Mangsit** and **Klui** both have great beaches, and in fact their cosy boutique hotels and villas have replaced Senggigi's high-rise resorts as the west coast place to be. Passing Malimbu, Nippah and Teluk Kodek, all with stunning white-sand bays, you arrive at Teluk Nara, the port for private fast boats to the Gilis and Bali, and with a pearl farm offshore. There are occasional *warungs* along the route, good for drinks and snacks, and there's nothing to stop you **swimming** off any of the lovely crescents of sand. Apart from Sundays, you'll likely be the only one in the water.

Pemenang marks the turn-off to Bangsal for public and shuttle boats to the Gili Islands. A couple of kilometres beyond Pemenang you reach the beautiful beach at **Sire** and its cluster of deluxe accommodation.

★ **Mama Bella's Retreat** Jl Arjuna Tiga No. 11; 0822 9709 8654. A short walk from the centre, but a world away in ambience, this delightful garden hideaway has gorgeous, very well-presented a/c rooms with minibars, satellite TV and verandas that face a central pool. It's run by a welcoming Australian couple; though no children under 12. Located up a narrow side road; turn right after the main mosque. $

Mascot Hotel Senggigi Jl Raya Senggigi No. 16; 0822 6654 8188. A central but tranquil place with cottage-style a/c and hot-water bungalows set around spacious sea-front lawns; the cheapest are fan-cooled and close to the road. There's a good restaurant and pool overlooking the sea. $

BATU BOLONG & SOUTHERN BEACHES

The swimming's good off the steeply raked grey-sand beach at Batu Bolong and it's just a 10min walk south of central Senggigi, via either the road or the beach (tide permitting).

Indah Homestay 500m off Jl Raya Senggigi, Kampung Loco; 0813 3710 3930. Tucked away down a lane, off the northern side of the main drag, this quiet homestay has six very neat, clean fan-cooled rooms and is run by a friendly Dutch lady who can arrange transport, motorbikes and laundry. $

★ **Sunset House** Jl Raya Senggigi No. 66; http://sunsethouse-lombok.com. Fronting the beach on Batu Balong, this well-managed place has enormous rooms with sea (and sunset) views, huge beds, contemporary decor and all the trimmings – a/c, satellite TV, big breakfasts and use of the generously sized beachside pool. $$

MANGSIT AND KLUI

With just half a dozen beachfront hotels, a couple of tiny shops and a mosque, the beach is the focus at Mangsit, 4km north of central Senggigi; it has a small reef for fair snorkelling at the northern end. *Bemos* shuttle into central Senggigi until 6pm. White-sand Klui, north over the headland from Mangsit, is very quiet.

Jeeva Klui Jl Raya Klui No. 1; http://jeevaresorts.com. Stylish boutique resort on lovely Klui beach with a stunning infinity pool, spa and fitness centre. Most of the "suites" have sea views through their picture windows, and there are fine vistas of Bali's Gunung Agung. Also check out their other property, *Jeeva Santai Villas*. $$$

Puri Mas Beach Resort Jl. Raya Mangsit; http://purimas-lombok.com. Originally a family beachside residence, the Puri Mas still exudes a welcoming atmosphere. Just 2km away set in a forest is their *Puri Mas Spa Resort* with two villas, a spa and an excellent restaurant. With free shuttle service, guests may use the facilities of either property. No children under the age of 12. $$

★ **Qunci Villas** Jl Raya Mangsit; http://quncivillas.com. Occupying a prime beach plot, this elegant, design-conscious hotel has rooms in separate zones divided by tropical gardens so intimacy is retained. Guests get the run of three shoreside pools, an excellent spa, lounge bar and a couple of restaurants. Rooms and suites are done out in cool, understated limestone and with original art on the walls. Staff are super-helpful, and the whole place ticks over as efficiently as a Swiss timepiece. $$

Villa Senang Jl. Wisata Alam No. 89, Mangsit; http://villasenangsenggigi.com. Set in a valley adjacent to a nature reserve with designated walking paths, Villa Senang has two 2-bedroom villas with a shared pool and one suite with private jacuzzi that can be connected to one of the villas. Units can be rented separately or as a whole. Gorgeous views of rainforest and only 5min by taxi to Senggigi. $$

EATING AND NIGHTLIFE

SEE MAP PAGE 250

Central Senggigi has several **restaurants**, but Batu Bolong, with its candlelit tables and flaming torches on the beach, is the most atmospheric place to eat after dark. On Sundays **local warungs** serve sate and seafood from the sea-view shacks near Batu Bolong temple, as they do all along the beach at Karandangan, and every evening at sunset, stalls sell grilled sweetcorn on the headland just north of the *Sheraton Senggigi*. **Senggigi nightlife** is mostly either restaurants with live music or dodgy karaoke places (not listed here) catering to male domestic tourists. During Ramadan all tourist places remain open. Many restaurants offer free shuttles within the Senggigi area in the evenings.

CENTRAL SENGGIGI

★**Asmara Restaurant & Lounge** Jl Raya Senggigi; http://asmara-group.com. This long-standing, family-friendly Senggigi favourite serves good international and Indonesian dishes including steak (with blue cheese sauce), great *Wiener schnitzel* and good kids' meals. There's a library and kids' toys too. $$

Happy Café Jl Raya Senggigi; https://instagram.com/happycafesenggigi. A popular friendly place to hang out and have good food and a few drinks in a relaxed atmosphere. Excellent live band in the evenings. The staff are always more than happy to please the patrons, living up to establishment's name. $

Square Restaurant & Lounge Senggigi Square Block B-10 Jl Raya Senggigi; http://squarelombok.com. Fine and casual dining and contemporary design make this Senggigi's destination restaurant. There's *begibung* (family-style eating), a mix of regional West Nusa Tenggara dishes, and the likes of slow-cooked lamb shank on mashed potato with caramelized shallot and mint oil – or splash out on the five-course gourmet set dinner. $$$

BATU BOLONG AND BATU LAYAR

Café Alberto Jl Raya Batu Bolong; http://cafealberto.com. Deservedly popular beachfront Italian restaurant with its own swimming pool and fantastic sunset views. The Italian menu includes home-made seafood spaghetti, small wood-fired pizzas, good bread and desserts. Round off your meal with a sip of complimentary limoncello. $

Warung Menega Batu Layar Beach; 0370 750 1649. Unpretentious *warung* selling fresh delicious seafood. Grilled lobster, prawns, crab, clams, barracuda and many more. Enjoy dinner on the beach with the best sunset views. $$

KARANDANGAN AND MANGSIT

★**Coco Beach Waroeng** Karandangan Beach; 0851 3733 2583. Excellent Indonesian home-style cooking in classy open-air dining huts on the edge of a coconut grove, just back from the dark-sand beach. Many ingredients are freshly picked from the adjacent garden, and highlights include *pelecing kangkung* (water spinach in a spicy chili sauce) and squid, either cooked in ink or with spicy *sambal* sauce. Food is served on banana leaves or from earthenware bowls. $$

Quali Jl Raya Mangsit (Qunci Villas); http://quncivillas.com. *Qunci*'s classy, romantic seafood restaurant is perfect for a memorable meal of grilled fish or expertly spiced and prepared local seafood. Dine by the shore below Lombok's dramatic evening skies, or with daytime views of Bali's Gunung Agung. $$

SHOPPING

SEE MAP PAGE 250

Anna's Gift Shop Jl. Raya Singgigi, Ruko Galeri Intan Toko V; https://facebook.com/Lombok. Annas.Giftshop. A great selection of good quality souvenirs with some unique pieces: sarongs, womenswear and handicrafts. Fixed prices; all items wrapped for travel.

Asmara Collection Jl Raya Senggigi; http://asmara-group.com. Good-quality handicrafts, jewellery and textiles, and a few antiques, all at fixed prices.

Bayan Lombok Handicraft Jl. Raya Senggigi Km.8; 0370 693 784. Hassle-free shopping with a wide selection of

STREET HAWKERS

Walk along the beach or eat at a streetside restaurant in central Senggigi and you'll be approached by one or more of the local **hawkers** selling sarongs, pearls, T-shirts, paintings, more pearls, tours, transport and yet more pearls. It can be irritating, but it's worth bearing a few things in mind. Despite the tourist gloss, many people in Lombok are poor. Employment opportunities are few, not least because you need either a considerable amount of money or well-placed connections to secure many jobs, from government positions to hotel and restaurant positions. Family land is often insufficient to support all the people dependent on it. Working as a hawker in Senggigi is a way of trying to escape the cycle – a reality that admittedly is not the first thing that comes to mind when you're faced with the umpteenth request of the day to "just have a look please".

handicrafts (eg rattan, wood, silver) at reasonable prices, all clearly marked. Will package large items for easier transport back home.

Pasar Seni Jl Raya Senggigi. Though small, the main tourist art market at the northern end of town has stalls and a few attractive shops selling beachwear, sarongs, pearls, jewellery and artefacts. If you don't like being hassled, you might want to skip this place.

DIRECTORY

ATMs There are many ATMs along Jl Raya Senggigi and in Batu Bolong but none in Mangsit.

Doctor The closest hospitals are in Mataram (see page 244).

Police Next to the Pasar Seni (see above). Call 0370 632733.

North Lombok

The focus of most visits to **north Lombok** is **Gunung Rinjani**, Lombok's highest and most sacred volcano. Climbing the mountain is a popular though very challenging undertaking that takes a minimum of two days, but there are plenty of alternative attractions in the area, not least the dramatic mountain scenery, several waterfalls that can be accessed on short hikes, a wildlife conservation park, deluxe resorts on the north coast and a couple of traditional Sasak villages. It's perfectly possible to visit the Rinjani area on a day-trip from Senggigi and surrounds, but if you're reliant on public transport you'll need to stay over – and you generally get the clearest views of the mountain in the early morning. There's accommodation in the villages at the start of the mountain trails, as well as some luxurious hotels on the beautiful **north-coast beaches**. Approaching Rinjani from the south, you'll find a couple of inviting villages in the foothills offering a chance to take in rural life, gentle treks and exhilarating mountain views.

Bangsal to Bayan

Gunung Rinjani is usually accessed via the **coast road** that runs north from Pemenang, near **Bangsal** (25km north of Senggigi and 27km north of Mataram), the harbour for public boats to the Gili Islands, and continues to northernmost Lombok. Five-star resorts occupy beaches along here and there are a couple of waterfalls, a traditional Sasak village and Lombok's oldest mosque, all of which can be woven into a day-trip from the Senggigi area.

Autore Pearl Farm

Teluk Nare • Tours charge • https://theautoregroup.com.au/pages/indonesian-farms

The **Autore Pearl Farm**, along the main road 4km west of Bangsal, is a working pearl farm (see page 244) with an enticing jewellery shop on stilts above the water. The fascinating one-hour **tours** (best booked in advance) take in the lab rooms where South Sea oyster larvae are hatched and fed with Tasmanian plankton and the racks where the small shells are placed to grow, and visitors also see the surgical operation whereby a pearl nucleus is placed inside a grown oyster and a grown pearl harvested from another.

Lombok Wildlife Park

Jl Raya Tanjung, Sire, 10min from Sire Beach • charge • http://lombokwildlifepark.com

Opened in 2017 with a handful of rescued critters and four elephants relocated from a Sumatra national park, this park has blossomed into a world-class conservation centre with 195 animals of 50 species whose aims include breeding and education. Visiting options include intimate experiences with animals including lunch or high tea, elephant mud baths, reptile encounters, an aviary and interaction with orangutans. There are two restaurants, a giftshop and a picnic area.

Pantai Sire

The longest white-sand **beach** on Lombok, **Pantai Sire**, 6.5km north of Bangsal, is a blindingly beautiful 2km strand of sand and coral, with ultra-calm waters, reasonable swimming at high tide (wear shoes to avoid sea urchins), lots of fish around the reefs about 100m offshore and fine sunrise views of Rinjani. The fairways of the nearby eighteen-hole **Sire Beach Golf Club** (http://sirebeachgolfclub.com) hug the shoreline.

Tiu Pupus and Gangga waterfalls

Beyond Pantai Sire, the coast road continues north via **Tanjung**, the district capital of north Lombok (with **ATMs**). Beyond is **Gondang**, the access point for **Tiu Pupus waterfall**, about 7km inland via a very rough track. The falls (the main water source for local farmers) are glorious, tumbling 50m down a semicircular, sheer rock face into a deep pool (swimmable but be careful of strong undercurrents). In the dry season (May–Nov), however, the water reduces to a trickle.

The trio of cascades at **Gangga waterfalls** on the northwest slope of Rinjani is about an hour's challenging trek beyond Tiu Pupas, through forest and rice fields and via the riverbed, crossed over by bamboo bridges and taking in a cave; guides will show you the way for a negotiable fee.

Segenter

West of Anyar, signs point inland and uphill to the traditional Sasak village **SEGENTER**, a 2km drive off the main road through dry expanses of cashew plantation; *bemos* drop off along the main road. The village is a more authentic and rewarding experience than the traditional villages around Kuta, and you will be guided round it (donation expected). The traditional part of the village comprises a grid of very simple, mud-floored bamboo-and-thatch huts and the occasional open-sided *bale* (general-purpose hut). You'll be taken inside one of the houses to see the eating platform, stone hearth and the *inan bale*, a small house-within-a-house where newlyweds spend their first night, but which is otherwise used to store rice.

Bayan

Four kilometres southeast of Anyar, **BAYAN** village, the centre for Wetu Telu believers (see page 258) is the site of Lombok's oldest mosque, **Masjid Kuno Bayan Beleq**, located on the eastern edge of the village, 1km east of the junction with the road to Senaru. Continuing east, the main road winds 8km through the Gunung Rinjani foothills, offering fine views of the volcano and soon giving way to the arid terrain of the east of Lombok. From the junction at **Kokok Putih**, also known as Kalih Putih, buses run to the Sembalun Valley, an alternative access-point for treks up Rinjani. The main road around the north coast continues for another 10km to Obel Obel and on to the east coast.

Masjid Kuno Bayan Beleq

Open only for special prayer ceremonies

Said to date from before 1700, around the time when Islam probably first arrived on Lombok, **Masjid Kuno Bayan Beleq** is strikingly simple in design, its profile reminiscent of a volcano, constructed entirely from timber, woven bamboo and palm thatch, atop a foundation of stones. It has been renovated of course, but apparently in the original style. You can't go inside but you can peek through the holes in the bamboo walls to see the mud floor and the bamboo torches, which light the interior during the few festival days when the mosque is used. This whole area, around the foothills of Gunung Rinjani and the sacred mountain itself, is a stronghold of the Wetu Telu branch of Islam (see page 258), and Masjid Kuno Bayan Beleq has a central role.

ARRIVAL AND DEPARTURE

By boat Bangsal is Lombok's main port for the Gili Islands. All public transport between Mataram and points around the north coast passes through Pemenang; from here it's a 1.5km *cidomos* (horse carts) ride or a shade-less walk to Bangsal's port.

By shuttle bus If you're coming from Senggigi to Bangsal, there's no *bemo* service so you'll either have to use Perama's shuttle bus (minimum 2 passengers) or take a taxi.

6

BANGSAL TO BAYAN

By bemo *Bemos* from Mataram or Pemenang terminate at the market in Anyar, on the main road beyond the Segenter turn-off. *Bemos* from here to Bayan and Senaru are most frequent in the morning, so you may have to charter one, or rent an *ojek*. Coming from Labuhan Lombok and the east, you'll change *bemos* at the turn-off in Bayan.

Destinations From Bayan: Mataram (Mandalika; 2hr 30min); Pemenang (2hr); Senaru (20min).

ACCOMMODATION AND EATING

PANTAI SIRE AND PANTAI MEDANA

The Legian Sire Lombok Sigar Penjalin; http://lhm-hotels.com. *This new ultra-luxury resort* opening in 2022 offers 46 high-standard stylish suites and 15 lovely villas on Lombok's most pristine beach with magnificent views of the Gili Islands. Three dining options, including Indonesian and Mediterranean cuisine, as well as the excellent *Wellness by the Legian* spa and infinity pools. $$$$

The Lombok Lodge Jl Pantai Medana; http://thelombok lodge.com. An exquisite beachfront hotel overlooking Pantai Medana offering a more intimate experience than its neighbours, with just nine villas set in a lush garden around a stunning pool. The in-house Frangipani Spa is one of Lombok's best, and yoga sessions can be organised for guests. An all-day breakfast and gourmet meals at the excellent restaurant are included in the rates. $$$$

The Oberoi Beach Resort http://oberoihotels.com. Luxury landmark hotel with accommodation in huge, beautifully appointed thatched villas, all with courtyard dining areas and many with private pools. Park-like palm-filled grounds edge the shore of Pantai Medana beach and there's a dive centre, spa, gym, generous pool and offshore reef. $$$$

★ **Tugu Lombok** Jl. Pantai Sire; http://tuguhotels.com. An astonishing creation, this fantasy hotel with a towering temple-like restaurant fronts Pantai Sire and is the perfect romantic getaway. Its suites and rooms fuse colonial, village and Chinese aesthetics and there's a huge infinity pool and vast grounds to explore. Their impressive *Kukuk Pletok* restaurant serves outstanding Indonesian and western food. $$$$

TANJUNG

Rinjani Beach Eco Resort Jl Raya Tanjung; http://rinjani-beach.com. A kilometre beyond the Pantai Medana turnoff, this tranquil if isolated place enjoys a beachfront location with good diving directly in front, and its thatch-and-bamboo bungalows are priced for mere mortals compared with its luxury neighbours. There's a small pool and restaurant. $–$$

Gunung Rinjani and around

The **climb** up majestic, forested **GUNUNG RINJANI** (3726m), taking in the magnificent **Danau Segara Anak** crater lake, is the most taxing and rewarding trek on either Bali or Lombok. Most climbs start from either **Senaru** or **Sembalun Lawang**, on the northern slopes. However, two new access points have opened at Aik Berik, near Benang Stokel waterfall, and Timbanuh both on the southern slopes. If you want to reach the summit, Sembalun Lawang is the best starting point. If you just want to see Danau Segara Anak from the crater rim, the easiest access is from Senaru. Other upland villages south of Rinjani, notably, south of Sembalun Lawang at **Sapit** and **Tetebatu**, in the Aik Berik region, make pleasant rural bases with opportunities for gentle hikes as well as facilities for arranging Rinjani climbs. The entire area was established as a UNESCO Global Geopark in 2018.

Climbing Gunung Rinjani

The 3726m **summit** of **Gunung Rinjani** is reached by relatively few trekkers; the majority are satisfied with a shorter, less arduous hike to the **crater rim** (2641m). From here there are fabulous views of the vast turquoise crater lake, **Danau Segara Anak**, which measures 8km by 6km, and the perfect, sometimes smoking, cone of **Gunung Baru** rising from within the lake. It is also possible to descend to the lakeside and ease aching muscles in scalding **hot springs**. The lake is considered to be the abode of the gods, and Wetu Telu pilgrims come on nights of the full moon, while Balinese Hindus make offerings to the lake during the Pekelem festival (at the full moon of the fifth Balinese month, often in November).

Having only intermittent activity since 1847, Gunung Baru **erupted** in August 1994, closing the mountain for several weeks, and there have been several smaller eruptions since; a larger series of eruptions occurred in 2010. The Gunung Rinjani cone itself has been inactive since 1901, apart from a few periodic puffs of smoke. However, the mountain should be treated with respect, and its weather is notoriously unpredictable.

WETU TELU

Followers of **Wetu Telu** – which translates as "three times", possibly referring to the number of daily prayer-times – adhere to the central tenets of Islam, such as belief in Allah as the one God and Muhammad as his prophet, but diverge significantly from the practices of orthodox Muslims, who, because they pray five times a day, are known as "Wetu Lima".

For the Wetu Telu, the older traditions of **ancestor worship and animism** persist and there are many similarities with Balinese Hindu beliefs and practices; both worship at Pura Lingsar, and Wetu Telu believe that **Gunung Rinjani** is the dwelling place of the ancestors and the supreme god, and make pilgrimages to the mountain. There are many Wetu Telu villages around Rinjani, including **Bayan**, whose ancient mosque is especially important. Many Wetu Telu observe a three-day fast rather than the full month of **Ramadan**. The most important Wetu Telu rituals are **life-cycle ceremonies** associated with birth, death, marriage and circumcision, as well as rituals connected with agriculture and house-building. Their central annual festival is **Maulid**, Muhammad's birthday.

Throughout their history, the Wetu Telu have been subjected to varying degrees of pressure to conform to mainstream Islamic ideas. During the civil unrest in 1965, anyone less than scrupulously orthodox was in danger of being regarded as communist and there were attacks against the Wetu Telu. These days many Wetu Telu profess to follow orthodox Islam while also carrying out their Wetu Telu observances under the label of *adat*, customary practices.

Despite clean-up efforts by park rangers and volunteers, sadly trash is a huge problem on all routes up the mountain and the situation gets worse every year. All campsites are a mess, the human waste and discarded food attracting scavenging mice, rats, flies and monkeys.

The routes

The shortest trek is **from Senaru to the crater rim** (two days, one night). This starts at the top of the village (601m) and ascends through forest to **Pos II** (1500m) and **Pos III** (2000m); you then leave the forest for the steep slog up to the rim (2641m). Most people take six to seven hours to reach the sheltered camp area where you overnight; from where it's about thirty minutes to the rim the next morning for sunrise, with classic views across Segara Anak to Gunung Baru. You can return to Senaru the same way.

The most popular trek is a longer version of the above: **from Senaru to the crater rim and down to the lake** (three days, two nights). From the crater rim, a path (2hr) descends into the crater to the lake (2050m). It is steep and scary at the top, with metal handrails and occasional ropes, but gets better. You can bathe in the lakeside hot springs if there are no religious ceremonies going on and will probably camp nearby, walking back to Senaru the next day.

You can also combine **the lake and summit from Senaru** (four days, three nights). From the lake, a different path (3hr; pretty steep) climbs to the rim on the Sembalun side and a site called **Plawangan II** (2639m), where everyone aiming for the summit overnights. From here it's an extraordinarily steep haul up to the summit of Rinjani (3726m; another 3–4hr, usually done for sunrise, then 2hr back down to Plawangan II). Trekkers usually descend via the shortest route, to Sembalun Lawang.

The **shortest route to the summit** is to climb **from Sembalun Lawang** (two days, one night). It takes seven to eight hours from Sembalun Lawang (1156m) to Plawangan II and you attack the summit the next morning (if you've any energy left!) before returning to Sembalun.

The most complete exploration of the mountain involves a round trip **from Sembalun Lawang to Senaru, via the summit and the lake** (three days, two nights). This gets the most exhausting ascent over while you are fresh and enables you to soak tired muscles in the hot springs afterwards. Longer trips of up to six days, featuring the "milk caves" and hot springs around the lake as well as the summit, are also possible.

Senaru and Sembalun Lawang are by far the most common trailheads, but hardcore hikers can also take a route up the southwestern flank **from Aik Berik,** the site of two well-known waterfalls about 28km northeast of Mataram. In the 2018 earthquake, the trail to the crater rim, via dense forest (6hr) and then down a very steep path to the southern side of the lake (3hr), was obliterated, making the rim

6

PLANNING A RINJANI TREK

The mountain is **closed to trekkers** during the wettest months of the year, usually from late December to late March, and may be out of bounds at other times if the authorities consider conditions to be too risky, though some unscrupulous companies simply take hikers up via illegal entrances. Be advised that trekkers have disappeared – or even died – here, so choose your guide carefully. Trekking at any time of year is not for the frail or unfit. A guide is essential and must be licensed by the Rinjani National Park authorities. Ask to see your guide's official license before agreeing on any guide. Upon arrival at any of the four trailheads you must **register** with the national park authorities and pay the national park admission fee (included in organized hikes) before you set off. A photocopy of your passport photo page is required. You can do this at Senaru at the Rinjani Trek Centre or at the Rinjani Trekking Center at Sembalun Lawang.

It is highly advisable to bring your own **walking boots** (trainers aren't suitable, though locals manage in flip-flops!). Other essential equipment includes a seriously **warm, windproof jacket** (summit temperatures can drop to freezing at night), a hat and gloves, a head torch that leaves your hands free, and loads of snacks and sweets (even if food is provided). Pack lists can be found on trekking operators' websites. Some trekking companies rent clothes and gear, or you can buy your own at Epicentrum Mall. Make sure that a mobile phone is available in your party for emergencies.

BOOKING A TREK

Agents in every tourist centre on Lombok, including Gili Trawangan and Senggigi, and even some on Bali, will offer to sell you a Rinjani trek. But choose carefully: this is a serious climb and there have been fatalities due to poor equipment (including lack of sufficiently warm gear) and reckless disregard for safety. As there have been reports of fake agencies on Bali and the Gili Islands copying the names of established operators to sell inferior packages, it's best to deal directly with reputable trek organizers, which you can do at **Senaru** and **Sembalun Lawang** trailhead villages via their websites.

The **Rinjani Trek Management Board** (RTMB; http://rinjaninationalpark.com) coordinates and licenses trekking facilities on the mountain and is supposed to clear litter and train porters. On its website it posts when the park is officially closed. The price of **organized treks** depends on the number of people in the group and the **level of service** – budget, standard or deluxe. There's plenty of competitive pricing going on, though corners are likely to be cut if you bargain too hard; insufficient food and unbearably thin sleeping bags are common complaints. Whatever your chosen service level, you should get a guide, porters, sleeping bags, tents, meals and water. Before you book, be sure to get specific details of exactly **what is included** in the price.

TREKKING GUIDES

Senaru is by far the busiest trekking centre, with hundreds of local guides and porters. **Sembalun Lawang** is much quieter and has far fewer trek organizers.

Green Rinjani Trekking Senaru; http://greenrinjani.com.

John's Adventures Senaru; http://rinjanimaster.com.

Rinjani Women Adventure Sembalun Lawang; http://rinjaniwomenadventure.com.

Rudy Trekker Senaru; http://rudytrekker.com.

inaccessible, but its scenery and waterfalls make trekking worthwhile and are likely to be a lot quieter than the main routes. The return route is the same, unless you want to tackle the summit, in which case you need to arrange to get paddled across the lake to the Sembalun side. The second new trail, at **Tibanuh**, is the steepest of the four. As with the Aik Berik, as of the time of research the summit is not reachable from here.

Batu Koq and Senaru

The small, contiguous villages **BATU KOQ** and **SENARU**, south of Bayan (about 80km from Mataram), are one of two main centres for Rinjani treks, full of guesthouses and trekking organizers. With cool temperatures and fine views of the mountain, they're also a pleasant destination in their own right.

Other than Rinjani itself, Senaru's main attractions are its waterfalls. The impressive 25m-high **Sindang Gile falls** (charge includes a guide and Tiu Kelep falls) is reached via a twenty-minute hike along a path that begins just south of *Pondok Senaru* bungalows. Another hour's challenging uphill slog gets you to **Tiu Kelep** falls, where the water pours down in a double horseshoe. You should probably take a dip here; local belief is that you become a year younger every time you swim behind the falls. Longer local treks such as the **Senaru Panorama Walk** (3hr) take in the falls and are guided by Rinjani Women Guides, who were born and raised here. You can arrange tours with them online or through the Rinjani Trek Centre.

Within a fenced compound a few metres from the Rinjani trailhead, at the end of the road and almost next door to the Rinjani Trek Centre, is Senaru's original **Sasak village** (entry by donation), whose residents still live in simple, traditional houses of bamboo and thatch, similar in design to those at Segenter. A villager will show you around.

Sembalun Lawang

Thirty kilometres southeast of Senaru, set in a high, flat-bottomed mountain valley filled with market gardens growing potatoes and chillies, **SEMBALUN LAWANG** is a very quiet village that's known chiefly as the other major trailhead for one of the main routes up Gunung Rinjani. The Rinjani Trekking Center can organize climbs. There are several more gentle local **treks** in this area as well as including a leisurely stroll through Sembalun village to Mangku Sakti Waterfall near Sajang village, a wildflowers walk (seasonal), and a full-day jungle hike over Pegasingan Hill to Obel Obel on the north coast. If you'd like to see the mighty volcano up-close but don't care to hike, drive to Taman Wisata Pasuk Sembalun where there is a bamboo walkway above the treeline. The area is also known for **handweaving**, and it's possible to visit local weavers. For all activities, ask at one of the village **guesthouses**.

Sembalun Bumbung

As you continue south from Sembalun Lawang towards Sapit, market gardens proliferate until the valley closes in (think yummy hill-grown strawberries). Some 4km south of Sembalun Lawang, **SEMBALUN BUMBUNG** clusters round the mosque in the shadows of the surrounding mountains. From Sembalun Bumbung, the mountain road winds south for 15km across Gunung Pusuk to Pesugulan, the turn-off for Sapit. There's a fine valley viewpoint at the pass, then it's mostly forest, inhabited by grey macaques and rare ebony leaf monkeys. Rockfalls are common, so the road is sometimes closed.

Sapit

Situated on Gunung Pusuk's southern slopes, 10km south over the pass from Sembalun Bumbung and a refreshing 800m above sea level, small **SAPIT** village makes a quiet retreat with views down to the east coast and over to Sumbawa.

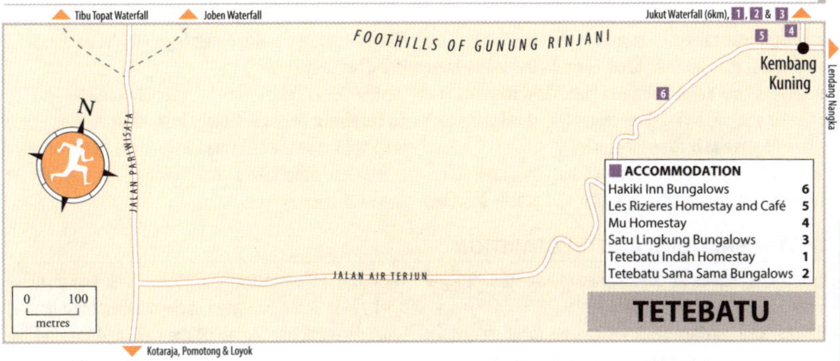

Tobacco-growing is the main industry round here, and Philip Morris the big employer; fields are dotted with red-brick drying towers. With basic **guesthouses** in the village, this is a good chance to get away from tourist crowds; staff will fill you in on **trails** to nearby waterfalls and natural swimming pools and can organize Rinjani treks.

Tetebatu and around

Scenically situated on the southern slopes of Gunung Rinjani, 50km east of Mataram (11km north of the main cross-island highway), **TETEBATU** enjoys fine views of the mountain across terraced fields lush with rice in the rainy season and tobacco in the dry; tall, red-brick drying towers for the tobacco are visible at every turn. At an altitude of about 600m, the area is cool but not cold and Tetebatu makes an excellent base from which to appreciate small-town life and explore the centre of the island. You can also arrange ascents of Rinjani here.

Tiny Tetebatu has no sights of its own, though on a clear morning the views north to Rinjani are exhilarating. The main street has plenty of small *kios* to browse, mostly selling everyday necessities and fresh food.

The waterfalls

The main local attraction is the **trek** through terraced ricefields to the local monkey forest and **Jukut waterfall** – also called Jeruk Manis – (charge for national park entry), where the water streams down a towering jungle-clad rock face into a pool 20m below. Any guesthouse can organize this as a six-hour return trip for an additional charge. With your own transport you can also travel by road to the falls car park (6km), from where it's 1.5km on foot that includes a steep and often slippery climb rewarded by a dip in the pool below. The twin cascades at **Tibu Topat**, northwest of the village, are a pretty alternative, with a sunlit pool for swimming. Also to the northwest, **Joben waterfall**, or Otak Kokok Gading, is small (only 5m tall) and much less impressive.

Kotaraja and Loyok

With transport you can explore **Kotaraja** town, about 5km south of Tetebatu, which is known for its **blacksmiths** and for its traditional **stickfighting**, *peresean* (see page 251), held in August, and nearby **Loyok**, a centre for **bamboo basketware**.

ARRIVAL AND DEPARTURE

GUNUNG RINJANI AND AROUND

BY SHUTTLE BUS

Perama offers shuttle transport from Senggigi and Mataram to Tetebatu, with a minimum of two passengers (http://peramatour.com).

BY BEMO OR BUS

To Senaru *Bemos* along the north-coast road stop at Anyar or Bayan for connections to Senaru.

To Sembalun Lawang You can reach Senaru via a steep

and badly maintained 16km road from Kokok Putih on the north-coast road, or from Sapit 16km to the south. There are *bemos* from Kokok Putih and from Sapit. There are also irregular pick-ups plying these routes (you stand in the back with villagers and hold on for dear life).
Destinations Aik Mel (2hr); Kokok Putih (1hr); Sapit (1hr).
To Sapit Sapit is served by *bemos* and a daily bus from Mataram; there are also *bemos* from Aik Mel on the cross-island highway (17km).
Destinations Aik Mel (1hr); Sembalun Lawang (1–2hr).
To Tetebatu *Bemos* and buses from Mataram will get you to Pomotong on the main road, from where it's about 10km to Tetebatu: either take a *bemo* to Kotaraja then an *ojek*, or an *ojek* all the way.

GETTING AROUND AND INFORMATION

In Tetebatu inquire at guesthouses to arrange motorbike rental, cars with driver or bicycle rental.
Banks and exchange ATMs can be found at regular intervals along the main cross-island highway. There are no ATMs in Senaru.
Tours In Tetebatu, Jonny Tour Guide (Jalan Pariwisata; http://jonnytourguide.com) is a recommended organiser of hikes to the waterfalls or beyond.
Trekking information The Rinjani Trek Centre (0819 0741 1211) at the trail-head at the southernmost limit of Senaru has information about the treks and maps of the mountain. In Sembalun Lawang, the go-to guys are at Rinjani Trekking Center (http://rinjanitrekkingcenter.com), which is a different group, and Rinjani Women Guides (http://rinjaniwomenadventure.com).

ACCOMMODATION AND EATING

BATU KOQ AND SENARU, SEE MAP PAGE 257

Accommodation, with one notable exception, is spread for several kilometres along the road through Batu Koq and Senaru. Places on the east of the road generally have the best views towards the mountain. Most can arrange local hikes and trekking guides and will store your stuff while you climb.
Ila Homestay Jl. Pariwisata Senaru; 0853 3753 3889. Run by a friendly husband and wife team, this little place is in a great location; only a 10min walk to Sindang Gile and Tiup Gelap waterfalls and an ideal base for Rinjani treks, which owners can arrange. Basic, clean rooms and good food. $
Pondok Senaru Cottages Jl. Pariwisata Senaru; 0818 0362 4129. The biggest place in the area, often thronged with hikers in high season. Offers a range of decent bungalows, some with hot water, in a pretty garden with good views and easy access to the waterfalls. Has a large restaurant with panoramic views too. $
Rinjani Lighthouse Cottages Jl. Pariwisata Senaru; http://rinjanilighthouse.com. Rebuilt after the 2018 earthquake, this German-owned, eco-friendly guesthouse at the quiet southern end of Senaru is the most relaxed guesthouse in the village, with mountain views from the garden and lovely wooden rooms with hot water and verandas. There's also a good restaurant and a traditional family house, sleeping six people. $
Rinjani Lodge Jl. Pariwisata Senaru; http://rinjanilodge.com. Enjoying sweeping views of the volcano down to Lombok's coast strip, this upmarket lodge has very smart rooms, trimmed with modish wooden panelling and boasting limestone-walled bathrooms. There's an infinity pool (which is opened to non-guests, making things noisy on weekends). $$
Tiu Kelep Homestay Jl. Pariwisata No. 2; 0878 6450 6965. Situated literally in front of the entrance to Sindang Gile and Tiup Gelap waterfalls, these spotlessly clean simple bungalows are excellent value. Owner can arrange treks and there are restaurants, a bar and shops nearby. $

SEMBALUN LAWANG, SEE MAP PAGE 257

Lembah Rinjani Jl. Taman Nasional Gunung Rinjani No. 10; 0877 6709 6368. A good base with clean, if plain, twins and doubles with verandas facing the mountain, located 200m along the Rinjani trail. The cheaper cold-water rooms are supplied with hot-water buckets for bathing. There's a restaurant too, with Indonesian and international dishes; give them notice and they'll provide cold beers so you can celebrate the end of your trek. $
Radiya Guesthouse Jl. Raya Sembaluan Lawang; 0812 3735 4646. A choice of clean, stilted bungalows or small but comfy and cosy rooms with cold shower hosted by a lovely family. This guesthouse is on the busy main street, so convenient to shops and food, but you might want to request a room at the back to escape daytime traffic noise. $
Sembalun Agro Jl. Raya Sembalun Lawang; 0853 3777 0606. The best accommodation in the valley is just north of the village along the main road; the modern rooms in this hotel all have sweeping views, hot water and satellite TV. The restaurant serves tasty beef sate and *gado-gado* and has a small shop with trekking food. $
Sembalun Kita Cottage Jl. Raya Sembalun Lawang No. 16; 0819 9994 1399. Simple rooms with great views of farmland and mountains with excellent hosts, clean rooms, tasty food and a campfire every night. $

TETEBATU AND AROUND, SEE MAP PAGE 261

Hakiki Inn Bungalows Jl Air Terjun; 0818 0373 7407.

A very rustic set-up with eight bare-bones *lumbung*-style bungalows and a few single huts set in a garden encircled by paddy fields, about 1km from the village centre. $

★ **Les Rizieres Homestay and Café** Kembang Kuning; http://les-rizieres.com. Charming French guesthouse with a warm ambience and plenty of activities to keep you busy, if you wish. Rooms are simple yet attractive, the owners serve delicious meals, and there's a large garden and views of ricefields and Rinjani. $$

Mu Homestay Jl. Kembang Kuning; https://instagram.com/mu_homestay. Modern rooms in a ricefield, each with veranda. Owner Mu and his family are excellent hosts and can take you to pottery and weaving villages, on treks, or whatever your heart desires. $

Satu Lingkung Bungalows Jl. Pariwisata Tetebatu; http://satulingkung.com. This friendly family-run homestay has four bungalows with terraces located in the ricefields and enjoying lovely views of the fields and forests. You can also climb a bamboo lookout tower for wider vistas. Authentic local food is served at the on-site *warung*. Cooking classes possible. $

Tetebatu Indah Homestay Jl. Monkey Forest Km.49, north side of village; https://tetebatuindahhomestay.com. A very welcoming homestay owned by Bram, an English-speaking local and his family, who really look after guests and can organize tours at fair rates. Rooms are basic but clean with *mandi*-style hot-water bathrooms. It's a great place to learn about village life in Lombok. $

Tetebatu Sama Sama Bungalows Kampung Orong Gerisak; 0356 7966 3940. Situated in a ricefield, clean simple but spacious bungalows owned by two brothers who are also excellent at arranging tours and extend courtesies beyond the call of duty. They serve fresh, grilled seafood; ask to taste their homemade rice wine. $

6

DIRECTORY

Banks and exchange There's a BNI ATM in Senaru just up from *Pondok Senaru*. John's Adventures in Senaru (see page 259) can exchange money; some trek organizers will take credit cards. On Rinjani's southern slopes there are BNI ATMs in Kotaraja and Aik Mel.

East Lombok

With an arid climate, sparse population and few facilities, **east Lombok** doesn't entice many visitors, although if you're heading to or from Sumbawa to the east you'll pass through **Labuhan Lombok** port (75km east of Mataram). One reason to linger is the prospect of good snorkelling at the uninhabited islands off **Labuhan Pandan**. Beyond the radar of most foreign tourists, the isolated little **Pantai Pulo Lampu** beach,13km north of Labuhan Lombok, near Transat village, is popular with locals at weekends but otherwise very quiet. Its main attraction is access to the two groups of uninhabited **islands** just off the coast. In the most southerly group, **Gili Lampu**, **Gili Kondo** and **Gili Bidara** have sandy beaches as well as coral walls and attract plenty of fish. Further north, the larger **Gili Sulat** and **Gili Lawang** islands are surrounded by coastal mangrove but have lots of coral.

Another reason to spend some time here is to see the giant *Ficus albipila* forest (locally called *pohon lian*) by the side of the road at Pringgabaya. Villagers say the towering 50m trees pre-date Dutch colonization.

Continuing south on the coastal highway is **pottery-producing Penakak** village, whose road is lined with large and small outlets selling a vast array of earthenware from throughout Lombok.

In **Masbagik**, 1.5km west, is the impressive principal **mosque** Masjid Al-Jami Al-Akbar: it's on the main trans-Lombok highway, in the heart of this busy town, and is one of the largest in Lombok. Across the road, cash-starved travellers staying in Tetebatu or Sapit will find an **ATM**. From Masbagik you can go back to the coastal road and continue to south Lombok or go west to Mataram.

ARRIVAL AND DEPARTURE — EAST LOMBOK

By bus Buses travel the length of the trans-Lombok highway from Mataram's Mandalika terminal to Labuhan Lombok; some continue to Labuhan Kayangan or Lubuhan Lombok, the ferry terminal for boats to Sumbawa.

Destinations Bayan (2hr); Kopang (for Praya; 1hr); Mataram (Mandalika; 2hr); Sembalun Lawang (2hr 30min).

By bemo *Bemos* from Labuhan Lombok to Pantai Pulo Lampu will drop you on the main road for the 500m walk down to the beach.

ACCOMMODATION

There are no recommendable places in Labuhan Lombok itself, so it's best to head just north up the coast to Labuhan Pandan or push on to Mataram or Tetebatu.

Pondok Gili Lampu Jl Raya Sambelia; 0878 6336 5666. Basic wood-and-thatch bungalows and smarter Deluxe options in a garden behind the restaurant and beach. The enthusiastic manager arranges boat trips to the islands for snorkelling or fishing, and can organize "desert-island" camping trips too. $

Pondok Siola Jl Raya Sambelia, Labuhan Pandan; 0819 9776 9364. Excellent beachfront place with dreamy views over a black-sand beach east towards Sumbawa. Well-built concrete bungalows are equipped with verandas and quality beds, mattresses and linen. The family owners can set up good snorkelling trips and there's tasty local grub served in the restaurant. $

6

South Lombok

Interest in the utterly spectacular **south coast** of Lombok is starting to take off and the varied accommodation range is already ahead of the game. It's extraordinarily beautiful, with kilometre upon kilometre of white-sand bays backed by wild, forested hills and washed by some of the most rewarding surf on the island. **Kuta** is the main tourist centre, centrally positioned for exploring the fabulous coastline to the west and east. **Inland**, there are worthwhile textile workshops at Sukarara, plus a couple of traditional Sasak villages at **Sade** and **Rembitan**.

Two major influences for growth here are the expansion of the **Lombok International Airport**,15km north, which has channelled travellers to this coast in ever-growing numbers and will further increase its capacity by 2028. The other is the construction of a new resort area, **Mandalika**, to the east of Kuta village, home to the five-star Pullman Lombok Mandalika Beach Resort along with chic cafés, eateries and a glamorous beach club. The world-class Mandalika International Street Circuit was inaugurated in November 2021 with the World Superbike Championship and in 2022 hosted its first MotoGP Grand Prix.

Outside the peak periods of July, August and late December, Kuta and the south are still relatively quiet but development is flourishing and it surely won't be long before the tourist boom hits Lombok's south shore.

Praya and around

PRAYA market town, 22km southeast of Mataram and 26km north of Kuta, is a transport hub for the south, though with the modern airport highway, buses from Mataram to the airport and shuttle buses to Kuta bypass the town completely.

NYALE FESTIVAL

Celebrated on Lombok and the more distant Sumba and Savu islands, the annual Bau Nyale, or **Nyale Festival**, is all about the sea worm, *Eunice viridis*, known locally as **nyale**. The worms live attached to rocks in the ocean, but at roughly the same time every year, on the nineteenth day of the tenth Sasak month (Feb or March), they begin their sexual cycle and release brightly coloured male and female sexual parts, which rise to the surface ready for fertilization, turning the ocean into a seething mass of fluorescent spaghetti. The number of worms is believed to indicate the success of the next rice harvest and draws huge crowds to celebrate their arrival. Around a hundred thousand people travel to Kuta's Seger beach and other south-coast beaches to gather the worms – which are believed to be aphrodisiacs – and to enjoy traditional singing, dancing, poetry and a re-enactment of the Putri Mandalika **legend**. This tells how the beautiful Princess Mandalika, distraught because of the number of suitors who were fighting over her and loath to upset any of them and risk plunging her country into war, flung herself into the sea where her hair was changed into *nyale* sea worms.

Sukarara

SUKARARA village, about 8km west of Praya, produces the widest range of textiles on Lombok, weaving highly coloured *songket* cloth on backstrap looms and ikat cloth on foot looms (see page 149). A sarong-and-scarf set can take up to five months to weave and designs are so numerous and complex that girls (and now boys too) start learning at the age of seven; young women must be skilled weavers in order to be considered marriageable. There are a number of textile shops in Sukarara and in neighbouring Puyung.

ARRIVAL AND INFORMATION — PRAYA AND AROUND

By bemo or bus Buses and *bemos* from Mataram's Mandalika terminal drop off at the bus terminal, 3km northwest of the centre, where there are onward buses to Sengkol and Kuta.

Destinations Kuta (1hr); Mataram (Mandalika; 30min).

Banks and exchange There are several ATMs in Praya.

Kuta and around

Youthful, laidback and surferish, **KUTA** is growing up fast – not too long ago, the south coast hub was little more than a scruffy fishing village with guesthouses, tourist restaurants and a few upscale alternatives. Today, the pace of change is definitely increasing, with more upmarket accommodation and dining options available than ever before and extensive construction taking place on the outskirts of town.

For the moment there is plenty for all to enjoy. **Surfers** return year after year to pursue the perfect wave, most famously at **Gerupuk**, **Mawi** and, more remotely, at **Ekas**. The **beach** at Kuta has been cleaned up – but still has very persistent hawkers – and is dotted with little shacks selling food and renting water activity equipment. For a swim and a sunbathe you're better off heading to the breathtakingly gorgeous sandy bays nearby, notably **east** at **Tanjung Aan** and west at **Mawun**, though always ask locally about currents, which can be treacherous. To access the beaches and get the best out of the area you need a car or motorbike – the north-south road to the airport is good but the east-west coastal road is still cursed by potholes.

Sade and Rembitan traditional villages

Rembitan admission by donation and charge for compulsory guide; Sade admission by donation, guides charge

North of Kuta on the Sengkol road are a couple of traditional **Sasak villages** that welcome tourists. Of the two, the northernmost, **REMBITAN**, 7km from Kuta, is the more authentic and the less grasping; with a good guide you may learn a lot. As

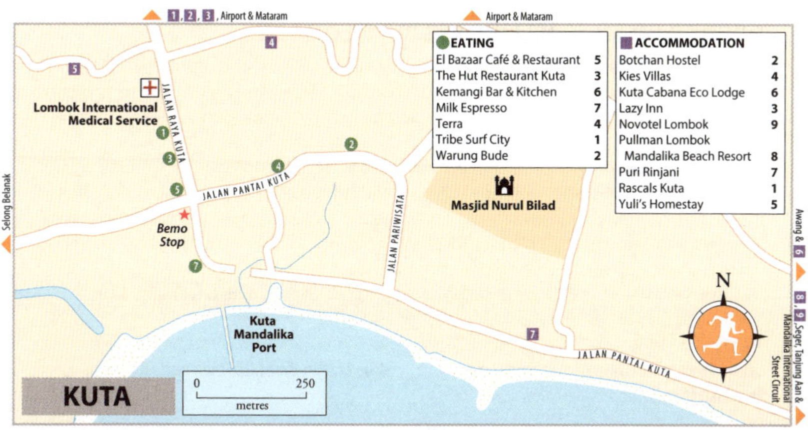

with other such villages in north Bali, the thirty homes here are simple, low-roofed, windowless constructions, with mud and buffalo-dung floors, bamboo walls and thatched roofs. Some have satellite TV but bathrooms are communal. Villagers farm soya beans and rice and weave cloth and make basketware, some of which is for sale.

The other traditional village is **SADE**, 1km south. It sees hordes of visitors, is more of a shopping and photo opportunity, and has a reputation for hassle.

ARRIVAL AND GETTING AROUND

KUTA AND AROUND

6

By plane See page 240

By shuttle bus Perama (http://peramatour.com) operates a shuttle service to Kuta from the Gili Islands, Senggigi, Lembar and Mataram (minimum two people). Other travel agency bus transfers are widely advertised in Kuta.

By bus and bemo Buses and *bemos* serve Kuta from Mataram's Mandalika terminal with a change at Praya's bus station; the number of *bemos* has declined in recent years however.

Destinations Praya (1hr); Sengkol (30min).

By motorbike, car or bike Motorbikes are available to rent everywhere: try Lombok Scooters (Jl. Mawun 2; https://lombokscooters.com) and many hotels offer bike rentals or car hire. It's important to avoid a widespread local scam for fake damage claims from freelance rental touts by only renting from your accommodation or other reputable agency.

By taxi or ride-share Ride-sharing apps Gojek and Grab are both now available in Lombok. Note that if you take a ride-share from the airport, you will need to walk outside of the airport to meet them. Alternatively, taxis are widely available.

ACTIVITIES

Kuta Bay's protective coral reef makes the calm waters an ideal spot for learning or having fun with all sorts of watersports, such as kayaking, standup paddleboarding, tubing, paragliding, jet ski, wakeboarding and kiteboarding.

Adventure sports Sky Lombok Paragliding (Jl. Mawun 33; https://skylombokadventure.com) offers tandem paragliding experiences along the coast. Ocean Addicts (Jl Pariwisata Pantai Kuta; https://oceanaddictslombok.com) is a one-stop-shop for water activities, including kiteboarding, wakeboarding, banana boating, and water-skiing. Mimpi Sup Club (https://mimpisupclub.com) rents stand-up paddleboards; lessons and yoga paddle are also available.

Fitness Several gyms and fitness centres have now opened up in Kuta, but Xeno Fit (Aik lengis, Dusun Mengalung; http://xenolombok.com) is by far the most stylish with a large open-air studio shaded beneath a bamboo roof. There's cross-fit, a climbing wall, and free weights plus classes and personal training available.

Fishing Kuta Lombok Fishing (https://kutalombokfishing.com) runs half and full-day fishing charters around Kuta Bay.

Surfing This is the main deal in Kuta and is possible year-round. Selong Blanak is sandy and good for beginners, and novices can also usually surf Gerupuk; Mawi is a swell magnet. Several surf shops can repair and rent boards and offer lessons for beginners (charge includes board rental) and trips to Mawi or Are Goling, including boat. They can also arrange surf-and-stay packages to Desert Point.

Yoga Mana Yoga Studio (at *Mana Retreat*) Jl. Baturiti, Kuta http://manalombok.com offers yoga classes including slow

DIVING AND SNORKELLING IN SOUTH LOMBOK

There are several dive spots in the Kuta vicinity, including at Gerupuk to the east and Mawun and Tampah to the west, and most are good for novices. Depending on skill levels and depths explored, sightings can include soft corals, colourful reef fish, shrimp and in deeper waters octopuses, lobsters, seasonal mantas, Napoleon wrasses and barracudas.

Further west, remote Belongas Bay is for advanced enthusiasts only due to its strong currents and unpredictable weather. At Magnet and Cathedral, barracudas, tunas and other pelagics are spotted throughout the year, with mobula and eagle rays making an appearance in August and September. At Magnet, there are hammerheads June through early November, white and black-tip sharks, sea snakes and untouched corals.

Most dive centres run PADI certification courses, fun dives and some offer night dives.

DIVE CENTRES

Scuba Froggy Kuta, http://scubafroggy.com.

Two Fish Divers http://twofishdivers.com

Blue Marlin Dive http://bluemarlindive.com/

flow, vinyasa, surfers yoga and several others (packages available) and also retreats of varying lengths that include spa treatments. Rascals Yoga (Jl Raya Kuta; https://yogakutalombok.com) has a daily schedule of yoga and mobility classes.

ACCOMMODATION

SEE MAP PAGE 265

There's almost no on-the-beach accommodation and no real sea views but most places are an easy stroll from the water. Theft from rooms is an occasional problem: always lock your room and outside-bathroom door, including when you're asleep inside. Accommodation options are expanding quickly, with many new places under construction. Try to book ahead for July and August and late December, when rooms are harder to find.

Botchan Hostel Jl Raya Kuta; 0852 3496 4222. Cheap and cheerful, centrally located hostel with six-, eight- and ten-bed a/c dorms, along with a handful of private rooms. Breakfast is included and there's free parking, shared kitchen and lounge areas, and a garden pool. $

Kies Villas Jl. Sawe-Baturiti; http://kiesvillaslombok.com. Changing the game in Kuta, these very upmarket studios, suites and villas tick all the right contemporary boxes with stylish interiors and sleek design including original art and gorgeous outdoor showers. Book a Sasak-style *lumbung* if you want more of a local feel. There are two pools. $$

Kuta Cabana Eco Lodge Jl. Raya Awang, Rangkap 1; https://facebook.com/KutaCabanaLodge. A bit off the beaten path, these simple but charming budget bamboo bungalows are set on a hilltop overlooking ricefields and Kuta Bay. Chill-out areas with hammocks add to the ambience. Restaurant serves excellent food and is open to non-guests. It's a 5min drive from Seger beach but if the walk is too much you can rent a scooter onsite. $

Lazy Inn Jl. Sawe-Baturiti; https://instagram.com/lazyinnlombok. You can't beat the location of this recently renovated B&B, right in the heart of Kuta. There's a pool, café and six spacious rooms with a/c, hot water, free Lombok coffee and bike hire. Good value and fabulous owners. $

Novotel Lombok Pantai Putri Nyale; http://novotellombok.com. Four-star resort stunningly located on its own stretch of white-sand beach, a 15min walk from Seger beach and 3km by road from central Kuta. It's designed to resemble a thatch-roofed village, with over 100 tastefully decorated rooms, some with private pools. There are two pools, one of them seafront, and a spa, plus lots of activities such as diving and a kid's club. $$

Pullman Lombok Mandalika Beach Resort ITDC Mandalika Tourism Complex; https://pullman-lombok-mandalika.com. This upscale beachfront hotel offers five-star luxury with two restaurants, *Aer* and *Sgara Seafood Restaurant, plus* a swim-up bar, a wellness centre, and a huge freeform pool. All of the 257 rooms and suites have private balconies while villas boast private pools with garden or beach access. $$$

Puri Rinjani Jl Pantai Kuta; 0370 615 4849. Right by the beach these clean, good-quality bungalows all have hot water and a/c. There's an inviting pool and a large restaurant with sea views. $

Rascals Kuta Jl. Sawe-Baturiti; http://rascalskutalombok.com. Friendly and smartly decorated in a quiet area but near local eateries, this Australian-owned boutique resort also has a day spa, gift shop and onsite ATM. All rooms have a/c and some have direct pool access. $$

★**Yuli's Homestay** Jl Pariwisata, http://yulishomestay.com. An extremely well-run and well-maintained popular place that constantly expands and refurbishes. It's owned by a charming New Zealand-Lombok couple and has spotless rooms – all with a/c and cold-water bathrooms – dotted around a huge grassy plot with three pools. There's a shared hot shower block and a communal kitchen too. Breakfast is cooked to order, filling and delicious. $

EATING

SEE MAP PAGE 265

Kuta's restaurant and café scene is ever-expanding and by far the most exciting in Lombok. **For nightlife**, expats and locals gather at Milk Espresso's Rooftop Bar for happy hour and live music before migrating to Surfers Bar Kuta Lombok (http://facebook.com/surfersbarkutalombok) to enjoy best cocktails and lovely views of Kuta beach.

★**El Bazaar Café & Restaurant** Jl Raya Kuta No. 5; https://instagram.com/elbazarlombok. *El Bazaar* offers excellent, healthy Middle Eastern food including tagines and kebabs as well as an outstanding meze platter which takes in pita bread, hummus, couscous, carrots with honey and mustard dressing, cumin potatoes in olive oil and *baba ganoush*, and is almost enough for two. Also serves espresso coffee. $$$

The Hut Restaurant Kuta Jl Raya Kuta No. 5; 0818 610 695. presented international and Asian fare is served in a nice little restaurant decorated with eclectic art. Thick hearty curries served with freshly baked pittas, big-bowl salads, and scrumptious desserts. $

Kemangi Bar & Kitchen Jl. Pariwisata; http://kemangilombok.com. Interestingly attached to a B&B, this chic restaurant serves un-ordinary Kuta fare. Billing its cuisine as "modern tropical", try the Ahi Tuna with lettuce, capers, orange slices and avocado for lunch or something heavier, such as Slow-Cooked Lamb Shank or Four-Cheese Risotto, at dinner. $$$

Milk Espresso Jl. Raya Kuta 3; https://instagram.com/milk.lombok. All the usual brunch suspects–fluffy pancakes, eggs benedict, smoothie bowls and chia pudding–are executed to perfection at this trendy café. There's also great coffee, fresh juices and tempting baked treats. $$

Terra Jl. Pariwisata; http://terra.health. Terra's tag line "Food That Loves You Back" says it all; menu is all vegan and gluten- and dairy-free with an emphasis on raw cuisine and gut-friendly grub. Design your own smoothie bowl, dine in or take away or try their Experimental Dinners. $$$

6

Tribe Surf City Jl Raya Kuta; https://instagram.com/tribepark.lombok. One of the more recent additions to Kuta's dining scene, this cool hangout is a restaurant and skate park in one. Burgers and bowls are the focalpoint of the menu with generous portion sizes, Look out for special events with happy hour cocktails or free skate passes. $$

Warung Bude Jl Pariwisata Pantai Kuta. Straightforward, homely *warung* that's as popular with locals as it is budget travellers. The *nasi goreng* and *nasi kuning* are bursting with flavour and come in plentiful portions. $

DIRECTORY

Banks and exchange Kuta has several ATMs and many hotels will change cash.

Clinic Lombok International Medical Service is a private clinic and pharmacy with English-speaking staff 550m north of the village centre on Jl Pariwisata No. 100X (081 835 3343). The nearest hospital is in Praya.

Police 500m north of central Kuta, near *Yuli's Homestay*.

Post *Segara Anak* hotel, Jl. Raya Pantai Kuta, is a postal agent; the nearest post office is in Sengkol.

West of Kuta

The coast **west of Kuta** has some of the loveliest beaches on Lombok, though to explore it, you'll need your own transport. For the time being, it's still mostly wilderness alongside the road towards Sepi, peppered with occasional hamlets; as you near Selong Blanak there are tobacco and ricefields too. But that is likely to change as development continues. All **beaches** are signed and all charge for parking. Except where stated they all have some **shade**, in *bales*, plus at least one tiny **stall** selling water, soft drinks and perhaps packet noodles. Most are quiet during the week.

Are Goleng and around

The road west out of Kuta climbs for a couple of kilometres, passing the *Ashtari Restaurant & Lounge* and its panoramic vistas. Some 7km out of Kuta a rough 2km-long dirt track heads to the coast and the **ARE GOLENG** village. The beach here is about 400m long and known for its excellent right-hand reef break, but a river empties into the bay and it's not one for sunbathers or sightseers.

The next beach west from Are Goleng is the awesomely beautiful **Mawun**, 9km from Kuta, a fabulous semicircular bay embraced by green headlands. It's usually calm and great for swimming and snorkelling, but has limited shade.

West from Mawun, **Tampah**, one of south Lombok's dive sites, and the surf breaks at **Mawi** are some of the most famous, most challenging and busiest in the area. The beach is small, however, and not as pretty as many, and you wouldn't come here for swimming. The turn-off is about 12km from Kuta; the road to the beach is very rough, degenerating into a gnarly dirt track for the final 500m. Even on a trail bike it's tough going, scooter riders should take it easy. Along the dirt road west of Kuta you'll likely see farmers herding their buffaloes and other signs of daily life.

Selong Belanak

The magnificent beach at **SELONG BELANAK**, 15km from Kuta, is a vast sweep of empty sand that stretches 2km west from the fishing village of the same name. Backed by green hills and framed by fine views of **Tomangomang** and **Serangan** beaches (both accessible by tracks), it offers excellent swimming and safe surfing for novices, who appreciate its sandy bottom. There is a long row of surf shacks by the blindingly white sand where local instructors rent boards and offer lessons as well as *warungs* serving simple food and drink to folks relaxing on sunloungers protected by umbrellas.

Sepi and Belongas Bay

Up to Selong Belanak the road is fine, but further west to Pengantap (18km), where seaweed-farming is a source of income, and on to **Sepi** (23km), it requires four-wheel-drive during the rainy season and great care at all times.

From Sepi another road takes you 11km north to Sekotong Tengah south to the sea, but the easiest access to **Belongas Bay** is by boat. Belongas offers challenging diving (see page 266) and isolated accommodation. The "road" marked on several maps west to Teluk Mekaki is a very rough track, more suited to a trail bike.

GETTING AROUND

WEST OF KUTA

There are no buses or *bemos* along this route. If you're travelling between Kuta and Sekotong, it's faster to drive via the airport highway and Lembar than via Selong Belanak. Occasional robberies of motorbikes have occurred on the road beyond Selong Belanak, and though incidents have decreased in recent years, check the situation first in Kuta. Always pay the parking fee (which offers some security) and consider taking a local guide with you as driver or passenger.

ACTIVITIES

Watersports At Mawun beach, kayaking, tubing, jet skiing and wakeboarding are popular. Contact Lombok Playground for details. Kura Kura Surf Camp (Palm Green Homestay, Jl. Mawun; http://kurakurasurfcamp.com) offers one-night/one-day surfing rates and longer stay packages.

Yoga The *Ashtari* hotel (3km west of central Kuta on the Mawun road, http://ashtarilombok.com) has up to six daily yoga classes in three locations, in hatha, yin, restorative and other styles. The yoga deck overlooking the ocean at its restaurant is truly spectacular.

ACCOMMODATION AND EATING

There are several rooms, bungalows and a few villas on the road to Selong Belanak, some of them budget accommodation catering to surfers and some higher-end ones perched on rugged cliffs overlooking the bay. A few of them have surprisingly good eateries attached.

Ashtari http://ashtarilombok.com. Occupying a spectacular panoramic hilltop position, the *Ashtari* hotel offers just one comfortable modern loft apartment with two beds and one simply furnished room with one bed, both with terraces. An excellent restaurant on the spot. $$

Ashtari Restaurant & Lounge Ashtari; http://ashtarilombok.com. Enjoying stunning views over the Kuta coastline, this boho hangout is a great place to chill. The (fairly healthy) menu lists fine breakfasts, snack platters to share, grilled fish and salads, juices and cakes. Seating is on cushions, and board games and magazines are available. They also run a cooking school and excellent yoga sessions here. $$

★ **Laut Biru Bar & Restaurant** Jl. Datuk Lopan Selong Belanak; http://sempiakvillas.com/laut-biru-bar-restaurant. *Sempiak Villas* runs this stunning open-sided shore-side café-restaurant, with tasteful white furniture and a hip feel. There are good breakfasts, seafood and all the espresso coffee options you'll need to recharge after a session in the surf offshore. $$$

Sempiak Villas Jl. Datuk Lopan, Selong Belanak; http://sempiakvillas.com. A tiny upmarket boutique enclave of octagonal wooden villas set on a steep hill overlooking the beach. The villas vary in size but all have a/c, a laptop for watching films, stereo and kitchenettes, and there's a pool, spa and restaurant. $$

East of Kuta

Few travellers venture east of Kuta and Mandalika due to bad roads and poor infrastructure, but if it's away-from-the-crowd getaways you yearn for, take a look here. Beyond the *Novotel*, the road **east of Kuta** is bad in places but for sunbathers the beach at Tanjung Aan is well worth the trip, while surfers head further on to Gerupuk for world-class wave action and there is good diving too.

A fifteen-minute walk from the *Novotel* beach takes you across the inlet and via the grassy-hummocked headland grazed by local cows to the white-sand beach at **Seger**. It's a popular surf spot, currents permitting, with a *warungs* and some shade; further south down the beach are a couple of bars that also serve grilled fish. Seger can also be good for swimming. In a different league, though, are the gloriously pretty twin crescents of **Tanjung Aan**, 5km from Kuta. The usually calm **Aan**, on the west side of the offshore outcrop, is perfect for swimming and (partially shaded) lounging. There are several *warungs* and cafés that offer shaded parking, grilled fish, parasols and drinks, plus the occasional sarong hawker.

6

Beyond Tanjung Aan, **Gerupuk** fishing village, 8km east of Kuta, sits on the western shores of Gumbang Bay. Lobster-fishing is the main source of income here, but with five good **surf breaks** within a fifteen-minute boat ride, surf-tourism is also important. From Gerupuk, you can look across the huge bay to **Awang** and **Bumbang** on the eastern shore of Lombok's largest bay, where there's a small selection of hideaway accommodation and a boutique hotel, and rent a boat for snorkelling. **Awang** and **Bumbang**, thriving fishing villages 16km east of Kuta, are worth the trip to play on the beach or surf (safe for beginners) at scenic **Awang Bay** (also known as **Ekas Bay**) with views east across to Ekas village and south to the open sea. See (Ekas below for further information).

ACTIVITIES

Watersports Gerupuk and Awang/Bumbang are surfing and diving spots. See Accommodation below for details.

ACCOMMODATION AND EATING — EAST OF KUTA

GERUPUK AND AWANG

Aussy Homestay and Café Beach-front Gerupuk; 0878 4040 0212. Enjoy a laid-back Aussie welcome at this beachside homestay, which also organises surf lessons and boats. Basic a/c rooms, terrace bar overlooking the ocean and free parking. $

Dome Lombok & Restaurant Sengkol Kecamatan Pujut Gerupuk; https://dome-lombok.com. Cosy hobbit-hole style dwellings with views across the lush southern hills and Tanjun Aan beach. Each stylishly furnished dome has its own quirky nooks and crannies, some with rooftop terraces and all enjoying access to the garden pool. $$

Gerupuk Homestay Jl. Raya, Gerupuk village; 0818 0360 8305. A simple but clean homestay on the main street 50m from the beach with a bar and shared chill-out area. Owners are Tommy, who is an accredited surf instructor, and Ben, a certified PADI dive instructor, the best of both worlds under one roof. $

Inlight Lombok Jl. Raya, Gerupuk village; http://inlightlombok.com. A chic option combining the owners' passion for surfing, free-diving, yoga, healthy food and spirituality, Inlight has smartly decorated villa-studios, gardens and sun terrace near a popular surf spot. It's Ayurveda Restaurant serves vegetarian, vegan and gluten-free dishes from Russia, India and Indonesia. $$

Ekas and the southeast peninsula

Getting to Lombok's little-visited southeast peninsula is via the Pray-to-east-coast highway, turning south at **Keruak**. At **Tuktuk** there are three options: the southwest road takes you to **Ekas**, due south goes to Kaliantan, and east ends at Tanjung Ringgit.

Across Awang/Ekas Bay on the west side of the southeast peninsula, Ekas' two surf breaks are well known as suitable for beginners and upwards. The waves are good here year 'round. Ekas is also good for standup paddleboarding and snorkelling.

Kaliantan's flat water and constant wind makes it ideal for learning kitesurfing, and there are two schools here. Best winds are April–Sept.

Tanjung Ringgit's *crème de la crème* resort entices with its trekking and biking opportunities in a 55 ha forest reserve with snorkelling trips to the nearby spectacular pink beach as icing on the cake.

ARRIVAL AND DEPARTURE — EKAS AND THE SOUTHEAST PENINSULA

By bemo or boat Irregular *bemos* link Ekas and the main road at Sepapan but the most comfortable way to get there is by boat from Awang.

ACTIVITIES

Lombok Kitesurfing School Kaliantan, http://kitelombok.com. Locally owned school with very basic accommodations. Runs three stages of beginner lessons (2hr each) as well as longer packages and advanced courses. Also offers snorkelling, standup paddleboarding and long- and short-board surfing.

ACCOMMODATION

Heaven on the Planet Ekas Bay; http://heavenontheplanet.com. This remote, deluxe resort consists of two sections, 20min walk apart: a variety of clifftop chalets and villas with fantastic views, and six further rooms and a beautiful spa at beach level near the Inside Ekas surf break. Both areas have a pool and restaurant, for guests only. Full-board rates include transport from the airport, watersports equipment (including kite- and wind-surfers) rental, boats to the waves and a massage every second day. $$

Jeeva Beloam Beach Camp Tanjung Ringgit; http://jeevaresorts.com/beloam. You can't get further away from things than at this stunning beach camp in a private cove at the southeastern point of Lombok. The eleven large cabins are made with recycled wood and *alang-alang* thatch, with open-air bathrooms and a/c in the evening. A few are set on the beach, the rest on the hillside. Apart from watersports, hiking and biking, the only thing you can do is relax. Room rates include full board and airport transfers, a 1hr 30min drive away. No wi-fi or TV. $$$

6

The Gili Islands

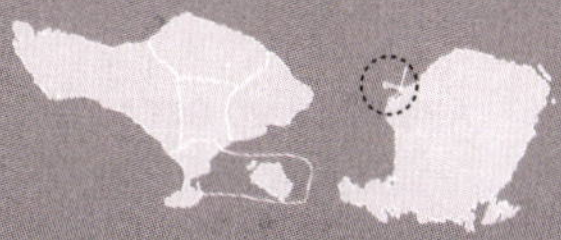

The Gili Islands

Fringed by dazzling white-sand beaches, turquoise waters and reefs that teem with turtles and fish, the trio of the tiny Gili Islands just off Lombok's northwest coast are strikingly beautiful and have exploded in popularity. With no motorized vehicles allowed on any of the islands (just horse carts and bicycles), and swathes of the dusty interiors still taken up with coconut plantations and sandy tracks, the Gilis are as close as you can get to living the tropical dream. Island life here can be incredibly seductive, and most visitors revel in long days spent snorkelling the reefs, eating fresh seafood and enjoying the spectacular views, with the volcanic profiles of Bali and Lombok filling the horizon.

Gili Trawangan, the most developed of the three, has become a premier tourist destination with its stunning white sand beaches, easy access from Bali and mass of affordable yet quite sophisticated places to eat, drink and party. Families, honeymooners and backpackers are all well catered for, though budget travellers should note that ultracheap **accommodation** is scarce on any of the islands. Prices soar from June to September and over Christmas; booking ahead is essential during these periods. Overdevelopment is also an issue, and you can expect to encounter noise (and debris) from the island's construction frenzy.

Diminutive **Gili Meno**, next east from Gili Trawangan, is the smallest and quietest of the Gilis, with a limited number of places to stay and no nightlife except a laidback bar or two. East again, **Gili Air** falls somewhere in between, with plenty of restaurants and bars but a much larger population of islanders to balance out the tourist influx.

Prices on the islands are generally higher than on Bali and mainland Lombok due to the high transport costs of importing practically everything and are continuing to increase as local land prices boom and more luxurious hotels open.

All three Gili Islands – *gili* means "small island" in Sasak – have only really been settled since the 1970s, mostly by Sasaks from mainland Lombok and Bugis fishermen from Sulawesi. Island culture reflects these roots and all three islands have predominately **Muslim** populations. Alcohol is for sale throughout, though you should be culturally sensitive near mosques (avoid boozing outside) and expect nightlife to be toned down a notch during Ramadan. Local people are very used to seeing scantily clad Westerners but you should cover up when you move away from the beach.

The tourism influx has altered Gili culture in other ways, too. In a bid to preserve marine life, scuba diving schools pay the islanders not to fish over the coral, and this has led to a return of top predators, including white- and black-tip reef sharks and the year-round presence of turtles. Biorock, a reef regeneration project, has also been a great success, and the Gilis' coral is now in better condition than it was back in the 1990s.

ARRIVAL AND DEPARTURE — THE GILI ISLANDS

Frequent boats run to the Gili Islands from Bali and Lombok; depending on the operator, you may need to change on Gili Trawangan for Gili Meno and Gili Air. Public and charter boats between the Gilis are plentiful. Though the islands have jetties, most boats dock on the beach, so you'll probably get your feet wet. Flying to Lombok and taking a boat across to the islands costs roughly the same as the fast boats, and is the only option in rough weather; between December and February all boat traffic from Bali can be suspended for days. Note that arrival and departure taxes apply for all travellers to the Gili Islands; fees vary depending on the island and transport method.

SUNSET VIEWS OF MOUNT AGUNG

Highlights

❶ **Scuba diving** The Gili's reefs are a delight to explore underwater, with healthy coral, dramatic drop-offs and prolific sealife at dive sites such as Secret Reef. See page 277

❷ **Other watersports** The Gilis are not exclusively about scuba: learn to freedive, take out a kayak – or there's even some surf from time to time. See pages 277 and 280

❸ **Sunset watching** The islands' west coasts are a dream at sunset; from bars such as *Malibu Beach Club*, the great cone of Bali's Agung volcano and setting sun is a spellbinding sight. See page 283

❹ **Partying in Gili T** Bar hop along the island's east coast then hit one of the designated party venues for dancing until (nearly) dawn. See page 283

❺ **Mellow Meno** To experience the Gilis of yesteryear you don't need to time travel: just hop on a boat to easy-going Meno, a Gili without the crowds. See page 284

❻ **Lounging by the shore** Kick back on the beach: either horizontal in a hammock or reclined in a beanbag at somewhere chilled like *Mirage Sunset Bar*. See page 288

HIGHLIGHTS ARE MARKED ON THE MAP ON PAGE 276

7

FROM BALI

BY PLANE

The most comfortable and safest option from Bali is to fly to Lombok's international airport (30min), then take a taxi to either Teluk Nare harbour (2hr) and charter a private boat (15min) to the Gilis or to Bangsal harbour where public boats await to make the crossing when the 10-passenger boats fill up.

BY FAST BOAT

The quickest way to get to the Gili Islands from Bali is to take one of the many fast boat services. Keep in mind that the channel between Bali and Lombok is open ocean, and that it can get very rough in bad weather, so beware of rogue operators that risk the crossing with substandard equipment; only book with trusted companies. Morning departures are usually calmer; in the afternoon choppy seas can make the crossings uncomfortable.

Fast boats depart from several harbours around south and east Bali – Benoa, Sanur, Serangan, Padang Bai, Nusa Lembongan and Amed – and tickets usually include transfers from hotels all over southern Bali. The sea crossing takes 1hr 30min–2hr in a fast boat; in low season prices go down considerably.

Operators Tickets can be bought online or at any tour agent in any tourist centre. Alternatively, the websites http://gilibookings.com and http://gili-fastboat.com have links to most companies, though dealing directly with the operator can be cheaper. Reliable fast-boat companies include: Blue Water Express (http://bluewater-express.com); Gili Getaway (http://giligetaway.com); Gili Gili (http://giligilifastboat.com); and Scoot Fast Cruised (http://scootcruise.com).

BY SLOW BOAT

The cheapest but most time-consuming option (and possibly most dangerous) is to take the public car ferry from Padang Bai to Lembar port in west Lombok, then continue by *bemos* to Bangsal for the public boat to the Gilis. Perama shuttle buses make use of this connection, linking Bali's main tourist centres to those on Lombok.

FROM LOMBOK

On Lombok, the main port for the Gili Islands is Bangsal where you'll find the cheapest and most frequent service to and from all three islands, but it's renowned for its hassle. Keep your cool – the Gilis are worth it. Taxis and shuttle buses stop at the car park and barrier 500m from the harbour, from where you can either walk or take a *cidomo*. The ticket office for all boats to the islands is on the seafront, to your left once you reach the harbour; ignore all other sellers and only buy your ticket from this large, clearly signed building, which displays a printed price list covering

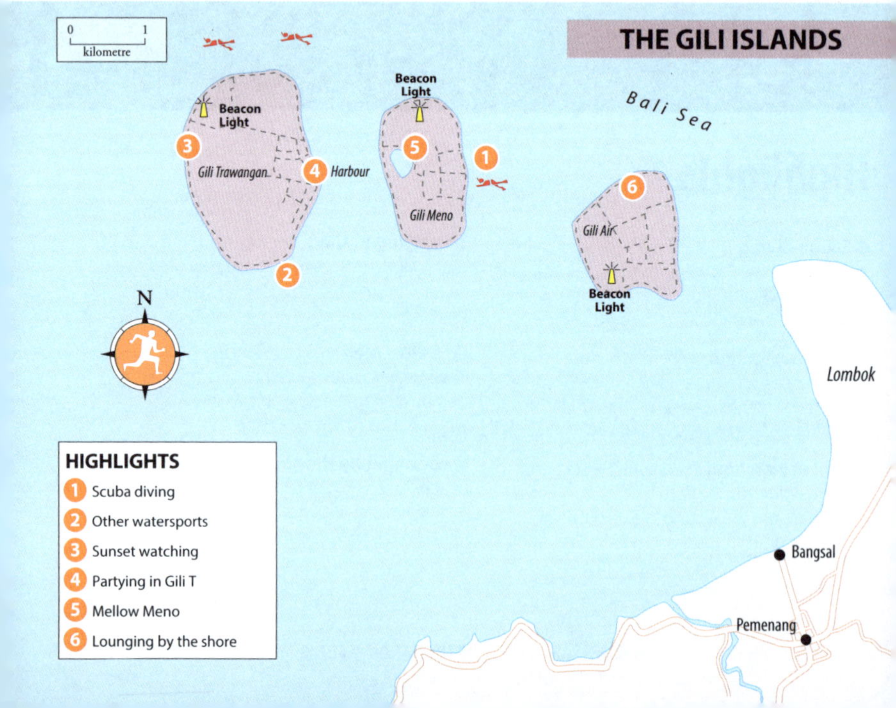

DIVING AND SNORKELLING OFF THE GILI ISLANDS

The **snorkelling** and **diving** around the Gili Islands is rewarding and accessible, with good snorkelling from the beaches and two dozen sites within half an hour's boat ride, including drop-offs, slopes and drift dives. The islands are fringed by **coral reefs**, and the Biorock coral regeneration programme has created house reefs throughout the Gilis (see page 278); visibility averages 15–25m. **Turtles** are common and the prolific **fish** life includes reef sharks, cuttlefish, moray eels, lobsters, wrasses and bumphead parrotfish. Among the most popular dive **sites** are Shark Point, Meno Wall, Halik, Manta Point and Hann's Reef; as they're so close, dive centres tend to send boats to at least three different sites a day, which gives lots of choice and flexibility.

There are also some **freediving** schools. Breath-hold diving (without tanks or scuba gear) is an exhilarating sport, with no bubbles between you and the fish, though you should always take a course with professionals before attempting it yourself.

Off Gili Meno is "The Nest", an undersea sculpture garden accessible to both snorkelers and divers.

7

DIVE CENTRES

Dive centres on the Gili Islands charge similar **prices**, though standards do vary; a list of established centres is below. Most offer dive-and-stay packages and many sell good-quality dive gear. All divers and snorkel-trippers off the Gili Islands are requested to pay a one-off **reef tax** to the Gili Eco Trust (http://giliecotrust.com), which works to protect local reefs (see page 278). There is a **recompression chamber** in Mataram at Kantor Kesehatan Pelabuhan, Jl Adi Sucipto No. 13B, Apenan (0370 616 2145). The hyperbaric chamber at Sanglah Public Hospital in Denpasar (see page 89) is larger, and there's a newer one at Kasih Ibu General Hospital (http://kih.co.id) in Saba, east Bali (see page 150).

Dive companies can take accompanying **snorkelers** or you can join one of the daily glass-bottomed boat trips to sites around all three Gilis, with a stop for lunch on Gili Air (price includes mask and snorkel); many shops, especially those on Gili Trawangan, sell tickets. Backpackers' liveaboard boat trips from Gili Trawangan to Komodo are widely advertised and last three or four days. For a more casual shore-based snorkel, gear is readily available almost everywhere. If you're snorkelling or swimming off the beach, be warned that local **offshore currents** are hazardous and can carry you further than you intended. Though the islands look temptingly close, do not attempt to swim between them; there have been drownings.

Blue Marlin Dive Dive shops in all three islands: Gili Trawangan, Gili Meno and Gili Air; http://bluemarlindive.com. The Gili's original dive school. Known for technical diving and tri-mix and rents out closed-circuit rebreathers.

Divine Divers Gili Meno; http://divinedivers.com. In a great, quiet spot on the west coast; offers PADI courses up to Divemaster.

Freedive Gili Gili Trawangan; http://freedivegili.com. Asia's foremost freediving school, run by UK record holder Mike Board with SSI courses. Has a 25m-long practice pool and is also home to Gili Yoga.

Lutwala Dive Gili Trawangan; http://lutwaladive.com. Based on the north coast, this 5-star PADI centre has small groups and does lots of instructor training.

Manta Dive Gili Trawangan and Gili Air; http://manta-dive.com. Offers both PADI and SSI courses.

Trawangan Dive Gili Trawangan; http://trawangandive.com. Works with the Gili Eco Trust and can offer conservation specialities.

public boats, shuttles and charters. Ideally, get your own bag onto and off the boats; if you can't, negotiate with the porters before you let them touch the bags – and be clear whether you're talking about rupiah or dollars, and for one bag or for the whole lot. Since public services are now so frequent, few people these days bother with the expensive option of chartering a boat.

By public boat to the Gilis Public boats to Gili Air (25min), Gili Meno (30min) and Gili Trawangan (45min) leave from Bangsal throughout the day, setting off when full (about 40 passengers) between 8am and 5pm. Public fastboats have scheduled departure times. Public speedboat charter services to the Gilis are also available.

Returning by public boat from the Gilis Returning

from the Gilis, Perama shuttle buses (minimum 2 people; must prebook) go to Mataram/Senggigi, Kuta, Lombok. Perama also has fastboat-bus shuttles from the Gills to various points in Bali. In Bangsal, shuttle buses and metered taxis wait near the barrier, a short walk or *cidomo* ride away. If you plan to travel by metered taxi (Blue Bird, 0370 627000, http://bluebirdgroup.com; Express 1500122, http://expressgroup.co.id), it's a good idea to phone ahead and reserve.

GETTING AROUND AND INFORMATION

By boat The island-hopping boat service between all three Gili Islands does one circuit (Air–Meno–Trawangan–Meno–Air) in the morning 8.30–10.15am, and another in the afternoon 3–4.15pm, which makes day-trips straightforward; the islands are 10–20min apart. The tickets are sold at each harbour. If you don't want to wait for a boat, charters are available in all the islands; ask around at each harbour.

Police There are no police on the islands, although Satgas (island security) on Gili Trawangan has a role in tourist security: it's the job of the *kepala desa*, the headman who looks after Gili Air and Gili Meno, and the *kepala kampung* on Gili Trawangan, to deal with any problems. Ask at your accommodation or one of the dive centres. If you need to make a police report (for insurance purposes, for example), go to the police on the mainland (at Tanjung or Mataram).

7

Gili Trawangan

The largest and most built-up of the islands, with a permanent population of around fifteen hundred, **GILI TRAWANGAN** (Gili T) is enjoyably buzzy; in parts on its east coast, it's even a little congested. Once a backpackers' party island, it now appeals to all ages and budgets, with simple accommodation at the bottom end of the scale and – as land prices increase rapidly – an increasing number of private villas and boutique

BIOROCK: THE DIY REEF

Gili Trawangan has seen intense development since tourists first arrived in the 1980s, and inevitably, the escalating demand on island resources has come at a price. The **Gili Eco Trust** was established in 2002 to address the most pressing environmental and social issues, and to involve islanders, business owners, expats and tourists in a sustainable future for the island.

The trust's most high-profile project to date has been the planting of **Biorock** installations to **regenerate the reef** around Gili T and Gili Air, counteracting degradation caused by anchor damage, fish-bombing, bleaching, and hindering erosion. Biorock frames are steel-grid structures that are fed a continual low-voltage electric current; this causes the minerals in the seawater to crystallize into limestone, and coral then begins to grow along the steel bars at up to six times faster than normal, further stimulated by the grafting of live coral fragments. It's possible to take a special dive course in Biorock and underwater conservation at a couple of Gili T's and Gili Air's dive centres.

Biorock and the other work of the Gili Eco Trust is financed in part by a small, one-off **reef tax** that every diver and snorkel-tripper on Gili Trawangan must pay (usually included in dive shop prices). The trust works alongside Satgas, the local island security organization. Another important initiative has been the forging of an agreement with fishermen that restricts fishing to designated zones and uses boat moorings. The trust has also instigated improvements in rubbish collection and **recycling**, environmental education at island schools and the treatment of *cidomo* horses. Divers also clear (illegally) discarded fishing nets from corals to prevent reef fish getting entangled. A weekly (Friday at 5pm) **beach cleanup** is run in conjunction with the dive centres and island headman, offering a free beer to those who participate. Larger-than-life marine critters with gaping mouths fashioned from plastic waste encouraging everyone to dispose of trash responsibly are also a trust project.

To find out more about the Gili Eco Trust, drop by the office just inland from the night market, or visit the website (http://giliecotrust.com).

resorts at the top. There are dozens of beachside restaurants and bars to choose from, and tour agents can organize everything from kayaking and horseriding to diving and snorkelling and trips to Komodo Island. Or you can simply go for the sybarite's option: lazing on the beach by day, living it large in the party venues by night.

A sandy track encircles the island and a tangle of paths crisscrosses it, with a few sections concreted. As the island is just 2.5km long by 1.75km wide you can **walk**

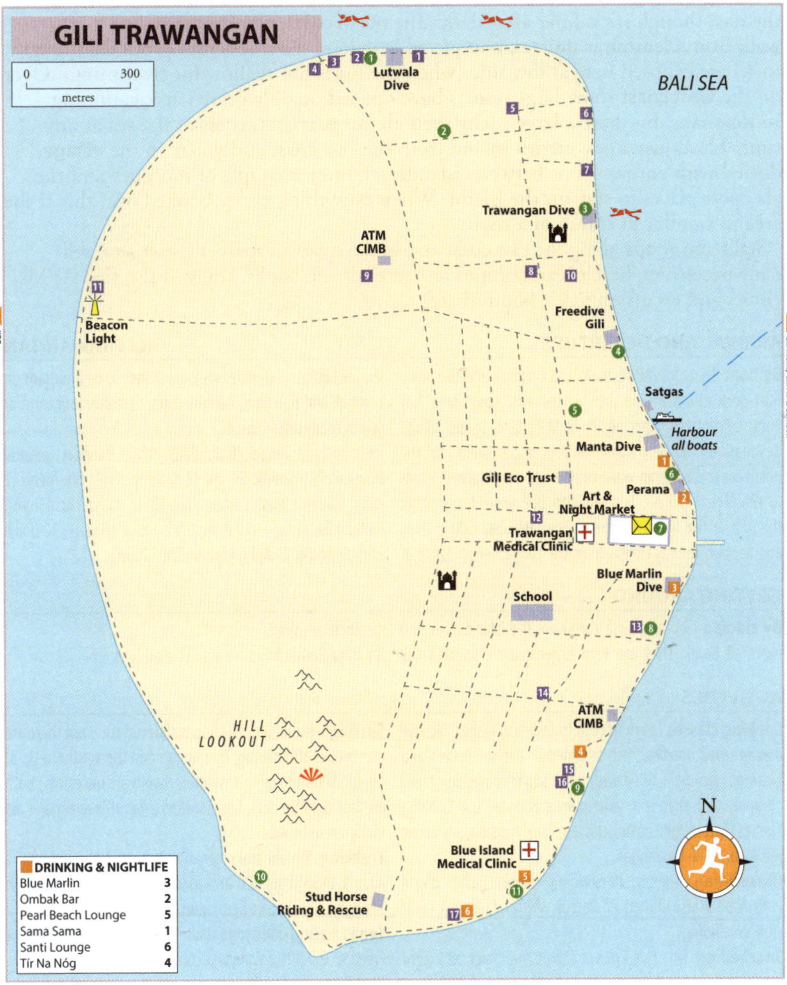

7

ACCOMMODATION
- Alam Gili 1
- Broken Compass Diver's Hostel 8
- Desa Dunia Beda Beach Resort 4
- Gili Beach Bum Hotel 10
- Gili Nyepi 12
- Jali Resort 5
- Karma Kayak 2
- Marta's 14
- Natya Hotel 15
- Pera ONE Villas 9
- Pesona Beach Resort & Spa 13
- Pondok Santi Estate 17
- Samba Villas & Wellness 7
- Scallywags Resort 16
- Villa Almarik 6
- Villa-Gili-Bali-Beach 11
- Wilson's Retreat 3

EATING
- The Banyan Tree 4
- Fat Cats Bar & Restaurant 3
- Karma Kayak 1
- Kayu Cafe 6
- Kiki Novi 7
- Ko-ko-mo 11
- Malibu Beach Club 10
- Pesona Restaurant & Sheesha Lounge 8
- Regina Pizzeria 5
- Scallywags Seafood Bar & Grill 9
- Tiki Grove Bar & Restaurant 2

around it in about two hours, or **cycle** it in less than an hour (pushing through the occasional stretches of deep sand). Development is encroaching inland, but there are still wide areas of dry scrub and coconut plantations. The 100m **hill** in the southwest has fine views of Gunung Agung on Bali, though trees obscure things somewhat.

The liveliest area to stay is the **east coast**, in particular the strip south of the harbour, known as **Central**, which is wall-to-wall bungalows, restaurants and dive shops. The lush white sands, clear waters and plentiful fish along the built-up east coast north of the harbour make it busy with snorkellers and sunbathers during the day, though it's calmer after dark. The **north coast**, about twenty-five minutes' walk from Central, is quieter, and places here have more spacious grounds, though rocks are exposed here at low tide (when the sea is too shallow for swimming). Over on the **west coast** some large resorts have opened, mainly geared at vacationing Indonesians, but here a large rocky shelf all but prevents access to the sea at any time. Head just a few metres inland from the east coast and you're in the **village**, dotted with corner shops between islanders' homes, a couple of mosques and the cheapest places to stay on the island. When everything else is booked out, this is the area to wander in search of a room.

7

Stalls and **shops** along the east coast and in the small art market (*pasar seni*) sell daily necessities, beachwear, fashions and secondhand books. You will also find ATMs, clinics and excursion ticket booths here.

ARRIVAL AND DEPARTURE — GILI TRAWANGAN

By boat Boats from Bali, mainland Lombok and the other Gilis dock either at the pier on the east coast or a few hundred metres further north. Most east-coast and village destinations can be reached on foot in 5–10min and the north coast is a 25min walk; or else hop on a *cidomo*. Boats to Gili Meno, Gili Air, Lombok and Bali leave from either the pier or the nearby harbour. Buy fast-boat tickets from agents, public-boat tickets from the Karya Behari office at the harbour, and shuttle bus/boat tickets to destinations on Lombok and Bali from Perama (http://peramatour.com) or one of many other agents.

Destinations Amed (Bali; daily; 1hr); Bangsal (several times daily; 45min); Gili Air (2 daily; 40min); Gili Meno (2 daily; 20min); Nusa Lembongan (Bali; daily; 1hr 45min); Padang Bai (Bali; 4–10 daily; 2hr); Sanur (Bali; 4–10 daily; 2hr); Senggigi (3 daily; 45min–2hr 30min).

GETTING AROUND

By cidomo *Cidomo* (horse carts) are the island taxis and meet all boats. They are very expensive considering the distances involved.

By bike Rental bikes are available all over.

ACTIVITIES

Cooking classes Learn to cook Indonesian dishes like *mie goreng (fried noodles)*, fish steamed in banana leaves and glutinous rice balls filled with palm sugar coated in grated coconut, and then eat your own creations. Gili Cooking Classes (https://gilicookingclasses.com), runs classes on on Gili Air and Gili Trawangan.

Horseriding There's horseriding around the island with Stud Horse Riding & Rescue (http://facebook.com/studhorseriding).

Snorkelling Bali Hai Cruises (http://balihaicruises.com) runs two daily snorkelling cruises; both include a BBQ meal cooked onboard.

Surfing The Gilis are not a big surf destination but there are reef breaks off Kokomo, Trawangan and the southern tip of Gili Air. Southern or southwestern swells are necessary; both are fast righthanders. Local surfers around Trawangan's art market rent boards.

Trekking Rinjani treks can be organized through Gili T agents, though are best arranged via reputable operators in Senggigi, Senaru and Sembalun.

Yoga Excellent daily yoga classes are offered by Gili Yoga at Freedive Gili (http://giliyoga.com).

Watersports Fly Gili Watersports (http://facebook.com/Flygilparasailing) offers parasailing and wakeboarding.

ACCOMMODATION — SEE MAP PAGE 279

There are very few hotels right on the beach. Those that do enjoy a shore-side location rarely have rooms with direct sea views; nowhere, however, is more than a few minutes' walk away from the sea. Note that many places along the east coast and in the village are **noisy**, whether from late-night bars or the mosques' early-morning calls to prayers – head north or west for more peace. The groundwater on Gili T is brackish so showers are often salty; however upmarket

SWIM WITH SEA TURTLES

While sea turtles everywhere struggle to survive, the Gilis seem to attract them. Endangered green turtles appear in greater numbers, but occasionally critically endangered Hawksbill Turtles are also spotted. Both snorkelers and divers can encounter these amazing animals if they know where to look.

On Gili T, snorkelers can swim along the north coast beach starting in front of *Karma Kayak* and on the east coast starting at *Villa Almarik*. Divers: check out Halik Reef, Shark Point and Goodheart Reef. Gili Meno's giant creatures congregate around the old Bounty jetty wreck, where snorkelers can see them. Divers can usually spot them at Meno Wall and Meno Slope. On Gili Air, the east coast from *Gili Air Santay* hotel to the boat harbour in the south is usually good for snorkelers, with Haan's Reef and Gili Air Wall for divers.

It goes without saying, don't try to interact with them in any way.

hotels and guesthouses import **fresh water**. Despite the growing number of places to stay on Gili T, accommodation is at a premium, and most places charge wildly inflated prices during the peak periods. Renting a **private villa** for a week or two is becoming increasingly popular. Note that hostels are officially banned in Gilis, due to opposition from guesthouse owners, though some places remain hostels in all but name. **Dorms** are permitted, but with no more than three beds in one room.

CENTRAL, THE EAST AND THE SOUTH COASTS

Gili Beach Bum Hotel East coast; https://gilibeachbum.com. Popular backpackers' lodge, by the beach and close to all the action. The very spacious a/c en-suite dorms and private twin rooms have good security (doors are secured by a pin-coded lock), lockers and clean facilities and there's a pool and a rooftop bar with regular movie screenings and parties. A decent breakfast buffet is included. $

Natya Hotel Gili Trawangan Central; http://natyahotel.com. Interestingly decorated hotel with splashes of bright colours complemented with Lombok pots, weavings and wood, there are 21 rooms here, a pool and a restaurant, and next door is a handy convenience store. $

Pesona Beach Resort & Spa East coast; http://pesonaresort.com. A contemporary resort with an Indian flair, there are 25 a/c rooms with fresh-water showers, including poolside rooms furnished with reclaimed Java teak. Two pools with bar and restaurant are complemented by a sheesha lounge. Also owns Villa Mimpi in north-central Gili T. $

Pondok Santi Estate South coast; http://pondoksanti.com. A stunning collection of oh-so spacious villas, set well back from the coastal road in expansive grounds shaded by coconut trees – perfect for those who enjoy their privacy. There's gourmet dining, a gorgeous pool area, yoga, and staff are efficient and helpful. They also host very classy sunset boat trips on a 25m wooden cruiser. $$$

Samba Villas & Wellness East coast; http://sambavillas.com. A compound with large, stylish rooms overlooking an attractive garden planted with native fruit trees, and lovely three-bedroom villas, family suites and rooms. There's a small pool and a spa. $$

Scallywags Resort South beach; http://scallywagsresort.com. A well-designed little hotel where each room has a/c, DVD player and contemporary furnishings; some have private plunge pools and ocean views. Showers are solar-powered and a desalination system produces drinking water for the sinks. A good-sized pool, a spa and a highly popular waterfront restaurant complete the picture. $$

Villa Almarik East coast http://almarik-lombok.com. More of a traditional hotel than most on the island, with large, Bali-style cottages and rooms, all with a/c and hot fresh-water showers, the brightest and most modern being the "superior", mid-priced ones. There's a big pool, a dive centre and sunloungers on the beach across the track. $$

INLAND

Broken Compass Diver's Hostel Jl. Ikan Hiu, Inland east coast, a few min. walk from beach; http://the-broken-compass.com. Attached to Compass Divers, where dive-stay discounts are given. Air-conditioned dorms with or without en suites and private rooms have hot water, pool, bar and restaurant, and bean bag chill areas. Bonus is it's not only clean, it's quiet. $

Gili Nyepi Inland east coast; http://gilinyepi.com. Just a short stroll from the harbour, these four delightful bungalows are set in a pretty garden and have private verandas, a/c, attractive furnishings and spacious bathrooms. It's owned by a welcoming Dutch-Indonesian couple who look after their guests well and is deservedly popular – book ahead. $

Jali Resort Jl. Nautilus, inland east coast, 4 min walk from beach; http://jaliresortgilitrawangan.com. Its tropical frangipani-filled garden adds to the relaxed vibe at Jali Resort, which has 24 standard, superior and deluxe rooms, all with a/c, a fresh-water lap pool and a restaurant serving delicious Mediterranean and Indonesian cuisine. The in-house dive centre offers one complimentary dive in the resort's pool to non-divers. $

Marta's Inland east coast, 2min walk from beach; http://martasgili.com. Joanna (from the UK) and her Sasak husband Marta run this welcoming guesthouse. The great-quality two-storey bungalows that sleep from two to five and standard rooms have attractive wooden carvings and all come with a/c and hot water. Verandas with day beds look onto the garden and pool. It is close to the village mosque, however, so be prepared for the early-morning call to prayer. $

Pera ONE Villas Inland Jalan Ikan Kotak; https://peraonevillas.com. Hidden away in the heart of the island, these luxury villas all have their own private garden and pool. Bright, modern décor, comfy beds and bathtubs come as standard, bikes are available for all guests and there are plenty of optional extras from in-room massages to romantic dinners. $$$$

7

THE NORTH AND WEST COASTS

Alam Gili Northeast coast; http://alamindahbali.com. Delightful wood-and-thatch a/c bungalows, including one fabulous seaview room, all with attractive Balinese-style furnishings in a quiet garden. Most have fans, all have hot freshwater showers and there's a tiny pool. $

★ **Desa Dunia Beda Beach Resort** Northwest coast; http://desaduniabeda.com. This fine hotel's huge plot of land is dotted with salvaged 150-year-old traditional Javanese *joglo* and *kampung* (village) homes: the supremely spacious wooden bungalows come with antique furniture and four-poster beds, though only some have a/c and most have saltwater showers. There's a pool and you're steps from the shore, with good snorkelling on your doorstep. $$

Karma Kayak North coast; https://facebook.com/GiliTrawangan.accommodation.restaurant.KarmaKayak. Run by two welcoming Dutch women (one a champion kayaker), this place has attractive, individually styled rooms with hot freshwater showers. It's across from the beach, with loungers and beanbags on the sand, and kayaking trips are available. The beachside restaurant is beautifully set up, and serves great tapas and sangría. $

Villa-Gili-Bali-Beach West coast; http://villa-gili-bali-beach.com. A lovely selection of beach bungalows, sea and sunset view suites and a private villa with a swimming pool. Snorkelling, diving and cycling available as well as massages. $$

Wilson's Retreat North beach; http://wilsons-retreat.com. Named after the volleyball in the *Cast Away* film, this gorgeous small resort has eight spacious suites and two villas with private pools and stunning interior design. Its location on the north shore makes it possible to view sunrise and sunset from the beach. $$

EATING

SEE MAP PAGE 279

With a mass of restaurants to choose from, half the fun is wandering slowly down the main drag, trying to decide which to go for. Alternatively, from sunset onwards, head for the popular **night market** in front of the art market, where *kaki lima* handcart stalls serve up cheap and authentic food – *ayam bakso* (chicken soup), *nasi campur*, seafood and *nasi goreng* are all on offer – which you can eat at the tables set out in front.

CENTRAL, VILLAGE AND THE EAST COAST

The Banyan Tree East coast; https://www.facebook.com/thebanyantreegili/. Attached to *Freedive Gili* and *Gili Yoga*, a great spot for a budget-friendly vegetarian feed, with an excellent *nasi campur* and salad bar. The (more pricey) healthy-eating menu features dishes like peanut and tofu stir-fry, dip platters and smoothie bowls that include lots of berry goodness. $$

Fat Cats Bar & Restaurant East coast; http://trawangandive.com. This establishment, attached to *Trawangan Dive*, is an ideal place to have a healthy meal inside the bistro-style restaurant (many veggie options) or a romantic dinner on the beach. In the evening enjoy *Fat Cats'* great cocktails. $$

Kayu Cafe East coast; http://facebook.com/kayucafe. Charming café with paninis, salads, pasta, healthy juices, smoothies and snacks plus some of the best bread and cakes in the Gilis – try their Oreo cheesecake. There's fine coffee and the interior is a/c. $$

Kiki Novi Jl Bintang Laut, East coast. A vivacious grey-haired lady cooks up ten pots or so of cheap and delicious local food every lunchtime and sells it from her small cornershop *warung* by the art market. There are plenty of vegetarian choices. $

Ko-ko-mo Southeast coast at Ko-Ko-Mo Resort; http://kokomogilit.com. A fine choice for a special meal, *Ko-ko-mo* offers gourmet dining on crisp white tablecloths and a terrific menu that takes in lots of seafood (oysters are usually on the menu) as well as tenderloin beef, rack of lamb and lobster; also serves breakfast and lunch. $$$$

Pesona Restaurant & Sheesha Lounge East coast at Pesona Beach Resort; http://pesonaresort.com. A popular Indian place that includes tandoori dishes, naan bread and papadums, rogan josh, biriani and dosas. You eat on low tables with cushions for seating and shisha pipes are available too. $

Regina Pizzeria East coast; 0877 6506 6255. An Italian chef offers a wide selection of delicious homemade pasta and wood oven pizzas. Large portions and a nice and friendly atmosphere. $$

Scallywags Seafood Bar & Grill South Beach; http://scallywagsresort.com. Fantastic seafood barbecues in the evenings – buy the fish at market price and get potatoes

MUSHROOMS AND MOONSHINE

After some bad **accidents with bootleg alcohol** containing poisonous methanol – including several deaths – the bars and restaurants that are members of Gili Trawangan's entrepreneur association **APGT** have tightened purchasing policies for alcoholic drinks, only buying from trusted suppliers; look for the acronym on the menu. It's still wise to be wary of cocktails that are too cheap to be true – or simply stick to beer, which is always safe. The **drugs scene** of a few years ago has quietened down and doesn't dominate all island nightlife, though (questionably) magic mushrooms are frequently offered. Be aware that penalties for the possession, use or trafficking of illegal drugs in Indonesia are severe and include death (see page 44).

and unlimited salad to go with it – plus open sandwiches, innovative salads, good tapas platters and steaks. Candlelit tables are set on the beach in the evening. $$$

Tiki Grove Bar & Restaurant Inland east coast, Jl. Vila Kelapa, 300m from the beach; https://facebook.com/tikigrovegilit/. Bringing the flavours of other tropical destinations, the Canadian owners serve up delights such as Pulled Chicken Sandwich and Pork Chorizo Sausage Tacos with the best cocktails on the Island. Try the Maui Wowie Chicken, too. $$

THE NORTH AND WEST COASTS

Karma Kayak North coast https://facebook.com/GiliTrawangan.accommodation.restaurant.KarmaKayak. Right on the beach, under the trees, this is a great place to chill out for a few hours and is a prime spot for sunset viewing from May to mid-September. There are beanbags, loungers and tables on the sand, and good tapas on the menu, along with burgers, salads and mains such as Vegan Poke Bowl. Wash it all down with a jug of sangría. $$

Malibu Beach Club Southwest coast http://malibuclubgili.com. This laid-back beachfront bar and restaurant is mainly popular for its mouthwatering burgers, Asian comfort food, good cocktails and several sangrias. Seafood paella is especially worth a try. It's also a perfect place to enjoy the sunset. $

NIGHTLIFE AND ENTERTAINMENT

SEE MAP PAGE 279

The west and southwestern sides of the island are wildly popular for drinks around sunset when big crowds gather for photos at the beach. For a mellower vibe at sundown head north to *Karma Kayak*. As the evening wears on, the southeast coast (which is away from the village, protecting them from the ruckus) becomes the party scene that Gili T is known for. Gili T's **famous nightlife** revolves around a handful of venues which take turns to host large parties a few times a week (from about 10pm till 3am or later), though there are plenty of alternatives.

Blue Marlin East coast; http://bluemarlindive.com. The big upstairs dancefloor above the dive centre is the popular Monday-night party venue. There are several bars, and DJs play deep house and trance. $

Ombak Bar East coast near night market; http://ombakbar.com. A hoppin' place after sundown, drink in the bar where there are games and Beer Pong, or settle on the beach where there's a nightly fire dance. Good music, DJs, great happy hour prices. $$

Pearl Beach Lounge Southeast coast; http://pearlbeachlounge.com. This lavish oceanfront establishment serves high-end cocktails, long drinks and wine (the list is quite extensive) plus delicious meals and snacks. An ideal place to take in romantic ocean views. $$

Sama Sama Southeast coast; 0812 3763 650. Known for its good live music, especially reggae, this bar is recommended for its great atmosphere, service and parties on Saturday. Bands play nightly at 9pm. $$

Santi Lounge South coast at Pondok Santi Estate; http://pondoksanti.com. Uber stylish yet relaxed lounge with the best cocktails in the Gilis, well-selected electronic tunes and a cool crowd. It makes a wonderful escape from the madness up the coast. $$$

Tír Na Nóg Southeast coast; http://tirnanogbar.com. Yes an Irish pub in the tropics is a cliché, but the "land of youth" is a perennially popular and lively beachside bar. Four bars in one venue with bottled Guinness, darts, movies and sports TV plus Aussie comfort food. There are nightly DJs (usually cheesy) from 10pm and it's the main party venue every Wednesday. $

DIRECTORY

Banks and exchange There are ATMs all around the island. Changing money is possible, but rates are better on the mainland. Some dive companies offer advances on Visa and MasterCard, but you'll pay up to ten percent for this.

Clinic There are several clinics on the island, all on the east coast. Most reliable are Trawangan Medical Clinic (0853 3811 0348), signposted down the alley south of the art market, is open 24hr and Blue Island Clinic (0819

9970 7705, http://blueislandclinic.com) located at Gili Indah Village, Pemenang District. The nearest hospital is in Mataram (see page 244).

Post There are postal agents in the art market.

Gili Meno

GILI MENO, 2km long and just over 1km wide, is the smallest and most tranquil of the islands, with a local population of around five hundred. There's plenty of space for horizon-gazing, some gorgeous deserted beaches and a delightfully mellow, barefoot vibe pervades. It takes about two hours to gently stroll around the island, with views across to Gili Air and Lombok from the east and to Trawangan and Bali's Gunung Agung to the west. As on the other Gilis, there's no motorized transport, just a few *cidomos* (horsecarts); bicycles aren't widely available, but ask at your accommodation. Gili Meno is now connected to mainland Lombok for fresh water and electricity via undersea pipes, making both available most of the time.

7

The **snorkelling** is arguably the best of the Gilis. Check locally for advice on currents (see page 277). There's a mesmerizing undersea sculpture garden off the west coast commissioned by *BASK* Gili Meno (http://baskgilimeno.com). Environmentalist and sea-sculptor John deCaires Taylor created "Nest", 48 human forms moulded from actual people with unique features, standing and lying in a circle. While merely an odd tourist attraction now, the statues will eventually be covered in corals, creating a clever house reef. To get there, look for the large BASK sign; "Nest" is about 20m from the shore at about 3m below the surface. You'll need water shoes to cross the rocks before entering the water. Note that all the snorkel tours stop here, so for a solitary look-see best to go at sunrise before they start at 8am, at noon while they're having lunch, or after 4pm when most tours end.

ACCOMMODATION		EATING	
BASK Gili Meno	4	Ana Warung	2
Biru Meno	8	Diana Café	3
Breathe Villa Meno	3	Escobar 2	5
Fantastic Cottages	6	Jizzy (JZ) Warung	1
Karma Reef	5	Karma Reef	4
Mahamaya	2		
Meno Dream Resort	7	DRINKING	
Villa Ottalia	1	Malfina Beach Bar	1
		Sasak Café	2

ARRIVAL AND DEPARTURE GILI MENO

By boat The harbour is on the southeast corner of Gili Meno, within walking distance of the main cluster of accommodation options; *cidomos* provide transport. Buy tickets for the island-hopping boat at the harbour office and for fast-boat connections at harbour-side outlets. You can also charter a local boat owner to take you to another Gili. Shuttle bus/boat tickets to destinations on Lombok and Bali can be bought from Perama (based in the *Kontiki* hotel, south of the harbour); other shuttle-bus tickets are also widely advertised.

Destinations Bangsal (3–4 daily; 30min); Gili Air (2 daily; 20min); Gili Trawangan (2 daily; 20min).

ACTIVITIES

Cooking classes You can take a public shuttle boat to *Gili Cooking Classes* on Gili Air, leaving Gili Meno at 9.45am (15min).

ACCOMMODATION SEE MAP PAGE 284

Accommodation on Meno is less flashy than on Trawangan: few budget places have a/c and there's some roughness around the edges, so things can feel quite rustic even though you're mostly paying well above backpacker prices. Prices fluctuate dramatically and in high season (June–

Sept and over Christmas), you need to book ahead.

BASK Gili Meno west point; https://baskgilimeno.com/. If you want to rub shoulders with the island's high-flyers and influencers then this sleek beachfront design hotel is the place to do it. The glamourous beach club is home to Jason deCaires Taylor's famous NEST underwater exhibition, while the lavish studios, suites and villas are set around a magnificent 35-meter infinity pool. $$$$

Biru Meno http://birumeno.com. Balinese-owned and -designed bungalows, just back from the beach near the southern tip of the island, a 10min walk from the harbour. All ten bungalows have large verandas, a/c and cold-water bathrooms. $

Breathe Villa Meno Inland; 0877 6528 3498. Two spacious thatched villas with a/c and ceiling fans, one with a private pool, are owned by an English-French couple who are dive instructors and know what visitors like. Scrupulously clean with a lovely garden and quiet elegance, a la carte breakfast is included along with free bicycle use. $

Fantastic Cottages East coast near harbour; 0819 1705 8139. Their location and good value prices make these cottages…well, fantastic. Right in the thick of things near eateries, the harbour and a 100m walk to the beach, each cottage has a/c, terraces and fresh-water shower. Adults and cash only. $

Karma Reef East coast; http://karmagroup.com. The excellent *lumbung* bungalows and sea front or sea view tents at this friendly place all have thoughtfully equipped a/c or fan interiors, open-air living rooms and comfy verandas with hammock chairs. There's also a movie night. $$$

Mahamaya Northwest coast; http://mahamaya.co. A stylish, family-friendly resort on the western side of the island, with beachfront villas and seven spacious pool-view rooms, all with modern artworks and a/c. Service is great, there are two pools (one for kids) and guests get gratis access to snorkelling gear, bikes and kayaks. $$$

Meno Dream Resort Southwest coast; 0878 6516 2045. Warm hospitality in addition to cleanliness draw many to Meno Dream. Its bungalows in a variety of sizes have minimalist, serviceable décors with TV and a/c. Cooking courses, a small saltwater pool and free bicycle use are added attractions. Only drawback is it's near neighbours; if you need soundless nights to sleep, this place might not be right for you. $$

Villa Ottalia Inland; http://lesvillasottalia.com. Each of the lovely bungalows and villas has access to a garden and a private or shared swimming pool. There is a good restaurant serving up Indonesian and Western dishes and free bikes for guests. $$

7

EATING

SEE MAP PAGE 284

Ana Warung Northeast coast; http://anawarung.com. This friendly laid-back *warung* has offered excellent traditional Sasak dishes for many years now and it has become very popular. The fresh fish dishes are very good. They also have four simple bungalows. $

Diana Café West coast; 0813 5355 6612. A totally chilled feet-in-the-sand experience with hammocks, cushions and fine views. The basic menu of Indonesian standards has curries and good seafood, such as grilled tuna steak, as well as cocktails with local liquor. Popular for sunset-viewing drinks. $

Escobar 2 South coast; 0812 4663 5647. Not much more than a beach shack decorated with seashells and orphaned flipflops, this place is literally a chairs-on-the-sand-under-a-tarp kind of place. It doesn't need to be more than that because the focus is on fish straight from the sea and onto the grill. Good drinks at reasonable prices make it an ideal sundowner venue too. $$

Jizzy (JZ) Warung Jl. Gili Meno, inland, northeast; https://instagram.com/jizzywarung/. A simple bamboo open-air pavilion, this family-run place turns out some of the best local food on the island at great prices. Although everything they lovingly prepare is delicious, their spicy chicken rendang gets raves. $

Karma Reef East coast, http://karmaroyalgroup.com. This gorgeous bamboo pavilion (at the *Karma Reef* hotel) is right by the beach and has a menu of Mediterranean and Asian food such as Sugar Cane Chicken Skewer Salad, wood-fired pizzas and a wine list. $$$

DRINKING

SEE MAP PAGE 284

Malfina Beach Bar Northwest coast. Plastic waste washed up on the beachside has been scrubbed clean and transformed into quirky, fluroescent-painted artworks that dangle from the ceiling at this laid-back beach bar. It's a relaxed spot for snacks and sundowners while you dig your toes into the sand. $

Sasak Café West coast, not far from the saltwater lake. This reggae bar and restaurant is a perfect spot to lounge the day away and snorkel on the reef right in front. The food (curries, sandwiches) is not remarkable but the cocktail list is worth dipping into; many creations are named after Marley songs – try a *Stir it Up* (with dark rum, lime and ginger ale). $

DIRECTORY

Banks and exchange There are a few ATMs on the island, and you can change money in the harbour area, where Blue Marlin also does credit card cash advances.

Clinic Blue Island Clinic (0819 9970 5702, http://

blueislandclinic.com) is 50m south of the harbour.
Shopping A minimarket at *Rust Bungalows* sells basic necessities, including a few over-the-counter medicines but prices are high.

Gili Air

Closest to the Lombok mainland, **GILI AIR** stretches about 1.5km in each direction and has the largest permanent population of the three islands (less than two thousand people). Though tourism is important here, and increasingly so, village life and homes dominate the heart of the island, giving Gili Air a more Indonesian atmosphere than Gili Trawangan, while still being more sociable and livelier than Gili Meno. **Accommodation** is spread around most of the coast and inland. The southeast has the most popular beach and excellent snorkelling; ask locally about currents, which can be strong. Countless tracks, some of them paved, cross the interior and allow you to explore beyond the tourist perimeter into the many coconut plantations and *kampung* (villages) with their mosques, flower-filled gardens and grazing cows.

If you're coming to Air just for the day, a good place to head for is the lovely stretch of **beach** on the southeast side of the island, around *Scallywags Beach Club*, which is less than ten minutes' walk east of the harbour. The restaurants in this area make

enjoyable places to spend the day, with shaded lounging *bale*, fine views across to Lombok and snorkel gear for rent.

The island is ringed by a partially paved road, shadeless and very soft in some places. It takes a couple of hours to complete a circuit on foot, and doing it by **bicycle** is also a lot of fun. As with the other Gilis, there's excellent **diving** offshore.

ARRIVAL AND DEPARTURE — GILI AIR

By boat Boats cover routes to and from Bali, Lombok and the other Gilis; they arrive and depart from the harbour in the south. You can buy boat tickets at the harbour counter and Perama tickets from their office nearby, opposite *Villa Karang Hotel* (http://peramatour.com).
Destinations Bangsal (roughly hourly; 20min); Gili Meno (2 daily; 20min); Gili Trawangan (2 daily; 40min).

GETTING AROUND

By cidomo These horse carts meet all boats.
By bicycle Ask at your accommodation for the nearest bike-rental outlet.

TOURS AND ACTIVITIES

Cooking courses Gili Cooking Classes (http://gilicookingclasses.com). Three daily classes are offered, allowing you to get a feel for Indonesian cuisine.
Diving Reputable dive centres include Blue Marlin Dive (http://bluemarlindive.com), Dream Divers (http://dreamdivers.com) and Manta Dive (http://manta-dive-giliair.com). All three have training pools.
Snorkelling Snorkelling trips to offshore reefs are widely advertised.
Subwing A fun water sport to view reef life; you hold onto a wing-shaped device with or without snorkel and a boat tows you through the water. Subwing Gili Islands (http://subwinggiliislands.com).
Yoga Classes including Hatha, Yin and flow at H20 Yoga (http://h2oyogaandmeditation.com) are held in their bamboo pavilion, just inland from *Gili Air Santay*. Multiple-class packages are available.

ACCOMMODATION — SEE MAP PAGE 286

7Seas Cottages Southeast coast; https://7seascottages.com/. Large shore-side resort offering a wide selection of accommodation: attractive a/c rooms, cottages, fan-cooled backpacker dormitories and a two-bed luxury villa. There's a gym, pool, dive school and restaurant by the beach. $

Captain Coconuts Jl. Sunset, west coast; http://facebook.com/captaincoconutsgili. This is no ordinary hostel, with beds in the Bamboo Lodge suspended from the rafters, each with its own privacy screen, fan and locker. There are also private a/c rooms with TV in Javanese joglo style. Hot water showers are solar powered. $

Fantastic Bamboo Huts South coast; 0877 2966 6957. Built almost entirely from bamboo, this popular hostel has smallish ceiling-fan-cooled dorms (with three or four beds) and rooms, all with mozzie nets, some with a/c. It's a short walk from the harbour, and the staff running the place are helpful and offer good island info. $

Jago Gili Air Jl. Mojo, inland east coast; http://jagogiliair.com. A boutique hotel with a chic-tropical feel and bamboo architectural features in public spaces. Rooms are bright and cheery, all have a/c and TV; all face the pool with terrace and sunloungers. Breakfast included. $

The Mandãna Suites & Villas Inland, east coast; http://themandanagiliair.com. The décor here has a modern-traditional feel using natural fabrics with wood and stone accents creating a lovely effect. One of the suites has a private pool. Check out the restaurant's healthy five-course breakfast prepared to order. $$$

Mola2 Resort Southwest coast; http://mola2resorthotel.com. Lovely beachfront bungalows in a peaceful part of the island where you can enjoy amazing sunset views. There's a restaurant, bar and spa as well as bicycle rental. Diving and snorkelling possible to arrange. $$

PinkCoco Gili Air Northwest coast; http://pinkhotels.com. Billing this funky group of rooms, cottages and villas (some with a/c) as the sexiest hotel on Gili Air entices you to at least have a look, right? Perhaps it's the pink colour they're referring to, which is featured in all rooms. $$

Segar Village East coast, 0818 0526 2218. Attractive a/c bungalows set around a huge garden (complete with grazing cows!) and a pool. Breakfast is served on the roof of the reception building by the beach. $

Villa Bulan Madu http://bulan-madu.com. Six luxurious and spacious villa-style cottages, decorated with textiles with a/c, freshwater bathrooms, kitchenette, and verandas. Each has its own generous private flower garden, complete with *bale* and dining table. There's also a full-service spa and a restaurant. Minimum 2 nights required. $

Villa Tokay West coast; https://www.villatokay.com/. A veritable palace sculpted out of bamboo, this luxury 4-star is one of the island's newest offerings and well worth the splurge if you're seeking a romantic showstopper. Each of the four villas has its own private garden and pool (complete with floating breakfast served to your taste) alongside unique touches like the hammock floor overlooking the pool and cosy nooks to cuddle up in. $$$$

EATING

SEE MAP PAGE 286

Chill Out Bar Southeast coast; http://chilloutbargiliair.com. A beachfront restaurant and bar serving all Indonesian staples, pasta, salads, and fresh seafood. A nice spot to hang out during the day between the swims. $$

Dolcemare Italian Restaurant Inland, southwest at Dolcemare Resort; 0819 0722 1519. Authentic Italian food in a cosy, romantic atmosphere with only six tables earns this restaurant a place on your bucket list. Freshly caught fish are magically transformed into carpaccio; the pastas and breads are made under the watchful eye of the Italian chef-owner. They also have a wine list and pressed juices. $$$$

7

Firda Warung Inland, south; 0878 6596 6127. Local food is served up with a flare in this simple *warung* attached to a homestay with the same name. That it's away from the busiest tourist areas makes it seem even more authentic. Recommended are any of the curries, especially chicken, or mie goreng dishes. $

Musa Cookery Inland, east; http://musagiliair.com. What a surprise to find such a delightful, healthy menu under a thatched joglo roof on such a tiny island. Vegan and gluten-free are the specialities here in dishes such as Chakra Salad and Jackfruit Gyros. For breakfast try French toast or pumpkin bread with a latte. $

Scallywags Seafood & Bar At Scallywags Beach Club, south coast; http://scallywagsresort.com. A well-run establishment with comfy seating and a prime beach plot serving lip-smackingly good sandwiches, salads, grilled meats, pasta dishes and fresh seafood barbecues every night. $$$

Sunrise Beach Club http://sunrisegiliair.com. A stunning beachfront location with tables directly facing the aqua blue sea. It's a perfect setting for a Greek salad, Mediterranean kebab or chicken quesadillas. There's also a large, covered café area where you'll find a dangerous cake cabinet (try the white chocolate mousse). $$$

Warung Sasak East coast; 0878 6016 7491. A family-run beachside *warung*, and one of the last locally owned shorefront places on the island. Try *ikan parapek*, fish with spicy yellow curry, or grilled snapper. $

DRINKING AND NIGHTLIFE

SEE MAP PAGE 286

★ **Legend Bar** North coast, http://legendbargiliair.id. Chilled bar and restaurant whose coral mobiles, *bale* seating and regulation Rasta accessories make it a nice, quiet spot to while away an afternoon. On Wednesday night this is the main party venue, with live music or trance DJ until late. On the food side, expect hearty portions of Indo and Euro standards, including an especially good *nasi goreng*, and there's barbecued seafood too. $

Mirage Sunset Bar Jl. Pelangi Sunset, north coast. As the name suggests, there's good sunset-viewing at this bar, with beanbags and seating angled for the best panoramas. Musically they keep things subtle and relaxed with ambient soundscapes and electronica. Also has a pool table. $

DIRECTORY

Banks and exchange There are several ATMs by the harbour; money can be changed at some shops but rates are poor; some dive shops can forward cash from credit cards for a 6–10 percent fee.

Clinic The Blue Island Clinic is just inland from the harbour (24hr; 0819 9970 5703, http://blueislandclinic.com); the closest hospital is in Mataram.

Post There's no post office on the island.

PURA SARASWATI TEMPLE

Contexts

History

Bali and Lombok, two tiny islands, have been buffeted by powerful empires throughout history, and their fortunes have often been tied to those of their larger neighbours, Java and Sumbawa. More recently, they have been subsumed in the fate of the vast Indonesian archipelago. Historically, relations between Bali and Lombok were turbulent, and the origins of their present cultural, religious and economic differences and similarities are firmly rooted in past events.

Beginnings

Homo erectus, a distant ancestor of modern man, arrived in Indonesia almost two million years ago during the **ice ages**. At this time glaciers advanced from the polar regions and the levels of the oceans fell, exposing **land bridges** between the islands and the land masses of Southeast Asia and Australia. Homo erectus moved across these land bridges into and through Indonesia. The fossilized bones of "Solo Man" and later "Java Man" from this period were found in Central Java and stone axes and adzes have been discovered on Bali.

Homo sapiens appeared around forty-five thousand years ago and were cave-dwelling hunter-gatherers whose rock paintings have been found in the far east of the archipelago. The **Neolithic** era, around 3000 BC, is marked by the appearance of more sophisticated stone tools, agricultural techniques and basic pottery. Remains from this period have been found at Cekik, in the far west of Bali. More recently, the remains of a diminutive humanoid were discovered; this *Homo foresiensis,* about 700,000 years old, has been dubbed "the Hobbit".

From the sixth century BC until the sixth century AD, the **Bronze Age** spread south from southern China. Many examples of bronze casting have been found in the Indonesian archipelago. In Bali is the largest single-cast decorated drum found anywhere in Southeast Asia, the **Moon of Pejeng**, nearly 2m long and housed in a temple near Ubud. **Stone sarcophagi** from this period are on display in the Bali Museum in Denpasar and the Museum Arkeologi Gedung Arca in Pejeng.

Early traders and empires

From at least 200 BC, **trade** was a feature of life across the archipelago. The earliest written records in Bali, metal inscriptions, or *prasasti*, dating from the ninth century AD, reveal significant Buddhist and Hindu influence from the Indian subcontinent, shown also by the statues, bronzes and rock-cut caves at Goa Gajah and two centuries later at Gunung Kawi.

The most notable event in early Balinese history occurred towards the end of the tenth century when an East Java princess, **Mahendradatta**, married the Balinese king **Udayana**. Their marriage portrait is believed to be depicted in a stone in the Pura Tegeh

1.81 million years ago	45,000 years ago	500 BC–500 AD
Homo erectus, "Solo man", arrives in Indonesia	Homo sapiens appear; their rock paintings have been found in Sulawesi	The Bronze Age spreads from China into Indonesia; bronze drums from this period include Bali's Moon of Pejeng

Koripan near Kintamani. Their son, **Airlangga** (also spelt Erlangga), born around 991 AD, later brought the two realms together until his death in 1049.

Intensive rice farming was possible from the ninth century onwards in Bali as a network of *subak* water channels were established, connecting communities and under the supervision of priests in water temples. This system, uniquely Balinese, is still in use today and has been named a UNESCO World Heritage Site.

In the following centuries, control of Bali was won by the Javanese, then wrested back by Balinese rulers, only to return to Java again. By 1300 Bali was being ruled domestically by **King Bedaulu**, based in the Pejeng district east of Ubud.

Little is known of **Lombok's** ancient history, although it is known that its mightiest empire, Selaparang, controlled the east of the island and Sumbawa in two waves; the first was a Hindu kingdom that ruled from the 13th century until 1357 and the second, Islamic, from the 16th century until 1740.

The Majapahit

One of the most significant dates in Balinese history is 1343 AD, when the island was colonized by **Gajah Mada**, prime minister of the powerful Hindu **Majapahit** kingdom of East Java. Establishing a court initially at Samprangan in eastern Bali and later moving to Gelgel, he introduced a caste system and Balinese who did not accept this established their own villages. Their descendants, known as the **Bali Aga** or Bali Mula, the "original Balinese", still adhere to ancient traditions and primarily live in separate villages, such as Tenganan near Candidasa and Trunyan on the shores of Danau Batur.

To the east, Majapahit defeated the reigning Lombok Selaparang kingdom in 1357; however, when the soldiers departed, Selaprang reemerged.

Throughout the fifteenth century, **Islam** gained influence on Java and when Majapahit fell in 1515, many of its Hindu followers – priests, craftsmen, soldiers, nobles and artists – fled to Bali, flooding the island with **Javanese cultural ideas** and reaffirming Hindu practices.

It is unclear why Islam did not expand to Bali, especially as it moved further east to Lombok, Sulawesi and Maluku. It could be that Islam spread along trade routes: with poor harbours and few resources, Bali was largely bypassed (although there are small Muslim communities on the island).

An ancient text detailing the history of the Majapahit dynasty lists **Lombok** as part of its empire, and the villages in the Sembalun valley on the eastern flanks of Gunung Rinjani consider themselves directly descended from the Majapahit dynasty, claiming the brother of a Majapahit raja is buried in the valley.

Bali's Golden Age

During the reign of **Batu Renggong**, who became king, or **dewa agung** (literally "great god") in 1550, the Gelgel kingdom ruled an empire from Blambangan in Java in the west to Sumbawa in the east. This period coincided with a cultural renaissance in Bali and, as a result, is often referred to as the **Golden Age**. The Javanese Hindu priest **Nirartha** achieved a great following on Bali at this time.

Eventually, the glory faded and other kingdoms within Bali rose to prominence, most notably **Gianyar** under Dewa Manggis Kuning in the seventeenth century.

Ninth century AD	Ninth century BC	Tenth century
Bali's earliest written records reveal Buddhist and Hindu influences	A network of water channels (*subak*) is developed across Bali, allowing intensive rice cultivation and indicating close village cooperation	Princess Mahendradatta of East Java marries the Balinese king Udayana. Their son brings the two realms together until 1049

Foreigners and trade

Lacking the spices of the eastern isles, Bali appears not to have been in the mainstream of the archipelago's early trading history. The **Chinese** visited Bali, which they knew as Paoli or Rice Island, in the seventh century, but by this time trade had been established on nearby islands for a thousand years. Bali became known to **Europeans** in the sixteenth century when Portuguese, Spanish and English explorers came in search of the lucrative Spice Islands. They marked Bali on their maps as Balle, Ilha Bale or Java Minor, but sailed on by.

The first documented contact between Europeans and the Balinese occurred later in the sixteenth century. The **Portuguese**, having won the race for the Spice Islands, dispatched a ship from Malacca in 1585, aiming to construct a trading post on Bali. The ship hit a reef just off Bali and sank. The survivors were treated kindly by the *dewa agung* but not permitted to leave the island. Portuguese attempts at establishing contact were not repeated.

On February 9, 1597, four **Dutch** ships under the command of Commodore Cornelis de Houtman anchored off Bali and three sailors landed at Kuta. Among them was Aernoudt Lintgens, whose report of his experiences is the first account by a Westerner of the island. The other two crew members were reportedly so entranced that they did not return to the ship.

The Dutch came again in 1601, when Jacob van Heemskerck arrived with a letter from the prince of Holland requesting **formal trade relations**, which the *dewa agung* accepted. The VOC, or **Dutch East India Company**, was formed in 1602, and its headquarters founded in Jayakarta kingdom, changing its name to Batavia (modern-day Jakarta) in 1619, from where the Dutch trading empire expanded as far as Sumatra, Borneo, Makassar and the Moluccas.

From then until the beginning of the nineteenth century, Bali was largely ignored by Europeans, as it produced little of interest to them. The exception was **slaves**, who were sold through Kuta to Dutch merchants from Batavia and French merchants from Mauritius.

17th to 19th century Lombok

During the seventeenth century, western Lombok was invaded by the **Balinese** from Karangasem in far eastern Bali; **Makassar**'s (Sulawesi) Gowa kingdom, which had conquered Sumbawa in 1618, also invaded eastern Lombok. The first major conflicts between these two outside powers occurred in 1677 when the Balinese, assisted by the indigenous **Sasak** aristocracy, defeated the Makassarese.

From the end of the seventeenth to the mid-nineteenth century, the Balinese struggled to secure control over Lombok. In 1775, **Gusti Wayan Tegah**, who had been placed on the throne by the Karangasem raja, died, and disagreements over the succession resulted in four rival principalities in the west vying for control: Pagasangan, Pagutan, Mataram and Cakranegara. Meanwhile, the Sasak aristocracy in the east of the island faced little interference in their affairs.

Eventually, in 1838, the Mataram raja, **Ratu Agung K'tut**, triumphed over the other principalities and brought eastern Lombok under his control. Astutely, he also provided four thousand troops to support the Dutch in their fight against Karangasem in eastern

1343	Sixteenth century	1550	1585
Bali is colonized by East Java's Hindu Majapahit kingdom. Texts indicate that Lombok was part of the Majapahit empire during this period	Islam gains in influence on Java, and when the Majapahit kingdom falls in 1515, many Hindus flee to Bali	The beginning of Bali's Golden Age	Portuguese sailing ship reaches Bali but is shipwrecked offshore

Bali. This ensured the defeat of the ruling dynasty in Karangasem, for which service the Dutch gave him the right to put his own nominee on the Karangasem throne.

Dutch incursions

By the mid-1830s, the Dutch interest in Bali had intensified. Bali was ruled by that time by a number of kingdoms, recognizable today as the regencies named after them: Badung, Bangli, Buleleng, Jembrana, Karangasem, Klungkung, Mengwi and Tabanan. The Danish trader **Mads Lange** had set up a trading post in Kuta supplying rice to British-held Singapore. The Dutch started trading with Bali, with the aim of gaining political control before the British. In 1839 they established an agent in Kuta with the agreement of the raja of Badung. In 1840, the Dutch envoy, **Huskus Koopman**, began a series of visits with the long-term aim of gaining Dutch sovereignty over the island.

The Dutch also wanted to abolish Balinese *tawan karang* or reef rights, which had been a long-term grievance. The Balinese had always asserted their right to goods salvaged from shipping wrecked on the island's reefs, much of which was Dutch. The plundering of the Dutch vessel *Overijssel*, wrecked on the Kuta reef on July 19, 1841, particularly outraged the Dutch.

By 1843 Koopman had made **treaties** with the Badung, Klungkung, Buleleng, Karangasem and Tabanan kingdoms, agreeing to a Dutch trade monopoly. The rajas failed to realize that they had also given the Dutch sovereignty over their lands and surrendered reef rights. Following Koopman's retirement, a new commissioner arrived in 1844 to finalize the treaties, but it soon became apparent that there were huge differences in Dutch and Balinese understandings. Most kingdoms did ratify the treaties, but **Buleleng** and **Karangasem** stood firm. A further Dutch mission came the following year, including a military officer whose brief was to assess the Buleleng defences. At a meeting in Singaraja in May 1845, Gusti Ketut Jelantik, brother of the Buleleng and Karangasem rajas, stated, "Not by a mere scrap of paper shall any man become the master of another's lands. Rather let the *kris* decide."

The First and Second Dutch Military Expeditions

On June 26, 1846, the **First Dutch Military Expedition** arrived off the Buleleng coast with 3500 men. On June 28, the military force landed and marched into Singaraja. The Buleleng and Karangasem rajas eventually surrendered, agreeing to Dutch sovereignty and to paying costs for the victor's military expedition.

The Dutch departed, believing they had achieved their objectives, and left behind a small garrison until the compensation was paid. However, this fitted in with Jelantik's plan, and he continued to prepare for future battle. Meanwhile, nothing was paid to the Dutch, and ships that foundered continued to be plundered. On March 7, 1848, the governor-general of the Dutch East Indies sent ultimatums demanding compensation, payment of war debts, the destruction of defence works and the delivery of Jelantik to them. These were ignored, and the **Second Dutch Military Expedition** arrived off the northern coast at Sangsit on June 8, 1848, with almost three thousand troops. Having quickly overcome the defences on the coast, the well-armed force marched towards **Jagaraga** where Jelantik had organized his army of around sixteen thousand, armed largely with *kris* (daggers) and lances. The Dutch

Seventeenth century	**1601**	**1677**
The Golden Age fades and other regional kingdoms rise to prominence	Bali accepts the Dutch request for formal trade relations	Western Lombok is invaded by the Balinese, while the Makassarese of Sulawesi attack eastern Lombok. In 1677, the former, helped by the Sasak aristocracy, defeat the latter

were eventually put to flight and around two hundred Dutch soldiers were killed or wounded. The Balinese suffered more than two thousand casualties but on June 10, 1848, the Dutch sailed back to Batavia.

The Third Dutch Military Expedition

The following year, during the **Third Dutch Military Expedition**, the Dutch used almost their entire military force in the Indies to overcome the Balinese. Around seven thousand troops landed in Buleleng on April 4, 1849. Negotiations failed and on April 15 the Dutch attacked the fortress at Jagaraga and defeated the Balinese with the loss of only about thirty men to the Balinese thousands. Jelantik and the Buleleng and Karangasem rajas fled east. With four thousand additional troops from Lombok, the Dutch attacked Karangasem first. On their arrival at the palace on May 20, Gusti Gde Ngurah Karangasem, the Karangasem raja, along with his family and followers, all committed **puputan** (ritual suicide). The Buleleng raja, accompanied by Jelantik, fled to the mountains near Seraya, where they were killed in further fighting.

Dutch troops then headed west towards Semarapura where the local king, the *dewa agung*, signed an **agreement** on July 13, 1849. The Balinese recognized Dutch sovereignty and accepted that *tawan karang* was prohibited, while in return the Dutch agreed to leave the rajas to administer their kingdoms and not to base garrisons on the island. A feast on July 15 sealed the agreement.

The strengthening of the Dutch position

The Dutch regarded themselves as having sovereignty over the whole island but initially left the kingdoms of the south and the east largely alone, basing themselves in the north and placing Dutch controllers over the Buleleng and Jembrana rajas.

From their administrative capital in **Singaraja**, the Dutch improved irrigation, planted coffee as a cash crop, and outlawed slavery and the tradition of *suttee*, whereby widows would throw themselves on their husbands' funeral pyres. They also quelled **local rebellions**, such as the 1864 uprising in Banjar village, close to modern-day Lovina.

With the Dutch concentrated in the north, the Klungkung, Badung, Gianyar, Mengwi, Bangli and Tabanan kingdoms in the south were weakened by internal conflicts and fighting one another. The rajas increasingly turned to the Dutch for protection from their neighbours.

Rebellion and the Dutch in Lombok

In Lombok, meanwhile, Ratu Agung K'tut continued to rule. The **west** of the island was relatively harmonious, but in the **east** the frustrated Sasak aristocracy deeply resented their Balinese masters and there were failed rebellions in 1855 and 1871. In 1872, Ratu Agung K'tut was succeeded by his younger brother, **Ratu Agung Ngurah**.

The **rebellion of 1891** was more successful. For many years, Ratu Agung Ngurah had vied with the *dewa agung* of the Balinese Klungkung kingdom over claims to the title of Supreme Ruler of Bali. In 1891 he decided to take action, but his demand for several thousand Sasak troops was met with resistance in **Praya**, and a local Sasak aristocrat was executed. On August 7, 1891, several thousand Sasaks surrounded and burned

1775	1830–45	1846–49	1855–91
Lombok monarch Gusti Wayan Tegah dies and four different factions fight to gain control	Dutch interest in Bali intensifies; the Balinese lose their land and reef rights	After three bloody conflicts, in 1849 the Dutch eventually secure sovereignty over northern Bali	After a series of failed rebellions, in 1891 the Sasak aristocracy in eastern Lombok overthrow their Balinese rulers

the palace of the Balinese district chief and rebellion spread quickly. By September 22, 1891, Balinese rule had been overthrown throughout eastern Lombok.

Hostilities between the Balinese and the Sasak aristocracy dragged on, gains being made and then lost, until 1894, when the Dutch army landed in West Lombok.

On the night of August 25, 1894, Balinese forces attacked the Dutch camp in the **Mayura Palace** at Cakranegara, where around nine hundred soldiers were camped. The Dutch escaped with heavy casualties, but they soon received reinforcements and, aided by the Sasaks from the east, proved too strong for the raja. Mataram was razed to the ground. Some members of the royal family surrendered while others committed *puputan*. The Dutch took control of the entire island, including the Karangasem district on Bali, which had been under the raja's control.

Further confrontation in south Bali

The Dutch had wanted to emphasize their control of the **south of Bali** for many years, but it wasn't until the beginning of the twentieth century that they made their move. On May 27, 1904, a schooner, the *Sri Kumala*, under Dutch protection, hit the reef just off Sanur. The owner complained to the Dutch Resident in Singaraja that copper and silver coins had been stolen from the ship. The Resident decreed a **blockade** of Badung and ordered that the Badung raja, Gusti Gede Ngurah, should pay compensation.

The confrontation continued until July 1906, when the Dutch threatened military action. Dutch forces landed at Sanur, and by September 20, 1906, had advanced to **Badung** (modern-day Denpasar). Gusti Gede Ngurah realized defence was useless and arranged the traditional **puputan**. An eyewitness account from a Dutch observer, Dr van Weede, in his book *Indies Travel Memories*, describes the event:

The ruler and the princes with their followers, dressed in their glittering attire, with their krises girded on, of which the golden hilts were in the form of Buddha statues and studded with precious stones; all of them were dressed in red or black and their hair was carefully combed, moistened with fragrant oils. The women were wearing the best clothes and accessories that they had; most of them wore their hair loose and all had white cloaks. The prince had his palace burned down and had everything that was breakable destroyed.

When at nine o'clock it was reported to him that the enemy had penetrated Denpasar from the North, the tragic procession of 250 people started to move; each man and woman carried a kris or long lance, also the children who had the strength to do it, while the babies were carried in their arms. Thus they walked to the north along the wide road bordered by tall trees, meeting their destruction.

The prince walked in front, carried on the shoulders by his followers according to custom, and silently … until all of a sudden, at a turning in the road, the dark line of our infantry was visible before them. Immediately a halt was commanded and Captain Schutstal ordered the interpreters to summon the arriving party to a halt with gestures and with words. However, these summons were in vain, and in spite of the repeated warnings the Balinese went over to a trot.

Incessantly the Captain and the interpreters made signs, but it was in vain. Soon they had to realize that they had to do with people who wanted to die. They let them approach to a

1894

The Dutch take over Lombok; forced labour, harsh taxes and many cases of virtual starvation follow

1904–09

The Dutch attack southern Bali, provoking mass *puputans*. By 1909 the Dutch rule all of Bali

1924

The arrival of a steamship line heralds the start of Western tourism in Bali

hundred paces, eighty, seventy paces, but now they went over to a double quick step with couched lances and raised krises, the prince always in front.

A longer delay would have been irresponsible in view of the safety of our men, and the first salvo was given; several killed men remained at the place. One of the first to fall was the ruler; and now one of the most horrible scenes one could imagine took place.

While those who were saved continued the attack, and the shooting on our part for self-defence remained necessary, one saw lightly wounded give the death-blow to the heavily wounded. Women held out their breasts to be killed or received the death blow between their shoulders, and those who did this were mowed down by our rifle fire, other men and women got up to continue the bloody work. Also suicides took place there on a big scale, and all seemed to yearn for their death: some women threw as a reward for the violent death which they desired from them gold coins to the soldiers, and stood straight up in front of them, pointing at their heart, as if they wanted to be hit there; if no shot was fired they killed themselves. Especially an old man was busily stepping over the corpses, and used his kris left and right until he was shot down. An old woman took his task and underwent the same fate, however, nothing helped. Always others got up to continue the work of destruction.

This scene was repeated later the same day at the palace of the **Pemecutan** prince. Estimates of the number of people killed that day vary between four hundred and two thousand. Having defeated Badung, on September 27, the Dutch marched on to **Tabanan**, where the raja and crown prince surrendered and were imprisoned, where they both committed suicide rather than face exile.

The completion of Dutch control

On April 28, 1908, Dutch troops in **Klungkung** witnessed a scene similar to the Badung *puputan* two years earlier. Reports tell how the *dewa agung* stabbed his royal *kris* into the ground expecting its power to rent the ground asunder or bring torrential rain to destroy the enemy. Nothing happened and around two hundred members of the royal household committed suicide that day; the remainder were exiled. At this point the **Bangli** raja realized a pretext would soon be found to attack him and, in October 1908, requested that his kingdom should have the same status as Gianyar and Karangasem and become a Dutch Protectorate. When this was approved in January 1909, the whole of the island of Bali came under **Dutch control**.

Colonial rule

The *puputans* of 1906 and 1908 caused a stir in Europe and the United States and pressure was put on the Dutch to moderate their policies. They ruled with a philosophy they called the **Ethical Policy**, which was claimed to uphold Balinese values. Traditional rulers remained as regents under Dutch authority, although not all of the old royal families were amenable to this; in Buleleng, it was not until several generations after the Dutch conquest that an obliging member of the royal family could be found.

Under the Dutch, engineers, doctors and teachers were introduced to the colony and Bali was spared the less enlightened **agricultural policies** that had turned large

1942–49	**1949**	**1963**
Japanese forces occupy Bali during World War II, and the Dutch are expelled. In 1945, President Sukarno declares independence for Indonesia, resulting in a prolonged armed conflict	The Indonesians achieve independence by UN resolution, having made the declaration in 1945	The Balinese stage a major purification ceremony while Gunung Agung rumbles in the background

parts of Java into plantations. Big businesses were discouraged from Bali, although the Dutch steamship line KPM began encouraging **tourism** on the island from 1924 onwards.

Lombok under the Dutch

Conditions on **Lombok** deteriorated markedly following the Dutch victory in 1894, and brought the population to the point of starvation more than once. The Dutch were determined to rule profitably: they taxed the population harshly and introduced **compulsory labour** for projects such as road-building. In addition to land tax, there were **taxes** on income and on the slaughter of animals. These were initially payable in local currency, but eventually they were demanded in Netherlands Indies currency (NIC). The Chinese rice-exporters were one of the few groups on the island who traded in NIC, and increasing amounts of rice needed to be sold to raise money for taxes. Consequently, a high proportion of food grown on the island was exported, and local rice consumption dropped by a quarter. By 1934, it was estimated that a third of the population were **landless and destitute**.

World War II and independence

Following the bombing of the US Pacific Fleet in Pearl Harbor on December 7, 1941, Japan entered **World War II** and moved quickly through Asia. The **Japanese** fleet that arrived off Sanur on February 18, 1942 were unopposed on their march to Denpasar – Indonesian leaders believing that Japan could free them from Dutch rule – and took control of Bali without a fight. Java and Sumatra had fallen by March 9 and the Dutch were expelled from the country.

The Japanese **occupation** was hard but it showed the occupied islanders that the Dutch colonialists could be defeated. Throughout the war years, the idea of liberation grew and, on August 17, 1945, three days after the Japanese surrender, Indonesia made its **Declaration of Independence** in an announcement by President **Sukarno**. Some Balinese were strong supporters of independence but many were uncertain about joining a republic dominated by Islamic Java.

The fight for independence

Returning to their Dutch East Indies colony in March 1946, the **Dutch** faced ferocious fighting on Java. On Bali, guerrilla forces, the most famous of which was led by **I Gusti Ngurah Rai**, harried the Dutch relentlessly, despite suffering immense losses in a battle near Marga in Tabanan. Ngurah Rai is remembered as a hero: Bali's airport is named after him.

However, the Dutch were also under a different sort of attack. The US questioned the Dutch expenditure of Marshall Plan aid (money allocated to European countries for reconstruction after the war) on fighting to keep the Indies. Finally, in January 1949, the UN Security Council ordered the Dutch to negotiate. In December 1949, the United States of Indonesia was legally recognized, dissolving the following year to form the **Republic of Indonesia**, with Sukarno as president. Today, Indonesia continues to celebrate its independence annually on August 17, marking the original date of the 1945 Declaration of Independence, without Dutch acknowledgement of that date.

1965

Suharto seizes power, unleashing a bloodbath across Indonesia. Around 150,000 people on Bali and Lombok are killed. As president, Suharto holds power for thirty-one years

Late 1990s

Indonesia suffers during the Asian economic crisis. Following widespread unrest, Suharto resigns in 1998

2001

Megawati Sukarnoputri becomes Indonesia's first (and only) female president

The Sukarno years

The early years of independence were not kind to Indonesia. Indonesia's economic position was disastrous as inflation, corruption and mismanagement ran riot. Martial rule was instituted and 1963–1966 saw a catastrophic war against The Federation of Malaysia.

Although Sukarno's mother was from Bali, the Balinese felt neglected by the government in Jakarta, which, in turn, was suspicious of the islanders' Hinduism. Sukarno visited his palace at Tampaksiring (Bali) regularly, with a huge entourage that demanded to be fed, entertained and then sent back to their homes with gifts. During the 1960s, a groundswell of resentment against the government grew in Bali. The Balinese began to believe that a state of spiritual disharmony had been reached, and a huge purification ceremony, **Eka Dasa Rudra**, was held in 1963 against the backdrop of a rumbling Gunung Agung (see page 157), which eventually erupted and laid waste to much of the east of the island.

Later events in Jakarta piled disaster upon disaster in Bali. In 1965 **Major-General Suharto** seized power after a mysterious attempted coup that was blamed on the communist party (PKI). It unleashed a bloodbath in the country with actual or suspected members of the PKI and their sympathizers the main targets, along with the Chinese population. At least half a million people were killed across Indonesia: an estimated hundred thousand on Bali and fifty thousand on Lombok. Around two hundred thousand were imprisoned or exiled, mostly without trial, more than half of them for ten years or more while their families were stigmatized well into the 1990s. Suharto officially became the second president of Indonesia in March 1968, a position he held for over thirty years.

Indonesia under Suharto

Suharto's **New Order** policy of attracting foreign investment, curbing inflation and re-entering the global economy was largely successful. It was helped enormously by Indonesia's massive **natural resources** of copper, tin, timber and oil. The country's **economy** improved and the material prosperity of the average Indonesian rose.

However, the economic benefits came with a price as alongside this the government acquired almost complete control. **Political opposition** was crushed and the **media** silenced. Corruption was rife and a transmigration policy, which moved landless people from Java and Bali to outlying, less-densely populated Indonesian islands, caused enormous ethnic strife. In every election from 1971 to 1997 the government party, Sekretariat Bersama Golongan Karya, known as **Golkar**, won the majority of seats in the House of Representatives and then re-elected Suharto as president.

The **economic crisis** of the late 1990s that decimated the economies of Southeast Asia savaged Indonesia as well. Prices of imports (including food) rose sharply, and a series of riots in early 1998, centred on Java, targeted Chinese businesses – long the scapegoats of Indonesian unrest. The violence spread to Lombok, where there were many deaths during days of rioting and several churches (many Chinese Indonesians are Christian) were torched in Mataram and Ampenan. Gradually, Indonesian anger turned against President Suharto and his family, who were seen to have been the biggest winners in the Indonesian economic success story.

2004

Susilo Bambang Yudhoyono wins the country's first direct presidential elections

2002–09

In 2002, Islamic militants carry out bombings in Bali. Further attacks take place in Jakarta in 2003, 2004, 2009 and 2016 and in Bali in 2005

2014

Joko Widodo elected Indonesian president on a mandate to tackle corruption and modernize economy and infrastructure

Student rioting in May 1998 led to more widespread unrest and, eventually, to **Suharto's resignation** on May 21. He spent the ten years until his death on January 27, 2008, dodging corruption charges – in 2000, he was judged as unfit to stand trial. Transparency International, an international anticorruption NGO, estimates that he stole $15–35 billion, possibly topping the worldwide list of corrupt politicians. Suharto's influence still endures across Indonesia, with his sons and daughters having controlling interests in many industries such as oil and gas, telecommunications and toll roads across the nation. The family also own vast chunks of prime real estate in Bali and Lombok including luxury tourist hotels in Nusa Dua, Jimbaran and Sanur. Indonesia has managed to recover some of the embezzled properties, but it's only the tip of the iceberg.

After Suharto

Following Suharto proved a tough job. The next two presidents, **B.J. Habibie** and **Abdurrahman Wahid**, lasted only short periods of time and on July 23, 2001 **Megawati Sukarnoputri** became president. Megawati – darling of the Balinese, to whom she is known simply as Ibu Mega – was regarded in Bali with something approaching fanaticism, based on the fact that her maternal grandmother (Sukarno's mother) was Balinese. Starting her presidency on a wave of optimism, she proved an ineffectual leader.

Indonesia hit the world headlines on **October 12, 2002**, when **bombs** planted in the heart of tourist Bali, at the *Sari Club* and *Paddy's Irish Bar* in Kuta, exploded, killing more than two hundred people, the majority of them tourists but with dozens of Indonesian victims also. A third bomb exploded outside the US consulate in Denpasar. The attacks were carried out by members of the Islamic militant organization Jemaah Islamiah. After hugely public and drawn-out trials, three men were executed in November 2008 and in 2012 bombmaker Umer Patek was sentenced to twenty years in prison for his role in the attacks. Further bombings in Jakarta in 2003, 2004 and 2009 and Jimbaran and Kuta in 2005 emphasized to Indonesians and the wider world that anti-Western jihadi forces represented an ongoing threat in the nation with the largest Muslim population in the world.

Whatever Megawati's failings, she did lay the foundations for Indonesia's first-ever **direct presidential election** in 2004, in which 114 million voters across almost fourteen thousand islands voted her out of the job in favour of **Susilo Bambang Yudhoyono**, commonly known as **SBY**.

With 61 percent of the vote in a run-off election Yudhoyono was the clear winner, and outside the country he received international approval for his peace deal with Aceh (Sumatra) separatists. He was re-elected with another landslide victory in 2009, as Indonesia weathered the global financial crisis far better than many of its neighbours, though corruption remained endemic.

Indonesia elected a relatively youthful Javanese businessmen-turned-politician **Joko Widodo** (best known as Jokowi) in 2014, on a mandate to tackle corruption. The first president not from an elite political or military background, Joko was faced with a difficult balancing act trying to stimulate the country's economy while facing reduced income from the key commodity and mining sectors.

2018	**2019**	**2020–21**
Lombok is struck by two devastating earthquakes that destroy 80 percent of the structures in the north, with damage in Bali and Java also	Joko Widodo is elected to a second term as Indonesian president. He announces plans to build Indonesia's new capital, Nusantara, in the East Kalimantan province, on Borneo island	Covid-19 pandemic spreads in Indonesia with widespread impact on the island's tourism industry

In 2019 Joko was reelected for his second (and last) five-year term following a divisive election by standing firm on religious pluralism, economic development and improving human resources and infrastructure. The protracted trade war between the US and China, two of Indonesia's biggest trade partners, poses another challenge but has forced Indonesia to develop relations with other countries, and, as more factories leave China, Indonesia is a likely new home.

The global Covid-19 pandemic in 2020-21 strongly affected Indonesia, including Bali and Lombok whose economies are largely based on tourism. By February 2022, 4.7 million coronavirus cases were reported in Indonesia with the death toll reaching almost 145,000. Interestingly enough, however, the World Bank report of December 2021 was quite optimistic for the country: Indonesia's economy grew by 3.7 percent in 2021 despite Covid-19 and it's expected to accelerate to 5.2 percent in 2025.

2022	2024	2025
In February, Bali reopens to direct international flights after two years' freeze and tourism slowly returns	Post-Covid travel booms and Bali welcomes a record number of annual tourists	After many setbacks, plans for the construction of a new North Bali airport are back on the agenda. Construction of Indonesia's new capital, Nusantara, begins

Religion

Some eighty percent of Balinese are Hindus, with Islam the dominant minority faith, practised mostly in the west and north by migrants from Java. The reverse is true on Lombok, where around 85 percent of the population is Muslim, with Balinese Hinduism followed mainly in the west by those of Balinese heritage. There are also small numbers of Buddhists and Christians, mostly from the Chinese community.

Religious activity permeates almost every aspect of **Balinese** life. Each morning, tiny palm-leaf offerings are laid down for the gods and spirits who need twenty-four-hour propitiation; in the afternoons, processions of people parade the streets en route to temple celebrations, towers of fruit and rice cake offerings balanced on their heads.

While Islam is as pervasive on **Lombok** as Hinduism is on Bali, it has a much more austere presence. You'll hear the call to prayer five times a day, and streets are often deserted on Fridays around noon, when a large proportion of the male population go to the mosque. Marriage and circumcision are celebrated, but the exuberant festivals of Balinese Hinduism have no Muslim equivalents.

Balinese Hinduism

Though it's not a proselytizing faith, **Balinese Hinduism** is a demanding one, which requires participation from every citizen. Despite certain obvious similarities, Balinese Hinduism differs dramatically from Indian and Nepalese Hinduism. Bali's is a blend of theories and practices borrowed from Hinduism and Buddhism, grafted onto the far stronger indigenous vision of a world that is populated by good and bad spirits.

Early influences

The **animism** of the Stone- and Bronze-Age Balinese probably differed very little from the beliefs of their twenty-first-century descendants, who worship sacred mountains and rivers, and conduct elaborate rituals to ensure that the souls of their dead ancestors are kept sweet. In among these animist practices are elements borrowed from the **Mahayana Buddhism** that dominated much of Southeast Asia in the eighth century – certain Buddhist saints, for example, some of which are still visible at Goa Gajah, and a penchant for highly ornate imagery. The strongest influences arrived with the droves of **East Javanese Hindu priests** who fled Muslim invaders en masse in the early sixteenth century. High-caste, educated pillars of the Majapahit kingdom, these strict followers of the Hindu faith settled all over Bali and quickly set about formalizing the island's embryonic Hindu practices. Balinese Hinduism, or **agama Hindu** as it's termed in Indonesia, became the official religion, and the Majapahit priests have, ever since, been venerated as the true Balinese ancestors.

As Bali's Hinduism gained strength, so its neighbouring islands turned towards Islam, and Bali is now a tiny Hindu enclave in an archipelago that contains the biggest Islamic population in the world. Hindu Bali's role within the predominantly Muslim Indonesian state has always been problematic. As part of its code of national law, or **Pancasila**, the Jakarta administration requires that all Indonesian faiths be monotheistic and embrace just one God – a proviso that doesn't sit easily with either Hindu or animist tenets. The compromise decided on by Bali's Hindu Council was to emphasize the role of the supreme deity, **Sanghyang Widi Wasa** (who manifests himself as the Hindu Trinity of Brahma, Siwa and Wisnu); this convinced the Ministry of Religion that Bali was essentially monotheistic, and in 1962 Balinese Hinduism was formally recognized by Jakarta.

The beliefs

At the root of *agama Hindu* is the understanding that the world – both natural and supernatural – is composed of opposing forces. These can be defined as good and evil, positive and negative, pure and impure, order and disorder, gods and demons, or as a mixture of all these things, but must in any event be balanced. The desire to achieve **equilibrium** and harmony in all things dictates every spiritual activity. **Positive forces**, or *dharma*, are represented by the gods (*dewa* and *bhatara*), and need to be entertained and honoured with offerings, dances, beautiful artworks, fine earthly abodes (temples) and ministrations from devotees. The **malevolent forces**, *adharma*, which manifest themselves as earth demons (*bhuta*, *kala* and *leyak*) and cause sickness, death and volcanic eruptions, need to be neutralized with rites and special offerings.

Ritual uncleanliness (sebel)

To ensure that malevolent forces never take the upper hand, elaborate purification rituals are undertaken for the exorcism of spirits. Crucial to this is the notion of **ritual uncleanliness** (*sebel*), a state which can affect an individual (during a woman's period, for example, or after a serious illness), a family (after the death of a close relative, or if twins are born), or even a whole community (a plague of rats in the village ricefields, or a fire in village buildings). The whole island can even become *sebel*, and **island-wide exorcisms** are held every new year (Nyepi) to restore the spiritual health of Bali and all its people. The 2002 Kuta bombing caused the whole island to become ritually unclean, and as well as a huge purification ceremony at Ground Zero a month after the attack, exorcism rites were performed simultaneously across the island. Other regular, very elaborate island-cleansing rituals are performed every five, ten and 25 years, climaxing with the centennial *Eka Dasa Rudra* rite, which is held at the mother temple, Besakih. In addition, there are all sorts of **purification rituals** (*yadnya*) that Balinese must go through at various significant stages in their lives (see page 321).

Holy water

The focus of every purification ritual is the ministering of **holy water** (*agama Hindu* is sometimes known as *agama tirta*, the religion of holy water). Ordinary well or tap water can be transformed into holy water by a *pedanda* (high priest), but water from certain sources is considered to be particularly sacred – the springs at Tirta Empul in Tampaksiring and on Gunung Agung, for example, and the water taken from the lakeside Pura Danu Batur.

As the main sources of these life-giving waters, Bali's three great **mountains** are also worshipped: the highest, and the holiest, of the three is Gunung Agung, site of Bali's most sacred mother temple, Besakih; Gunung Batur and Gunung Batukaru also hold great spiritual power. Ever since the Stone Age, the Balinese have regarded their mountains as being the realm of the deities, the sea as the abode of demons and giants, and the valleys in between as the natural province of the human world. From this concept comes the Balinese sense of direction and **spatial orientation**, whereby all things, such as temples, houses and villages, are aligned in relation to the mountains and the sea: **kaja** is the direction towards the mountains, upstream, and is the holiest direction; **kelod** is the downstream direction, the part that is closest to the sea and therefore impure.

Karma, reincarnation and enlightenment

Finally, there are the notions of karma, reincarnation and the attaining of enlightenment (*moksa*). The aim of every Hindu is to attain **enlightenment**, which unites the individual and the divine, and brings liberation from the endless cycle of death and rebirth; it is only attainable by pure souls, and can take hundreds of lifetimes to attain. Hindus believe that everybody is **reincarnated** according to their **karma**, a kind of account book that registers all the good and bad deeds performed in the past lives of a soul. Karma is closely bound up with caste and the notion that an individual should accept rather than challenge their destiny.

The gods

All Balinese **gods** are manifestations of the supreme being, **Sanghyang Widi Wasa**, a deity who is often only alluded to in abstract form by an empty throne-shrine, the *padmasana*, that stands in the holiest corner of every temple. Sanghyang Widi Wasa's three main aspects manifest themselves as the Hindu trinity: Brahma, Wisnu and Siwa.

Brahma and Wisnu

Brahma is the Creator, represented by the colour red and often depicted riding on a bull. His consort is the goddess of learning, **Saraswati**, who rides a white goose. As the Preserver, **Wisnu** is associated with life-giving waters; he rides the Garuda (half-man, half-bird) and is honoured by the colour black. Wisnu also has several avatars, including **Buddha** – a neat way of incorporating Buddhist elements into the Hindu faith.

Siwa, Durga and Ganesh

Siwa, the Destroyer, or more accurately the Dissolver, is associated with death and rebirth, with the temples of the dead and with the colour white. He is also represented as a phallic pillar or lingam, and sometimes in the manifestation of **Surya**, the sun god. Siwa's consort is the terrifying goddess **Durga**, whose Balinese personality is the gruesome widow-witch **Rangda**, queen of the demons. The son of Siwa and Durga is the elephant-headed deity **Ganesh**, generally worshipped as the remover of obstacles.

Lesser deities

Among the many lesser deities or *dewi* (*dewa* if male) are **Dewi Sri**, the goddess of rice, worshipped at tiny shrines in the paddy fields and celebrated at significant stages throughout the agricultural year; and **Dewi Danu** (more formally known as Ida Batara Dewi Ulun Danu), the goddess of the crater lakes. Dewi Danu is honoured with temples at lakes Bratan, Batur and Tamblingan, and is so important to rice growers as a source of vital irrigation that annual pilgrimages are made to all three temples.

The demons

Demons also come in a variety of manifestations. The forces of evil are personified by a cast of **bhuta** and **kala**, invisible goblins and ghosts who inhabit eerie, desolate places like the temples of the dead, cemeteries, moonless seashores and dark forests. Their purpose is to wreak havoc in the human world, causing horrible lingering illnesses, ruinous agricultural and economic disasters and entering villagers' minds and turning them insane. But they are not invincible and can be appeased with **offerings** just as the gods can – the difference being that the offerings for these demons consist mainly of dirty, unpleasant, unattractive and mouldy things, which are thrown on the ground, rather than placed respectfully on ledges and altars. Demons are notoriously greedy, too, and so the Balinese will often waste a dash of *arak* (rice liquor) on the ground before drinking, or drop a few grains of rice to the floor when eating.

Various other strategies are used to repel, confuse and banish the *bhuta* and *kala*. Most entrance gates to temples and households are guarded by fierce-looking statues and ugly demonic images designed to frighten off even the boldest demon. Many gateways are also blocked by a low brick wall, an **aling-aling**, as demons can only walk in straight lines, and so won't be able to zigzag around it. *Bhuta* and *kala* get particular pleasure from entering a person's body via their various orifices, so certain temples (especially in the north) have covered their walls in pornographic carvings, the theory being that the demons will have so much fun penetrating the carved simulation orifices on the outside walls that they won't bother to try their luck further inside the temple compound.

The leyak

In addition to the unseen *bhuta* and *kala*, there are the **leyak**, or witches, who take highly visible and creepy forms, morphing into headless chickens, bald-headed giants, monkeys with rows of shiny gold teeth, fireballs and riderless motorbikes. *Leyak* can transform themselves effortlessly, and most assume the human form during the daytime, leading outwardly normal lives. Only at night do they release their dark spirits to wreak havoc on unsuspecting islanders, while their human shell remains innocently asleep in bed. Even in their human form, *leyak* cannot be killed with knives or poisons, but they can be controlled by harnessing the white magic practised by shamanic *balian* (traditional healers) and priests.

The temples

The focus of every community's spiritual activity is the **temple**, or *pura*, a temporary abode for the gods that's open and unroofed to invite easy access between heaven and earth.

To outsiders, Balinese temples can seem confusing, even unimpressive: open-roofed compounds scattered with shrines and altars, built mainly of limestone and red brick, and with no paintings or treasures to focus on. But there are tens of thousands of temples on the island and many do reward closer examination. Every structure within a temple complex is charged with great symbolic significance, often with entertaining legends attached, and many of the walls and gateways are carved with an ebullience of mythical figures, demonic spirits and even secular scenes. Note that when **visiting a temple**, you must be appropriately dressed (see page 38), even if there's no one else in the vicinity.

Every *banjar*, or neighbourhood, in Bali is obliged to build at least three temples. At the top of the village – the *kaja*, or holiest end – stands the **pura puseh**, the temple of origin, dedicated to the community's founders. For routine spiritual activities, villagers worship at the **pura desa**, the village temple, which always stands at the heart of the village. (In some communities, the *pura puseh* and the *pura desa* are combined within a single compound.) The trio is completed by the **pura dalem**, or temple of the dead, at the *kelod* (unclean) end of the village, which is usually dedicated either to Siwa or to the widow-witch Rangda.

Bali also has nine directional temples, or **kayangan jagat**, which protect the entire island and all its people. They're located at strategic points across Bali, especially on high mountain slopes, rugged cliff faces and lakeside shores: Pura Ulun Danu Batur is on the shores of Danau Batur (north); Pura Pasar Agung on Gunung Agung (northeast); Pura Lempuyang Luhur on Gunung Lempuyang (east); Pura Goa Lawah near Candidasa (southeast); Pura Masceti near Lebih (south); Pura Luhur Uluwatu on the Bukit (southwest); Pura Luhur Batukaru on Gunung Batukaru (west); Pura Ulun Danu Bratan on the shores of Danau Bratan (northwest); and Pura Besakih on Gunung Agung (centre). The most important of these is **Besakih** – the mother temple – as it occupies the crucial position on Bali's holiest and highest mountain, Gunung Agung; the others are all of equal status, and islanders are expected to attend the anniversary celebrations (*odalan*) of the one situated closest to their home.

Temple layout

Whatever the size, status or particular function of a temple, it follows a prescribed layout. All Balinese temples are oriented *kaja–kelod*, and are designed around two or three courtyards, each section divided from the next by a low wall punctuated by a huge, and usually ornate, "split" gateway, the **candi bentar**.

COCKFIGHTS

Certain Hindu rituals require the shedding of fresh sacrificial blood to placate evil spirits, so every temple's purification ceremony is prefaced by a **cockfight** (adu tajen), which attracts massive crowds and even larger bets. Although gambling is illegal under Indonesian law, it is "permitted" as a religious ritual in this case. Providing you wear suitable temple dress, tourists are welcome to attend, but make sure you can stand the gore.

Prize cocks can earn both their owners and the temple tidy sums of money – and plunge losing gamblers into debilitating debt – and you'll see men of all ages and incomes preening their birds in public. When not being pampered, the birds are kept in bell-shaped bamboo baskets, often in quite noisy public places such as by the roadside, to train them not to be scared or distracted when in the ring.

Fights generally take place in the temple's special cockfighting pavilion or *wantilan*. Complicated **rules** written on ancient manuscripts specify the days on which fights may take place, and describe the detailed classification system under which the birds are categorized. Before the fight, a lethal 11- to 15cm-long blade, or *taji*, is attached to the left ankle of each bird. This is considered a sacred weapon and cockfights are meant to be won and lost by skilful use of the *taji*, not just by brutish pecking. Fights last for a maximum of five rounds, and the winning bird is the cock who remains standing the longest – even if he drops dead soon after. The owner of the winning cock gets the body of the losing bird plus his opponent's share of the central fund.

In many temples, particularly in northern Bali, the **outer courtyard** (*jaba*) and **middle courtyard** (*jaba tengah*) are merged into one. These courtyards represent the transition zone between the human and the divine worlds, containing thatched pavilions or **bale** (pronounced "ba-leh") for the preparation of offerings, cockfights (see box opposite) and the less sacred dance performances (such as those for tourists). The **kulkul** or drum tower is also here, housing the wooden bell ("drum") used to summon villagers to meetings and festivals. Entry to the extremely sacred **inner courtyard**, *jeroan*, is via an imposing covered gateway, the three-doored **kori agung** or **paduraksa**, whose central door is kept locked, opened only for the deities at festival times. The *jeroan* houses all the **shrines**: the small, thatched, red-brick structures dedicated to a particular deity or ancestor are *gedong*; the distinctive, elegant pagoda-style towers with multitiered roofs thatched with thick black sugar-palm fibre are **meru**, after the sacred Hindu peak Mount Meru (the tip of which is locally believed to be Mount Semeru, in East Java), home of the gods. A *meru* always has an odd number of roofs (three, five, seven, nine or eleven), the number indicating the status of the god to whom it is dedicated. All offerings are brought to the inner courtyard, the most sacred dances are performed within its confines, and prayers are held in front of the shrines. The *jeroan* is quite often out of bounds to the lay community and opened only during festivals.

Temple festivals

Aside from the daily propitiation of the household spirits, *agama Hindu* requires no regular act of collective worship, daily mass or weekly service, and so, for much of the year, Bali's thousands of temples remain deserted, visited only by the village priest (*pemangku*) and perhaps the occasional curious tourist. But this all changes on the occasion of the temple's anniversary celebrations, or **odalan**, a three-day devotional extravaganza held at every temple either once every 210 days – every Balinese calendar year – or once every 354–356 days (the *saka* year). As there are at least three temples in every community, any visitor who spends more than a week on the island will be certain to see some kind of festival. Most temples welcome tourists to the celebrations, provided they dress respectably (see page 38), wear the temple sash and don't walk in front of praying devotees.

The more important the temple, the more dramatic the *odalan* celebrations. But whatever the size, the purpose is always to invite the gods down to earth so that they can be entertained and pampered by as many displays of devotion as the community can afford. In the days before the *odalan*, the *pemangku* dresses the temple statues in **holy cloths**, either the spiritually charged black-and-white *kain poleng*, or a length of plain cloth in a symbolic colour. Meanwhile, community's women begin to construct their offering towers, or *banten*, and to cook ceremonial food.

Odalan are so important that everyone makes a huge effort to return to their home village for their own temple festival, even if they live and work far away; most employers will automatically give their Balinese staff time off to attend. **Celebrations** start in the afternoon, with a procession of ceremonially clad women carrying their offerings to the temple. Sometimes the gods will temporarily inhabit the body of one of the worshippers, sending him or her into a trance and conveying its message through gestures or words. Elsewhere in the temple compound, there might be a cockfight and some gamelan music, and sacred dances are regularly performed. After dark, a shadow play, *wayang kulit*, is often staged.

As well as the temple anniversary celebrations, there are numerous island-wide religious festivals, the most important of which are Nyepi and Galungan-Kuningan.

Offerings

The simplest **offerings** are the ones laid out every day by the women of each house, and placed at the household shrine, at the entrance gate, and in any crannies thought to be of interest to *bhuta* and *kala*. These offerings, called **canang**, are tiny banana-leaf trays, pinned together with bamboo splinters and filled with a symbolic assortment of rice, fruit, flowers and incense. The flowers are always red or pink, to represent the Hindu god Brahma, and white for Siwa, with the green of the banana leaf symbolizing Wisnu. Though it's still common for women to make their own *canang*, an increasing number buy theirs at the market. Offerings for the gods are always placed in elevated positions, either on specially constructed altars or on functional shelves, but those meant for the demons are scattered on the ground. When the devotee places the gods' offering, she sprinkles holy water over it and wafts the incense smoke heavenwards. This sends the essence of the *canang* up to the appropriate god and ensures that he comes down immediately to enjoy it. Once the essence has been extracted, the *canang* loses its holiness and is left to rot.

In the run-up to festivals and celebrations, the women of each *banjar* band together to create great towers of fruit and rice cakes, tiny rice-dough figurines and banners woven from palm fronds. The most dramatic of these are the magnificent **banten**, built up around the trunk of a young banana tree, up to 3m high. *Banten* cannot be reused, but once they've done service at the temple they can be dismantled and eaten by the families who donated them.

On the occasion of major island-wide festivals, such as Galungan-Kuningan, or at the Balinese New Year, Nyepi, Bali's villages get decked out with special banners and ornamental poles, designed to attract the attention of the deities living on Gunung Agung and to invite them onto the local streets. The banners, known as **lamak**, are amazing ornamental mats, often up to 3m long and woven in bold symbolic patterns from fresh green banana leaves. The most common design centres round the **cili** motif, a stylized female figure thought to represent the rice goddess Dewi Sri, with a body formed of simple geometric shapes and wearing a spiky headdress. Seven days before the great Galungan festival begins, special bamboo poles, or **penyor**, are erected along the streets of every village, each one bowed down with intricately woven garlands of dried flowers and palm leaves, which arch gracefully over the roadway. Attached to the *penyor* are symbolic leafy tassels, and offerings of dried paddy sheaves and coconut shells.

Lombok and Islam

Indonesia has the largest **Muslim** population in the world, and almost ninety percent of its population follow the faith. On Lombok, eighty-five percent of the islanders are Muslim, and most of the remainder are Balinese Hindus. A tiny minority of Lombok's Muslims adhere to **Wetu Telu** (see page 258) but as it is not officially recognized, numbers of followers are unknown.

On Lombok, most women dress modestly, wearing a *hijab* (headscarf which covers the head and chest, called *jilbab* in Indonesia), but may combine this with anything from Arabian-style ankle-length robes to tight-fitting jeans. The centre and east of the island are more conservative and devout, but even here you'll see some women without head-coverings and relatively few with their entire body covered. The **mosque** is the centre of the Muslim faith, and prayers on Friday at noon pretty much empty the villages of men (women often do not attend this service). Those planning to visit a mosque should be aware of the expected etiquette (see page 38). Many new, extremely grand concrete mosques are under construction throughout the island and driving around the interior you'll be regularly stopped by bucket-shakers asking for donations for mosque renovations. Thousands of islanders every year manage to afford the many millions of rupiah needed for a pilgrimage to Mecca that's required by Islam.

It's generally accepted that **Islam came to Indonesia** via Arab traders in north Sumatra, becoming established there by the end of the thirteenth century. By the seventeenth century Islam had reached Lombok through traders arriving from Sumbawa. Traditionally, the arrival of Islam in **Java** is thought to have more exotic roots, brought by nine fourteenth-century Islamic saints or *wali sanga*, one of whom is believed to be buried near Rembitan in southern Lombok.

The most influential modern-day **Islamic social organization** on Lombok is Nahdlatul Wathan, which was founded in east Lombok by Maulana Sueikh (popularly known as Guru Pancor) in Pancor in 1953. It now runs madrasas (Islamic colleges) throughout Indonesia and at one time had many adherents among government officials. However, after the deaths of Suharto and Maulana, its influence has waned due to internal disputes. Interestingly, the former provincial governor, Zainul Majdi (popularly known as Guru Bajang, or "Young Teacher"), is Guru Pancor's grandson.

Traditional music and dance

Music and dance play an essential part in daily Balinese life, and as a visitor you can't fail to experience them, either at a special tourist show, in rehearsal or at a temple festival. Ubud and its neighbouring villages have long had a reputation for their superb dance troupes and gamelan orchestras, and villagers supplement their incomes by doing regular shows in temple courtyards and village compounds. Although not exactly authentic – most shows comprise a medley of highlights from the more dramatic temple dances – the quality is generally high and spectators are given English-language synopses. Ubud is also the place to take lessons in the performing arts. To see wholly authentic performances you'll need to find out about imminent temple festivals or attend rehearsals, most of which take place in the local *banjar* after sundown; you'll probably be welcome to watch. Lombok also has a vibrant tradition of music and dance, rarely witnessed by casual visitors to the island, since it's associated almost exclusively with religious practices.

Balinese performing arts

Traditionally, **Balinese** dancers and musicians have always learnt their craft from the experts in their village and by imitating other performers. Since the 1960s, however, arts students have also had the option of attending a government-run high school and college dedicated to the performing arts. Denpasar's month-long **Bali Arts Festival** (see page 32) showcases the best in the performing arts, staging both new and traditional works by professional arts graduates, village groups and international artists.

Balinese gamelan music

Bali's traditional music is **gamelan**, a jangly clashing of syncopated sounds described by the writer Miguel Covarrubias as being like "an oriental ultra-modern Bach fugue, an astounding combination of bells, machinery and thunder." The highly structured compositions are produced by a group of twenty-five or more musicians playing a variety of bronze percussion instruments – gongs, metallophones and cymbals – with a couple of optional wind and stringed instruments and two drums. All gamelan music is written for instruments tuned either to a five- or (less commonly) a seven-tone scale, and most is performed at an incredible speed: one study found that each instrumentalist played an average of seven notes per second.

"Gamelan" is derived from the Javanese word for striking bronze instruments with a mallet, and the music probably came over from Java around the fourteenth century. The Balinese adapted it to suit their own personality, and now the sounds of the Javanese and Balinese gamelan are distinctive even to the untrained ear. Where Javanese gamelan music is restrained and rather courtly, Balinese is loud and flashy, boisterous and speedy, full of dramatic stops and starts. This modern Balinese style, known as **gong kebyar** (*gong* means orchestra, *kebyar* translates, aptly, as lightning flashes), has been around since the early 1900s, emerging at a time of great political upheaval when the status of Bali's royal houses was irreparably dented by Dutch colonial aggression. Until then, Bali's music had been as palace-oriented as Javanese gamelan, but in 1915 village musicians from northern Bali gave a public performance in the new *kebyar* style,

DISCOGRAPHY OF TRADITIONAL MUSIC

All the following are available to download or order. Alternatively, try any of the tourist CD shops on Bali or Ganesha Books in Ubud (http://ganeshabooksbali.com).

Angklung 1 Sidarkarya (Maharani; http://bali-maharani.com). Ceremonial classics played by a small, light, processional gamelan orchestra.

Bali: Gamelan and Kecak (http://discogs.com). A fine cross-section, including *gong kebyar, gender wayang*, Kecak and *genggong*.

Bali-Balinese Music of Lombok (http://farsidemusic.com). From the Smithsonian Folkways collection.

Dancers of Bali (http://discogs.com). Gamelan played by an ensemble from Peliatan village (1952).

Gamelan Semar Pegulingan: The Heavenly Orchestra of Bali (CMP; http://discogs.com). Sonorous recording of the gentle, older gamelan from Kamasan.

Jegog: The Rhythmic Power of Bamboo (MCM; http://discogs.com). Fast-paced music from western Bali played on **jegog,** gamelan sets fashioned from bamboo.

and the trend spread like wildfire, with whole orchestras turning their instruments in to be melted down and recast in the new, more exuberant, timbres.

Gamelan orchestras are an essential part of village life. Every *banjar* that can afford to buy a set of instruments has its own *seka* or **music club**, and there are said to be 1500 active *gong kebyar* on the island. In most communities, the *seka* is open only to men (the all-female gamelan of Peliatan is a rare exception) but welcomes players between the ages of eight and eighty. There's special *gong* music for every occasion – for sacred and secular dances, cremations, *odalan* festivities and *wayang kulit* shows – but players never learn from scores (few *gong* compositions are ever notated), preferring instead to have it drummed into them by repetitive practice. Whatever the occasion, *gong* players always dress in the ceremonial uniform of their music club, and make appropriate blessings and ritual offerings. Like dancers, musicians are acutely conscious of their role as entertainers of the gods.

Although the *gong kebyar* is by far the most popular style of music and orchestra in Bali, there are more than twenty different ensemble variations. The smallest is the four-piece **gender wayang**, which traditionally accompanies the *wayang kulit* shadow-play performances; the largest is the old-fashioned classical Javanese-style orchestra comprising fifty instruments, known as the **gamelan gong**. Most gamelan instruments are huge and far too heavy to be easily transported, so many *banjar* also possess a portable orchestra known as a **gamelan angklung**, designed around a set of miniature four-keyed metallophones, for playing in processions and at cremations or seashore ceremonies. There are also a few "bamboo orchestras", particularly in western Bali, where they're known as **gamelan joged bumbung** and **gamelan jegog**, composed entirely of bamboo instruments such as split bamboo tubes, marimbas and flutes.

Traditional dance-dramas of Bali

Most Balinese **dance-dramas** have evolved from **sacred rituals**, and are still performed at religious events, with full attention given to the devotional aspects. Before the show, a *pemangku* sprinkles the players and the performance area with holy water, and many performances open with a Pendet, or welcome dance, intended for the gods. The exorcist Barong-Rangda dramas continue to play a vital function in village **spiritual practices**, and the Baris dance re-enacts the traditional offering up of weapons by village warriors to the gods to invest them with supernatural power. Some of the more secular dance-dramas tell ancient and **legendary stories**, many of them adapted from the epic Hindu morality tales, the *Ramayana* and the *Mahabharata* (see page 311), which came from India more than a thousand years ago. Others are based on **historical**

events, embellishing the romances and battles of the royal courts of Java and Bali between the tenth and the fourteenth centuries.

There are few professional **dancers** in Bali; most performers don costumes and make-up only at festival times or for tourist shows. Dancers learn by imitation and repetition and personal expression has no place, but the skilful execution of traditional moves is much admired and trained dancers enjoy a high status.

Female dancers keep their feet firmly planted on the ground, their legs and hips encased in restrictive sarongs that give them a distinctive forward-angled posture. They express themselves through a vocabulary of controlled **angular movements** of the arms, wrists, fingers, neck and, most beguilingly, the eyes. Each pose and gesture derives from a movement observed in the natural rather than the human world. Thus, a certain type of flutter of the hand may be a bird in flight, a vigorous rotation of the forearms the shaking of water from an animal's coat. Dressed in pantaloons or hitched-up sarongs, the **male dancers** are much more energetic, emphasizing their manliness by opening shoulders and limbs outwards, keeping their knees bent and their heads high.

Most dramas are performed either within a temple or palace compound. The **costumes and masks** give immediate clues to the identity of each character – and the action that is to follow. Some are performed in a combination of contemporary Bahasa Indonesia and the ancient literary Kawi language, while others stick to modern speech, perhaps with a few humorous English phrases thrown in for the tourists.

Baris

The **Baris** or **Warrior Dance** is most commonly performed as a solo by a strutting young man who cuts an impressive figure in a gilded brocade cloak of ribboned pennants. He enacts a young warrior's preparation for battle, goading himself into a courageous mood, trying out his martial skills, showing pride at his calling and then expressing a whole series of emotions, much of it through his eyes.

Barong-Rangda dramas

Featuring the most spectacular costumes of all the Balinese dances, the **Barong-Rangda dramas** are also among the most sacred and important. Essentially a dramatization of the eternal conflict between good and evil, they take various forms but nearly always serve as ritualized exorcisms.

The mythical widow-witch character **Rangda** represents the forces of evil, and her costume and mask present a frightening spectacle. The **Barong** is much more lovable, a shaggy-haired creature with bug-eyes and a mischievous grin, a cross between a pantomime horse and a Chinese dragon. The Barong Ket (lion) is his most common persona, but you might also see Barong Macan (tiger), Barong Bangkal (wild boar) and Barong Celeng (pig). All Rangda and Barong **masks** are invested with great sacred power and treated with extreme respect.

Barong-Rangda dramas can be self-contained, as in the Calonarang, or just one symbolic episode in the middle of a well-known story. Whatever the context, the format tends to be similar. Rangda is always called upon by a character who wants to cause harm (unrequited love is a common cause). She generally sends a minion to wage the first battles, and is then forced to appear herself when the opposition calls in the Barong, the defender of the good. In this final confrontation, the Barong enters first, occasionally joined by a monkey who teases him and plays tricks. Suddenly, Rangda appears, fingernails first, from behind the central gateway. Flashing her magic white cloth, she harasses the Barong, stalking him at every turn. When the Barong looks to be on his last legs, a group of village men rush in to his rescue, but are entranced by Rangda's magic and stab themselves instead of her. A priest quickly enters before any real injury is inflicted. The series of confrontations continues, and the drama ends in a typically Balinese stalemate: the forces of good and evil remain as strong and vital as ever, ready to clash again in the next bout.

THE MAHABHARATA

Like its companion piece the **Ramayana**, the **Mahabharata** is an epic moral narrative of Hindu ethics that came to Indonesia from India in the eleventh century. Written during the fourth century AD by the Indian poet Vyasa, the original poem is phenomenally long – more than a hundred thousand verses. The **Balinese version** is translated into the ancient poetic Kawi language written on sacred *lontar* books kept in the Gedong Kirtya library at Singaraja. Its most famous episodes are known to every Balinese and reiterated in paintings, sculpted reliefs, *wayang kulit* dramas and dances.

THE PANDAWAS AND THE KORAWAS

At the heart of the story is the conflict between two rival branches of the same family, the Pandawas and the Korawas, all of them descendants of various unions between the deities and the mortals. The five **Pandawa brothers** represent the side of virtue, morality and noble purpose, though they each have their own foibles. The eldest is **Yudhisthira**, a calm and thoughtful leader with a passion for justice, whose one vice – an insatiable love of gambling – nonetheless manages to land the brothers in trouble. Then comes **Bhima**, a strong, courageous and hot-headed fighter, whose fiery temper and earthy manner make him especially appealing to the Balinese. The third brother, **Arjuna**, is the real hero; not only is he a brave warrior and an expert archer, but he's also handsome, high-minded and a great lover. Arjuna's two younger brothers, the expert horseman **Nakula** and the learned **Sahadeva**, are twins. Their rivals are their cousins the **Korawas**, who number a hundred in all, and are led by the eldest male **Durodhana**, a symbol of jealousy, deviousness and ignoble behaviour.

AN EARLY EPISODE

An early episode in the Mahabharata tells how the Pandawa boys are forced by the usurping Korawas to give up their rightful claim to the throne. Banished to the mountains for a minimum of thirteen years, the Pandawas grow up determined to regain what is theirs. Meanwhile, both families engage in countless adventures, confrontations with gods and demons, long journeys, seductions and practical jokes. A particular favourite is the exploit known as **Bhima Swarga**, in which Bhima is dispatched to Hell to rescue the souls of his dead father and stepmother. While there, he witnesses all sorts of horrible tortures and punishments, many of which are graphically depicted on the ceilings of Semarapura's Kerta Gosa. When Bhima returns to earth with the souls of his relatives, he's immediately sent off to Heaven in search of the holy water needed to smooth his dead parents' passage there. This episode is known as **Bhima Suci** and features the nine directional gods, as well as a dramatic battle between Bhima and his own godly (as opposed to earthly) father, Bayu.

Finally, a full-scale battle is declared between the two sets of cousins. On the eve of the battle, Arjuna suddenly becomes doubtful about the morality of fighting his own family, and confides as much to his friend and charioteer Krishna. Actually an avatar of the Hindu god Wisnu, Krishna then launches into a long theological lecture, in which he explains to Arjuna that the action is the all-important factor, not the result, and that because Arjuna is of the warrior caste, his duty is to fight, to act in a manner that's appropriate to his destiny. This episode of the Mahabharata is known as the **Bhagavad Gita**, and encapsulates the core Hindu philosophy of caste, and the notions of karma and destiny. Duly persuaded, Arjuna joins his brothers in battle, and at the end of eighteen bloody days the Pandawa brothers are victorious.

The **Calonarang** is an embellished version of the Barong-Rangda conflict, grafted onto an ancient legend about the daughter of a witch queen whom no one will marry because they're scared of her mother. The witch queen Calonarang is a manifestation of Rangda who, furious at the lack of suitors for her daughter, demands that her followers wreak destruction in all the villages. This drama is acted out on a regular basis, whenever there are considered to be evil forces and impurities affecting the community, and sometimes the whole neighbourhood takes part, the men parading with hand-held *kulkul* drums and the women filing in to make offerings at the temple shrines.

There's also an unusual human version of the Barong, called **Barong Landung** ("Tall Barong"), which feature two huge puppets. The forbidding male puppet represents the malicious giant from Nusa Penida, Jero Gede; the far sweeter-looking female is the smiling Jero Luh. Together they act out a bawdy comic opera, which also has exorcist purposes.

Kecak

Sometimes called the **Monkey Dance** after the animals represented by the chorus, the **Kecak** gets its Balinese name from the hypnotic chattering sounds made by the a cappella choir. Chanting nothing more than "chak chak chak chak", the chorus of fifty or more men uses seven different rhythms to create the astonishing music that accompanies the drama. Bare-chested, and wearing lengths of black-and-white-check *kain poleng* cloth around their waists and a single red hibiscus behind the ear, the men sit cross-legged in five or six tight concentric circles. The **narrative** itself is taken from a core episode of the Ramayana, centring around the kidnap of Sita by the demon king Rawana, and is acted out in the middle of the chorus circle, with one or two narrators speaking for all the characters.

Although frequently attributed to the German artist and musician Walter Spies, the main creative force behind the Kecak was the famous Baris dancer **I Wayan Limbak**, who lived in Bedulu in Gianyar. In 1931, he developed the chants from the Sanghyang trance dances, in which the chorus chants the "chak chak chak" syncopation as part of the trance-inducing ritual, and created accompanying choreography to flesh out the episode from the Ramayana.

Legong

Undoubtedly the most refined of all the temple dances, the **Legong** is an acquired taste, characterized by the restrained, intricate weavings of arms, fingers, torsos and heads. It's always performed by three prepubescent girls who are bound tightly in sarongs and chest cloths of opulent green or pink, with gilded crowns filled with frangipani blossoms on their heads. The Legong is considered the acme of Balinese femininity and Legong dancers have always enjoyed a special status, a reputation that endures long after they retire at the onset of menstruation. In the past, many a Legong dancer has ended up as a raja's wife or, later, as an expatriate artist's muse.

The dance evolved from a highly sacred Sanghyang trance dance and takes several different forms. By far the most common is the **Legong Keraton** ("Dance of the Royal Court"), based on a classical twelfth-century tale from Java. It tells the story of King Laksem, who is holding a princess, Rangkesari, captive against her will. Rescue is on the way in the form of Prince Daha, who plans to wage battle against King Laksem. The princess tries to dissuade the king from going to war, but he sets off anyway. As he leaves he is attacked by a raven, an extremely bad omen, after which he duly loses the battle and is killed.

The **performance** begins with a solo dance by a court lady, known as the *condong* (dressed in pink and gold). She picks up two fans from the ground in anticipation of the arrival of the two *legong* (literally "dancer"). Dressed identically in bright green and gold, the two *legong* enact the story, adopting and swapping characters with no obvious distinction. The *condong* always returns as the raven, with pink wings attached to her costume. The final fatal battle is never shown on stage.

Sanghyang: trance dances

The **trance** state lies at the heart of traditional Balinese dance. In order to maintain the health of the village, the gods are periodically invited down into the temple to

THE RAMAYANA

Written in Sanskrit around the fifth century BC, the 24,000 verses that comprise the **Ramayana** have since fired the imaginations of writers, artists, dramatists and theologians right across Southeast Asia. Like the other great Hindu epic, the **Mahabharata**, the **Ramayana** has been translated into the classical Javanese Kawi language and transcribed on to sacred *lontar* texts.

GOOD AND EVIL

It's essentially a morality tale, a dramatization of the eternal conflict between the forces of good (*dharma*) and the forces of evil (*adharma*). The forces of good are represented by Rama and his friends. **Rama**, the hero, is a refined and dutiful young man, handsome, strong and courageous, who also happens to be an avatar of the god Wisnu. Rama's wife, **Sita**, epitomizes the Hindu ideals of womanhood – virtue, fidelity and love – while Rama's brother, **Laksmana**, is a symbol of fraternal loyalty and youthful courage. The other important member of the Rama camp is **Hanuman**, the general of the monkey army, a wily and athletic ape who is unfailingly loyal to his allies. On the opposing side, the forces of evil are mainly represented by the demon king **Rawana**, a lustful and devious leader whose retainers are giants and devils.

The story begins with Rama, the eldest son of the king, being banished to the forests for thirteen years, having been cheated out of his rightful claim to the throne by a scheming stepmother. Sita and Laksmana accompany him, and together the trio have various encounters with sages, giants and seductresses.

SITA'S ABDUCTION

The most crucial event in the epic is the **abduction of Sita** by Rawana, a crime that inspires the rather unwarlike Rama to wage battle against his enemy. A favourite subject for dances and carvings, the episode starts with Sita catching sight of a beautiful golden deer and imploring her husband Rama to catch it for her. The golden deer turns out to be a decoy planted by Rawana, and the demon king duly swoops down to abduct Sita as soon as Rama and Laksmana go off to chase the animal. The distraught Rama determines to get Sita back and, together with Laksmana, he sets off for Rawana's kingdom. En route he meets Hanuman, the monkey general, who agrees to sneak into Sita's room at Rawana's palace and **give her Rama's ring**. Eventually, Rama, Laksmana, Hanuman and his monkey army all arrive at Rawana's palace and, following a big battle, Sita is rescued and Rawana done away with.

help in the exorcism of evil and sickness-inducing spirits. The deities reveal themselves by possessing certain individuals, sometimes communicating through them with words, which may have to be interpreted by a priest, and sometimes taking over the whole physical being so that the medium is moved to dance or to perform astonishing physical feats. The chosen medium is put into a trance state through a combination of priestly chants and protective mantras, intoned exhortations by the a cappella choir, and great clouds of incense wafted heavenwards to attract the gods' attention. Trance dances are traditionally only performed when the village is suffering from a particularly serious bout of sickness or ill fortune – the versions that are reproduced at tourist shows have none of the spiritual dynamism of the real thing, though it is said that performers do sometimes slip into trance.

One of the most common trance dances is the **Sanghyang Dedari**, in which two young girls become possessed and perform a complicated duet with their eyes closed; though they have never learnt the steps, the girls usually perform in sync, sometimes for up to four hours. In the Sanghyang Dedari performed at tourist shows, however, the girls have almost certainly rehearsed the dance beforehand and probably do not enter a trance state at all. They wear the same tightly bound green and gold sarongs as the Legong dancers, and perform to the haunting backing vocals of an a cappella chorus of men and women.

In the **Sanghyang Jaran** (Horse Deity), one or more men are put into a trance state while the temple floor is littered with burning coconut husks. As they enter the trance, the men grab hold of wooden hobbyhorse sticks and then gallop frantically back and forth across the red-hot embers as if they were on real horses. The all-male Kecak chorus fuels the drama with energetic a cappella crescendos until, finally, the exhausted hobbyhorse riders are awoken by the priest.

Topeng: mask dances

In the **Topeng** or **Mask Dance**, the performer is possessed by the spirit of the mask (see page 136). Before every entrance, the Topeng actor sprinkles holy water on his mask and recites a mantra. Women never participate in Topeng: female roles are played by men.

Topeng **storylines** usually centre around popular folk tales or well-known historical episodes, and the characters are immediately recognizable. One of the most popular is the **Topeng Tua**, a touching solo in which an elderly retired first-minister recalls his time in the king's service. His mask is fringed with straggly white hair and beard, and his gait is frail and wavering. Another favourite tourist Topeng is the **Frog Dance** – performed to the evocative music of the Balinese jew's harp or *genggong* – which tells how a frog turns into a prince. In the **Jauk**, the soloist portrays a terrifying demon-king who leaps mischievously about the stage as if darting from behind trees and pouncing on unsuspecting villagers. His red or white mask has bulging eyes and a creepy smile and he flashes his long fingernails menacingly throughout.

Wayang kulit: shadow-puppet shows

Wayang kulit or **shadow-puppet shows** are typically staged as entertainment following weddings, cremations or temple *odalan*. The stories are often taken from *Mahabharata*, but improvisation and topical jokes keep the art alive and a skilled and witty *dalang* (puppeteer), nearly always a man, can attract huge crowds and keep them entertained into the early hours. The performance takes place behind a white cloth screen illuminated by flaming torches and may star as many as sixty different **wayang** (puppets), generally made from buffalo hide and mounted on a stick. Visitors can see the workshops of some well-known *dalang* in Sukawati.

Amazingly, the **dalang** not only manipulates each of his many *wayang* himself, but speaks for each one of them as well, displaying an impressive memory for lines and an extraordinary range of different voices. At the same time he also conducts the special four-piece orchestra, the *gender wayang*. Unsurprisingly, *dalang* are greatly revered and considered to have great spiritual power.

The torchlit **screen** represents the world in microcosm: the puppets are the humans that inhabit it, the torch represents the sun, and the *dalang* acts as god. Puppets representing good characters always appear to the right of the *dalang*; evil ones appear on his left. A leaf-shaped fan-like puppet, symbolizing the tree of life, marks centre stage and is used to indicate the end of a scene as well as to represent clouds, spirits and magical forces.

Lombok music and dance

Lombok has a rich heritage of music and dance. The indigenous Sasak traditions have been subject to many influences, both Hindu and Islamic, direct from Bali and Java, and through Buginese and Makassarese traders. The resulting melange of puppetry, poetry, song and dance is varied, but largely inaccessible to tourists. **Cultural shows**

are very rare, except during the annual **Senggigi Festival** (see page 251), held in September, but you may stumble across a wedding or other celebration.

Lombok's gamelan music

Lombok's traditional **gamelan** music is similar to Bali's, though some of the orchestras are different. The **gamelan gong Sasak** resembles the *gamelan gong*, but may be combined with the bamboo xylophones of the **gamelan grantang.** The **gamelan oncer** accompanies the Gendang Beleq ("Big Drum") dance.

Gamelan tawa-tawa has the usual gongs and drums accompanied by flutes and cymbals with the addition of *tawa-tawa*, small kettle drums that set the cadence of the music. **Gamelan barong tenkok** is almost the same except that one of the instruments is covered with a *barong* costume, representative of Barong's protective powers. Both are used In processions such as weddings and circumcision ceremonies.

At one period, over a century ago, staunch religious leaders on Lombok banned the use of bronze instruments as un-Islamic (this ban has since been lifted), and new types of gamelan began to appear. One example is **Gamelan rebana** which includes as many as twenty large-headed drums that mimic the traditional sound of gamelan music, but without the use of bronze instruments. Another type (very rarely seen today) is **gamelan klentang**, made up entirely of iron instruments.

Other musical ensembles that are seen on the island include **kecimol** and **cilokaq**, consisting of an oboe (*preret*), flutes, lutes, violins and drums, and are often played to accompany Sasak poetry.

Lombok's performance and martial arts

In contrast to the huge academic interest in Balinese performing arts, Sasak **dances** have been studied far less.

Of the various **public dances**, the **Gendang Beleq** was traditionally used to send off soldiers heading into battle and to welcome them home again. It is performed to the distinctive rhythm of two huge drums (*gendang*) with their players facing each other in confrontational poses. These days it is staged to welcome VIPs and for tourists. The **Batek Baris**, which is performed in Lingsar and elsewhere, has dancers wearing costumes mimicking Dutch army uniforms and carrying wooden rifles while they lead a procession to the sacred springs. At the Nyale Festival near Kuta the Putri Mandalika legend is re-enacted to large crowds (see page 264); the popular **Kemidi Rudat** retells the *Thousand and One Nights* stories, complete with colourful characters and clowns; the **Telek** is based on the tale of a princess who falls in love with a humble man; and the **Kayak Sando** (with masks) dramatizes the Panji stories from Java in which a prince undergoes numerous adventures while searching for his lost bride.

Local, village-based dances include the **Gandrung** of central Lombok, a demonstration of love performed by a solo female dancer who selects a man to join her, and the **Tandak Geroq**, staged in east Lombok to celebrate the end of the harvest. There are also **trance dances** such as the **Suling Dewa**, accompanied by flutes and song, which is particular to north Lombok and used to induce spirits to enter the local shaman and bless the village. The **Pepakon**, from east Lombok, causes the sick to become possessed so that their illness can be removed from them.

More a martial art than a performing art, but still a massive spectator draw, **peresean**, or **stickfighting**, involves two men attacking each other with long rattan canes, with only a goatskin shield to defend themselves. The aim is to draw blood to ensure a good harvest – and it's all for real, as the injuries show. Every schoolboy learns the *peresean* art and contests are staged between village teams. The best time to see a stickfight is on August 18, the day after Independence Day: Narmada, east of Mataram, and Kotaraja near Tetebatu are both well-known centres. You can also see *peresean* at the Senggigi Festival (see page 251).

Modern Balinese music

The last twenty years has seen an explosion in the popularity of modern Balinese music – in Bali itself, throughout Indonesia, and even abroad. Uniquely in Indonesia, Balinese musicians no longer need to go to Jakarta to make their name, but can use Bali as a gateway to national and international recognition. More and more relatively small local bands, musicians and DJs are now playing overseas without first hitting the big time in the Indonesian capital.

There are two main genres of modern Balinese music: **Balinesia**, in which indie Balinese artists sing in Indonesian or English, and **Balibali**, in which they sing in Balinese. Albums by musicians from both genres outsell their Western competition in Bali, and concerts are often as well attended as those of the major national (mainly Javanese) bands. The cultural impact of this boom has been significant. Instead of feeling marginalized and crowded out by Java, Balinese youth now have a channel through which they can express themselves and their disappointment with politics, corruption and environmental concerns. There is also a renewed pride in the Balinese language, whose "cool" status has been given a big boost by artists singing in Balinese.

The **indie scene** actively encourages creativity, especially in the young (a big contrast with the repressively conformist years under Suharto's rule), and has opened people's eyes to the possibility of doing something different from the Balinese norm. This is reflected in the trend for all things punk and alternative, from independent clothing shops (*distros*) selling original fashion and music-related paraphernalia, to chopper-style motorbikes and low-rider pushbikes.

Balinesia

Balinesia emerged in the mid-1980s with rock bands that favoured covers – AC/DC, Rainbow and Def Leppard were all popular in Bali – and drew large crowds.

But the Balinesia breakthrough came in 2003 when the first big Balinese band, punk-rock-styled **Superman Is Dead (SID)**, released their debut album, *Kuta Rock City*, with a major label, Sony Music Indonesia. They were the first Balinese band to make it big outside Bali and the first to record mostly in English (with about thirty percent of their songs in Indonesian). Having toured Australia, and participated in the legendary Warped Tour around the USA in 2009, they went on to break into the US Billboard chart.

Grunge band **Navicula** is the second-biggest Balinesia band on the island and one of the most successful grunge/alternative bands in Indonesia. Their focus on social and environmental issues and flower-power fashion style has them tagged as new hippies. Their *Tatap Muka* album is largely acoustic and was recorded at Ubud's Setia Darma museum.

Another star is virtuoso guitarist **Balawan** and his band, Batuan Ethnic Fusion. They skilfully combine jazz and Balinese music, using gamelan instruments, *kendang* (traditional drums) and bamboo flutes alongside guitars, modern drums and keyboards. A master of finger-tapping, Balawan is the only guitarist in Indonesia who plays a double-neck guitar with two independent hands (eight-finger touch style). He frequently performs overseas, mainly in Europe and Asia. Balawan is also involved in a Hindu/spiritual project called **Nyanyian Dharma**, in which he and other popular Balinese musicians sing in Sanskrit and promote peace and love around Indonesia and abroad.

One of Balawan's collaborators on Nyanyian Dharma is the increasingly recognized world music singer **Ayu Laksmi**. She began as a "lady rocker" in the late 1980s but has since embraced jazz fusion. Her 2011 world music album, *Svara Semesta*, on which she sang in five languages – including Sanskrit, Kawi and Balinese – was a nationwide hit and rated as one of Indonesia's best albums of the year.

Other notable local music artists include pioneer rockabillies **The Hydrant**, who have a significant fanbase in Bali and Java and are an exciting band to see live, with European tours under their belt. There's also the amazing trumpeter **Rio Sidik**, "psychobilly" band **Suicidal Sinatra** (mixing punk and rockabilly) and punk collective **Scared of Bums**. They are all massive in Bali and have enjoyed a similarly positive reception nationwide – especially Rio, who, with his world music band **Saharadja**, has already travelled the world and can sometimes still be heard playing in Kuta, Seminyak and Ubud.

Balibali

The **Balibali** phenomenon is unique in Indonesia: its artists sing exclusively in Balinese, and the music tends to be edgy and controversial. Its appeal is not as limited as you might expect, as there are tightknit Balinese communities also in Lombok, Kalimantan, Sumatra and Sulawesi. Interest in Balibali peaked between about 2003 and 2008, but its big-name artists still attract significant audiences.

DISCOGRAPHY

Modern Balinese music is hard to find outside Indonesia, but within Bali the best sources are local music shops, *distros* and streaming (http://discogs.com). The following are popular albums from major local artists.

PUNK ROCK/ALTERNATIVE ROCK

The Hydrant *Bali Bandidos* (Balinesia; a few lyrics in English)
Lolot *Pejalan Idup* (Balibali)
Nanoe Biroe *M3tamorforia* (Balibali)
Painful by Kisses *The Curse of…* (Balinesia; some lyrics in English)
Superman Is Dead *Sunset di Tanah Anarki* (Balinesia; Sony Music Indonesia)

GRUNGE/METAL

Navicula *Salto* (Balinesia; some lyrics in English)
Parau *Somatoform* (Balinesia; a few lyrics in English)

JAZZ/WORLD MUSIC

Ayu Laksmi *Svara Semesta* (Balinesia; some lyrics in English)
Riwin *My Sexy Life* (Balinesia; a few lyrics in English)

REGGAE

Joni Agung & Double T *Melalung* (Balibali)

HIP-HOP

XXX *Sangut Delem* (Balibali)

ELECTRONICA

Discotion Pill *Amphetamine* (Balinesia; lyrics mostly in English)

POP

Dek Ulik *Rindu Ngantosang Janji* (Balibali)

Balibali began with folk-style bands in the 1960s and came of age in the mid-1980s, when several artists released pop-rock-style albums in Balinese and began writing more risqué lyrics, perhaps due to new Western influences. But the big shake-up came in 2003 when Lolot 'N Band released *Gumine Mangkin*. **Lolot**, the singer, was a complete original of the genre with his punk-rock attitude and confrontational Balinese lyrics, totally unlike the plaintive style common to the genre. He invented so-called alternative rock in Bali and pushed the boundaries with songs such as *Bangsat* (Bastard), a social protest anthem against the grasping Indonesian authorities.

Nanoe Biroe is another Balibali rock star, commanding a legion of fanatical followers known as "Beduda" who see him as a hero, or even a prophet. All over Bali, you'll come across young men wearing "President of Beduda" T-shirts, bearing a Nanoe version of the famous Che Guevara silhouette. "Beduda" is Balinese for dung beetle and so the dreadlocked Nanoe has cleverly positioned himself as the leader of marginalized people.

But perhaps the biggest of them all are **XXX,** Balibali's first hip-hop band. Their unique approach, Balinese rapping and great voices have made them an enduring act. The island's top reggae artists are **Joni Agung & Double T**; their records go down well all over Bali and Joni is a local celebrity. Pop diva **Dek Ulik** is especially popular with Balinese women. Her 2005 debut album, *Rindu Ngantosang Janji*, sold more than fifty thousand copies, a first for a Balinese female soloist.

Venues and festivals

The main live music **venues** for Balinese bands are in Kuta and Denpasar, and are detailed in the relevant accounts in the Guide. For gig **listings** check the free fortnightly English-language magazine *The Beat* (http://thebeatbali.com). You can also hear Balinesia and Balibali artists on the many dedicated local music radio stations.

Modern music **festivals** in Indonesia used to depend solely on corporate sponsorship but now get a little more support from regional government. Among the highlights, **Soundrenaline** always involves lots of local bands. The annual Denfest (**Denpasar Festival**), held in downtown Denpasar (Dec 28–31), has a special stage presenting the best local bands, while **Kuta Karnival** (on Kuta Beach) is usually held in October (see page 32) and features a stimulating mix of Bali and national band line-ups.

Village life and traditions

Most people on Bali and Lombok live in villages. People employed in the cities or tourist resorts may well commute and even those whose villages are far away still identify with them and return for particular festivals each year.

Balinese village layout

Orientation in Bali does not correspond to the compass points of north, south, east and west. The main directions are **kaja** (towards Gunung Agung, dwelling place of the gods) and **kelod** (away from the mountain). The other directions are *kangin* (from where the sun rises), and its opposite, *kauh* (where the sun sets).

All Balinese villages are oriented *kaja–kelod* and the locations of the three village temples, *pura dalem*, *pura puseh* and *pura desa*, are determined on this axis.

House compounds

Each traditional Balinese **house compound** is built within a confining wall. When a son of the family marries, his wife usually moves into his compound, so there are frequently several generations living together, each with their own sleeping quarters, but otherwise sharing the same facilities. Most domestic activities take place outside or in the partial shelter of **bale** (raised platforms with a roof). The different structures of the compound are believed to reflect the human body: the family shrine (*Sanggah Kemulan*) is the head, the *bale* are the arms, the courtyard is the navel, the kitchen and rice barn are the legs and feet, and the rubbish tip, located along with the pig pens outside the *kelod* wall, is the anus. The Traditional Balinese House museum in Tabanan is a good example of a typical compound.

TYPICAL BALINESE HOUSE COMPOUND

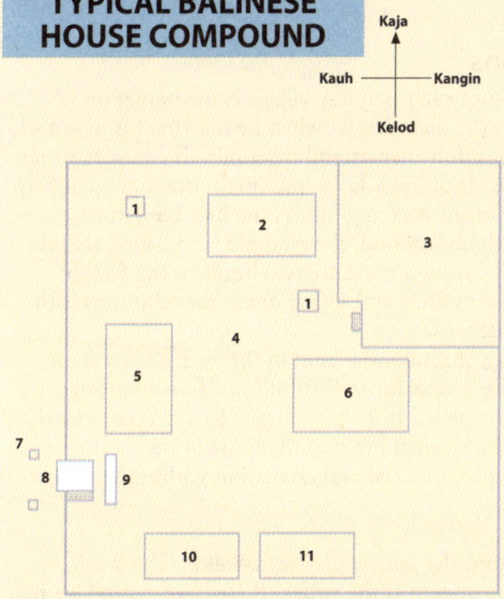

Note: House compounds in the north of the island are a mirror image of this

1. tugu and **pengijeng** Small shrines.

2. bale daja Pavilion of the head of the household and storehouse for family heirlooms.

3. Sanggah Kemulan Family temple, in the *kaja–kangin* corner, with the main shrine dedicated to the souls of the ancestors.

4. natah Open courtyard.

5. bale dauh Guest pavilion.

6. bale dangin Used for ceremonies such as marriage and tooth-filing.

7. apit lawang Gate shrines.

8. lawang Entrance, ideally situated in the *kauh* wall towards the *kelod* end.

9. aling-aling Short wall inside the entrance to prevent evil spirits from entering.

10. paon Kitchen, usually towards the *kelod–kauh* corner.

11. lumbung Rice storage barn.

Initially all prospective house-builders consult an expert in the Balinese calendar to choose auspicious days for buying land and beginning construction. The architect or master builder (*undagi*) follows rules laid down in ancient texts, taking a series of **measurements** from the body of the **head of the household** and using these to calculate the exact dimensions of the compound. Before building starts, offerings are placed in the foundations so that work will proceed smoothly. When the building work is finished, further ceremonies must take place before the compound can be occupied. The final ceremony is the **melaspas**, an inauguration ritual that "brings the building to life".

Lombok's Sasak villages

Balinese people living on Lombok retain their traditional house compounds, as do the Bugis people, who have settled along Lombok's eastern and southern coasts and live in wooden houses constructed on tall piles. The indigenous **Sasak** people of Lombok also have their own architectural style.

Traditional Sasak villages, such as those at Segenter and Senaru in northern Lombok, and Rembitan and Sade in southern Lombok, are walled enclosures, with a gateway that is closed at night. **Houses** are made of bamboo with a thatch roof that slopes almost to the ground and floors of mud and dung; they may have none or only a few windows, with a veranda on at least one side. Traditionally, the cooking hearth and eating area are inside the house; a walled-off room, the *inan bale*, is used for storage but is also the place where newlyweds spend their first night.

The symbol of Lombok, the **lumbung rice barn**, with its bonnet-shaped roof, is a feature in the south of the island. They are built in rows, on four piles, with a thatch roof and a single opening high up. A circular wooden disc, the *jelepreng*, on each post stops rats climbing up to the rice. Underneath each post, old Chinese coins (*kepeng*) are buried for good luck and protection.

Thatched *lumbung*-style cottages have become wildly popular as (faux-traditional) tourist bungalows in the Gili islands, and even in Bali and Lembongan, though many hoteliers equip them with a/c and mod cons rather than devices to keep out rodents.

Balinese Village organizations

The smallest unit of social organization in each Balinese village is the **banjar** or neighbourhood. Each adult male joins the local *banjar* when he marries; his wife and children are also members but only the adult men attend meetings. The largest *banjar* in Denpasar may have five hundred heads of household, the small rural ones just fifty.

Typically, the *banjar* meets monthly in the meeting house, the **bale banjar**, to discuss anything of relevance to the neighbourhood, for example land issues, temple ceremonies or the gamelan orchestra. Although there are two heads of the *banjar* (*kliang adat*, who looks after customary matters and *kliang dinas*, the administration head), all decisions are reached by consensus.

The *banjar* has considerable authority. If residential land in the area is left vacant for a period of time, it will revert to the *banjar* for redistribution. If members neglect their duties, they can be fined or even expelled from the village. This is a particularly powerful threat among people where communal life is at the heart of their existence. Expulsion also means the loss of the right to burial and cremation within the village.

The subak

Much of village daily life revolves around the *sawah*, or wet **ricefields**. The local organization controlling each irrigation system is the **subak**; these have existed on Bali since the ninth century, and are made up of all the farmers who use the water in that system. The maintenance of the irrigation system, along with complex planning that ensures every farmer gets an equal share of water, is coordinated by the *kliang subak*, a priest in the regional water temple. Any *subak* with plans that have a wider impact or cause potential conflict with another *subak* – such as changing dry fields to wet – consults the *kilang subak* and, ultimately, the **Jero Gede**, chief priest of Pura Ulun Danu Batur, whose decision is final.

The **Subak Museum** is well worth a visit for more information on this unique aspect of Balinese life. In 2012, UNESCO added the Balinese *subak* system to its World Heritage list as being of outstanding value to humanity. Interestingly, attempts to duplicate the *subak* organization in other countries have all failed. It works in Bali due to communal spirit and belief in the Tri Hita Karana philosophy of the relationship between humans, the earth and the gods.

Balinese life-cycle celebrations

On **Bali**, rituals and ceremonies are carried out at important points in an individual's life for purification and to ensure sufficient spiritual energy for good health.

The first life-cycle ritual, **pegedong-gedongan**, takes place about six months after conception, when the foetus has a human form, and emphasizes the hope for a long, healthy life. Subsequent **birth rituals** focus on the placenta, which is buried inside a coconut wrapped in sacred white cloth near the gateway of the parents' household. A rock is placed over the spot to protect it, and regular offerings are made there.

Following the birth, the parents and child are regarded as unclean (*sebel*), and cannot participate in religious practices. For the mother and baby, this lasts 42 days; for the father, it lasts until the baby's umbilical cord drops off, when the **kepus pungsed** ritual is carried out. The cord is wrapped in cloth, placed in an offering shaped like a dove and suspended over the baby's bed, along with a small shrine dedicated to Sanghyang Panca Kumara, son of Siwa, who is invoked as the child's protector. There are further ceremonies at twelve and 42 days and then, after 105 days, it's time for **telubulan**, a large, elaborate ceremony at which the child is named and may be given an amulet to guard against evil spirits.

The child's **first birthday**, *oton*, occurs after 210 days – a Balinese year in the *pawukon* calendar. This is the first occasion that the child is allowed contact with the ground, and it may be accompanied by a ritual hair-cutting ceremony. The next ceremony, **maketus**, takes place when the child's milk teeth fall out. Sanghyang Panca Kumara, who has been protecting the child since birth, is relieved of his duties, and the child is now guarded by the family ancestors.

Tooth filing

The **tooth-filing ritual**, *matatah*, which preferably takes place before marriage, is a huge celebration with guests, music and lavish offerings. It is considered vital, and the elderly, and even the dead, have been known to have their teeth filed if they have never had it done previously. The aim is to remove coarse behaviour from the person and rid them of lust, greed, anger, drunkenness, confusion and jealousy, in order that they will lead a better life and be assured a more favourable reincarnation. The upper canine teeth or fangs and the four teeth in between are filed down.

Marriage

There are three **marriage** options. Although rarely done these days – especially in cities – arranged marriages still occur. However, the optimum method is *mamadik*, when the marriage is agreed between the two sets of parents and a huge financial outlay for lavish ceremonies is involved. Much more common is *ngerorod* or *malaib* – elopement. The man and woman run off and spend the night together, not so secretly that nobody knows, but with sufficient subterfuge that the girl's parents can pretend outrage. The following morning the couple are married in a private ceremony. More elaborate rituals and a reception may be hosted later the same day by the boy's parents. The girl's parents will not be invited as there is supposed to be bad feeling between the two sides. However, three days later the two sets of parents meet at the *ketipat bantal* ceremony and are reconciled.

Cremation

The ceremony that visitors to Bali are most likely to witness is **cremation** (*pengabenan* or *palebonan*). The Balinese believe that the soul inhabits a temporary receptacle, the body, during life on earth. After death, the body must be returned to the five elements of solid, liquid, energy, radiance and ether to ready the soul for reincarnation.

Following death, the body is usually buried, sometimes for years, while the **preparations** for the cremation are made. Poorer families often share in the cremation ceremonies of wealthier families as costs are crippling. The entire extended family and *banjar* is involved in preparations and all must be fed by the host family until the work has been completed. Animals are slaughtered, holy water acquired and gamelan, dancers and puppet shows organized. An animal-shaped, highly decorated sarcophagus is built to hold the body. The cremation tower, representing the Balinese universe, supported by the turtle, Bedawang Nala, and the two *naga*, Basuki and Anantaboga, is also built, with tiers similar to the roofs on the *meru* in temples. A *bale* at the base of the tiers houses the body or an effigy of the dead person.

Accompanied by the bamboo **gamelan angklung**, the sarcophagus and cremation tower are carried to the cemetery and twirled around many times en route to ensure that the soul is confused and cannot return home to cause mischief for the family. If the deceased has been buried, the cleansed body (or bones) is placed in the sarcophagus. At the cremation ground the sarcophagus and tower are burned and the ashes taken to the sea or to a stream that will carry them to the ocean. Further ceremonies are needed after three days and twelve days to release the soul to heaven, finishing with the *nyagara-gunung* ritual when the family take offerings to important sea and mountain temples.

Sasak life-cycle ceremonies

Some of the ceremonies performed in Sasak communities on **Lombok** are associated with the more orthodox adherents to Islam, while others are associated only with Wetu Telu followers (see page 258). The Wetu Telu **birth ceremony**, *adi kaka,* is similar to the Balinese one involving the placenta. A few days after birth, the **naming ceremony** of *buang au* or *malang mali* takes place. After the baby is born, burning charcoal is placed under its bed for warmth; when the charcoal has turned to ash (*au*) it is ritually disposed of (*buang*). A **hair-cutting ceremony**, *ngurisang*, is also obligatory for a young child, although the age it takes place varies between six months and twelve years. It is a cleansing ceremony to prepare children for later coming of age rituals.

TRADITIONAL HEALERS

Known as *balian* in Bali and *dukun* in Lombok, **traditional healers** are a vital adjunct to Western medicine on the islands. On both islands, illlness is believed to stem from a lack of balance between the patient and the spirit world; for example, a patient may have paid insufficient respect to a god. There are many different kinds of *balian* including the practical and medical like *balian tulang* (bonesetters), *balian manak* (midwives) and *balian apun* (masseurs). More spiritual healers include *balian taksu*, mediums who enter a trance to communicate with the spirit world and *balian kebal*, who work with charms and spells, making love potions and magical amulets to protect the wearer against spiritual attack. *Balian* are also consulted to find out which ancestral souls have been reincarnated in the bodies of newborn babies, and which days are auspicious for certain events.

The most important ceremony for a Muslim boy is his **circumcision** (*nyunatang*), which often takes place in the Muslim month of the Prophet Muhammad's birthday, accompanied by much ceremony and feasting.

There are three **marriage** options in Sasak culture: a marriage arranged by the families, one between cousins, or an elopement. Whichever occurs, the man's family pays a price for the bride, who moves to their house. During the wedding ceremony, the couple are often carried on a sedan chair and accompanied by a gamelan orchestra.

Under the laws of Islam, the dead are **buried**, rather than cremated. According to Wetu Telu custom, the dead are ritually washed and wrapped in a white sarong, carried to the cemetery and buried with the head towards Mecca. A death in the family sets in motion a whole cycle of rituals. The most important is **deena nitook**, seven days after the death, **nyatus** after a hundred days, and the final event, **nyiu**, a thousand days after death, when the grave is sprinkled with holy water, commemorative stones are placed on it and offerings such as toothbrushes and clothes are made to ensure the deceased is comfortable in heaven.

The impact of tourism

Debates about the effects of tourism on Bali and Lombok have been running for almost a century. In the 1920s and 1930s, soon after the first tourists arrived, some local commentators decried visitors who took photographs of bare-breasted Balinese women and damaged island roads with their motor cars. In fact, nostalgia for a more peaceful Bali is even older; a Javanese mystic who visited Bali in 1500 complained that it was no longer quiet enough to practise meditation.

The history of tourism

Tourism in Bali effectively started in 1924 when KPM, the Dutch Royal Packet Navigation Company, established weekly **steamship services** connecting Bali with Batavia (Jakarta), Singapore, Semarang, Surabaya and Makassar, with visitors to Bali using the government rest-houses dotted around the island. Bali received 213 visitors that year, and the numbers, with a few blips, have continued to rise ever since; the island had almost five million foreign visitors in 2016, plus similar numbers of Indonesian tourists.

In 1928, KPM opened the island's first **hotel**, the *Bali Hotel* in Denpasar; an air link between Denpasar and Surabaya began in 1933; a daily ferry between Java and Gilimanuk launched in 1934; and the airport at Tuban opened in 1938. By the 1930s several thousand tourists were visiting Bali each year, some of whom settled there. Artists, such as Walter Spies and Miguel Covarrubias, and anthropologists, including Margaret Mead and Gregory Bateson, focused on the artistic and religious aspects of Balinese life and, through their writing, painting, photography and filmmaking enhanced the worldwide image of Bali as a paradise.

The Japanese occupation during World War II, followed by the struggle for independence, halted the tourist influx, but under President Sukarno and later President Suharto, tourism **promotion** became official government policy. The inauguration of **Ngurah Rai Airport** in 1968 marked the beginning of mass tourism; it is now Indonesia's second-busiest airport after Jakarta.

In 1972, the government-owned **Bali Tourist Development Corporation (BTDC)** was formed and built the **Nusa Dua** resort aimed at closeting high-spending tourists away from local people on in-arable land. However, the tourists didn't all stay hidden away. By the 1970s, **Kuta** had become a surfing hub and local villagers turned their homes into small hotels. Not everyone was happy; the surfers were labelled as hippies, drug addicts and practitioners of free love, and the negative impact of tourism on the island was contemplated fearfully.

There was also concern about the **over-commercialization** of arts and culture for tourist consumption. Dances, for example, were shortened and changed to suit tourist tastes; it was a rare visitor who could enjoy a five-hour performance. In 1979 the annual Bali Arts Festival was inaugurated to encourage the Balinese to appreciate their own culture.

Nevertheless, tourism continued to advance. In 1971, about 33 percent of the island's income was derived from tourism; by 2016, it was approaching 70 per cent, boosted by the success of the film *Eat Pray Love* and booming numbers from China, Malaysia and Australia. Bali is one of Indonesia's wealthiest provinces, with average income exceeding that on neighbouring Java.

In 2017 the Bali Tourist Development Corporation was rebranded Indonesia Tourist Development Corporation (ITDC) and charged with fashioning land in Lombok called Mandalika (which includes Kuta, Seger and Tanjung Aan beaches) into a Nusa Dua-type resort area.

The global Covid-19 pandemic in 2020-21 strongly affected Indonesia, including Bali. It had a devastating effect on the tourism industry with just 1.07 million foreign tourists arriving in 2020 and only 51 in 2021, compared to 6.28 million international arrivals in 2019. While Bali's international airport only reopened in February 2022 after the pandemic closure, tourist arrivals in 2024 have already overtaken pre-pandemic figures and are on track to reach 6.5 million foreign tourists in 2025.

Brand Bali

Bali has an extremely high **global profile** and is regularly voted one of the top island destinations in the world. This image, however, was sorely tested by the terrorist attacks of 2002 and 2005. Without Bali's high profile and the international interest in the island, it is unlikely that it would have held any interest for the bombers.

Following the Kuta bombing on October 12, 2002, the island emptied of tourists overnight. However, when it was discovered that the bombers were Muslims, the Hindu population of Bali made no moves against Muslim communities or individuals on the island. Many Balinese interpreted the bombing as an indication that the gods were angry and on November 15, 2002, a huge purification ceremony was carried out. The annual commemoration ceremony has always been an interfaith service.

With an estimated eighty percent of the population relying on tourism for their living in some way or another, the economy nosedived. By June 2003, a World Bank report estimated that the average Balinese income had dropped by forty percent. The fate of Lombok, inextricably linked to that of its more famous neighbour, mirrored Bali's exactly. However, within a year there were signs of recovery aided by messages to the world that Bali was safe and needed tourists to return and support the island. When bombers struck again on October 1, 2005, in Kuta and Jimbaran, tourist arrivals plummeted again. Still, once again, Bali recovered and tourist numbers now far exceed those before the bombs. Indeed, such is Bali's worldwide appeal that the challenge is now managing the millions, a crisis of popularity shared with the likes of Venice, Rome and Barcelona in Europe or Angkor Wat in Cambodia.

Economy versus culture

Whatever the **economic benefits** to the island, in studies by Universitas Udayana (Bali's premier university), some Balinese people described tourism as a tempest. Particular concerns related to tourism damaging **religion**; they condemned the desecration of temples by tourists and the fact that Balinese involved in the industry neglected their religious duties.

Even when tourism is thriving, the financial advantages are unevenly spread and there remain significant pockets of poverty on the island. Similarly, profits from multinational hotel chains flood out of the island. Equally concerning to many Balinese, the island is now a magnet for migrants from across Indonesia. Some people describe Kuta Beach as *universitas pantai*, the beach university. Although many of the traders from all across Indonesia have no formal education, they end up as skilled, multilingual communicators with sales skills second to none. Some tourist businesses prefer to employ non-Balinese rather than cope with Balinese staff needing to take time off to attend religious ceremonies.

However, as families grow, many people in Bali can no longer earn a living from agriculture; the tourist sector offers opportunities at all levels, and Bali is now an exporter of skilled staff for the hospitality industry. Commentators have noted that the increased wealth of the Balinese is very often spent in highly traditional ways – in particular, on elaborate religious ceremonies.

RESPONSIBLE TOURISM ORGANIZATIONS

Many organizations are working to raise awareness of the impact of tourism throughout the world and to encourage responsible travelling.

Ethical Traveler http://ethicaltraveler.org
Global Sustainable Tourism Council http://gstcouncil.org
Indonesian Ecotourism Network http://indecon.id
Responsible Travel http://responsibletravel.com

Environmental concerns

Tourism also generates major **environmental concerns**. It is estimated that ten square kilometres of agricultural land are lost to tourist development every year. Rice cultivation, so prevalent in Bali, depends heavily on water; one five-star hotel room is estimated to consume five hundred litres of water each day. Recent fears relate to the Balinese water table being polluted by saltwater due to overuse and uncontrolled development.

Global awareness of the environmental problems of **golf courses** is established, while particular concerns have arisen about the effects of tourist developments on the island's **coral reefs**. Perhaps the most pressing concern is the poor air quality and pollution that affects the Denpasar-Kuta-Legian-Seminyak conurbation in southern Bali. Thousands of new **vehicles** head out onto a woefully inadequate road network each month and at times the entire region is gridlocked. Few Balinese choose to ride public transport, and with cheap loans virtually everyone can afford a motorbike. The **rubbish** problem is another huge issue and visible for every visitor to see; many villagers simply chuck plastic into rivers, which end up dumping waste onto the island's beaches and into the ocean, while discarded construction materials fringe roadsides. Several organizations both locally and abroad are working hard to raise awareness of plastics and ocean pollution, while plans have been made for new roads and infrastructure around the island. Since 2024, all international travellers visiting Bali are subject to a one-time Bali Tourism Tax Levy to fund new conservation and sustainable tourism initiatives.

Social changes

Social change has inevitably followed the influx of tourism. Michel Picard, author of *Bali: Cultural Tourism and Touristic Culture*, suggests Bali has now become a "**touristic culture**" whereby the Balinese have adopted the tourists' perceptions of themselves and their island as their own, and have "come to search for confirmation of their 'Balinese-ness' in the mirror held to them by the tourists".

Tourism in Lombok

A trickle of tourists started arriving on **Lombok** in the 1980s and local people set up small *losmen* around Senggigi, the Gili Islands and, later, around Kuta. By 1989, there were over 120,000 visitors annually and, though the figures are now over 800,000, many of those only stay in the Gili Islands, and numbers are still a fraction of those visiting Bali.

Lombok's fortunes are closely tied with those of Bali, and visitor numbers plummeted following the 2002 and 2005 bombings. As on Bali, however, Lombok tourism later revived. Indeed, one tiny, atypical corner – the **Gili Islands** – is once again booming following the 2018 earthquakes, raising widespread concern about the social and environmental sustainability of unregulated development on its tiny land mass. Islanders and expats are actively addressing this under the auspices of the impressive Gili Eco Trust, and the island has become the subject of a surprising number of academic studies on island tourism.

The opening of Lombok's **airport** in 2011 near Kuta in south Lombok was part of a master plan to, in part, relieve Bali of some of its crowds but also to spread tourism revenue to other parts of the country. The airport, which brought more flights to Lombok, also inspired the much-needed upgrading of roads across south Lombok. In the new resort area called Mandalika that includes Kuta, Seger and Tanjung Aan beaches, several five-star resorts have opened post-pandemic, while chic cafés and boutiques are popping up everywhere. Also, the world-class Mandalika International Street Circuit was inaugurated in November 2021 and has since hosted the World Superbike Championship and the Indonesian MotoGP Grand Prix.

The completion of the grandiose Mandalika Mosque is expected to increase the growing numbers of Islamic travellers who come from Europe, Asia, and the Middle East. In 2019, Lombok surpassed Jakarta and Aceh as Indonesia's top "halal tourism" destination and ranked fourth globally. Although Lombok's tourism industry suffered greatly as a result of the Covid-19 pandemic, it's experienced a rapid rise in tourism and investment ever since. How Lombok's myriad tourism realms will mesh together in the future remains to be seen.

Books

While plenty has been written on the culture, temples and arts and crafts of Bali, there has been little coverage of Lombok. We have included publishers' details only for books that may be hard to find outside Indonesia. Ganesha (http://ganeshabooksbali.com) in Ubud offers an online ordering service. Titles marked ★ are particularly recommended; "o/p" means out of print.

TRAVEL

Elizabeth Gilbert *Eat, Pray, Love*. This insightful, funny journey of self-discovery, now a bestseller and a film, climaxes in Ubud with various life-changing encounters of the sensual and spiritual kind.

★ **William Ingram** *A Little Bit One O'Clock: Living with a Balinese Family*. Warm, funny, warts-and-all portrait of the author's life with an Ubud family in the 1990s. Both the author and his adoptive family still live in Ubud.

★ **Louise G. Koke** *Our Hotel in Bali* (o/p). The engaging true story of two young Americans who built the first hotel on Kuta beach, in 1936. Some of the book's photos are displayed in Ubud's Neka Art Museum.

★ **Elizabeth Pisani** *Indonesia, Etc.: Exploring the Improbable Nation*. A terrific state-of-the-nation account of Indonesia today from a fluent Indonesian speaker and on-off resident. Pisani explores virtually every nook and cranny of the country and debates all the important issues in an engaging, often humorous manner.

Adrian Vickers (ed) *Travelling to Bali: Four Hundred Years of Journeys* (o/p). One-stop anthology with accounts by early Dutch, Thai and British adventurers, excerpts from writings by the expat community in the 1930s, and the musings of late twentieth-century visitors.

CULTURE, SOCIETY AND HISTORY

Susan-Jane Beers *Jamu: The Ancient Indonesian Art of Herbal Healing*. Captivating look at the role of herbal medicine (*jamu*) in Indonesia.

Kathryn Bonella *Hotel Kerobokan: The Shocking Inside Story of Bali's Most Notorious Jail*. Extraordinarily revealing exposé of Kerobokan Prison, the corrupt system that sustains it and the tourists and locals who end up doing time there. Bonella followed it up with a wider exposé of the Bali drugs world, *Snowing in Bali*.

★ **Miguel Covarrubias** *Island of Bali*. An early classic (first published in 1937) in which the Mexican artist and amateur anthropologist explores everything from the daily routines of his adopted village household to the philosophical significance of the island's arts, drama and music.

★ **Dr A.A.M. Djelantik** *The Birthmark: Memoirs of a Balinese Prince* (o/p). Engaging autobiography of the son of the last raja of Karangasem, who was born in east Bali in 1919, became Bali's most influential doctor, and lived through Dutch rule, World War II, the eruption of Gunung Agung and the communist killings.

Fred B. Eiseman Jr *Bali: Sekala and Niskala Vols 1 and 2*. Seminal, essential, wide-ranging anthologies of cultural and anthropological essays by an American expat.

Cameron Forbes *Under the Volcano: A story of Bali*. A compelling picture of Bali from a former foreign correspondent based on interviews with islanders and foreign settlers. Covers the ritual suicides of the colonial era as well as the twentieth-century bombings.

David J. Fox *Once a Century: Pura Besakih and the Eka Dasa Rudra Festival* (Penerbit Sinar Harapan, Citra, Indonesia). Fabulous pictures and a readable text make this an excellent introduction to Besakih. The book includes accounts of the 1963 Eka Dasa Rudra festival and the eruption of Gunung Agung.

Gregor Krause *Bali 1912* (January Books, New Zealand). Reprinted edition of the original black-and-white photographs that inspired the first generation of arty expats to visit Bali. The pictures were taken by a young German doctor and give unrivalled insight into Balinese life in the early twentieth century.

Jeff Lewis and Belinda Lewis *Bali's Silent Crisis: Desire, Tragedy, and Transition*. Especially interesting on the unresolved trauma of the 1965 massacres and Bali's troubled relationship with the greater Indonesian state.

Anna Mathews *The Night of Purnama* (o/p). Moving description of village life focusing on events in the Iseh area in the 1960s, including the Gunung Agung eruption. Written with a keen realization of the gap between West and East.

Michel Picard *Bali: Cultural Tourism and Touristic Culture*. Interesting, readable but ultimately depressing analysis of the effects of tourism on the Balinese.

★ **Robert Pringle** *A Short History of Bali*. An incisive history from the prehistorical era to the 2002 bomb, focusing on society, culture and the environment.

★ **K'tut Tantri** *Revolt in Paradise*. The extraordinary, if embellished, story of Glasgow-born Muriel Pearson, aka Surabaya Sue, who became an active member of the Indonesian independence movement between 1932 and

1947, for which she was tortured by the Japanese.

Adrian Vickers *Bali: A Paradise Created*. Detailed, intelligent and highly readable account of the outside world's perception of Bali, the development of tourism, and how events inside and outside the country have shaped the Balinese opinion of themselves as well as outsiders' view of them.

ART, CRAFTS AND MUSIC

Edward Frey *The Kris: Mystic Weapon of the Malay World*. Small but well-illustrated book outlining the history and making of *kris daggers*, along with some of the associated myths.

John Gillow and Barry Dawson *Traditional Indonesian Textiles*. Beautifully photographed and accessible introduction to Indonesia's *ikat* and batik fabrics; a handy guide if you're thinking of buying cloth in Bali or Lombok.

Brigitta Hauser-Schaüblin, Marie-Louise Nabholz-Kartaschoff and Urs Ramseyer *Balinese Textiles*. Thorough and gloriously photographed survey of Balinese textiles and their role within contemporary society.

★ **Garrett Kam** *Perceptions of Paradise: Images of Bali in the Arts* (Yayasan Dharma Seni Neka Museum, Bali). Ostensibly a guide to Ubud's Neka Art Museum, this is actually one of the best introductions to Balinese art.

Jean McKinnon *Vessels of Life: Lombok Earthenware*. Exhaustive and fabulously photographed book about Sasak life, pottery techniques and the significance of the items they create in the lives of the women potters.

Idanna Pucci *Bhima Swarga: The Balinese Journey of the Soul*. Brilliantly produced guide to the Mahabharata legends. Illustrated with glossy colour photographs and including descriptions of the stories.

Anne Richter *Arts and Crafts of Indonesia* (o/p). A guide to the fabrics, carvings, jewellery and other folk arts of the archipelago, with some background on the practices involved.

Michael Tenzer *Balinese Music*. Well-pitched introduction to the gamelan.

LIFESTYLE

Gianni Francione and Luca Invernizzi Tettoni *Bali Modern: The Art of Tropical Living*. A celebration of modern Balinese architecture, from the tasteful to the ostentatious.

Rio Helmi and Barbara Walker *Bali Style*. Sumptuously photographed paean to all things Balinese, from bamboo furniture to elegant homes.

William Warren and Luca Invernizzi Tettoni *Balinese Gardens*. This exploration of the role of the garden in Balinese culture is gorgeously photographed.

Made Wijaya and Isabella Ginanneschi *At Home in Bali*. The beautiful homes of Bali's beautiful (mainly expatriate) people.

FOOD AND COOKERY

Heinz von Holzen *Street Foods of Bali*. The longtime Bali resident, chef and restaurateur provides a beautiful evocation of Balinese food including plenty of background information, pictures and recipes.

Janet DeNeefe *Fragrant Rice*. The Australian cofounder of Ubud's *Casa Luna* paints an enticing picture of life with her Balinese husband and family, interweaving her observations with recipes for local dishes.

NATURAL HISTORY

John MacKinnon *Field Guide to the Birds of Borneo, Sumatra, Java and Bali*. The most comprehensive field guide of its kind.

★ **David Pickell and Wally Siagian** *Diving Bali: The Underwater Jewel of Southeast Asia*. Beautifully photographed and detailed account.

FICTION

★ **Nigel Barley** *Island of Demons*. Delightful, fictionalized account of the early expats in Bali told in the distinctive (imaginary) voice of Rudolf Bonnet, by turns sad, petulant, generous and tetchy, but never boring.

★ **Diana Darling** *The Painted Alphabet*. Charming reworking of a traditional Balinese tale about young love, rivalry and the harnessing of supernatural power.

Garrett Kam *Midnight Shadows* (o/p). A teenage boy's life in 1960s Bali is turned upside down first by the devastating Gunung Agung eruption and then by the vicious, divisive, anti-communist violence that swept the island.

Odyle Knight *Bali Moon: A Spiritual Odyssey* (o/p). Riveting tale of an Australian woman's deepening involvement with the Balinese spirit world through her romance with a young Balinese priest. Apparently based on true events.

Christopher J. Koch *The Year of Living Dangerously*. Set in Jakarta in the last year of President Sukarno's rule, leading up to the 1965 takeover by Suharto and the subsequent violence, this story compellingly details ethnic, political and religious tensions that are still apparent in Indonesia today.

Putu Oka Sukanta *The Sweat of Pearls: Short Stories about Women of Bali* (o/p). Though all the stories in this collection were written by a man, the vignettes of village life are enlightening, and the author is a respected writer who spent many years as a political prisoner.

Language

You'll hear an exciting mix of languages in Bali and Lombok: the national language of Indonesia, known locally as Bahasa Indonesia and in English as Indonesian, as well as the indigenous languages of Balinese and Sasak (on Lombok), which are just two of more than seven hundred native languages and dialects spoken throughout the Indonesian archipelago. In practical terms, Indonesian will help you to communicate effectively, and everyone on the islands is at least bilingual, but a few words of Balinese or Sasak used appropriately will get you an extra warm welcome.

Bahasa Indonesia

Until the 1920s, the lingua franca of government and commerce was Dutch, but the independence movement adopted a form of Bahasa Malay as a unifying language and by the 1950s this had crystallized into **Bahasa Indonesia**, which is taught in every school and understood throughout Bali and Lombok.

Bahasa Indonesia is written in Roman script, has no tones and uses a fairly straight-forward grammar, making it relatively easy to get to grips with. There are several pocket-sized **phrasebooks**, including one published by Rough Guides, and any number of apps. Among many downloadable **teach yourself** courses, you could try Talk Now DL Indonesian (http://eurotalk.com). A good **dictionary** is the *Tuttle Concise Indonesian Dictionary*. The best Indonesian language schools are Yogyakarta (Java), but there are also schools in Denpasar and Ubud.

Grammar and pronunciation

For **grammar**, Bahasa Indonesia uses the same subject-verb-object word order as in English. The easiest way to make a question is simply to add a question mark and use a rising intonation. **Nouns** have no gender and don't require an article. To make a noun **plural** you usually just say the noun twice; thus *anak* (child), *anak-anak* (children). **Adjectives** always follow the noun. **Verbs** have no tenses: to indicate the past, prefix the verb with *sudah* (already) or *belum* (not yet); for the future, prefix the verb with *akan* (will).

VOWELS AND DIPHTHONGS

a as in car or far

e as in along; or as in pay; or as in get; or sometimes omitted (eg *selamat* is pronounced "slamat")

i as in boutique; or as in bee

o has two sounds: as in hot; or as in cold

u as in boot

ai has two sounds: as in fine; or pronounced individually, for example, *lain* (other)

au as in how

CONSONANTS

Most consonants are pronounced as in English, with the following exceptions:

c as in cheap

g is always hard, as in girl

k is hard, as in English, except at the end of the word, when you should stop just short of pronouncing it. In written form, this is often indicated by an apostrophe; for example, beso' for *besok*.

GREETINGS AND BASIC PHRASES

The all-purpose greeting is **Selamat** (derived from Arabic), which communicates general goodwill. If addressing a married woman, it's polite to use the respectful term **Ibu** or **Nyonya**; if addressing a married man or a gentleman older than yourself use **Bapak**.

Good morning (5–11am) Selamat pagi

Good day (11am–3pm) Selamat siang

Good afternoon (3–7pm) Selamat sore

Good evening (after 7pm) Selamat malam

Good night Selamat tidur

Goodbye (to the person staying) Selamat tinggal
Goodbye (to the person leaving) Selamat jalan
See you later Sampai jumpa lagi
Welcome Selamat datang
Enjoy your meal Selamat makan
Cheers (toast) Selamat minum
How are you? Apa kabar?
I'm fine Bagus/Kabar baik
Please (requesting) tolong
Please (offering, as a seat) silakan
Thank you (very much) Terima kasih (banyak)
You're welcome Sama sama
Sorry/excuse me Ma'af
Never mind/no worries Tidak apa apa
What is your name? Siapa nama anda?
My name is … Nama saya …
Where are you coming from? Dari mana?
What is your home country? Asal dari mana?
I come from … Saya dari …
Do you speak English? Bisa bicara bahasa Inggris?
I don't understand Saya tidak mengerti
Do you have …? Ada …?
I want/would like … Saya mau …
I don't want it/No thanks Tidak mau
What is this/that? Apa ini/itu?
another satu lagi
beautiful cantik
big/small besar/kecil
boyfriend or girlfriend pacar
clean/dirty bersih/kotor
cold dingin
expensive/inexpensive mahal/murah
fast/slow cepat/lambat
foreigner turis/orang asing
friend teman
good/bad bagus/buruk
hot (water/weather) panas
hot (spicy) pedas
how much/many? berapa?
hungry/thirsty lapar/haus
ill/sick sakit
married/single kawin/bujang
men/women laki-laki/perempuan or wanita
no (with noun) bukan
not (with verb) tidak (or tak)
open/closed buka/tutup
tired lelah
very much/a lot banyak
what? apa?
when? kapan?
where? dimana?
who? siapa?
why? mengapa?
yes ya

DIRECTIONS AND GETTING AROUND

Where is the …? Dimana …?
I'd like to go to the … Saya mau pergi ke …
How far? Berapa kilometre?
How long (time)? Berapa jam?
How much is the fare to …? Berapa harga karcis ke …?
Where is this bemo going? Kemana bemo pergi?
When will the bus leave? bemo/ Bila bemo/bis berangkut?
Where is this? Dimana ini?
Stop! Berhenti!
here disini
right kanan
left kiri
straight on terus
airport bandara
bank bank
beach pantai
bemo/bus station terminal
bicycle sepeda
bus bis
car mobil
city/downtown kota
to come/go datang/pergi
to drive mengemuda
entrance/exit masuk/keluar
ferry ferry
fuel (petrol) bensin
horse cart dokar/cidomo
hospital rumah sakit
hotel/homestay hotel/losmen
market pasar
motorbike sepeda motor
motorbike taxi ojek
near/far dekat/jauh
pharmacy apotik
phone office kantor Telkom
police station kantor polisi
post office kantor pos
restaurant restoran/rumah makan/warung
shop toko
taxi taksi
ticket karcis
tourist office kantor turis
village desa
to walk jalan kaki

ACCOMMODATION AND SHOPPING

How much is ...? Berapa harga ...?
a single room kamar untuk satu orang
a double room kamar untuk dua orang
Do you have a cheaper room? Ada kamar yang lebih murah?
May I look at the room? Boleh saya lihat kamar?
to sleep tidur
to buy/sell membeli/menjual
money uang
is there ...? apakah ada...?
air-conditioning ac (pronounced "ah say")
bathroom kamar mandi
breakfast makan pagi
fan kipas
hot water air panas
mosquito net kelambu nyamuk
swimming pool kolam renang
toilet kamar kecil/wc (pronounced "waysay")

NUMBERS

0 nol
1 satu
2 dua
3 tiga
4 empat
5 lima
6 enam
7 tujuh
8 delapan
9 sembilan
10 sepuluh
11 sebelas
12, 13, 14, etc duabelas, tigabelas, empatbelas
20 duapuluh
21, 22, 23, etc duapuluh satu, duapuluh dua, duapuluh tiga
30, 40, 50, etc tigapuluh, empatpuluh, limapuluh
100 seratus
200, 300, 400, etc duaratus, tigaratus, empatratus
1000 seribu
2000, 3000, 4000, etc duaribu, tigaribu, empatribu
10,000 sepuluhribu
20,000, 30,000, 40,000, etc dua puluhribu, tiga puluhribu, empat puluhribu
100,000 seratusribu
200,000, 300,000, 400,000, etc dua ratusribu, tiga ratusribu, empat ratusribu
1,000,000 sejuta
2,000,000, 3,000,000, 4,000,000, etc dua juta, tiga juta, empat juta

TIME AND DAYS OF THE WEEK

What time is it? Jam berapa?
When does it open/close? Kapan dia buka/tutup?
3.00 jam tiga
4.10 jam empat lewat sepuluh
4.45 jam lima kurang seperempat ("fifteen to five")
6.30 jam setengah tujuh ("half to seven")
... in the morning ... pagi
... in the afternoon ... sore
... in the evening ... malam
minute/hour menit/jam
day hari
week minggu
month bulan
year tahun
today/tomorrow hari ini/besok
yesterday kemarin
now sekarang
not yet belum
never tidak pernah
already sudah
Monday Hari Senin
Tuesday Hari Selasa
Wednesday Hari Rabu
Thursday Hari Kamis
Friday Hari Jumaat
Saturday Hari Sabtu
Sunday Hari Minggu

MENU READER

GENERAL TERMS

to eat makan
breakfast makan pagi/sarapan
lunch makan siang
evening meal makan malam
menu daftar makanan
I am vegetarian Saya seorang vegetaris
I don't eat meat Saya tidak makan daging
knife pisau
fork garpu
spoon sendok
plate piring
glass gelas
drink minum

without ice, please tolong tanpa es
without sugar, please tolong tanpa gula
cold dingin
hot (temperature) panas
hot (spicy) pedas
sweet-and-sour asam manis
fried goreng
delicious enak
I want to pay Saya injin bayar

MEAT, FISH AND BASIC FOODS

ayam chicken
babi pork
bakmi noodles
bebek duck
buah fruit
es ice
garam salt
gula sugar
ikan fish
kambing goat
kare curry
kecap asam sour soy sauce
kecap manis sweet soy sauce
kelinci rabbit
kepiting crab
nasi rice
petis ikan fish paste
sambal hot chilli sauce
sapi beef
soto soup
tahu tofu
telur egg
tempeh fermented soya bean cake
tenggiri mackerel
udang prawn
udang karang crayfish

EVERYDAY DISHES

ayam goreng fried chicken
bakmi goreng fried noodles with vegetables and meat
bakso meatball soup
botok daging sapi spicy minced beef with tofu, tempeh and coconut milk
cap cai mixed fried vegetables
es campur fruit and shredded ice dessert
gado-gado steamed vegetables with a spicy peanut sauce
ikan bakar grilled fish
ikan goreng fried fish
ikan pepes spiced fish steamed in banana leaf
jaffles toasted sandwiches
kangkung water spinach
kerupuk rice or cassava crackers, usually flavoured with prawn
lalapan raw vegetables and sambal
lontong steamed rice in a banana-leaf packet
lumpia spring rolls
nasi campur boiled rice served with small amounts of vegetable, meat, fish and sometimes egg
nasi goreng fried rice
nasi pecel steamed green vegetables with a spicy peanut sauce and rice
nasi putih plain boiled rice
nasi sela steamed rice and sweet potato
pisang goreng fried bananas
rendang spicy coconut curry with beef, chicken or pork
rijsttafel Dutch/Indonesian spread of six to ten different meat, fish and vegetable dishes with rice
rujak hot, spiced fruit salad
rujak petis vegetable and fruit in a spicy peanut and shrimp sauce
tahu goreng telur tofu omelette
sate meat or fish kebabs served with a spicy peanut sauce
sayur bening soup with spinach and corn
sayur lodeh vegetable and coconut-milk soup
urap-urap/urap timum vegetables with coconut and chilli

BALINESE SPECIALITIES

ayam betutu steamed chilli-chicken
babi guling roasted suckling pig
betutu bebek spicy smoked duck
lawar minced meat, vegetables, blood and spices
megibung Balinese shared meal
sate lilit ground fish, coconut, spices and sugar wrapped on a bamboo stick and grilled

SASAK SPECIALITIES

ayam taliwang fried or grilled chicken served with a hot chilli sauce
beberuk raw aubergine and chilli sauce
bubuh injin black rice pudding
cerorot rice-flour, palm-sugar and coconut-milk sweet, wrapped into a cone shape
gule lemak beef curry
hati liver
jeroan ayam chicken offal
kelor *Moringa* leaves
lapis legit rice-flour, coconut-milk and sugar dessert, wrapped in banana leaves
olah olah mixed vegetables and coconut milk curry
paru lungs
plecing kangung water spinach with spicy chilli sauce

sate pusut minced beef and coconut *sate*
sayur nangka young jackfruit curry
sumsum bone marrow
usus intestines
wajik sticky rice and palm-sugar sweet

FRUIT

apel apple
buah anggur grapes
jeruk manis orange
jeruk nipis lemon
kelapa coconut
mangga mango
manggis mangosteen
nanas pineapple
nangka jackfruit
pisang banana
semangkha air watermelon

DRINKS

air jeruk orange juice
air jeruk nipis lemon juice
air minum drinking water
arak palm or rice spirit
bir beer
brem local rice wine
kopi coffee
kopi bal black coffee
kopi susu white coffee
susu milk
teh tea
tuak rice or palm beer

Bahasa Bali

The Balinese language, **Bahasa Bali**, has three main forms: High (*basa ketah*), Middle or Polite (*basa madia*) and Low (*basa singgih*). The form the speaker uses depends on the caste (see page 39) of the person he or she is addressing and on the context. If speaking to family or friends, or to a low-caste (Sudra) Balinese, you use **Low Balinese**; if addressing a superior or a stranger, you use **Middle or Polite Balinese**; if talking to someone from a high caste (Brahman, Satriya or Wesia) or discussing religious affairs, you use **High Balinese**. If the caste is not immediately apparent, then the speaker traditionally opens the conversation with the euphemistic question "Where do you sit?", in order to elicit an indication of caste. However, in the last couple of decades there's been a move to popularize the use of Polite or Middle Balinese and to disregard the caste factor. In fact, relatively few speak High Balinese these days and a translator is needed if speaking to a priest.

Despite its numerous forms, Bahasa Bali is essentially a **spoken language**, with few official rules of grammar and hardly any textbooks or dictionaries. However, there is *Tuttle's Practical Balinese*, available internationally. All phrases and questions given below are shown in the Middle or Polite form, unless otherwise stated.

USEFUL WORDS AND PHRASES

What is your name? Sira pesengane?
Where are you going? Lunga kija?
Where have you been? Kija busan?
How are you? Kenken kebare?
How are things? Napa orti?
(I'm/everything's) fine Becik
I am sick Tiang gelem
What is that? Napi punika?
bad corah
big ageng
child putra, putri
to come rauh, dateng
delicious jaen
to eat ngajeng, nunas
family panyaman, pasa metonan
food ajeng-ajengan, tetedan
friend switra
to go lunga
good becik
house jeroan
husband rabi
no tan, nente
rice pantu, beras, ajengan
to sleep sirep sare
small alit
wife timpal, isteri
yes inggih, patut
0 kosun
1 siki, adiri
2 kalih
3 tiga
4 papat
5 lima
6 nem, nenam

7 pitu
8 kutus
9 sia
10 dasa

Sasak

The language of Lombok is **Sasak**, a purely oral language that varies quite a lot from one part of the island to another. However, even a few words of Sasak are likely to be greeted with delight. The following should get you started.

There's no Sasak equivalent to the Indonesian **greetings** *Selamat pagi* and the like. If you meet someone walking along the road, the enquiry "Where are you going?" serves this purpose even if the answer is blatantly obvious.

USEFUL WORDS AND PHRASES

Where are you going? Ojok um bay?
Just walking around Lampat-lampat
I'm going to Rinjani Rinjani wah mo ojok um bay
Where is …? Um bay tao …?
How are you? Berem bay khabar?
I'm fine Bagus/Solah
And you? Berem bay seeda?
What are you doing? Upa gowey de?
How many children do you have? Pira kanak de?
See you (I'm going) Yak la low
No problem Nday kambay kambay
Go away! Nyeri too!
big/small belek/kodek
brother/sister semeton mama/ semeton nine
child/grandchild kanak/bai
dark/light peteng/tenang
daughter/son kanak nine/kanak mame
delicious maik
fast/slow betjat/adeng-adeng
friend kantje
frightened takoot
heavy/light berat/ringan
hot beneng
hungry lapar
husband/wife semame/senine
nothing ndarak
thirsty goro
tired telah
today djelo sine
tomorrow djema
yesterday sirutsin
none ndarak
0 nol
1 skek
2 dua
3 telu
4 empat
5 lima
6 enam
7 pitook
8 baluk
9 siwak
10 sepulu

Glossary

adat Traditional law and custom.

alang-alang Tall, tough, sharp-edged *Imperata cylindrical* grass widely used for thatching roofs.

aling-aling Low, freestanding wall built directly behind a gateway to deter evil spirits.

Airlangga (sometimes **Erlangga**) Eleventh-century East Java king, son of Rangda.

Arjuna The hero of the *Mahbharata* epic; one of the five heroic Pandawa brothers.

bale Open-sided pavilion found in temples, family compounds and on roadsides, usually used as a resting place or shelter.

bale banjar Village *bale* used for meetings.

balian (or **dukun**) Traditional faith healer, herbalist or shaman.

banjar Neighbourhood. Also refers to the neighbourhood association or council to which all married men are obliged to belong; membership averages one hundred to five hundred.

Barong Ket Mythical lion-like creature who represents the forces of good.

Barong Landung Ten-metre-high humanoid puppets used in temple rituals and dances representing distinguishing good from evil.

bemo Local minibus transport.

berugaq The Sasak equivalent of a Balinese *bale*: an open-sided "resting" pavilion in family compounds and on roadsides and beaches.

Bhoma (or **Boma**) The son of the earth and repeller of evil spirits.

bhuta (and **kala**) Invisible demons and goblins, the personification of the forces of evil.

Calonarang Exorcist dance-drama featuring the widow-witch Rangda.

candi A Buddhist or Hindu temple or shrine.

candi bentar Split gateway in a temple compound.

cidomo Horse-drawn cart used as a taxi on Lombok.

dalang Puppet-master of *wayang kulit* shadow plays.

danau Lake.

desa Village.

dewa/dewi God/goddess.

Dewi Pertiwi Earth goddess.

Dewi Sri Rice goddess.

dokar Horse-drawn cart used as a taxi.

dukun See *balian*.

dulang Wooden stand/pedestal used for offerings.

endek Ikat cloth in which the weft threads are dyed to the final pattern before being woven.

Galungan Balinese New Year. The most important Bali-wide holiday, held for ten days every 210 days in celebration of the triumph of good over evil.

gamelan Orchestra or music of bronze metallophones.

Ganesh Hindu elephant-headed deity, remover of obstacles and god of knowledge.

gang Lane or alley.

Garuda Mythical Hindu creature, half-man and half-bird, and the favoured vehicle of the god Wisnu.

gedung Building.

genggong Crude bamboo wind instrument, played like a jew's harp.

geringsing Weaving technique and cloth, also known as double ikat because both the warp and the weft threads are dyed to the final design before being woven.

gunung Mountain.

Hanuman Monkey-god and chief of the monkey army in the *Ramayana* story; Rama's ally.

Ida Batara Dewi Ulun Danu (also just **Dewi Danu**) The goddess of the lake Danu Batur.

ikat Cloth in which the warp or weft threads, or both warp and weft threads, are tie-dyed to the final pattern before being woven: see also *endek* and *geringsing*.

jalan (Jl) Road.

joglo Traditional Javanese wooden house, usually made from teak

jukung Traditional wooden fishing boat with outriggers.

kain poleng Black-and-white checked cloth used for religious purposes, symbolizing the harmonious balancing of good and evil forces.

kaja Crucial Balinese direction (opposite of *kelod*), which determines house and temple orientation; towards the mountains, upstream.

kala See *bhuta*.

kantor pos Post Office.

kantor Telkom Government telephone office.

Kawi Ancient Javanese courtly language.

kayangan jagat Highly sacred directional temple.

keben Square-lidded basket used for offerings or storage.

Kebo Iwa Mythical giant credited with building some of Bali's oldest monuments.

Kecak Spectacular dance-drama often referred to as the Monkey Dance.

kelod Crucial Balinese direction (opposite of *kaja*), which determines house and temple orientation; towards the sea, downstream.

kepeng Old Chinese coins with holes bored through the middle.

ketu Terracotta crown-shaped roof ornament.

kori agung See *paduraksa*.

kris (also spelled keris)Traditional-style dagger, with scalloped blade edges, of great symbolic and spiritual significance.

kulkul Bell-like drum made from a large, hollow log slit down the middle and suspended high up in a purpose-built tower in temples and other public places.

Kumakarma Brother of the demon king, Rawana, in the Ramayana story.

Kuningan The culmination day of the important ten-day Galungan festivities.

Legong Classical Balinese dance performed by two or three prepubescent girls.

leyak Witches who often assume disguises.

lontar Palm-leaf manuscripts on which all ancient texts were inscribed; also the local name of the *Palmyra* palm from which the leaves are taken.

losmen Homestay or guesthouse.

lumbung Barn used for storing rice in Lombok, raised high on stilts above a platform, and with a distinctive bonnet-shaped roof.

Mahabharata Lengthy Hindu epic describing the battles between representatives of good and evil, and focusing on the exploits of the Pandawa brothers.

mandi Traditional scoop-and-slosh method of showering, sometimes in open-roofed bathrooms.

meru Multitiered Hindu shrine with an odd number of thatched roofs (from one to eleven), which symbolizes the cosmic Mount Meru.

moksa Spiritual liberation, freedom from reincarnation, for Hindus.

naga Mythological deity, a cross between a snake and a dragon.

nusa Island.

odalan Individual temple festival held to mark the anniversary of the founding of every temple on Bali.

ojek Motorcycle taxi.

padmasana The empty throne that tops the shrine-tower, found in every temple and dedicated to the supreme god Sanghyang Widi Wasa.

paduraksa (or **kori agung**) Temple gateway to the inner sanctuary, like the *candi bentar,* but joined together rather than split.

Pancasila The five principles of the Indonesian constitution: belief in one god; the unity of the Indonesian nation; guided democracy; social justice and humanitarianism; and a civilized and prosperous society. Symbolized by an eagle bearing a five-part crest.

paras Soft, grey volcanic tuff used for carving.

pasar Market.

pasar seni "Art market" selling fabrics and non-foodstuffs, artefacts and souvenirs.

pawukon (also wuku) Complex Balinese calendar system based on a 210-day lunar cycle.

peci Black felt or velvet hat worn by Muslim men.

pedanda High priest of the Brahman caste.

pemangku Village priest.

perada Gold, screen-printed material used for ceremonial garb and temple decorations.

prahu Traditional wooden fishing boat.

prasasti Ancient bronze inscriptions.

pulau Island.

puputan Suicidal fight to the death.

pura Hindu temple.

pura dalem Temple of the dead.

pura desa Village temple.

pura puseh Temple of origin.

puri Raja's palace, or the home of a wealthy nobleman.

raksasa Mythical Hindu demon-giant with long teeth and a large club, often used to guard temple entrances.

Rama Hero of the *Ramayana* and an avatar of Wisnu.

Ramayana Hugely influential Hindu epic, essentially a morality tale of the battles between good and evil.

Rangda Legendary widow-witch who personifies evil and is most commonly depicted with huge fangs, a massive lolling tongue and pendulous breasts.

Rawana The demon king who represents the forces of evil (Rama's adversary in the *Ramayana*).

raya Main or principal ("Jalan Raya Ubud" is the main Ubud road).

ruko A shophouse; building with living space upstairs and shop space on ground floor.

saka Hindu calendar, which is divided into years made up of between 354 and 356 days and runs eighty years behind the Western Gregorian calendar.

Sanghyang Widi Wasa The supreme Hindu god; all other gods are a manifestation of him.

Saraswati Goddess of science, learning and literature.

sarong The anglicized generic term for any length of material wrapped around the lower body and worn by men and women.

sawah Wet ricefields, as opposed to *ladang*, non-irrigated ricefields.

sebel Ritually unclean.

Siwa (Shiva) Important Hindu deity; "The Destroyer" or, more accurately, "The Dissolver".

songket Silk brocades woven with gold or silver-coloured thread.

subak Irrigation committee or local farmers' council.

suttee Ancient Hindu practice of widows choosing to burn themselves to death on their husbands' funeral pyres.

swastika Ancient Hindu and Buddhist symbol representing the wheel of the sun.

teluk Bay.

Topeng Masked dance-drama, performed with human masks; also the masks themselves.

tuak Rice or palm wine.

wantilan Large pavilion, usually used for cockfights and dance performances.
warung Food stall or tiny streetside restaurant.
wayang kulit Shadow-puppet play.
Wisnu (Vishnu) Important Hindu deity – "The Preserver". Usually shown with four arms, holding a disc, a conch, a lotus and a club, and often seated astride his vehicle, the Garuda.

Small print and index

Rough Guide credits

Editor: Kate Drynan
Cartography: Katie Bennett
Picture Manager: Tom Smyth
Layout: Pradeep Thapliyal
Publishing Technology Manager: Rebeka Davies
Production Operations Manager: Katie Bennett
Head of Publishing: Sarah Clark

MIX
From well-managed forests
FSC® C164814
www.fsc.org

Publishing information

Eleventh edition 2025

Distribution
UK, Ireland and Europe
Apa Publications (UK) Ltd; mail@roughguides.com
United States and Canada
Two Rivers; ips@ingramcontent.com
Australia and New Zealand
Woodslane; info@woodslane.com.au
Worldwide
Apa Publications (UK) Ltd; mail@roughguides.com

Special Sales, Content Licensing and CoPublishing
Rough Guides can be purchased in bulk quantities at discounted prices. We can create special editions, personalized jackets and corporate imprints tailored to your needs. mail@roughguides.com.

roughguides.com

EU Representative
LOGOS EUROPE, 9 rue Nicolas Poussin, 17000, LA ROCHELLE, France; Contact@logoseurope.eu; +33 (0) 667937378

Printed by Elma Basim in Turkey

ISBN: 9781835292358

This book was produced using **Typefi** automated publishing software.

A catalogue record for this book is available from the British Library.

Help us update

We've gone to a lot of effort to ensure that this edition of **The Rough Guide to Bali & Lombok** is accurate and up-to-date. However, things change – places get "discovered", transport routes are altered, restaurants and hotels raise prices or lower standards, and businesses cease trading. If you feel we've got it wrong or left something out, we'd like to know, and if you can direct us to the web address, so much the better.

Please send your comments with the subject line "**Rough Guide Bali & Lombok Update**" to mail@roughguides.com. We'll send a copy of the next edition (or any other Rough Guide if you prefer) for the very best emails.

Acknowledgements

Thanks to Bali Tourism Board, Love Bali, Rene Schultz, Mike Miler, Nadine Leroy, and Amy Thomas.

ABOUT THE AUTHOR

Zoë Smith is a travel writer and digital editor who has written for Rough Guides titles including France, Dordogne & the Lot, Turkey, and Istanbul. She backpacked solo around South America and Southeast Asia and travelled to 50+ countries before settling in her childhood second home of France. She enjoys seeking out local cultural experiences as well as outdoor adventures like hiking, scuba diving and horse riding, and can't resist an unusual place to stay.

Photo credits

(Key: T-top; C-centre; B-bottom; L-left; R-right)

Alamy 5, 15T, 55, 109, 213, 272/273
Dreamstime 13C, 13B
Shutterstock 1, 2, 4, 9, 11T, 11B, 12, 13TL, 13TR, 14B, 14T, 14C, 15B, 16T, 16B, 17T, 17BR, 17BL, 18B, 18T, 19T, 19C, 19B, 20, 22, 52/53, 106/107, 142/143, 145, 184/185, 187, 210/211, 234/235, 237, 275, 289

Cover: Tegallalang Rice Terrace **iStock**

Index

M

N

O

P

V

W

Y

Samsonite
ECODIVER
samsonite.co.uk

Map symbols

The symbols below are used on maps throughout the book

- Chapter division boundary
- Motorway
- Road
- Pedestrianized road
- Steps
- Ferry
- Footpath
- Bemo/bus stop
- International airport
- Point of interest
- Parking
- Post office
- Information centre
- Hospital
- Fuel station
- International ATM
- Golf course
- Snorkelling
- Viewpoint/lookout
- Gate/park entrance
- Spring
- Waterfall
- Surf break
- Mountain peak
- Mountain range
- Lighthouse
- Reef
- Cave
- Statue/memorial
- Boat
- Park HQ
- Museum
- Birdwatching
- Balinese temple
- Chinese temple
- Mosque
- Monastery
- Church
- Market
- Building
- Park/forest
- Beach
- Mangrove swamp/marsh

Listings key

- Accommodation
- Eating/beach club
- Drinking/nightlife/live music
- Shopping